UNDER THE GUARDIANSHIP OF THE NATION

# Under the Guardianship of Guardianship of the Nation

THE FREEDMEN'S

BUREAU AND THE

RECONSTRUCTION

OF GEORGIA,

1865–1870

## Paul A. Cimbala

THE UNIVERSITY OF GEORGIA PRESS   ATHENS AND LONDON

© 1997 by the University of Georgia Press

Athens, Georgia 30602

All rights reserved

Designed by Erin Kirk New

Set in 10 on 14 New Caledonia by G&S Typesetters, Inc.

Printed and bound by Maple-Vail Book Manufacturing Group

The paper in this book meets the guidelines for

permanence and durability of the Committee on

Production Guidelines for Book Longevity of the

Council on Library Resources.

Printed in the United States of America

01  00  99  98  97  C  5  4  3  2  1

Library of Congress Cataloging in Publication Data

Cimbala, Paul A. (Paul Alan), 1951–

Under the guardianship of the nation  :  the Freedmen's Bureau

and the reconstruction of Georgia, 1865–1870 / Paul A. Cimbala.

p.   cm.

Includes bibliographical references and index.

ISBN 0-8203-1891-4 (alk. paper)

1. Georgia—Race relations—Government policy.   2. United

States. Bureau of Refugees, Freedmen, and Abandoned

Lands.   3. Freedmen—Georgia—History—19th century.

4. Reconstruction—Georgia.   I. Title.

F291.C56   1997

975.8′041—dc20      96-31225

British Library Cataloging in Publication Data available

FOR ELLY

# Contents

# Acknowledgments

Malcolm Call of the University of Georgia Press has perfected a most effective method for shaming an author into delivering a long-overdue manuscript. I am sure that I have tried his patience, but I will always appreciate his interest in my work. Along the way to meeting his expectations, I have accumulated many more debts to individuals and institutions than I could possibly repay in a historian's lifetime. Archivists at the various repositories noted in my bibliography made my research a pleasure, but none were more helpful than Bowdoin College's Susan Ravdin. Without her assistance, I would not have made such good use of the Oliver Otis Howard Papers. Several photographic repositories, including the Archives of the State of Maine and the Library of Congress, helped to put a human face to the Freedmen's Bureau by providing photographs of men associated with the agency, but Michael J. Winey and his efficient, helpful staff at the U.S. Army Military History Institute proved to me that his institution is a Civil War era historian's treasure trove. Mary Ellen Brooks and her staff at the Hargrett Rare Book and Manuscript Library at the University of Georgia came to my aid by locating at the last minute photographs of Charles J. Jenkins and Rufus Bullock, two Georgia governors who had important dealings with the Bureau.

Emory University, the University of South Carolina System, Fordham University, and the National Endowment for the Humanities provided funds that allowed me to visit the manuscript collections that I used in completing this book. When I could not travel, reference and interlibrary loan librarians helped me keep up the momentum of my research. I have been fortunate to have had the help of many of these fine service-oriented professionals, but Eric Nitschke, Marie Morris Nitschke, and the other librarians at Emory University went beyond the call of duty during the critical initial stages of my research. They accepted each of my questions as a challenge and refused to give up in the search for even the most obscure references.

Some of the research with which these individuals assisted me first appeared in journal articles. My tentative and earliest ideas about Davis Tillson first appeared in "The 'Talisman Power': Davis Tillson, the Freedmen's Bureau, and Free Labor in Reconstruction Georgia, 1865–1866," *Civil War History* (June 1982). Chapters 3 and 5 are much-revised and expanded versions of "On the Frontline of Freedom: Freedmen's Bureau Agents and the Reconstruction of Georgia, 1865–1868," *Georgia Historical Quarterly* (fall 1992), and "Making Good Yankees: The Freedmen's Bureau and Education in Reconstruction Georgia, 1865–1870," *Atlanta Historical Journal* (fall 1985). Chapter 7 appeared pretty much as it now is as "The Freedmen's Bureau, the Freedmen, and Sherman's Grant in Reconstruction Georgia, 1865–1867," *Journal of Southern History* (November 1989). I thank John Hubbell, John Inscoe, Bradley Rice, and John Boles for allowing me to use this material.

Over the years I have been fortunate to have discussed my ideas about the Freedmen's Bureau with many fine historians. Jerry Thornbery first suggested to me that the Georgia Bureau would make a good subject for study. Barry Crouch, Lee Drago, Paul Escott, Richard Fuke, and Donald Nieman read all or parts of the manuscript; Clarence Mohr carefully reviewed the earliest versions of the chapter on the Sherman Reservation. While I have not taken all of their suggestions to heart, I know that the book is better than it would have been without their constructive criticism. While I was working as an assistant editor at the Black Abolitionist Papers Project at Florida State University, Peter Ripley's witty skepticism forced me to sharpen my arguments about the Bureau. I am sure that I did not change his mind about anything, but the effort was an education unto itself.

My colleagues in the Social Sciences Division at the University of South Carolina at Aiken and in Fordham University's History Department patiently listened to me talk about the Bureau and Reconstruction. At Fordham, my American history colleagues Elaine Crane, Robert Jones, and Robert Himmelberg set high standards, while providing a congenial environment in which to meet them.

The Social Science Division at Aiken was a beehive of activity, populated by an interdisciplinary group of scholars who encouraged each other to think more clearly about our own disciplines. It was a fortunate thing for a new assistant professor to fall into such an environment. I will always be particularly grateful to two of my Aiken colleagues, Robert Botsch and Valdis Lumans, above all others, for the support and the friendship that they have offered to me over the years even after I moved north to study the South.

Years before I began researching the Freedmen's Bureau, my teachers at Saint Joseph's College (now University) taught me about the joys of doing history. More than any of the other faculty, however, David Burton and Randall Miller were responsible for convincing me that being a historian could be a noble and exciting profession, although given the gloomy academic job market, I am sure that that was not their intention at the time. Randall Miller, now as a friend and a collaborator on other projects, remains a source of encouragement, ideas, and high standards.

My good fortune in finding fine teachers continued in the history department of Emory University, certainly one of the most gracious, humane, and lively departments in the country. Robert Smith, the late Bingham Duncan, John Juricek, Harvey Young, Jack Rabun, and Jonathan Prude were all more than excellent teachers; they were good, caring people. Harvey Young and Jack Rabun deserve special thanks for reading the earliest version of this book.

My mother and stepfather, Betty and Ken Terryberry, have offered much emotional support over the years. I appreciate all that they, the rest of my family, and my friends have done for me, but I never would have completed this project if I had not been fortunate to have crossed paths with three people. Dan T. Carter, my adviser at Emory University, is a rigorous scholar who tempers his serious side with a gentle sense of southern humor and a genuine concern for his students that cannot be matched. His kind encouragement over the years and his willingness to take time out to talk to an old student helped to keep me focused on my goals. Equally important were my stepson's timely distractions. Peter has reminded me that life without play cannot be full or satisfying. Finally, my wife, Elly, has reminded me that there is much to life that cannot be found in dusty archives. She has made everything worthwhile, and I owe her more than she can imagine.

# Introduction

Soon after Abraham Lincoln issued his Emancipation Proclamation on January 1, 1863, an increasingly vocal segment of the Republican Party argued that some sort of agency of the federal government should take responsibility for guiding the South's slaves from bondage to freedom. Eventually, on March 3, 1865, Congress legislated and Lincoln signed into existence the nation's first regulatory and social welfare agency, to which the government charged "the supervision and management of all abandoned lands, and the control of all subjects relating to refugees and freedmen from the rebel states." Legislative language gave the agency its formal title—the Bureau of Refugees, Freedmen, and Abandoned Lands—but its more commonly used name—the Freedmen's Bureau—reflected its primary concern.[1]

This Freedmen's Bureau was an extraordinary agency born of the expansion of federal power during the Civil War and the Union's desire to do something for the South's emancipated slaves. There was no precedent for such an agency potentially capable of actively influencing a wide range of affairs previously left outside Washington's sphere. The Bureau's charge to oversee all subjects relating to the ex-slaves presented its officers and agents with the opportunity to challenge old notions of labor, civil rights, politics, and other aspects of the South's racial status quo. Consequently, the Bureau was in a position to play a crucial role in the implementation of Reconstruction policy, translating directives, laws, and constitutional guarantees into the reality promised by emancipation.

Years after the Bureau's passing, one Georgia freedwoman succinctly described what she and probably most freedpeople had expected at the least from the agency: "to get things to going smooth after the war."[2] That was no easy task given the circumstances. In Georgia, state commanders of the Freedmen's Bureau supervised anywhere from a handful of men to over two hundred officers, field agents, clerks, medical personnel, and special agents—all with very limit-ed resources—who on a daily basis dealt with potentially combustible prob-lems concerning labor, education, relief, politics, and civil rights.[3] Their au-thority spread over 132 counties and almost 59,000 square miles of diverse topography in the largest state east of the Mississippi. Their agency's jurisdic-tion included isolated cotton plantations where freedpeople had belatedly learned of emancipation as well as the riverside rice plantations and coastal barrier islands of an exclusive black reservation where ex-slaves had established independent communities months before Appomattox. By the time of the Georgia Bureau's demise in 1870, their agency had become the personification of the North's level of commitment to Reconstruction for over 545,000 black Georgians and for almost 639,000 whites, who had petitioned, cooperated with, challenged, or simply ignored the Bureau at one time or another during its ex-istence.[4] Needless to say, their efforts at coping with what Rufus Saxton, the Georgia Bureau's first commander, called the agency's "peculiar and delicate duties" did not please everyone.[5]

The Georgia Freedmen's Bureau elicited mixed assessments from its own and later generations that reflect the larger debate over the role of the agency in the reconstruction of the South. From its inception, the Bureau at all levels aroused controversy. Its contemporaries North and South argued about the agency's propriety and efficacy, damning it for doing too little and damning it for doing too much. Older scholarly works condemn the Bureau for forcing an unjust Reconstruction on the white South, but most recent historians have been critical of the agency for failing to push hard for the physical and eco-nomic security of the freedpeople within the context of civil and political rights. These critics have argued that the officers and agents of the Bureau lacked real commitment to the freedpeople's cause and either did not care to or were too timid to challenge the basic racial assumptions of the day. Accused of being concerned primarily with reestablishing social and economic order and a profit-able agricultural system under the control of white employers, the men of the Bureau, so its critics have argued, more often than not aligned themselves with white Southerners or simply failed to take into consideration the aspirations of the former slaves.

There are exceptions to this interpretation. Some scholars have attempted to understand the Bureau's methods and goals within the context of nineteenth-century America, which is a much more fruitful approach than trying to mea-sure its agents and officers against the social and political yardsticks of the post–civil rights era of the present century.[6] Despite the very real flaws of the agency, its men deserve better than a summary dismissal of their work as being no more than the efforts of a racist society attempting to define a subordinate kind of freedom for the ex-slaves.

Critics of the Georgia Bureau tend to focus their negative assessments of the agency especially on the tenure of Davis Tillson, the state's second assistant commissioner. Tillson is best remembered for his aggressive pursuit of a contract system that returned the freedpeople to the status of laborers under the supervision of their former masters, his use of native white Georgians as agents, and his supervision of the dispossession of the freedpeople who claimed land along Georgia's coast. Thus the change of Bureau command from Rufus Saxton, who was arguably of all the assistant commissioners the most sympathetic to the greater aspirations of the freedpeople, to Tillson could be viewed as a shift from a radical officer who had acted in the ex-slave's best interests to, according to his Bureau commander and his critics, "a conservative and harmonizer, leaning possibly to the side of the white employers" and the policies of Andrew Johnson.[7] In this assessment, Tillson turned the Bureau into the planters' procurer of black labor, unconcerned with the freedpeople's ambitions beyond having a place to work. The change in administrations in January 1867 supposedly reversed this trend; Tillson's successors, Caleb C. Sibley and John Randolph Lewis, in part because of their emphasis on the importance of education, redeemed the promise.[8]

This neat compartmentalization of events and attitudes, however, distorts the complexity of the men, their ideas, and the circumstances in which they functioned. More than anything else, a change of administration shifted the Bureau's priorities and tactics, but it altered neither the basic assumptions these Bureau men brought to their jobs nor the Bureau's ultimate goal. In fact, the administrations of Georgia's assistant commissioners had much in common. All hoped to secure justice for the freedmen; all hoped to leave Georgia's ex-slaves with the ability to advance in life on their own once the agency withdrew from the state; and all had an ideological framework within which they could push for an expanded definition of black freedom.

In some respects, the Bureau's work, especially the contract system it advocated, appeared to be directly descended from the wartime policies of the Union army in the Mississippi valley. However, to draw a line from those earlier efforts designed for coping with contrabands while fighting a war to the work of the Georgia Bureau, including the administration of Davis Tillson, would be a mistake. Bureau men had a different purpose.[9] Furthermore, they were sufficiently sensitive to the rapidly changing conditions they encountered in Georgia to adjust to the new challenges before them. In the process, Bureau officers developed a sense of what had to be done to obtain justice for the freedpeople and to leave them better able to cope with the challenges of freedom on their own. If the men of the Bureau drew on previous experiences to help bring meaning to their work, they looked beyond wartime contraband policy to the antebellum ideals that had nurtured the free-labor ideology embodied in the Republican Party.

There were, however, limits to how far the agency could or would go in implementing a reconstruction that would have a lasting impact on black and white Georgia. Nineteenth-century perceptions concerning, among other things, the power of moral suasion, the developmental impact of slavery on black character, the role of work and charity on shaping the free individual, and the necessity of the participation of white Georgians in Reconstruction limited the Bureau's effectiveness. Too often, closely held beliefs proved to be contradictory in their implementaion, and conceptual restraints lessened the impact of the good intentions of the Bureau men. These limitations were important, but recent scholarship that emphasizes Yankee ideology's internal weaknesses and the racism of Northerners diminishes the importance of the very real obstacles— most notably its limited resources but especially white intransigence—the Bureau encountered in its work.[10]

The Freedmen's Bureau's commitment to such ideas as individualism and equality before the law as well as the positive effects of hard work and education provided its assistant commissioners as well as a number of its officers and Yankee agents with potent weapons of change. Such values as these were not empty "shibboleths," especially when one realizes that what the Bureau men did in the name of their ideals frequently risked alienating or provoking the white population that their critics accused them of courting.[11] It is an examination of the ideas that established the intellectual parameters of action that become the starting point for understanding the Freedmen's Bureau in Georgia.

The intellectual parameters of action, of course, physically shaped the agency as assistant commissioners strove to establish a bureaucracy that could implement their ideas, the subject of the second chapter of this study. The circumstances surrounding the appointments of Georgia's assistant commissioners, the reasons for changes in administrations, the reorganization of the agency, and the impediments placed in the way of the assistant commissioners as they tried to establish functional and effective chains of command, including the sometimes difficult relationship that the Georgia Bureau had with the army—all reveal much about the nature of Reconstruction and the prospects of the Bureau's success.

The Georgia Bureau's organizational changes are perhaps best illustrated by the types of men upon whom the assistant commissioners relied to carry out their agenda. Chapter 3 focuses on those appointees' service with the agency. Reformers, white Georgians, and Union veterans all significantly influenced the ranks of the agents and field officers. Their experiences reveal not only the impact that they had on the outcome of Reconstruction but also the impact that Reconstruction had on their lives. Granted, not all of these men best embodied the ideals that motivated their commanders, but those who worked for the Bureau's goals, regardless of geographic nativity, found themselves living a harried, lonely, and often dangerous existence.

Congress and Bureau headquarters expected these men to oversee a variety of charges that could have given significant substantive meaning to emancipation: providing emergency relief and medical care, assisting educational enterprise, regulating labor and guiding the freedpeople in their quest for homesteads, and supervising the processes whereby blacks claimed their civil rights and political privileges. Through the examination of these various functions in subsequent chapters, it becomes clear that the apparent weaknesses in their ideological assumptions played only a secondary role in limiting the Bureau's impact on postbellum Georgia. Congress, too, worked within ideological limits, and politicians found it difficult to expend resources on an agency that was by legislative definition only a temporary and extraordinary manifestation of federal power. The Bureau's commitment to such concepts as justice and civil rights and to traditional American views concerning the power of work and education, even when hampered by self-imposed ideological limits, could have worked to the freedmen's advantage if the agency had had the material resources and military force to implement the promise of those beliefs in what turned out to be an extremely hostile environment created by white Georgians.

Unfortunately for black Georgians, the number of officers and agents always seemed inadequate, and on too many occasions a freedman's share of the harvest was lost—literally—for want of a horse. Consequently, before one criticizes the Georgia Bureau for failing to enforce contracts or failing to provide adequate medical attention for the freedpeople or failing to offer more assistance with their educational endeavors, one must ask what was actually possible for the Bureau to accomplish given the resources at its disposal. Moreover, it leads one to ask what would have been necessary to convince or to force white Georgians, who had their own distinct ideas about Reconstruction, to accept a postwar settlement based on what the Bureau hoped to accomplish.

Bureau activity obviously did not take place in a vacuum. Georgia's emancipated slaves and their former owners faced freedom with expectations of their own. Their different visions of what the new order should be and where they coincided with and contradicted the Bureau's vision provides a recurring theme for the present study. The weaker party in the postwar confrontations, the freedpeople, experienced more than their share of frustration and disappointment, but they never were simply pawns in the game. They were neither easily duped by white Southerners nor easily controlled by Yankees. Still, although they never fully accepted the role sketched out for them by their former masters, they did move cautiously toward accepting some of the notions that the agency men brought to the South, including the potential benefits of the contract-regulated free-labor system.

The flawed consequences of the Bureau's efforts to help guarantee a truly free status, however, did not flow from the agency's intentions. A subservient black population was not what the Bureau had expected to leave behind in Georgia. Rather, it was what white Georgians preferred and worked to establish. Reconstruction for white Georgians meant a Reconstruction defined not by Yankees or freedpeople but by whites who claimed to know what was best for their state, an attitude that goes far in explaining why the Freedmen's Bureau failed to accomplish much in a lasting way for Georgia's ex-slaves.[12]

This failure was perhaps most bitterly experienced by freedpeople who had tasted complete political, social, and economic independence along the coast of Georgia, the focus of chapter 7. Briefly in 1865 and 1866, a small portion of Georgia's black population held on to parcels of land along the Savannah River, in the Ogeechee district of Chatham County, and on the barrier islands along the coast. Encouraged by General Sherman's Special Field Orders, No. 15, which in January 1865 had set aside the land for their exclusive use, these ex-slaves organized communities and planted rice and cotton free from the commands of old masters or new white bosses.[13]

For an even briefer moment a handful of federal agents, first under the authority of Sherman's orders and then under Rufus Saxton's Freedmen's Bureau, seemed to confirm the former slaves' claims to their Civil War inheritance. The promise appeared bright, but the freedpeople abruptly learned that neither a special field order nor Bureau agents could provide anything but tenuous authority for land redistribution in the face of planter protest and capital politics. The land was restored to its white claimants before the ex-slaves had even one full season to test their new status, and the Freedmen's Bureau served as the agent of their dispossession.

The Freedmen's Bureau mediated the restoration process, thereby playing a central role in the resolution of the land question on the Georgia coast. Consequently, the agency provides a clear focus for understanding both the process by which the government rescinded the promise of land and the coastal freedpeople's increasing estrangement from their northern emancipators. The Bureau, as the government's enforcer of an unpopular policy, does not fare well in most assessments of its performance in the coastal drama, whether contemporary or modern, history or fiction.[14]

A reading of the events that transpired within the Georgia reservation, the area of land set aside for the freedmen, suggests that criticism of the Bureau was not unwarranted. Needs defined by strangers were inadequate substitutes for black aspirations; the Bureau's officers and agents clearly believed that they knew what was possible and what was best for the freedpeople. Nevertheless, the Bureau, like the people it claimed to help, deserves more than a one-dimensional caricature. A broader, more detailed picture does more than polish the agency's reputation; it illustrates the tension that was inherent in the Reconstruction process.

The confrontation between the Bureau and the freedpeople in the reservation was one that neither party could have won. Certainly, Bureau views concerning land and labor limited the amount of sympathy the agency held for the reservation freedpeople. However, the Bureau's commitment to justice allowed the agency to be more than simply the harsh executor of an insensitive policy. Regardless, the Bureau, no matter how tolerant of the freedmen's foot-dragging compliance with orders from Washington, D.C., could not give their black charges what they had come to expect as their Civil War inheritance—land. Decisions made in Washington forcing the Bureau to remove those who claimed land deprived the agency of the ability to compromise with the freedmen.

Although freedpeople within the reservation harshly judged the Bureau because of these events, elsewhere Georgia's blacks developed less uniformly negative views of the agency. They understood that the Bureau was an important ally in their quest for security through alternatives to land ownership. Some complained about the insensitivity of individual agents and officers, but a significant number by their very actions reaffirmed their belief that the agency remained *their* Bureau. Down through the last days of the Bureau's existence in Georgia, freedpeople laid before their agents complaints ranging from mistreatment at the hands of their employers to community disputes and family problems. And when the agency wrapped the last of its red tape around the tri-folded papers that documented its activities, Georgia freedpeople mourned. White Georgians, however, were glad to see the agency go.

Moods of hostility and submission swung with the shifting realities of Reconstruction politics, but there were significant limits to white Georgia's acceptance of the Bureau's mission. At first, white Georgians might have considered the Bureau an ally, a perception influenced by the agency's talk of the necessity and benefits of hard and regular work as well as its assumption that a successful reconstruction must include the defeated in the process of rebuilding the state. But white Georgians changed their minds when they realized that the Bureau's views of justice required them to respect black rights. They aggressively challenged the Bureau and contributed mightily to its failure.

Any study of the Freedmen's Bureau that deals with these issues must rely heavily on the voluminous records produced by the agency. Certainly, those records have their flaws, especially because the Bureau archive is foremost a repository of complaints. Yet one wonders how many ex-slaves and ex-masters actually lived beyond the conditions that prompted those complaints during the troubled years immediately following the war. As other sources confirm, racism, violence, and fraud were all part of the landscape of Reconstruction Georgia. Disappointment was a fact of life among the freedpeople in the state's cotton fields and rice fields, and the Bureau's records are essential for chronicling this difficult life.

Another apparent flaw of the Bureau records may be found in their provenance. Since the Bureau records are an institutional archive, they necessarily make those officials who generated so much of the paperwork of the agency the central figures in Georgia's Reconstruction drama. But because the foremost purpose of this study is understand how the Freedmen's Bureau worked in Georgia, the archive's focus on officers and agents is crucial. The extensive archive provides the Bureau men with ample opportunity to speak for themselves.

In the end, though, the Bureau's archive, despite its weaknesses, illuminates much more than the history of an institution. The contracts, petitions, and letters from white and black Georgians reveal a great deal about their own expectations as well as the strengths and weaknesses of the Yankee referees who responded to them.[15] Furthermore, what one can learn from the operation of the Georgia Bureau is far greater than the agency's own institutional significance. The record left behind by the Freedmen's Bureau helps to illuminate why Reconstruction failed to take lasting hold and suggests that to understand Reconstruction one must start by understanding the Bureau.

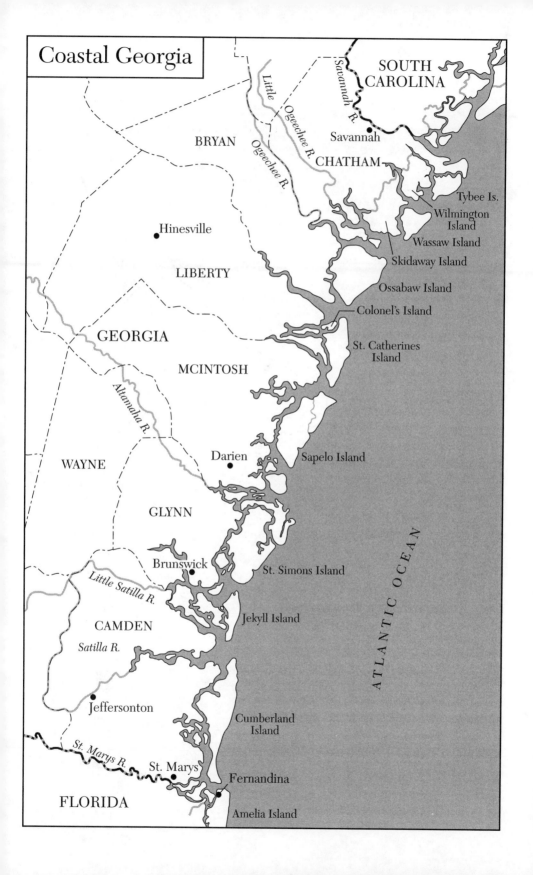

## Coastal Georgia

SOUTH CAROLINA

*Little Ogeechee R.*

*Savannah R.*

Savannah

BRYAN

CHATHAM

Tybee Is.

Wilmington Island

*Ogeechee R.*

Wassaw Island

Skidaway Island

Hinesville

LIBERTY

Ossabaw Island

Colonel's Island

GEORGIA

St. Catherines Island

MCINTOSH

*Altamaha R.*

Darien

Sapelo Island

WAYNE

GLYNN

Brunswick

St. Simons Island

*Little Satilla R.*

Jekyll Island

CAMDEN

*Satilla R.*

ATLANTIC OCEAN

Jeffersonton

Cumberland Island

*St. Marys R.*

St. Marys

FLORIDA

Fernandina

Amelia Island

# Georgia Counties circa 1860

DADE

WALKER

CHATTOOGA

CATOOSA

WHITFIELD
• Dalton

MURRAY

FANNIN

GILMER

GORDON

CASS

• Rome
FLOYD

POLK

PAULDING

HARALSON

CARROLL

HEARD

TROUP
• Lagrange

COWETA
• Newman

MERIWETHER

CAMPBELL

FAYETTE

CLAYTON
• Jonesboro

COBB
Marietta •

FULTON
Atlanta •

DEKALB
Decatur •

HENRY
McDonough •

SPALDING
Griffin •

PIKE

UPSON

BUTTS

MONROE
Forsyth •

JASPER

NEWTON

MORGAN

PUTNAM
Eatonton •

JONES

BALDWIN
Milledgeville •

HANCOCK

WASHINGTON

WARREN

JEFFERSON

GLASCOCK

GREENE
Greensboro •

TALIAFERRO
Crawfordsville •

COLUMBIA

RICHMOND
• Augusta

BURKE

WILKES
Washington •

LINCOLN

OGLETHORPE

CLARKE
Athens •

WALTON

GWINNETT

MILTON

FORSYTH

DAWSON

CHEROKE

PICKENS

LUMPKIN

UNION

TOWNS

RABUN

HABERSHAM

WHITE

HALL

BANKS

JACKSON

MADISON

FRANKLIN
Carnesville •

HART

ELBERT
Elberton •

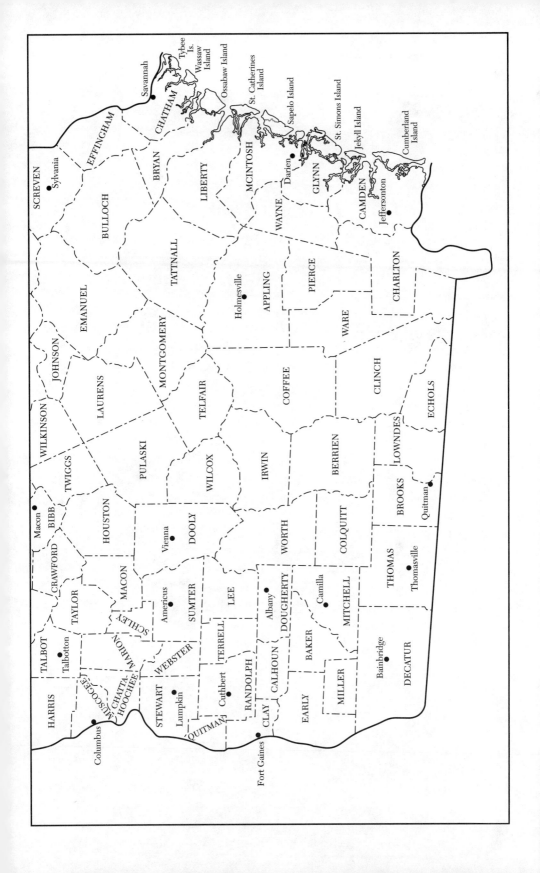

UNDER THE GUARDIANSHIP OF THE NATION

# 1

## Under the Guardianship of the Nation

ASSISTANT

COMMISSIONERS

AND THE

INTELLECTUAL

PARAMETERS

OF ACTION

On May 12, 1865, the Freedmen's Bureau found its guiding spirit in the appointment of its first and only commissioner, Major General Oliver Otis Howard. Howard, the "Christian General" from Maine and former commander of the Army of the Tennessee, conscientiously oversaw the agency, a bureau in the War Department, until its demise in 1872.[1] Howard's sympathy for the freedpeople and his dedication influenced the course of the agency, but more than one individual gave the Bureau its shape and direction. The Freedmen's Bureau became essentially an organization of men with varying degrees of commitment to Howard's vision who interpreted the commissioner's directives in response to the situations they confronted in their state and local jurisdictions. Howard's assistant commissioners and their own appointees were on the frontline of change, facing and adapting to many situations about which the national office could only read in various reports. At the state level, it was Howard's assistant commissioners who did much to define the nature of the agency. In Georgia, they wrestled with the problems of Reconstruction from the spring of 1865 into 1870, setting the tone for Bureau activity in this important jurisdiction.[2]

### The Initial Promise of Land and Labor

The Bureau officer who first attempted to guide Georgia into the uncharted waters of a postemancipation South was Brigadier General Rufus Saxton. On May 20, 1865, Commissioner Howard informed Saxton, a forty-one-year-old native of Greenfield, Massachusetts, that he was now in charge of the agency's efforts in South Carolina, Georgia, and temporarily Florida.[3] Saxton was clearly an accomplished soldier whose background meshed nicely with Howard's expectations for the agency.

Saxton's father espoused Unitarianism, advocated Garrisonian abolitionism, and exhibited an interest in social experiments like George Ripley's Brook Farm. Saxton, however, gave no indication before the war that he was anything but committed to his duty and to the slow advancement that the peacetime service offered its personnel. After graduating from the United States Military Academy in 1849, he served with the artillery fighting Seminoles in Florida. He then engaged in more peaceful pursuits such as surveying and teaching artillery tactics at West Point.

At the outset of the war, Saxton commanded the artillery that helped to disperse Missouri rebels at Camp Jackson and then acted as quartermaster with various commanders, the branch of the service to which he would return upon the conclusion of his Reconstruction duties. After becoming a brigadier general of volunteers in April 1862, Saxton commanded the defenses of Harpers Ferry for a short but critical period during Stonewall Jackson's Valley Campaign. That assignment earned him the Medal of Honor.[4]

Saxton's accomplishments before and during the early months of the war indicate that he was a competent officer, willing to fight but also capable of dealing with the logistical problems that readied an army for battle.[5] Later in life he would joke about how it was the custom of commanding officers to turn over all of their "knotty questions" to their quartermasters.[6] What led him to that conclusion was neither fighting rebels nor tackling supply duties but one of his assignments with the ex-slaves on the southeastern coast. There he engaged in his real preparation for Bureau duty.

In July 1862, Rufus Saxton assumed command of the abandoned plantations and their black occupants on the sea islands of South Carolina centered at Port Royal. He reluctantly accepted this assignment, not because of any strong sense of mission but because of his commitment to duty. However, time among the contrabands transformed Rufus Saxton into a firm supporter of the freedpeople's cause.[7] By the end of 1864, he characterized himself as "being charged with a mission of justice and atonement for wrongs and oppressions the race had suffered under the sanction of national law."[8]

At Port Royal, Saxton, whose supporters found him to be "an honest, pure, and capable man,"[9] undoubtedly was influenced by the people for whom and with whom he worked, including the Yankee schoolteacher who became his wife. He quickly perceived the faults of the old antebellum plantation routines, accepted measures whereby blacks could tend their own plots of land, doggedly fought against tax commissioners and speculators for land division and sale favorable to the freedpeople within his jurisdiction, and lobbied for the just treatment of the black troops he actively recruited.[10]

His experience at Port Royal shaped a favorable impression of the ex-slaves and led him to conclude optimistically that they were seizing hold of the opportunities of freedom and not shirking its responsibilities. That experience convinced Saxton that the former slaves could rise to the challenges of independent farming. It also impressed upon him "that to lay a sure basis for the substantial freedom and permanent improvement of the negroes, that they should be owners of the land they cultivate." As far as Saxton was concerned, they had already paid for it many times over.[11]

At the beginning of 1865, Rufus Saxton expanded this work when he became General Sherman's "inspector of settlements and plantations" for a swath of land extending down the southeastern seaboard, including the barrier islands off the coast of Georgia.[12] He now supervised agents on the Georgia sea islands and in the Ogeechee district in Chatham County near Savannah, vigorously pursuing his charge to settle freedpeople on abandoned property. At war's end, he planned to do the same for the rest of the state.[13] After such service, a position with the Freedmen's Bureau was a natural step in a career that had already become closely identified with helping emancipated slaves.

When Saxton accepted his appointment in the Bureau, he believed he had no reason to discontinue his land policy, and he urged his subordinates to locate freedpeople on any available property.[14] For Saxton, then, the distribution of land to the ex-slaves had become an important component of a lasting Reconstruction, even if it would be just the start of the freedpeople's journey. "When he is made a landholder," Saxton wrote about the freedmen in August 1865, "he becomes practically an independent citizen, and a great step towards his future elevation has been made."[15]

Despite his enthusiasm for land redistribution, the assistant commissioner was confronted with practical concerns that prevented him from implementing such a program beyond the boundaries of the Sherman Reservation: the agency controlled no land outside that strip along the coast.[16] Even if Saxton could obtain more property, he could advocate no plan more radical than that outlined by the Bureau's enabling legislation, which promised the freedpeople opportunities to rent and eventually purchase abandoned or confiscated property.[17] At the same time, however, Saxton endorsed a satisfactory alternative for securing the economic promise of emancipation that did not compromise his beliefs about land for the freedpeople: a free-labor system guided by written contracts that recognized the rights and obligations of both ex-master and ex-slave.[18]

While at Port Royal, Saxton had come to accept labor contracts to which he held both whites and blacks "rigidly to the bargain" as a means by which he could protect freedpeople from exploitation.[19] Now as a Bureau officer, his labor message to black and white Georgians was one that would become a common refrain for Bureau officials throughout the agency's existence. In June 1865, Saxton, assuming the roles of missionary and prophet, admonished recalcitrant planters to sign "fair and equitable" contracts, promising that the benefits of free labor would be demonstrated beyond a doubt when they observed "the rules of exact justice" in their labor relations.[20] The assistant commissioner believed that these documents would help him protect the freedpeople of Georgia from fraud and unfair work arrangements as well as ensure a degree of agricultural stability, but they were also a means to more far-reaching ends.[21]

Saxton's faith in the free-labor system prompted him to preach a message to his black charges that stressed their obligations, urged patience, but also held out the promise of a better future brought about by hard work. In mid-August, he informed the freedpeople, "Your first duty is to go to work at whatever honest labor your hands can find to do." Saxton also took this opportunity to remind them that their new status required that they honor their contracts and respect the obligations to which they committed themselves.

Freedom, therefore, meant that the ex-slaves had to shoulder significant responsibilities and prove themselves deserving of their new status. "Try to show by your good conduct, that you are worthy of all," Saxton beseeched them. "Freedmen, let not a day pass ere you find some work for your hands to do, and do it with all your might. Plough and plant, dig and hoe, cut and gather harvest. Let it be seen that where in slavery there was raised a blade of corn or a pound of cotton, in freedom there will be *two*."

The freedpeople, Saxton also warned, should be patient in their expectations, if all for which they wished at first eluded them: "If you do not obtain all your rights this year, be content with part, and if you act rightly all will come in good time." But even in urging patience, he reassured the freedpeople that they should have faith in God, the Bureau, and the system, that the rewards of honest labor, including moral uplift and economic security, made all of the obligations of freedom worthwhile. As Saxton explained, "Labor is ennobling to the character, and if rightly directed, brings to the laborer all the comforts and luxuries of life." Henceforth, freedpeople were no longer bound by the static confines of slavery; they now had the opportunity to shape their own destiny.[22]

By August 1865, the lack of abandoned and confiscated property and presidential initiatives prevented Rufus Saxton from aggressively pursuing his desire to lease and sell land to the freedpeople.[23] Nevertheless, his sincere message concerning the promise of free labor was by no means a retreat from a more radical position, if only in its assumption that the freedpeople would take charge of and improve their lives. Unfortunately for Saxton, he had little opportunity to put his ideas into operation in Georgia. Appointed in late May, on leave from late June until early August, plagued with controversial subordinates, and lacking ample resources, he failed to establish a strong Bureau presence throughout the state. Consequently, Commissioner Howard appointed another assistant commissioner to deal with the area outside the Sherman Reservation. Saxton remained in charge of South Carolina and for a short time parts of coastal Georgia.[24]

## The Challenge of the Work Ethic

The officer responsible for establishing the Bureau's presence throughout Georgia was Brigadier General Davis Tillson. Like Rufus Saxton, Tillson brought significant experience when he assumed command of the Georgia agency on September 22, 1865.[25] The thirty-five-year-old native of Rockland, Maine, and scion of an old New England family attended West Point, where he first met his future Bureau commander, O. O. Howard. Tillson, however, never received his commission. An accident, which resulted in the amputation of part of a leg, forced his resignation from the military academy in September 1851. Despite his handicap, he continued to lead a busy life initially as a civil engineer and then as a Republican politician. In 1857 he won a seat in Maine's legislature, and in 1858 he became adjutant general of the state. His political connections also led to his appointment to the position of customs collector for one of Maine's revenue districts.

During the war, Tillson served as an artillery officer, becoming a brigadier general of volunteers by early 1863 and earning increasingly responsible commands. He also raised and organized the First Regiment of U.S. Heavy Artillery Colored. After Appomattox, he was prepared to resign from the service, but he accepted a position as superintendent of the Freedmen's Bureau's District of

Western Tennessee, an assignment made, by his own guess, because of his wartime efforts to prevent injustice to blacks in eastern Tennessee as well as his interest in recruiting black troops.[26]

Once involved in Reconstruction, it became clear that despite this experience Tillson was no egalitarian. The transplanted Down-Easter brought some conservative views in his intellectual carpetbag, which to an extent were influenced by class prejudices as much as by race. He did not believe that the Freedmen's Bureau should or could secure political rights for the South's blacks, at least not in 1865 or 1866. But then he saw nothing wrong with depriving Yankee women of the vote, and he once publicly questioned the wisdom of allowing the "uneducated" Northern masses to exercise the franchise. Social equality, which for Tillson meant the unquestioned right to associate with others, black or white, against their wishes, was out of the question for the freedpeople. Social arrangements were selective by their very nature, and social equality, after all, had "never existed among white people."[27] However, in other areas, Tillson offered the freedpeople a clear opportunity to break with the past.

As with Rufus Saxton, Davis Tillson's early Reconstruction experiences influenced his views on how best to proceed through the thicket of problems posed by emancipation. His background as an engineer predisposed him to bring order and system where there appeared to be neither; without these qualities, it would be impossible, he believed, "to educate" the freedpeople "to habits of neatness thrift and industry."[28] It was in Memphis, Tennessee, his first Bureau command, where he began to implement ideas about labor and contracts that would follow him to his Georgia posting.

The seemingly chaotic movement of freedpeople to Memphis during the spring and summer of 1865 confirmed Tillson's assumption that he had an obligation to bring stability and confidence to the new labor system. Troubled by the destitution he witnessed in his district, he first unsuccessfully explored the possibility of settling freedpeople on abandoned property farther south along the Mississippi. Tillson's effort in this case indicated the direction that he would take in these matters in the future. He was motivated by a very pragmatic concern: he wished the freedpeople to have an opportunity to support themselves.[29] When Memphis became crowded with unemployed freedpeople, including those who had abandoned their contracts, Tillson asked them to return to the countryside to honor their agreements or find work with white employers. Displeased with the results, he then felt compelled to take more forceful measures to remove idlers from the city, arresting contract violators and finding employers for apparent vagrants.[30]

Throughout his brief tenure in Tennessee, Davis Tillson worked hard to impress on the ex-slaves and planters of his district that freedom required order and that prosperity would come from respecting mutual obligations and privileges in the new free-labor system. In August 1865, planters from Fayette County, Tennessee, complained to Tillson about the problems they were having with their workers. In replying, the general sounded themes—mutual obligations and mutual rights, the rewards of honest work, and equal treatment before the law—that he would repeat time and again in Georgia. Freedpeople must work, and black vagrants "will be arrested & punished in the same manner and to the same extent to which a white man would be liable for similar offenses." At the same time, it was the responsibility of employers to patiently cultivate faithful labor by "implanting in the freedman a desire for a home of his own, with all its blessings and security, [and] by holding out before him the inducements and motives which impel other men to labor."[31] Once in command of the Georgia Bureau, he continued to emphasize the need to establish mutually beneficial working arrangements, because he believed much was at stake. "The material salvation of the white people of this state," he once reasoned, "as well as the black depends upon the success of the freed labor system."[32]

At least in part, Tillson accepted an environmentalistic approach—the idea that slavery had limited the freedpeople's intellectual development—in explaining what he believed was the freedpeople's slow adjustment to the new economy.[33] Consequently, the freedpeople, who Tillson at first assumed would be the reluctant participants in free-labor arrangements, would need special attention. Preaching to the choir, the assistant commissioner explained this point to his white audience at the Georgia state constitutional convention in October 1865, noting that the freedpeople's "dense ignorance, their inability to understand or comprehend the meaning of freedom, its rights and duties, is what makes it so extremely difficult to influence and manage them."[34]

No doubt these views in part roused him to issue a challenge to the freedpeople of Georgia that was, in fact, not much different from the labor message of his predecessor. In January 1866, he addressed a meeting of freedpeople in Augusta, using a rhetoric that was in harmony with the pronouncements of Rufus Saxton and with antebellum free-labor ideas. Stressing the moral obligation of every individual to work and the responsibility of each freedperson to assume the burden of proving that the work ethic could take root in the South, Tillson outlined the free-labor philosophy that guided his actions throughout his tenure in Georgia. "Remember," he told his audience, "that labor is not imposed by the white man, but by your Creator; that it is not a curse but a

blessing and that it can only be avoided at the expense of misery and degrada-
tion." He warned his listeners that their future was in their own hands, that they
were "on trial before the country." If they failed to rise to the challenge, if they
failed to accept their new obligation, they would "bring shame and mortifica-
tion upon your friends, and sorrow and suffering upon yourselves."[35]

This was certainly an awesome challenge, phrased in a dramatic rhetoric,
which placed a significant burden on the freedpeople to prove that they were
worthy of their new status. But the greater the challenge, the greater the rewards. "A single year of patient, honest, steady work and the fortunes of your
people are established forever," the assistant commissioner promised the Augusta convention.[36]

Tillson's vision of a successful transplantation of free labor to Georgia, in fact,
meant more than steady employment for the freedpeople at fair wages. To be
sure, some Northerners believed that was a sufficient goal. Tillson's Atlanta subassistant commissioner, Colonel George Curkendall, subscribed to what was
becoming the modern perspective on work. Basing his assessment on his own
experience, he told a visitor that he had been a "working man" all his life and
"he supposed that they [the freedmen] too would be working men as long as
they lived."[37] If by "working man" Curkendall meant a wage earner, he was expressing a view more realistically in tune with the changing circumstances of
the industrializing North.[38] However, at this place and time, he was out of step
with Yankees like Tillson, who continued to believe that work could bring more
than just a living wage.

Obligations and responsibilities, which Tillson stressed so dramatically to the
1866 Augusta freedmen's convention, did not contradict the expectations that
work brought power and rewards. The free-labor ideology espoused by men
like Tillson and his predecessor, Saxton, made the freedpeople's position in society a dynamic one, a concept that was a revolutionary alternative to the sti-
fling permanence of slavery even if the Bureau cast the freedpeople as junior
partners in its implementation. With hard work and the help of their Yankee allies, the freedpeople could remove the economic and moral vestiges of the institution of slavery. The freedpeople may be working under contract now, Tillson argued, but change was possible for the industrious. Work was the "talisman
power," according to Tillson, "which can remove your poverty and ignorance
and replace them with wealth, knowledge and happiness."[39]

Playing on the antebellum and wartime themes of individualism and self-
control, Davis Tillson also assured the freedmen at the Augusta convention, "All

you can earn is your own, you have the same right with all other men to accumulate, hold, and enjoy property; the right to be as rich as you can make yourself by your own energy, industry and economy."[40] In other words, work fairly paid would build up their fortune, their character, and their lives just as surely as slavery had torn them down.

For Davis Tillson, the just rewards of labor were powerful incentives, and land ownership was the logical end in an agricultural society to the wage earner's toil.[41] Because of his belief in these dynamics, Tillson's views on land for the freedpeople were not dissimilar to those held by Saxton. But unlike his predecessor, he believed that no one should claim property who had not earned the right to purchase it. He honored no debt owed to the freedpeople by a nation that had sanctioned slavery; he saw no injustice in withholding property from a population that had had no control over its own labor for generations while the nation had extracted significant wealth from its toil. Nevertheless, Tillson's view of the freedpeople's potential was a break with Georgia's past.[42]

For his predecessor, Rufus Saxton, landholding could bring out the best qualities in the freedpeople—"industry, sagacity, and prudence"—but for Davis Tillson, ex-slaves needed to learn these same qualities before striking out on their own as propertied individuals, or the experiment would end in disaster. The key for Tillson was the accumulation of capital, which was a sure sign that freedpeople had overcome a history that had deprived them of the opportunity "to exercise care, economy and forecast." These virtues needed "cultivation," and for Tillson the best possible system in which the ex-slaves could learn responsibility was the Bureau-supervised contract system.[43]

## The Power of Education

Davis Tillson served as Georgia's assistant commissioner until January 14, 1867, at which time he retired from the Bureau to plant cotton in coastal Bryan County, Georgia.[44] He turned over command to Colonel Caleb C. Sibley, previously the "gentlemanly" post commander at Savannah. A Massachusetts native, a West Point graduate of the class of 1829, and a veteran of the Mexican War as well as western service, the sixty-one-year-old regular army officer probably accepted his new assignment expecting it to be his last. His long, uncontroversial career offered no hint of any ambition higher than the performance of his duty, perhaps in part because of health problems. In fact, the most unusual aspect of his Civil War service was also his most embarrassing: on April 26,

1861, while en route to Matagorda Bay, Texas, Sibley was forced to surrender his battalion to Confederate General Earl Van Doren. Thereafter, the colonel commanded troops at posts far removed from the fighting while other officers secured their brigadier's star in combat or through political maneuvering in the volunteer service.

Sibley's relative isolation also meant that he lacked firsthand initiation into the problems of Reconstruction before coming to Georgia. Before his arrival at his Savannah post in November 1866, he spent only a few months in Nashville. He then completed a leave of absence that lasted through the summer and into the fall. He was by far the most reticent Georgia assistant commissioner. He rarely offered strong personal views on Reconstruction policy, at least if he had to put them in writing. His circulars were routine and typically regular army in style; they lacked the imagination—for good or naught—that those of his predecessors had expressed when confronting significant problems.[45] All told, Sibley was foremost a soldier who followed orders. During almost two years of Bureau service he avoided personal controversy as easily as Rufus Saxton or Davis Tillson had stirred it up. In the process, he reorganized the Georgia Bureau and did his best to carry out the requirements of Military Reconstruction, while enforcing contracts in much the same way that his predecessor had.[46]

In January 1867, Commissioner Howard, probably concerned with his new assistant commissioner's inexperience in freedmen's affairs as well as his waning influence in his own organization as signified by Sibley's regular army background, made an important appointment to Sibley's staff. Howard assigned Colonel John Randolph Lewis to the position of assistant inspector general for the Georgia Bureau. Unlike Sibley, Lewis was an amateur soldier. Although he had campaigned with the Army of the Potomac, he did not receive his commission as a major in the regular army until after he assumed his duties in Georgia. Also unlike Sibley, Lewis was young, thirty-two years old, and obviously concerned with his future prospects, especially since the war had destroyed his ability to practice his chosen profession of dentistry. A musket ball had shattered his left arm in May 1864 in the Wilderness, and Lewis would suffer from lingering pain and abscessing decades after his September 1864 transfer to the Veteran Reserve Corps.[47]

Lewis differed from Sibley in an even more significant way when he arrived in Georgia. Since December 1865, he had been serving with the Bureau in Tennessee, first as assistant inspector general, then as assistant commissioner.[48] It was in Tennessee that Lewis confronted the unreconstructed whites who helped to shape his views about the relative value of free-labor contracts and education. Contracts, Lewis explained near the end of his stay with the Tennessee Bureau, were useful documents, if the Bureau could rigorously enforce their intent upon the white population. The agreements "serve to fix the freedmen in permanent homes, keep families together, enable them to calculate and make plans for the future, and increase the amount saved at the end of the year." He was not as enthusiastic as Tillson was about the system's ability to secure the freedpeople's rapid economic progress, but he assumed that a successful contract system would decrease pauperism and destitution. Furthermore, it would allow the freedpeople to accumulate property at a steady rate.[49] Lewis's frustration with the documents, however, grew from his realization that employers would never honor them and that the freedpeople could not depend on local officials to protect their rights.

Lewis also realized that the Bureau, without a substantial increase in power, could do little in the face of white opposition. On one occasion, Lewis found himself helpless in a confrontation with Tennessee civil authorities who had allowed labor contractors to gather up freedpeople for an Arkansas plantation after maliciously accusing the ex-slaves of vagrancy. An appeal either to law or to Bureau authority could not prevent the injustice.[50]

Such experiences, therefore, convinced Lewis that although the major Reconstruction questions concerned civil rights and labor, education would provide the "controlling element" in their final settlement. The freedpeople, Lewis concluded, "must have intelligence and Education—nothing else will secure their rights."[51] It was education, Lewis believed, that would have an enduring impact on the freedpeople and the South long after the Bureau's demise. "The schools established and the school-houses built and freedmen educated," he poetically explained before leaving Tennessee, "are the seed sown in this land of oppression that shall spring up soldiers strong and mighty to resist the oppressor and strive for their rights."[52]

Lewis's presence in Georgia meant that Howard would have an officer in the state who was familiar with the major problems of Reconstruction and sympathetic to his own views concerning education.[53] And while Sibley also warmly supported the Bureau's education work, Lewis, in fact, superseded his assistant commissioner in influence, becoming Howard's most valued officer in the state. Unsurprisingly, the commissioner placed Lewis in charge of the shrinking state agency on October 16, 1868, when Sibley assumed exclusively the duties of military commander of the District of Georgia.[54] In that position and in the role of the Georgia Bureau's chief education officer, Lewis continued his dedicated effort to educate the freedpeople. By the end of his association with the Bureau, however, Lewis probably concluded that Reconstruction in Georgia needed even more than educated freedpeople to guarantee its durability beyond the agency's termination: the state required the right politicians to continue to guide the process, which for him meant the Rufus Bullock wing of the Republican Party.[55]

The invigorated emphasis on educational matters that John Randolph Lewis infused into Bureau activity did not mean that the agency abandoned the contract system or the ideological commitment to free labor so fully expressed during Davis Tillson's administration.[56] Yankees designed the freedpeople's schoolhouse and the labor contract to convey the values that they expected the ex-slaves to use to maintain their new status. The messages included in Bureau pronouncements since the summer of 1865 were expressions of ideas that went beyond specific agency personnel.

Educators, also steeped in the intellectual and ideological developments of the antebellum and wartime North, wove those concepts of industriousness, self-discipline, respect for property, and the rewards of work, among other themes, into the very fabric of freedmen's education.[57] In December 1865, for example, the American Missionary Association's Ira Pettibone informed freedpeople that "they should carefully avoid the impression that *freedom* means liberty to be idle & *wild* or *lawless*[;] that it is the privilege of working for themselves & their families to use & lay by their earnings for their own benefit & improvement."[58] Also, in early 1867 William J. White, a black special agent for education in the Georgia Bureau, easily combined his efforts to convince black communities "to do all they can to support their own schools" with encouraging words about "procuring homes" (that is, signing labor contracts) and exercising economy.[59] And John R. Lewis himself saw no conflict when he mentioned in his 1868 address to the freedpeople at the dedication of the Beach Institute in Savannah a list of virtues that Davis Tillson had earlier attempted to convey to the ex-slaves. The freedpeople of Georgia, he declaimed, "were not thoroughly emancipated or free until they emancipated themselves from vice and immorality, and became educated, and fit to enjoy the rights which had been conferred upon them, and became law abiding, honest, and industrious people, that would be so looked upon by people everywhere, and be respected and trusted."[60]

The Bureau accepted the belief that education could influence all of the freedpeople's habits, including industry and economy,[61] and considered its own encouragement of hard work and the acquisition of education to be complementary. Davis Tillson, even though he left most matters in this area to his education superintendent, believed that education would "inculcate, among them [the freedpeople], the principles of virtue, industry, and morality."[62] Others agreed with his agenda. Furthermore, although education might ultimately protect the freedpeople's independence and even prepare them to be responsible voters,[63] they would still have to conform to Yankee notions of labor if educational efforts were to succeed. After all, they would have to pay for their own schools.

As Gilbert L. Eberhart, the Georgia Bureau's first superintendent of education, explained, such a requirement was essential for achieving the Bureau's purpose. "One of the most important objects to be obtained," he wrote in November 1865, "is to place these people in a condition to support themselves, and control all their own interests."[64] Free education would only hinder those goals. Certainly, education, like the contract system, could be viewed as a conservative force, a means to preserve order and economic recovery by training the freedpeople to be disciplined workers. But the potential for change was clearly a part of the Yankee syllabus, as Eberhart's rationale for requiring black support of their schools promised.

Education continued to give the Bureau some meaning in its waning days, a time when white Georgians were paying little attention to the agency. As of January 1869, Lewis's Georgia Bureau had to limit its activities to nurturing the freedpeople's schools and to securing bounty claims for black veterans. The assistant commissioner retired from the agency in April 1870 to become the state's first school superintendent. The Bureau lingered on after Lewis's departure under Acting Superintendent of Education Edmund A. Ware, an abolitionist and a veteran of the American Missionary Association and the agency's education department, until August 1870.[65]

## The Bureau as Guarantor of Justice

The views of the assistant commissioners of the Georgia Bureau, while shaped by specific individual experiences, had much in common because the men shared intellectual touchstones firmly secured in antebellum ideals of work, individual responsibility, and justice. Antebellum Northerners, including abolitionists, had nurtured a strong commitment to a work ethic that in theory made the region open to initiative and advancement, specifics clearly related to those broader ideals of democracy, individualism, egalitarianism, and self-control that became central to the ideology of the Yankee war effort. Before the Civil War, the work ethic had become a widely accepted icon of American life in the North and an important part of Republican Party ideology.

For writers, ministers, philosophers, teachers, and politicians, work loomed large as the key ingredient for living a moral life. Work involved significant responsibilities and obligations, but also won for the diligent the rewards of economic success and personal independence. The rewards of work, however, went beyond personal moral development and individual economic advancement; the ability to earn was a requirement of responsible citizenship and, consequently, also a public matter.[66]

Given the civic significance of work, it is not surprising to find that the antebellum North had developed a legal system that accepted certain controls on work and idleness. Northerners had an abundant record of court cases affirming that employers could legitimately impose labor discipline with long-term contracts and that society had a legitimate right to regulate the idle with vagrancy laws. Furthermore, except for the most radical among them, Northerners assumed that these regulatory instruments in no way compromised the promise of the free-labor message.[67]

As Yankees revered free labor, they also revered the free institutions, such as the schoolhouse and the ballot box, that guarded liberty. Education, one of the Bureau's primary concerns, had significant implications beyond literacy. Schooling could very well help an individual advance economically in a free-labor society. But education was also considered essential for maintaining a virtuous citizenry, the bedrock of republicanism.[68] When in 1868 the Reverend E. N. Kirk, then president of the American Missionary Association, expounded on the important interconnectedness of education and labor, he noted that workers who became "educated laborers" not only improved their own conditions but also became "a portion of the moral, intellectual and political strength of their country."[69]

The views that Bureau men held concerning labor and education were reinforced by a broader conception of justice based on the freedpeople's claims to their constitutional rights. Bureau men believed that the freedpeople were always entitled to equal treatment under the laws of the land. By the commencement of the war, at least within the Republican Party, men were abandoning the basest assumptions about race and were assuming that the government should protect blacks in certain fundamental rights. By no means did this perspective suggest that antebellum Republicans or Freedmen's Bureau officials after them advocated complete equality for the races. Rather, the enlightened opinion was that, as human beings, blacks were entitled to the natural rights embodied in the Declaration of Independence and should expect the Constitution to provide them with the means to guard those rights. Political and social equality remained debatable claims for black Americans, but by Appomattox, Northerners began to accept the idea that if slavery had deprived black Southerners of their rights as human beings, then freedom must restore those rights.[70] Northerners, including Bureau officials, could hold these beliefs even if they continued to accept the concept of black political and social inferiority.[71]

The Bureau, therefore, understood its obligation to protect the freedpeople's rights even as it tried to convince white Georgians to recognize them. The message was clear: as Tillson explained, the freedpeople must "stand upon the same footing before the law with white people."[72] As long as the freedpeople worked and avoided running afoul of the law, "they are their own masters."[73]

The assistant commissioners of the Georgia Bureau certainly understood that economic justice and a system of black education could not long survive if this point did not register first with their subordinates and then with the white people of Georgia. In May 1867, John R. Lewis chastised an agent who had apparently forgotten that black and white Georgians "must be treated exactly alike." Lewis was most explicit. "Whatever the law and orders will allow you to do in cases of white persons, you can do in these [black] cases and no more."[74]

Thus, the intellectual parameters of Reconstruction set by the Georgia Bureau's assistant commissioners had the potential to propel the freedpeople and the state well beyond the boundaries once set by the institution of slavery. But parameters bespeak of limits, too, and Bureau men often contradicted broader assumptions about black independence when confronted with specific problems. Eloquent paeans to the promise of work and education and to black rights were accompanied by assumptions that Georgia's black population needed close supervision and that the freedpeople had to be exhorted onward to prove that they were worthy and capable of freedom.[75] Davis Tillson, for example, believed that freedmen had as much right to exercise control over their families, including apprenticing their children, as did their white counterparts. However, a paternalistic Bureau had to watch over them to prevent whites from taking "advantage" of their "ignorance."[76]

Tillson was not alone in holding these views. John R. Lewis also told freedpeople they would earn respect and trust only by their industry and moral behavior.[77] Even the sympathetic and optimistic Rufus Saxton believed the freedpeople needed his guidance not only to clarify the promise of hard work but also to prevent them from selling corn to distillers, to stop them from running back and forth "without any special object" between the sea islands and the mainland, and to encourage them to abandon the ways of slavery and to honor their marital commitments.[78] Both Saxton and Lewis accepted the principle of black independence, and yet they could not shake the feeling that the freedpeople still required a benevolent but firm hand to direct their progress.

The Bureau's goal of instituting black self-sufficiency also implicated nineteenth-century views concerning the negative impact of charity on individual character. If the Bureau were to teach the freedpeople, as Rufus Saxton noted, that "they must get rid of the idea of dependence upon the Government for anything as soon as possible" and if the agency were to "encourage industry, frugality and independence," then it was imperative that the government "bestow as little charity as possible, consistent with the plainest dictates of humanity."[79]

The fear that charity would almost certainly sap an individual's initiative and permanently damage his character limited experimentation and precluded the implementation of imaginative programs that might have helped freedpeople achieve greater economic independence.[80] That fear also put a sharp edge on Bureau rhetoric and action and at times made it appear that the agency was most concerned with coaxing freedpeople back into the fields under white supervision. Thus, Rufus Saxton could admonish freedpeople to "bear in mind that a man who will not work should not be allowed to eat."[81] And Caleb Sibley could conclude that the withdrawal of Bureau relief "had the good effect of forcing many [freedpeople] to successful exertions to obtain support, who (under other circumstances) would have lingered on in idleness as long as there was a chance to subsist on the bounty of the Government."[82]

Equally important in defining the limits of Bureau action was the fact that the agency was by law a temporary institution, one that was an aberration to the normal way of doing the federal government's business. The agency's existence was marked by an uncertainty about its future—or rather a certainty that it would not last very long—that had an impact on its effectiveness. Congress limited the resources it was willing to commit to the Bureau's task, and white Georgians believed that if they persevered they would outlast their Yankee tormentors. The March 1865 Bureau law, which failed to provide for sound financing, would have closed down the agency one year after the end of the war—at the best June 30, 1866, by Commissioner Howard's reckoning. The second law of June 16, 1866, passed over a disruptive presidential veto, added two years to the agency's existence and gave it its first congressional appropriation. But the July 6, 1868, law, which continued the agency beyond the election of 1868, also authorized the secretary of state to discontinue the Bureau in states that were reconstructed, unless he believed that its presence was necessary. Commissioner Howard discontinued most of the agency's activities on January 1, 1869, and the agency was of little consequence thereafter.[83] In other words, the Bureau's officers and agents never had the luxury of knowing that they had unlimited time in which to secure the promise of Reconstruction.

The implications here went beyond Congress's unwillingness to provide more resources to an agency that was marked for termination as soon as it had been established. Despite the triumph of the Union over states' rights, federalism had not died in the war. Bureau men therefore understood that it was important to convince whites that the new order of things would be good for them as well as for their ex-slaves. After all, sooner or later the Bureau would have to turn over its functions to state and local authorities.[84]

Because of these circumstances, Davis Tillson assumed that a lasting Reconstruction required white Southerners to accept and embrace the Yankee ideals essential to the process. A confrontational relationship with white Georgians might "purchase a cheap popularity with certain well-meaning newspapers," but in the long run, it would only hurt the freedpeople's chances for advancement by stirring up a debilitating resentment for the Bureau and anyone associated with it.[85] Also, even as he petitioned Howard for more military power in December 1865, Tillson feared that, without white acceptance, no amount of troops could protect the freedpeople.[86]

Thus, the assistant commissioner, who at first believed in the reasonableness of white Georgians, realized that the Bureau's success would depend at least in part on his ability to "act in concert" with the local authorities "to promote the public good" and to remove "from the public mind . . . the grave misapprehension which existed as to . . . [the Bureau's] objects and purposes."[87] On a more concrete level, the belief in the need for white acceptance of Reconstruction led Tillson to bring white Georgians—especially, he hoped, "the best men," those who "alone have it in their power to modify or change public opinion in favor of the freedman"[88]—into the process by using them as agents, with the hope that those so engaged would convince their neighbors to look upon the Bureau and its goals with respect.[89] Unfortunately, this attempt to encourage positive white participation in Reconstruction also prematurely encouraged white Southerners to reassert themselves, thereby depriving the freedpeople of real safeguards for their newfound rights before they had been established on firm ground.

Self-generated limitations, therefore, restricted and contradicted the Bureau's grand rhetoric. The belief that the Bureau knew what was best for the freedpeople, the fear of charity, limited time and resources to enforce acceptable goals, and the desire and need to include white Georgians in the Reconstruction process certainly affected Bureau performance. Self-generated limitations, however, did not mean that Bureau assistant commissioners would be no more than accommodating servants of the ex-masters' appetite for cheap, docile labor. Nor did they mean that the agency would readily abandon distressed freedpeople who suffered at the hands of their employers. Freedmen's Bureau officials may have assumed that they knew what was best for their black charges, but they took seriously their obligation to see that the freedpeople started off on the right track. If white Georgians obstructed them, the Bureau would interfere, because the freedpeople were "under the guardianship of the Nation."[90]

Davis Tillson, for example, believed that protecting the freedpeople's economic rights was at the heart of his contract system and required white recognition of the freedpeople's claims to economic justice. "Start wrong, fail to secure for the freed people fair compensation for their labor," he once warned Commissioner Howard, "and the system of free labor, upon which almost every thing depends, will be a certain failure."[91] Although Tillson admitted that his objective was "to restore the supremacy of civil law," he understood that such a restoration must also "secure justice to all classes of citizens, irrespective of color or condition."[92]

Tillson believed that the people of the state had the right to enforce their own laws, but he had no problem claiming that the supremacy of the federal government allowed him to circumvent local institutions and laws if such actions were necessary for securing justice for the freedpeople at least until whites learned to enforce them in an equitable manner without distinctions made by race.[93] "This experiment is now being made under the inspection of Military Officers of the United States who are willing and anxious to do everything in their power to make it a complete success," Tillson informed a Miller County judge who was infringing on the rights of freedpeople to testify in his court. "The Government of the United States has not relinquished its right to interfere for the protection of the freed people whenever it shall become evident that such interference is necessary to secure justice."[94] Tillson always understood that even the most conciliatory gesture must be backed with the real possibility of the use of force, at least until both blacks and whites became accustomed to their new roles in postwar society.[95] Indeed, in February 1866, Andrew Johnson's veto of the Freedmen's Bureau bill caused Tillson to fear that further presidential interference would destroy what ability he had to secure justice for the freedpeople. If he could no longer protect the freedpeople, he informed Commissioner Howard, he would resign, because "it would be too mortifying to be endured."[96]

Throughout the Freedmen's Bureau's tenure in Georgia, its officers used familiar Yankee ideals to construct an intellectual context in which they tried to come to grips with the problems that confronted them. Their views were not static. Some, like Tillson, even changed their minds about which segment of the population would be more receptive to their message and adjusted their policies accordingly. But generally Yankee Bureau men believed that the agency as the protector of the freedpeople had the power to secure justice for the ex-slaves, whether in the cotton fields or in county courthouses.

That Bureau men had an ideological commitment to justice does not absolve them from being fallible and from confusing their decisions by indulging in poor judgment, jealousy, personal animosity, pettiness, or any of the other less endearing qualities that were indications of their humanity. Davis Tillson's clash with former Augusta Bureau agent John Emory Bryant during the spring of 1866 suggested as much. On this occasion the assistant commissioner revealed a malicious side that was irritated by Bryant's own poor judgment and political ambition.[97]

Tillson believed that Bryant was obstructing him in his duty, particularly when he, along with Augusta's Yankee schoolteachers, refused to follow his advice to postpone their April 28 memorial service for Union war dead. Bryant and the teachers had defiantly scheduled the event on the spur of the moment to take place two days after a Confederate memorial service at the same local cemetery. Tillson, concerned about provoking confrontations with white Georgians, believed this decision to be unwise. He disappointed Bryant and the teachers by asking them to delay their demonstration. When they refused to accept his advice, the assistant commissioner refused to recommend an armed guard to help them carry out their program.[98]

This confrontation ignited deeper resentments, for as Unionist Jacob R. Davis, Bryant's successor at the Augusta agency, noted, "No one at the time believed that such a great importance could have been given to so trifling an affair."[99] Regardless of Davis's opinion, Bryant raised the controversy to another level when he publicized Tillson's "disloyalty" in his paper, the *Loyal Georgian*. Northern newspapers and politicians paid attention to Bryant's claims that the assistant commissioner was pandering to the ex-rebels while defiling the memory of the Union war dead, an accusation that the assistant commissioner considered a serious insult to his five years of military service.[100]

Probably more annoying to the assistant commissioner was Bryant's move into political activism after he had left the Bureau. Tillson concluded that Bryant was attempting to position himself to challenge Tillson's authority among Augusta's freedpeople, which on one occasion embarrassed the assistant commissioner during a public meeting with officers on an inspection tour of the Bureau.[101] The bad blood led to Bryant's slanderous attacks on Tillson and Tillson's ill-advised attempt at censorship ostensibly to prevent the publication of a "threatening letter" directed at Tillson that might provoke violence. Tillson stationed soldiers at Bryant's office on the night of June 6 to carry out his intent, which led to more bad press for him in the North.[102]

In early July, Tillson vented his anger to George Whipple of the American Missionary Association, blaming Bryant for "nearly all the difficulty here." Tillson accused his nemesis of stirring up strife between the races "in order to obtain mean personal advantages."[103] Earlier, Tillson had warned Commissioner Howard that Bryant was "living off the negroes" by "collecting money in the colored churches for his private use."[104] Now the assistant commissioner explored his suspicions by looking closely at accusations that Bryant was engaged in questionable practices of fund-raising for his newspaper among the freed communities of the state, which indeed had prompted some complaints from the freedpeople themselves. He also denounced Bryant as a swindler in front of an assembled meeting of the Georgia Equal Rights Association.[105]

The tempers of the principals never cooled, and for the remainder of his tenure Tillson forbade his wife and his officers to associate with Bryant and his wife. In fact, he threatened to have Augusta subassistant commissioner W. F. White mustered out if he continued to disregard this request. In Tillson's mind, keeping company with Bryant degraded the Bureau.[106] This temperamental response to Bryant's challenge rightly embarrassed Tillson in the Northern press, among Washington politicians, and at Bureau headquarters, but it neither defined his views on Reconstruction nor exemplified how his administration implemented them. Bad judgment and pettiness in this particular instance did not define Tillson's Reconstruction ideology.

Some critics of the Bureau's policies have argued that Tillson and other Yankee Bureau men were simply helping the freedpeople exchange an old master for a new one—the Northern middle-class values of the victors—in their efforts to turn the ex-slaves into right-thinking Yankees. Perhaps. But given the ideological context of the agency's work, Bureau men believed that these northern ideals held out the best promise for securing liberty for the freedpeople. Hard work, discipline, frugality, and education in a cooperative environment could very well lead to economic advancement and an expanded role in the civil life of a society. What was problematical for these Bureau men was that they were not working in a cooperative environment. Their best intentions were weak weapons in the face of the active resistance posed by white Georgia.

# 2

## A Real Blessing to the Inhabitants of the State

THE

ORGANIZATION

OF THE

FREEDMEN'S

BUREAU

IN GEORGIA

Throughout his short tenure as Georgia's Bureau chief, Rufus Saxton believed that the best system of Freedmen's Bureau agents would result from selectively recruiting individuals who would be in full sympathy with the agency's charge.[1] Saxton desired a Freedmen's Bureau staffed with Yankees whom he could trust and who shared his own views about Reconstruction. Neither local citizens nor most army officers, he argued, would make good agents, given their questionable sympathies toward the freedpeople.[2] Despite these intentions, necessity in the form of a lack of funds for hiring Yankee agents determined policy and left the Georgia Bureau more a promise than a power in the critical early months of Reconstruction.

### The Uncertain Summer of 1865

Rufus Saxton initially preferred to use men who had been associated with his earlier assignments and therefore were familiar with his agenda for the freedpeople. For example, the Reverend William F. Eaton, a native of Maine and a minister associated with the Free Will Baptists, had been a missionary on the South Carolina coast where Saxton had commanded the Port Royal experiment. He first took up residence on the Georgia coast to assist Saxton in executing General Sherman's Special Field Orders, No. 15, and continued on with the Bureau.[3] Another Port Royal associate, John Emory Bryant, had earned Saxton's praise for his skill and bravery fighting with black troops under his command. After the war, Saxton appointed him to the position of "general superintendent of the freedmen" in the Augusta area; Bryant stayed on as the Bureau's officer in the city.[4] And shortly after the establishment of Sherman's coastal reservation, Saxton appointed as his representative in Savannah N. C. Dennett, the man who would become his Bureau agent in that city.[5]

On June 16, Saxton, recognizing a need for closer supervision of the expansion of the Georgia Bureau than he could personally give, appointed Brigadier General Edward A. Wild as acting assistant commissioner for an area west of the jurisdictions of the Augusta and Savannah agents.[6] Although Saxton had not worked with Wild before, he undoubtedly was aware of the officer's credentials, which would have pleased even the most radical of Reconstructionists. Of good New England stock, Wild had studied at Harvard and earned a medical degree in 1847 from Jefferson Medical College in Philadelphia. His war service won him a reputation for personal courage; his maimed hand and an empty sleeve offered testimony to his bravery at the battles of Seven Pines and South Mountain. More important, in 1863 he had helped recruit black troops first in Massachusetts and then in North Carolina. Wild's service record also provided ample evidence of his characteristic rashness and insubordination. Twice brought before courts-martial, once convicted, he had a public record of harsh and violent treatment of rebels, perhaps in part because of the physical reminders of their treachery that he carried with him.[7]

At the outset of his service with Saxton, Wild encountered an uncertainty about the scope of the Bureau's power that would trouble the agency throughout its existence in Georgia. After arriving in Augusta on June 30 to assume his duties as acting assistant commissioner, Wild decided not to move on to Macon as originally planned. He thought it best to wait until Saxton, who was absent from his command from late June into early August, conveyed to him the outcome of a conference with Howard. Wild expected that conference to clarify the extent of the agency's authority. Making this matter all the more imperative was the jurisdictional dispute in which he found John Emory Bryant embroiled with the army's Augusta post commander. Wild determined that he "had better fight it out on this line" and resolve the problem "before getting any deeper into the country." "In other words," he reasoned, "if I could not set up Capt. Bryant firmly at Augusta, then I could not set up another man at Macon, Atlanta, [or] Columbus."[8]

The Bureau won this particular round in what would become the recurring questioning of the nature of its authority. Nevertheless, despite Saxton's talk with Howard, as late as mid-August uncertainty remained.[9] Wild had arrived in Georgia without specific instructions, and when he did move out into the countryside, he approached the problems of Reconstruction from his own expansive interpretation of the Bureau's role.[10]

In mid-July, General Wild traveled into Wilkes County, not far from Augusta in the northeastern part of the state, to investigate charges that planters were still treating their freedpeople as slaves.[11] While at Washington, the county seat, the general seized several buildings, including the county courthouse, claiming them for the educational advancement of the freedpeople. Not stopping there, Wild topped off his vigorous confiscation campaign by appropriating the home of Wilkes County's famous native son, Confederate politician and soldier Robert Toombs, and he evicted Mrs. Toombs in the process.[12] Also, by his own admission, he tortured members of a Wilkes County family to gain information about some specie stolen from a cache of Confederate gold that had been shipped south from Virginia to avoid capture at the end of the war.[13] He next planned to seize all state property and perhaps Georgia's railroad system, because it had been used to aid and abet the rebellion.[14]

In August, even as evidence accumulated attesting to Wild's overzealousness, Saxton expressed his faith in his subordinate by increasing his jurisdiction to all of mainland Georgia except the Savannah district. As far as Saxton was concerned, Wild was an "earnest and energetic" man still deserving of his trust.[15] Yet Wild's dedication to a vigorous and punitive Reconstruction accomplished little by way of helping Saxton expand his Bureau into Georgia's interior. Because Saxton was Wild's superior, their fates were commingled, and blame for this failure, however undeserved, ultimately came to rest with the assistant commissioner.

In early August, there was no Bureau organization beyond Augusta and Savannah to supervise freedpeople's affairs at a critical time when ex-masters and ex-slaves were beginning to explore the boundaries of their new relationships.[16] As late as September 1, there were only three army officers serving as subassistant commissioners with headquarters at Albany, Columbus, and Macon.[17] Furthermore, Wild's inability to establish the Bureau at Atlanta at this time was a cause of embarrassment for Saxton. In early September a neighboring officer, Brigadier General Clinton B. Fisk, assistant commissioner of the Bureau in Tennessee and Kentucky, complained to O. O. Howard about the disorganized state of affairs there; he unsuccessfully proposed to annex the city to his jurisdiction.[18]

By the end of Saxton's tenure as commander of the Georgia Bureau, the agency was hardly much more of a presence. Outside the Sherman Reservation there were two agents, one at Augusta and another at Savannah, along with eight army officers on detached service with the Bureau scattered throughout the state. Within the Sherman Reservation, Saxton continued to rely on his adjutant general and former Port Royal associate, Captain Alexander P. Ketchum, to supervise three agents. Saxton had also been able to recruit two army surgeons to tend to the freedpeople's medical needs and to appoint a superintendent of education, who did not assume his duties until after the assistant commissioner was relieved of his Georgia command.[19]

Commissioner Howard later excused Saxton's failure to establish a strong Bureau presence in Georgia by explaining that a serious illness had forced the assistant commissioner to be absent in midsummer, which indeed deprived Wild of close supervision.[20] But Lieutenant Colonel Joseph S. Fullerton, at this time Howard's adjutant general, placed the blame for the Bureau's inauspicious start squarely on what he considered to be Saxton's inept shoulders, accusing him of sins of commission rather than omission. Fullerton, who was on an inspection tour of South Carolina and Georgia in July 1865, believed that Saxton "has but little administrative ability and he has too much to do, so but very little has been done." Furthermore, when Saxton did do something, it was the wrong thing. The assistant commissioner, according to Fullerton, ignored his "legitimate" Bureau duties while squandering his time making speeches to the freedpeople on the subject of suffrage and encouraging them to pursue "imaginary 'rights.'"[21]

Fullerton's judgment of Saxton's administrative abilities was unduly harsh and, in fact, unfair given the general's successful military experience. His unflattering assessment of the assistant commissioner's commitment to freedmen's rights originated more in his own conservative perception of the Bureau's task than in Saxton's pronouncements to the freedpeople, which generally balanced discussions of the privileges of freedom with its accompanying obligations. Furthermore, Fullerton was influenced by hostile reports he received from the military authorities. The army's views of Saxton's Bureau were tainted by an increasingly strained relationship between the two agencies of Reconstruction, a most unfortunate situation because the army was the source to which Saxton had to turn to solve his staffing problems.[22]

Although Saxton preferred known quantities for his agents, he did not have at his disposal congressional appropriations for hiring the civilians who would fit his requirements.[23] He urged Howard to have the politicians correct this situation, but nothing changed during his tenure. He also came to the conclusion that "to do the work that is required, I need a small army." Consequently, despite their reservations, both he and Wild, who also preferred to hire good Yankees, were sufficiently realistic to understand that their best hope for obtaining suitable personnel remained the occupying army.[24] This approach required a cooperative relationship with the military commander of the department that failed to last beyond the first weeks of Major General James B. Steedman's tour of duty.

The Georgia Bureau had every reason to expect assistance from Steedman, the former printer and Ohio Democratic legislator who at the end of June assumed command of the Department of Georgia.[25] Not only had the congressional legislation that established the Bureau authorized the army to detail officers to the agency from their regular duties, but Steedman upon arrival at his new post gave the impression that he was sympathetic to the freedpeople. Furthermore, his own orders, which were in harmony with the Bureau's charge, indicated his willingness to assist the Freedmen's Bureau.[26]

Indeed, Steedman's relations with the Bureau were at first quite cordial. In mid-July, the Reverend Mansfield French, Saxton's unofficial agent-at-large in Georgia, praised Steedman's "generous support" of the Bureau after the general had taken a "noble stand" in settling the jurisdictional dispute between Bryant and the Augusta post commander.[27] Even as late as mid-July, General Wild was confident of Steedman's willingness to help the Bureau help the freedpeople.[28] However, in August after Saxton returned from his leave, the assistant commissioner found Steedman unreceptive to his requests for officers to serve on detached service with the Bureau or to act as Bureau officials while they continued to perform their military duties primarily because of Steedman's low opinion of the Georgia agency.[29]

Certainly, a number of factors were at work here. Steedman had staffing problems of his own because of the rapid muster out of personnel. He also believed the alternative to detaching men for exclusive Bureau service, which was to have his officers answer to both him and Saxton, to be impracticable. Furthermore, Wild found it difficult to convince competent army officers who remained on duty in Georgia to volunteer for Bureau service; many of them were less than enthusiastic about being detailed to the agency, finding the assignment to be detrimental to their military careers, too taxing a job, or simply a disagreeable duty.[30] Steedman's support of Wild's efforts might have encouraged his officers to shed their reluctance; however, he apparently had become convinced that sharing his scarce resources with an organization supervised by Wild, a man he considered to be lacking in judgment and unfit for duty, would not be a productive use of his already inadequate command.[31]

During Saxton's absence, problems quickly arose between Steedman and the Bureau's most aggressive representatives on the Georgia mainland, Bryant and

Wild. Steedman perceived these officials to be overstepping the authority that he believed they could legitimately exercise. Steedman assumed that the Bureau had the right to supervise freedmen's affairs to the extent that the agency was the primary adjudicator of matters concerning work. Other matters became the province of the Bureau, as far as Steedman was concerned, only in areas where military tribunals and civilian courts were lacking or where civilian courts failed to give the freedpeople justice. Steedman made these views clear to Wild shortly after the Bureau official had arrived in the state, also noting that he believed that the agency had no authority to become involved in matters concerning abandoned or confiscated property other than as the executor of military or judicial decisions.[32] Wild chose to ignore Steedman, challenging the legality of the military's plans for returning property within the Sherman Reservation to its white owners.[33]

Despite his initially favorable dealings with the Augusta Bureau, Steedman closed Bryant's freedmen's court of claims ostensibly because the agent was overreaching the prescribed limits of Bureau authority by adjudicating criminal matters.[34] Consequently, Bryant found it impossible for the Bureau to work harmoniously with army commanders "unless they [the Bureau] yield everything to the military." "Men love power," he complained, and he presciently warned Saxton, "The military authorities will swallow up the Bureau if possible."[35]

General Wild's activities in Wilkes County, which circumvented Steedman's presumed limits of the Bureau's power, did little to encourage the department commander's confidence in him or the agency. Furthermore, Wild's enthusiasm, which led him to appoint army officers to supervise Bureau affairs in Columbus and Albany without the approval of the military, gave Steedman the impression that he was trying to do the department commander's job. In August, Steedman complained to Fullerton that Wild was playing hell in Georgia. Only his respect for Howard and his desire not to disgrace the Bureau kept Steedman from arresting Saxton's acting assistant commissioner. To make matters worse, Fullerton's own efforts to educate General Wild in the limits of his authority, although somewhat successful, left him dubious about the general's ability to carry out his duties. "But there is no telling what he may do," he warned Commissioner Howard. "I really believe that he is a little crazy." In the end, Fullerton offered a damning assessment of the Georgia Bureau. "But little has been done by the agent of the Bureau in Georgia," he concluded, "and that little had better not have been done for it has given us a bad name with all classes of persons in the state, civil & military."[36] A month later, Howard, realizing Wild had done more harm than good, ordered his removal.[37]

In large part because of the tension between the agency and the army, Steedman spared only a handful of officers for Bureau duty, preferring to have his provost marshals supervise the freedpeople until Saxton established his own network of subordinates or until the state reorganized its civil courts. Steedman now believed that it was best to keep the freedpeople's affairs under his jurisdiction until the Bureau was fully operational in Georgia.[38] But this approach would have mixed results because the confusion that characterized Reconstruction in the state during the summer of 1865 demanded a group of individuals dedicated to this singular task.

Army officers were concerned first with maintaining order in a very disorderly state, not with supervising the establishment of new social and economic systems. Furthermore, as Saxton had worried, they might not be overly concerned with the freedpeople's rights and would at least need close supervision from the Bureau. In July 1865, as if to support Saxton's concerns, David Young reported to the American Missionary Association that the freedpeople of Burke County were plagued not only with tyrannical ex-masters but also with military authorities who had "but little sympathy towards them."[39] Finally, as future Bureau officers and agents would learn, an army officer also looking after freedmen's affairs could very well be consumed by the assignment, which, as Carl Schurz determined on his inspection tour of Georgia in August 1865, "will require all his time and will leave him not a minute for other business."[40]

Even where local commanders and provost marshals acted in good faith, they needed better direction in their duties than the military department provided. By early September 1865, a frustrated Colonel William Kimball had been stationed at Blackshear in Pierce County for nearly three months and had become thoroughly confused about how to deal with the freedpeople. He supervised a jurisdiction in the military department that included sixteen counties. Like a good soldier, he had tried to do his duty by conforming to all regulations. Unfortunately, the orders that he had "accidently" received from various commanders in Georgia and Florida were "so *conflicting*" that he could not rely on them for direction. He feared the freedpeople's condition would be much worse, however, with the expected withdrawal of his regiment, and he urged O. O. Howard to have the Bureau take up the responsibilities that were properly its own.[41]

Needless to say, Steedman's policy decision essentially guaranteed Saxton's failure to establish at least the framework for a fuller Bureau presence in Georgia. It would be impossible for the assistant commissioner to make real progress in organizing a viable agency without additional congressional funding or a change of heart about using native white Georgians. No wonder Saxton hoped Howard would understand his predicament so that he "may not be held responsible for any seeming failures."[42]

Complicating matters for Saxton were the rumors circulating in mid-August, which turned out to be true, that Howard would soon relieve him of his Georgia duties and give the state its own assistant commissioner.[43] Howard undoubtedly realized that a state as large and as significant as Georgia deserved the undivided attention of its own Bureau chief. At first he hesitated to appoint an independent assistant commissioner, because the Bureau authorization act limited the agency to only ten state officers.[44] However, in early August, reports of General Wild's activities confirmed the necessity of having a man of "common practical sense" in complete charge of the state. Howard found that quality in Davis Tillson, "a good man for Georgia," according to Major General George Thomas.[45] On August 31, the commissioner directed Tillson's commander, Clinton B. Fisk, to relieve him of his duties with the Bureau in Tennessee, explaining, "I wish to give him a state."[46]

## The Establishment of the Bureau

On September 22, 1865, Davis Tillson officially assumed command of the Georgia Bureau at his headquarters city of Augusta, where he found no real organization and much hostility toward the agency among white Georgians.[47] Consequently, the new assistant commissioner became determined to organize the Bureau "in such a shape that it will work promptly and efficiently and prove a real blessing to the inhabitants of the State both black and white."[48] To fulfill this purpose, he had to expand as rapidly as possible Saxton's small contingent of ten field officers now stationed within Tillson's command, eight of whom were on detached service from the army and subject to being mustered out on short notice.[49]

As had Saxton before him, Tillson understandably turned to officers he knew and trusted to assist him with this task. Major William Gray, for example, became Tillson's inspector general, an important office that would review the service of and deal with complaints about the Bureau's field agents. Before his Georgia assignment, Gray had served as an officer with the First United States Colored Heavy Artillery, which Tillson had organized, and had been a member of Tillson's staff when he had been in charge of the Bureau's western Tennessee district.[50] Captain William W. Deane, Tillson's right-hand man and adjutant general for the Georgia Bureau, had also served the general in that capacity when Tillson was a divisional commander and a Bureau superintendent.[51]

Tillson completed the selection of his staff officers in early October and immediately began to use them to help compensate for the lack of information left to him by his predecessor. Throughout October and November, his adjutant general, quartermaster, inspector general, chief surgeon, and superintendent of education traveled around the state, busily surveying the extent and progress of Reconstruction in Georgia.[52] At the same time, the assistant commissioner visited various locations within his new jurisdiction to explain the Bureau's purpose and make his own observations.[53] One of those stops was the state capital, Milledgeville, where he publicly proposed his plan for implementing a grassroots, Bureau-supervised Reconstruction in every county of the state, employing local residents as his agents. Despite the potential for problems, Tillson concluded that local leaders—justices of the peace, court ordinaries, and prominent citizens—would act in the best interests of all concerned.[54] It was among this group of Georgians that Tillson assumed he would find "high minded, honorable men—who had sufficient manly pride and courage to disregard the prejudice of the people and do justice to all men irrespective of condition or color."[55]

Realizing that the Bureau eventually would "give place to the authority of the state," Commissioner Howard cautiously approved Tillson's proposed use of native white agents as a means to "test the spirit of the civil officers."[56] On October 27, 1865, after first receiving the endorsement of Georgia's provisional governor, James Johnson, Tillson presented his plan to delegates at the state constitutional convention then in session at Milledgeville. The assistant commissioner did not officially need their approval or support, but he considered this a wise and pragmatic gesture. If his agents acted with the convention's endorsement and thus cloaked themselves in the authority of the provisional state government as well as the federal government, they would command a legitimacy, Tillson optimistically believed, that the local courts could not disregard. Indeed, because Tillson expected to appoint men who had served as inferior court justices, justices of the peace, and ordinaries, he expected harmony to exist between his men and sitting local officials.[57]

Davis Tillson's views about who should represent the Bureau at the local level were quite different from his predecessor's, but he did not develop his policy to purge the agency of Saxton's handful of Yankee appointees. N. C. Dennett,

Saxton's Savannah agent, for example, requested a leave of absence, and Tillson replaced him in October 1865. William Tiffany, Saxton's Ogeechee District agent, could no longer stand the summer weather and asked to be relieved in November 1865. Also, it was Saxton who recognized Tillson's right to choose his own agents when he discharged William F. Eaton and Tunis G. Campbell in early 1866 after Tillson assumed control of the coastal reservation. Sapelo Island's Eaton, however, continued to serve as an agent through most of Tillson's tenure until he chose to resign. Tillson also allowed Campbell to continue to function as an agent until he removed him in May 1866 when it became clear that the agent would not cooperate with federal policy concerning the restoration of the Sherman Reservation land grants. Earlier in December 1865, Tillson had removed John Emory Bryant, possibly because he could not keep a paid agent on his books, but more likely because Saxton's Augusta agent had a bad relationship with the Georgia district's military officers.[58] The assistant commissioner, however, replaced him with a New Jersey–born ironclad Georgia Unionist, Jacob R. Davis, who remained with the Bureau into April 1868 and became a Republican politician.[59] Tillson, in fact, appointed several Georgia Unionists and fellow veterans to staff local agencies, but his vision of Reconstruction required that he take a chance on the native agents who came to make up the overwhelming majority of his men.[60]

After the adjournment of the convention, the delegates dispersed to implement this new experiment in self-reconstruction and consulted with their constituents in the selection of their new Freedmen's Bureau agents.[61] Tillson found the response encouraging.[62] One delegate assured Tillson that the use of civilian agents "will produce a formidable impression upon the minds of the citizens of this state generally."[63] Two others informed him, "Your proposition to appoint a citizen to the agency of the Bureau in the various counties of the State met our hearty approval. Upon our return to Newton County, we find our citizens inclined to meet in good faith the new and as yet untried experiment in hired labor."[64] Tillson's message at the convention so impressed one delegate that he sang his praises to Andrew Johnson, informing the president that he "endorse[d] every word."[65]

No doubt these Georgians were so kindly disposed to Tillson's plan because they believed that it was "fortunate for the country that these things are being turned over to Southern men and men who understand something of the Negro character," an attitude that unfortunately would hurt Tillson's operations in the future.[66] Still, the assistant commissioner believed that white Georgians must be brought into the Reconstruction process. Based on the recommendations that these delegates sent to him, as well as petitions from their communities, Tillson was able to confirm his initial selection of citizen agents on the first day of December, only a month after the Georgia constitutional convention had approved his plan.[67] Over the next four months, he appointed 194 civilians to agencies throughout the state.[68]

Because Tillson expected nominees for Bureau agencies to be, as one reference noted, "men of highest social position and intelligence,"[69] he ended up appointing individuals who had enjoyed antebellum wealth, slave property, and good social standing among their peers. Thomas H. Blount and William Morris, who became agents in Burke County, were among their county's largest slaveholders before the war, with Blount owning forty-one slaves and Morris fifty.[70] Park E. Arnold enjoyed a similar position in Coweta County, where he had been one of the four largest slave owners before he lost his one hundred chattels to emancipation.[71] And although Benjamin F. Willis could not have matched the holdings of a planter like Arnold, he had been among the larger slaveholders residing in Franklin County.[72] Indeed, a significant number of the 252 agents appointed by Tillson could probably trace their community standing back to their prewar wealth in property and slaves.[73]

The longtime residency of a number of these agents also underscored the desire of citizens to have familiar individuals involved in what they considered to be a chancey experiment. H. D. Williams, who became the agent of Harris County in December 1865, had resided for thirty years within the boundaries of his new jurisdiction. More significantly, both George N. Forbes and Samuel Crawford had held public office for twenty years before accepting Bureau agencies.[74]

Because Tillson had requested such nominations, a record of public service often accompanied the recommendations of other agents. Lewis Burwell of Floyd County, "a conservative during the war," had been an inferior court judge for four years, and Adam Robinson of Gwinnet County, a "moral and popular man" despite his "violent" opposition to secession, had been a state legislator, justice of the peace, and judge of the inferior court.[75] To be sure, justices of the peace, prime candidates for Tillson's agencies, were not always the wealthiest men or the most prominent citizens of the state. However, they were respected by their neighbors and probably had good connections with the local squirearchy. Micajah Jones, a sixty-year-old blacksmith and longtime justice of the peace, for example, was poor "but has the character of being a just and upright man," or so vouched his kinsman Alexander H. Stephens.[76]

Those Georgians who nominated Lewis Burwell and Adam Robinson not only pointed out their candidates' records of community service but made it clear to the assistant commissioner that their nominees had not been rabid secessionists. The committee that nominated James Beland also belabored this point. Beland, a man "of good business and moral habits," Newton County petitioners assured Tillson, "was not actively engaged in the late rebel[l]ion neither in bringing it on, nor in prosecuting it after commencing."[77] The convention delegates from Clay County who nominated Seaborn McLenden did not make the same claim about their candidate, but they assured Tillson that their man was a loyal citizen, he having "long since subscribed to the oath of Amnesty."[78]

Such nominations offered dubious if any evidence of the agents' potential to do right by the freedpeople; those communities or individuals who pursued that tack usually went on about their candidates' paternalism or "humane & just . . . dealings with all classes."[79] They do suggest, however, that some Georgia communities might have gone out of their way to find individuals who appeared to be more acceptable to the Yankees because of their reluctance to support secession, their conditional acceptance of the Confederacy, or their apparent acquiescence to defeat. No matter what their reasons for making this effort, they encouraged the assistant commissioner's optimism and initial belief in the reasonableness of the "better sort" who understood that white Georgians also had a vested interest in making Reconstruction work.[80]

Obviously, Tillson's approach to building his Bureau meant that the freedpeople would not have much to say about whom the agency would appoint to supervise the transition to free labor. Tillson suggested that white Georgians consult with the "more intelligent" freedmen of their counties before making recommendations for agencies.[81] But it would have been the rare ex-slave who made his dissenting voice heard at the courthouse meetings often used to nominate agents. Nevertheless, as the freedpeople of Catoosa County learned, the assistant commissioner was willing to listen to the recommendations of ex-slaves that did reach him. Tillson appointed John M. Combs to an agency in their county less than two weeks after he received their petition putting Combs's name before him.[82] The freedpeople of Clarke County also had reason to appreciate the assistant commissioner's attention when it appeared that the worst of the old order was about to take charge of their agency.

In late November 1865, the white citizens of Clarke County nominated William H. Dorsey for a Bureau agency. Before forwarding the recommendation to Tillson, Lieutenant Colonel Homer B. Sprague, the subassistant commissioner stationed at Athens, consulted with the local freedpeople. "Mr. Dorsay [*sic*] is no friend of the Freedmen," replied Madison Davis, a future state legislator, and other black community leaders. Dorsey had been a slave trader and an overbearing marshal in Athens where "it was his chief delight to defraud the Colored Citizens while in servitude." The freedpeople had no desire to see the Bureau give him more power over their lives, and they suggested James Lyle in his stead. Tillson appointed Lyle, not Dorsey, to the Clarke County agency.[83]

Civilian agents became the Georgia freedpeople's first recourse for settling disputes with their white neighbors, but the power allocated to those agents appeared to circumscribe their actions from the start. The actual jurisdiction of Tillson's civilian agents was similar to that of minor county officials. Tillson limited the agents' individual actions to cases between freedpeople and whites involving sums not exceeding fifty dollars, exclusive of interest, or punishment for offenses committed by or against freedpeople not exceeding a fifty dollar fine or a thirty-day hard labor jail term. For more serious cases, the litigants were to select one disinterested person each to sit in judgment with the agent. Such a tribunal could adjudicate cases in which the sum involved did not exceed one hundred dollars or the possible sentence for an offense did not exceed a fine of one hundred fifty dollars or imprisonment at hard labor for sixty days. Most important, Tillson authorized the three-man panel to settle all contract disputes.

Tillson, in keeping with his philosophy of Reconstruction, advised his agents to present important cases to the civil courts on the condition that the magistrates allow the testimony of the freedpeople. If the civil authorities refused to concede this right to the freedpeople, the agents were to "request" that the magistrates involved discontinue the hearing and turn the case over to the military. If they refused this request, the agents were to contact the nearest Bureau or army officer to suspend any judgment rendered. Furthermore, agents were to see that civil courts did not impose any cruel or unusual punishments—specifically whipping—upon the freedpeople. Punishment for crime, Tillson advised, must be administered without distinction of color. For all of this, the agents were to receive fees comparable to those received by justices of the peace, ordinaries, and other county officers for similar services. Also, agents were permitted to charge one dollar for the first ten persons covered by a supervised labor contract and an additional ten cents for each individual over that number.[84]

If the authority of Tillson's agents appeared insignificant, it was sufficient to keep them at the heart of the Reconstruction process in towns and counties throughout the state. The dollar amounts of the cases agents could initially adjudicate were large enough to cover a majority of the freedpeople's common complaints. More important than the specific jurisdiction, however, was the general charge that the assistant commissioner issued to his appointees, which placed the agents' duty within a larger context that reflected the spirit of the Bureau's purpose. The agents were to protect the ex-slaves "in their freedom; in the security of their labor, and the peaceable enjoyment of the fruits thereof; and in their right to testifying in cases where freedmen are parties interested."[85] In other words, although these men were arbitrators, mediators, and observers, always watching over the shoulders of Georgia's civil authorities, they were in fact the eyes and ears of Reconstruction, the nation's first line of defense in its efforts to protect the freedpeople's rights. How well they performed their duties would certainly influence the definition of the freedpeople's new status.

Tillson was aware of this important relationship between his Bureau's performance and the lasting impact of Reconstruction. Consequently, his initial optimism concerning white Georgia's acceptance of his Bureau and Reconstruction did not blind him to the fact that his civilian agents would need guidance. He recruited several army officers, Homer Sprague among them, to act as his subassistant commissioners to watch over the more numerous county-level agents, usually with the assistance of a noncommissioned officer and a few enlisted men.[86]

Sprague, the post commander at Athens, volunteered for Bureau duty after meeting Tillson and listening to his views. General Steedman allowed Sprague to act as a Bureau officer in addition to his regular military duties, which suggests that Steedman's earlier objections to such arrangements when proposed by Saxton were the consequences of personal prejudices as much as practical concerns. Indeed, Tillson happily reported that the general "grants all my requests and shows a disposition to aid me."[87] However, rapid demobilization and the unwillingness of the government to keep officers on duty with the Bureau after their units had been mustered out of the service kept the army an unreliable source of men. In April 1866, for example, the muster out of troops deprived Tillson of six officers, half of the subassistant commissioners at his disposal.[88]

To avoid future disruptions, Tillson eventually relied on Veteran Reserve Corps officers such as Captain George T. Crabtree, a fellow native of Rockland, Maine, who had been severely wounded during the war, to fill these positions. This unit, formerly known as the Invalid Corps, was an organization of war-disabled but still capable army men. Although the second Bureau law of July

1866 stabilized the situation by authorizing the secretary of war to keep officers on duty with the agency after their regiments were mustered out, the Georgia Bureau continued to rely on the Veteran Reserve Corps. Tillson never believed that he had enough of these men on duty, but by December 1866, he supervised twelve officers from the Corps stationed in the larger cities throughout the state.[89] This lack of manpower influenced the way Tillson structured the Bureau.

Tillson did not set up a rigidly hierarchical chain of command once he had begun to recruit his officers because he believed that he did not have the necessary manpower at his disposal to establish the extensive network of subassistant commissioners needed for the supervision of the citizen agents. The agents were "to consult, advise, and act in concert with the nearest officer of the bureau in this state," but they were not under the direct command of subassistant commissioners. They were subject only to orders originating at Tillson's headquarters. At best, the agents were to comply with "requests" from the officers as a matter of courtesy.[90]

The lack of hierarchy in the Georgia Bureau would leave Tillson open to criticism in the future. From the outset the Washington Bureau headquarters believed that civilian agents needed close supervision, something that Tillson's Bureau failed to provide.[91] Also, the informal relationship between the subassistant commissioners and agents caused some confusion within the Georgia command.[92] However, the assistant commissioner did not view his organization as beyond alteration. In fact, he hoped for changes that would strengthen his hand in pursuing justice, which indicated that although he believed white Georgians must accept Reconstruction for it to be a success, he was not above using more than moral suasion to help them reach that point.

On December 20, 1865, Tillson forwarded to Howard what amounted to a plan for the establishment of Military Reconstruction in the South in which the Bureau would play a prominent role.[93] Although the plan was fairly much a representation of his own state organization, it also indicated that Tillson hoped to have more military officers in his command to allow him to place agents directly under their control to increase the efficiency of the agency. Furthermore, although he expected to give citizens the opportunity to administer justice under the supervision of the federal authorities, his proposed bill provided for the continuation of military tribunals to consider matters beyond the authority of his agents as well as the power to remove civilian officials who failed to perform their obligations in a just way.

Tillson understood that by emphasizing the role of military instead of civilian power to enforce Reconstruction policy he was deviating "from the theory of our Government." Nevertheless, he reasoned that theories must be shaped by reality. "No man who has had sufficient opportunities for observation will for a moment assert that the Bureau organized upon a purely civil basis could accomplish its object or exert any great or controlling influence," he explained to Commissioner Howard. "It would certainly be found inefficient, useless and impotent." And although there were Georgians who were well disposed to see justice done to the freedpeople, there were many others who were not. Consequently, the government needed to keep troops in the state because "these people ought to have for a time at least the experience and education of military law, they ought to be taught some regard for the law and . . . order, otherwise loyal white men to say nothing of negroes, would find it extremely unpleasant living South."[94]

Tillson never received permission to reorganize the Bureau according to his plan. In fact, the agency's authority became somewhat more restricted in the spring of 1866. In March the Georgia legislature passed a series of laws defining the rights of the state's freedpeople.[95] As a result, the army department commander, recognizing the progress of the legislature, issued an order that limited military authority and consequently the Bureau's power to use the military.[96] In April, the assistant commissioner ordered agents to turn over all cases beyond their jurisdiction to civilian courts, avoiding the three-man panels, although they continued to observe procedures to make certain that the courts administered impartial justice.[97] For some white Georgians, the legislation signaled the end of the Bureau's constitutional legitimacy, a signal confirmed in their minds by actions of the highest executive authority in the land.[98]

At about the same time as the passage of Georgia's legislation, Washington politics intruded into Tillson's routine, causing confusion and hurting the Bureau's ability to fulfill its purpose. The fact that the agency required renewal in 1866 and that Andrew Johnson, who had already established a record of leniency toward the South, successfully delayed that renewal had an impact on the Bureau's authority in Georgia. His February 1866 veto of the Bureau bill, which embodied his conservative constitutionalism as well as his racism, made it clear that he believed military authority had no place in the peacetime South.[99]

On April 2, 1866, President Johnson further aggravated the problems facing Tillson when he declared the insurrection subdued and again attacked the

Bureau and military power in the South. Undoubtedly complicating matters was the April 3 Supreme Court decision concerning the Milligan case, which confirmed the jurisdiction of civil courts and the rights of citizens to be tried in them where they were functioning to the exclusion of military tribunals except in areas actually plagued by war.[100]

Because the presidential proclamation and the court decision followed so closely the enactment of the March legislation and Tillson's own tentative recognition of civil authority, white Georgians celebrated the end of "official insolence" and the "satrapy of the sword," as well as the right to reclaim control of their affairs without any regard for Bureau policy.[101] Reports from Tillson's officers and agents confirmed the ill effects of the president's premature proclamation. Not only was Subassistant Commissioner F. A. H. Gaebel now confused about the Bureau's status, but the whites within his southwest Georgia jurisdiction believed that they had "the right to do as [they] pleased," thanks to the president.[102] Joseph Taylor, the agent in Randolph County, found that the president's proclamation "aroused the *vindictive feelings* of the South and induced them to believe that they . . . could annihilate the Freedmen's Bureau and take the management of business into their own hands."[103] Much to Tillson's dismay, the proclamation also influenced General John Brannan, military department commander to whom Tillson had to turn for troops to enforce his orders. Brannan now did not feel competent to arrest civilians.[104]

In less than two weeks, Commissioner Howard and President Johnson clarified the actual intent of the proclamation. Howard also reaffirmed Tillson's power to act in the interest of the freedpeople, and Governor Charles Jenkins issued a proclamation making Georgians aware of the Bureau's continued authority.[105] Tillson could also take heart in the actions of Congress, which in April passed the Civil Rights Act, giving the Bureau the power to pull cases from Georgia's courts into federal courts, and later, in July, passed the second Bureau law, restoring the threat of the use of military tribunals.[106] Furthermore, in May, the assistant commissioner assumed the duties of military commander of the District of Georgia, a change that gave him greater authority for dispatching troops in response to the needs and duties of the Georgia Bureau.[107] This increase in his authority was a clear sign that the joyful but unreconstructed citizens were very wrong about the Bureau's demise.[108] As if these developments did not send a strong enough message to white Georgians, on July 6, Ulysses S. Grant issued General Orders, No. 44, which gave Tillson as an army commander the authority to arrest and detain for trial lawbreakers who avoided justice at the hands of the civil officials.[109]

Despite these indications, the damage was done and white Georgians across the state continued to believe what they wished about the Bureau. On April 28, agent Taylor, again blaming the presidential proclamation, reported a *"fanatical disposition* on the part of the citizens to disregard the authority of the Freedmen's Bureau." In May, Henry County residents assumed that the Bureau "will be done away with soon." And as late as December 1866, the prevailing opinion in places like Taylor County was that the president's proclamation had "deprived the Bureau of *all* jurisdiction whatever."[110]

Undoubtedly, white Georgians remained optimistic and defiant because further conflict between Howard and the president along with another presidential peace proclamation issued in August continued to sow confusion over the exact extent of the Bureau's authority.[111] More immediate and reassuring to white Georgians, however, was an inspection tour begun in April 1866 sponsored by the president and conducted by James B. Steedman and Joseph S. Fullerton, a tour that Howard believed was designed "with the armed purpose of ruining" him. He was correct. President Johnson, desiring to advance his own Reconstruction agenda, wished to stop all congressional efforts to strengthen the Bureau by discrediting it in the eyes of the nation.[112]

During the spring and summer of 1866, Steedman, Tillson's former Georgia associate, and Fullerton, Howard's former subordinate, chipped away at the Bureau's credibility. In late May, for example, Herschel V. Johnson expressed his pleasure over the fact that Steedman had reassured him that the Democratic Party in "the Northern states will cordially coalesce with the Conservative republicans and sustain Johnson."[113] Reports from and about Steedman and Fullerton published in local and Northern newspapers further drew into question the Bureau's authority by challenging even the limited judicial power that agents attempted to exercise, by criticizing the contract system in which Tillson placed so much faith, and by accusing officers of malfeasance.[114] Steedman and Fullerton confirmed the impression of white Georgians who believed that the Bureau "had been a swindling scheme"; others drew the conclusion that "they can now do as they please" because the Bureau "is done away with."[115] Tillson did his best to show these Georgians that the Bureau still had a purpose and some power to fulfill it.

Even as Tillson modified what his agents and officers could do and even as he faced white Georgians who believed that his men could do nothing, the assistant commissioner held to his general philosophy of Reconstruction and expected his men to do the same. Tillson continued to believe that the Bureau was a power in Georgia and that his agents could continue to function within

their limited area of authority as they had done from the beginning of his administration. He advised his subordinates to turn over all cases that could not
be compromised to civil authorities to give them the opportunity to prove
themselves worthy of the trust of the federal government and the freedpeople
before the Bureau interfered with the judicial process, but he never gave up his
belief that his Bureau, as a representative of the federal government, could intervene to correct injustices.[116]

Although Tillson was reluctant to revive the regular use of the three-man tribunals as a substitute for civil justice, he did not hesitate to advise his subordinates to remind white Georgians of the Bureau's role in the state's continuing
reconstruction when they believed that civilian courts failed to give freedpeople
justice. In November, he advised an agent to solve nettlesome labor problems
between employers and freedpeople in Randolph County by resorting to the
*voluntary* use of a three-man board of referees. If the planters refused to participate in this process, "you will arrest them and if released by writs of Habeas
Corpus, rearrest them and continue to do so until such time as they will meet a
just settlement with the Freedpeople."[117]

There obviously remained limits to Tillson's willingness to allow Georgia's
civil government to function without reference to his own authority. In July
1866, for example, Rome subassistant commissioner Carlos A. de la Mesa informed Tillson that a planter's lawyers told him to ignore the Bureau because
the Civil Rights Act had "done away with all [Bureau] authority." The assistant
commissioner made it clear that the attorneys were wrong. Although he now
advised de la Mesa to present a specific case involving a freedman to the local
authorities, he authorized the subassistant commissioner to step in and settle
the case at the point where civil law failed to do justice to the freedman. Tillson
also promised him military power to enforce his decision and in November
gave him the authority to arrest and imprison an individual without first con-
tacting the civil authorities.[118] On other occasions and as late as the end of his
relationship with the Bureau, Tillson referred to Grant's General Orders, No. 44,
and authorized his men to use military force to arrest individuals who perpetrated crimes against the freedpeople. They could then turn the prisoners over
to the civil authorities for trial or hold them until the courts were willing to pursue justice.[119]

By the end of October 1866, Tillson, concerned about the extent of the Bureau's ability to enforce the contract settlement decisions of its agents and
officers, advised Howard to have Congress clarify and strengthen the agency's

judicial authority, lest the civil authorities continue to ignore his men.[120] However, he did not assume that his agents and officers were now powerless in the pursuit of their duties. In December, for example, Tillson authorized Major John Leonard, his subassistant commissioner at Atlanta, to arrest all whites who were implicated in the murder of three freedpeople and hold them until the civil authorities were willing to bring them to trial.[121] He also authorized other subordinates to arrest an employer to force a contract settlement, to hold an alleged white criminal until the civil authorities took action in the case, to use force to compel an employer to give up a freedwoman's property, and to advise a freedwoman in the pursuit of a case against the white father of her child.[122] Tillson had not built an agency to see it languish as he himself prepared to leave the military for civilian life.

Even as Tillson attempted to establish the Bureau on firm ground, he, like Saxton before him, found himself subjected to censure.[123] As early as the summer of 1866, there were indications that Howard might require Tillson to reorganize the Georgia Bureau because of the criticism leveled by Generals Steedman and Fullerton. Their reports printed in Northern newspapers were filled with allegations which suggested that the Bureau was in need of reform.[124] But if the summer brought criticism, it also brought opportunity in the passage on July 13 of the Army Appropriations Act, which for the first time assigned the Bureau funds for hiring agents, and on July 16 of the law to extend the life of the Bureau for an additional two years. Howard convened a commission, which included Davis Tillson, to address the criticism of the agency and to explore the opportunities for making the Bureau more effective.[125]

This drive for greater efficiency, combined with the opportunities presented by the new legislation, should have been sufficient to prompt alterations in the Bureau's organization in Georgia. Nothing came of it during the remainder of 1866, probably because Tillson, who moved his headquarters to Savannah at the end of October, was deeply involved with the problematic duty of restoring the freedpeople's Sherman Reservation to white claimants.[126] The real impetus for change in Georgia, however, was the critical December 1866 report of F. D. Sewall.

Sewall, Howard's inspector general, drew the commissioner's attention to the lack of hierarchy and the use of native agents in Georgia with charges that went beyond inefficiency. His observations led him to conclude that Tillson's "administration is not altogether satisfactory to the colored people, and I think so far as I have seen, they have some cause for complaint."[127] Civilian agents, Sewall reported, received their appointments based on recommendations from their neighbors without any special vetting of "their political antecedents and loyalty to the government." In his opinion, such men needed closer supervision than that offered by Tillson because not all were doing a good job.

Although Tillson had done his best to guard against abuses, his efforts had not impressed Sewall. In fact, there were some glaring examples of incompetent agents that marred the Georgia Bureau's record. The circumstances, according to the inspector general, demanded a complete reorganization—"an entirely new system"—which would place a reduced number of truly loyal agents under the direct control of the Yankee officers acting as subassistant commissioners.[128] The opportunity to implement these changes came after Tillson's departure.

## The Reorganization of the Bureau

Caleb Sibley, a man accustomed to working within the bureaucratic confines of the military's chain of command for over thirty years, recognized the validity of Sewall's criticism. Within a few weeks of assuming command in January 1867, he discovered that it was "inconvenient and unsatisfactory" to supervise agents from his headquarters. To ease the burden, Sibley divided the state into ten subdistricts and placed his civilian agents directly under the command of the ten army officers who were his subassistant commissioners. The arrangement, he hoped, would free his office of "trifling and unimportant" routine and allow it to maintain better control over the entire organization.[129]

Initially, the change was not a radical one as far as personnel was concerned. In February 1867, seven of Sibley's ten subassistant commissioners had served under Tillson. All those veteran Bureau officers remained on duty throughout the summer, and it was only with the coming of the fall that they began to leave the agency's service. Likewise, several members of Tillson's headquarters staff remained on duty into the summer, helping Sibley become acquainted with his new duties; however, John R. Lewis joined the Georgia Bureau as inspector general shortly after Sibley's appointment.[130] Lewis's Tennessee service had not only convinced him that education was the key to the freedpeople's future. It also led him to conclude that a fee system, whereby planters paid agents to witness their labor contracts, actually discouraged employers from bringing them in for approval by the Bureau. Salaried agents who depended on the Bureau, not the planters, for their money, Lewis believed, would serve the agency and the freedpeople more effectively.[131] Lewis's views paralleled, if not influenced, Howard's plans for reorganizing the Bureau. In January 1867 the commissioner abolished contract fees and by doing so began to change significantly the roster of the Georgia Bureau.[132]

When Caleb Sibley first arrived in Georgia, he did not expect organizational changes to go beyond those that would strengthen the agency's bureaucratic structure. In January, probably confirming Tillson's plans, he even appointed a few native Georgians to act as agents.[133] When he learned of Howard's new fee policy, he recognized that its implementation would "very nearly" destroy his organization. In a rare letter of protest, Sibley asked Howard to allow the fee system to continue in Georgia. The assistant commissioner knew that his agents, most of whom could not take the ironclad oath attesting to past as well as future loyalty required of salaried government employees, would not continue to serve without compensation. No matter, Howard replied; the agents on duty could no longer collect fees after February 20. If their exodus from office occurred as Sibley predicted, the remaining men "you have under pay must extend their field adding whatever others may be necessary." Loyal men who could sub-scribe to the oath must take the places of those who resigned, he advised. By the end of February, Sibley realized that he would have to appoint a consider-able number of new agents if the Bureau were to retain any influence in the state.[134] In March and April, Sibley searched his rosters for men who could take the required oath of office, but discovered that he would probably have to re-lieve almost all the civilians who had not yet resigned.[135]

If at first Sibley protested the forced reduction of his complement of agents, he soon accepted and supported his superior's plan. By March the assistant commissioner had decided that he could make do with a sizably reduced con-tingent of agents. In fact, by then the number of agents that he believed to be necessary for carrying out the Bureau's charge was about one-fourth the num-ber employed by Tillson. Sibley estimated that he would need only forty-five men. Throughout his tenure, the number of paid and unpaid agents never ex-ceeded that March estimate by many, and in 1868 it actually fell below it.[136]

Sibley "pushed" the desired change "as rapidly as possible," but the old Bu-reau lingered on into the new planting season.[137] Over 150 of Tillson's agents remained on duty at the beginning of April either supervising new contracts and old settlements or, because of their uncertain status and lack of fees, ig-noring their duties, while Sibley identified those who could take the required oath. When he received negative replies to his queries, he relieved the agents concerned. At the beginning of May over one hundred citizen agents were still on duty, but by the end of June only a handful of certifiably loyal ones remained.[138]

In June, when his work finally appeared ready to bear fruit, Caleb Sibley looked to the future with optimism. "It is hoped that much greater efficiency may be secured and the work of this office greatly simplified," he reported to Howard, "while the purposes for which it was established shall be accomplished with a force and certainty not heretofore obtained."[139] The assistant commissioner accepted Lewis's and Howard's opinion that the reduced number of agencies would provide better service to the freedpeople not only because of the Bureau's new hierarchical organization but also because of the type of men who were replacing Tillson's old agents.

Ex-Union soldiers, Yankees, and loyal Southerners applied for positions with the Bureau throughout the spring and summer of 1867 and into 1868.[140] In place of Tillson's agents Sibley appointed men like James L. Dunning and C. W. Chapman. Both had remained staunch supporters of the federal government despite the secession of their state, no doubt in part because they both had Northern roots. Dunning was a Connecticut Yankee and a "practical mechanic" who had migrated south in the late 1840s to become a proprietor of the Atlanta Machine Works. During the war he had been an "uncompromising Union man"; after the war he continued to support his country's interests as Davis Tillson's Fulton County agent. Sibley kept him on the rolls until the end of 1867, when he became a member of the constitutional convention.[141]

C. W. Chapman, another New England–born Georgian, had established a high school for young ladies in Columbus before the war. In 1863 a local vigilance committee had him arrested and imprisoned for a time. Chapman served as an agent at Columbus until the end of November 1868.[142]

In addition, Sibley looked for Georgia-born Union men like Howell Flournoy of Clarke County. Flournoy, a man who had maintained his "sterling loyalty" at the risk of his life, had been reported to the Confederate authorities on numerous occasions for his Union sentiments. He served with the Bureau until the end of November 1868.[143]

Now permitted to hire salaried agents, Sibley was able to add to the Georgia Bureau's ranks the men for which Saxton and Wild had only been able to express their preferences: Northerners and Union veterans. Although these Yankees never held all or even a majority of the local agencies, they became an important new component of the Georgia Bureau. By August 1, 1867, out of a total of forty-four agents, there were twenty Northerners—twenty-three if men who had come south before the war are included. Of these Yankees at least fifteen were Union veterans. The assistant commissioner supplemented this number with three army officers, in addition to his ten subassistant commissioners, titled with the military's usual precision and flair for the prosaic "assistant subassistant commissioners." These officers were superior to regular paid civilian agents, performed duties delegated by their subassistant commissioners, but also acted as agents within a defined jurisdiction of counties. This Yankee presence was the norm for the remainder of the Bureau's existence in Georgia. Out of the eighty-two agents who served in the Georgia Bureau during Sibley's and John R. Lewis's tenures, at least twenty-seven were veterans, at least thirty-seven were antebellum residents of the wartime Union states, and at least three were antebellum Yankee transplants to Georgia.[144]

Within this new organization, however, there was one group of loyal men that remained unrepresented. Caleb Sibley did not appoint blacks to the state's vacated civilian agencies, probably aware that such action would only antagonize an already uncooperative white population and place such agents in extraordinarily dangerous positions. An exception was William J. White. An Augusta resident and son of a white father and a black and Indian mother, White had organized illegal schools for slaves before the war. He received a commission to act as an "agent-at-large" in Sibley's Bureau, but his duties consisted solely of educational activities. His job, controversial enough for many white Georgians, safely distanced him from direct confrontations with white employers, although he still felt the sting of discrimination as he traveled the state on his educational duties.[145]

Edwin Belcher was the only other Bureau official with African blood, and Sibley appointed him unaware of his racial background. Belcher had been raised in Philadelphia, had served as a lieutenant colonel in a Pennsylvania regiment, and had been wounded and captured at Chancellorsville. He moved to Georgia after the war and was teaching at a freedmen's school in Augusta when he received his appointment with the Bureau. Unaware that he had been born in South Carolina, he came to grips with his mixed racial heritage only after he received his appointment and then only after he had "it continually thrown in my face that I am a negroe [sic] when I do not know whether it is a fact or not." Presumably Sibley did not know about his racial background until Belcher later wrote to him after his appointment. In October 1867 he resigned, planning to return to Pennsylvania to "enter into some more congenial Employment."

However, he experienced a change of heart, accepted his racial heritage, and went on to become an active Republican politician in Georgia.[146]

As with Saxton and Tillson before him, Sibley and his men had to contend with a degree of confusion concerning their authority, something that the advent of Military Reconstruction did not resolve. Nevertheless, after March 1867, the relationship between the Bureau and the army became clear. Both Georgia and Colonel Sibley were subject to the authority of General John Pope, the commander of the Third Military District. Caleb Sibley would remain in charge of the district of Georgia, an officer in Pope's hierarchy as well as Howard's.[147]

Sibley's role in Military Reconstruction was in fact an indication of O. O. Howard's creeping loss of control over his own bureaucracy.[148] In Georgia, the shifting of the Bureau's headquarters was symbolic of that reality. In early March 1867, before Congress initiated the new phase of Reconstruction, Sibley had moved the Bureau's headquarters from Savannah to Macon, probably because of the city's central location.[149] The next move, however, was to Atlanta, Pope's headquarters since early April. In July Pope ordered Sibley to move the Georgia military district headquarters to the city, which obviously meant the Bureau moved as well. Sibley asked for Howard's permission to move the Bureau headquarters more out of courtesy than anything else.[150] Atlanta remained the Georgia Bureau's headquarters city until it closed its operations.

Now that Military Reconstruction was upon the state, Bureau men expected their authority and power to expand. Albany agent O. H. Howard, tired of old "rose-water processes" like moral suasion, expected to be able to take more forceful measures to encourage incorrigible white Georgians to "keep good faith with their credulous fellow citizens the freedmen."[151] Subassistant Commissioner J. Murray Hoag also believed that the Reconstruction laws now made the Bureau's power when used for obtaining justice for the freedpeople "absolute."[152] The reality, however, was something quite different. When the Bureau witnessed injustice, it could call upon the military to intercede; however, the military's role remained a cautious one.

Military authorities continued the practice of allowing the civil authorities to prove their commitment to provide justice for the freedpeople, including in the new area of electoral politics, with the Bureau men keeping close watch before interfering with the process.[153] General Pope's personal beliefs about Reconstruction confirmed that arrangement. In July 1867, Pope encouraged Ulysses S. Grant to allow much latitude in dealing with the issue of free speech in the South. "I need scarcely repeat," he argued, "that reconstruction, to be in the spirit of the acts of Congress and to be permanent must be the act of the people themselves, after the fullest and freest discussion." Yet he also cautioned that the government needed to be careful about protecting the gains made by the freedpeople and "to guard jealously against any reaction which may and will check this most desirable progress of the colored race."[154]

That reaction to which Pope referred, however, had to be extraordinarily aggressive. In July 1867, for example, Sibley's adjutant assured the Macon sub-assistant commissioner that he had the authority to arrest perpetrators of violence against the freedpeople and that he had a right to call for a military commission to try them. However, the Bureau and presumably the military did not believe such action was "advisable" unless there was "sufficient evidence to convict."[155] Furthermore, after General George Gordon Meade assumed command of the Third Military District in January 1868, the army showed little tolerance for Bureau men who exhibited initiative in asserting Bureau power. In April 1868 the commanding general learned that agent J. M. Robinson had asked a magistrate to dismiss a case, a request that, according to Meade, was "virtually an order, or if not an order an unwarranted interference." Robinson had to follow procedures that included allowing a case to take its course in the civil arena before appealing to the military commander to step in. Meade would "not permit any of his subordinates, agents of the Freedmen's Bureau included, in assuming to interfere with, or exercise control over the civil authorities on their judgment alone, of what the said authorities ought to do." Sibley did not need further clarification of his Bureau's authority; his men could not interfere with local officials "in any manner" except under Meade's orders.[156]

In the area of protecting the freedpeople's economic rights, the Bureau also found itself subordinate to and limited by the military. The Bureau could seize the crops of employers bent on cheating their workers out of the fruits of their labor. However, Sibley could not initiate proceedings for the sale of those crops without the permission of the commander of the Third Military District.[157] During Military Reconstruction, the last hope for a positive resolution of a freedman's claim rested on an appeal to the army.

As Military Reconstruction restricted the Bureau's independent authority, it also increased the duties of its agents and officers by inaugurating black participation in electoral politics. In April 1867, General Pope called for the registration of eligible black and white voters to participate in an October 1867 election for delegates to Georgia's constitutional convention, the product of which they would then approve or reject, along with the selection of state legislators, in April 1868.[158] Caleb Sibley as military commander of the District of Georgia was drawn into the registration process when Pope ordered the superintendent of registration in Georgia as well as the boards of registrars to report to him.[159] This duty was officially an army assignment that involved Sibley in his capacity as a military commander, but Bureau agents and officers were to render all possible assistance to the process, even acting as registrars or managers of elections if the Military District of Georgia's chief of registration, Brevet Colonel Edward Hulbert, requested such assistance.[160] Bureau men, who were to observe all electoral activity, could arrest individuals who violated the freedmen's right to vote and hold them for trial by military commission. Nevertheless, Bureau men, more than anything else, acted as the freedpeople's first line of defense against electoral fraud by investigating how well Georgia was adjusting to biracial electoral politics.[161]

In the end, the military's influence was limited, short-lived, and, once it was removed, fleeting. In July 1868 the newly elected government of Rufus Bullock provided the occasion for restoring the state to civilian control, and the military began to concentrate its troops in Atlanta, Savannah, and Dahlonega. Sibley explored the possibility of resorting to the "quasi" authority of justices of the peace that the provisional legislature had given to Tillson's agents as a way to hold on to some power for his Bureau, but he decided that the rush of events and legislation had rendered it anachronistic. After July 1868, Bureau agents could no longer directly interfere on behalf of the freedpeople. Their only proper course of action, until the assistant commissioner removed them or confined their primary activities to assisting with freedmen's education and bounties, was to serve as the next friends or attorneys of wronged freedpeople, at best helping the freedpeople avoid expensive court hearings by acting as arbitrators, if necessary assisting the freedpeople in making use of the 1866 Civil Rights Act, or gathering information concerning the violation of their rights. Given these circumstances, Sibley warned, "suffering and difficulties for the freedmen are to be expected . . . and I believe are unavoidable."[162]

For the remainder of 1868, Assistant Commissioners Caleb C. Sibley and John Randolph Lewis supervised some forty-five field officers and agents to carry out this work, but by the end of January 1869 Lewis had only nine officers and civilians assisting him at his headquarters and in the field. Although the Bureau lingered on in its emaciated form into the summer of 1870, it would be hard-pressed to protect its own staff, let alone the freedpeople.[163]

In the end, the reorganization of the Georgia Bureau, initiated by O. O. Howard and carried out by Caleb C. Sibley, addressed only a few of the agency's problems. While some of their number were as disappointing as the men they had replaced, Sibley's new agents brought new life to the Bureau. However, Caleb Sibley needed more than new faces to eliminate the conditions that caused the failures experienced by his predecessor. The assistant commissioner's new men quickly learned that dedication to simple justice was an inadequate weapon when hampered by small resources employed in a determinedly hostile environment.

# 3

## Laborious, Vexatious, and Dangerous Service

Georgia's three generations of Bureau agents were men who accepted their assignments for a variety of reasons. Consequently, they had varying degrees of commitment to Reconstruction's larger goals. Saxton's reform-minded civilian subordinates embodied the most radical motivation for working with the freedpeople. Drawn to the South before the end of the war, they had come to help the ex-slaves achieve the fullest expression of freedom possible given the conditions of the times and the parameters of nineteenth-century thought. They were, in fact, assisting in God's plans for "overturning old systems, old practices to give place to new and . . . better"; they acted as missionaries and teachers as well as government agents.[1]

Tunis G. Campbell, Saxton's one black agent, William F. Eaton, and William H. Tiffany were all northern ministers serving within Sherman's Reservation. They actively interceded for the freedpeople, helping them to form local governments, organize militias, and withstand challenges from planters and less sympathetic Yankees. They also conducted their wedding ceremonies, preached, and taught Sunday school.[2] As the Reverend Eaton explained, he was "engaged in the work of elevating the oppressed" in a South that was "not subdued but simply overborne."[3]

The best officers assigned to Rufus Saxton by General James Steedman at least accepted their posting as good subordinates. For instance, Colonel Hiram F. Sickles reported to Saxton with the understanding that the Bureau would decide "questions of great importance"; he assured his new superior, "I am a soldier and . . . my highest ambition has been, and is now, to do my duty."[4] The few army men who actually volunteered to associate themselves with Saxton's agency during the spring of 1865, however, clearly had a commitment to seeing their commander's brand of Reconstruction take hold in the state. Captain Alexander P. Ketchum, Saxton's Port Royal colleague and chief officer in Georgia's Sherman Reservation throughout 1865, was committed to making freedpeople landholders.[5] So, too, was General Edward A. Wild.

General Wild, who was constantly reminded by his mangled hand and amputated arm that he had sacrificed his ability to practice medicine for the Union cause, envisioned his service with the Bureau to be part of a broader mission to secure the fruits of victory. Wild nurtured a strong distrust of erstwhile Confederates, whom he believed to be nursing "schemes of future treasonable resistance." He therefore advocated a lengthy, firmly supervised Reconstruction, "else peace will be only temporary and precarious."[6] Perhaps his efforts were tainted by revenge, but by one sympathetic assessment he was a *"splendid man, heart & soul* in the cause."[7]

That favorable assessment was probably based on an observation of the constructive side of Wild's radical views. Upon his arrival in Georgia, Wild planned to make every effort to eliminate discriminatory treatment of the freedpeople. He even tried to eliminate the word *colored* from copies and newspaper reports of Bureau claims proceedings, understanding that discrimination began at the point of publicly separating people by this racial feature.[8] Furthermore, his plans for the property that he confiscated in Wilkes County involved transforming the courthouse at Washington into a freedmen's school and the Toombs estate into black homesteads.[9]

Neither Saxton nor his successors had many agents committed to pursuing the aggressively radical course set by Wild. In fact, most of the Yankees who later became involved with the Bureau would be more like Captain John Emory Bryant, Saxton's more moderate Augusta agent. By his own admission Bryant, a native of Maine, mixed personal motives for serving as a Bureau agent with philanthropic ones, the former certainly not necessarily rendering the latter any less significant. During his association with the Bureau he acted as a missionary for free-labor ideology and justice for the ex-slaves, while he also made a living for his family and a reputation that would launch him into state politics.[10]

If Saxton's men found much of their motivation in their desire to reform the South, many of Tillson's native civilian agents found theirs primarily in a more conservative form of self-interest. Some white Georgians volunteered their services or accepted appointments because they professed a desire to see justice done,[11] but others scrambled for a sinecure because they were either "destitute of employment and very anxious to have something to do" or handicapped and unable to find work.[12] J. G. McCrary was quite plain about why he took on his Lee County agency when he offered his resignation. "It is the poorest office I ever had," he groused with unabashed honesty. "I do no good for the office & the office does no good for me."[13] When many of McCrary's colleagues learned that Colonel Caleb Sibley had been ordered to abolish the fee system by which they were paid, they clogged the mails with complaints well into March 1867; when they learned, however, that there were prospects for collecting regular salaries, they eagerly wrote to headquarters asking to be included on the new payroll.[14]

A number of these agents accepted their appointments with the Bureau because they shared the concerns of their white neighbors, particularly the desire to direct the course of their state's reconstruction. Brien Maguire, a resident of Washington, Wilkes County, probably decided to serve as an agent because of what his community had experienced at the hands of General Wild. As he later explained, he volunteered for Bureau duty "to render a public service . . . for we wanted to get the management of affairs in our own hands, and we wanted to be rid of U.S. Soldiers."[15] Others agreed that cooperating with the federal authorities would be the best way to speed the return of their state to civilian control, "the only means by which industry can be revived and the ravages of war repaired."[16]

Still others, more specifically, saw cooperation as a means by which they could preserve the old racial and economic hierarchy. Responding to Assistant Commissioner Tillson's request for nominations for civilian agents, white Georgians, who had not come into contact with Saxton's fledgling Bureau and knew little about the agency, put forward names of possible agents with the assumption that the Bureau's purpose was primarily one of keeping the freedpeople "straight."[17] The labor contracts, approved by a number of these civilian agents, that placed freedpeople in unfavorable situations suggest that they agreed with their white neighbors.[18]

Sibley expected his new agents to bring purer motives to their positions, but he would have had a difficult time ascertaining from his appointees' letters of application whether the freedpeople's cause was foremost on their minds. Most letters stressed Unionism or military service, the ability to take a loyalty oath, or a Northern state of residence as qualifications for their appointments. Sibley apparently judged many of the candidates by these criteria, for rarely did a letter of application plead a special concern for the plight of the ex-slaves. To be sure, Unionism, military service, or Northern nativity could indicate a greater commitment to seeing Yankee ideals take root in the South, but most applications contained explicit evidence of a problem that troubled many postwar Americans, regardless of region of residence. Like a number of Tillson's civilian agents, these men were looking for a way to earn a living.[19]

The Georgia Unionists who served with Sibley's Bureau believed that they should now have a larger voice in determining the direction of their state, but their unhappy wartime circumstances placed them in a position, as Columbus, Georgia, resident and former teacher C. W. Chapman lamented, of "almost daily dependence." The Massachusetts-born Chapman, who had been imprisoned during the war, believed that a government job would alleviate his condition. Subassistant Commissioner Frederick Mosebach agreed. "He is in need," Mosebach wrote to headquarters, "and deserves some return for the many sacrifices he made on account of loyal principles." Chapman secured an agency that paid the standard salary of $1,200 per year in the subdistrict of Columbus.[20]

Veterans, too, made their claims on the Bureau, hoping, as one put it, that "my past services as a Soldier may entitle me to the favor I ask."[21] Some of these men, Albany agent O. H. Howard among them, brought greater weight to their applications than civilians could by soliciting recommendations from some impressive military connections. In February 1867, shortly before he received his appointment, Howard had his old friend, the Bureau commissioner, remind Caleb Sibley of his wartime service. Still, these military men needed the Bureau for many of the same reasons that their Unionist counterparts did. In February 1868, P. J. O'Rourke, a veteran of the Pennsylvania volunteer service, asked his former commander, General George G. Meade, to intercede for him with the Bureau because his business in Louisville, Kentucky, was foundering. He tapped the right reference and became an agent in northeastern Georgia.[22]

Max Marbach, who became the agent for Jefferson and Burke Counties, also needed help, but he went directly to the Georgia Bureau with his problems. Marbach had commanded black troops during the war and presumably had some knowledge of the plight of the freedpeople. Nevertheless, when he wrote to the Bureau in February 1868, he had already resigned from his position at an English firm because of ill health, and he explained that he needed a job. His colleagues Andrew Clark, Alvin Clark, and William Pierce, all former Union officers of the Kentucky volunteer service, applied for Bureau agencies, and all similarly stressed their need for employment. For Alvin Clark, who was residing in southwest Georgia at the time, a government job was just about his last hope. Disabled, he could not do hard manual labor; although he had tried his best to secure employment, he pointed out that he could "not expect assistance from the people here." The agency complied with his and the other Kentuckians' requests, helping these veterans in their efforts to adjust to postwar civilian life.[23] Indeed, the plight of these veterans was not extraordinary. A number of Sibley's appointees probably had come south for economic or health reasons and only after an initial false start turned to the Bureau as a way to salvage their efforts to find a competence in their new homes.[24]

The Bureau staff officers and subassistant commissioners who were members of the Veteran Reserve Corps were especially vulnerable to the vagaries of the labor market. Their very presence in the Corps meant that they were partially disabled and therefore had limited opportunities in their peacetime communities, a common concern expressed by these Yankee job seekers during all Georgia Bureau administrations.[25] Veteran Reserve Corps officers also suspected that the Bureau was the only chance for continued military service for those Corps members who wished to remain in uniform. Frederick Mosebach, who served under Tillson as a subassistant commissioner at Albany and at Columbus, understood that the Bureau was "the last hold" that the Veteran Reserve Corps officers had on military employment. Although he admitted that he did not feel very sorry about it, he realized that he and his fellow Reserve Corps officers would be quickly discarded once the army reduced its ranks and the Bureau was abolished.[26]

Of course, there were any number of other reasons beyond finding a job that would prompt a veteran to solicit a Bureau position, none of them having to do with patriotism or higher moral motives. An assignment with the Bureau might provide a convenient opportunity, as Maine native and Veteran Reserve Corps officer George Crabtree hoped, to see if "the country out south" was a suitable place to put down new roots. For Martin Archer, a former Ohio resident and colonel of a black regiment, it was the opportunity to escape from a shotgun marriage, the consequence of a youthful antebellum indiscretion. The Bureau and Georgia must have lived up to both of their expectations because Crabtree eventually went into planting and Archer soon became a bigamist.[27]

Self-interest was common among the Unionists and Yankees who sought positions with the Bureau, but self-interest and a commitment to the Bureau's goals were not mutually exclusive. Since most of the army officers who remained on duty with the Bureau from 1866 on were from the Veteran Reserve Corps, at least many of Georgia's subassistant commissioners were constantly reminded of the price they had paid for victory.

Many Veteran Reserve Corps members continued to suffer from battle wounds and camp diseases long after the flags had been furled. For instance,

Oliver B. Gray, on duty as a subassistant commissioner at Marietta from January 1866 through December 1867, had lost an arm because of a wound sustained at Gettysburg; he suffered severe phantom pain, and the amputation never fully healed, continuing to abscess until just before his death in 1870. William F. Martins, Sibley's subassistant commissioner at Newnan, had been wounded in the right elbow and had lost his left foot and his right leg below the knee; he continued to endure pain long after he left the Bureau. And Frederick A. H. Gaebel, who served as a subassistant commissioner in southwest Georgia for Tillson and Sibley, had been wounded at Malvern Hill, at Antietam, and at Fredericksburg; he carried around in his back a lead ball that was a constant reminder of his military service. Although they might exaggerate their pain and discomfort in order to receive sympathy, Bureau appointments, and government pensions, these wounded veterans certainly had valid reasons to look on their Reconstruction work as something that would give lasting value to their personal losses.[28]

John J. Knox, Sibley's officer at Athens, lived with chronic respiratory and throat problems, the consequences of a neck wound that had also disabled his right arm. Perhaps his physical discomfort caused by the rebellion reinforced his commitment to Reconstruction. Perhaps it also prompted his criticism of President Andrew Johnson's policies, which threatened the safety of the one group of citizens that held to the values for which he had fought. "Every action of the President's in the way of apologizing for and strengthening the hands of the Rebels," he warned, "is but an excuse for additional outrages on the col'd man who stand nobly by the principles union Liberty and equal rights to all."[29]

In a similar manner, perhaps F. A. H. Gaebel's experiences in the war accounted for his concern about losing the peace. Like E. A. Wild before him, Gaebel's contempt for traitors was sharpened by his wartime encounters. For three months during the last winter of the war, he had commanded the 16th Regiment of the Veteran Reserve Corps, which had combed the forests and mountains of western Pennsylvania breaking up camps of deserters, capturing draft dodgers, and making sure convalescents returned to duty. Also like Wild, he worried that erstwhile Confederates were keen on renewing the sectional conflict as soon as they could. These same dormant rebels, he warned, could not be trusted to participate in government for years to come and consequently needed military supervision if the freedpeople were to receive any justice. He also formulated a retributive prescription for dealing with the unreconstructed "chivalry," lest the federal government's conciliatory approach to Reconstruction be perceived as weakness. He proposed establishing a prison pen at Andersonville for the "cruel Cavaliers"; their guards would be ex-slaves serving under the command of former Union prisoners of war.[30]

Knox, Gaebel, and others like them clearly needed the Bureau, but their actions revealed a genuine concern about the outcome of the enterprise for which they had volunteered. Personal concern undoubtedly motivated Max Marbach when he found himself unemployed because of his poor health; however, money alone could not explain why he faced down a drunken, threatening planter while working out a crop settlement. When the planter asked him if he "would die in the attempt to give a *nigger* his right," Marbach replied, "Yes."[31]

The presence of veterans and Reserve Corps officers in the Bureau from Tillson's administration through Lewis's seeded the agency with individuals who shared a commitment to the views publicly espoused by their superiors. Captain C. C. Richardson, for example, arrived in southwest Georgia during the fall of 1865 intending to "conciliate as much as possible without compromising the honor of . . . God & the rights of the Freedmen." Lieutenant Douglas Risley, who had been wounded leading black troops during the war, also understood that his duties included protecting the rights of the freedpeople and preventing suffering among those unfortunate ex-slaves who caused his heart to ache. He also believed that the freedpeople, despite an ignorance bred in slavery, would see through their ex-masters' protestations of friendship and continue to look to the North "for their advisers, their helpers and their friends" because of his work. The Bureau, Risley believed, could indeed shape the political future of the South.[32]

Like Davis Tillson, many of these Yankee Bureau men perceived the freedpeople to be initially qualified to act only as junior partners in Reconstruction because of the ignorance imposed on them by their past condition. Nevertheless, as Lieutenant Colonel Ira Ayer explained, the ex-slave "is a *free man*, and those who seek to render his condition otherwise must be made to feel the power of the government to protect them in their freedom."[33] The fact that these officers and agents understood themselves to be the freedpeople's guardians gave balance and direction to their work. John Emory Bryant, Carlos de la Mesa, and Douglas Risley all assumed at one time or another that the freedpeople should be treated as minors. Yet these men were all committed to advancing the ex-slaves' cause.[34]

These Bureau men also recognized that because of the perceived weaknesses of the newly freed slaves, white Georgians had to be tolerant, responsible, and just, all qualities that employers too often lacked. Lieutenant Colonel Homer B. Sprague, who had been a subassistant commissioner under Tillson for a few months, made this point while criticizing the excessively negative manner in which Georgia newspapers depicted the condition of the ex-slaves. "Now the negroes are bad enough, Heaven knows, without exaggerating—idle enough, vicious enough, ignorant enough—just as slavery had left them." But the freed-people must "be protected in their rights as well as punished for their mis-deeds, to be instructed in their duties and treated as men with immortal souls rather than as beasts of burden or machines for pulling cotton. They need a guardian rather than a jailor or a hangman."[35]

With these attitudes in mind, many a Yankee agent or officer arrived at his posting, assessed the situation, and committed himself, even at the risk of his personal comfort and his life, to do nothing less than his duty and at least to see that simple justice prevailed. As army veteran William C. Morrill, who went to southwest Georgia after the war to earn a living as a planter and stayed on to serve as a Bureau agent, testified, "I tried to do as near right as I knew how."[36]

## Flawed Performances

When Sibley reorganized the Bureau during the first five months of his tenure, he worked under the assumption that Tillson's civilian appointees had served the agency and the freedpeople in an unsatisfactory manner. Several of his new agents reinforced that belief when they protested that either their predecessors or neighboring agents had failed to watch after the freedpeople's interests. Andrew Clark, recently settled in Newton, Georgia, to supervise Mitchell and Baker Counties, learned shortly after his arrival in the spring of 1867 that citizen agents had continued to approve poor contracts despite Tillson's efforts to stop them.[37] Other newly appointed agents echoed Andrew Clark's complaints. Alvin Clark, stationed at Quitman near the Florida border, reported that the freedpeople in the counties adjoining his jurisdiction had been unable to secure assistance from the local agents. And O. H. Howard, the Albany agent, realized that his heavy caseload was the result of earlier negligence. Southwestern Georgia citizen agents had paid insufficient attention to the freedpeople's interests, Howard reported, "as a majority of the cases which came before me are those which should have been settled by my predecessors." The freedpeople had postponed complaining about their situation because they were waiting for the arrival of a "Yankee Bureau."[38]

In many cases these complaints were justified. Some civilian agents under-estimated the work involved and might have chosen to give priority to their own planting or business interests or to the duties of the local offices they held.[39] Others volunteered not realizing that their duties could become "unpleasant" or render them "odious" if they forced them into confrontations with friends and neighbors, which would be ample justification for some to approach their Bureau obligations in a halfhearted manner.[40] Still others succumbed to the pressure of their neighbors, who "prevent them doing simple, manly justice to the freedpeople."[41]

Some white Georgians sabotaged the Bureau by duping Tillson not only by nominating individuals who agreed with their views but also by nominating individuals whom they could easily manipulate or ignore. Taylor County agent James T. Harmon, for example, was an old invalid, barely able to move about let alone actively pursue justice. He had been accused of punishing a freedman by hanging him by his thumbs and of conspiring with a planter to defraud freedpeople. Although he had used corporal punishment, he appeared to have been incapable of actually scheming to cheat freedpeople. Tillson's inspector general, George Walbridge, determined that he was only guilty of being "a weak minded imbecile and undetermined old man, one who tries to please all parties and consequently does justice to none."[42]

Other agents had similar experiences for similar reasons. W. B. Carter, the agent for Putnam County, had good intentions, but ended up approving poor contracts. Major William Gray, the previous inspector general, concluded, "If I judge correctly he had no fixed purpose to carry out the requirements of the Bureau so necessary in holding his position . . . he has been overcome by the representations of the citizens." Subassistant Commissioner Frederick Gaebel found some of the agents in his subdistrict to be no better. After a tour of counties in his southwest Georgia jurisdiction, he could only grouse about pliable civilian agents who "have no nerve."[43]

The complaints leveled by Sibley's new appointees, however, did not reveal the entire story of Davis Tillson's Bureau. The problematic agents were more a reflection of white Georgia's unwillingness to accept the new order and Tillson's misplaced trust than of Tillson's lack of desire to secure justice. "Let me assure you," the assistant commissioner informed a quartermaster officer, "it is the firm determination of the Govt. to stand by the freedpeople in their just rights and that wherever I find an agent who from indisposition or lack of Courage, fails to do this he will be removed and some other person placed in his stead."[44] Indeed, Tillson kept his promise when agents' inadequacies came to his attention, as was the case in Pike County, where an agent had whipped a freedman, and in Cattoosa County, where another had sat in judgment on a case in which he had been an interested party.[45]

Most important, Tillson seriously considered complaints coming from the freedpeople themselves, investigated their accusations, and did not hesitate to act decisively when the evidence warranted it. In Polk County, the freedpeople had lost all confidence in their agent at a time when planters were depriving them of justice. Their complaints led to his removal.[46] In Baker County, two agents were overcharging freedpeople for their services and requiring planters to deduct the costs from their employees' wages. The freedpeople were prepared to make a formal complaint against one of the agents. When Tillson learned of their grievance, he canceled the excessive fees and removed the agent.[47]

Unfortunately for the freedpeople, although the assistant commissioner did his best to respond to complaints made about his civilian agents, his limited resources prevented regular inspections of all agencies, which were necessary to root out problems that were not immediately reported. In the case of the Cattoosa County agent, Tillson required a little over a month from the date of the complaint to resolve the case, but it took the Bureau almost one year to discover James T. Harmon's inadequacies.[48]

Ironically, Tillson was reluctant to remove the beleaguered and ineffectual J. R. Phillips, not because he was insensitive to the concerns of the freedpeople of Henry County, but because he wished to encourage their confidence in the Bureau. During a personal interview, Phillips gave Tillson the impression that he had "neither the intellectual vigor nor moral or physical courage necessary to the proper performance of his duty." Nevertheless, the assistant commissioner avoided taking action against him because white Henry County residents had recently petitioned for Phillips's removal and such a move "would be misunderstood by the freedpeople." Tillson believed that if he acted now, the county's ex-slaves would assume that he had been influenced by the demands of the same disgruntled whites who were oppressing freedpeople and doing violence to their agent. Instead, the assistant commissioner dispatched troops to Henry County to prove his commitment to the Bureau's goals. It was only after Bureau headquarters ordered him to act that Tillson replaced Phillips with another Georgia native, George Nolan, an agent who had been sufficiently loyal to the Union to qualify for an appointment in Sibley's reorganized Bureau.[49]

Tillson's more fortunate appointments tempered their actions with a practical desire to see justice done for both employer and employee, as if they had accepted Tillson's argument that the future of both races depended upon it. Elias Yulee, for example, considered the freedpeople to be "different fundamentally, both spiritually and morally from the white race." They were indeed a dependent people and required the Bureau's guardianship because the prejudices of many whites would not allow for equal protection under the state's laws. Fair play, however, had a very pragmatic consequence for Yulee. "I believe that if the negro does not have justice done him," he explained, "it will make him reckless & in the end those very planters [who criticized the agent's defense of the freedpeople] will be the serious sufferers."[50]

Although this type of motivation fell short of the altruism of Saxton's agents, it did reveal a willingness to make some compromises that benefited the freedpeople in order to speed both political and economic recovery. Greensboro agent James Davison's expectations for the new system took account of its perceived flaws. Some freedpeople, he observed, "violate & quit their contracts, others will doubtless do likewise. White men would probably do the same. And the Negro is by no means more perfect."[51] Yet acceptance of the need for some sort of Reconstruction prompted Davison, who had been a local official, to pursue his charge with vigor, lecturing black and white residents of Greene County and correcting his mistakes along the way. In supervising agreements for the 1865 season, Davison made the error of accepting some contracts that were below minimum wage guidelines established by Davis Tillson. Informed of his lapse in judgment, by the beginning of March 1866 he had revised those documents to conform to Tillson's expectations.[52] The Bureau eventually lost the fine services of Davison, even though Caleb Sibley commended him for his "eminently satisfactory" performance, because he could not subscribe to the oath of past loyalty that the reorganized agency Bureau required of its paid employees.[53] Davison and other Bureau men who shared his views were no match for Saxton's small group of reformers when it came to advocating a wide range of freedmen's rights, but the very fact that they could accept the revolutionary notion that blacks should be paid a fair wage indicated that they were willing to acknowledge that a new order had settled upon their state.

Yulee and Davison were not alone among the civilian Bureau agents who saw the need to pursue simple justice, but even the most conscientious of them could be foiled by circumstances beyond their control, including white intransigence and a lack of resources for combating it. Consequently, even as they tried to do their jobs, they earned the displeasure of their black constituents. George Washington Jones, for example, was not the most able agent, but after joining

the Bureau in January 1866 he obeyed orders and tried to do his job. However, he had the "worst set of men in the country to deal with" in Bainbridge
County.[54] In Perry County, J. D. Harris, another Tillson appointee, found himself stymied in his efforts to secure contract settlements for the freedpeople because the civil authorities refused to provide him with any assistance.[55]

Given these circumstances, freedpeople could become impatient for justice
and could give an agent a bad name, even if the official had done his best to
protect their interests. In Baldwin County, Agent T. W. White, a citizen appointed by Tillson, clearly understood the implications of a case he could not
settle because the planter had absconded. "The freedmen, relying upon the
promise I had made them in signing their contracts felt that in not collecting
their wages that I have deceived them," he reported in January 1867. "The result is that this single case, if allowed to pass, will not only discourage these particular Freedmen, but, will effect the Confidence & energy of many others."[56]

Also, policy matters that were beyond the Bureau agents' control led to complaints that agents simply could not resolve because of their lack of authority or
power. In March 1867, freedpeople complained about the lax efforts of the citizen agent of Walker County. However, Carlos A. de la Mesa, the area's subassistant commissioner, investigated and learned that the charges were unfounded.
The freedpeople's cases were already before a civil tribunal. According to established policy, the agent could do nothing unless the final outcome deprived the
freedpeople of justice. "The agents in many instances would do more when
called upon if they had power," explained de la Mesa, "but they summon parties
who refuse to appear and will not recognize their authority."[57]

A number of Tillson's agents bemoaned their inability to secure justice for
the freedpeople.[58] They realized that without more weight placed immediately
behind their decisions, they could not do much to further the Bureau's ends.
General Tillson, however, had been restrained by his belief that his own authority was inadequate to increase the agents' jurisdiction or executive power
without congressional action first defining the new limits.[59] Furthermore, a lack
of military resources, especially cavalry, limited the assistant commissioner's
ability to accomplish what even he believed was within his range of authority.[60]
Because of rapid demobilization, by January 1866 there were only 2,764 infantry left to patrol the largest state east of the Mississippi. But by April the
number dropped to 520, increasing only to 850 in October. The numbers did
not match the Bureau's needs, but infantry alone would not solve the Bureau's
problems.[61] Subassistant Commissioner Gaebel understood the significance of

the lack of mobile force when in March 1866 he argued that a small troop of regular cavalry would far surpass in effectiveness a much larger contingent of volunteer infantry in part by bringing "more energy" to the citizen agents.[62]

As Sibley's agents would discover, freedpeople, who had their own short-comings, unfairly tarred more than one agent. William C. Morrill admitted that sometimes the freedpeople exaggerated their claims, although at other times they were perfectly reliable.[63] Lieutenant O. H. Howard believed that they, "like most other human beings," overemphasized their own rights and privileges and claimed "in many instances an independence and freedom of action, totally incompatible with the proper and faithful discharge" of their contractual obligations.[64] Consequently, as agent James R. Smith learned, there was always the possibility that proper decisions against black employees who violated contracts could have given some agents undeservedly bad reputations.

Dr. Smith, a physician who taught a freedmen's school, faithfully served as one of Tillson's agents in Washington County, thereby earning an appointment in Sibley's Bureau. Smith was known as a friend to the freedpeople, and Tillson in fact had appointed him because the agent's black neighbors urged him to take the position. Because of his habit of speaking his mind as an advocate for the freedpeople's cause, he had "been reduced to penury, and almost completely ostracized for the position he has taken," to the point where he believed that he would need to find a new home after his retirement. Yet in November 1867, the Loyal League of the county petitioned for his removal. "I found soon after I accepted the agency that no conscientious Honest Man can please [the freedpeople]. . . . If the Testimony of the white People was taken they would say that to befriend & assist the Negro I have sacrificed myself and the action of the League is the return that has been made." The charges did not result in his removal, and he remained with the Bureau until the agency prepared to close its operations.[65]

In the end, Sibley's reorganized Bureau shared the same problems that Tillson's had experienced and did not fare much better in resolving them. Like a number of Tillson's agents, Union veteran Anthony Pokorny, the agent at Columbus, did his best but simply lacked influence with his white and black constituents.[66] A few of Sibley's job-hungry agents were lazy, incompetent, or drunk and neglected their duties.[67] Others like F. C. Genth, who disappeared without a trace from his Fort Gaines headquarters to avoid his local creditors, permitted their finances to embarrass the Bureau.[68]

Not all of Sibley's men escaped the white influence to which Tillson's men had been accused of submitting. The citizens of Americus, Georgia, an unreconstructed group of rebels who held Northerners in contempt, as Yankee traveler Sidney Andrews observed firsthand, probably appreciated J. M. Robinson, their agent, for all the wrong reasons. Robinson, a Pennsylvania native who served the Americus area for a year, was besotted in every sense of the word, with serious consequences for the freedpeople under his jurisdiction. As early as June 1867, two months after his appointment, an anonymous writer claimed that Robinson was a drunk, and Robinson's successor learned that "when parties came in he would settle a claim for a drink of whiskey, no matter what it was." In January 1868, the Albany subassistant commissioner, O. H. Howard, confirmed the agent's lack of fitness for duty, the consequence of his "long continued and constant use of stimulants," which "impaired his mental faculties." Since Robinson had "no decision of mind whatever," he frequently relied on the white men of Americus for advice, and they frequently took advantage of him.[69]

The most serious example of the agent's deficiency surfaced after he left the Freedmen's Bureau in April 1868 to visit his aged parents. Robinson's superiors discovered that forty bales of cotton he had seized to secure freedpeople's earnings were missing. Clearly, Sibley should have removed the agent after receiving Howard's warning, for although Bureau headquarters in Washington found the agent innocent of fraud, the evidence suggested his weak character. Eliphalet Whittlesey, the former North Carolina assistant commissioner now acting as one of Commissioner Howard's staff officers, believed unscrupulous whites had taken advantage of the agent's incompetence to deprive the freedpeople of their cotton.[70] Regardless, William C. Morrill, Robinson's successor, found that the agent had also left behind numerous unjust settlements that had deprived freedpeople of a significant portion of their wages.[71]

There were other instances of malfeasance and incompetence that marred Sibley's administrative record. Also, some subassistant commissioners continued to find it necessary to remind their agents that, if they wished to remain on the government payroll, they must accept the full spirit of the Bureau's charge.[72] However, the complaints of the Bureau's inability to satisfy the needs of the freedpeople were more often than not beyond the control of Sibley's men. The emphasis placed on moral suasion and arbitration as well as the requirement to allow cases to follow their course in civil courts delayed speedy action. Also, reorganization did not solve the problem of the Bureau's inadequate power for protecting black Georgians, a task made all the more difficult during 1867 and 1868 as agents and officers supervised the freedmen's entry into electoral politics.[73]

As Tillson's men had learned, the Bureau needed the constant presence of troops to enforce justice at a time when the number of soldiers in the state was in decline. Although the number of troops increased by about three hundred between October 1866 and October 1867, within a year the military's presence again dropped to under a thousand men. Furthermore, because the department commander concentrated his forces at three garrisons by the fall of 1868 instead of the six used a year earlier, key locations—Athens, for example—lacked a military presence.[74]

The consequences were indeed serious. In April 1867, O. H. Howard complained from Albany about the citizens' contempt for his office and his impotence to act without military aid. If he were to have nothing more than his personal influence to enforce Bureau policy, "the government had better save the salary of such Agent, or place him upon some other duty."[75] As had been the case with Tillson's better appointments, no matter how dedicated an agent might have been, he still found himself overworked and underprotected in the face of an uncooperative and at times violent white population.

## A Heavy Workload

A significant contribution to the derailing of the Freedmen's Bureau's pursuit of justice in Georgia was the sheer volume of each agent's or subassistant commissioner's caseload, as the freedpeople of Calhoun understood. In August 1867, they petitioned the assistant commissioner because "their rights are neglected" by Agent C. B. Blacker, a former officer of black troops. The problem arose not because of Blacker's neglect, unconcern, or incompetence but because he simply did not have the time to cope with the extraordinary amount of work presented to him by the freedpeople.[76]

From the commencement of Bureau activities in Georgia, officers, agents, and observers acknowledged the agency's busy and difficult jobs.[77] Throughout the agency's history, especially at the beginning and at the end of the planting year, freedpeople arrived at offices before sunrise and began petitioning agents even before they were dressed. Attempts to compromise individual cases could involve hours of talk. Consequently, during the busy seasons, Bureau men could be employed night and day, fourteen hours a day, seven days a week, their lives consumed by agency work.[78] In June 1866, this type of schedule led James Davison to admit, "I am *tired out* and *broke down.*" Indeed, Davison had been busy. "Every day for 6 months, day after day, I have had from 5 to 20 complaints, *generally trivial* and of no moment, yet requiring consideration & attention coming from both Black & White. . . . The result is my time is consumed, and I virtually become a 'pack horse' for the whole county."[79]

Other Bureau men had similar experiences. In December 1865, Major G. A. Hastings, a veteran soldier plagued by debilitating chills and chronic diarrhea, wondered if he could stand his job much longer because he had "to do two men's work here."[80] In September 1866, Lieutenant William Mitchell, a subassistant commissioner stationed in Marietta, found white and black petitioners presenting cases to him before breakfast and after supper, through his window while he tried to complete his paperwork, and on his way into stores as he tried to run his errands.[81] In April 1867, O. H. Howard noted that his days were filled with work that required more "tact" and "ability" than any other position of public service that he had held in the past ten years.[82] And even as the Bureau prepared to terminate its work in Georgia, Subassistant Commissioner de la Mesa maintained a dizzyingly busy travel agenda that sent him throughout his Rome subdistrict. Over any period of time during the latter part of 1868, de la Mesa found himself inspecting schoolbuildings and agents' offices, collecting rents, facilitating freedmen's bounty claims, investigating labor complaints against employers and employees, investigating charges of child molestation, abandonment, and bigamy within the freedmen's community, investigating charges against civil authorities, consulting with the assistant commissioner, and advising freedpeople on how to collect their pay after the Bureau left the state.[83]

Indeed, some of the complaints made by Caleb Sibley's subassistant commissioners about their subordinates reflected not a lack of concern for justice on the part of the agents but rather the inability of the Georgia Bureau's diminished complement of overworked appointees to keep up with its increasingly bureaucratic nature. Reorganization was designed to bring greater efficiency to the Bureau and better service to the freedpeople, but it also brought a demand from headquarters for more paperwork from the reduced contingent of officers and agents, including numerous reports that went along with the Bureau's greater involvement with education.[84] Christian Raushenberg, who was also acting as a Bureau surgeon at the time, begged for an office clerk to alleviate the burden of paperwork at his Cuthbert agency while he tended to his most pressing tasks. "Complaints and settlements occupy more than the office hours of each day," he explained, "and leave little time and less freshness of mind for corresponding & bookkeeping."[85]

A number of Bureau men also found that their work was not made any easier by the public insults and lack of cooperation shown by the local authorities. H. F. Mills was harassed by the local overseer of the public highways; the official refused to accept the Stockton agent's exemption from road work and attempted to fine him. Thomas Holden, Sibley's agent at Warrenton, was annoyed by the sheriff of Warren County, himself a former agent who "embarrasses him in the performance of his official duties." And George Ballou was insulted by a local jurist, an action that the Cuthbert agent understood went beyond the personal to be a challenge to his office. This lack of official cooperation only encouraged citizens to defy Bureau decisions.[86]

Unreconstructed local officials made it especially difficult to summon parties to arbitration, a situation that left agents with only the ineffectual course of using freedpeople—often the complaining parties—as their bailiffs.[87] C. A. de la Mesa received a blunt response from a planter transmitted to him by the freedman who had carried the officer's summons to the offending party: "Tell the Captain to go to Hell and be damned. . . . If he wants a settlement he can come to me."[88] Savannah agent A. W. Stone also learned that using "colored men that no one will obey" to execute his orders was a futile endeavor. "Give me *power* or please *relieve* me," he pleaded in his frustration. "I feel like a fool to pass judgment & then be told I can't enforce it."[89]

Agents and officers not only found themselves stymied by unresponsive local and county officials but at times found their own freedom jeopardized by actively obstructionist grand juries, judges, and sheriffs. Lieutenant William F. Martins, Tillson's Waynesboro subassistant commissioner, was presented to the county court by a grand jury as a nuisance.[90] Worse still was the situation in Stewart County, where well into 1867 citizen agent E. F. Kirksey faced arrest every time he tried to do his duty; nevertheless, although he worried that his authority was "lame" and that the Bureau might become a "farce," he was "resolved to meet the worst" as long as he had troops to back him. As in other cases with other Bureau men, Kirksey's authority was "fully vindicated" when those troops were present to enforce his decisions.[91]

Quasi-official obstructionism existed throughout Military Reconstruction down to the Bureau's last days in the state, when, without military protection, agents were confronted by increasingly brazen acts of defiance by local officials. In September 1868, Daniel Losey was accosted by drunks at Perry and wound up being charged by the authorities with rioting in the streets.[92] Two months later civil authorities indicted Subassistant Commissioner de la Mesa on charges of "seizing and detaining the property of a citizen of Georgia." As far as he could ascertain, the accusation was the consequence of his effort to follow orders to collect rents on some abandoned property.[93]

## Political Commitments

After March 1867, busy Bureau men assumed the additional political duties laid on their shoulders by the requirements of Military Reconstruction. However, before Military Reconstruction, the Bureau's role in engaging the freedpeople in organizational politics was limited. During Saxton's administration, Bureau agents and officers encouraged black political activity in Sherman's Reservation, but beyond that coastal region the agency did not have the resources or the time to devote to politicizing the freedmen. Saxton's men apprised the ex-slaves of their rights and obligations, and the assistant commissioner encouraged individuals to hold meetings to organize Union Leagues anywhere in his jurisdiction.[94] Nevertheless, even John Emory Bryant spent most of his time organizing labor, settling disputes between freedmen and ex-masters, and arguing with the military.[95] It was only after Bryant left the Bureau that he identified his future with a politicized black population.[96]

Neither Davis Tillson nor his native white agents considered it imperative or wise to politicize the freedpeople.[97] Any agent who did attempt to "radicalize" the ex-slaves risked running afoul of the Bureau hierarchy, as did the one exception that proved the rule. In October 1866, Tillson asked William Gaulden, a former slaveholder, antisecessionist, early Reconstructionist, and Liberty County agent, to resign from the Bureau because his political activities promoted a "bad temper" toward the agency within his jurisdiction.[98] Gaulden flaunted his power as agent and engaged in a disruptive feud with his colleague Elias Yulee, but his ability to exercise an inordinate amount of influence over the Hinesville freedpeople, an ability about which he bragged, caused much of the ill will. On one occasion, for example, he called from the fields a large number of freedpeople, many of whom were armed. Gaulden might or might not have planned to use this influence for his own benefit, but Tillson's inspector general believed that "he has entire control over them" and that "he will stir up an insurrection among the blacks that will eventually cause bloodshed."[99]

Regardless of Gaulden's plans, civilian agents as a rule did not consciously see their Bureau association as a means of enhancing their own political careers. Indeed, Warren Moss, a county ordinary when he accepted his appointment with the Bureau, concluded after almost a year of service that if he wished to secure his reelection he had "better resign as there is more opposition to the agency here this year than last year."[100]

Most of Tillson's civilian agents, who frequently were already involved in local office holding before they received their appointments, probably viewed Bureau service as a continuation of their earlier official duties. They might not have been as concerned about their connections as agent Moss had been, but they probably did not see any particular advantage for their political futures in their Bureau associations. If they continued to hold local offices or renewed their involvement in local politics after they had entered the Bureau's service, it was because they found it natural to do so.[101] Agent George Forbes, for example, was elected judge of the county court because the people did not want to lose his services if Washington disbanded the Bureau; however, he had been elected to local offices over the past two decades.[102] He most likely would not have had much difficulty winning an election without his connection with the agency.

Despite the lack of official political activity, the Bureau's work before Military Reconstruction was not devoid of political implications; there were aspects of the Bureau's policies concerning education, contract labor, and civil rights that encouraged and facilitated the freedpeople's larger political aspirations. Nevertheless, during this period, the agency lacked a specific official political charge. Commissioner Howard might privately ask Davis Tillson to urge his men to subscribe to newspapers with Republican sympathies, but that request did not make a policy.[103]

Sibley's reorganized Bureau, however, became an integral component in the politicization of Georgia's freedmen. Charged with assisting with voter registration and with observing and reporting electoral activities within their jurisdictions while maintaining peace at elections, agents and officers educated the freedmen in their new political rights and obligations even as their ex-masters tried to keep them ignorant of them.[104] Bureau men recommended sound, loyal individuals for positions as voter registrars, justices of the peace, and notary publics. They warned their superiors about individuals residing within their jurisdictions who held unreconstructed ideas about black electoral participation. Furthermore, they attended Republican meetings (an act that could reassure freedpeople of the Bureau's support), investigated fraud, gathered affidavits, and supervised elections sometimes with soldiers at their elbows, all the while producing the necessary paperwork to keep their superiors informed of their efforts.[105]

In 1867 and 1868 officers and agents challenged and investigated employers who discharged or threatened to discharge freedpeople for registering to vote or for voting the Republican ticket.[106] Subassistant commissioners visited and "scrutinized" as many of the registration boards in their subdistricts as possible.[107] And after the November 1868 election they traveled through their jurisdictions to inquire into the fairness of voting procedures.[108]

Some agents and subassistant commissioners also assumed the duties of voter registrar and election manager, earning extra money for their troubles.[109] Money might have accounted only partially for their efforts, however, for Sibley's men often revealed a plain understanding of the connection between the durability of their work and the success of the Republican Party.[110] In June 1867, Brunswick subassistant commissioner Douglas Risley expressed his belief that Union Leagues would prevent the freedpeople from suffering from white intimidation and "that their self protection is better insured by conferring upon them the elective franchise and their self-respect greatly increased thereby."[111] In October 1867, Captain William F. White warned ex-slaves that the exercise of the ballot was essential for preserving the fruits of victory.[112] And in 1868 agent William Morrill, who frequently found himself in harm's way as he carried out his Bureau duties, revealed his own commitment to Republicanism and Reconstruction in his high expectations for the good consequences for the freedpeople in labor and politics that would flow from the successes of his party throughout the nation.[113]

At the local level, Morrill was willing to put his life on the line to further that success. When the polls failed to open in Americus for the 1868 election, he "went up and demanded that a room be furnished so the people could vote." White men confronted him and "swore the colored men shouldn't hold election & swore that they would prevent it showing me their pistols & alluding to it— but it started them up and now they are opening the polls." At least the brave Morrill accomplished something, but even he could not prevent the exclusion of large numbers of black voters from the polls once they were opened.[114] An equally determined H. de F. Young, the agent at Irwinton, achieved little in the face of Democrats who threatened freedmen with the loss of work or bribed them with free-flowing liquor, and Albany subassistant commissioner O. H. Howard admitted that he had been completely unprepared for the Democrats' peaceful ballot stuffing, which characterized the election in his jurisdiction.[115]

In May 1867, Oglethorpe County Unionist agent Joseph McWhorter did all he could to impress upon the freedmen "the importance of registering and voting for a convention"; at the same time, he urged them "to be careful who they vote for." In this instance, McWhorter's enthusiasm revealed a personal interest in the freedpeople's political activism. He expected to run for the new legislature when the opportunity presented itself, and he was already trying to control the black vote in his section of the county.[116]

McWhorter was a rare Bureau agent in his use of his office for personal political gain; those who became involved in politics usually followed the paths of John Emory Bryant and his partner, C. C. Richardson, waiting until their official connections had been cut. In fact, McWhorter was almost alone in his willingness to trade his agency for state or local office, because that is exactly what Commissioner Howard expected his men to do if they chose to become politically active.[117] Howard, who now believed that an agent's duties were sufficient to consume his time, considered it improper and "always objectionable for Bureau officers to be mixed up in political matters."[118] Consequently, he would not allow his men to hold elected office while still on his Bureau's roster. Most of Sibley's agents and officers, men who had lobbied hard for their appointments, apparently decided not to risk their livelihoods but to pursue their Reconstruction work from their paid positions within the Bureau; few actually left the Bureau to pursue political office.[119]

It was at times difficult to keep the agency as free of politics, or at least the public expression of politics, as Howard might have wished simply because of the nature of the Bureau's work and the type of men who staffed the agency during the Sibley and Lewis years. Also, the message of emancipation, which Bureau men were to promulgate, was intimately connected with the Republican Party, whereas the opposition to the Bureau's task was clearly identified with Democratic clubs similar to the one that obstructed black voting in Athens in November 1868.[120] Furthermore, black politicians invited Bureau officers to attend "Radical" meetings. At the same time, the assistant commissioner's office ordered them to visit and observe Republican gatherings. These activities placed them in situations where their efforts to answer requests for information could be misinterpreted as political discourse.[121]

Gilbert L. Eberhart, for example, was reprimanded by Commissioner Howard for making a political address, but the school superintendent believed that white Georgians unfriendly to the cause misrepresented him. At the request of the leaders of the Athens freed community, Eberhart had gone "into politics so far as to tell them what party passed and sustained the Emancipation Proclamation, the Civil Rights, Freedmens Bureau and Sherman Bills." Eberhart might have escaped censure if he had been more discreet, but discretion was not one of his virtues; his real offense probably was his casting doubt on the Bureau's impartiality when he allowed the local white press to hear and reprint his words.[122]

Eberhart was alone neither in his sympathies nor in their manner of expression. When Andrew B. Clark commented on the November 1868 election from his Dawson, Terrell County, post, he did not report that the Republicans had gone down in defeat; rather, he told John R. Lewis, "We are beat hear [sic]." Lewis undoubtedly appreciated the implications of Clark's message; he could not well hide his own Republican sympathies, which became increasingly visible as the Bureau's operations contracted. During 1869 and 1870, Lewis expressed partisan leanings that reflected his vision of Reconstruction and his concern for the Georgia freedpeople or, as he once referred to it, "the cause for which we labor."[123]

Lewis engaged in vigorous, if discreet, political activity. In 1869, for example, he opposed a call for another of what he considered to be John Emory Bryant's self-serving conventions. He also threw his support behind Republican governor Rufus Bullock's candidate for a place on the U.S. Supreme Court. Later in 1870 he personally encouraged support for Bullock while on a visit to Washington. In March 1870, as he prepared to wind down the Bureau's educational activities, he also urged his education officers "to strengthen Bullock as much as you can" because "he can & will do more for us & our work than any other man."[124] Nevertheless, the Bureau at least expected to maintain the appearance of nonpartisanship, which was one reason why ex-Bureau agent John Emory Bryant's efforts to depose education superintendent Eberhart failed.

In June 1867, Bryant petitioned Commissioner Howard for an appointment in the Georgia Bureau as its superintendent of education, criticizing Eberhart and his abilities. Subassistant Commissioner Sibley successfully opposed the appointment because Bryant, whom Sibley believed was full of himself, was too "intimately associated with political affairs" in Georgia and "so ardent a politician" that his appointment would be injurious to the Georgia Bureau's reputation.[125]

The Bureau's political duties were never fully accepted by white Georgians as they came to realize the full implications of Reconstruction. The agency's political activity aggravated the uneasy relationships that agents and officers had with their white neighbors, but H. de F. Young learned a lesson that many of his colleagues knew all too well: an agent need not be actively engaged in educating the freedpeople in their political rights to run afoul of white Georgians. "I have not expressed a single political opinion to black or white, but have only done my simple duty," he complained, "& in doing that have become obnoxious to these latter day rebels."[126]

## An Inhospitable Environment

The life of a conscientious Bureau man was often an unpleasant one, too frequently with common creature comforts and cordial social intercourse gone wanting. Some agents and officers put up with minor inconveniences, such as the "perfect old dilapidated crib" that passed for an office in Carnesville or residences that were "very poor and expensive at that."[127] Yankee officials battled the unfamiliar oppressive summer weather, which restrained their effectiveness by aggravating the health problems that many had acquired during the war; the discomfort was significant enough to force some of them to resign.[128] Additionally, the inhospitable social climate, which could be every bit as unpleasant as a humid August day in Savannah, took its toll. Bureau men endured treatment that ranged from indifference to chilly receptions, contemptuous insults, verbal intimidation, and outright physical violence. Understandably, agents and officers could feel quite isolated in their positions.

Some Yankee Bureau men, like O. H. Howard, were fortunate to have their wives and families join them at their posts. Domestic comforts allowed these men to place their arduous duties in some kind of perspective as they watched the normal routines of life unfold. Subassistant Commissioner J. Murray Hoag courted and married a New York woman who was visiting her sister at Savannah and won his first leave in almost three years to go on his honeymoon. John A. Rockwell, an American Missionary Association teacher connected with the Bureau as an unpaid special agent-at-large for educational matters, planned to move into a new house that he purchased for himself and his bride-to-be. New Yorker Carlos de la Mesa, made additionally foreign to the natives by his ethnicity and his Catholic faith, had the pleasure of seeing two newborn daughters baptized in an Atlanta church while he was serving at Rome, Georgia.[129]

But, as de la Mesa learned, although families might provide islands of tranquility, they, too, existed in a larger sea of isolation. Agent Morrill recalled that people at times treated him courteously, but he also admitted that "not much" of society had been open to him and his family.[130] Similar circumstances prompted Stockton agent Horace F. Mills's wife to instigate his resignation when she expressed her desire to return to Middletown, New York, "to be with friends."[131]

Other Bureau men, for one reason or another, deferred their pursuit of domesticity and more keenly felt their isolation. Bureau surgeons Thomas R. Clement and George O. Dalton both complained about the loneliness of their lives in Georgia. Lieutenant George Wagner, a Veteran Reserve Corps officer who served the Bureau at Macon, Augusta, and Americus, was occasionally entertained by the freedpeople's frolics, visits with other officers, and a few social occasions with his white neighbors, but by the time he applied for a leave in July 1868, he had been on duty in Georgia for two years and he missed his family. Although there were white Georgians who accepted the presence of agents with a degree of hospitality, agent H. de F. Young acknowledged that they could ill afford to be too neighborly. Within his jurisdiction, his opponents made it clear "that no man's life was safe who attempted to befriend me."[132]

The inhospitality or social indifference experienced by some Bureau officials turned into more vexatious and dangerous circumstances for others even when they attempted to enjoy a recess from their duties. In August 1867, upon arriving at Carnesville, agent J. W. Barney found only one other Union man in the county. As soon as he began his duties he "became obnoxious to the citizens of Carnesville and the surrounding country." He thus found himself isolated, complaining that he "had no society whatever." Curious about his new home, he had looked forward to exploring the nearby scenic places, but even that recreation was marred by white resentment of his office. When he and his wife arrived for an outing at the resort at Franklin Springs, the agent was warned to leave because his business was "objectionable to southern gentlemen."[133] And even when whites chose to socialize with agents and officers, the events they attended did not necessarily fill them with genuine cordiality. "Last night we had company—'a *genuine Radical*' Bureau officer," a white Georgian recounted. "He only had one arm. [I]t is a pity that it wasn't his head."[134]

One white Georgian admitted in a circuitous way that not only did his neighbors approach Yankees with less than gracious courtesy but Bureau men particularly deserved such treatment. "One of the sad mistakes of our people has been their standing off—and uncourteousness to the Army officer," Iverson Harris explained. "Much might have been accomplished by *politeness*." Bureau men were another matter. "The distinction between the Freedmen's bureau set—and the real Army men is wide. We should never confound the two sets."[135]

Such hostility easily erupted into insults and open expressions of ridicule when Bureau men and their families mingled with local residents in public. If Davis Tillson, his wife, and daughter endured disrespectful treatment from the people of Augusta, Bureau officials elsewhere in the state could not expect much better acceptance by their neighbors.[136] Carlos de la Mesa, tagged as an excitable foreigner by a local jurist, confronted acts of defiance on a regular basis, including those directed at him at a public exhibition in Rome. "In one tableaux not only the Flag of the Confederacy was displayed but there was an officer and a squad of soldiers, all armed and in full confederate uniform at 'Present Arms,'" recounted the Yankee veteran who had fought at Gettysburg. "I could do nothing but pocket the insult[,] put on my cap, take my family, and walk out amidst the applause and Hisses of the audience, the latter without doubt intended for myself."[137] Men associated with the Bureau in Athens experienced a more straightforward approach: they could not even walk the streets of the town without one resident following in their paths, haranguing them about the Ku Klux Klan.[138]

A defeated people found satisfaction in insulting Yankees, but citizens who indulged in the verbal abuse that followed agents and officers through the streets and towns where they lived had the more practical purpose of ridding their communities of the Bureau. Not all men were as determined as William Morrill, who discovered a plot against his life by a "party of lawless men." Although Morrill vowed not to "flinch one hairsbreadth or deviate" his course from what he believed "to be right," threats of violence terrorized other Bureau men, inhibited their ability to do their jobs, and led them to admit defeat.[139] In late 1867 agent T. J. Herbert of Carnesville was subjected to "intimidation and threats" that "so frightened the poor fellow that he left and has not been heard from since."[140]

Inhospitable behavior, verbal abuse, and threats were only barely removed from outright violence in the rough culture of postwar Georgia where in some areas "the man who can best flourish a knife or pistol is a gentleman."[141] Bureau men, therefore, risked suffering grave consequences for exerting themselves in their duty, consequences that made their stay in Georgia too hazardous to take their commitment to Reconstruction with anything but the seriousness that it deserves.

## A Dangerous Job

It was not remarkable that General Edward A. Wild would have an attempt made on his life, but even pursuing a course less radical than his had its risks in postwar Georgia.[142] By advocating something as basic to Northern goals as simple justice in labor relations, Bureau agents put their lives on the line for the freedpeople and for Reconstruction; that they provoked violence from white Georgians was one indication of the threat that their enemies believed they posed to the status quo.[143] In July 1865 the Reverend Eaton incurred the wrath of planters in the southeastern part of the state with his efforts to secure the wages of black workers and consequently placed himself in a dangerous position. "Southern Georgia is moved with indignation," he wrote after presenting accounts to twenty planters for wages due to freedpeople. "They are very angry . . . and talk big things among themselves." His experiences led him to conclude that "were it not for the force of our Military arm, we . . . would lose our heads very soon."[144]

Up the Savannah River at Augusta, agent John Emory Bryant, a "vile abolitionist" according to one of his critics, promulgated a free-labor contract system, established a court of appeals to assist the freedpeople in securing their wages, and received numerous death threats.[145] Augusta malcontents, however, did more than talk; on August 30, 1865, they murdered one of Bryant's assistants. Returning to his quarters after a long day at the office, Captain Alex Heasley was attacked by three Confederate veterans who fired three equally deadly balls into his body and then made sure of their work with their knives.[146] No wonder the Reverend William Tiffany carried a revolver as he went about his business in the Ogeechee district.[147]

As early as December 1865, Tillson understood that loyal men as well as the freedpeople could come under attack from unreconstructed white Georgians unless military power backed Bureau pronouncements.[148] His fears were not unfounded, for white opposition to the Bureau placed his active agents and officers in as much danger as Saxton's reformers. During Tillson's administration, agents and officers found themselves in life-threatening situations on a number of occasions. Major William Gray, Tillson's inspector general, was almost mobbed when trying to arrange for freedpeople to leave the Eatonton area for better labor arrangements elsewhere.[149] Captain C. A. de la Mesa, the Rome subassistant commissioner, postponed travel after being warned by freedpeople of a probable assassination plot.[150] Henry County residents abused their agent, J. R. Phillips, threatened to murder him, fired into his office, and besieged him there until Tillson stationed a detachment of troops in the county.[151] William C. Riddle, agent for Washington County, had to use his fists against a white man who drew a pistol on him.[152] And a disgruntled planter pummeled E. J. Jackson, the agent for Campbell County who never had the "moral support" of his community, into a "cowed and powerless" state.[153]

Violence continued to stalk Bureau men into Sibley's administration and Military Reconstruction. Both Andrew B. Clark and D. A. Newsom were in gunfights with disgruntled whites.[154] Dr. Christian Raushenberg, who eventually survived about two and a half years of dedicated service with the Bureau in southwest Georgia, was almost shot on the street.[155] And Union veteran Henry W. Kearsing, the agent stationed in Bartow County, in June 1868 reported that "it was a common thing to have pistols fired off at his feet" by hidden assailants. During the spring of 1868, men habitually surrounded Kearsing's house at night firing their guns to warn him of their intentions, and on one occasion they stole his flag halyards, with which they threatened to hang him and "his damn Yankee *Bitch*." Although there was some question about Kearsing's sobriety (he explained to one visitor that the appearance of drunkenness was "caused by his head being affected by Quinine which he takes for fever & ague in a little whiskey" or a patent medicine), his predecessor, William O. Moffit, confirmed the dangers. From the safety of Dutchess County, New York, he warned Kearsing that there had been attempts on his life, too, "and but for my extreme watchfulness they would have succeeded." He also advised Kearsing to take action against the one most troublesome villain. "If he comes into your office as he did into mine on divers occasions to abuse the Government and insult you personally," he cautioned, "shoot him in his traitorous tracks and you will be upheld by the Government."[156]

The political contests of Reconstruction only aggravated these circumstances. Andrew Clark believed that his situation began to worsen in 1867 with the commencement of the registration of the freedpeople.[157] In November 1868, Major John J. Knox, the Athens Bureau subassistant commissioner, barely escaped injury because of a confrontation that originated in his conscientious performance of his political duties, but the consequences for the Bureau were just as grave as if he had been murdered. Since his appointment in February 1867, he had made friends among the city's freedpeople because he took the time to visit their churches and schools and, as one of their teachers acknowledged, because he "insisted on making known to the colored people their rights as Freedmen."[158] The political excitement of the 1868 campaign brought things to a head. Knox received numerous insults and threats when he spent the November election day monitoring the polls. Afterwards, he learned that white sentiment was that he should never leave Athens alive. Knox, who "never did scare worth a cent," paid little attention to this threat, but before the month was over he discovered that at least one Athens Democrat was serious about its implementation.[159]

Tom Frierson had had a confrontation with Knox at the polls in which the young Confederate veteran drew a pistol on the Bureau man. On November 21, after allowing his anger to fester for a while, a drunken Frierson took it upon himself to rid the city of Knox because, as one white Clarke County resident later explained, "the agents of the Freedmen's Bureau were at that time very obnoxious to our people." The murder attempt failed, and Knox earned the wrath of the locals because he wounded his assailant, who was, according to the unreconstructed informant, "a very popular young man, beloved by the whole community."[160]

Knox surrendered to the authorities, but his moment of danger was not yet over. A mob gathered, and the assistant commissioner feared for his life until a large crowd of freedmen appeared and threatened to torch the town if anyone molested him. Knox, a most dedicated Bureau man, was soon acquitted of any wrongdoing, but the assailant still accomplished his task. The Michigander, feeling as if his life was not worth much in Athens, resigned and went home as soon as the troops sent to protect him were withdrawn.[161]

Knox could leave town to find peace and quiet in his native state, but for the Bureau men who remained in Georgia, disassociating oneself from the agency did not necessarily bring safety. Violence followed some conscientious Bureau men into private life. Thomas Holden, Sibley's agent at Warrenton, was ostracized, threatened, and denounced as a traitor by his neighbors; the first crop that he harvested after he left the Bureau went up in smoke, burned after the local "Rascals" set fire to his barn.[162] C. C. Richardson, who had served under Tillson from the fall of 1865 into the early spring of 1866 as a subassistant commissioner in southwest Georgia, remained in Thomasville. A little over two months after he had left the Bureau, he was ordered to leave town by a man on whom he had passed judgment for defrauding and abusing freedpeople. "No such negro scoundrel as you can live here," the man warned Richardson and then fired at the former agent in front of a crowd of twenty witnesses. "Must one submit to be persecuted, hunted & shot like a dog in the streets, because of doing his duty to the government while an officer," Richardson asked. "Perhaps if I had been false to my trust while here as an officer, I would have been welcomed back with open arms."[163]

One can only speculate about how the experience of serving with the Bureau in such a hostile environment under such frustrating circumstance influenced the emotional lives of these men. The drunkenness that prompted some complaints against Bureau agents might have stemmed from the pressure and isolation of the position. In December 1867, the intoxicated agent Robinson, who had only been on duty since April, begged for military assistance, explaining that he was "worn out."[164] Bureau surgeon George O. Dalton, although not constantly in conflict with intransigent employers, was a "hardworking Agent of the Bureau," a symbol of Yankee occupation, and another drunken embarrassment to the agency. Stationed in Albany in that most unfriendly region of southwest Georgia, he lived a lonely existence and "got into the habit of drinking to excess."[165]

Agent Andrew Clark, who laid part of the blame for the unsettled state of affairs in Georgia on the White House doorstep, lived in fear for his life for almost his entire duty in Georgia, which could not have been an emotionally healthy situation.[166] Such pressure apparently pushed Subassistant Commissioner Carlos A. de la Mesa over the edge. De la Mesa had worked hard for the agency and the freedpeople, but spent his last days in an insane asylum in Washington, D.C., where the Catholic veteran believed he was a high-ranking military officer or the pope. He had suffered from lingering injuries received at Gettysburg, where he had fallen and had been trampled by his company. Still, his wife believed that those injuries had little to do with his condition. "The remote cause of insanity," she explained, "was vexatious duties under the Freedmen's Bureau in the Southern States," a diagnosis confirmed by an examining physician.[167]

For some Bureau men, the termination of the agency presented them with an honorable opportunity for preserving their own sanity and safety. After the summer withdrawal of their military support in 1868, their lives had become increasingly uncomfortable and dangerous. By early fall, agents were complaining about their inability to secure the necessities of life in the midst of a hostile population; some even had to resort to sleeping in tents for want of better shelter.[168] In Irwinton, citizens boycotted the store of H. de F. Young's landlord and forced the agent to procure new lodgings three miles from their town. The Lancaster, New Hampshire, native, however, was a stubborn man and swore to do his duty to the end if his superior would grant his unfulfillable request for military support. "I only ask protection," he wrote to Bureau headquarters, "and if these people have not had a sufficiency of war why I would give them another dose."[169]

The threat of white violence, however, took its toll on Bureau men not as fearless as the Irwinton agent. In October 1868, fear prompted Subassistant Commissioner O. H. Howard to refuse to investigate a report of violence without a military escort.[170] In August 1868, Hawkinsville agent Lieberman resigned because he feared for his life.[171] Also at this time, J. W. Barney admitted that his situation was becoming increasingly dangerous and that he had become "powerless to do the people (col'd) any good." Threatened, ordered to attend Democratic meetings, attacked, and warned to leave town, Barney rightly concluded that it would be impossible to remain at Carnesville "with any degree of safety." Less determined than his Irwinton colleague, probably because his wife was with him, Barney resigned. "I have endured this as long as mortal men can," he wrote in August 1868, and now he wished to return to the company of "civilized men and in a country where life is protected by law." "The great mystery to the many," explained the Delaware native, "is that a man of my stamp could live in that section of the country for one year."[172] Barney and other Bureau men understood that the Bureau had a valuable role to play in the Reconstruction of Georgia, but because of the intensity of white opposition and their inability to counter it, they conceded defeat. They knew that their own safety required that they leave Georgia.

# 4

## None but the Very Destitute

Davis Tillson, Caleb Sibley, and John R. Lewis, along with a good number of their subordinates, expected their Bureau to have a lasting impact on Georgia by reshaping the ways in which its residents thought, worked, and resolved their disputes. The goal of a reconstructed state well tutored in Yankee ideals, however, foundered not only upon the conscious resistance of individuals who had their own visions of the future but also upon the unprecedented physical problems left behind in the wake of a great war. Ex-masters and ex-slaves alike suffered from widespread and lingering destitution, the consequence of refugeeing, Sherman's march to the sea, poor harvests, and the less dramatic economic manifestations of the war's conduct.[1] Georgia's destitution, though not of the proportions of history's great famines, disrupted social order, caused individual hardship, and stymied economic recovery. For freedpeople just embarking on their new lives, these hard times deflated the opportunities promised to them by the proselytizers of free labor; for ex-masters, who believed that the past held the solutions to stability and renewed prosperity, they encouraged a desire to restore as much of the old order as possible.

In the spring of 1865, chaotic events emphasized the need for a speedy distribution of relief to alleviate the immediate suffering that followed the end of the war. The disorganized state of civil affairs and the disrupted transportation system aggravated the shortage of essential supplies, prompting thievery and pillaging. In Augusta returning soldiers, freedpeople, and even "white women and boys" robbed private larders and plundered stockpiles of stores formerly owned by the Confederate government. Similar incidents occurred elsewhere in the state as hungry veterans and citizens took what they needed, leading James A. Blackshear of Sumter County to conclude that "lawlessness has begun."[2]

For white Georgians, this sense of chaos was heightened by another sign of the breakdown of civilized society that lasted throughout the summer of 1865—roads clogged with black pilgrims. White observers were correct to view this black mobility as evidence that their state's old economic system had collapsed. Crops abandoned in the fields by ex-slaves were indeed a new phenomenon and, to white Georgians, a harbinger of future disasters. Also, in the months following Appomattox, Georgia's cities swelled with black refugees from the rural counties who congregated in camps and shantytowns to try city life or simply to find an alternative to cotton planting, another example of the unsettled times. Clearly, black mobility, regardless of the freedpeople's legitimate motives, contributed not only to white fears but also to the state's hardships. The irony, however, was that from the perspective of the ex-slaves, intrastate migration was in part prompted by their need to search for a way to relieve their own hunger.[3]

The 1865 agricultural season, so thoroughly disrupted by the last convulsions of the war, did not solve the problem of Georgia's widespread destitution. In the spring of 1866, freedpeople from Floyd County in the northwestern corner of the state, for example, petitioned President Andrew Johnson for aid because both Union and Confederate armies had marched, camped, and foraged over their land, contributing to the poor 1865 harvest that left them without adequate provisions.[4] Georgia, especially its northern counties, had not yet fully recovered from the war well into 1866, and the impecunious nature of the state's population threatened to ruin yet another season even before it had begun. Consequently, some residents would not only suffer for the immediate want of food but also risk falling into a cycle of poverty because they lacked the resources necessary for producing the abundant harvests that could come with fair assistance from the heavens.[5]

Even if all other conditions had been ideal, Georgia's farmers still would have had to cope with the uncooperative weather, which provided either too much or not enough rainfall to suit their corn and cotton.[6] Consequently, Georgia's troubled agricultural economy continued into 1867, forcing many residents into destitution.[7] This convinced O. H. Howard, the agent at Albany, that a crisis would be upon southwestern Georgia before the year's end "unless the people learn to eat cotton."[8]

Compounding the problem of hunger were the diseases that so often followed in the wake of war and delayed economic recovery. In 1866 freedpeople died from cholera, but it was smallpox that reached epidemic proportions. During the fall and winter months of 1865 and 1866, the disease, which in some areas lingered on into the spring, further debilitated an already weakened portion of the population, especially in the newly congested cities where freedpeople congregated in close quarters and squalid conditions. Indeed, the serious public health conditions and disease that Davis Tillson observed within the black settlements of the Sherman Reservation probably influenced his views about the wisdom of allowing the freedpeople along the coast to continue on their independent course without Bureau supervision. In April 1866, after learning of the smallpox problem on St. Catherines Island, he ordered his chief medical officer to "send one of the best surgeons you have at Savannah by first boat" with as much medicine as needed to contain the disease on that island.[9]

Smallpox continued to infect the black population in 1867 along with fevers, respiratory ailments, venereal diseases, and other illnesses. Such health problems obviously could take a toll on the freedpeople's economic progress, especially for blacks who lacked the stamina to earn a living and the families who had to care for them. As Bureau surgeon James Laing pointed out in his worried description of the treatment of pneumonia in the Albany area, a poor diet extended the length of time to recovery, and a poor diet was clearly a consequence of an inadequate livelihood.[10]

The difficult economic conditions of postwar Georgia clearly had serious negative consequences for advancing the goals of free labor. Economics prevented some planters from engaging in full agricultural operations and placed the harvests of others in jeopardy because they might not be able to continue to feed the workers they had hired. As late as March 1868, a Richmond County planter pleaded destitution and claimed he was unable to feed his workers, who suffered from conditions that forced them to scavenge and steal. "Instead of orderly, industrious citizens," he warned Caleb Sibley, "they become thriftless vagabonds."[11]

For freedpeople who were working hard and attempting to follow the tenets of free labor, the state's poor economic conditions could quickly destroy their hopes of becoming successful farmers, especially if their profits were tied to the size of the harvest. In August 1866, the Marietta subassistant commissioner observed that "the very dry season has ruined the crops, and those who have worked on shares have made little or nothing." To the east in Oglethorpe County, in October another Bureau agent predicted that freedpeople working for shares "will make little or nothing." But even before harvest time, the problem of inadequate resources to sustain those more independent freedpeople who had been able to set out on their own posed a conundrum for the advocates of the new free-labor system.[12]

Many of those freedpeople of Floyd County who had petitioned Andrew

Johnson in the spring of 1866 had rented land; they needed help because they had "not provision enough to carry them through till the wheat is harvested— and only want a little assistance." In Morgan County, freedpeople who had been working their own lands found their progress disrupted by "the scarcity of provisions [that] keeps them away from their fields hunting provisions for their families." Similar circumstances forced some renters and sharecroppers to abandon their fields, leaving their families to fend for themselves while they took on work to earn food, a problem that did not abate during the next season.[13]

In the spring of 1867, there remained freedpeople who had ambitiously negotiated themselves out from under the constant supervision of white men only to be hard-pressed to feed themselves until they harvested the fruits of their labors.[14] In the Rome region in the northwestern part of the state, freedpeople renting land or working on shares could not secure supplies because merchants would not accept a lien on crops that they assumed the freedpeople did not completely control.[15] In the Athens area, a similar situation existed. "Many of the colored people, are trying to make a crop upon their own hook, they have been mistaken in their calculations they thought they had meat and bread to make a crop upon, but are now out," explained an area resident. "They have their crops in good condition, but right at this time when the crops need them most they have to leave it, to work 3 or 4 days for a bushel of corn, to feed their families."[16] Freedpeople such as these, individuals who exhibited the kind of behavior that made liars of their skeptical former masters, turned to their Bureau for the assistance they required to carry them through their difficult times. Unfortunately, the Bureau could not help them in any meaningful way that would have long-term consequences without discarding beliefs about charity that were central to Yankee ideas about work, government, and human nature. This was a step that most of its officers could not take.

## The Bureau's Response to Destitution

The destitution of the freedpeople in the erstwhile Confederacy was by statute the Freedmen's Bureau's concern.[17] The agency's response to this charge was certainly limited by its lack of substantial resources. More important, however, its chronic worry that all but short-term charity would do more harm than good determined its policy. Furthermore, its officers and agents understood that eleemosynary activities were properly the concern of families, private associations, or the state and local governments, which should quickly resume their responsibilities, not the federal authorities. When the Georgia Bureau did respond to suffering, it did so with the limited resources of a temporary agency concerned with resolving an immediate crisis, not the long-term structural problems that might demand innovative approaches to meet the needs of the extraordinary times in which the agency existed.[18]

Almost as soon as the Bureau began to function as a relief agency, it planned its withdrawal from the field. On May 31, 1865, Oliver Otis Howard informed his assistant commissioners that relief would be discontinued as rapidly as possible, and on June 20, he specifically restricted the issuance of rations to individuals for not more than seven days.[19] Georgia's assistant commissioners and their subordinates generally agreed with Howard's policy. The consensus was that a little help was necessary, given the postwar circumstances, but too much would almost certainly sap a man's initiative and lead to chronic dependence. Even the sympathetic Rufus Saxton saw danger in the dole. Before he assumed his duties as assistant commissioner, he instructed his subordinates "to encourage industry, frugality and independence and to bestow as little charity as possible, consistent with the plainest dictates of humanity."[20] This same attitude prompted his Augusta subordinate, John Emory Bryant, to promulgate labor regulations that made it the responsibility of the working freedpeople to support their unproductive family members and to approve contracts that allowed employers to deduct the expenses of feeding and caring for nonworkers from the earnings of workers.[21] Such terms simply recognized one of the many responsibilities of freedom.

For Davis Tillson, who on October 3, 1865, prohibited the distribution of rations to able-bodied freedpeople, government handouts provided only "subsidiary" and "temporary" relief. Indeed, among his first official acts as Georgia's assistant commissioner was his successful effort to rein in what he considered to be the extravagant amount of relief distributed in Savannah, where in September 1865 the agent there had issued almost 120,000 rations.[22] His policy also became apparent at the commencement of the 1866 season when he ordered the Atlanta contraband camp to discharge all able-bodied freedpeople.[23] His agents always had to be cautious in their distribution of aid, for "much mischief may be done by issuing rations to persons who are really able to take care of themselves."[24] Throughout his tenure, Tillson always assumed that the best solution to destitution was moving freedpeople away from the blighted areas of Georgia to plantations within and outside the state where they could find profitable employment.[25]

Officers like Americus subassistant commissioner George Wagner, Cuthbert subassistant commissioner F. A. H. Gaebel, and Athens subassistant commissioner J. J. Knox carried such concerns to their own commands; all worried that prolonged issues of rations would bring out the worst in those who had access to free food. Indeed, Major Knox made a direct connection between the Bureau's commencement of the issuing of rations and the increase in the number of claims of destitution. When people saw that relief was available, Knox explained, they raised a cry for it, which soon made the officer "heartily sick of this 'Draw' business."[26]

The notion of self-help also carried over into the medical relief activities of the agency. In the fall of 1865, the Atlanta Bureau surgeon "had a great deal of trouble" with the local authorities who attempted to turn over to the Bureau's care all of the city's smallpox-infected freedpeople. The surgeon coped with this abdication of responsibility, but he also encouraged the founding of a freedmen's benevolent society to help with the medical expenses he incurred while treating black Atlantans.[27]

Even toward the end of the Bureau's life, after witnessing the vicissitudes of postwar Georgia agriculture, Bureau attitudes about relief had changed little. In June 1868, Assistant Commissioner Caleb Sibley concluded that the withdrawal of Bureau assistance "had the good effect of forcing many to successful exertions to obtain support, who (under other circumstances) would have lingered on in idleness as long as there was a chance to subsist on the bounty of the Government."[28] Despite this commitment to extricate the Bureau from charitable endeavors, both Sibley and his predecessor, Tillson, recognized crisis situations in 1866 and in 1867 and responded to them. Nevertheless, their actions represented diversions from their policies, not changes of heart that would lead the federal government in new directions.

Throughout the Bureau's existence in Georgia there were a few agents and officers who came to recognize that there were problems with a Bureau policy that was rooted in antebellum ideas about charity. Some Bureau men even suggested discarding old ideas about the negative impact of economic assistance to confront the extraordinary circumstances of the times. New Jersey native, wartime Georgia Unionist, and Augusta agent Jacob R. Davis, for example, urged Commissioner Howard to provide capital to his fellow Unionists who had lost all but their land because of the war. Their only difficulty now in producing all that they and their neighbors needed, he explained, was their inability to feed their animals and their workers. If the government assisted them and took a lien on their crops, disaster could be avoided at least in Richmond County.[29]

Davis's plan excluded ex-rebels, for whom he had no sympathy, and made no mention of the freedpeople besides their role as agricultural hands, but other Bureau men had ideas for the ex-slaves with whom they worked. Augustus Mitchell, a Bureau physician at St. Marys, Georgia, proposed that those freedpeople who sought out government lands in Florida under the terms of the Southern Homestead Act of 1866 should be capitalized until they harvested a crop, not simply for the unrealistic term of one month as provided by the Bureau.[30] A more modest proposal, but a diversion from commonly held beliefs nonetheless, could have logically followed from a simple observation made by the Reverend William Tiffany. In September 1865, he suggested that the freedpeople under his supervision in the Ogeechee district would have raised a much better crop if they had been provided with seed.[31]

Apparently, other Bureau men, though not as direct as Dr. Mitchell, talked around the issue of the agency's role as an investor in the freedpeople's economic success. In May 1867, Savannah subassistant commissioner J. Murray Hoag expressed the tension that could exist between holding to policy and divining workable solutions to the problem of destitution. The officer watched Liberty County freedpeople, who "did all in their power to make a good crop" on land that they were renting, hurt their prospects because, short of provisions, they had to neglect their fields in order to find food. Hoag understood that the Bureau could salvage the situation by advancing provisions to these freedpeople. However, these people were able-bodied, labor commanded decent wages in his district, and Bureau policy prevented him from taking on the role of a banker. "Extreme suffering," which was O. O. Howard's condition for issuing relief at this time, "cannot well exist among the able bodied when labor commands fair wages," he reasoned. "An advance would no doubt in many instances result advantageously to the freedpeople yet it would virtually amount to a loan of capital."[32]

Hoag stopped short of recommending action that would contradict Bureau policy as he understood it, but there were other agents and officers who recommended that the Bureau should provide rations for those black petitioners who were working land on their own until they harvested their crop and could repay the agency.[33] At times, the Georgia Bureau responded positively to these latter suggestions, but only in ways that fit its preconceived ideas about its charitable role. In May 1866, for example, Davis Tillson approved the distribution of a limited amount of rations to the Floyd County petitioners, after the lapse of a month during which time Bureau officers investigated their situation to determine the legitimacy of their request.[34] Also, during the spring of 1867, Caleb Sibley was inclined to assist two freedmen's colonies, one in McIntosh County and the other in Camden County, by providing a limited amount of rations after they had agreed to give the agency first lien on their harvests.[35] The Bureau was ever reluctant to give anything beyond a loan of provisions to the ex-slaves; even when Captain Alexander Ketchum distributed rations to freedpeople in the coastal reservation lands in 1865, he took a lien on their crops.[36]

Advancing rations to freedpeople was an ad hoc activity directed at immediate needs and never developed into anything like a coherent comprehensive policy. Caleb Sibley was just as inclined to turn down such requests as to honor them, lest "we should be flooded with them, if it is known we furnish rations to carry on plantations, taking a lien on crops." Commissioner Howard agreed, although he allowed his assistant commissioners to act at their own discretion in judging the circumstances of each petition. Still, the guidelines were clear. Bureau rations were distributed "to prevent extreme suffering and not to lend capital to any planters."[37] Consequently, the Bureau's role in this area would remain temporary and limited.

As the Bureau distanced itself from functioning as a charitable organization, it pressured freedpeople, ex-masters, and local government officials to shoulder their responsibilities to the destitute. Davis Tillson preferred to see, and Caleb Sibley was pleased to witness, freedpeople caring for their own.[38] But if the freedpeople could not bear this economic burden or if the destitute, particularly the elderly, had no family to care for them, their proper primary avenue for assistance was white Georgia.

In 1865 and 1866 Davis Tillson explained to ex-masters who complained about being burdened by unproductive freedpeople that they must provide for them, an obligation that was, according to the assistant commissioner, the consequence of the implied contract of slavery and one that would stand until the civil authorities could assume the burden.[39] White Georgians, however, made the Bureau's task a hard one by acting on the assumption that Tillson's implied contract had died with the institution. The editor of the *Columbus Daily Enquirer* provided what ex-masters must have considered a logical and just protest to Tillson's policy when he argued that the destruction of slavery deprived planters of the "prop that upheld the whole system." Without "efficient workers," planters could not "provide for those who could not provide for themselves."[40] Now many of these ex-masters, who were aware that their county coffers were impoverished and who had abandoned any pretense of paternalism, expected the Bureau to assume the burden of caring for unproductive ex-slaves even as the agency began to limit its activities. As late as May 1868, a Griffin resident noted that there were a "good many" black paupers in Spalding County; because his county government had no funds, he saw no reason to assume that anyone but the Freedmen's Bureau should care for them.[41] During the fall of 1868, the Bureau surgeon in Macon tended to insane, aged, sick, and blind freedpeople, some of whom had lived with their last master more than thirty years before being deposited at the agency's Sibley Hospital.[42]

Beyond dealing with extreme cases of hardship and finding good positions for the able-bodied, the Bureau's primary relief role nevertheless remained constant: to convince or force the civil authorities of Georgia to shoulder the responsibility of caring for the destitute of both races.[43] The assumptions that Bureau officials held concerning these authorities and white Georgians in general were hardly different from their views on the freedpeople when it came to assessing the impact of Washington's largess on their initiative. White Georgians also would willingly "defraud" the federal government, an act considered by some, according to one Bureau officer, to be "meritorious."[44] Indeed, on one occasion a Bureau officer accused both black and white Georgians in the southwestern part of the state of "playing starving," accepting Bureau rations, and then trading the food for various nonessential items at local shops.[45] Bureau officials, therefore, assumed that an early withdrawal of relief, whether it be rations, clothing, or medical assistance, would have the positive effect of forcing whites as well as blacks to greater exertions, with the added benefit of leaving the civil authorities with no alternative but that of assuming their rightful responsibilities.

Chief surgeon J. W. Lawton's draconian reaction to the outbreak of smallpox in Savannah during the fall of 1865 was extraordinary in its harshness but still one that most Bureau officials would have at least understood if not wholeheartedly accepted. "If the result of the war has been to throw an extra burden upon cities South by the freedom of these millions of slaves," he explained to his medical officer in the afflicted city, "they must meet it—the time *must* come, when the United States Government will withdraw from the care of the Freedmen and force their care upon local (Town or County) Authorities—this may as well be done, if possible, now as months or years hence, and the aid of the Bureau is to be rendered only until the authorities can make proper provision." The extent of assistance he was willing to proffer was in accord with this assessment: some tents to shelter the suffering. "I cannot help thinking that as

long as we will do for them, the authorities will be quite willing to allow it."
Withholding assistance would force the authorities to act "or let the disease run
riot in the city—a choice to which they are welcome and the results also."[46]

The Georgia Bureau's response to disease and hunger was more charitable
than Lawton's suggestion, and Lawton himself assumed a more cooperative approach to dealing with the civil authorities, but the underlying assumptions remained in place.[47] Lawton's successor, J. V. De Hanne, advised against extending the Bureau's medical services because such a course would encourage the
civil authorities to ignore their responsibilities. And Caleb Sibley, eager to extract his agency from the relief business, provided the same rationale for limiting the distribution of rations, even if suffering resulted. "Nothing but extreme
want and severe experience," he explained, "will induce the Civil Authorities to
assume the responsibilities belonging to them, and take the necessary steps to
obviate these difficulties."[48]

Needless to say, the Bureau's efforts to alert the civil authorities to their obligations met with mixed results. White Georgians with good intentions found
that the magnitude of the problem facing them strained a system designed to
deal with only the handful of paupers that had been the antebellum norm; now,
suffering the consequences of the bad harvests and inadequate tax revenues,
local officials, who had always been the custodians of the poor, found their
resources stretched to the limits by unprecedented destitution in their counties.[49] In 1868 in Burke County, destitute individuals were housed in the
county jail because there was no poorhouse.[50] And in 1866 Muscogee County
officials could not even afford to bury the black paupers who died within their
jurisdiction.[51]

At times, the Bureau and local officials worked together to bring relief to the
freedpeople, as was the case during the smallpox epidemic of 1865 and 1866.
The Bureau furnished some of the municipalities with extra assistance with
which to battle the disease by supplying food, medicine, and clothing to hospitals that admitted freedpeople.[52] Yet, although crisis and necessity prompted
several instances of cooperation between the agency and local officials, Bureau
surgeon Lawton discerned a general unwillingness on the part of the civil authorities to assume the expense of administering social services to blacks.[53]
Consequently, during the fall and winter of 1867, Sibley and his subordinates
found it necessary to continue to survey local government's willingness and
ability to assume the responsibilities of caring for the sick and destitute.[54] If
agents presented cases for the attention of the local authorities and they refused

to act, the Bureau, following the procedures prescribed by Military Reconstruction, took steps to have them removed for being delinquent in their duties.[55] In 1868 as the Bureau began its withdrawal from the state, it reminded civil authorities of their obligations by making arrangements to transport paupers residing in its hospitals to their home counties for relief and by closing its medical facilities or negotiating with city governments to assume their control.[56] But the agency's efforts to make a serious impression failed. Obviously, civil authorities understood that they had one great tactical advantage over the Bureau: they simply could refuse to act if they wished to stymie the agency's plans, shortchange the freedpeople's needs, and escape responsibility.

On more than a few occasions, the Bureau found its job made all the more difficult when officials did not act in good faith and either refused to accept their responsibilities or obstructed the attempts of the ex-slaves to secure relief. During the early fall of 1866, for example, the Bureau offered to hire a physician to care for the freedpeople of Sumter County if the inferior court there assumed the burden of paying for medicine. The court officers refused this partnership, claiming poverty.[57] Earlier, in December 1865, the Savannah city health officer agreed to provide for the sick of both races who had been residents of the port before Sherman's arrival on the Georgia coast but no others; blacks who had arrived in the city with or after Sherman were freedpeople and therefore not his but the Bureau's responsibility.[58] Although the city of Savannah eventually contributed funds for the maintenance of the Bureau hospital, this earlier attitude persisted even as the Bureau attempted to reduce its services. After being notified that the Bureau hospital could no longer accept patients, the city officials abandoned helpless freedpeople at the hospital's gate.[59]

Local officials had been the source of charity for paupers in antebellum Georgia, but because of the extreme circumstances in the fall of 1866 state officials intervened by passing a relief law that addressed the needs of Confederate widows and orphans but ignored freedpeople.[60] This state policy remained in effect during the hard times of the spring of 1867, and a few local officials used it as an excuse to deny freedpeople relief regardless of the source of the food that they had at their disposal.[61] Other local officials failed to give the problem of relieving destitution "practical, energetic attention," performed their duties in a "dilatory manner," or tangled the process in "red tape."[62] To meet these and other aggravating circumstances, such as the difficulty caused by a railroad station agent who refused to release a shipment of rations until someone paid the freight charges, the Bureau prodded, threatened, and promised to issue rations only to the freedpeople and whites who were neglected by local officials.[63] For Atlanta subassistant commissioner Fred Mosebach, the latter course of action was only right when whites made "worthless assurances and professions of good will, but they think and act differently." In June 1867, when he learned that once again Henry County residents were pursuing a "heartless course" toward the freedpeople, treating the suffering less than fairly, Mosebach ordered agent George Nolan to stop issuing recently arrived provisions to whites. If Henry County officials "make distinction of race or color[,] very well; let us do the same," he instructed Nolan. Recognizing the Bureau's obligations to the truly needy, he advised Nolan to "allways give the preference to the freedmen, those that are really unable to work and to make a support and consequently suffering—if we don't care for them nobody will."[64]

Bureau policy combined with the hard times and the white reluctance to assume the burdens of relief meant that the most vulnerable freedpeople could become the victims of abstract pronouncements about the benefits of withholding aid or of a stubborn military or civil bureaucracy. On occasion, individual initiative staved off disaster as local Bureau officers assumed responsibility for the suffering humanity confronting them in their jurisdictions and worried about the financial consequences later. In May 1867, Quitman agent Alvin B. Clark quarantined freedpeople with smallpox, and only after he secured a doctor to care for them did he ask his superiors if there were funds to pay for the medical care.[65] The following year Americus agent William C. Morrill paid the doctors' bills of some freedpeople because the county could not and the physicians refused to treat patients without pay.[66] In April 1868, Athens subassistant commissioner John J. Knox discovered that the county poor fund could not help a destitute freedwoman, so he bought her corn, bacon, and sugar.[67] And in May of the same year, Columbus subassistant commissioner John Leonard gave his personal security to obtain rations to feed thirty paupers in the county poorhouse, left to fend for themselves after the inferior court justices of Muscogee County all resigned.[68] Rome subassistant commissioner C. A. de la Mesa best explained these charitable actions when he rescued a family of freedpeople from freezing and secured medical attention for them. De la Mesa believed that something had to be done to alleviate the suffering. The civil authorities refused to act, so he, the freedpeople's last resort, assumed responsibility.[69]

On other occasions rigid adherence to bureaucratic procedures led to delays and increased suffering. In May 1866, for example, Atlanta freedpeople could not secure assistance from either the city officials or the Bureau; many were widows with children, handicapped, or elderly "at wits end to contrive to keep soul and body together" and found succor at the hand of the American Missionary Association representative in the city.[70] In May 1867 agent Alvin Clark learned that his request for clothes for those freedpeople leaving smallpox quarantine would be delayed because he had not applied for them through proper channels.[71] And in July 1868, because of the Bureau's withdrawal from relief activities, agent Christian Raushenberg kept transferring cases to the Inferior Court of Dougherty County, even though the county lacked funds to care for the freedpeople.[72] But most distressing was the stubborn commitment to policy that had fatal consequences in Wilkes County.

In January 1866, agent Brien Maguire confronted Wilkes County officials with cases of smallpox in need of treatment. They refused to act, contending that sick freedpeople were the Bureau's responsibility. Maguire then applied to Tillson's adjutant, Captain W. W. Deane, for assistance. Deane referred him back to the civil authorities, who pleaded their own poverty. In the meantime, charity compelled Maguire to assume the expenses of caring for two of the suffering freedpeople. It was a case of too little too late; the delay led to the death of an elderly freedwoman and contributed to the death of an elderly freedman, who had crawled off into the woods after learning of a threat to burn down his cabin.[73]

Even when things moved smoothly through bureaucratic channels, the time wasted in confirming cases, securing transportation costs, and receiving permissions could have serious consequences. In February 1867, following proper channels delayed the admission of a Waynesboro freedman into the Augusta Bureau hospital. By the time the subassistant commissioner received permission to transport the freedman to the hospital, the patient was dead.[74]

As much as the Bureau wished to distance itself from any form of relief activity, be it the distribution of rations or the administration of health facilities, it could not ignore completely the needs of a destitute postwar Georgia. There were times when its officers and agents accepted the fact that the federal government had to act as the last resort of many petitioners and expended what limited resources were available to them, even as Bureau officials in Washington urged them to continue to contract the Bureau's operations in this area. Their approach was nothing if not spasmodic, but within a narrowly defined sphere of action—providing a limited amount of short-term relief as a last resort in critical situations—the agency helped to alleviate some of the hardship of a substantial number of black and white Georgians.

## Relieving Destitution

Although Congress charged the Bureau to supervise the distribution of relief, it failed to provide the agency with an independent appropriation for purchasing the necessary supplies. Income from confiscated property was nonexistent in Georgia during the summer of 1865, so the Bureau became dependent on outside sources. Rufus Saxton appealed to Northern aid societies to supplement the rations furnished by the army's commissary general and the clothing allocated from the quartermaster's stores.[75] The imperfect organization of the Bureau in Georgia prohibited it from assuming complete responsibility for the destitute, but its officers did their best to meet the demands placed on them. By June 11 John Emory Bryant had made heavy drafts on the commissary stores at Augusta and had begun to worry that he would not have enough supplies to relieve all the suffering that he confronted.[76] Over a four-month period, the Augusta agency issued 61,713 rations.[77] The Savannah agency, the only other agency that functioned outside the Sherman Reservation for the entire summer, distributed in September alone almost 120,000 rations.[78]

The resources available to Tillson for attending to destitution initially were not much better than his predecessor's. When his quartermaster, Captain Charles T. Watson, assumed his duties on October 15, 1865, he found no property in the Bureau's possession and no funds available even to meet routine expenses. Watson, a Maine native who had entered the war as a private, energetically pursued his duty and secured for the Georgia Bureau thirty-one acres of land outside the Sherman Reservation as well as 149 buildings for the Bureau's use. The agency sold some of this property but also was required to turn over much of it to the Ordnance Department or return it to its former owners. Those transfers of property left the agency with seventeen acres of land and eighty-five buildings, "a large portion of which are of little value," to use to produce income. The Bureau finally received funding that could be expended on relief through the Army Appropriations Act of July 1866, with over half of the funds set aside for clothing and rations for freedpeople.[79]

At first Tillson was wary of accepting at face value the reports of extraordinary destitution in the northern portion of the state.[80] However, the assistant commissioner, despite his concerns about prolonged and unnecessary issues of relief, was sufficiently flexible and realistic to recognize a legitimate crisis. In the spring of 1866, with the approval of Congress and Commissioner Howard, the Bureau surveyed the needs of the state and from June through

September distributed emergency relief.[81] By mid-June Tillson was urging the military, his source of supply, to act quickly to curb the "great and severe" destitution in the state. Firsthand reports from his own subordinates had convinced him that northern Georgia could absorb from 100,000 to 200,000 rations each month until harvest time. By the beginning of July, Tillson believed that blacks and whites in the suffering counties would need at least 150,000 rations, and the assistant commissioner urged the army to send him the food as rapidly as possible.[82]

The task of the actual distribution of these rations further complicated the chores of the Bureau's agents and officers, who were already fully engaged in the time-consuming task of supervising labor arrangements. Not only did they have to deal with the logistical problems but they had to take care to screen all applicants to make certain that only those worthy of assistance received rations.[83] To relieve his agents' workload, Tillson hired temporary special agents to deal exclusively with the problems of destitution, and he appointed New York native and Veteran Reserve Corps officer Captain Eugene Pickett. who officially joined Tillson's staff in June 1866, to supervise the Georgia Bureau's relief operations.[84]

By mid-July Captain Pickett discovered that the Bureau had already distributed 115,000 rations to blacks and whites, exhausting its supplies in the state. Appeals to the military brought an additional 150,000 rations into Georgia from Chattanooga on July 29. Within a week Pickett had distributed another 110,000 rations to northern Georgia counties. Despite such efforts, his inspection of the area revealed continuing destitution with little prospect for salvation from a bountiful harvest.[85] Although reports from other sources reached Tillson suggesting that the crops would be inadequate to support the full needs of the people, the Bureau no longer intended to issue the extraordinary relief beyond the summer. In August, after conducting an inspection tour, Commissioner Howard's acting assistant inspector general recommended that all distribution of relief be discontinued in Georgia "as a measure of economy and true kindness."[86] By August 30, Pickett had discharged his special agents, allowing them to distribute whatever supplies they had on hand; however, on September 10, after further consideration, the captain concluded that real suffering would result from the crop failure. Unfortunately, Howard had instructed Tillson to turn over all requests for aid to the civil authorities.[87]

Tillson, proving that he was neither without a mind of his own nor blind to reality of the freedpeople's condition, did his best to convince Commissioner

Howard that there remained a real need for federal assistance to alleviate the suffering of destitute blacks in Georgia. In late September, he made it clear to the commissioner that the troubles of northern Georgia could not be attributed to "improvident habits and laziness of the people, but to the past season." Three days later, he again reminded the commissioner that, although it was proper to return the responsibility of relief to the state, the legislature had yet to provide for the relief of the freedpeople. Even if local officials accepted such a responsibility, Tillson admitted, the destitution was so great in some parts of the state that they would not be able to meet the needs of all the hungry.[88] Nevertheless, during the last months of Tillson's tenure, the Bureau did not return to a general program of relief based on large distributions of rations. By the order of the secretary of war, Tillson stopped all issuances on October 1, 1866, except to relieve the most extreme cases ignored by the civil authorities.[89] In November Tillson received permission to draw on commissary stores only to relieve documented cases of dire distress.[90] Despite these and all other practical and ideological limitations, Tillson's Bureau had distributed 683,206 rations in one year, including 177,942 rations for white consumption.[91]

Caleb Sibley's administration experienced a similar pattern of charitable activities. The Bureau was initially reluctant to distribute rations only to find itself scrambling to deal with a springtime emergency. Once it accepted the need to feed Georgians, it worked hard to remove itself from the relief business as quickly as possible. The assistant commissioner, already beginning his effort to reorganize the Bureau, did his best to follow Washington's directives and extricate the agency from the general relief process by encouraging the civil authorities to assume their legitimate responsibilities to the destitute of both races and by limiting relief offered by his office. In February, for example, the Georgia Bureau fed only 1,543 whites and 1,917 blacks; in March, only 1,300 whites and 2,142 blacks.[92]

In all likelihood, the Georgia Bureau during this period of transition, which involved phasing out the use of Tillson's native white Georgians and replacing them with loyal men, failed to develop a complete picture of the problem of destitution within its jurisdiction. Along with the break in administrative continuity, in some counties the civilian agents not yet relieved were "unwilling to exert themselves to any extent without compensation."[93] However, there were alert subordinates who reported serious destitution, the inability of local jurisdictions to cope with the problem, and the unwillingness of some civil officials to deal impartially with black as well as white paupers. These reports prompted

Sibley to increase the Georgia Bureau's relief activities once again to meet the specific crisis.

In March, reports from various counties began to illustrate the danger inherent in the Bureau's premature attempt to withdraw the charitable crutch it had offered Georgians and to allow them to stand on their own amidst crippling destitution.[94] Washington, however, was aware of the situation. In early March, Commissioner Howard reported to Congress the projected needs of his agency if it were to assume a significant role in assuaging a summer of suffering. The figures he presented, which included an estimated 7,500 whites and 5,000 blacks from Georgia who presumably would need 375,000 rations to sustain them for five months, prompted Congress on March 30 to give Howard the authority to deal with the problem. The lawmakers, refusing to allocate to the agency new resources, gave the Bureau permission to purchase supplies with funds already designated for other purposes.[95]

Various Northern aid societies also rallied to meet the needs of the destitute, and the corn they provided relieved some of Georgia's needs during the spring of 1867. Organizations like the New York Southern Famine Relief Commission and the Philadelphia Famine Relief Commission contributed almost 47,000 bushels of corn to assist Georgia's indigent before the middle of May 1867. And it was Sibley's Bureau that supervised its distribution.[96]

To oversee the relief process, Sibley tapped the experienced Captain Eugene Pickett, who again relied on several special agents to assist him in the distribution of supplies in the counties.[97] Unsurprisingly, the monthly salary of one hundred dollars was especially appealing to out-of-work veterans and Georgia Unionists like Martin Hinton, who had "suffered extreme persecution at the hands of the Confederate authorities" losing "nearly all of his property on account of the war."[98] The Bureau also tried to move some supplies through the county inferior court system, but it found several judges partial in their response for aid or at best slow to meet the pressing demands of the situation.[99] Some of the agency's own men also hindered its relief efforts with their negligence or inefficiency, but few were actually guilty of knowingly defrauding the Bureau of its supplies. Union veteran Azra A. Buck, for example, was convicted of selling corn placed in his charge. He admitted the charge was true, but he also argued that it was a necessary step for bringing relief to distant places where he could not transport bulky freight. Nevertheless, Sibley removed him.[100]

Buck claimed that he was a victim of his lying enemies, who informed the Bureau that he was an embezzler. His protestations of innocence did not faze his superiors, but a similar case involving the misuse of rations suggests that selfish motives could prompt neighbors to lodge complaints against agents. Agent George W. Selvidge's situation serves as a reminder that personal antagonisms and personal gain could instigate attacks on Bureau agents and officers. Tillson had appointed Selvidge in December 1865, and Sibley carried him on the rolls as a paid agent stationed at Dalton until May 1866, when an investigation found him guilty of "gross incompetence and serious dereliction of duty."[101] Most of the charges, including the selling of rations and clothing, were false as far as the investigating officer, Subassistant Commissioner C. A. de la Mesa, could determine. Selvidge failed to monitor his assistants and his wife, who actually stole the property, but he was not guilty of theft. Nevertheless, although de la Mesa found that Selvidge did not use the promise of rations to seduce an innocent woman as charged, he discovered that the agent had "criminal intercourse" with her, a woman of "abandoned character," in his office. This activity was sufficient to have the agent dismissed, but this case was more involved than the crimes of negligence and lust indicate. One of his accusers, Dr. L. P. Gudger, the president of the local Union League, hoped to assume Selvidge's duties as tax collector; another, a Union veteran who worked closely with Gudger, applied for Selvidge's Bureau position even before the case was decided; and a third was angry with Selvidge for recommending someone else for the position of voter registrar. Consequently, de la Mesa concluded that the charges made against Selvidge were motivated by personal prejudice; the Rome subassistant commissioner "was unable to find but one colored citizen who had any fault to find with him."[102]

There remained some confusion concerning Selvidge's incomplete relief accounts after he left the Bureau owing to his quick exit from Dalton to visit an ailing relative in Tennessee. His books showed a serious deficiency in the number of rations actually distributed when compared with the amount received. This discrepancy, however, provided another example of the need for caution when judging accusations against Bureau agents. Selvidge had balanced his books. He had turned his papers over to another agent who had mislaid them, but it took about a month to straighten out the record.[103]

Despite these troubles, the Bureau's relief efforts continued throughout the summer, allowing the agency to help a significant number of white as well as black destitute. Under the authority granted by the March 30 resolution, Sibley issued relief in May to 14,754 whites and 8,574 blacks.[104] A large number of women and children especially benefited from the relief. In June, the Bureau provided aid to 18,046 whites, including 11,343 women and children, and 12,320 blacks, including 5,750 women and children. When the Bureau's relief efforts peaked in July, of the 22,376 whites who accepted assistance, 13,921 were women and children; of the 19,318 freedpeople, 9,792 were women and children.[105]

In July, however, Captain Pickett reminded Georgia of the temporary nature of Bureau relief when he began to give notice that the government would no longer distribute rations.[106] Consequently, although substantial issuances of the supplies on hand continued into August, in October the Bureau fed only 112 whites and 94 freedpeople. Thereafter, in conformity with directions from Washington, Bureau relief activities were extraordinary and confined to emergency situations; after the crisis of the spring and summer of 1867, the Georgia Bureau never again became involved in extensive relief efforts. If circumstances once again prevented freedpeople from caring for their own, their relief would become the responsibility of the local civil authorities. The Bureau's immediate role in the area of relief became one of an overseer committed to convincing or forcing those authorities to accept their legitimate obligations to the poor of both races.[107]

## Medical Care for the Freedpeople

Keeping within the understood limits of its assignment, the Bureau did not design its medical program to be anything but temporary. Bureau medical assistance, like its distribution of rations, dealt with emergencies and the immediate suffering of freedpeople who would eventually become the charges of their families or the civil authorities. Nevertheless, despite some bureaucratic blunders, Bureau-employed doctors and Bureau-supplied medicines helped a number of ailing freedpeople who otherwise would have gone unattended.

The Bureau's medical efforts during the early months of Reconstruction were as limited as its organization. During the summer of 1865 almost three hundred cases of smallpox received treatment thanks to two doctors the Bureau had hired at Macon. But when surgeon J. W. Lawton arrived on September 1 to assume his duties as the Georgia Bureau's chief medical officer, he found no organized medical relief except for John Emory Bryant's poorly equipped hospital in Augusta.[108]

Bryant had established his hospital shortly after he had arrived at his post and it, too, reflected the Bureau's slow entry into Reconstruction work. Located in an old government workshop, an "unfit" building but the best that Bryant could secure, it consisted of one large room which by early August housed about one hundred men and women. Bryant's help included one steward, one clerk, and several cooks as well as a doctor who was not yet under contract with the Bureau. The hospital was poorly supplied and lacking all medicines because Bryant could not obtain the cooperation of the army's medical director in Georgia.

Despite these limitations, Bryant's plans were still more ambitious than the Bureau medical department would later accept. The officer had established asylums for the aged and orphaned freedpeople. He also was providing shelter for unwed pregnant women who were close to giving birth, which by August 1865 had made him a foster father many times over. "I have already quite a family of children who have lately come into the world," he informed Rufus Saxton.[109]

Lawton's interpretation of his assignment was not so wide-ranging. After touring the state, he softened his earlier response to the medical crisis in Savannah and concluded that the Bureau could best serve the population by locating medical facilities at central and easily accessible points throughout the state. Lawton believed a dispensary system would provide the most economical means for distributing medical relief. All that it would require of the Bureau was a supply of drugs placed at the disposal of a locally contracted physician who would be willing to prescribe them to freedpeople. Perhaps Davis Tillson saw this type of approach as a way to begin to draw the county authorities into providing relief; he proposed that the government hire physicians for each county, provide them with medicine, and then try to convince the local authorities to pay part of the cost for maintaining the physicians. However, in early 1866 and again in October, when Lawton asked Howard to permit him to employ generally a system of dispensaries, the commissioner believed that even that expansion of the Bureau's activities was inadvisable.[110]

As a result, the Bureau never established more than a handful of dispensaries. Lawton supplied physicians at Brunswick, St. Catherines Island, St. Marys, and Stone Mountain, but by the end of September 1866 only the latter two remained in operation.[111] Lawton's successors opened some medical outposts and closed others. Army surgeon J. V. De Hanne, who assumed Lawton's duties on October 24, 1866, closed dispensaries at Stone Mountain, St. Marys, and Americus. His civilian successor, James M. Laing, who assumed the position of chief surgeon on July 26, 1867, reported that by the beginning of October 1867, the

Bureau's medical department supplied dispensaries only at Albany, Brunswick, and Darien.[112]

The Bureau's medical efforts were in fact concentrated in several of Georgia's larger towns. During Lawton's tenure and afterwards, until the Bureau began phasing out its medical operations, the agency maintained regular hospitals at Atlanta, Augusta, Columbus, Macon, and Savannah. Confiscated rebel property conveniently provided the Bureau officials with adequate if not entirely appropriate hospital buildings. In Augusta the hospital had previously seen service as a Confederate machine shop; in Macon the first hospital building had been a rebel chemical laboratory. The subassistant commissioner at Columbus probably did not endear himself to the freedpeople of his jurisdiction when he seized their church in October 1865 so that they might have "a fine hospital," but the Bureau eventually found an erstwhile Confederate armory there suitable for the medical needs of the city's black community. The Savannah buildings, which housed the largest Bureau facility, had actually been a Confederate hospital, but in Atlanta, a city devastated by the war, tents eventually gave way to newly erected buildings and rooms rented from the local medical college.[113]

At its peak during the winter of 1866–67, the Georgia Bureau's medical department employed thirteen physicians, including the chief surgeon, to staff these facilities.[114] Several of these doctors were army surgeons, but from the outset the Bureau relied heavily on the contracted services of civilian physicians, especially because rapid demobilization was thinning the ranks of qualified officers.[115] By December 1865, for example, only three medical officers were on duty with the Bureau, while the agency employed seven private physicians; by June 30, 1867, only one army doctor remained on duty with the Bureau, while the agency employed eight civilians. By June 30, 1868, all of the Bureau's Georgia doctors were civilians.[116]

This was not a large staff, but the Bureau had no intention of becoming the primary provider of medical care to the freedpeople of Georgia, whether they were solvent or destitute. Consequently, physicians were overworked and their facilities were strained as the Bureau continued its efforts to convince civil authorities to assume the burden. Even when conditions demonstrated a pressing need for Bureau intervention, as they did at the busy dispensary at Albany, the general belief that a contraction of services would force others to assume the responsibility continued to direct Bureau actions. Both Dr. De Hanne and Dr. Laing pleaded for the expansion of the Bureau's hospital network by opening a freedmen's hospital at Albany. The dispensary there had treated two thousand patients between January and May 1867, sometimes serving one hundred a day. At one point George Dalton, the "most faithful," overworked, and lonely Albany physician who succumbed to drink, was treating 760 patients a week, even as their masters tried to discourage them from seeking the assistance of a "stranger." Freedpeople called on him day and night, with some coming "in from the country with newly discovered ailments, for the sake of seeing a live Yankee, he is such a rare animal." Indeed, his superior believed that overwork contributed to the drinking problem that cost him his position.[117]

The Albany dispensary was, in fact, the only relief available to some 31,000 freedpeople of the eight surrounding counties. To make matters even more pressing, the civil authorities did nothing to ease the burden. Nevertheless, Assistant Commissioner Sibley could not respond favorably to the request to establish a new hospital in the city. Under "existing circumstances it is not deemed advisable for the Government to assume" the burden.[118]

Despite a few lapses, such as the intemperance of Dalton and the drunkenness and misconduct of Dalton's successor, army surgeon Charles Lodge,[119] these physicians generally acquitted themselves well. Like Dalton, they often worked "under very disheartening circumstances."[120] They shared in the loneliness and danger that other Bureau officers and agents experienced. Furthermore, when no other Bureau man was in the neighborhood, they acted as a symbol of Reconstruction and adviser for the freedpeople.[121]

Dr. Augustus Mitchell, the surgeon for a time at St. Marys, did his job only to have whites threaten his life. Dr. Dalton believed that even if the Bureau found it appropriate to establish a hospital at Albany, the same whites who interfered with his practice would not allow it to remain open.[122] Bureau doctors A. T. Augusta, C. H. Taylor, and T. L. Harris all shared additional risks and embarrassments because they were blacks.[123] Dr. Taylor, for example, was delayed in reaching his post at the dispensary at Brunswick in the spring of 1867 because the captain of the steamer sailing there refused to take him on board as a passenger.[124]

Still, even as the troubled Dr. Dalton "stuck nobly to his work," so, too, did most Bureau surgeons. Dr. Mitchell, for example, was on the verge of resigning from his St. Marys post because of the burden of having to act alone as an ombudsman for the freedpeople "until I am tired of the matter." After reconsidering, the transplanted Down-Easter and Georgia Unionist again committed himself to carrying on his efforts "in the redemption of the colored, and the establishment of justice, Equity, and order."[125]

Dr. Lawton reported that his doctors did commendable work, even the ex-Confederate surgeon at Macon "who deserves great credit for his faithful and laborious services" but who received a discharge owing to his former connections.[126] Chief medical officers praised their subordinates for keeping clean, well-managed establishments "as far as the means are available," although at times the surgeons themselves complained about inadequate facilities and overcrowding. But J. V. De Hanne discovered one disturbing fault common to all of his hospitals, an evil which appeared "insurmountable" even by his most talented subordinate: the hospital food was terrible. His doctors could not find suitably trained cooks "who will always prepare the food in a palatable form and manner suitable to sick persons," and those on duty "could not be cured of vicious modes of cookery." Indeed, finding qualified cooks was not the only personnel problem encountered by the Bureau. Poor salaries could not attract sufficient numbers of clerks, meaning that paperwork distracted the already busy doctors at the Bureau's hospitals.[127]

Despite foul food, paperwork, and exhausted doctors, Bureau facilities prevented suffering and saved lives. For example, from September 1, 1865, through September 30, 1866, 5,611 freedpeople received treatment at the Bureau's hospitals. In October 1865, to help the state cope with the smallpox epidemic, Dr. Lawton opened special facilities to deal with the disease in Georgia's major cities and distributed supplies to municipalities that admitted ill freedpeople to their hospitals. Also, the Bureau vaccinated 20,000 freedpeople before the end of September 1866.[128] During the next report period, October 1, 1866, through September 30, 1867, the figure of freedpeople treated by the Bureau's facilities almost tripled. The Bureau provided medical care for 14,145 freedpeople, including 486 who had remained in the Bureau's hospital wards from the last report period.[129] For the overlapping report period of July 1, 1867, through June 30, 1868, the Georgia Bureau provided medical care for 16,955 freed men, women, and children.[130]

Even though physicians did their best, they discovered that Bureau hospitals had significant mortality figures. Dr. Lawton, for example, recognized that the mortality rates in his hospitals were noticeably high. From September 1865 through September 1866, of the 1,374 patients treated at the Savannah hospital, 345 died; of the 942 treated at Macon, 214 died.[131]

White Georgians found this information unsurprising, linking it to the consequences of emancipation. As one editor explained, there were fewer deaths "when the negroes were taken care of."[132] In a way, the Bureau agreed. The high mortality rate at his hospitals, Dr. Lawton explained, reflected not on the quality of care patients received but on the type of patient left in their wards— the jetsam of the labor market. Most patients were old and infirm, destitute and orphaned freedpeople because "the great change in the social systems had thrown them upon the charity of the General Government for support." The resulting deaths, however, should not be blamed on black freedom. No longer profitable hands, "their former owners were unable and in most cases unwilling to provide for them longer," a situation that would only worsen as the Bureau began to wind down.[133]

By the spring of 1867 Sibley already was reducing the population of the Bureau's hospitals by transferring orphans, who often wound up on the agency's doorsteps, to a home at Atlanta. He was also closing down dispensaries of "doubtful utility."[134] At the end of August, he commanded his subordinates to turn over insane freedpeople to the civil authorities who could forward the patients to the state asylum at Milledgeville.[135] By the end of the year, the assistant commissioner had reduced operations at Augusta to the extent that the hospital could move to smaller quarters, and the hospital at Columbus closed its doors after paupers in its care were turned over to the civil authorities.[136] A dispensary would serve the sick at Columbus for the time being, but the Bureau's message was clear. It was time for Georgia to care for its own.

During the last year of full Bureau operations, assistant commissioners across the South who wished to disengage the agency from welfare duties continued to "unburden the bureau by turning over to civil authorities all its sick, insane included, for future care and treatment."[137] Preparatory to closing the hospitals at Macon and Atlanta, Bureau officers located the home counties of pauper patients remaining in their care and contacted the appropriate civil authorities, alerting them to their duty.[138] Dr. Laing tried to make the proposition more palatable to Macon city officials by offering to sell them the Macon Bureau hospital equipment at nominal cost if they would maintain an infirmary for indigent sick and disabled freedpeople.[139] There were no alternatives. Howard's adjutant had informed Sibley that when the Bureau's authority in most areas expired at the end of 1868, there would be no funds for relief institutions.[140] The Bureau might distribute some medical supplies to physicians to tend to the needs of the destitute during its waning months, but by the new year, if the county officials would not help the freedpeople, Georgia's blacks would have to care for their own.[141] After all, as Dr. Laing believed, "the probabilities are that the colored people are as fully prepared now, as they ever will be, to shift for themselves." Nevertheless, amidst this urgency to clear its books by December 31, the Bureau's medical department still found the time to treat 4,525 freedpeople during the last three months of its operations.[142]

For Tillson, Sibley, Lewis, and other Yankees, all forms of relief issuing from Washington were, as O. O. Howard explained, "abnormal to our system of government."[143] Too much assistance for too long a time would only result in "much mischief."[144] Although these men willingly met the challenge of particular crises, they never forgot that their charitable enterprises were temporary expedients. Within that limited context they achieved much, but they always believed that the permanent solution to poverty and sickness—indeed, the best service that they could perform for the freedpeople—was to teach them, as Rufus Saxton's brother Willard clearly explained during the early days of the agency's work, to "get rid of the idea of dependence upon the Government for anything as soon as possible."[145] For these men, the most appropriate avenue down which they could direct their energies when dealing with Georgia's ex-slaves was that of establishing habits and attitudes within the freedmen's community that would continue to guarantee black initiative and independence after the Bureau was long gone from the state.

Oliver Otis Howard, commissioner of
the Freedmen's Bureau (Massachusetts
Commandery, Military Order of the
Loyal Legion, and the U.S. Army
Military History Institute)

Rufus Saxton, Georgia's first assistant
commissioner (Poyouhniak Collection,
U.S. Army Military History Institute)

John Emory Bryant, the first Augusta
Bureau officer, newspaper editor, and
Republican politician (Maine State
Archives)

Edward A. Wild, Saxton's chief Bureau officer for most of mainland Georgia during the summer of 1865 (Massachusetts Commandery, Military Order of the Loyal Legion, and the U.S. Army Military History Institute)

James B. Steedman, commander of the Department of Georgia during the Bureau's early days and later one of Andrew Johnson's officers sent south to investigate Howard's agency (Massachusetts Commandery, Military Order of the Loyal Legion, and the U.S. Army Military History Institute)

Davis Tillson, the Georgia Bureau's second assistant commissioner (Massachusetts Commandery, Military Order of the Loyal Legion, and the U.S. Army Military History Institute)

William W. Deane, Davis Tillson's long-time adjutant (U.S. Army Military History Institute)

Charles J. Jenkins, Georgia governor
during Tillson's administration
(Hargrett Rare Book and Manuscript
Library, University of Georgia
Libraries)

Caleb C. Sibley, the Regular Army man
who replaced Tillson as assistant
commissioner (Massachusetts
Commandery, Military Order of the
Loyal Legion, and the U.S. Army
Military History Institute)

John Randolph Lewis, Georgia's last
Bureau assistant commissioner
(Massachusetts Commandery, Military
Order of the Loyal Legion, and the U.S.
Army Military History Institute)

Rufus B. Bullock, Georgia governor and
Republican ally of John R. Lewis
(Hargrett Rare Book and Manuscript
Library, University of Georgia
Libraries)

Union wounded and amputees near Fredericksburg, Virginia, after the Battle of the Wilderness in May 1864, where John R. Lewis lost an arm. These were painful experiences shared by many of the Yankee Freedmen's Bureau agents and officers who served in Georgia. (LC-138184-740 and LC-138184-B462, Library of Congress)

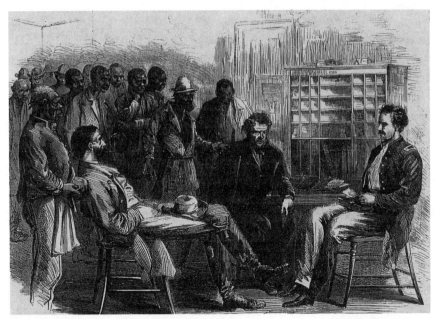

Office of the Freedmen's Bureau, Memphis, Tennessee, almost a year after Davis Tillson left that city. The crowded scene was common in Bureau offices throughout Georgia and the South. (*Harper's Weekly,* June 2, 1866, LC-USZ62-32013, Library of Congress)

"The Freedmen's Bureau" by A. R. Waud, an idealized version of the Bureau's efforts to negotiate the meaning of freedom between ex-masters and ex-slaves (*Harper's Weekly,* July 26, 1868, LC-USZ62-18090, Library of Congress)

# 5

## The Seed Sown in This Land

**FACILITATING**

**EDUCATION**

The very nature of the Bureau's genesis guaranteed that it would be involved with the education of the freedpeople. Its enabling legislation gave the agency "the control of all subjects" concerning the ex-slaves.[1] Furthermore, the sentiment of many Georgia Bureau officials, including John Randolph Lewis, William F. Eaton, John J. Knox, Daniel Losey, and O. H. Howard, encouraged the agency to promote its educational mission. Nevertheless, along with authority and enthusiasm came practical and ideological limitations. The federal government failed to provide the Bureau with sufficient financial resources to do great things for education, and commonly held beliefs about the proper extent of federal intervention in areas long considered the province of local government reinforced the Bureau's reliance on private philanthropy from the North and local action from within the freedmen's community.

In May 1865, Commissioner Howard instructed his subordinates to "systematize and facilitate" the work of the Northern benevolent associations already cultivating the intellectual development of the freedpeople.[2] It was a message that Davis Tillson passed along to his subordinates when in the fall of 1865 he informed his Savannah subassistant commissioner, "We simply intend to give what incidental aid we can and to be the medium of distributing the charity of benevolent individuals and societies."[3] The Bureau would not supersede those groups nor would it absolve the ex-slaves of their own obligations.

Even those men most committed to the Bureau's educational mission assumed that if the freedpeople truly desired education, they would manage to contribute to its support. In part, the Bureau found that its own limited resources necessitated black financial contributions for education; on more than one occasion its officers pleaded poverty when responding to a request for aid and urged the freedpeople to "do what they can to help themselves."[4] Furthermore, the assistance that the Northern benevolent societies directed to their educational missions in Georgia was never so generous as to absorb the entire cost of the freedmen's schooling beyond the Bureau's modest subsidies.[5] The ideological rationale behind the Bureau's efforts to encourage the freedpeople, however, had an even greater impact on the Bureau's approach to financing black education: even when resources were available, the agency expected the freedpeople to make an effort to support their own schools, an obligation commensurate with their new status. In March 1866, Davis Tillson promised to provide a subvention for a teacher's salary in Darien if the freedpeople's initial efforts did not meet the entire expense, but those initial efforts were undoubtedly important to an officer so concerned with black self-sufficiency.[6]

Gilbert Eberhart's approach to securing financial support for the freedmen's schools was in line with Tillson's ideas and typical of the Bureau's attitude during Sibley's and Lewis's administrations. Eberhart was a thirty-five-year-old native of Beaver County, Pennsylvania, when he joined Davis Tillson's staff in early October 1865 as the Georgia Bureau's chief education officer. He had a background in engineering, public education, and the Yankee army.[7] Like many of his contemporaries, his need for work drew him to the Bureau, and he remained with the agency until the end of July 1867.[8] From the outset, his views on the financing of black education were clear. He planned "to exact such amount of money *in all cases* as they [the freedpeople] are able to contribute to the support of their schools," a message that he personally carried to all corners of the state during his first several months on duty.[9] Eberhart's desire to have the freedpeople pay their own way, which he believed was a necessary part of their lesson in self-sufficiency, was neither unique nor short-lived. In April 1867, the education superintendent argued that "colored people who are unwilling to help educate their children do not deserve to have schools."[10] This attitude was common among Bureau officers. In August 1869 John R. Lewis indignantly responded to a belated request for assistance with paying the rent for a freedmen's schoolhouse. "The colored people must raise the rent. If they will not make an effort and do this I must recommend that the School be discontinued," he warned the petitioner. "If they can not & will not make this effort they must not expect to be aided any longer."[11]

Eberhart's and Lewis's subordinates concurred. Subassistant Commissioner Douglas G. Risley, a supporter of black education in his Brunswick subdistrict, helped freedpeople establish schools and procured teachers and books for them while "encouraging the people to direct effort in their own behalf to procure and sustain these advantages." "I do not believe in free schools for these people," he wrote in July 1867. "They should be taught to prize their privileges[;] to learn this their privileges must cost them effort." By the end of the year, he found that the best way to deal with financially apathetic freedpeople was to threaten to close their schools, harsh though that might be. The tactic, he later concluded, was "a good purse string laxative."[12]

In 1867 and 1868, under the direction of Caleb C. Sibley and John R. Lewis, the Georgia Bureau's involvement with black education expanded. On February 20, 1867, Commissioner Howard ordered his assistant commissioners and their agents to pay particular attention to school affairs while performing their other duties. On a relatively regular basis, agents and officers of the Georgia Bureau visited schools, observed their operations, noted their defects, suggested improvements, detected obstacles to their development, and discovered areas devoid of educational opportunities. Orders also required agents to induce teachers to report to the Bureau on approved forms in an effort to promote the "efficiency and usefulness" of the schools.[13]

To assist and encourage continued black participation in the educational endeavor, Sibley and Lewis urged their officers and agents to meet with the freedpeople and help them establish education associations. Both hoped to encourage the freedpeople to donate sufficient funds through such associations to allow their schools to function without the need for burdening the most hardpressed scholars with tuition payments that might discourage their attendance.[14] Consequently, Bureau men did what they could to alert the freedpeople to their educational responsibilities, responsibilities that were intimately linked, as special agent William J. White himself noted, to the freedpeople's need to accept the Bureau's free-labor message. In early 1867, White organized educational societies in Thomasville, Bainbridge, Albany, Georgetown, Cuthbert, and Americus in pursuit of this end.[15]

The Bureau's involvement in establishing educational associations was reinforced by Caleb Sibley's desire to have his agency cooperate more closely with the Georgia Education Association. Formed at a January 1866 meeting of freedmen in Augusta as the Georgia Equal Rights Association, the organization changed its name and its tactics before the year ended to avoid the heated native white opposition to its political agenda. Despite—or, perhaps, because of—the lasting political ambitions of its first president, former Bureau agent

John Emory Bryant, and its more prominent members, the organization committed itself to establishing a grassroots educational movement, certainly not devoid of political motivation, as a means of advancing the freedpeople's rights. Before Sibley's arrival in Georgia, the personal animosity between Davis Tillson and Bryant along with Tillson's views about black political participation at the time when the Georgia Educational Association was advocating such activity had limited the Bureau's cooperation with the association. However, even before Tillson had left the Bureau, his education officer, most likely without the assistant commissioner's knowledge, had written directly to O. O. Howard to secure the appointment of William J. White as an agent for organizing schools in cooperation with the Equal Rights Association, an appointment favored by Bryant. Also, by the spring of 1867, John R. Lewis was serving as president of the association's board.[16]

Since the Georgia Education Association proposed to work in harmony with the Bureau and the Northern aid societies, Caleb Sibley in July 1867 urged his subordinates to carry out its designs and to continue helping the freedpeople organize local educational associations.[17] As one subassistant commissioner noted, "Agents should devote their utmost unremitting labor and attention to this duty."[18] Now, building on their earlier work, whenever they traveled through their districts, they met with freedpeople and urged those who had not yet done so to organize school associations.[19] By October 1867, Alvin Clark, the Quitman agent, had organized school associations throughout Clay County in southwest Georgia. Indeed, Clark's work was not extraordinary, as agents across the state pursued similar goals with equal vigor.[20] In November 1867, agent C. B. Blacker of Cartersville met with heads of black families in Dawson County to urge them to organize an educational association, and before the end of 1867 Bartow agent William Moffit helped to organize six schools.[21] The agency's two agents-at-large for educational matters, the Reverend White and American Missionary Association teacher John A. Rockwell, spread the Bureau's educational message.[22]

Even as the Bureau began to terminate its other major Reconstruction activities, its men continued to encourage the freedpeople's educational efforts with a vigor that seemed to suggest they wished to leave behind some kind of legacy. In August 1868, when L. Lieberman, the Hawkinsville agent, learned of a group of freedpeople who wished to establish a school, he voiced his enthusiastic approval and promised to do all he could to assist them. Lieberman could not follow through on his commitment because white Georgians ran him out of town, but some of his more determined colleagues continued to encourage the freedpeople to make their own educational opportunities.[23] As late as August 1868, agent M. R. Archer of Dahlonega arranged meetings with "prominent colored people" to talk about organizing educational associations.[24] Also during the summer of 1868, Lieutenant H. L. Haskell, the subassistant commissioner at LaGrange, spent much of his time trying to secure support for freedmen's schools among his black charges, and Carnesville agent J. W. Barney "organized schools under adverse conditions."[25] During the summer and fall of 1868, the ever-busy subassistant commissioner at Rome, Carlos de la Mesa, met with freedpeople to assess their prospects for supporting schools of their own.[26] Throughout 1869 and into 1870 John R. Lewis and Edmund A. Ware continued the Bureau's efforts with a greatly reduced staff, now dedicated almost exclusively to forwarding educational goals.

The Bureau's actions as a booster of black schooling encouraged freedpeople and their teachers to identify the agency as an important element in the educational process and as the proper channel for all sorts of requests for assistance. Consequently, demands for teachers, books, rent assistance, and buildings passed into the files of school superintendent Eberhart and his successor, Edmund Asa Ware. The agency did its best to satisfy these needs, but it continued to consider its role to be that of a coordinator of the educational activities of the primary participants—the freedpeople and the Northern benevolent societies.

## The Freedpeople's Response

Some Bureau agents and officers complained about "indifferent" freedpeople or freedpeople who expected their education to be free and wholly subsidized by the Bureau, Northern benevolence, or the state. But Georgia's ex-slaves generally recognized their educational obligations.[27] In fact, black communities across Georgia actively demonstrated that they did not require their white allies to remind them of the important role that education could play in their lives. Because Rufus Saxton failed to establish an extensive Bureau organization in Georgia, much of what the freedpeople accomplished at the outset of Reconstruction was done with insignificant material support from the agency. In Macon and Savannah, black churches and black teachers, not the Bureau, provided the rallying points for the earliest school activity.[28] By the end of the first summer of freedom in Atlanta, before the arrival of Bureau officers or the American Missionary Association, the benevolent organization that would make the city one of its particular fields, 180 students sat in classes conducted by two black men.[29] And elsewhere in Georgia during the summer of 1865, freedpeople, not waiting for Yankee direction, hired their own black teachers to conduct schools for their communities.[30]

Georgia's ex-slaves translated this enthusiasm for education into a significant financial commitment for a people newly entering a free-labor workplace. By the end of 1866, the state's freedpeople who reported their efforts to the Freedmen's Bureau owned 57 school buildings and wholly or partially supported 96 of 127 schools in the state. By May 1867, the contributions of the freedpeople sustained 104 schools and teachers and 3,045 students, the Bureau supported 44 schools, 50 teachers, and 3,093 pupils, and the Northern aid societies supported 84 schools, 78 teachers, and 7,125 students. In addition, the freedpeople helped pay the expenses of 45 schools.[31]

Despite an increasingly hostile economic and political climate, the freedpeople continued to support their schools. During the first six months of 1868, black Georgians assumed the expenses of 45 schools and assisted in the support of 62 more, out of a total of 132 day and night schools carried on the Bureau's records.[32] In June 1869, John R. Lewis could report that the freedpeople continued to "contribute more and more liberally from their scanty means."[33] And by July 1870, of the 204 schools that regularly filed reports, freedpeople sustained 35 and contributed to the expenses of 134.[34]

The freedpeople of Georgia were willing to make sacrifices to support these schools because they understood the value of education. At one level, they viewed the school as a means by which they could independently nurture their newly freed communities, which in part explains their desire to hire their own people, individuals who had a better sense of their greater aspirations, to teach their children whenever possible. This was a practice that led to some tension between the freedpeople and Bureau officials, who worried about incompetence, unnecessary competition, and the squandering of limited resources.[35] Georgia Bureau school superintendent E. A. Ware, for example, was quite irritated to learn that Allan Clark, a black minister and president of the local education association at Madison, Georgia, "did not want any of 'Mr. Ware's Pets' there." Presumably Clark preferred finding his own black teachers.[36] Because of a similar situation in Columbus, John R. Lewis feared that the Northern-supported school in the city was in danger of closing because the freedpeople appeared to favor their own school.[37]

On another occasion, Lewis was especially put out by the willingness of freedpeople to pay a premium for black teachers while his own agency was struggling to find assistance for schools staffed by the missionary societies. In July 1869, he complained that "false pride" prompted freedpeople in Macon and Augusta to send their children to several independent schools in those cities paying "from 50cts to one dollar p[e]r month tuition rather than send them to the free Society Schools where they are asked if able to pay only 10cts p[e]r week and where they have far better accommodations and better teaching." Lewis believed that this situation was "mainly due . . . to the influence of their ignorant but influential teachers."[38]

The Bureau officials opposed the use of black teachers when they believed that the freedpeople were squandering their limited resources on inferior tuition or challenging the wisdom of the agency's efforts to coordinate some kind of rational educational plan. Lewis and other Yankees, however, recognized the need to have properly trained black teachers available to expand their educational work, and they supported preparing them for the task.[39] In late June 1870, E. A. Ware sent out twenty-five normal school students to teach freedpeople during the summer, desperately hoping to find Bureau funds to pay them just weeks before he was to close down the Georgia agency's educational operations.[40] Indeed, in 1869 John R. Lewis committed Bureau resources to the completion of facilities for an American Missionary Association–sponsored normal school at Atlanta for the training of black teachers; such a building, he believed, would "be the crowning work of the Bureau in Georgia."[41]

Ultimately, the freedpeople enjoyed the services of approximately two hundred black Georgians between 1866 and 1870, individuals who would be most familiar with and sympathetic to the concerns and hopes of the black community.[42] One might suspect, however, that if these black teachers had any formal education, they, like Georgia's black preachers and politicians, had absorbed and were passing on the same free-labor values to which the white Yankee schoolteachers and their Bureau allies adhered.[43] Georgia's ex-slaves should not have had any problems with such a focus. Freedpeople understood that pursuing an education that conveyed those middle-class values meant seizing a weapon by which they could challenge the racial hierarchy and the white monopoly of power.[44]

The education brought south by Yankee schoolteachers and encouraged by the Bureau could help the freedpeople deal with their employers on more equitable terms when, at the end of the planting season, it came time to settle their contractual obligations.[45] In a more general sense, the Yankee curriculum also provided Georgia's freedpeople with the opportunity to broaden their understanding of the world beyond the limits defined by their ex-masters, which in turn expanded their liberty and their confidence or, as planter Howell Cobb believed, their "impudence."[46] The Yankee liberal values of individual responsibility, temperance, and the work ethic that were central to the teachers' lessons encouraged freedpeople by taking into account the fact that they *could* advance, an obvious challenge to old white Southern notions of limited black potential and the static place of blacks in Southern society.

Ultimately, ex-slaves understood that Yankee-sponsored education gave them at least some leverage in protecting their freedom and all that it implied. One freedman applied this notion to land acquisition. "Negroes had to go to school first and git larnin'," he observed, "so they would know how to keep some of them white folks from gittin' land away from 'em if they did buy it."[47] Granted, it was the kind of message that a middle-class Yankee teacher or a Bureau officer might have promulgated. Nevertheless, it still made sense to nineteenth-century black Georgians, some of whom also understood education to be essential preparation for intelligent political activity, a notion encouraged by their teachers and Bureau allies.[48]

O. O. Howard's chief education officer, John W. Alvord, discouraged partisan politics in the Bureau, and Eberhart told Macon freedpeople that "he did not want politics mixed up with the schools."[49] Eberhart's successor, E. A. Ware, also expressed the Bureau sentiment that "no teacher is expected to give direct instruction in political, or at least partizan [*sic*] matters."[50] At the same time, Bureau officials were well aware of the political implications of their education program. Even the more cautious Bureau men suggested that Yankee education, along with hard work, "would soon put the ballot into the hands of every Negro in the South."[51] And Georgia's school superintendents, despite their warnings to teachers to be discreet, made it clear that they knew what black education held in store for the future of the state and the Republican Party. After Tillson left the Bureau, Eberhart's civic lessons to the freedpeople were sufficiently political in content to anger white Georgians and earn him a reprimand from Commissioner Howard.[52] E. A. Ware also made it perfectly clear in several letters written in September 1867 that although teachers he solicited must avoid partisan politics, they would be working with a black "voting population." In the end, Ware understood that the teachers need not be politically didactic; the freedmen themselves were intelligent enough to equate the benefits of education with the "great progressive party of the Nation."[53]

Teachers, however, were less cautious than the Bureau would have preferred and reinforced the freedpeople's understanding of the political nature of education. Despite the paternalistic attitude of many of them, the Yankee teachers helped politicize the freedpeople by teaching them patriotic songs and professing the equality of the races. They also encouraged them to become politically active and assisted in the formation of Union Leagues and Grant Clubs, which often met in schoolhouses.[54] Consequently, the freedpeople's schoolhouses became "centers of influence and interest" of the black community as well as symbols of black independence that drove some of their ex-masters to violence.[55]

Even the most naive freedpeople probably developed some appreciation of education's real worth and power when they considered that their masters had withheld it from them during slavery and continued to oppose it or try to control it in freedom.[56] Nonviolent opponents to their schools simply ignored them, withholding much needed community support. Some white Georgians promised assistance but never rendered it. A few offered to support black schools if they could control them, thereby preventing the possibility that teachers would ruin their labor with unsound political ideas. Others offered help if the freedpeople would turn away from their Yankee teachers or refuse to report their progress to the Bureau's agents. Some whites hindered the freedpeople's educational efforts by refusing to sell or rent land to ex-slaves for school purposes and threatening those white neighbors who would. Still others refused to allow their workers' children to attend school, or they drove off workers who tried to organize school associations.[57] In Newton, whites, who had yet to put a stop to the local freedpeople's school, monitored the teachers' efforts by opening their mail.[58]

Opponents to black education also did their best to discourage the freedpeople and their teachers by interrupting classes, annoying students, hissing at teachers on the street, throwing rocks at schoolhouses, threatening teachers and their students with violence, and assaulting pupils. In one instance an individual who took exception to black education fired a pistol into a schoolhouse; in another, whites burned a school's desks.[59] Threats of violence discouraged some freedpeople from organizing educational societies and encouraged others to close down schools already established. Mob violence drove away teachers, and on at least one occasion, violence persuaded some freedpeople that they would be better off without their militant Yankee schoolteacher.[60] In Cherokee County in December 1868, a mob actually pulled down a schoolhouse after threatening the teacher, but arson was the favorite quick method of removing what many whites considered to be a cancerous growth on the community.[61] In a short period during 1866, Griffin freedpeople watched three schoolhouses go up in flames.[62]

Assaults on their schoolhouses must have had an impact on the freed-people's understanding of the value of education, which for some probably re-inforced their commitment to maintaining schools. Nevertheless, enthusiastic freedpeople sooner or later strained their resources in their efforts to support their schools and teachers. The same Freedmen's Bureau reports that showed the results of an impressive black effort to support education also illustrated the need for outside assistance. In January 1869, shortly before he assumed the re-sponsibilities of the Bureau's assistant superintendent of schools for the Bain-bridge subdistrict, W. L. Clark informed Edmund A. Ware that their "friends at home need not stop giving yet."[63]

Some schools failed when funds became scarce, and the freedpeople could not launch others because of their chronic poverty.[64] In the spring of 1867, a Davisboro man found the freedpeople he observed working well and under bet-ter circumstances than during the previous year. However, they were still too poor to establish schools on their own. "Time will be required before they can devote any portion of their scanty earnings to the education of their children," he warned Eberhart.[65] And in Bainbridge, where William J. White had orga-nized an educational association in 1867, poverty prevented the freedpeople from fulfilling its promise. In July 1868, a Bureau agent reported, "Prospects for building [a] school house in B[ainbridge] are about as poor as the freedmen."[66]

Even the more successful freedpeople needed continued assistance in sup-porting their schools, whether it was in the form of additional funds, teachers, books, or buildings. Agent H. F. Mills, for example, discovered that two groups of freedpeople residing within his Stockton jurisdiction could cover the board of teachers but not their salaries, and a third could support a teacher for only a few months at a time. In January 1869 Bureau agent and AMA educator John A. Rockwell closed down the freedmen's school in Cuthbert because the "people could meet only about half the expenses."[67]

The Bureau's own limited resources precluded wide-ranging contributions from its coffers to these freedpeople and others like them, but it was still able to assist their educational agenda in meaningful material ways. It helped to con-struct school buildings and contributed to the support of teachers with what-ever funds were available, and it acted as a clearinghouse for requests for aid and a coordinator of Northern benevolence. Identifying the needs of the freed-people, alerting Northern aid societies to those needs, coordinating the distrib-ution of the resulting philanthropy, and helping teachers and their students cope with a hostile environment were worthwhile contributions to the growth of freedmen's education in Georgia.

## The Bureau's Schoolhouses

Rufus Saxton's subordinate, Edward A. Wild, provided a fleeting glimpse at what aggressive action and a liberal interpretation of confiscable property might accomplish for education. Before he concluded his campaign in Wilkes County, he called up from Augusta W. P. Russell of the American Missionary Association and charged him with encouraging the freedpeople to establish schools in the buildings he had confiscated. The missionary teacher wasted no time and on August 3 reported the freedpeople busily cleaning out the county seat's town hall, which Wild had confiscated, for their promised school.[68]

Wild's superiors quickly reined in his grand plans, but the general had at least tried to address a significant need of the freedpeople. During the fall of 1865, the shortage of schoolhouses was critical.[69] To correct this situation, the Georgia Bureau could only draw on the confiscated and abandoned property under its control and the fines it imposed on whites who violated the freedpeople's peace, both sources being quite small because of the agency's limited presence in the state.[70] Wild's solution was to take an aggressive approach to expanding the agency's resources, but Davis Tillson's more moderate approach was indicative of the role that the agency would play in the future.

In November 1865, Colonel Hiram F. Sickles, the subassistant commissioner at Savannah, asked for funds with which he proposed to rent buildings for educational purposes. Tillson refused the request. Explaining his position, Tillson informed the officer, "We simply intend to give what incidental aid we can and to be the medium of distributing the charity of benevolent individuals and societies." Tillson, however, also recognized the Bureau's obligation to do something to assist the Savannah freedpeople. As an alternative to direct funding, he authorized Sickles to use available resources, including idle soldiers, to lend the freedpeople a hand in constructing the needed facilities. Exhibiting a concern for preserving what the freedpeople and his subordinate would accomplish, he also warned Sickles, "Take care to locate them [the school buildings] on *land* that the colored people will be able to control and keep possession of hereafter."[71] By mid-November Sickles was moving abandoned buildings to Savannah for use as freedmen's schools and had detailed soldiers to help the freedpeople construct additional classrooms. In the meantime, Eberhart's assistant had secured rooms in some of the city's black churches to provide additional classroom space.[72]

Davis Tillson's response to Sickles's request was not unusual. In November 1865, he secured an abandoned building in Albany for a freedmen's school, and in May 1866, he received authorization to use a frame building in Augusta for the same purpose. This solution to the space problem, however, was not the perfect one. Although Tillson tried to secure the much needed schoolhouses upon request, he sometimes failed owing to the reluctance of military commanders to give up property in their possession.[73] Furthermore, although the Yankee aid societies could use abandoned buildings turned over to them by the agency, the property remained under the control of the Bureau and therefore was subject to restoration to its owners.[74]

Tillson exhibited a concern for black scholars even as he carried out his restoration duties. Additionally, when he did have funds at his disposal, he was willing to help pay building rents. In December 1865, he authorized the return of a Savannah house to its white owner, with an important restriction. The freedpeople who were holding school on the property would be protected by the Bureau in their right to continue their educational activities there until they found another suitable structure. In the meantime, Tillson agreed to pay rent to the building's owner.[75]

After mid-July 1866, the Bureau was able to give substantially more material assistance to education. The Army Appropriations Act, approved on July 13, gave the Bureau its first appropriation. Not only did this piece of legislation provide $21,000 for the salaries of state school superintendents, but it also allowed the agency $500,000 for renting and repairing schoolhouses and asylums. Meanwhile, on July 16, 1866, Congress overrode President Johnson's veto of the bill to extend the life of the agency for an additional two years. Included in this new law was the express charge of Congress to the agency to "seize, hold, use, lease, or sell" property belonging to the former Confederate states for the benefit of freedmen's education. The act also required the Bureau to cooperate with the benevolent associations and their agents and teachers. Furthermore, the Bureau was to lease buildings for educational purposes whenever the associations provided teachers to staff them without cost to the government.[76] Thus in October, when the Reverend E. P. Smith of the American Missionary Association asked the Bureau for $4,700 for rental and repair of school buildings in Atlanta, Davis Tillson could approve the request as long as the AMA promised to use the buildings for the education of "all classes, irrespective of color or condition." And as long as the Bureau had resources to distribute, its policy remained, as E. A. Ware later noted, to "give no aid to *white* schools—no aid to *black* schools; but aid only to schools open to *all*."[77]

For the remainder of its existence, the Bureau expended funds at its disposal to help provide facilities for the freedpeople's education, but again the agency helped those who helped themselves. The Georgia Bureau encouraged freed-people to secure land and begin the construction of schoolhouses, pledging its assistance once they presented evidence of their good intentions and future support, lest the Bureau's efforts be wasted.[78] Agent L. Lieberman, for example, exhorted freedpeople: "Go to work at once[,] raise your school & rest assured you shall have all the assistance in my power, in your good undertaking."[79] Lieberman failed to make good on his commitment because whites ran him out of town, but the Bureau's school superintendents made similar promises and tried to follow through with them. G. L. Eberhart, E. A. Ware, and J. R. Lewis all pledged to help with school construction costs or rents, making a general commitment, which at times the Bureau could not meet because of its ever lim-ited resources, to those freedpeople who showed some initiative in securing land titles, buildings, and funds to house and board teachers.[80]

When building projects proved to be worthy, the Bureau did what it could to help them to completion. It even suggested the proper dimensions and re-viewed construction plans to make certain that the schoolhouses would be "built in a good substantial manner, plain but neat so as to be an ornament to the city."[81] Such a commitment led the Georgia Bureau to expend $22,305.75 between January 1 and June 30, 1867, primarily for educational purposes, in-cluding the construction and rental of school buildings.[82] At the beginning of Eberhart's last summer as school superintendent, the Bureau planned to erect buildings at Savannah, Macon, Athens, and Atlanta, while paying for repairs at LaGrange, Americus, Monticello, and elsewhere. The sums earmarked for these projects suggested the extent of the agency's commitment when it had re-sources at its disposal. The school building at Savannah would, according to the estimate, cost the Bureau $10,000 by the time its students sat on its benches. Caleb Sibley believed the school at Athens would cost about $4,000, at Atlanta $2,500, at Macon $10,000, and at Brunswick between $3,000 and $4,000.[83] By the spring of 1868, E. A. Ware noticed significant educational benefits resulting from this construction program. "Improved facilities in the erection of the new buildings," he explained, "has made it possible to grade the schools thoroughly, and to introduce the more improved methods of study."[84]

By loosely interpreting the Bureau's authority to repair school buildings, the agency actually erected a number of them, while allowing local trustees and missionary societies to maintain title to them. The Bureau usually required the freedpeople or a benevolent association to make some sort of effort to present it with the beginnings of a structure to repair. During the fall of 1869, the freedpeople at Quitman and at Camilla requested Bureau assistance in building their schoolhouses. Lewis, now acting as the Georgia Bureau's school superintendent, agreed to help as long as the school trustees recognized the Bureau's sole right to construct and then dispose of the buildings. However, if they raised enough money to lay a foundation and put up a frame, such an agreement would be unnecessary. Black initiative, in these cases, gave the Bureau sufficient cause to consider the building to be the property of the trustees and, hence, only in need of repair.[85]

By July 1, 1869, despite the uncertainty of its future, political disturbances, and limited resources, the Georgia Bureau had expended for construction and repairs of school buildings since its establishment $104,003.86, which helped to provide facilities for 4,690 pupils. In addition, the Bureau spent $10,471 on repairs for buildings used only part of the time for school purposes, providing accommodations for 3,725 additional scholars. The Bureau continued to involve itself in construction projects throughout the remainder of 1869 into 1870, and by the time of its withdrawal from Georgia, it could claim to have assisted with the building of some fifty schools.[86] These schoolhouses would be, as Bartow agent William Moffit predicted, "the monuments of the Bureau."[87]

## An Advocate for Black Education

Building schoolhouses was but one activity that placed a demand on the resources of the Bureau. Staffing those buildings and supplying teachers and students required additional expenses, and while the agency contributed to the advancement of black education in these areas, it expected the freedpeople to shoulder much of the responsibility. Beyond the freedpeople's own efforts, the agency expected and actively solicited assistance from private sources.

At first the Bureau hoped to receive the cooperation and the financial assistance of the freedpeople's ex-masters. Superintendent Eberhart appealed to white Georgians for help, assuming that at least their own self-interest would prompt them to see the benefits in encouraging the education of their ex-slaves. The superintendent reminded them that education "is likely to teach the freedman his duty to himself and the community; and to render him an intelligent, honest and industrious member of society."[88] Nevertheless, when Eberhart asked local Georgia clergymen to help him establish a school system, he received only one affirmative reply. After almost a year, he still could report only two white ministers affiliated with Southern religious denominations who were cooperating with the Bureau.[89]

Such an underwhelming response in 1865 and 1866 should not have surprised Eberhart. Postwar poverty acknowledged no racial boundaries. Also, white preachers shared or at least were aware of the fear ex-masters had of such a radical experiment that was not completely under their control. Charles Howard, the Bureau commissioner's brother, discovered at the end of 1865 that whites in Georgia's coastal counties generally opposed education. Some of the Georgians he encountered argued that schooling wasted valuable time better spent at labor, but others opposed it on a more general principle: "It was injurious to all working classes to be taught from books." These ex-masters probably also shared the views of Charles Colcock Jones Jr., who believed that, because of the unsettled nature of the times, schools on their property would only be "an opening to complications."[90]

Eberhart's successors did not fare much better in their own efforts to elicit white Georgia's assistance.[91] Whites, if they did not openly oppose black schools, too frequently paid no more than lip service to their support. In 1868, one Athens teacher noted that the area's educators "have no direct opposition here by the whites." Yet, although white Georgians were "willing and anxious that the Blacks be educated . . . they render little or no aid." Still, the teacher found some benefit in this lack of attention: "If they let us alone we feel glad."[92]

Sometimes towns provided plots of land on which freedpeople built school-houses, and individuals, from time to time, assisted their workers in meeting the expenses of education.[93] Such generosity, however, could come at a steep price for teachers and freedpeople, because often it came with strings attached. For those white Georgians who might concede some benefit in the teaching of freedpeople, it was the fact that they, not Yankees, controlled the process that made the business palatable.[94] In 1867 Bainbridge businessmen offered to give the freedpeople all the money they needed to maintain their school if they first drove off the Yankee veteran who was acting as their teacher.[95] The generous offer of one Camden County resident was less overtly malicious but came from the same motivation.

In April 1867, Duncan F. Clinch asked the Bureau for financial assistance in erecting a school and a church on his land for the enrichment of his workers' minds and morals. He would repay the agency's expenses, an offer that was difficult to refuse. A Bureau officer inspected Clinch's plantation, recognized the need for a school in the area, but advised against cooperating with the planter. The officer concluded that Clinch's place was in a poor location for these institutions and consequently would not serve the best interests of the freedpeople in the neighborhood. More important, he discovered that Clinch was primarily concerned with using the school as an instrument of labor control. Clinch desired "a teacher who would do his whole duty, and 'not disturb the present pleasant relations existing' between Mr. C. and his hands." Despite the planter's promise to repay the Bureau's outlay, the officer refused to recommend assistance.[96] Although the Bureau had no objections to using education to inculcate the freedpeople with the values of discipline and hard work, it understood the difference between Yankee ideals and simple labor control.

Freedmen's education also received little general assistance from local civil authorities owing to their indifference to, suspicion of, and open hostility toward the concept. In fact, some Georgia counties taxed black land owners to support schools for the children of indigent residents, but barred black children from attending them. In late 1868, eight teachers in Augusta, Macon, and Liberty County actually received financial support from county poor school funds, but these funds were the first that Bureau-associated teachers received. By the end of June 1869, past performance had made John R. Lewis, then acting in the capacity of the Bureau's state school superintendent, so pessimistic that he expected no general assistance from the civil authorities in the near future. By 1870, E. A. Ware could rightly claim that the progress in black education witnessed in Georgia was a consequence of the Bureau's ability to coordinate educational activities of the freedpeople and Northern philanthropists without the assistance of state or local governments.[97]

With white Georgians reluctant to respond to the Bureau's call, the agency relied most heavily on Northern benevolence to supplement its own and the freedpeople's contributions to education. In 1865 and 1866, for example, the Bureau's educational efforts received assistance from the New England Freedmen's Aid Society, the American Missionary Association, and the National Freedmen's Aid Society as well as the Society of Friends. By June 1866, such Northern benevolence sustained the bulk of the cost of 125 teachers attending to the needs of 8,000 pupils in 113 schools at forty-five locations.[98]

Despite these accomplishments, the Bureau's educational officers constantly urged the agency's Northern friends to exert even greater efforts on behalf of the freedpeople. When Gilbert Eberhart took leave to visit his home in Pennsylvania at the end of 1866, for example, he also planned to visit New York to talk with AMA officials about enlarging the society's work in Georgia.[99] Just before the October 1867 opening of the school term, E. A. Ware embarked on a letter-writing campaign in an attempt to alert his correspondents to the tutorial and material needs of the freedpeople; the school superintendent "begged" the Northern aid societies to increase their efforts while writing "to all quarters of the north for teachers & books." [100]

Individual agents and officers like Lieutenant Douglas Risley and the Reverend W. F. Eaton also wrote directly to the aid societies and especially to the AMA, keeping the needs of their districts before the charitable organizations's officers. Eaton, desperate for an additional teacher, even tried to allay the concerns of sojourners about the strange climate in which they would have to work, using himself and his wife as examples of how well Yankees could adapt to the Georgia sea islands where he was stationed. "These islands are on most parts as healthy as the northern climate in summer," he optimistically reassured the AMA's George Whipple. "A teacher who will exercise due caution can teach the year round as well as in Boston." [101]

Unfortunately, even when persistence satisfied a particular need, other needs quickly came to the Bureau's attention. While congratulating the AMA's E. P. Smith for his decision to supply Albany and the surrounding area with teachers, E. A. Ware also pointed out the lack of schools south of that town. And W. F. Eaton's plea to the same association came in the wake of the successful opening of a school by a Boston teacher at the north end of his Sapelo Island jurisdiction; he still needed another to tend to nearly one hundred children on the southern part of the island. [102]

Sometimes a society's broken promise or a tardy fulfillment of a pledge sparked urgent reminders directed northward from the Bureau's school superintendents. In early 1868, for example, after the Bureau had constructed a schoolhouse in Rome, the facility lay dormant awaiting the arrival of teachers promised by the aid society of the Methodist Episcopal Church. In the fall, the political excitement that corresponded with the opening of the school term convinced the American Missionary Association to delay sending teachers to Georgia until after the elections. In both cases, E. A. Ware pressed these organizations to honor their obligations. [103]

When Northern aid societies were feeling the financial strain of their commitments during 1867, Superintendent Ware directed his pleas beyond the benevolent societies' offices to friends and pastors "to rouse the good people of the North to a sense of the magnitude and pressing necessity of this work." [104] During the later critical phase of Yankee educational efforts, the Bureau was able to secure and distribute assistance to freedmen's schools from the Peabody Fund, which during the 1868–1869 and 1869–1870 school years provided the

agency with $8,000 for teachers' salaries, which otherwise would have gone un-
paid.[105] During the 1868–1869 school year, J. R. Lewis found it necessary to
use this source to keep several much needed AMA teachers in the field who
had lost their sponsor's financial support before the school term had ended.[106]
Additionally, Peabody money encouraged freedpeople in some places to renew
their own contributions to education.[107] The Georgia Bureau continued to distribute this money until the very day that its office closed in July 1870.[108]

Although the Bureau planted its "monuments" throughout the state and
Northern aid societies staffed them with teachers, the resources the agency and
organizations directed to cities like Macon, Savannah, and Atlanta revealed an
urban bias that ultimately limited the impact of their programs on black education in Georgia. According to Commissioner Howard's chief education officer,
violence prevented the Bureau-sponsored school system from reaching into the
interior of Georgia.[109] Although safety was a real concern, the benevolent associations upon which the Bureau and freedpeople depended generally favored
working in urban areas where their scarce resources would reach more pupils
in larger classes and where the concentration of population could support a
system of schools that extended from the elementary to the collegiate level.
The Freedmen's Bureau supported this plan as the most economical approach
to educating the freedpeople.[110] Also, as E. A. Ware explained, urban schools
did more for establishing a permanent system of education by becoming centers of influence and giving "to all the people some idea of the public school
system of America." Small schools scattered over the countryside usually employed poor teachers and did little good except to give testimony to the need
for competent teachers and the freedpeople's desire to learn.[111]

The consequence of this policy was significant. In 1867 Northern teachers in
the state's five major cities (Atlanta, Augusta, Columbus, Macon, and Savannah) instructed almost half of the black population enrolled in Georgia's schools.
Between 1865 and 1870, aid societies sent over 70 percent of their teachers to
Georgia's largest cities, which contained only 15 percent of the black population of the state. By 1870, in part because of the severe reduction of the Freedmen's Bureau's activities during the summer, organizations retrenched and
redirected their priorities, further limiting black opportunities. The American
Missionary Association, the society that remained most active beyond the Reconstruction years into the late nineteenth century, for example, concentrated
its resources on urban-based normal schools, a few secondary schools, and Atlanta University.[112]

## The Bureau and the Teachers

The American Missionary Association was by far the leading Northern contributor to black education in Georgia in part because of its relationship with the Freedmen's Bureau. At the outset of Reconstruction, the Bureau identified its educational interests with the AMA and acted accordingly. In December 1865, for example, Superintendent Eberhart received approval of his superiors at Augusta and at Washington to place all educational activity in Savannah under the AMA's supervision.[113] The AMA, which responded aggressively to the needs of freedmen's education, by its deeds helped to seal the relationship.[114]

There were few official connections between the society and the agency, but one was significant in helping sustain the AMA's position. Edmund A. Ware, G. L. Eberhart's successor, was one of the AMA's own. The Massachusetts-born, Yale-educated abolitionist, who would become the first president of the AMA's Atlanta University, had begun his Georgia Reconstruction work in 1866 organizing schools in Atlanta before becoming an unpaid Bureau agent there in April 1867. No wonder Ware could write that the "interests of the A.M.A. are our [the Bureau's] interests."[115]

Other benevolent societies working in Georgia suspected that they might be slighted because of Eberhart's and Ware's favoritism, and they jealously complained about the AMA's close relationship with the Bureau.[116] Some rival associations even tried to avoid E. A. Ware's supervision by making special appeals to O. O. Howard, which perhaps accounted for Ware's efforts to guard the Georgia Bureau's acknowledged role as the primary coordinator of all educational enterprises in the state that looked to the federal government for assistance.[117] The Bureau's favored view of the AMA, however, was understandable and not unjustified. Because the AMA had responded early and generously to Georgia's educational needs, Bureau officials like Eberhart, who had no official connections with the AMA, found it easy to reward its labors and encourage its prominence. By giving the AMA the foremost role in Georgia, Bureau officials hoped to prevent unproductive competition and the inefficient duplication of effort, something that would have drained the resources available to the Bureau for educational assistance.[118]

John R. Lewis, who assumed direct control of the Georgia Bureau's educational affairs in January 1869, clearly exhibited the desire to avoid the inefficiency that might result from unbridled competition.[119] A fair individual and not simply an AMA booster, he favored an orderly approach to education even

when individuals or organizations moved into the established and acknowledged teaching fields of other societies working in Georgia. In January 1870, he
protested the attempts of another society to encroach on the Augusta field of
the Baptist Home Missionary Society, explaining that such activity would only
"interfere with their general plan, divide the work and seriously interfere with
the prosperity of the school work there." Indeed, Lewis's efforts to be impartial
in his efficiency led E. A. Ware to worry that rival societies would win Lewis's
favor at the expense of the AMA.[120]

On occasion, Georgia Bureau education superintendents and AMA officials
discussed formalizing their relationship. In November 1865, Eberhart suggested all AMA agents be given official Bureau status as his unpaid assistants,
and in early 1868 E. A. Ware suggested that Bureau officers be appointed AMA
school superintendents. Nothing came of these suggestions, perhaps because
the AMA, though appreciative of the Bureau's assistance, did not wish to become "too much mixed up" with the agency. Ira Pettibone, for example, understood that there was a negative side to having the Bureau's favor. "Many of the
people here hate the 'Nigger Teachers' as they are called," Pettibone observed
about the climate in Savannah, "but they hate the *Bureau more*." Take the Bureau's help, he reasoned, "but it is no benefit to have it go out as it frequently
does that our schools are sustained and our teachers paid by the Bureau." Another AMA official, E. M. Cravath, feared that if joint appointments did not
work out, the failure could cause friction between the AMA and the Bureau
and thus hinder the larger goals of both organizations.[121]

Such a concern was not unreasonable given the few significant breaches that
the Bureau and some AMA-sponsored teachers experienced. Usually, when Bureau men clashed with teachers it was because of personal differences, or because teachers believed that the agency was not giving them sufficient support,
or because of the teachers' desire to implement a political or social agenda
more radical than a particular officer's. During the spring of 1866, all of these
things, to varying degrees, played a role in the breach between Davis Tillson
and the Augusta teachers who had planned to march on the local cemetery,
with students and flowers in tow.

When he requested that the teachers postpone their memorial service, Tillson was already aware that they had no reservoir of goodwill stored up among
the white citizens of Augusta; he believed that even if the teachers did not intend their procession to be provocative, white Augustans would consider it to
be so. Aside from the fact that they were freedmen's teachers, the sharp-tongued

Yankee women had in the past unhesitatingly responded in kind to insults hurled at them on the streets of Augusta. It was probably asking too much for unreconstructed rebels who had already shown themselves prone to violence to remain calm in this situation. The teachers who failed in their mission concluded that Tillson was pandering to the ex-rebels of Augusta, and their breach with the assistant commissioner went festering, aggravated by an escalating personal feud between their supporter John Emory Bryant and Davis Tillson.[122] One of the Augusta teachers openly insulted Tillson at a picnic, despite the fact that he was a guest of the freedpeople who had organized it, and even one of their own admitted that some of them were "improperly critical & even insulting" to Tillson. These confrontations did nothing to cool Tillson's temper; on one occasion he referred to his nemeses as *damned old maids* and *damned whores*."[123]

In the spring of 1868, Subassistant Commissioner Douglas Risley also had an ugly falling-out with the AMA teachers at Brunswick, who were politically more radical than he. Personal matters contributed to the souring of his relationship with the local teachers; one teacher, Risley believed, was a gossip who spread rumors that there was "something wrong" between him and his wife before they were married. Conditions did not improve with time, and the officer attempted to assert his authority over the teachers, whom he believed were trying to undermine his influence with the freedpeople in his jurisdiction. He unsuccessfully tried to convince the AMA to make him a superintendent so "that all *official* communications to & from the teachers be sent through [his] office." Finally, in December the teachers, "very much discouraged" because they allegedly received inadequate support from Risley, left town. They also left the subassistant commissioner to explain to his superiors what the Bureau would now do with an expensive, newly constructed school building at a time when good Yankee teachers were increasingly difficult to come by.

Clearly, some matters were beyond Risley's control. The freedpeople, with whom Risley had had difficulty in encouraging contributions to education, contributed to the lack of support about which the teachers complained. Also, one of the teachers implied that Risley was hurting their efforts because he apparently could not stop the freedpeople from building a new church, a project that diverted funds from the support of the teachers and a construction decision that was the freedpeople's, not Risley's, to make. In the end, however, E. A. Ware investigated this conflict and concluded that the teachers were at fault.[124]

A more serious schism developed between teachers and School Superintendent Eberhart, with repercussions that reached all the way back to Washington
and cost the Bureau official his job. At the outset of his tenure, Eberhart developed a cordial relationship with the American Missionary Association. He had
encouraged their dominant role in the state and, on a more personal level, he
had stood by the Augusta teachers in their confrontation with Davis Tillson
during the cemetery battle, an act that earned him a dressing-down by the
assistant commissioner.[125] Except for his support of the Augusta teachers' cemetery march, his vision of Reconstruction was more compatible with Davis Tillson's free-labor ideology than with more radical political approaches; nevertheless, through 1866 he earned the praise of some AMA people who witnessed his
work.[126] In 1867, however, as Reconstruction became more politically complicated, the ideological and the professional became mixed up with the personal
to create a situation that led to Eberhart's removal.

In April 1867, reports began to reach AMA headquarters that Eberhart was
showing less sympathy for the freedpeople's advancement than was necessary
to do his job well. In part, that impression might very well have come from
Eberhart's views about the freedpeople and Reconstruction, which were well
within the parameters of nineteenth-century Republican Party ideology. In November 1865, shortly after assuming his duties as school superintendent, he attempted to reassure wary white Georgians that education was not a threat to
them; rather, it could only improve the economic positions of all residents of
the state because the interests of blacks and whites were "nearly identical." "No
effort or expense [should] be spared which is likely to teach the freedman his
duty to himself and the community, and to render him an intelligent, honest,
and industrious member of society," Eberhart believed.[127] Later, in a May 1867
address to the Georgia Educational Association, he urged the freedpeople to
muster their own resources for expanding their network of schools and to be
"industrious and self-sustaining." [128]

Eberhart also made it clear that the educational mission of the Bureau and
the Yankee teachers demanded discretion. That was why in the fall of 1865 he
attempted to head off violent opposition to black education by reassuring white
Georgians that social equality and suffrage were not part of the program.[129]
And that was why in the spring of 1866 he argued that Yankee teachers should
not invite trouble by kissing black babies, proclaiming belief in black equality,
or replying in kind to white insults on the streets of Augusta. He also urged the
teachers to be prudent, wise advice given the already hostile environment in

which they worked and the limited resources available to the Bureau for policing white violence. Probably having these views reinforced by Tillson's lecture
after the cemetery incident, Eberhart acknowledged that the teachers had a
right to do many things, but they should defer doing them so as not to endanger
their primary goal of educating the freedpeople. Furthermore, Eberhart believed that the teachers should set an example for white Georgians to follow. If
subjected to insults, they should "*bear* them," thus showing "our enemies that
we are above every impulse of malice and vindictiveness, and that no insult
they can give is sufficient to induce us to so far forget our dignity."[130]

Eberhart's beliefs might easily clash with those of idealistic Yankee teachers,
who typically found their way south accompanied by a missionary zeal that
made it easier for them to accept their small fifteen-dollar-a-month salary.[131]
Nevertheless, although Eberhart's views did not provoke criticism in 1865 and
1866, the shift in national Reconstruction policy, new opportunities in state politics, and different personal circumstances, all developing in 1867, put the
school superintendent at odds with his former allies even as his publicly expressed allegiance to the Republican Party caused him difficulty with Commissioner Howard. Julia A. Shearman, an Augusta teacher with legitimate complaints about male superiors as well as a talent for spreading vitriolic gossip,
believed that Eberhart's newfound fortune—his wife had recently inherited an
estate in England—encouraged in him an unbearable arrogance. The Bureau
school superintendent, she said, a "small & mean" man, now went about informing freedpeople that he need not support himself by working to help them
and that he could readily toss some money their way to boot. Shearman also
hinted that a replacement, a real man who knew what it meant to work for a living, would be welcomed. "I do think, woman as I am, I could fill the post better
than he." She favored E. A. Ware.[132]

Aggravating Shearman's dislike for Eberhart was the Bureau man's break
with her friend, ex-Bureau agent John Emory Bryant, who in fact coveted
Eberhart's position. Bryant soon reinforced Shearman's brief against the school
superintendent with complaints of his own.[133] As late as mid-July 1866, Eberhart was vouching for Bryant's honesty, but within a few months, the school
official, agreeing with Tillson's concerns or at least now trying to placate his superior, questioned Bryant's use of funds donated by freedpeople to his newspaper.[134] Also, in May 1867, Eberhart, who was not a shy Republican, called
a convention with the endorsement of the Georgia Equal Rights Association
at which he became involved in some unsuccessful politicking designed to

influence the meeting and remove Bryant from the GERA's presidency. Bryant's maneuvering was much more sophisticated and effective. He reorganized the association, co-opted his opponents (including Eberhart) by having them elected to the organization's board, and had J. R. Lewis elected president of the board. Also, Bryant took the opportunity presented by the convention to circulate the rumor that AMA field secretary E. P. Smith had no confidence in Eberhart.[135]

Reports of disharmony in the Georgia educational community eventually reached Bureau Commissioner O. O. Howard, who ordered Eberhart's removal in July 1867. John R. Lewis assured Eberhart that Assistant Commissioner Sibley had nothing to do with Howard's action, even though Lewis believed that Eberhart's "influence was weakened and efficiency impaired by the personal difficulties into which [he] had been led, and the wide spread and growing animosities arriving from alleged interference on your part in political affairs."[136] Commissioner Howard, in fact, had determined to remove Eberhart "without consultation" with the Georgia Bureau. Apparently, the American Missionary Association had ignored Sibley's office and had taken Shearman's and Bryant's complaints directly to the top of the Bureau hierarchy.[137]

Despite these specific instances of conflict, Yankee Bureau men generally worked well with teachers because of their own interest in the educational advancement of the freedpeople. Along the way, officers and agents earned the respect and praise of the teachers. According to one AMA correspondent, Lieutenant J. Murray Hoag was a "cordial & earnest co-worker."[138] In Athens, the teachers named their school after Major John J. Knox, the Bureau subassistant commissioner there, because he had shown them "much kindness & should receive the thanks of the Association."[139] And in Macon, the American Missionary Association named a high school after J. R. Lewis, who was recognized as a well-placed friend of the society even while serving as Sibley's inspector general.[140]

Once teachers arrived at schools organized by the freedpeople and the Bureau, the agency continued to assist them in their efforts regardless of their affiliations, which, if all went smoothly, further enhanced their personal associations. Although the Bureau neglected to secure rooms in Columbus in which five teachers could conduct their fall 1868 classes, elsewhere its men dutifully scouted new terrain for suitable schoolrooms and housing accommodations for the Yankee sojourners who arrived at their destinations courtesy of the transportation that the agency had provided for them.[141] Once settled in, when the educators encountered miscellaneous expenses such as blackboard repairs, they turned to the Bureau.[142] When freedpeople fell behind in their financial obligations to their teachers, schoolmistresses asked the Bureau for assistance in securing their promised living, and officials responded by advancing funds or even trying to track down the pupils who were in arrears of their fees.[143] When teachers' salaries were late in arriving from Northern associations, they could expect the Bureau to advance funds to them as well as to mediate complaints leveled by them against their sponsors.[144] And when native whites proved to be less than gracious hosts, teachers looked to the Bureau for protection.[145] In June 1868, a Bartow County teacher who had encouraged the freedpeople to participate in politics found himself homeless, friendless, and constantly threatened; his only recourse for obtaining "the necessities of life" was to turn to the local Bureau agent.[146] No wonder a former AMA employee and Bureau school official believed that there was a role for the Bureau to be played in looking after teachers.[147]

Teachers at times did not make the Bureau's job any easier by failing to listen to Eberhart's advice about discreet behavior. At Greenville, the seat of Meriwether County, the freedpeople actually asked for the removal of a Fannie Randall, who was causing them great concern by her aggressive reaction to the white opposition she and the freedpeople were encountering. On one occasion, she stood out on the street and promised to have the town razed if anyone threatened her, or garrisoned with black troops if anyone insulted her. Randall's problems fell into the lap of Lieutenant Harry Haskell, the LaGrange officer. Haskell had no intention of making good her imprudent threats, but he did what the Bureau was supposed to do in these situations: he traveled to Greenville to investigate, interviewed Miss Randall along with a half dozen freedpeople, and decided that the freedpeople offered the best solution to diffusing the increasingly tense climate in which one freedman had already been severely beaten. He recommended Fannie Randall's removal.[148]

The Freedmen's Bureau received and investigated teachers' complaints against their white neighbors, used the powers at its disposal to try to resolve them, and urged the civil authorities to protect the teachers. During Tillson's tenure, officers and agents issued numerous threats to impose a harsh justice on any Georgian who violently opposed education. When the citizens of Pike County appeared to be growing rambunctious, the Bureau warned them that "the parties so opposing [the school] will be arrested and held responsible for the future safety and protection of the Freedpeople and their children."[149] Tillson's Atlanta officer also warned the citizens of Henry County that the freedpeople's children "must be allowed to obtain and pursue their studies, and the teacher to pursue his avocation as Instructor without any molestation or threats."[150] A few months later troops stationed in Henry County put armed force behind that threat.

As with most things, however, the Bureau's power and influence with the most recalcitrant segment of the white citizenry were limited. In Cuthbert, the presence of a Bureau subassistant commissioner protected the teacher there until the summer of 1866, when the officer had business out of town. Shortly after he left, a mob forced the teacher to follow him.[151] And in the spring of 1867, when a second schoolhouse disappeared in flames at Jonesboro, Major Frederick Mosebach investigated. Finding no evidence against the suspects, all he could do was to "set several persons watching them."[152]

In dealing with teachers' complaints, the Bureau encountered the same limitations that it experienced with its other duties. During Military Reconstruction, the Bureau monitored the way civil authorities dealt with cases involving schoolteachers, urging its agents to pressure the authorities to bring offenders to justice. Only after this channel proved to be a failure could the agency turn to the military authorities.[153] Consequently, the Georgia Bureau's inspector general, John R. Lewis, had limited options when in July 1867 he investigated the case of a Forsyth teacher who had been shot in both legs. Lewis discovered that the local constabulary had charged the teacher as the offending party. Although the teacher had been drunk at the time of the shooting, Lewis believed he was innocent of any offense, but he could only urge that the Bureau have someone aid in his defense.[154]

All things considered, the Bureau's ability to stop violence directed at black education was limited, short-lived, and certainly ineffectual in changing the minds of white Georgians. After the end of Military Reconstruction, the Bureau acted as informal counsel to its oppressed friends. In August 1868, Captain Nathan Sellers Hill's best effort in a case of violence against a black educator was to assist the teacher in taking out a warrant to bring his assailants to justice.[155] And when in September 1869 a teacher turned to the Bureau for help, E. A. Ware could only suggest that he take the matter up with the civil authorities. "The Bureau," he wrote, "is now unable to give you protection."[156]

# 6

## The Talisman Power

FREE LABOR,

CONTRACTS,

AND PROTECTING

THE ECONOMIC

RIGHTS OF THE

FREEDPEOPLE

According to O. O. Howard, the Freedmen's Bureau's "first business was to regulate labor"—in other words, to oversee the successful planting of the new free-labor system in the South.[1] That duty was one of the most crucial aspects of the Bureau's charge and an essential element in the plan for securing a lasting Reconstruction. In fact, Davis Tillson was not too far from the truth when he argued that "almost everything" else depended on free labor's success.[2]

The Bureau's preferred tool for facilitating this educational and regulatory task was the written labor contract, a piece of paper well known to antebellum Yankee farmers and their hired hands but heretofore unnecessary in the economic relationships between the South's ex-masters and ex-slaves.[3] It was through the use of these contracts that the Bureau expected to reassure dubious white employers and cautious black employees that free-labor agriculture would succeed. The documents, Bureau men expected, would help to persuade ex-masters and ex-slaves of the fairness of the new system by guaranteeing the rights and obligations of both parties. Significantly, the actual process of signing these agreements would present the agency with the opportunities it required for teaching Southerners not only about Yankee economics but also about the ways of freedom.

During the spring and summer of 1865, Georgians required this type of instruction because ex-masters and ex-slaves were formulating their own contradictory definitions of freedom. These developments made it all the more imperative for the Bureau to act quickly if it were to succeed in establishing its contract-labor system. The fear and resentment nursed by white Georgians and the unrealistic optimism held by black Georgians should have given the Freedmen's Bureau fair warning of the difficulties that lay ahead. The Bureau would need more than lectures and circulars to convince Georgians of the benefits of the contract system. And as Bryant, Tillson, Lewis, and other Bureau men learned, even when individuals agreed to accept contract-regulated labor, the documents alone were inadequate guarantors of an orderly execution of the new free-labor system.

## Initial White Concerns, Black Expectations, Bureau Efforts

In the spring of 1865, white Georgians gave little indication that they would eagerly embrace the intellectual underpinnings of the new social and economic order. Some white Georgians still questioned the finality of emancipation. Some hoped that, if emancipation were indeed the reality, the federal government would have the good sense to allow it to come in a gradual fashion, and so some neglected to tell their workers about the results of the war, planning to make one more crop with bound labor.[4] But even as whites came to accept their fate, they considered how they might reassert control over their laborers and make their hands "go on with their work and obey as usual."[5] An editorialist in southwest Georgia summed up the more liberal white views when he wrote, "Those [freedmen] who are willing to work for fair wages—work as they did before they were freed—may remain [on the plantations], but we want it distinctly understood that no 'airs' about 'freedom and equality' are going to be tolerated here. . . . They must know their proper sphere and not turn to the right or the left."[6]

Planters were concerned about their farming operations and their livelihoods because they feared that unrestrained black labor would be undisciplined and, therefore, unprofitable. Throughout the early months of freedom, they grumbled about the need for compulsion to make their freedpeople work, continued to complain about the policy of abolishing the one institution that brought order and discipline to their fields, and watched bewildered as footloose freedpeople left them stranded with unharvested crops in the fields.[7] For pessimistic planters such as these, the seemingly unrestrained and pandemic desire of their ex-slaves to take to Georgia's roads provided sufficient testimony to prove their gloomy prognosis for a race war in the near future, unless at least a speedy restoration of civil government occurred.[8]

Ex-masters viewed black mobility as proof of the need to reassert control over their ex-slaves, but for black Georgians it symbolized the essence of freedom. Leaving the old fields of former masters was the unambiguous seizing of one's destiny.[9] Freedpeople also understood the pragmatic side of movement and crowded Georgia's roads in their quests to reunite families, return to old homes, look for new opportunities, and explore town life. Those freedpeople who had been displaced by the war and now walked back to their old homes perhaps traveled with the greatest of expectations as well as a clear understanding of what was essential for the confirmation of their freedom. Liberty County matriarch Mary Jones sensed the eager anticipation of her former slaves as she prepared to return to her plantation with her hands, and it worried her. "I think they have an idea of possession," she warned her son, advising him to make it clear to their former slaves that they must "be subject to control."[10] As Jones feared and as Bureau officer Alexander P. Ketchum confirmed, "the negro regards the ownership of land as a privilege that ought to be co-existent with his freedom."[11]

E. A. Wild's midsummer confiscation campaign in Wilkes County falsely alarmed some whites that the Bureau would be an ally in the freedpeople's quest to dispossess them of their property. Earlier in June, some procrastinating employers scrambled to make contracts because Rufus Saxton threatened to confiscate the land of whites who refused to recognize the economic freedom of their black workers by mid-August. But this unenforced—indeed, unenforceable—threat was like Wild's campaign: extraordinary.[12] During the early months of Reconstruction the agency's activities were designed to educate Georgians about its own expectations for the new economy and to encourage them to accept the wisdom found in Yankee ways. Saxton and his representatives in Georgia, men who came of age at a time when reformers proclaimed the power of moral suasion, expected that reasonable men, black and white, would find their exposition on the logic of free labor to have an appeal of its own.

In late May, John Emory Bryant and Saxton's old Port Royal colleague, the Reverend Mansfield French, began the Bureau's free-labor campaign in Georgia. They addressed freedpeople and employers in Augusta, articulating ideas about labor relations that would be part of the Bureau's message for the duration of its stay in Georgia. Bryant made it clear that black freedom was unquestionable and that the Bureau would adjudicate labor disputes. However, while both he and French stressed the rights and obligations of employers and employees, they also impressed the white listeners in the crowd with their desire to bring order back to the state by urging freedpeople to remain at work at their old homes.[13]

After sharing the podium with Bryant, the Reverend French carried the Bureau's message into central and southwestern Georgia, spending the spring and summer traveling from Augusta to Atlanta, Columbus, Albany, Macon, Milledgeville, and points in between. Concerned with the disorganized state of agricultural affairs that he witnessed during his trip, he heavily emphasized the need to reestablish order and discipline among Georgia's laborers. In Atlanta he lectured freedmen on the benefits of remaining and cultivating "amicable relations" with their old owners.[14] Visiting communities in central and southern Georgia, he continued to encourage freedmen to remain at their old homes and to regard their newly signed contracts as sacred. The Bureau, he assured them, would look after their interests. French also disappointed many freedpeople when he disabused them of the belief that the ex-slaves would receive land from the government. The army chaplain told his black audiences that the only way they would come by property would be to earn enough cash to buy it.[15]

Bryant codified these views when on June 12, 1865, he issued regulations that alerted employers and employees well beyond his jurisdiction to the Bureau's expectations.[16] Bryant confirmed the right of ex-slaves to choose their employers and the power of the Bureau to intercede when employers failed to deal justly with their workers. He also suggested guidelines for wages. In addition to "wholesome food, comfortable clothing, quarters, fuel and medical attendance," top male fieldhands should earn seven dollars per month and top female hands should earn six dollars. At the same time, however, Bryant stressed the usual obligations of workers: support families, honor contracts, and avoid idleness and vagrancy. Bryant made it clear that freedpeople were bound by the laws of free labor, as were their ex-masters. They had to learn how to support themselves as soon as possible, and "if they desire to become the owners of lands, they must buy them" as all other free individuals do.[17] Later in the summer after his return to the South, Saxton failed to endorse Bryant's explicit wage guideline.[18] However, his own message to black and white Georgians alike confirmed the free-labor exhortations of his subordinates.[19]

Planters' reactions to the Bureau's proselytizing during this initial phase of contract labor were ambivalent and inconsistent. There were ex-masters— those who perhaps had not yet grasped the full implications of the Bureau's message—who willingly, if not enthusiastically, accepted labor contracts. These individuals, though concerned about federal intrusion into their private affairs, conceded that there were aspects of the program that could be put to good use in speeding forward their own agenda. As an editorialist from central Georgia admitted, a contract system could be beneficial if it included provisions for forcing unwilling blacks to work.[20]

Another reason for the willingness of some employers to accept contracts was their misinterpretation of the documents' purpose. Employers unfamiliar with northern free-labor ideals misread the intentions of the Bureau and heard in the speeches of men like French and Bryant a promise to restore employer control and worker discipline. Without close supervision by the Bureau, something that the agency's short personnel roster did not permit during the summer of 1865, planters could use French's and Bryant's words to calm their own fears. The Augusta newspaper, for example, favorably reviewed French's May 1865 speech.[21] In June, a group of planters meeting at Albany thought it a humane policy that government officials should encourage freedpeople to "reside at the house of their former owners, and contract with them as to their wages."[22] And in August a Macon editorialist noted that French "has succeeded in this locality, at least, in disabusing their minds of many erroneous ideas, and expectations, which are calculated to prove hurtful to them, and dangerous to us."[23]

The impression that the federal government might be a useful ally was reinforced by army personnel who appeared to be sympathetic to the planters' requests for assistance in subduing willful freedpeople.[24] Also, the contracts approved not only by army provost marshals but also by John Emory Bryant and other Bureau officials during the spring and summer of 1865 might have further encouraged white expectations of federal assistance in their efforts to restore discipline to Georgia's fields.[25] To be sure, at the least, signing contracts forced planters to accept the abolition of slavery, to recognize their workers as economic free agents, and to acknowledge the supervisory role of strangers; nevertheless, those planters who decided to cooperate with the new order also realized that contracts presented them with the opportunity to remind freedpeople that they had once been slaves and should act accordingly.[26]

Bryant's Augusta office unwittingly encouraged the expectations of these planters by approving contracts that made it clear that the employer was the responsible and ultimate authority for determining and supervising farm chores.[27] This requirement alone was not unusual in agricultural work relationships, but the Bureau agent also allowed planters to outline the social obligations of their workers and to set behavioral standards for them as well. Planters, who might have found their freed slaves to be impertinent, now bound their employees not only to be industrious but also faithful, sober, courteous, respectful, and even submissive.[28]

There were other Georgians who signed contracts but remained dubious converts to the mechanics of free labor. They were uncertain that the documents would be of any use in keeping the freedpeople in the fields, but at this time assumed that they had no other alternative.[29] John McCrary best summed up their feelings when he scrawled his assessment across the bottom of a contract to which he was a party in August 1865: "This is a yankey humbug to harass the Southern people."[30] Yet, while people like McCrary complained vociferously about the agency's meddling in their private affairs, they saw no need to act or think in a consistent way if they could benefit from being ideologically flexible, which is exactly how the Stiles family coped with the Bureau's contract system.

In July 1865, William Henry Stiles condemned the "Northern vandals" and pledged to "fight it out against tyranny, poverty & the minions of power." After an additional month of experience with free labor, his wife confirmed the family's opposition to Reconstruction. For Elizabeth Anne Stiles, the entire free-labor system was a great Yankee fraud; the Freedmen's Bureau and its contracts were simply the vehicles by which Northerners could steal Southern land if Georgia planters failed to meet their obligations to their workers. Yet within a month of Mr. Stiles's outburst, the family was conducting its agricultural business under the guidance of a labor contract. Furthermore, when his freedpeople abandoned his Terrell County plantation, Stiles did not hesitate to ask for "simple justice" from those very Yankee vandals he and his wife had condemned.[31] Thus, white Georgians could question the necessity, legality, and constitutionality of the Bureau, but still urge the agency to "be more energetic in its movements" in enforcing the contracts to which they had affixed their signatures.[32]

An early key moment for testing whether whites understood contracts to be something more than waivers to exercise labor discipline came at the end of freedom's first summer, from late July into early September 1865, when the freedpeople had completed the bulk of the work on the cotton crop.[33] This "lay-by time" revealed a cavalier attitude among employers who had no desire to honor contracts when they considered them to be unprofitable, inconvenient, or in some way contrary to their understanding of their prerogatives.[34] John Emory Bryant's workload was so pressing at this time because planters turned away deserving employees without pay "in hundreds of cases"; their labor was no longer needed, and planters had no desire to support them until the fall harvest.[35] Farther south, W. F. Eaton, the Bureau agent at St. Simons Island, discovered that planters on the mainland across from his island were also discharging workers for no legitimate cause but that "the crop for the season was made." Eaton estimated that planters in the southern Georgia counties of Glynn, Wayne, Camden, Ware, and Clinch turned off at least three thousand freedmen.[36]

When such planters came into contact with the few available agents who imposed upon them the concept that employers had obligations to their employees, they formed a less reassuring opinion of the fledgling agency compared with their peers who had yet to see a Bureau man. In late July, for example, Ella Thomas's husband had to respond to a summons from John Emory Bryant "to appear before him to answer to the demand of these Negroes for wages." By the fall, this and other examples of Bryant's activism led her to conclude that the agent had "broadcast the seeds of dissention between the former master and slave and caused what might have continued to be a kind interest to become in many cases a bitter enmity." For this Southern lady, Bryant was a loathsome character for presuming "to interfere in our domestic affairs," a complaint that would become all the more common about the Bureau during the next few years.[37]

By the time of Tillson's arrival at Augusta, Rufus Saxton not only had failed to organize the Bureau in Georgia but also had failed to impress upon the state's planters—despite his good intentions—that contract-regulated free labor was more than a new method of labor control. Although many whites remained confused about their future with free labor, others already were showing an inclination to use whatever tools were available to help them have their way with their former slaves. When Bureau agents informed them that they were in fact no longer masters, they worked hard to prove them wrong.

Georgia's freedpeople, who still clung to the hope that the end of the year would bring them land, had every right to remain wary of a system that appeared to give them so little protection and no property at the very commencement of their new way of life. Yet these ex-slaves, as Bryant's long workdays proved, were beginning to look to the Bureau and their contracts for help in protecting their economic rights. In southwestern Georgia, freedpeople were also evidencing an early faith in the federal government when they expressed their dissatisfaction with crop settlement procedures "unless some United States officer or bureau agent were present."[38] Consequently, Tillson took command of the Georgia Bureau at a critical time. Black and white Georgia's ambiguous views and erroneous expectations of free labor, the contract system, and the agency demanded clarification if the Freedmen's Bureau and Reconstruction were to have a lasting impact on labor relations in the state.

## Contracting during Tillson's Administration

At the outset of his tenure, Davis Tillson directed much of his initial efforts to reassuring white Georgians of the just and worthwhile aims of the Bureau and the forthcoming benefits of free labor. Through correspondence and public addresses he calmed anxious whites by promising that he would enforce all fair labor arrangements and that the freedpeople "will be required to perform in good faith their contracts."[39] These were optimistic times for Tillson because he believed that white Georgians were responding favorably to his message. Even the "rebel" newspaper at Washington in Wilkes County endorsed his labor objectives, and a visit to Athens "produced a very happy impression."[40]

Tillson was particularly pleased with his reception at Milledgeville, where on October 27, 1865, he informed the delegates attending the state constitutional convention about his plans for Georgia.[41] No doubt Tillson's announcement that he wished to use white Georgians as his agents contributed to that happy reception; his audience walked away with the impression that the Bureau had just turned over the implementation of Reconstruction to the delegates and their neighbors.[42] The assistant commissioner, however, should have been more circumspect, paying closer attention to the sobering symbolic reception that went beyond words. Ex-rebel generals, colonels, and politicians joined the delegates to witness the proceedings from the convention floor, but Tillson and Generals Steedman and Wilson "were obliged to find seats as best they could in the dirty and miserable gallery."[43]

Tillson also should have read with a critical eye the newspaper reports of his speeches. Commentators tended to emphasize his stern instructions to the freedpeople and to discount or miss altogether his words concerning the obligations of employers.[44] Davis Tillson at this point in his tenure, however, was less concerned with white Georgians than with the untutored freedpeople. Throughout the fall of 1865, there were examples of freedpeople who refused to sign contracts because they had no desire to work under the supervision of overseers, feared that the documents "would bind them forever," or continued to expect a general land division.[45] Some were quite aggressive about making their point. In Lincoln County, for example, freedpeople on Shelton Oliver's property not only refused to sign contracts but refused to leave the land, and in Bryan County on Thomas Arnold's plantation, freedpeople refused to contract, refused to leave, and refused to allow other workers on the place.[46] Planters could be expected to complain about such black intractability, but even Charles Howard, the Bureau commissioner's brother, observed on his visit to the Georgia coast in the fall of 1865 that the freedpeople exhibited a marked reluctance to go to work for wages.[47]

Tillson was aware and concerned about the labor implications of the freedpeople's expectation that they would have land by Christmas, a notion that he and his officers discouraged.[48] The general, however, had to look no further than the highly visible destitution of the freedpeople's congested refugee camps and shantytowns to confirm his unflattering impressions of the freedpeople. For the orderly, systematic engineer, the continued migration of unemployed freedpeople to Georgia's cities would only result in a winter of suffering and disease.[49]

On October 3, Tillson confronted the problem by directing his subordinates to "make immediate and vigorous efforts" to find employment for all idle freedpeople lounging about Georgia's towns.[50] Continued complaints from white Georgians concerning the unreliability of labor and the difficulty in securing contracts—as well as intelligence alerting him to the demand for labor—prompted Tillson to take an even firmer stand.[51] On December 22, while acknowledging the worker's right to choose his or her own employer, he set January 10, 1866, as the deadline for all freedpeople who had no means of support to make contracts or have the Bureau make the arrangements for them.[52]

In October, as he formulated his policies, Davis Tillson anticipated more difficulty "in inducing ignorant freedpeople to become law-abiding, peaceful and industrious citizens than in compelling the white people to refrain from cruelty and injustice toward them."[53] In late 1865, however, sufficient evidence crossed his desk to convince him that the freedpeople were willing to work, and in early February 1866, he admitted that there was no need for his earlier compulsory contract deadline. In his opinion, the freedpeople were signing fair contracts, whereas employers were trying to evade Bureau supervision.[54]

Tillson's growing awareness of the reality of labor relations in Georgia led him to acknowledge that planters had denied their workers reasonable wages either out of maliciousness or ignorance. Consequently, as he became more familiar with his jurisdiction, he altered his initial vision of a free-market labor economy to make sure employers fairly compensated the freedpeople.[55] In

October, Tillson had refused to "fix a price for labor," allowing "labor like any other commodity, to sell itself, in the open market to the highest bidder."[56] On December 22, however, Tillson took steps to remove any confusion about his own expectations concerning free labor's just compensation by establishing a wage guideline with which he expected all employers to comply.

The assistant commissioner instructed his agents to secure contracts paying twelve to thirteen dollars per month for a prime male hand and eight to ten dollars per month for a prime female hand in upper and middle Georgia. Along the coast and in southwest Georgia as well as in other areas with land more fertile than upper and middle Georgia, Tillson required fifteen dollars and ten dollars per month for first-rate men and women workers, respectively, an improvement over the suggestions of Bryant and Saxton. The employers were to provide food and lodging for the freedpeople. If a planter wished to pay with a share of the crop, Tillson required "from one-third the gross to one-half the net proceeds."[57]

In early January 1866, Tillson, who in the face of white protests refused to accept the assertion that Georgia's plantations and farms could not support his wage rates, admitted that not all contracts made since he had established his wage schedule met his standards.[58] He confronted the state's planters, warning them that they should not expect the Bureau to compel freedpeople to honor the agreements and that agents would find more suitable positions for the freedpeople where wages were more liberal.[59] This was the tack he took in February 1866 when a Milton County planter informed him that the freedpeople there preferred to stay in familiar surroundings for five or six dollars per month rather than move from their north-central Georgia homes to more prosperous lands. Tillson assured him that he would not deviate from the course set. The assistant commissioner warned him that the Bureau would not enforce contracts embodying these low wages but would continue to facilitate migration. If freedpeople who remained in the county later complained about low wage rates at settlement time, the Bureau would allow them "the highest rate of wages paid in the county . . . without reference to the contract claimed to have been made."[60]

Tillson if anything was consistent in his efforts to educate the people to his interpretation of free labor, regardless of the race or the status of his listeners. He challenged the state's governor and legislature, warning them that he would ignore any law that attempted to undermine the Bureau's ability to supervise contracts.[61] He vigorously defended his actions to the Bureau commissioner, who questioned the wisdom of his intrusive policies.[62] And he chastised his own men who had approved substandard contracts, voiding their inadequate handiwork.[63]

Some of Tillson's native civilian agents at times appeared to be more a hindrance than a help to the Bureau's labor program, justifying their actions with the same arguments used by their planter neighbors about poverty, laissez-faire economics, and labor value in local markets.[64] But the best of them—those who, like Greene County agent James Davison, acknowledged the need for some kind of adjustment to the new circumstances now confronting Georgia—accepted Tillson's instructions and became an extension of the assistant commissioner's efforts to convince whites of the value of contract labor. After his appointment in December 1865, Davison directed his initial efforts to bringing order to the labor market as Tillson had done: he focused on the freedpeople. The task was time-consuming. On January 8, 1866, he reported, "For the last 3 weeks I have bent every energy and given my whole time to advancing the general interest of the Freedmen," which meant convincing them to sign contracts and work for their old masters. He canvased his jurisdiction, which involved one-third of the county, speaking to ex-slaves wherever and whenever he could "find or get a Crowd." Soon freedpeople began to come to his addresses to hear the advice of the Bureau. "They always went away if not rejoicing—at least better informed." His efforts, he believed, produced quiet, industrious laborers.

Within a month, he discovered that many planters were hiring freedpeople but refusing to commit themselves to written contracts, "adopting the principle that no one has any rights to either enquire into or meddle with their business affairs." To counter this tendency, Davison held a meeting with planters at Greensboro and informed them that, if they wished the Bureau to protect their interests, they must comply with its regulations. Davison also had made the mistake of accepting some contracts that were below the minimum wage guidelines established by Tillson. By the beginning of March 1866, however, he had revised those documents to conform with Tillson's expectations and supervised others, which brought his total of agreements to 242 covering 1,450 hands. On March 14, 1866, Major William Gray, Tillson's inspector general, reported that nearly all of the freedpeople of Greene County were working industriously under the protection of contracts.[65]

Elsewhere, the Bureau did not hesitate to use more than its persuasive powers to convince employers to sign contracts. On January 30, 1866, Major Gray discovered that employers in Elbert County, where freedpeople had signed contracts for wages ranging from two to six dollars a month, were determined not to raise freedmen's wages. They had already informed the local agent that they would not submit to the wishes of the Bureau. Wasting no time, on January 31 Tillson requested troops for duty in the county. The next day Gray was on his way back to Elbert County with armed force to back up his orders.[66] The presence of blue uniforms had the desired effect; at the end of February, an officer touring the county informed Tillson that, in his opinion, "a majority of planters are sufficiently persuaded to make fair contracts with the freedmen."[67]

In Morgan County, the Bureau also resorted to using military force to impress upon employers "that the freedpeople shall have the protection of the strong arm of the Government" to support them in claiming their economic rights.[68] Morgan employers failed to offer freedpeople contracts that measured up to Tillson's standards and also prevented their ex-slaves from seeking work elsewhere. Tillson arranged to send a sergeant and six men to Madison, the county seat. The presence of a detachment of soldiers may not have changed any minds there, but at least the Bureau and the sergeant made a point by arresting some of those individuals who had attempted to limit their workers' freedom.[69]

The Bureau's effort to encourage contracting under its supervision continued through the remainder of Tillson's administration and ran headlong into continued white resistance from employers who denied the Bureau's authority to interfere in their affairs. Officers and agents still found the occasion to inform freedpeople that they were entitled to be paid for their labor.[70] And there remained employers who avoided Bureau supervision in order to take advantage of their workers' ignorance, like the planters in the Augusta region who inserted unfavorable terms into their contracts without informing their illiterate workers.[71]

Even those employers who complied with Tillson's policies failed to internalize the Yankee ideals preached by Bureau men. Some of them obviously used contracts not because they believed it to be right and just to do so but because the government required it of them.[72] Others once again considered the contracting process as a time for reminding the freedpeople of the necessity to be faithful laborers.[73] Those planters who still saw some value in soliciting assistance from the agency in disciplining their workers signed Bureau-approved contracts because Tillson had made it known that his men would enforce only written agreements that measured up to his standards.[74] Finally, there were planters who accepted the Bureau's contract policies because they saw future political advantage in temporary compliance; they expected their acquiescence to speed along the agency's termination by proving that there was no need for it.[75]

Despite some success on the part of the Bureau, many whites continued to avoid Yankee scrutiny whenever possible, and the Georgia legislature, despite Tillson's protests, made it all the easier to accomplish that end. On March 17, 1866, Georgia passed legislation that gave the state's county courts the authority to register yearlong contracts and to settle disputes arising from them without regard for the Bureau's system of supervision.[76] Now planters could use state law to legitimize their efforts to undermine the Bureau's authority. In July 1866, the Rome Bureau officer estimated that Floyd County planters had signed about one thousand contracts with their employees, but the local agent had approved only eighty-eight.[77] Later in January 1867, just as Tillson stepped down from command, James Davison, the Greene County agent who believed he had made headway earlier in the year, commented upon the ephemeral nature of the Bureau's successes. "There seems manifest, on the part of many of our *Farmers* & Employers, contracting with Freedmen, a disposition not to have their contracts submitted to the 'Bureau' for Examination, approval or Disapproval," he noted. "The majority from what I can learn seem disinclined so to do, and from what I learn from the 'freedmen' use every specious argument imaginable with them, to satisfy them, that no necessity, or order exist for so doing."[78]

Tillson's efforts to counter white intransigence did not endear him or the agency to Georgia's employers. By January 1867, for example, Carlos de la Mesa had been sufficiently active on behalf of the freedpeople to prompt farmer John Horry Dent to conclude that the Bureau "backs them [the freedpeople] in all their rascality and causes them to observe no contracts or obligations entered into." Georgia's ex-slaves, in Dent's opinion, were too free because the Bureau "overrides the state laws and makes the Negro independent and his own master."[79]

Other white Georgians agreed that the Bureau's meddling in contract arrangements was "arbitrary and despotic."[80] A committee of citizens of Oglethorpe County, where planters had contracted to pay freedpeople only three to eight dollars for a month's work, expressed its indignation over the assistant commissioner's insistence on higher wages.[81] Another citizen complained that planters had made contracts, primarily to protect themselves, but "no sooner were the contracts made (for which they had to pay[)] than here comes 'Old John Brown's soul marching on' with that *sweet scented* piece of furniture the Freedmen's Bureau & nullifies all contracts."[82] Tillson's altering of Baker County contracts led an editorialist to protest that the outsider had no sense of the freedpeople's abilities, and southwestern Georgia planters groused about the agency's "prying into the privacy of [their] family affairs."[83] Such protests about Tillson's policies became even more cacophonous when the assistant commissioner resorted to labor relocation to speed along compliance with his contract system.

## Tillson and Labor Relocation

Tillson in his efforts "to overcome the combination to keep the price of labor down" found that persuasion and threats were all the more convincing when accompanied by efforts to locate alternative employment for undervalued black workers. As early as October, the assistant commissioner admitted the benefit of having private "intelligence offices" assist his agency in relocating labor from subdistricts that enjoyed a surplus of hands to those that suffered from a shortage.[84] And throughout the months before the 1866 planting season began, he offered free transportation for freedpeople who sought work where they could receive the best possible wages, usually in southwestern Georgia or the Mississippi valley.[85] The Bureau offer attracted numerous requests for hands from employers during the winter months of 1865 and 1866 in anticipation of the upcoming planting season; Tillson obliged them as far as possible.[86] The assistant commissioner had his officers identify underpaid freedpeople, areas of surplus labor, and areas of need, and his inspectors general, Major William Gray and Major George Walbridge, as well as other officers, assisted labor contractors in recruiting hands.[87]

Tillson was concerned about unemployed freedpeople congregating in towns and contraband camps, and he was happy to encourage their relocation to more productive quarters where the Bureau did not need to concern itself with feeding them. In March 1866, for example, he endorsed the activities of the Liberty County Bureau agent who traveled to Atlanta to recruit workers from the contraband camp there. Tillson was willing to provide transportation for workers who accepted fair wages to relocate to the coast, but he also made it clear that able freedpeople who refused a reasonable offer must leave the camp.[88]

Many freedpeople who found themselves in unacceptable labor arrangements, however, did not need more encouragement than the prospect of better conditions and transportation to take advantage of relocation. In December 1865, Wilkes County freedpeople, plagued by Jayhawkers, contracted to work on a plantation in Tennessee.[89] In January 1866, some of Elbert County's ex-slaves decided to leave for better positions, despite fears that planters would resort to violence to keep them on their farms.[90] And in March in Putnam County, when Major William Gray presented the option to freedpeople laboring under miserable conditions, they flocked to his headquarters in Eatonton.[91] Later in the fall of 1866, freedpeople also considered emigration as an alternative to remaining in an area troubled by the season's poor harvest, and they turned to the Bureau for information and assistance.[92] In November 1866, M. H. Mathews, the leader of a group of freedpeople from the Griffin area, asked Tillson for information about prospects outside Georgia, and in December 150 freedpeople gathered at Thomasville, all wishing to go west where they expected to better their economic circumstances.[93]

The Bureau proved to be a useful guardian in the emigration of these freedpeople. Not only did the agency provide labor intelligence, coordination, and fares for these individuals but it made sure that the out-of-state contracts measured up to Davis Tillson's standards and that the freedpeople would indeed find "comfortable homes" awaiting them. The Bureau also did its best to prevent labor agents from leaving behind dependent family members.[94] And on at least one occasion it prevented railroad officials from treating the freedpeople with any less courtesy than white travelers. Railroad officials at Eatonton planned to pack 140 of the Putnam County freedpeople into boxcars for transportation westward before Major William Gray put a stop to it.[95]

Bureau officials did not record the exact number of freedpeople who took advantage of the opportunities presented by agency-sponsored contractors or by out-of-state planters. In November 1866, Tillson reported to Howard that he had issued only 381 orders for transportation, covering the needs of 2,947 adult freedpeople and 1,013 children. He believed that these figures exaggerated the actual number of Bureau-sponsored emigrants because some of the freedpeople failed to take advantage of the transportation issued.[96] Also, the Georgia Bureau's transportation program was sporadic, tapering off by February 1866 to resume later in the fall of that year. Consequently, some freedpeople or their employers assumed the costs of relocation.[97]

Black migration was sufficient to contribute to an interregional shift of the freed population within Georgia, particularly from older plantation areas to the newer lands of southwestern Georgia where wages were higher, and noticeable enough to spark fear of a labor shortage among planters throughout the state.[98]

Tillson believed this population shift and the white perception that freedpeople were leaving the state were key components in his plan for stimulating demand for labor and increasing the freedpeople's ability to secure good jobs.[99] Furthermore, although he might have exaggerated the benefits of emigration, Tillson understood the psychological impact of a policy that threatened to reduce Georgia's labor pool. "I have not yet sent off a thousand negroes out of the State," he remarked during the winter after his arrival in Georgia. "But I have sent off enough to alarm the people." In the end, the exact number of emigrants was less important than the worry it caused among Georgia's planters.[100]

The demographic consequences of Tillson's transportation policy became apparent as early as the beginning of 1866, when Bureau men could no longer satisfy requests for hands from outside and from within the state.[101] Indeed, as early as January 1866, Tillson's adjutant had turned down a request for transportation from parties hiring freedpeople for farms in southern Mississippi, explaining that Georgia's own labor needs, more noticeable with every passing day, took precedence.[102] Consequently, by March 1866, Tillson remained willing to provide transportation for freedpeople moving within the state, but the only assistance the Bureau offered western planters was its influence in trying to help employers obtain reduced rail rates to Atlanta or Chattanooga.[103]

After it became apparent that the 1866 harvest would be a poor one, the Georgia Bureau began to provide transportation for freedpeople to the borders of the state, and then, in late December 1866, with Commissioner Howard's encouragement, increased its efforts to remove destitute freedpeople by offering transportation for them to out-of-state planters who could prove their legitimate intentions. As far as Tillson was concerned, in such circumstances, a renewed effort in Bureau-sponsored transportation was economical and ideologically sound. It would be, he allowed in one case, "cheaper to send these people to points where they can obtain a livelihood by their own exertions, than to feed them here."[104]

By January 1867, however, the Georgia Bureau once again saw no need to assist in moving workers to other states. Caleb C. Sibley, in fact, discouraged requests for hands. "So many freedmen have already left the state, that it is with greatest difficulty that the planters can obtain sufficient numbers of hands to plant this year," he explained. Furthermore, "in some instances they [Georgia planters] have been obliged to go to neighboring states to procure them."[105]

During the remainder of the Bureau's existence, the involvement of its agents and officers in labor emigration was minimal. On at least one occasion, an agent tried to improve the working conditions of freedpeople when he "organized a stampede among the colored people" of Schley County because of the poor treatment they were receiving from employers there.[106] However, although freedpeople continued to find emigration to better locations within Georgia and beyond its boundaries an appealing alternative to bad treatment and economic oppression throughout the late 1860s and 1870s, they had to rely on their own or their new employers' resources to fund their travels.[107]

Georgia's planters found the Bureau's transportation policy a distasteful one, especially if the laborers were moving from their neighborhoods to someone else's. As far as they were concerned, it was difficult enough having to cope with free labor without worrying about competing for workers with planters cultivating more fertile soil or, worse yet, dealing with freedpeople who had their own sense of self-worth awakened by the competition. In Wilkes County, where Tillson had received a warm welcome when he had first arrived in the state, citizens now believed that, by encouraging their laborers to find more profitable employment elsewhere, he "meant to desolate" their county "unless they would raise the compensation according to his orders."[108] It was clearly unfair of the Bureau, another critic complained, to pit the "worn & thin" lands of upper Georgia against Mississippi.[109]

Georgia's employers were well aware of the consequence of losing their surplus labor, understanding that if sufficient numbers left their counties, freedpeople would be able to "hire themselves only to such farmers as would give them their price."[110] For the freedpeople, just knowing that there was a better price for their labor beyond their neighborhoods influenced their dealings with their former masters, as Howell Cobb Jr. discovered when he tried to hire workers who were now "high in their self-esteem."[111]

Editorialists generally agreed with Cobb and found it easy to blame Northerners for the troubles. In assessing the situation in Putnam County, one critic of Bureau policy noted that since the arrival of Bureau-protected labor contractors in the Eatonton area, the freedpeople, previously content with their lot, were now bitter and unhappy. "The negroes in this county," he concluded, "do very well when there are no Yankees about."[112]

Another editorialist from middle Georgia complained that the exodus of freedpeople in early 1866 had stopped work on many plantations, raising the grievance that labor contractors had hired away freedpeople with legitimate agreements. Although some Georgians decided that it would be best to alter their dealings with their workers to induce them to stay on, he suggested an occasional application of "Lynch Law" to stop the labor bandits.[113] Some whites needed little encouragement to follow this advice, and they resorted to trickery, threats, and violence to stem the tide of emigration from their neighborhoods.

In January 1866, Wilkes County planters cooled the wanderlust of local freedpeople by telling them that labor contractors planned to sell them into slavery in Cuba, as did Taylor County planters almost a year later, but other land owners often employed more vigorous tactics, especially when the planting season was at hand.[114] In Walton County, for example, local authorities arrested two labor recruiters, falsely accusing them of tampering with a legitimate contract.[115] A Putnam County mob threatened Major William Gray, the labor contractors traveling with him, and their ten escorts.[116] In Butts County, where citizens swore they could manage their freedpeople without the help of "any Yankee Bureau," they prohibited strangers from hiring black laborers there and beat a man who tried.[117] In Cowetta County, employers threatened to kill any freedperson who left his or her former owner.[118]

White Georgians, disturbed by the tampering with their labor supply, also attempted to sabotage Bureau-sponsored emigration by charging the agency with corruption. "The Slave Trade Revived by the Freedmen's Bureau," trumpeted one headline; the writer explained that the agency was promising good wages in the Mississippi valley but was actually selling freedpeople to the West Indies.[119] "Negro brokers" made exorbitant profits with the help of the "Radical negro-trading agencies," another critic claimed.[120] Freedpeople suffered "great hardships and cruelties" as Bureau agents, who skimmed their share of the profits, turned a blind eye to the activities of friends and relatives involved in recruiting labor, according to yet another. "I know of several of these local agents and their families, who, previous to their appointment in the bureau, could not borrow a dollar in the places where they live, are now rich, buy fast horses, smoke expensive cigars, wear flash[y] clothes, and get drunk daily," the writer explained. "Surely the legitimate remuneration of a bureau agent would not warrant the financial revolution."[121] In late 1866, word of speculation in transportation issued by the Bureau reached Washington, and Davis Tillson bore the brunt of local charges of malfeasance, including the allegation that someone "put several hundred dollars into . . . [his] pocket from the use of such transportation."[122]

Labor agents certainly made money at their work, and not all of them were as honest as they should have been, but the charges directed against the Georgia Bureau and particularly Davis Tillson had little substance. The assistant commissioner attempted to balance the rights of the freedpeople and those of employers with the requirements of the Bureau in implementing his policy of labor redistribution. He did not allow freedpeople or labor contractors to break legitimate agreements, but he always supported the freedpeople in their right to look for the best arrangements available within or outside the state before they signed contracts.[123] In March 1866, for example, Tillson ordered the arrest of a planter who had no contracts with his workers but was interfering with an emigration agent.[124]

Certainly, Tillson was not completely successful in implementing an unblemished emigration program, but it was not for want of effort. Although he allowed civilian agents to collect fees for recruiting hands, he attempted to keep track of how his subordinates used government-issued transportation.[125] Furthermore, he restricted his subordinates' actual involvement in the process and, in late 1866, the issuance of transportation because of charges of impropriety against the Bureau and some evidence of fraudulent use of government-issued transportation.[126] He also investigated cases involving labor contractors that came to his attention, arresting those transgressors who appeared to have violated Bureau policy.[127]

The case of J. Clark Swayze should have provided a good example to the agency's critics of how the Georgia Bureau dealt with charges of impropriety involving transportation and labor contractors. In November 1866, General Tillson suspected that Swayze and others were selling government-issued transportation; that suspicion led him to suspend temporarily the issuance of transportation. The investigation cleared Swayze, but—like so many of these types of complaints—personality, past politics, and ideological conflict converged to influence and confuse the accusations and the defense. The hapless Swayze was an ostracized Unionist, New York native, and former Bureau agent who had made violent enemies among his neighbors. He also ran afoul of the area's Bureau subassistant commissioner over emigration policy and had a falling-out with his partner in the labor business. The animosity generated by Swayze was such that later in February 1867 one Bureau officer on Sibley's headquarters staff recommended that he leave Griffin as soon as possible because he had alienated so many of his neighbors. Although the Bureau cleared Swayze of serious wrongdoing, Tillson's adjutant, probably speaking for his superior, urged the ex-agent to leave well enough alone and get out of the labor contracting business.[128]

As for Tillson and his administration, F. D. Sewall, Commissioner Howard's inspector general, discovered some abuses in the practice of transporting freedpeople, which he concluded benefited planters and "negro brokers" more than the freedpeople. Nevertheless, he found nothing that implicated the assistant commissioner or supported the charges leveled against him by angry white Georgians. Sewall, in fact, gave no indication that he had altered his earlier opinion that, although fraud had become part of the emigration business, Tillson was "endeavoring to prevent it." [129]

## Further Efforts to Promote Bureau Contracts

Caleb Sibley's reorganization of the Georgia Bureau did not solve the problem of white intransigence, but the new assistant commissioner had no intention of abandoning the contract system. When it came to work arrangements, Sibley, like Tillson before him, thought in terms of productive labor and fair, binding contracts. His agents and officers continued to act as his advocates for the contract system and as the free-labor instructors of black and white Georgians. Subassistant Commissioner J. J. Knox, for example, warned freedpeople during the summer of 1867 that the Bureau would not "countenance or sanction any dishonesty nor any breaking of contracts." [130]

Lieutenant O. H. Howard's commitment to the system prompted him to write a free-labor sermon that was reminiscent of the admonitions of Bryant and Tillson. "You must labor industriously, obeying all reasonable orders promptly and cheerfully," he informed the freedpeople. "Do your whole duty to yourselves and to your employers, remembering that your success in life depends upon yourselves, upon your own conduct, your industry, your honesty, truthfulness and frugality, and that he among you who is the most industrious, the most honest, truthful and frugal, will have the greatest measure of success." In the meantime, he reassured his charges, the Bureau would continue to supervise their employers to make sure that they offered fair compensation, the best guarantee for reliable and profitable labor. [131]

Lieutenant Howard understood that a successful contract system required more than black labor discipline. Such an assumption prompted him to warn the freedpeople's employers that the Bureau would not cooperate with those planters who failed to acknowledge the necessity of offering freedpeople adequate terms. [132] Captain W. F. White, the Thomasville subassistant commissioner, also warned planters that they were only hurting themselves by offering inadequate terms to their workers, who would become dissatisfied with their impoverished situations and leave for greener pastures. For White the best way to enforce contracts was for employers to give their workers good wages and good treatment. "If the laboring class are prosperous," he explained, "the country is prosperous and the Laborers are satisfied." [133]

White and his colleagues were kept busy by an abundance of unacceptable contractual arrangements that tried to shift power and control to the former masters. The planters' views of contracts were quite different from Captain White's, for employers still assumed that if they could keep the freedpeople poor, they could keep them subservient.[134] For Sibley's Bureau, however, contracts could neither give employers extraordinary power over their workers nor allow them to be the final or "sole judge" of their workers' performance. Such one-sided documents were "contrary to equity & justice" and gave employers the opportunity to discharge freedpeople without compensation.[135]

Captain White confronted the problem when he voided contracts that appeared to place an onerous burden of proof of the fulfillment of their obligations on the freedpeople.[136] Also, officers such as Carlos de la Mesa chastised agents who approved vague contracts that would allow planters to take "all kinds of advantages" of the freedpeople."[137] Because of these concerns, the Bureau continued a practice begun during Tillson's tenure that favored the freedpeople; the agency refused to approve contracts with forfeiture clauses that linked the dismissal of an employee with the loss of all rights to the crop regardless of how long the freedperson had worked on the crop.[138]

In March 1867, Caleb Sibley believed that the freedpeople of Georgia were working under better contracts for 1867 than they had been able to obtain during the previous season.[139] Sibley's optimism, however, was not entirely warranted. Planters had yet to accept the philosophy behind the system as described by the Bureau. In northwestern Georgia, for example, a renewed fear of confiscation, not a conversion, had land owners doing "any and everything they are told to do" to save their property.[140] Elsewhere in the state, although freedpeople were employed—indeed, employed to the point where Sibley could discourage the activities of out-of-state recruiters—the majority were working under verbal or unapproved written contracts, an indication that employers were learning how to secure labor, satisfy the formalities that freedpeople might require, and still bypass the Yankee Bureau.[141] Sibley and his inspector general, John Randolph Lewis, continued to urge agents to do all they could to induce blacks and whites to make written contracts before the Bureau. However, shortly after Sibley assumed command, he departed from Tillson's stricter policy by recognizing that fair verbal agreements were binding.[142]

Although the state legislation sanctioning court contracts had had an impact on Tillson's efforts in 1866, its ability to speed the erosion of the agency's supervisory role became all the more apparent in 1867. In late January 1867, just as the Bureau began its transition from one administration to the next, planters and local officials in Washington County and Clayton County were hard at work convincing freedpeople to register their agreements in the county court; in Clayton County officials resorted to lying to the freedpeople, telling them the Bureau would charge them "everything they made" to approve their contracts.[143] By September 1867 in Mitchell and Baker Counties in southwestern Georgia, few agreements were reaching the Bureau agent for review; those contracts that did not had forfeiture clauses intact and were registered with the county court.[144]

What made this system so damaging to the freedpeople's prospects was that local officials were not likely to go out of their way to protect the freedpeople's economic rights. In southwestern Georgia, county judges believed that the freedpeople should look after their own interests, while claiming no right and seeing no reason to interfere with agreements presented to their courts. The whole process, agent Christian Raushenberg concluded, "generally defeat[s] the object of the Bureau."[145]

Because the legislature's contract law allowed, but did not require, employers to have written contracts registered at the county seats and because the Bureau lacked the authority to force reluctant employers to bring contracts before its agents, white Georgians found it easier to saddle uninformed and agreeable freedpeople with unfair terms. In Subassistant Commissioner F. A. H. Gaebel's jurisdiction, judges referring to state law acceded to the verbal contracts— "*mostly frauds*," according to Gaebel—to allow employers to avoid the Bureau.[146] Employers in Alvin Clark's jurisdiction bypassed the agent and simply had witnesses sign their contracts. The agent also observed that if the freedpeople carried out their unapproved agreements, in some cases they would end up in debt "even if they should raise a good crop."[147] Andrew Clark discovered that the overwhelming majority of freedpeople in Mitchell and Baker Counties had court contracts that would make it easy for their employers to force the freedpeople's forfeiture of their rights to the crops if they failed to comply with the employers' interpretation of their terms.[148]

As for the next season, it was no better. In January 1868, Caleb Sibley urged his men to do their best to secure good arrangements for the freedpeople, but with the Bureau's demise expected, white Georgians felt little compulsion to look to the withering agency for the approval of anything.[149] In the fall of 1868 Daniel Losey, a New Jersey native and agent for Houston and Dooly Counties, discovered that the planters were already scheming to keep down the price of labor and warning the freedpeople to expect stern treatment now that the Bureau "is run out."[150]

## The Freedpeople's Response

As Davis Tillson learned during his first winter in Georgia, freedpeople will-ingly signed Bureau-supervised contracts. In part, the acceptance of contracts came from the freedpeople's resignation to circumstances that provided them with few options. During the spring of 1867, for example, labor in the Bruns-wick area was "more easily controlled," Douglas Risley explained, because the freedpeople had "abandoned the hope of realizing any thing from confiscation for the present."[151]

There was, however, a positive side to the freedpeople's acceptance of con-tracts. Once they understood that their immediate hopes of becoming land owners were ephemeral, they came to accept contracts as a valid alternative be-cause they recognized the potential of the documents. Ex-slaves believed con-tract negotiations embodied in signed documents confirmed their freedom and their autonomous identities, despite the fact that ex-masters tried to use those same contracts to reinforce their own authority. Also, dealing directly with planters—not their representatives—in a formal manner placed ex-slaves, so they believed, on an equal footing with their ex-masters.[152] Furthermore, by 1867 contracts appeared to be vehicles for asserting black individuality; more and more documents signed in that year and later were between individual heads of black households and employers, not between an ex-master and a gang of freedpeople as was common immediately after the war.[153]

The permutations of the labor agreements that followed these and other ex-slaves into freedom—wages, share wages, sharecropping, tenant farming, and numerous hybrids—ultimately limited their independence and contributed to the economic failure of Reconstruction.[154] Nevertheless, the freedpeople ini-tially believed that work brought advantages not known in slavery and that con-tracts could help to protect those advantages. Many of Georgia's ex-slaves al-most intuitively grasped important aspects of free labor, as did the ex-slaves on a Clarke County plantation who "went right out and left 'er [their mistress] and hired out to make money for deyselves."[155] For one freedman in the Ogeechee District, the consequence of hard work was also quite clear. Pounding away at some rice, he explained his exertion to a Yankee teacher by stating that "work brings the greenbacks now . . . [and] there's nothing better than greenbacks."[156]

Elsewhere, freedpeople forced employers to acknowledge their equality by refusing to accept blindly the compensation that former masters offered to them. In 1868 freedpeople along the coast delayed signing contracts "in hopes of better terms."[157] Earlier, in the fall of 1865, Muscogee County freedpeople threatened to strike for higher wages because they believed that white men "must now compete, as respects labor, on terms of equality" with them.[158] Indeed, white competition for black labor, a competition encouraged by the Freedmen's Bureau, initially reinforced the freedpeople's sense of self-worth. In December 1865, a frustrated Howell Cobb complained that freedpeople were refusing his good terms. "Grant them one thing," he complained, and "they demand something more and there is no telling where they would stop."[159]

Contracts made within this competitive framework ideally meant that the freedpeople and their employers came to terms through a process of bargaining; as whites competed for labor, the freedpeople tried to expand their autonomy through their labor agreements. Some were successful. In early 1866 in Emmanuel County the freedman Moses under the supervision of the Bureau bargained away the labor of his two sons in return for provisions, horse feed, and thirty acres of land.[160] Another freedman in Bullock County, also using the labor of his sons and a Bureau contract, secured among other things a lease to sixteen acres of land.[161]

Freedpeople like Moses understood that the Bureau's system at least provided them with opportunities to negotiate terms with their employers under the supervision of a friendly third party that could improve their immediate condition while protecting the one commodity that they had to sell—labor. Whereas some might accept unsupervised contracts, others insisted on Bureau protection. In late 1866, for example, when the freedpeople of Walton County learned that the county judge would be approving contracts for the next season, they objected because they preferred to have Bureau-supervised documents.[162] In 1867, LaGrange area freedpeople continued to distrust their old masters, but they accepted work arrangements with them under the Bureau agent's "assurance & promise of protection."[163] Later, in the spring of 1868, freedpeople in the Crawfordville area also evidenced their preference for Bureau-approved contracts. That they failed to sign Bureau contracts was less a matter of free choice than the persuasiveness of their employers who pointed out that the Bureau would not be around to enforce those documents at the end of the season.[164] At the end of the year, probably because of the Bureau's contraction, agent W. L. Clark of Bainbridge reported, "Very many—a majority I think, have worked this year without contracts altho[ugh] freedmen generally wanted to enter into writings."[165]

Freedpeople signed Bureau contracts because they assumed that the documents would commit the agency to helping them make the most of their situation. They did not accept their employers' assumption that such documents, Bureau-sponsored or not, necessarily placed severe limitations on their freedom. The freedpeople's interpretation of the various and diverse share arrangements, which became increasingly common during the 1867 season, provided the critics of free labor with numerous examples of this attitude.[166] Planters who came to rely on some type of share arrangement to attract workers did so for economic reasons, but freedpeople who accepted these terms also believed that their agreements gave them various privileges, not the least being the right to claim the status of coproprietors of the crop.[167] Some freedpeople argued that planters should receive only a share equal to that of an individual laborer.[168] And some freedpeople, like those ex-slaves near Valdosta who in November 1867 refused to work until their employer met their demands, claimed a right to control the marketing of their shares despite planter opposition.[169]

At times freedpeople, new to the ideas of free labor, interpreted their rights in absolute terms, failing to grasp the responsibilities of their new status. While many employers tried to use the Bureau for their own ends, some had legitimate grievances about freedpeople who had absorbed neither the full meaning of the Bureau's rhetoric nor the import of their contractual obligations.[170] As Bureau men understood, the freedpeople's noncompliance with their contracts could have serious consequences; the concerns of Yankees as well as ex-masters were not simply the unfounded worries of insensitive whites. Freedpeople who wandered away from their fields either for the day or for good left not only their employers shorthanded but also the more constant employees, thus threatening their coworkers' chances for economic success. During the 1866 season, for example, two freedmen in charge of a Screven County plantation allowed all work discipline to deteriorate. Despite a fair contract with the owner, "the freedmen have worked when they chose, and when they felt disposed to leave the plantation they did so for days and weeks together." The two foremen even prevented the more industrious freedpeople from working harder than they judged necessary. In December, the local Bureau agent replaced the foremen and in this case probably helped the employees secure the fair harvest that promised in his estimate to bring them profit and sustain them through the next year.[171]

During the spring of 1868, the irresponsibility of four Baker County freedpeople almost led to a less favorable resolution for their more reliable coworkers.

In May the freedmen abandoned their contract for better terms on a Calhoun County plantation. Agent Andrew B. Clark, who concluded that these workers left without just cause, realized that "the hands remaining are not able to make the crop unless those that left are made [to] return and comply with the contract which was read and explained by myself and it is a fair one." The Bureau ordered their new employer to return the freedpeople.[172]

In such situations, the message from Bureau headquarters was consistently clear: it was just as much a challenge to equitable work arrangements and just as dangerous to the success of the new system for freedpeople to ignore reasonable obligations accepted in good faith as it was for their ex-masters. Sibley's adjutant, Frank Gallagher, plainly confronted the problem of footloose freedpeople. To allow employees the absolute freedom to terminate their contracts on whim and move about until they found the most suitable contract terms, he explained, would "weaken the confidence" of whites in free labor. Furthermore, such license would "defeat the very objects of the contract system besides being contrary to all equity inasmuch as it would hold the contract binding on one party but not on the other." Gallagher's conclusion was the obvious one for a Yankee familiar with the culture of free labor. "Freedpeople must be taught & compelled to keep faith with their employers," he reasoned, "or we cannot in justice compel the latter to keep faith with them."[173] Bureau men, therefore, unhesitatingly investigated complaints against employees. Agents and officers, sometimes overstepping the bounds of legitimate authority, enforced compliance of contracts by allowing employers to penalize or even discharge contract violators after settling their accounts and by fining freedpeople, while also locating and compelling the return of absconding freedpeople to their rightful employers and calling on troops to support the Bureau's decisions.[174]

Freedpeople certainly placed demands on the Bureau's time, but their failings as participants in the new contract-labor system never matched those of their ex-masters. For whatever reasons, white Georgians might have initially accepted the new system, signed contracts, and planted their seed in the spring. But planting gave way to lay-by, harvest, and settlement time, all with their own perils for even the most diligent freedpeople and all with their own opportunities for hard-pressed, unreconstructed, or dishonest employers.

As O. H. Howard learned in southwestern Georgia, too many employers ignored the spirit of the system by acting tyrannically, demanding "implicit obedience and immediate and unconditional submission" because they "still presume they are masters."[175] Weighing his experiences with both races, Howard concluded that despite the freedpeople's sometimes irresponsible behavior, free labor was "in greater danger from the neglect or refusal of planters to pay their freedmen fully and promptly for their labor, than from any and all other causes."[176] George Ballou, another southwestern Georgia Bureau man, would later concur. It was his experience that planters were quite willing to make fair contracts with the freedpeople; what was problematical was convincing them to carry out those agreements.[177]

## White Rejection of the Contract System

Agents Bryant and Eaton had learned during the first summer of freedom that their hectic days were in no small part the consequence of white Georgia's lack of commitment to an honest trial of free labor. In 1866 and 1867 the difficulties encountered by freedpeople and the Bureau increased as employers became more adept at circumventing the wishes of the freedpeople and the goals of the Bureau. Complicating matters were the debts that planters owed to their factors after the poor harvests of the early postwar years; employers preferred to pay their creditors before their workers, a straightforward rejection of the Bureau's policy of recognizing the black employees' first lien on their crops and an almost certain guarantee of a delayed settlement for the freedpeople.[178] Also, planters understood that the freedmen's involvement with electoral politics during 1867 and 1868 raised the stakes in the contest over who would control their state, providing an additional reason to use employment and pay to assert their control over their workers.[179]

Tillson's administration was plagued with shortsighted planters who dealt with the agricultural problems of a bad season by running off their workers at lay-by time.[180] Beginning in late June 1866, reports of planters releasing freedpeople began to reach the assistant commissioner. The number of incidents grew during the summer, and freedpeople and agents continued to report difficulties into September. As Tillson himself admitted and as his agents confirmed, it was a common practice for planters to stage a quarrel and threaten their workers with violence. During the lay-by period freedpeople and agents reported an increased number of violent outrages committed by planters against freedpeople; fear prompted the freedpeople to abandon their homes, thus allowing employers to claim that they had violated their contracts and therefore forfeited their wages.[181] Planters must have found the tactic useful, for despite Tillson's intervention, a change of Bureau administration, and the coming of Military Reconstruction, they continued to create disturbances to force unwanted hands, "glad to escape with their lives," to abandon their year-long contracts and forfeit their claims on the crop.[182]

Even as Bureau men witnessed this rejection of their free-labor plans, they discovered that threats and beatings were not the only methods by which planters, some of whom did not wish to run off their workers, could defraud the freedpeople. Some planters withheld food to force their freedpeople to break their contracts, tampered with contracts that were unreadable to illiterate freedpeople, or had their workers arrested on trumped-up charges. Others skillfully balanced their ledgers, leaving freedpeople destitute after a year's labor, while some sold their crops without telling their workers or absconded with their profits. Still others shipped their harvests beyond the county or state line to avoid the freedpeople's claims.[183]

By the spring of 1867, planters in the Augusta area so regularly delayed honoring their contracts that it became the custom for freedpeople to sue for their wages in the civil courts before their employers would even consider settling with them. According to Augusta subassistant commissioner E. M. L. Ehlers, it was a practice that only increased the wealth of lawyers.[184] But impecunious freedpeople had difficulty finding lawyers who were more concerned with justice than with their fees.[185] And even if freedpeople found representation and presented their case in court, they risked having their cases dismissed and then being assessed court costs, an expense that they could hardly afford.[186] Furthermore, freedpeople, who had to take time off from their present jobs to appear in court, were placed at a particular disadvantage in cases involving employers who had legal residences outside the county in which they had hired the freedpeople; employees had to pursue their claims for wages in the counties in which the defendants resided.[187]

Courts could follow the letter of the law and still hinder justice, because routine cases could drag on for over a year, and dishonest planters used such delays to their advantage.[188] A citizen from Waynesboro recognized the serious implications of the court system's legal prolonging of the resolution of contract settlements. Recently released from slavery, the freedpeople who were pursuing claims in court were "wholly dependent upon what is now due them for this year's labor, and if they do not get this promptly, they must die or steal."[189] Unhappily for the freedpeople, even if they received favorable judgments, there was no guarantee that the civil authorities would vigorously enforce them.[190]

The Bureau's uncertain authority and limited power encouraged planters to act boldly even as they learned how to cope with assertive black labor or aggressive Bureau representatives. It became all too common throughout Georgia for employers to avoid making settlements for as long as possible and, as the Bureau's authority waned, to ignore the agents who summoned them to an accounting. In late 1867 and in early 1868, planters from Rome to Albany appeared none too eager to own up to their obligations; many of them waited until their employees filed complaints with the Bureau before they even began to consider settling their accounts.[191] Even after agents and officers entertained complaints from freedpeople, they often had to summon employers two or three times before they might appear for a hearing, delaying justice and sometimes circumventing it altogether.[192] As agent W. L. Clark learned, freedpeople, especially those who lived some distance from an agency, "frequently [did] not come the second time" if their employers failed to respond to an initial summons.[193]

Sometimes Bureau investigations concerning a settlement went on for months, with or without the employers' cooperation.[194] Employers, who might inflate their workers' debts by overcharging them for necessities, tried to deceive agents about the extent of their obligations to the freedpeople. There were those planters who covered themselves with a veneer of cooperation, hoping that delays would force the freedpeople to abandon or at least compromise their claims. Planters promised to appear before agents but failed to arrive at the appointed time; others requested postponements to secure new witnesses to support their cases; still others accepted a settlement while finding room for further delay by giving notes to redeem at some future date, which they then failed to honor and which the Bureau then tried to collect.[195]

At the end of the 1866 season, planters in the Rome subdistrict preyed on their workers' ignorance about money, easy credit terms, and the negative balance of their accounts to tie them to the land in debt peonage. Some employers required freedpeople to give their notes for the amount owed after an unfavorable settlement and renew their contracts as a way to ensure their payment. The freedpeople, who might have been quite naive when it came to financial matters, at least could rely on the Bureau to watch out for their interests. Subassistant Commissioner Carlos de la Mesa refused to approve the contracts that would institute debt peonage and discouraged the freedpeople from giving promissory notes to their employers until he examined their accounts.[196] In fact, it was Davis Tillson's policy to prohibit planters from binding over freedpeople who might have incurred debt under the previous season's contracts as long as white debtors were not subjected to such treatment.[197] Caleb Sibley also made it clear that the "same laws for collection of debt apply in cases of freedmen as in cases of white men"; employers could not have freedpeople imprisoned for debt.[198]

Bureau officials preferred that their agents settle contract disputes through arbitration, even if it meant compromising a claim. It was always best, they assumed, to keep the freedpeople out of the tangled games their employers played. Ideally, agents and officers acted as peacemakers, as Tillson's agent James Davison referred to himself. "Where parties fall out," he explained, "I frequently by producing this Course get them to 'make up' & 'fall in' again."[199] Still, compromise required the cooperation of both parties involved. Where white Georgians showed no desire to bend, the assistant commissioners were willing to use more forceful measures than reason to deal with their obstructionism.

If threats proved to be insufficient, Davis Tillson ordered agents to seize and hold crops until settlements were worked out.[200] If planters refused to make honest efforts to settle with their workers, he was prepared to have agents use force to hold them until they changed their minds. And if local authorities freed the jailed parties, Tillson was willing to ignore civil law to have the freedpeople paid. In late October 1866, Joseph H. Taylor, the Randolph County agent, complained that employers were forcing off freedpeople "for some frivolous complaint." He believed that the freedpeople should receive their rightful compensation, but the civil authorities promised to release anyone arrested by the Bureau. Tillson directed the agent to allow employers to make their cases in the usual suggested manner before a board of three referees, with one being selected by the planter, another by the freedperson, and the agent acting as the third. If employers refused to submit to the procedure, Tillson, relying on Grant's General Orders, No. 44, instructed the agent to "arrest them and if released by writs of Habeas Corpus, rearrest them and continue to do so until such a time as they will make a just settlement with the Freed people."[201]

During Tillson's administration, the threat of using military force on more than one occasion gave a Bureau agent or officer the opportunity to call an intransigent employer's bluff.[202] After Tillson became military commander of the Department of Georgia in May 1866, he had a greater freedom in committing troops to support Bureau decisions. In the fall of 1866 the Bureau officer in Thomas County used a detachment of eleven soldiers to help him with contract settlements.[203] Tillson stationed troops in Henry County, where during the summer of 1866 violence forced black workers off plantations in large numbers and prevented the intimidated agent from doing his job. In October 1866, after the military restored order, 137 freedpeople presented claims for collection to the local agent with more being brought to his attention daily.[204]

Henry County was not alone in its need for the presence of blue uniforms, but Tillson's aggressiveness had its practical limits in the small number of soldiers at his disposal. Furthermore, not only was the Bureau pressed by the army's policy of rapidly mustering out officers but so were the garrisons that were supposed to help the agency. During the summer of 1866, there had been complaints that the garrison at Atlanta was failing to support the Bureau. Tillson's inspector general, George Walbridge, investigated and discovered the source of the problem. "I do not think any officer is at blame for the seeming neglect as all that are able to do duty are absent executing orders previously received," he informed headquarters. "C. Co. are ready to move at once as soon as an officer can be furnished or one reports to take charge of them."[205] Consequently, although Tillson frequently responded affirmatively to agents' requests for military support, he almost as frequently amended such an answer with the phrase "as soon as possible."[206]

In 1867 and 1868, Sibley's small contingent of Bureau men continued to pursue the Bureau's constant charge to see that freedpeople with legitimate complaints received the pay that they deserved. The methods used to achieve that end also remained fairly constant, although during the period of Military Reconstruction the Bureau's ability to satisfy the freedpeople's claims technically improved. An agent or officer, after taking a freedman's statement, usually asked to see the employer along with his accounts and records, so that he could investigate the case and arrive at a fair determination. In some instances, agents continued to act in concert with two additional arbitrators selected by the involved parties. If all went according to plan, and perhaps after issuing appropriate threats and warnings, the agent settled the dispute and at least extracted the employer's promise to comply with the decision. The agent's arbitration, even if it meant compromising a claim, also kept the freedman away from long and fruitless proceedings in the civil courts.[207]

In its efforts to speed along settlements, the Bureau continued to pursue other avenues that could be effective in helping the freedpeople secure economic justice. Sometimes a visit from one of Sibley's men was sufficient to move a planter to settle with his employees, as was the case when agent Charles Holcombe personally worked out the division of the crops on a plantation where employers were attempting to defraud the freedpeople.[208] Often, a stubborn planter came to terms when Sibley's agency threatened his economic well-being by using military force to withhold his crop from the marketplace. In May 1867, for example, Lieutenant F. A. H. Gaebel seized the crop of a Stewart County employer, using the troops at his disposal. The procrastinating planter agreed to settle.[209] In December 1867, agent Christian Raushenberg protected some Cuthbert area freedpeople's interest in their crop by detailing four privates "to guard the corn cribs and ginhouses and keep account of the amount of bales ginned daily and see that no portion of the crop is removed."[210] And later, in January and February 1868, William Moffit, the Bartow agent, discovered that "the threats and bluster of disloyal citizens" in Johnson and Emmanuel Counties diminished when he confronted them with a small garrison by his side. Using his power, he seized crops to facilitate settlements, an action that had an influence beyond the planters directly affected "as others who had long withheld the money due to the laborers have been constrained by force of example in the other cases to settle with their hands."[211]

Not only did agents and officers press employers within their jurisdictions to settle fairly with their employees but they also actively confronted whites who ignored the freedpeople's first lien. Bureau men, for example, intervened on behalf of the freedpeople when local officials placed the interests of their white neighbors over those of the ex-slaves.[212] Also, when employers ignored the freedpeople's claims and shipped their crops to warehouses beyond the reach of the freedpeople, the network of Bureau agents and officers allowed black Georgians a sympathetic venue in which they could pursue their claims across county lines.

Agent Adolph Leers believed that the best way to stop "this game" of assigning crops to factors to pay off employers' debts while leaving "the poor freedmen . . . in the cold" was to keep the freedpeople ever vigilant. In September 1868, he warned his Screven County charges not to let their crops out of their sight until they received their full shares.[213] The Bureau, however, often had to do more than lecture the freedpeople, as Leers himself understood. Earlier, in March 1868, Hutchinson Island freedpeople would have had little chance of securing their pay if Leers had not intervened. The agent discovered that their employer had already shipped over $1,100 worth of rice to his factors in Savannah. Leers prevented the shipping of the remaining rice out from under the freedpeople until the involved parties resolved the dispute.[214]

Leers enjoyed some success in helping the freedpeople keep hold of their crops, but there were other planters who successfully eluded even watchful agents. In such cases, the Bureau interceded on behalf of freedpeople who did not have the time or the resources to follow their crops beyond their own neighborhoods. Georgia's network of Bureau officers and agents cooperated to track down and seize the crops that had been shipped out of the county, while intervening with warehouse merchants who were storing the crops and stopping those merchants from making payments directly to planters who still owed money to their workers.

In December 1867, for example, Augusta subassistant commissioner E. M. L. Ehlers intervened to prevent merchants from paying out the proceeds from a cotton crop in their possession until a freedman received his wages.[215] In January 1868, J. Murray Hoag, the Savannah subassistant commissioner, assisted William F. White, his colleague at Thomasville, by seizing crops stored at a warehouse at the port city, while White worked out a settlement.[216]

A few months later in another case that stretched from southwestern Georgia to the coast, the Bureau secured over $1,800 for freedpeople who had moved to Savannah.[217] Also, in January 1868, John Leonard, the Columbus subassistant commissioner, ordered the Butler agent to take and hold crops previously seized by a merchant in Macon, and the assistant commissioner shortly before that action had authorized Leonard's predecessor, George Wagner, to seize and hold cotton shipped there beyond the reach of sixty freedpeople who were waiting for a settlement in southwestern Georgia.[218]

Beyond seizing and withholding crops from the market, during Military Reconstruction the Bureau had to petition the army to sanction the sale of the impounded property, which the military commander allowed the agency to do on numerous occasions.[219] Selling planters' harvests under military authority remained an action of last resort, however, for the Bureau preferred to try to secure settlements before resorting to military force and the military authorities required it.[220] In fact, although Military Reconstruction improved the Bureau's ability to satisfy freedmen's claims and clarified the agency's power to enforce contracts and settlements, it, too, brought uncertainty and conflict in sufficient doses to encourage resistance among increasingly aggressive ex-masters.

Even though Sibley held a position in the military chain of command, he encountered conservative post commanders who questioned his orders, with unfavorable results for the freedpeople. In November 1867, Quitman agent Alvin B. Clark petitioned the Savannah post commander for assistance. He advised Clark to rely on civil officers.[221] In December 1867, Subassistant Commissioner Carlos de la Mesa pursued a claim only to be delayed by the post commander at Rome. The officer questioned Sibley's direct order to an agent to seize and sell an employer's cotton. The lapse in de la Mesa's authority permitted other creditors to ship the bales of cotton to New York and, although the Bureau officer eventually satisfied the freedpeople's claim, it took him almost two months longer than necessary.[222]

Such activities undoubtedly cast a shadow over de la Mesa's authority in northwestern Georgia, but the consequences of military timidity or conservatism and its relationship to white resistance were exemplified by the actions of Thomas Ruger, a brevet brigadier general whom Meade had appointed provisional governor of Georgia after removing Charles Jenkins. In the spring of 1868, Ruger visited southwestern Georgia and consequently provoked the citizens of Bainbridge agent W. L. Clark's jurisdiction to ignore the Bureau's claim to the right to seize crops. The people believed that Clark exceeded his authority in trying to tie up their harvest because Ruger had "expressed some doubt as to the legality or policy of doing it." The agent was stymied, even though Meade had approved his actions and Sibley had reassured him of his authority.[223]

Despite an improved military presence in the state, Sibley's Bureau faced the same personnel problem that had hindered Tillson's agency when it came to serving summons to and enforcing orders on intransigent whites.[224] During Military Reconstruction, civil authorities actively encouraged employers in their disregard for the agency.[225] They ignored the Bureau's policy of recognizing the freedpeople's first claim to the harvested crop, frustrated the Bureau's efforts to seize property, obstructed the completion of settlements, and advised citizens to ignore the Bureau's orders.[226]

White planters, who during the spring of 1868 were well aware of Bureau's imminent termination, chose to ignore the agency even during the months before the state's restoration in July; they were quite confident that the agency did not have enough power or time to discipline them.[227] Employers became even more audacious in flouting the Bureau and the rights of the freedpeople as the agency's authority waned. After July, as far as employers were concerned, the Bureau was a dead letter. In August 1868, planters near Atlanta refused to deal fairly with their freedpeople because the Bureau lacked military power and they did not fear civil prosecution.[228] About the same time in Greene and Dougherty Counties, planters were treating freedpeople and the Bureau with increasing disrespect after the military withdrew its support.[229]

Freedpeople also understood that they were losing an important ally in their efforts to hold on to what they had earned. In January 1868, the Athens agent reported his office "every day . . . crowded with freedmen women and children . . .

demanding justice."[230] Later in August 1868, the Bureau's change of status left the freedpeople in the west-central counties of Talbot, Taylor, and Macon "full of cares about their wages and part of the crop for this year."[231] Agents continued to record complaints and help present cases to the civil courts for these and other freedpeople, but the Bureau now lacked even toothless threats in its efforts to secure the economic rights of Georgia's ex-slaves.[232]

# 7

## The People Go to Their Work Early and Gladly

Unlike their counterparts in the interior of the state, the Georgia freedpeople who experienced the war and the early stages of Reconstruction on the coast had for a moment within their grasp the land that in their minds could guarantee their freedom. As early as the spring of 1862, Union naval guns kept abandoned plantations on the sea islands open to black refugees.[1] But it was in the wake of Sherman's famous march from Atlanta to the sea that ex-slaves came to consider the coast theirs for the future. For the freedpeople, Sherman's special field order of January 16, 1865, held out a formal if vague promise that their Yankee allies would recognize their desire for land of their own.

Sherman set aside land for the use of former slaves in an exclusively black reservation running along the Atlantic coast south from Charleston, South Carolina, down through land between the shore and the St. Johns River in the northeasternmost counties of Florida. He included in the reservation land along the rivers that nurtured the region's rice plantations up to thirty miles inland. Sherman specified that freedpeople could request permission to settle an island or an area of land within this reservation when "three respectable negroes, heads of families," came together for that purpose. Once Sherman's inspector of plantations and settlements approved the request, the freedmen could claim their land and subdivide it among themselves and any other freedmen who wished to settle near them, allotting no more than forty acres of tillable ground to each family.

Sherman's promise of homesteads for the freedmen, however, was intentionally limited. The freedpeople could not claim their land in fee simple, for Sherman ordered his officer-in-charge to give to the claimants "possessory titles," titles that acknowledged their right to work the land and enjoy the products of their labor but fell short of conveying ownership. Consequently, his order made no stipulations about how long the freedpeople would be able to stay on the land or how much they would have to pay in order to purchase it. Sherman wanted Congress to deal with such matters while he went about the business of fighting a war, now free of the troublesome train of black refugees who had followed him through the Georgia interior.[2]

Ill-defined possessory titles would cause problems in the near future. So, too, would the freedpeople's failure to carry out the requirements for claiming land in the neat, orderly fashion prescribed by Sherman. A majority apparently presented government officials with faits accomplis, forcing those officials to try to make the records agree with the reality of settlement in the reservation. Nevertheless, no matter what the titles actually conveyed to the freedpeople, they undoubtedly encouraged those who held one or hoped to receive one to assume that the government had acknowledged their right to the land. Furthermore, Sherman charged Brigadier General Rufus Saxton with executing the provisions of the special field order, an appointment that guaranteed a vigorous commitment to the spirit of the order.[3]

As inspector of plantations and settlements and then the Freedmen's Bureau assistant commissioner, Saxton vigorously pursued his charge. Before the summer of 1865 he had placed agents in the Ogeechee district (an area along the Ogeechee and the Little Ogeechee Rivers in Chatham County near Savannah), in Savannah, and on St. Catherines and St. Simons Islands. In June, when he first reported to General Oliver Otis Howard, he estimated that his efforts had settled forty thousand ex-slaves on four hundred thousand acres within the swath of land subject to Sherman's order. Saxton also hoped to secure abandoned property on mainland Georgia for the freedmen's use, taking his cue from the Bureau's enabling legislation that authorized it to rent and to sell abandoned or confiscated property to the freedmen.[4] By all indications Saxton meant to fulfill Sherman's promise.

Saxton's impressive settlement figures did not specify the actual distribution of ex-slaves within the boundaries of the Georgia reservation, but the number of grants recorded by Captain Alexander P. Ketchum, his officer in charge of freedmen's affairs on the Georgia coast, and the reports from Saxton's agents suggest that the population on the Georgia reservation should be numbered in the thousands. During the spring and summer of 1865 Ketchum registered 459 grants that located 1,846 freedmen on 9,486 acres of reservation land claimed by 48 planters. The captain's records, however, were not an accurate account of black settlement. Ketchum's figures underrepresent the number of freedpeople who claimed land on the sea islands from Ossabaw south to Cumberland. He recorded 62 grants for 242 freedpeople claiming 1,645 acres on Ossabaw, St. Catherines, Sapelo, and St. Simons Islands.[5] In August 1865, however, the Reverend William F. Eaton, whose agency included the islands from Sapelo south, had not yet been able to survey the land claims of the freedpeople within his jurisdiction. Nevertheless, Eaton reported 352 freedpeople residing on Sapelo, 606 on St. Simons, and 60 on Cumberland. Farther north on St. Catherines and Ossabaw Islands, the reports of the Reverend Tunis G. Campbell revealed a similar discrepancy. In December 1865, the agent reported 369 freedmen claiming four thousand acres of improved and unimproved land on St. Catherines. On Ossabaw there were 78 freedmen claiming two thousand acres of land.[6]

Ketchum had not been negligent in executing his duties. Rather, location and time explain the low number of sea island claimants in the official register. The jurisdictions of agents Campbell and Eaton were simply more difficult to reach from the captain's headquarters in Savannah. He therefore could not verify the claims of the settlers before a change of policy curtailed his activities in the fall of 1865.

In contrast, Ketchum's records for the Ogeechee district, the Savannah River plantations, and the islands near Savannah show that the officer had not been idle. In an easy radius from his base he recorded 1,592 freedpeople with 397 grants on 7,841 acres of land on 42 plantations, figures that may come closer to but still fall short of the actual population of freedpeople there. In February 1865, for example, there were more than 1,000 freedpeople living on Skidaway Island near Savannah, but only 408 ex-slaves were living on Sherman grants of 2,845 acres registered to 99 claimants.[7] The discrepencies between the records and the actual number of residents who were unregistered claimants would become problematical by 1866. But during the spring and summer of 1865, the freedpeople who took up their Sherman lands, whether duly registered or not, gave their former masters and the federal government sufficient notice by their actions that they intended to stay on the land. Furthermore, the handful of Freedmen's Bureau officials who supervised the transition from slavery to freedom encouraged the ex-slaves to explore the potential of their new status. Consequently, the federal agents strengthened the freedmen's belief that the government would support their cause.

Up and down the coast, black Georgians, supervised by Saxton's agents, organized governments and mustered militias to protect their freedom and the common good. In March 1865 the Reverend William H. Tiffany, the agent on the Ogeechee, oversaw the establishment of governments on the plantations in his district. Representatives elected by the freedmen from their neighborhoods formed a board of advisers to the agent. They also formed their own militia, the Ogeechee Home Guard, which at its most active mustered a strength of about forty men.[8] Later in May the men on St. Simons organized the island into a town, adopted a constitution, and selected officials to enforce the collective will, and the men in Tunis Campbell's jurisdiction formed similar institutions, including a 275-man militia to protect their islands from white encroachment.[9] On Skidaway Island, by November 1865, the freedpeople, with their own black governor "not only manage their secular interests with success, but also their civil affairs."[10]

With these institutions in place, the freedpeople became accustomed to looking to their leaders to carry out their decisions and to keep the peace of their communities. Black men accepted these responsibilities and in the process acquired skills that one day would be used against federal agents who challenged the expectations of their constituents. On the Ogeechee, for example, black guardsmen led by Captain William Joiner and his sergeants chased white guerrillas who threatened the safety of the freedpeople.[11] The Ogeechee Home Guard also enforced civil order among the black residents of the region, as it did when a guardsman arrested a freedman for attempted rape.[12] To the south on St. Simons, where townsmen passed a law initiating compulsory labor on the island's roads, the black sheriff and town guards responded to a challenge from those who refused to do the required roadwork. The confrontation led to an exchange of gunfire and to the death of one of the troublemakers, but Stephen Mayberry, a town commissioner who accompanied the posse, accepted the necessity of using force to protect the island's peace and quiet. "I saw at a glance," he later testified, "that to maintain order, those men must at once be subdued, or all order was at an end."[13]

In addition to organizing community affairs, the freedpeople established agricultural routines. In the spring and summer of 1865, the Ogeechee blacks cultivated the rice plantations in the district. They continued to farm the land quite productively "in concert" instead of working on the individual plots to which they were entitled. That productivity and the communal approach to labor reflected the freedpeople's sense of proprietorship. They were on land, most likely old plantation homes that they had formerly worked by the task system, that was now under their control. No wonder Agent Tiffany observed that "the people, not being driven by master or overseer, go to their work early and gladly, and the body shares the healthfulness of the mind."[14]

The freedpeople's approach to labor was not uniform throughout the reservation. Also, unlike the mainland Ogeechee blacks, by 1865 the sea islanders counted among their numbers strangers from the interior unused to the old coastal routines as well as returning natives who had experienced the most disruptive and liberating effects of having been removed by their owners from the progress of invading Union forces. At first observation, the sea island blacks appeared to be less committed to producing the area's staple crop, sea island cotton, than were their rice-growing Ogeechee cousins. In 1865 the sea islanders failed to cultivate more than a fraction of the available land. On Cumberland, St. Simons, and Sapelo, they worked an estimated 445 acres out of a reported total of 32,240 acres; on St. Catherines, they worked only 300 of 2,500 acres of cleared land.[15]

In part, the absence of easily measurable signs of productivity reflected the freedpeople's "great dislike" for the agricultural routines of slavery. As early as the spring of 1862, freedpeople on St. Simons Island exhibited a strong disinclination to do the work that, as one astute Yankee observer noted, "seems to make their condition the same as before." Freedpeople there avoided their fields, but "sit up all night and fish and catch crabs and go and catch horses and wild cattle and cross to the main in sculls and get corn and so on," practices that later would lead to clashes with their Yankee guardians.[16] Just as significant, however, was the impact of wartime dislocation and disruption, the lack of resources required for seeding and cultivating extensive tracts, and the fact that some residents had arrived too late in the season to begin planting a crop. Forced to improvise in order to survive, freedmen continued to go fishing and crabbing, they cut wood and hunted deer for the Savannah market, and they grew corn and sweet potatoes for their supper pots. In 1865 some returned to the mainland to work for wages, leaving their families behind to tend to their island parcels of land.[17] Given these circumstances, it was not clear that the reservation freedmen uniformly intended to use their grants to follow peasant lives outside the market economy.

In the meantime, they took advantage of whatever opportunities were at hand and assumed that the next season would find them cultivating their own land. Significantly, during the summer of 1865, Freedmen's Bureau representatives accepted the need to improvise; the agency encouraged the freedpeople to pursue whatever activities would sustain them in their present situations. In September, for example, Tunis Campbell, true to Yankee ideals, planned to put new arrivals to work cutting moss and fishing, not to allow them to escape labor but "to show them that they ought not to ask for anything now they have got Liberty."[18] Agent Eaton refrained from issuing full rations to latecomers "but compel[led] them to do something to sustain themselves." Freedpeople on his islands prepared fodder and fished. Eaton, in fact, proposed to have them sell wood in Savannah, repair tools, and manufacture furniture, thus further encouraging their economic independence.[19]

Apparently the tactics had some immediate success. Although a large number of the ex-slaves in Eaton's jurisdiction required assistance, the majority were able to support themselves. Also, the small number of rations for which Campbell accounted in his December 1865 report could not have sustained his charges in idleness even for a month. And in the Ogeechee district, at least in September 1865 after a summer during which the freedpeople had relied on government assistance, the entire population was well on its way to becoming self-supporting.[20]

In the Ogeechee district another kind of independence manifested itself during the fall of 1865, which gave some indication of what the Bureau—and the freedpeople—could expect when the agency's prescription for freedom diverged from the course plotted by the ex-slaves. At the same time the Bureau's response revealed the unwillingness of one of Saxton's agents to challenge the freedpeople's activities. Freedmen, under agent William Tiffany's direction, were operating the Habersham and Screven rice mills at a loss because many ex-slaves in the district continued to process the grain in the old way with mortar and pestle, threshing the product by hand. Certainly these freedpeople were conservative in their folkways, but in this case they were cleverly avoiding a mill toll and rice tax. The freedpeople also refused to leave their processed rice at the mills for the government to sell. They preferred to sell their crops on their own, apparently exchanging what the agent thought would be greater profit for the right to act independently in the marketplace.

Agent Tiffany attempted to discourage this activity by placing guards on the road to Savannah to stop the freedpeople on their way to market, but he failed to convince them to bring their rice to the mills. As late as mid-December 1865, the mills continued to operate at a loss. Tiffany hoped to resolve this difficulty by making it more attractive for the freedpeople to leave their crop with the agency. He suggested that the Bureau arrange to have cash on hand to pay for the freedpeople's rice and thus avoid a delay for them in receiving payment for their grain.[21]

Nothing came of Tiffany's suggestion because changes in policy concerning the reservation were already in motion and the freedpeople eventually had to pay the tax, which was used to cover the cost of milling and storage materials as well as to compensate the Ogeechee Home Guard. The agent's approach to the problem, however, indicated that during the Freedmen's Bureau's early existence in Georgia, blacks could readily accept or ignore the agency's direction because the local agents either reinforced or failed to challenge the freedpeople's expectations. This situation developed from more than "the want of personal attention," as a critic of Tiffany called it.[22] Rather, on numerous occasions the agents actually performed the role of advocate for the freedpeople's cause. Eaton, for example, challenged the navy's careless practice of letting its animals graze freely on reservation land, thus destroying the freedpeople's crops. He also refused to allow planters to bully him into making concessions that would compromise the freedpeople's land claims.[23]

The Reverend Tiffany was equally aggressive. He sought out additional abandoned property, argued against a liberal restoration policy for white property owners, and challenged whites who claimed crops on plantations that he considered to be abandoned. Also, when confronted with an order to disarm the Ogeechee freedmen, he objected, threatened to resign, and promised to be personally responsible for the proper use of firearms in his district. Furthermore, Tiffany and the reservation's other minister-agents became part of the freedpeople's lives by officiating at their weddings, teaching them in Sunday school, and conducting their weekly religious services.[24]

Not surprisingly then, these men acted as a positive force in helping the ex-slaves define their new status. Under Bureau supervision, the reservation blacks were able to "try on" freedom, tailoring it to their specifications. The freedpeople, however, were unwilling to comply readily with the government's policies when Washington failed to follow through with a sustained effort at land redistribution and when a new set of Bureau men approached their duties with new considerations.

Even as some refugees completed the construction of their log and tabby dwellings on the islands, there were indications that their claim to the reservation was not entirely secure. During the spring and summer of 1865, Saxton and his officers successfully sparred (for the time being) with the military authorities over the implementation of Sherman's special field order and the army's attempt to restore sea island property to white claimants.[25] The assistant commissioner, however, had no success in expanding the distribution of abandoned and confiscable property to the rest of Georgia in accordance with the provisions of the Freedmen's Bureau law. By the time Saxton's Bureau had even a minimal presence on the mainland beyond the reservation, there simply were no plantations available upon which Saxton's Bureau could duplicate the reservation experiment. Apparently, Georgia land owners had returned to their homes during the summer of 1865 before their property had come under Bureau scrutiny, thus frustrating Saxton's plans. In late August 1865, Howard's inspector general, Joseph Fullerton, undoubtedly aware of this situation, emphatically explained the agency's policy to Saxton. If owners reoccupied abandoned lands before any of his Bureau agents could lay claim to them, "they *cannot be taken by you*. They are no longer abandoned." [26]

More disturbing omens were the battles being waged in Washington. During the summer, Commissioner Howard engaged President Andrew Johnson in a paper duel over the definition of confiscable and abandoned property. By September 12 the president had effectively nullified the section of the Bureau's enabling law concerning the distribution of land to the freedmen.[27]

Changes were also taking place in the Georgia Bureau that would have an impact on the reservation. In August, Commissioner Howard began to consider giving the state its own assistant commissioner because of the difficulty the agency was experiencing in establishing a respected and effective presence outside the reservation; by the end of September Saxton's authority in Georgia was confined to the reservation, an arrangement that barely outlasted the year. In the meantime, Saxton clearly refused to believe that Howard's Circular No. 15 of September 12, which embodied the president's lenient land restoration policy, had anything to do with Sherman's grant.[28]

Not everyone accepted Saxton's interpretation of the signals coming from the nation's capital. Planters who during the war had abandoned lands now in the reservation believed that they were entitled to the same consideration as those who were regaining land that was unencumbered by Sherman's special field order. Once these planters made their acts of contrition, they expected restoration of their property.[29]

Unfortunately for the freedpeople, the numerous applications for the restoration of estates and the uncompromising fealty of Rufus Saxton to Sherman's orders did not escape the attention of the ever absolving President Johnson. In

October 1865 he ordered Commissioner Howard to proceed to South Carolina, Georgia, and Florida to bring about "mutually satisfactory" arrangements between planters and freedmen on the Sherman Reservation.[30] On October 19 Howard issued orders that recognized the right of the pardoned planters to petition for the restoration of their lands in the reservation, providing they pledged the current crop to the freedmen who had raised it and made equitable contracts with the freedmen for the next season.[31] Word of Howard's activities preceded him to Savannah, and by the time he arrived there in mid-October a white resident reported that the freedmen "are all in despair at not having any land. . . . Plantations are to be restored at once."[32] "At once," however, was a phrase open to interpretation; before Saxton lost his jurisdiction over the Georgia reservation, he continued to give the impression to white claimants that he was encouraging blacks in their desire to hold on to the land.[33]

## Davis Tillson and the Restoration

In January 1866, Captain Alexander P. Ketchum, the officer Howard had placed in charge of the restoration process, reported to his new superior, Davis Tillson, that upon receiving the applications of the plantation owners, the commissioner would arrange for the return of their lands. What Ketchum did not emphasize was that the stipulations the Bureau commissioner attached to restoration allowed for considerable delay. With the support of Howard and the secretary of war, Edwin M. Stanton, Ketchum pursued restoration much more slowly than the planters had expected in the hope that Congress would eventually confirm the freedmen's position.[34]

The planters' reluctance to offer reasonable contracts to the freedpeople and their inability to gain the trust of their former slaves hindered the progress of restoration, but the freedpeople also contributed to the delay. Reservation blacks were firmly committed to the land, and many expected Congress to respect their claims. Leaders, Aaron A. Bradley among them, encouraged the reservation residents to stand firm.[35] Whites considered Bradley, a Georgia black who had escaped to freedom before the war, to be "deranged" and his "harangues" that promised land and the franchise to be "seditious." Tillson came to consider him "a very mischievous person," but the former slaves felt his message confirmed their expectations. Consequently, the freedpeople refused to do anything that would prejudice their claims.[36]

Howard ordered Captain Ketchum to work out a compromise between the
two unyielding groups. Howard's reliance on Ketchum was a choice of officer
seemingly weighted in favor of the freedpeople because the Port Royal veteran
had earlier expressed his belief in the importance of black land ownership.[37] By
the fall of 1865, it was apparent that he had not changed his mind; he continued
to believe that the freedmen had valid possessory titles, that Howard's orders
did not apply to the Sherman grants, and that Congress still might take additional action favorable to the freedpeople. The complaints that reached Washington from the region's planters confirmed that Ketchum continued to support
the ex-slaves' interests.[38]

Ketchum's orders instructed him to resolve the difficulties between ex-
masters and ex-slaves by establishing boards of supervisors to represent all concerned parties. By January 1866 he had established only three: one on Skidaway
Island, one in the Ogeechee district, and one between the Ogeechee district
and the Savannah River. Ketchum also probably discovered that he could present the illusion of progress to complaining planters by giving them "informal
possession" of their property. In such cases, the Bureau did not restore their
lands but simply allowed the planters to reside on them until the government
reached a final decision concerning their disposition. Planters with informal
possession had no power to interfere with or remove the freedpeople without
the Bureau's permission. Consequently, although Ketchum had fully restored
all but eight plantations on the rivers, he had returned "only two or three" island properties, all located on Skidaway Island.[39] Furthermore, he and Saxton
failed, perhaps purposely, to notify Eaton of the change in policy, and Eaton
continued to settle freedmen on plots of land within his jurisdiction into the
month of December.[40]

Complicating the situation was the late return of coastal blacks who had been
displaced by the war. Arriving home without a means of support, they might
have expected a piece of the old plantation to accompany their freedom. That
option was now out of the question, and it was not possible to work familiar
fields for old masters who had not yet had their land restored. On St. Catherines Island by February 1866, Tunis Campbell had divided all of the available
land among approximately four hundred freedmen. About two hundred former
slaves of the island's antebellum owner had recently returned to their homes
but were too late to benefit from Campbell's division of the land. They were, according to Davis Tillson's observations, "in a very destitute condition."[41] One

planter, who was still unsure of the status of his property, wished to remove the strange freedpeople who had settled on his island lands to make room for his former slaves, "they being anxious to return." His advocate produced an appealingly simple argument for prompt action that paraphrased the assistant commissioner's foremost worry: "A month's delay at this season of the year may render [the planter's] efforts to make a crop fruitless."[42] Eventually someone or something would have to give way if all of the reservation blacks were to make a living. None of the alternatives would satisfy all concerned parties.

Davis Tillson found this situation unpromising.[43] It was not that he opposed black land ownership. On the contrary, he did not assume that the freedpeople were to become a permanent wage-earning class, and he did believe that they had every right to earn a homestead. One of his first projects as Georgia's assistant commissioner, for example, had been to explore the possibility of encouraging private enterprise aided by Northern benevolence to purchase large tracts of land that then might be subdivided for sale to freedpeople.[44] He also had offered Bureau advice and protection to a group of Wilkes County freedpeople who had accumulated seven thousand dollars and wished to purchase land in southwestern Georgia; circumstances required that the freedpeople establish themselves on a rented plantation in Dougherty County, but the assistant commissioner entertained a genuine interest in the success of the colony.[45] Also, after the passage of the Southern Homestead Act of June 1866, Tillson assisted freedpeople in their efforts to take advantage of the law, if they had the resources to keep from becoming a burden on the government.[46]

But the reservation was unique. Tillson was extremely wary of arrangements that failed to give the ex-slaves the opportunity to earn their stake in society and thereby deprived them of the opportunity to learn how to be frugal. Lacking Rufus Saxton's sense of compensatory justice, he failed to see the logic of paying freedpeople for generations of slave labor with coastal land, especially after his superiors had ordered him to do otherwise. Furthermore, the assistant commissioner and other Bureau men could accept a retreat from Sherman's orders because the federal government, for a number of reasons including constitutional concerns, had failed to pursue confiscation with any degree of vigor during the war.[47] Federal officials and politicians ignored the arguments of Congressman Thaddeus Stevens, who called for the confiscation and redistribution of land, and failed to devise a practical alternative to their faith in the boundless potential of hard work. Even agent William Tiffany's modest suggestion to aid black farmers already on the land, albeit temporarily, was never explored by the Bureau officers in any systematic way so as to ensure the success of reservation freedmen.[48]

In 1866, then, the Bureau approached its job within the confines of widely held assumptions and beliefs. Confiscation was unacceptable as a solution to the land question. The only alternative, as far as the Bureau was concerned, was to oversee the freedmen's entry into the market economy as wage workers, not proprietors. What was remarkable, given these circumstances, was Tillson's willingness to move as cautiously as he did in working out arrangements in the reservation.

Fearing that destitution and an unproductive season would extend the problem of hunger into the next year, Tillson proposed a moderate plan that would give dispossessed owners of land *unencumbered* by black titles temporary control of their property for the remainder of 1866. Those freedmen who had returned too late to claim land would be able to contract, and Congress would be able to take more time to study the reservation situation carefully. Howard thought Tillson's plan to be premature because he expected Congress to pass legislation resolving the problem in favor of the freedpeople on February 1. Nevertheless, Tillson, convinced that any resolution would follow a moderate course and worried about the ill effects of further delays on the state's agricultural prospects, set out to make the islands bloom.[49]

In February and March the assistant commissioner spent his days in the field campaigning to restore "that beautiful and fertile portion of the state to something of its former prosperity."[50] Traveling up and down the coast in an inadequate tug that could barely negotiate the shallow channels, winding creeks, and lagoons of the inland waterway, once traveling only forty miles in nine hours, the assistant commissioner escorted planters—many of them Yankee entrepreneurs—to several sea islands and attempted to work out compromises with the freedmen.[51] His first effort to bring capital and labor together and still respect the Sherman grants occurred on St. Catherines Island. There was some room for maneuvering here because Tillson doubted the validity of the grants then held by most of the freedmen. Only a handful of the black residents held registered grants. The rest had grants issued and signed by Tunis Campbell, who claimed to have "verbal authority" from Rufus Saxton to comply with Sherman's orders. Tillson found it grossly irregular that Saxton had delegated that kind of power to a civilian, especially since Sherman's orders specifically stated that the inspector of settlements and plantations was to "furnish personally . . . a possessory title in writing." Furthermore, Tillson discovered that Campbell had issued grants of land to himself, his sons, and "even men who were born free," contrary to the intent of the order.[52]

Tillson at first tried to convince the freedpeople that they would be better off working for planters who could provide for them until the harvest secured a profit for all. The islanders, turning to a committee of their leaders, informed the Bureau officer that they had no intention of giving up their independence for the supposed security of a contract. Probably sensing an impasse, the assistant commissioner decided not to dispossess those St. Catherines residents who claimed land by virtue of Campbell's grants. To settle the matter and to provide for those freedmen who held no title, Tillson accepted not only the validity of the grants issued by Saxton and signed by Ketchum but also, at discounted values, those issued by Campbell. He allowed the freedmen who held them not the forty acres originally allotted by Campbell but ten to fifteen acres. The amount was, according to Tillson's estimate, "as much land as [they] could work *well.*" Yankee entrepreneur John F. Winchester of Boston and his partner Schuyler from New York would plant the unclaimed portion of the island with the help of those freedmen who would sign their contract, allow them to use their agricultural machinery, and act as factors for the whole island. Finally, the freedmen with grants agreed to pay the rent if Congress failed to approve their titles. Probably feeling like Solomon, Tillson expected "that this arrangement will heal the wounds of the former owner, satisfy the freed people, combine labor and capital, and, with a good season, make success almost certain thereby producing crops and helping pay our National debt."[53]

After arranging the compromise on St. Catherines, Tillson sailed south along the coast past Sapelo Island and the mouth of the Altamaha River and went ashore at St. Simons. There he encountered similar problems on the islands within the Reverend William Eaton's jurisdiction. Most of the freedmen who claimed land on Cumberland, Jekyll, St. Simons, and Sapelo Islands had never received their titles from Saxton or Ketchum as specified by Sherman's orders, probably because of their distance from Savannah. Also, some freedmen had actually claimed their parcels after Howard had countermanded that order in October. These freedmen, although in possession of the land, lacked even the dubious titles assigned by Tunis Campbell, as well as his aggressive leadership. In this case Tillson strictly interpreted Sherman's orders. After consolidating legitimate claims on the various plantations, he presented the remaining freedpeople with a disappointing choice: sign contracts with planters under Bureau supervision or leave the islands.[54] The Bureau's new policy made one thing clear. The majority of freedmen who had hoped to own reservation land would be working for someone else for the remainder of 1866.

Still, a number of freedmen with valid grants continued to hold on to the promise and received the tepid support of the Bureau. After Tillson's tour of the coast, northern entrepreneurs soon controlled most of Sapelo Island, where their employees worked for two-thirds of the crop in accordance with Bureau guidelines. But Captain Ketchum had recorded valid grants for the island, and Tillson provided for them. On the properties of Thomas Spalding and Dr. A. M. Kenan, an undetermined number of freedpeople continued to cultivate their own land totaling approximately 550 acres out of an earlier total of 745 grant-secured acres. Some of the grant holders even hired other freedmen to assist them, much to the "injury" of the white planters.[55] A similar pattern emerged on the other sea islands. On Ossabaw, sixty were working under contract, but eleven freedmen held on to their grants through the summer. On St. Catherines, most of the freedpeople kept what they could. Although 147 freedpeople went to work for the Yankee planters, 420 others followed Campbell to the southern part of the island to plant on their own.[56]

Tillson's reservation settlement revealed much about his attitude toward the Sherman grant and, despite his own good intentions, his inability to understand the reservation freedpeople's own priorities. In his own way Tillson was pursuing his charge to look after the best interests of the freedpeople. Appalled by the lack of visible agricultural progress, he feared that the dearth of black resources would condemn the freedpeople to an unending cycle of poverty or, worse still, to the government dole, a debilitating alternative that would further erode their ambition to succeed. According to Tillson's logic, a poor crop would shame the race (and implicitly its Bureau advocates); a good harvest would prove conclusively that the freedpeople were dependable workers, even more productive now than before the war had removed the shackles of slavery. Tillson believed that men like Schuyler and Winchester would leaven the reservation not only with their capital but also with their right-thinking approach to free labor. At the same time, Tillson saw the black leaders who represented the freedmen as crafty manipulators of the ex-slaves because, probably more than anything else, they challenged the assistant commissioner's authority and his vision.[57]

In judging the Bureau's shift in policy from Saxton's advocacy to Tillson's intrusion into the black routine, one must keep in mind that the Georgia assistant commissioner had no authority to distribute land to freedpeople who lacked valid titles. In fact, by allowing those freedmen with good Sherman titles—and even the questionable ones issued by Campbell—to hold on to the land, he followed Saxton's and Ketchum's course of action and failed to satisfy the wishes of the president and white Georgians for complete restoration. Furthermore, he was not willing to abandon those blacks who chose to farm on their own. The St. Catherines freedpeople forced him by their firm stand to make concessions such as allowing them to use the interloping Yankees' equipment, but he did in fact concede to their demands. Furthermore, he made it clear that the planters would not have a free hand in arranging work agreements with their employees. And when planters challenged the valid grant claims of freedmen, Tillson supported the freedmen.[58]

At the same time, the politics of Washington, D.C., influenced the decisions Tillson made. The general sailed down the coast looking over his shoulder to the capital, ever concerned with what future government policy might be. In fact, Tillson's compromise did not conflict with the legislation that Commissioner Howard was expecting. As Tillson had assumed, the bill sponsored by Senator Lyman Trumbull was not a radical departure in the government's approach to the land question. If passed, there would be no lifetime grants to the former slaves, only three-year "possessory" titles given with the hope that Bureau officials would be able to convince planters to give or sell land to the freedpeople. The president vetoed the legislation. Nevertheless, Tillson still believed his compromise could stand, although he feared the disruptive consequences of the veto. It would, he argued, encourage the planters to become all the more unreasonable in dealing with the ex-slaves, to become "more unwilling to compromise as they hope to obtain every thing they now demand." Furthermore, the veto, Tillson believed, would discourage those freedpeople who were working their own parcels and make them wary of any future promises coming from the government.[59]

A few days after issuing his protest about the veto to Commissioner Howard, Tillson once again became optimistic about his compromise on the sea islands, but the actions of the planters on the reservation suggest that he had been correct in assessing the damage done by the president. In April, not even a month after Tillson had returned to his Augusta headquarters from the reservation, some planters began to fulfill his pessimistic predictions. On St. Simons, planters challenged the land claims of freedmen on two plantations and compelled the freedmen to work for them under contract. Even though the Bureau now considered the freedmen's titles "of very doubtful validity, and of very little value," the assistant commissioner ordered the Reverend Eaton to investigate, reminding him that whatever the claims were worth, they could not "be forcibly taken from the freed people."[60]

Eaton's problems with planters did not subside. In May the agent found them questioning the Bureau's right to interfere with their affairs. When the agent confronted a planter on Jekyll Island who had no Bureau-approved contract with his hands, the planter exhibited contempt for Eaton's authority. Even a junior member of the Yankee cotton planting firm of Marston and Rowe, a concern that leased land on St. Simons, told Eaton that "he did not care a damn for me nor the Bureau either as we had no soldiers to back us up and he knew how we would fare in civil courts." No wonder the agent concluded that there would "be some trouble securing the pay for the freedmen this fall." Troops were no longer stationed nearby. Tillson must have remembered his earlier predictions, but he was mortified to see Northern men fulfilling them. By September, Eaton had concluded that these Yankee planters, who had "so little regard for honor, or principle," would knowingly cheat the freedpeople if the Bureau did not carefully watch them.[61]

Despite his intention to define the freedpeople's status, Tillson unwittingly hampered the Bureau's effectiveness in dealing with the reservation blacks when he installed a new complement of agents, men who did not share the same values as the minister-abolitionists favored by Saxton. On February 14 he assigned as a salaried agent the trusted William A. Perry, his wartime aide-de-camp and a "consistent" member of the Baptist Church, to keep an eye on Tunis Campbell and to supervise Bureau affairs on Sapelo and other islands to the north. Also during February, March, and April, unsalaried agents for Skidaway, Wilmington, and Whitemarsh Islands near Savannah and Ossabaw and Sapelo Islands joined the Bureau's ranks to assist Perry, the veteran agent Eaton, and the suspect Campbell.[62]

Tillson was not purging the Bureau of Saxton's earlier appointees. The only agent he actually removed for what may be considered political reasons—his opposition to the government policy of restoration—was Tunis G. Campbell, and Tillson did not find Campbell guilty of "dishonest practices" until the end of May 1866.[63] Still, the Bureau in the reservation had new personnel by the spring. In mid-December 1865, Tillson had appointed a new agent for Chatham County after William Tiffany, concerned about his health, left the Ogeechee district, "this region of miasma, disease and death."[64] A. P. Ketchum turned over his records to Tillson in March 1866 and assumed new duties in

Washington.[65] Eaton was the last of Saxton's veterans to leave the agency. He remained at his post until he was relieved in October 1866, but in September he had expressed a desire to return north to tend to personal affairs.[66]

With the influence of their old friends now diluted, the freedpeople had to deal not only with new policies and planters that challenged their independence but also with new agents who had a very different perspective concerning the freedmen's place on the land. No longer would the Bureau and the freedmen harmoniously pursue the new challenges of Reconstruction as they had done in the first months after the war. The new agents were not like freedmen's advocate Eaton, who was unhindered by financial concerns tied to the agricultural activities of his charges.

Because the Bureau had no budget for hiring additional salaried agents in 1866, the only whites available to do the agency's work were those who had planting interests. Allen G. Bass, the agent for McIntosh County and Sapelo Island, was an in-law of the Thomas Spalding family as well as their wartime overseer. Tillson, however, showed a belated sensitivity to black concerns about old taskmasters, probably after learning about his past, and removed Bass within two weeks of his appointment.[67] Nevertheless, other agents maintained the connection. John C. Dickson, a Yankee who succeeded Bass in April, had relatives who rented property from the Spalding family on Sapelo. John W. Magill, who became the agent for Ossabaw in late April, was a partner in a firm engaged in planting on the island. Even Tillson's friend William Perry gave up his salaried Bureau position for an unpaid agency in order to go to work for the cotton planting firm of Schuyler and Winchester.[68]

While this kind of appointment was the norm throughout the rest of Georgia, on the sea islands it took on special significance. Because of the confrontation between returning or newly arriving whites and independent blacks, the appointments probably contributed to the freedpeople's loss of faith in the government in a stronger way than elsewhere in Georgia. When freedpeople on a St. Simons plantation learned that they had to give up their land, they understood "that their new friends the Yankees had deceived them." And when Toby Maxwell, a freedman from St. Catherines, later complained about the bookkeeping practices of the two entrepreneurs there who, he claimed, deprived him and his fellows of all they had made, he understood the Bureau to be an accomplice in the fraudulent assessments. "This stealing and outrage," he concluded, "was done by the direction of Gen'l Tilson [*sic*]."[69]

The complaints voiced by planters and agents concerning the freedpeople revealed the new antagonism between the reservation freedpeople and the

Bureau. The freedpeople's assertive behavior was more than anything else a reflection of a way of life established before the Bureau began to curtail their independence. As A. S. Dickson explained about the Sapelo freedpeople, "The fact of their having their own way last year it is hard to bring them into proper position & must be done with judgment & care."[70] But the "judgment & care" employed by the Bureau failed to convince the freedpeople to change their ways. Many refused to accept the decisions of the Bureau agents and continued to consider the land and its fruits to be theirs by rights.

On Sapelo Island, the freedpeople showed little respect for the new Bureau agent or their employers. At first they refused to sign a contract without the advice of Tunis G. Campbell, but even after they accepted terms they tried to maintain complete control of their lives. Despite the contract, they left the island whenever they pleased and refused to "raise a hoe on Saturdays." Despite Bureau orders, they continued to hunt the island's deer. Furthermore, there were indications that they were selling the island's products before the final division of the crop, which was contrary to their contract because it enabled them to avoid repayment of the advances in supplies their employers had made to them.[71]

The confrontation finally came when Davis Tillson responded to pleas for assistance from the agent and the planters on Sapelo Island. On September 5 he threatened to arrest Tunis Campbell, whom he blamed for the troubles on the island, if he returned to Sapelo. On the same day, Tillson ordered a small detachment of troops to Sapelo to settle the differences between the planters and the freedpeople. The two officers who led the expedition were treated contemptuously by the black residents. The soldiers arrested twelve of the freedmen's leaders, and Tillson jailed the prisoners at Fort Pulaski, hoping that a few days of hard labor would convince them to respect the contract and the Bureau. The assistant commissioner found them sufficiently reasonable after fourteen days' confinement and sent them home. The Bureau's actions, however, were too late to do much good for agent Dickson and the island's white tenants. Before late September Dickson resigned his agency, and by January 1867 the planters left Sapelo with little to show for their season's efforts. The freedpeople, according to one observer, were to blame for the failure of the free-labor experiment "because they have led a precarious kind of existence, fishing, hunting, &c—and laboring under no guiding head."[72]

The problems on Sapelo were not isolated examples of the deterioration of relations between the Bureau and the reservation freedmen. On Ossabaw the freedpeople refused to respect the authority or the contract of the agent and planter John Magill. Magill resorted to humoring the freedpeople in an attempt to gain their cooperation and apparently agreed to allow them to cultivate plots of their own. Still, they remained "impudent and intractable," which intimidated Magill. Throughout the season the freedmen worked at their own pace, but they were productive. In September 1866, a Bureau officer discovered that the freedmen who worked under contract would make money after they harvested the cotton, and the corn they were cultivating "on their own account" could bring each of them about two hundred dollars. To these freedpeople, however, there was something more valuable than profit. Their neighbors who were not under contract but were planting on land that they claimed to own would make only about a fourth of what those under contract would earn if they stayed through their term with Magill and his partners. Yet, when a Bureau officer asked how they felt about their circumstances, all but fifteen of the sixty employees believed they could have done better on land of their own.[73]

No doubt other reservation freedpeople shared that belief; some were willing to take steps to make it a reality. J. R. Cheves discovered how difficult it was to enforce his will on ex-slaves "who had for a year past been indoctrinated in the wildest theories of freedom & personal rights." At the outset of the season he had hired a hundred able-bodied freedpeople to work his Grove Point rice plantation in the Ogeechee district. In 1865, 108 freedmen had held thirty possessory titles to 390 acres of Cheves's land. In the meantime, the planter complied with the terms set forth by Ketchum's board of supervisors and had understood that Howard had restored his property. Nevertheless, questions arose about the status of the land.

Cheves's employees began to flout the contract almost immediately after agreeing to its terms. "They did not prepare the lands according to custom but in the rudest & most slovenly manner," the planter complained. More seriously, "finally taking umbrage at my presence among them, they assembled as a *Landsturm*, surrounded my house & drowning my voice with violent, insolent & contemptuous denunciations declared that there was no master on the plantation." The Bureau had tried to restore order, but the freedpeople still refused to allow Cheves to supervise their work with any authority. Now in September, Cheves begged General Tillson to do something. "These freedmen, in actual possession declared they 'would work for no man.' They would have the land & nothing but the land would satisfy them."

Tillson was not quick to use troops in this instance. He answered Cheves's plea by forming a board of arbitration to settle the difficulty and promised to employ military force to carry out the board's final determination only if the freedmen had a voice in the process.[74] Nevertheless, he knew that the board could not satisfy the freedmen's greatest desire even for those who held on to valid possessory titles. Congress had finally decided to restore all of the Sherman Reservation to its white claimants.

On July 16, Congress overrode another presidential veto and gave the Bureau additional time to cope with the problems of Reconstruction. Using that legislative opportunity, the federal lawmakers settled the future of the Sherman grants. The freedmen who still held valid possessory titles could harvest their crops, claim compensation for improvements on the land, and exchange their soon-to-be-worthless Georgia grants for the right to purchase twenty-acre parcels of coastal South Carolina land owned by the federal government. Those freedmen who had given up their grants to earlier acts of restoration still had a chance to become yeoman farmers once the available lands satisfied the needs of their more persistent neighbors.[75]

Tillson and the Bureau began to carry out the law's provisions during the fall of 1866. At the end of October, the assistant commissioner moved his headquarters to Savannah to supervise the restoration process. He was not pleased with what he discovered. Apparently, he now paid closer attention to the details of Sherman's original orders and probably allowed his unpleasant experience with the reservation freedpeople to influence his judgment. He concluded that every title that crossed his camp desk was inadequate. None of the land titles met all of the minimum requirements enumerated by Sherman; therefore, technically, none of the titles was valid. Nevertheless, Tillson decided to make "the Record agree with the facts." Freedmen who had taken the "initiatory steps" to comply with the order would be entitled to warrants for South Carolina land because, Tillson reasoned, Sherman had not stated a specific deadline for perfecting the process.[76]

Needless to say, not all of the involved parties willingly complied with restoration. Already moved once to make room for white planters, those freedpeople who objected to pulling up stakes again undoubtedly resented yet another governmental intrusion. Before Tillson left the Bureau in mid-January 1867, he issued warrants to 176 freedmen, significantly fewer than half of the 459 who held valid registered grants.[77] Of those who did not receive warrants, some had already abandoned their claims. As early as May 1866, Tillson had surmised that some of the freedmen had never occupied their valid grants, and others had abandoned them during the early months of Reconstruction. The lack of capital, the lure of Savannah, white intrusions, intimidation, and the uncertainty of government action probably influenced their decisions. By the spring of 1866, for example, some freedpeople in the Ogeechee district had become "disheartened" with their prospects and had voluntarily abandoned their legitimate claims in order to accept contracts. The freedpeople on Burnside Island, near Savannah, also deserted their grants, which allowed the owner to reclaim his land with the blessing of the Bureau, and freedpeople on Cumberland Island found work in Florida.[78]

Other freedmen, however, simply refused to be willing accomplices in their own dispossession. In the Savannah area, Aaron Bradley assumed the role of the freedpeople's guardian and urged them not to give up their grants. Some freedmen may have lost their chance to secure South Carolina land because of Bradley's advice. On Wilmington and Skidaway Islands, close to Bradley's Savannah base of operations, only a handful received warrants.[79]

The situation that developed on Ossabaw Island during Davis Tillson's last weeks with the Bureau in the spring of 1867 provides a good example of the course of action followed by the more militant freedmen. Counseled by Tunis Campbell, the Ossabaw freedmen refused to give up their grants for the new warrants. Bureau agent J. W. Magill, who brought the bad news to them, recognized their determination and feared they would resort to force in order to maintain their holdings. The Ossabaw Islanders, however, first peacefully petitioned the Bureau. Retaining as their attorney the militant Bradley, they reasonably requested the protection of their rights in the crop and the improvements made on the land. They also asked the impossible: an extension of their land grants for another two years.

On the island the freedpeople, probably aware of the futility of their request for an extension of their grants, continued to ignore the government's proposition, insisted on their right to the land, and acted forcibly to maintain it. To make their point, they convinced the freedpeople who had been working under contract to leave Agent Magill's cotton standing in the fields and arranged to have them plant on grant land. These freedmen also intimidated Magill's workers who did not go along with their plans; as late as January 1867, the dissidents were able to prevent Magill's hands from beginning the new year's chores.

By this time Tillson had left the Bureau, but his successor, Caleb Sibley, also believed in implementing the wishes of Congress. On January 25 he ordered an officer to proceed to Ossabaw with a detachment of soldiers to "arrange" the "difficulty" between planters and freedmen and to enforce the law. The troops met no opposition, the officer placed the owners in control, and apparently the freedmen in their disappointment still did not accept warrants for South Carolina land.[80] Caleb Sibley did not record the fate of the Ossabaw freedpeople, but those who remained on the island did so as employees or tenants.

The other freedpeople of the islands fared no better as the restoration of lands continued throughout 1867 and into 1868. In May 1867, for example, only a few freedmen on Sapelo continued to work for themselves, whereas the entire black population of St. Catherines was working under contract.[81] The more independent followers of Tunis Campbell, perhaps accompanied by some of the Ossabaw freedpeople, had left St. Catherines in early 1867 for the McIntosh County mainland, where they leased the Belle Ville plantation.[82]

There were probably others like the Ossabaw freedmen who refused to accept warrants, but even the militant ex-slaves on Cheves's Grove Point rice plantation who had registered grants finally acquiesced. Apparently they had decided that government-supported land titles in South Carolina were better than tenuous claims in Georgia. So, too, did a majority of Sapelo grant holders who had earlier looked to Campbell for advice.[83]

Obviously any displeasure aroused by the government's resettlement plan would burden the reputations of the men who executed its requirements, and Davis Tillson's reputation certainly was no exception. Radical critics such as Bradley, whom Tillson had once jailed, and Edward E. Howard, the adopted son of Tunis G. Campbell and a freedmen's teacher at Darien who shared the sympathies of Tillson's Augusta antagonist, John Emory Bryant, found Tillson guilty of all sorts of outrages. Howard, for example, accused Tillson of hustling the freedpeople off St. Catherines grants while as much as fifteen thousand pounds of ripe cotton stood in their fields.[84]

Howard's charges make little sense in light of Tillson's almost constant fear of poor crops and destitution. It is possible that the freedpeople to whom Howard referred, like their Ossabaw neighbors, left their fields in protest, but if Howard's accusations were accurate, no white man benefited from the cotton: the St. Catherines firm of Schuyler and Winchester went bankrupt before the end of 1867. In fact, Howard's remarks were slanderous. Davis Tillson, before leaving the Bureau, had initiated the arrangements with a Savannah cotton firm that allowed the agency to secure part of the freedpeople's share of the 1866 crop, despite Winchester's initial dissatisfaction with those arrangements.[85]

During the restoration period Tillson tried to secure what he considered to be the freedpeople's just claims. In December a planter disregarded the grant rights of some freedmen because they also worked for him on shares. Tillson determined that the planter had no right to claim any part of the crop raised on the grant land. The grants were legitimate, and the freedmen had every right to control their products.[86]

Although he conscientiously adhered to the law, Tillson by now found little that was positive about the sea island experiment. Unable to accept either what he perceived to be the uneconomical approach of the freedpeople to independent agriculture or their emotional desire for the confirmation of their Civil War inheritance, Tillson proclaimed that the experiment was a failure and that the restoration of the reservation property was the soundest course to follow. Tillson left the Bureau convinced that a contract system, closely supervised by the Bureau, would allow free labor to flourish in the reservation and throughout the South, would teach the freedpeople lessons of hard work and thrift, and finally would provide them with the resources necessary for securing land on their own account.[87]

Tillson's views about free labor in Georgia were overly optimistic, especially given the problems that he had encountered on the mainland. His assessment, made as he prepared to leave an agency to which he had devoted almost two years of his life and one that was supposed to help guarantee the Union's Civil War victory, was perhaps his best effort to put a flawed system into its best light. Given his commitment to the contract system and the emotional capital that he had spent promoting it, he had no choice but to remain optimistic about free labor. In the end, he simply could not conceive of an alternative.

## The Reservation after Tillson

When Davis Tillson left the Bureau, there was still work for his successor in the old Sherman Reservation. Some land owners had yet to comply with the legislative requirements of the restoration process, and some freedmen remained on their grants waiting for the final determination by the Bureau. But in the end the course first set by Tillson would play itself out unchanged.

As the freedmen on Ossabaw learned, Tillson's critics were wrong to assume that Caleb Sibley would be able to change policy made in Washington. Sibley was a professional, a career army man near retirement who followed orders, and his most influential staff officer and the man who would be his successor, John Randolph Lewis, could not change the law. Perhaps if either officer had become a vocal advocate of confiscation, the lonely voices in Washington who argued the justice of such a course would have found greater support for their cause. The ineffective arguments of strong supporters like Saxton and Ketchum suggest otherwise. In all fairness, the Bureau was an arm of the government, an executor of policy made somewhere far removed from the frontlines of Reconstruction. As long as the federal government failed to alter its land policy, the agency could do nothing.

The debate over confiscation and land redistribution continued in Washington into the spring and summer of 1867, but failed to advance the cause of the freedpeople on the reservation. Republicans continued to echo Tillson's fears about the effects of charity. They delayed consideration of new Reconstruction measures while they waited to see if old ones would succeed or fail. And they worried about political party building; Republicans feared that confiscation would alienate white Southerners who might otherwise enter the party's fold.[88]

At the state level, politicians also failed to change the direction of events on the reservation. Except for the radical advocacy of Campbell and Bradley, there were no calls from Georgia's elected black leadership for confiscation. Black politicians worked for civil and political rights, causes germane to the economic well-being of their constituents, but still not aimed at immediate and radical economic reform. Even if these leaders had been in favor of confiscation, they would have lacked the political power to implement the program. Comprising 20 percent of the membership of the state legislature, they needed white assistance to further their ends, and their white counterparts opposed land reform.[89]

Consequently, the Freedmen's Bureau continued to restore reservation land; there was little prospect for future reversal. Some freedpeople, like those on St. Catherines Island, accepted the necessity of signing contracts. In the process, they learned that they could squeeze some concessions from their white employers that allowed them to maintain some sense of autonomy within the new system. In the coastal counties, some freedmen leased land by paying either in cash, kind, or labor.[90] As early as January 1866, freedpeople residing on Joseph Waring's Skidaway Island plantation refused to sign any contract other than a lease arrangement for individual parcels of land. Waring agreed and leased over one hundred acres to twelve freedpeople for two dollars an acre.[91] Others preserved vestiges of the reservation in the garden patches and larger plots of land they arranged to cultivate in their off-time. Some freedpeople signed contracts that preserved the routines of the antebellum task system. Such arrangements could have reassured freedpeople native to the coast that at least they would be able to maintain the antebellum perquisites they had enjoyed under the task system, which had allowed them to work on their own after they had completed the day's assignment.[92]

Clearly, there were freedpeople in the reservation who understood that, although the Bureau's contract system failed to divide the land, it extended other opportunities for them to advance their interests. Frances Butler's frustrating experience with her workers suggests as much. In 1867, freedpeople from Butler's Hampton Point place on St. Simons, a sea island cotton plantation, refused to sign a contract unless she was present. As their mainland cousins understood, they, too, believed a contract to be an agreement sufficiently important to require the proprietor's presence; an agent for the mistress would not do if the freedpeople viewed the contract as an agreement between equal parties. Back on Butler Island, Frances Butler spent six hours one Saturday negotiating a contract with freedpeople. The following Monday was even more grueling. She bargained with potential employees from 10 A.M. until 6 P.M. and still had to deal with "stragglers" over the next two days. The desire to bargain failed to fade, for before the onset of the 1869 season Butler's employees were "all prepared again to make their own, and different, terms for the next year."[93]

The strong-willed Butler usually had her way with the contracts, but she at least seemed sufficiently fair-minded to pay her workers.[94] Much depended on the willingness of sea island employers to accept the notion that free labor involved mutual rights and obligations, something that became less likely as the Bureau reduced its presence in Georgia as it wound down most of its operations in 1868. As the Bureau came to play a role of less prominence, other reservation freedpeople unsurprisingly failed to place their trust in the contracts. Even if the contracts made economic sense to them, the agreements were a step backwards from Sherman's earlier promise. Some of these freedpeople were able to delay their dispossession; as late as the spring of 1868, there remained an area in the Ogeechee district where no whites ventured and freedpeople controlled two or three plantations. Other freedpeople avoided white control by moving to less desirable pine lands or "squatting" on neglected plots of island property.[95] Unfortunately, even isolation could not guarantee security on the land. In 1868 and in 1871 white planters on Cumberland Island and St. Simons Island forced squatters off their property.[96]

Freedpeople left to themselves, however, continued to sink roots into the land, making it difficult for whites to dislodge them when owners tried to regain control of their property. In the Ogeechee district, even as late as 1868, freedpeople who occupied a neglected rice plantation near Savannah reacted militantly when the land owner exercised his right to lease the property. Having been left "pretty much to themselves" until the end of 1868, a neighboring planter observed, the freedpeople believed that the owner had no right to dispossess them. The freedpeople also allegedly kept a substantial amount of rice claimed by the land owner. Violence erupted. Freedpeople mobbed authorities who had arrested several of their number and attacked other whites, causing panic in Savannah. Shortly after the new year, over two dozen freedpeople were charged with insurrection. Caleb Sibley accompanied the infantry that quelled the "Ogeechee Rebellion" to observe the freedpeople's situation firsthand, but the Bureau could not reverse government policy or intercede on behalf of the "black banditti."[97]

The best that the Bureau could do at times was to try to convince planters to allow squatters to remain on the land if the freedpeople agreed to accept some sort of contractual arrangement. In the spring of 1867, for example, Lieutenant Douglas G. Risley interceded for black squatters on Cumberland Island. He asked the white proprietor to allow the freedpeople to remain as tenants, which apparently he did. In January 1868, however, Risley's efforts on behalf of squatters in Glynn County were unsuccessful.[98] Ironically, the Bureau's effort to substitute contract labor for land grants as a means of introducing a free-labor economy to the reservation probably helped push those uncompromising freedpeople to the fringes of Georgia's postwar economy. Squatting on marginal land was an alternative to contracts, but it might not have been a freedman's preference if he had been able to preserve a reservation grant.

It was not clear that all reservation freedpeople expected to use their Sherman grants to subsist outside the marketplace. In 1866 John T. Trowbridge observed how situations beyond their control forced freedpeople to follow a course that might not have been their original intention. He believed that uncertainty concerning the final disposition of the Sherman lands led some freedpeople to approach agriculture halfheartedly. Freedmen faced with the possibility of restoration worried that they would not benefit from improvements they made to the land. The implication was that they would have pursued agriculture more vigorously if the government had confirmed their titles.[99]

Also, the Bureau's very limited assistance program for freedpeople who struck out on their own might have hurt the chances of ambitious independent communities of reservation freedpeople who wished to establish viable agricultural concerns in low-country Georgia.[100] In 1867 freedpeople purchased seven hundred acres of land at Elliot's Bluff plantation near the coastal town of St. Marys in the southernmost reaches of Camden County. Perhaps duplicating an earlier reservation experiment in which they had participated, they established their own set of laws and government. Furthermore, they impressed a Freedmen's Bureau doctor with their "perseverance, energy, and ambition." Also in 1867 freedpeople leased a plantation near the river town of Riceboro in Liberty County. Savannah subassistant commissioner J. Murray Hoag concluded "that the condition of the place and the amount of land under cultivation evinces a determination on the part of the . . . people to do all in their power to make a good crop." Both groups of freedpeople wanted more than subsistence, even if they pursued their ends as communities and not as individuals. Both groups found their progress limited by their small resources and, in the case of the Camden County freedpeople, the necessity to leave their fields to find food. If they failed to raise a marketable crop, it was not for want of effort on their part.[101]

The rice-planting Ogeechee freedpeople who tried to preserve their profits as well as their independence by avoiding rice tolls and middlemen were progressing beyond subsistence farming. The Sapelo freedmen who cultivated grants on the Spalding and Kenan properties hired extra labor, which they would not have needed had they wished to live a hand-to-mouth existence. One wonders if the freedmen who had returned to the mainland in 1865 to work for wages had hoped to earn the funds required for making their grants successful. Also, the freedmen who had signed leases and contracts in the coastal counties might have expected to profit from their labors; the system failed them, but that failure did not mean that they had failed to make use of the system. Furthermore, the poor land that Frances Butler's workers purchased—land that was suitable only for subsistence—might not have been the freedpeople's first choice, but it was the only type of land that whites would sell to them.[102] Obviously, not all of the reservation's black residents eagerly accepted the challenge to prove that free labor was as competitive as slavery had been in producing goods for the marketplace. However, some might have chosen a different economic path had the circumstances allowed. In the end, the consequences of restoration within the Sherman Reservation did not necessarily follow from the intentions of the Bureau or the freedpeople.

# 8

# The Same Footing before the Law

The Georgia Freedmen's Bureau's attempt to establish a free-labor system recognized that the freedpeople had rights that existed concurrently with their obligations as laborers. The Bureau expected white Georgians to respect those rights, which extended beyond the right to be paid for labor to include the right to choose employers, the right to travel to find work, the right to avoid debt peonage, and the right to avoid any type of confinement to places of employment after working hours. Davis Tillson's early anxiety over the labor situation had prompted him to threaten freedpeople with mandatory contracts, but otherwise he always believed that honest workers should be able to select their own employers.

Tillson also believed that ex-slaves had the right to freedom of movement even when not looking for work. He disallowed a request from Greene County planters to give them the authority to prohibit freedpeople from leaving their places of employment without passes. Although restraining wandering freedmen might produce some good in some cases, Tillson reasoned, it was a violation of state and federal law as well as Bureau policy. Passes were, he allowed, a restraint on the freedpeople's personal liberty.[1]

Clearly, many of the rights that the freedpeople could claim in the workplace or elsewhere were necessary for the success of the Bureau's new contract system. Tillson implemented his relocation program to address labor demand, for example, with the understanding that freedpeople had the right to select employers and the right to travel wherever the wages appealed to them.

Also, the agency's insistence that Georgia's judicial system treat blacks equitably was directly related to its concern for the freedpeople's economic well-being and the future of the new labor system. Agent

Christian Raushenberg, for example, believed that the dilatory manner in which the authorities attended to black justice in his southwestern Georgia jurisdiction undermined free labor and was the cause of the freedpeople's regression to their "old habits and old modes of thinking." According to Raushenberg, a judicial system that cheated the laborers out of their wages and allowed employers to take advantage of them encouraged the freedpeople to become indolent and dishonest because they had little to gain by being hardworking and honest.[2]

The Bureau's understanding of black rights, therefore, had a very pragmatic side that extended beyond the workplace into other aspects of its relationship with the freedpeople. The agency's efforts to encourage and enforce familial responsibility, for example, helped to extricate the agency from the relief business by forcing fathers to support their children and husbands to care for their wives. At the same time, however, Bureau men recognized that fathers had a "sacred right and privilege" to control their families.[3]

Consequently, the Bureau's efforts also reflected a belief that the freedpeople deserved the same consideration before the law as that received by their ex-masters. The Bureau made it clear that it expected white officials to respect the constitutional rights of freedpeople, regardless of their own race fears. The Georgia Bureau, therefore, expected to prepare white Georgia to give the ex-slaves fair access to justice when their basic rights were violated and, in the process, to preserve for the freedpeople something more than simply the right to earn a living.

## The Freedmen's Families and Apprenticeship

According to the earliest regulations of the Freedmen's Bureau, ex-slaves had an obligation as well as a right to control their family lives. During the summer of 1865, Rufus Saxton and his agency alerted the freedpeople to the need to reunite husbands and wives, sanctify slave unions, and support children while urging them to hold sacred the "domestic altar."[4] Other Bureau officials added their admonitions to Saxton's and did not hesitate to use their offices to try to impose stability on unions that lacked it and responsibility on individuals who rejected it.[5] Davis Tillson, for example, admonished parents to support their children and children to support their aged parents, while advising his officers and agents to be certain that the freedpeople abided by all of the state's laws concerning marriage.[6] Because the Bureau men believed in the importance of such obligations, they took an active role in reuniting families separated by slavery or the fortunes of war, lest more freedpeople become a burden on the agency's already strained resources. Corresponding across jurisdictional lines, they helped individuals locate family members and even procured transportation for those freedpeople who had to travel beyond Georgia to regain their families.[7]

At the same time, Bureau policy followed Tillson's assumption that the sanctity of marriage and the rights of the family could not be disturbed by the labor needs of whites. He considered it a "serious wrong" for employers to deprive a husband of his wife or a wife of her husband as well as to keep children from their parents.[8] Tillson and other Bureau men probably assumed that an intact family unit had a better chance of escaping economic dependency, but they also understood that there were larger issues at stake, including the civil equality of the ex-slaves. For Tillson and like-minded Bureau men, "the husband has the same right to control his wife and children that a white man has."[9]

Despite some exceptions, most freedpeople did not need the Bureau to remind them of their obligations to their families. Saxton's Augusta officer, John Emory Bryant, specifically commented on the numerous cases of family reunification that followed in the wake of emancipation.[10] Still, the disruptions experienced by the black community during and immediately after the war put pressure on weak unions that led to family difficulties. Rachael Lumpkin killed her husband in a fit of jealousy, but, more often than not, wronged freedpeople brought their troubles to the Bureau, expecting agents and officers to help them resolve problems of abuse and abandonment.[11] Mary Allen, for example, expected the Bureau to force her husband, who left her after the war, to contribute to the support of their children, and Silva asked the Bureau to give her protection from a husband who "beats her brutally & without provocation."[12]

In 1866, Washington agent Brien Maguire dealt with a half dozen domestic cases, all of which he decided in favor of the complaining party. In cases of abandonment, he ordered the wandering party to return to his or her spouse or, in the case of those who had no desire to do so, to pay child support.[13] In 1867 and 1868, Milledgeville agent J. D. Rogers listened to the complaints of eleven men and women who had been abused or abandoned and likewise tried to impose order and responsibility on the families before him. He commanded men and women to live together "peaceably" and demanded that fathers pay child support.[14]

Rogers revealed a common prejudice when he heard a custody case brought by a husband abandoned by his wife. The wife argued that she had been abused and had to find shelter for herself and her children with another man. Although the agent was generally sympathetic to victims of domestic violence, in this case he returned the children to their father, apparently assuming that a mother rendered herself less fit to raise her children if she had become involved in an adulterous relationship, regardless of the circumstances.[15]

In the resolution of domestic cases, the Bureau's authority only went so far, for much ultimately depended on the father's ability to secure his pay to contribute to his child's support or the resolution of the disputing parties to turn over a new leaf. In January 1868, Abraham Armstrong promised to return to his wife and support their five children "and to regard her and no other woman as a wife while she lives." An abusive Bill Jenkins was ordered to take care of his wife and "treat her kindly until she is delivered of a child." [16] The Bureau also ordered Billy Findley to support his wife, Barbara, even though he had run off to marry another woman, until she gave birth to their child. Furthermore, the agency required him to support the baby for several years thereafter.[17] But these were only orders and promises. The Bureau's ability to protect the rights of a wronged man or woman was at best weak if the offending parties failed to be convinced by the agency that they had to mend their ways.

In May 1866, agent Brian Maguire gave permission to a planter to discharge a freedwoman without pay if she failed to live with her legal husband. Also in May he jailed freedman Alick Burns's adulterous wife, Adaline, and the corespondent, freedman Dick Wingfield, after both pleaded guilty to the charges. However, earlier in January 1866, when he resolved a case of abandonment and child support by ordering the freedman George to marry the freedwoman Judy, the mother of his three children, his power was insufficient for protecting the wronged party. Just as the ceremony was about to be performed, George "bolted out of the courtroom, and left Judy to seek redress some other way." [18]

The agency's efforts to ensure a degree of stability and responsibility in troubled black personal relationships undoubtedly was influenced by its desire to prevent any more indigent freedpeople from becoming a burden on the agency's limited resources. Yet, the actions of its officers and agents in these cases went beyond looking for the simplest resolution of an aggrieved spouse's complaint; they were more in line with the Bureau men's views of how freedpeople should internalize the individual responsibility and personal discipline necessary to help make Georgia's new free-labor society a success. Just as important, however, was the determination of Bureau officials to protect the rights of the abused parties.

No complaint brought before the Bureau by the freedpeople dealing with domestic concerns more clearly indicated the sympathetic disposition of many of its agents and officers to the needs and the rights of the freedpeople than those involving illegal apprenticeship. Freedpeople believed that it was the Bureau's duty to protect their children from exploitation in unfair or unlawful apprenticeship arrangements, and the Bureau agreed. Consequently, although the problems surrounding apprenticeship at first appeared to be problems of labor control or charity, they also brought into focus the freedpeople's understanding that exercising control over their families was important for securing their economic independence as well as an expression of their fullest understanding of freedom.[19]

The freedmen who had their children work for planters in exchange for better contract arrangements for themselves understood the value of their youngsters' labor, especially when it brought them plots of land.[20] So, too, did the freedwoman who petitioned the Bureau to have her son, who had run off to Augusta, returned to her "to work out his contract for this year & assist her in making a living."[21] Freedman Arthur Reeves not only accepted that he had a right to his child's labor but assumed that the Bureau had an obligation to make his son understand his position; he dragged the fourteen-year-old boy before the Milledgeville Bureau expecting the agent to discipline him because he refused to hire out with his father.[22]

Indeed, the desire to control the labor of children could lead to abuse even within the freed community where an extra four dollars a month earned by an apprenticed child could make the difference between solvency and destitution.[23] Nevertheless, the real abuse to the apprenticeship system and consequently the freedpeople's rights to control their families came from white Georgians. In early 1867, the Georgia Bureau's inspector general discovered that whites in Emanuel County, avoiding the authority of black parents, also scrambled after the labor of children, whom they probably considered more pliable than their elders.[24] Planter William Henry Stiles was quite clear about this advantage. In September 1865, he explained to his wife that young freedpeople "would be exceedingly useful" on his Terrell County farm because "they would not have the run-away & fortune-making nature of the men." He intended to "try & get the best of the [former slaves'] children bound to me— such I mean as are now or will shortly be able to work."[25]

For Stiles as well as the freedpeople, controlling the labor of children had important economic consequences. But ex-slaves also understood that there was more involved in exercising control over their children than money. Their identity as free people required that they assert their right to determine the destinies of their families in the face of planters who were still trying to reassert their mastery by exploiting the most vulnerable segment of the freed population. They found an ally in this cause in the Bureau.

The Bureau had no difficulty accepting legitimate apprenticeship agreements and in fact encouraged them when appropriate. From the Bureau's perspective, apprenticeship relieved the agency of the burden of worrying about Georgia's population of black orphans, some of whom found their way into the Bureau's already overcrowded hospitals searching for food and shelter. The Bureau's options included either turning over children in its custody to the American Missionary Association's Washburne Orphanage in Atlanta or, as Atlanta sub-assistant commissioner Mosebach did, asking agents and officers throughout the state to locate suitable homes into which the freed children could be apprenticed.[26] Cases that did not involve orphans, however, were of a different sort, and the Bureau generally accepted the rights of the parents to determine whether they should apprentice their children. The abuses perpetrated by white Georgians and the freedpeople's demands for redress turned the common procedure into occasions for directing the agency's attention to black rights.

Official indication that white Georgians would not be able to have their way with the children came when Davis Tillson issued regulations concerning apprenticeship. His circular of October 14, 1865, which remained in effect for the duration of the Bureau's existence in Georgia, identified the proper subjects for apprenticeship (minor children without guardians or with parents who consented to the indenture) and the terms to which they would be subjected until they achieved their majority (eighteen years of age for girls, twenty-one for boys). Children fourteen or older could select their own masters and mistresses, but otherwise they had little say in the arrangements. Parents, relatives, or the Bureau acting as an orphan's guardian controlled their future.

The Freedmen's Bureau, however, did not ignore the needs of the children simply to relieve the government of its day-to-day obligations or to provide planters with cheap labor. Court ordinaries, who had previously had the power to bind out orphaned poor children, continued to record apprenticeship agreements, but the Bureau's agents had to approve the arrangements and investigate the character of the prospective masters and mistresses. Moreover, Bureau regulations required masters and mistresses to provide for more than their wards' physical needs in return for the agency's support in maintaining the children's faithful service. They had to teach the children to read, write, and cipher—a clear break with antebellum precedent—to prepare them for their day of discharge, when they would also give the former apprentices a stipend.[27]

In March 1866, the legislature passed Georgia's own guideline for regulating apprenticeship. The law in fact applied to white and black Georgians, but conditions suggested that it would be used most frequently to indenture the children of ex-slaves. Furthermore, its terms were not as favorable as the Bureau's, requiring masters and mistresses only to teach their charges to read and allowing them to bind girls until they turned twenty-one. Another aspect of the new law, however, provided ex-masters with ample opportunity for abusing the freedpeople's rights. County judges and ordinaries now had the power to execute agreements not only for orphans but also for all minors "whose parents reside out of the county" as well as those "whose parents, from age, infirmity or poverty, are unable to support them." By early 1867, Caleb Sibley determined whites had used this law to impose "Great injustice" upon the freedpeople.[28]

Throughout the Bureau's tenure, agents and officers received complaints from freedpeople who found whites, usually ex-masters, unwilling to allow them to reunite their families because of unfairly and illegally conceived indentures. Some planters did not bother to obtain indentures until parents appeared at their back doors.[29] Others took advantage of the freedpeople's ignorance and used violence, threats of jail, or protestations of legal form to hold black children with a determination that suggests the importance they placed on the arrangements.[30]

As if illegally conceived agreements were not enough, some white Georgians flouted the law and perjured themselves to keep freedpeople bound longer than allowed. In June 1868, the Cartersville Bureau agent discovered that an indenture listed three children to be at least four years younger than their actual ages.[31] Earlier in February 1867, the Georgia Bureau's inspector general discovered "a growing evil" in Emanuel County, where officials ignored all laws concerning apprenticeship and where "men grown are bound out to Employers for board & clothes." In one case, he annulled an agreement made by the ordinary of Burke County that bound out two "boys," one twenty-two years of age, the other twenty-four.[32] In a similar case, in March 1867, the Marietta subassistant commissioner investigated a case in which two freedmen in their early twenties had been listed on their apprenticeship agreements as being only fourteen and fifteen years old. He refused to enforce such a blatantly fraudulent agreement because "the whole affair is a high handed outrage to make those two persons slaves for six and seven years longer."[33]

What disturbed conscientious Bureau officers and agents was the willingness shown by some local authorities like those in Emanuel County to disregard regulations, the law, and the wishes of parents to "accommodate their friends willingly with cheap labor." Apparently, this was a real problem in Subassistant Commissioner F. A. H. Gaebel's southwestern Georgia jurisdiction where he had to confront "the rascalish county Judge of Stewart Co." After reviewing a case in April 1867, Gaebel concluded that abuse of the apprenticeship law "has already brought back into Slavery numbers of young men."[34]

In another part of the state, Edwin Belcher, the agent stationed at Forsyth in Monroe County, also discovered that planters were trying to reinstitute slavery on the backs of young freedpeople. He believed that the county ordinary had bound one-third of the black children in Monroe to planters. In some cases whites had driven off the fathers before approaching the court to swear that the men were out of the county leaving behind wives incapable of supporting their children. "The mother being ignorant," Belcher explained, "is easily duped." Gaebel and Belcher were not exaggerating, for even the Georgia Supreme Court found it necessary to warn local officials to take care when apprenticing black children.[35]

The procedures for pursuing complaints followed the usual bureaucratic routes that must have appeared overly cautious to anxious freedpeople. However, the Bureau willingly interposed its authority between civil authorities and the freedpeople when investigations documented clear cases of abuse and the local officials neglected to act. Davis Tillson considered it to be an injustice to separate children from parents, except when done according to his own prescribed guidelines.[36] Therefore, his action in an August 1866 Miller County case was not extraordinary; his intentions were clear even though he felt obliged to follow procedures when a freedwoman entered her appeal.

The black mother complained that the ordinary of Miller County told her that "the law" required her to bind out her children. The Bureau agent who investigated the case reported that the woman was industrious and that her two eldest sons were sufficiently mature to help support the family. The heartlessness of the arrangement was revealed when the new master refused to allow any contact between the mother and the children. In reply, Davis Tillson's adjutant general directed the agent to confront the ordinary and "demand that the Indentures be revoked and the children restored to their mother" because the Bureau considered the agreement "Null & void." If the ordinary refused, the agent had to report to headquarters once more before the Bureau could take further action.[37]

Usually, such a report prompted a letter and a threat from the assistant commissioner. "I am exceedingly anxious not to interfere with the civil officers of the State in the performance of their duties," Davis Tillson assured a troublesome Randolph County judge. However, he warned that law "gives me ample authority, and makes it my duty, to interfere for the protection of the Freed people, and to disregard the action of the civil courts of the State where I am convinced that it is necessary to secure justice." In this particular case, Tillson ordered his subassistant commissioner, F. A. H. Gaebel, to annul the indenture in question if his investigation called for it. Also, he instructed the officer to arrest anyone who interfered with the black family after its reunion.[38] In another case, after informing the agent of Twiggs County that he would ignore illegally conceived indentures, Tillson's adjutant reminded him that he was the guardian of the freed childen in his jurisdiction, thanks to federal law, which all states must respect. "Any action of the State Courts ignoring this right of guardianship will be treated as illegal and void."[39]

The case of John Calvin Johnson provided further illustration of Tillson's belief that a mother had the right to her children, even if her circumstances were questionable. At the end of the war a father, one of Johnson's former slaves, left two children with him. The father absconded in the fall of 1865—he had been accused of hog stealing—and in November 1866 the mother wished to reclaim her children. Apparently, the freedpeople had not been living as man and wife. Since Johnson was also a civilian Bureau agent, he forwarded the case to Davis Tillson for his decision. At the same time he pleaded his right to possession of the children, claiming that the mother had married an "improvident" man, an immoral "vagabond" no less, and that she, too, was "idle and profligate." If the children's natural father were present, the agent argued, he would certainly agree to bind them to him. "The children are horrified at the idea of leaving us," wrote Johnson. "What shall I do as a man and an agent[?]" The response of the assistant commissioner was clear and direct: the same law applies for whites and blacks. The Bureau had no authority to disregard the legal rights of the mother, even if the children would be better off in a white household.[40]

In 1867 and 1868, the Bureau continued to follow procedures established during Tillson's administration. Freedmen continued to make complaints about illegal indentures, and Bureau men continued to void irregular indentures made by local civil authorities and to look after the rights of children as well as their parents.[41] In February 1867, Subassistant Commissioner Mosebach of Atlanta finally acted on a case concerning two freed children in the hands of a white couple who had been mistreating them. As early as January 1866, he had been aware of the problem, but could gather no solid evidence. Later it became obvious. "The *numerous scars* on the back of the little boy will be the best evidence *against Mrs. Bellamy*," he contended. With this evidence, Mosebach did not hesitate. Using an armed guard, he removed the children from the Bellamy household and, acting as the children's guardian, he apprenticed them to more appropriate homes.[42]

Although the Bureau generally supported the claims of parents to their children, it acknowledged conditions to those claims, which unfortunately ignored the realities of slavery and the wartime confusion that might have led to involuntary separations. If Bureau investigation proved that parents had in fact abandoned their children, a situation that could easily have resulted from wartime separation, and that the children had become parties to an apprenticeship agreement, the parents could not reclaim them "without paying a reasonable allowance for the care and support during the time they have been provided for." Still, Tillson was willing to annul the indenture if the freed parents met the condition.[43]

Other relatives found it more difficult to claim children under these circumstances.[44] During Sibley's administration, in May 1868, Harriet and Seaborn Reeves claimed to be "next of kin" to a little girl whose stepfather had agreed to allow her to stay with a planter. The Milledgeville Bureau agent saw nothing irregular with the arrangement, probably because the girl's mother was dead and the stepfather had custody of the child. He denied the Reeves' effort to gain custody and allowed the planter to keep the girl.[45]

Earlier in September 1867, an old black man named Jack Gill tried to regain possession of his orphaned thirteen-year-old granddaughter, Alice. The old man, a resident of Marietta in Cobb County, had not tried to claim the girl until November 1866. In the meantime, the Bureau agent of Walton County approved an apprenticeship agreement that assigned to the girl's former owner—and reputed father—her services until she turned eighteen. Gill eloquently expressed his claim and his desire to have the girl educated in a Marietta school. "I think it very hard of the former owners for Trying to Keep My blood when I Know that Slavery is Dead," he protested. "Now they pretend to be union men but will Take advantage of Us & Bind our Children a Gainst our wishes & a Gainst all Law to be slaves until they are Twenty one years of age and then they will have no Education." The Bureau nevertheless decided against his claim. In October, Caleb Sibley's adjutant general explained that relatives who had abandoned childen "at a time when most in need of their protection" could not expect "the parties, who cared for her, in this emergency, to be deprived of her services, at a time when she can, in a measure recompense them, for their care." If Gill wished to pursue his claim, he would have to come to his own "amicable settlement" with the master.[46]

Every time a freedman like Jack Gill approached a Bureau officer or agent with a complaint, he gave testimony to his belief that the agency's purpose was to protect him in his new freedom. As in other situations, though, some agency officials betrayed the trust of the freedpeople or failed to help them through no fault of their own. Freedman Elbert Walker learned that Savannah subassistant commissioner J. Murray Hoag's order carried little weight; it was only when the Savannah officer enforced his order in person three months after Walker's first appeal for assistance that the freedman received his child.[47] The freedwoman Emily clearly understood the flaw in the agency's inadequate power and insufficient resources. When given a piece of paper to obtain the release of her child from an apprenticeship agreement, she pleaded for an armed escort: "I see no other chance to get my son."[48]

The troops that freedwoman Emily requested were probably just as necessary to protect her as to force the planter to turn over her son. Parents who tried to assert their rights over their own children at the expense of their ex-masters' authority could find themselves in difficult positions. In April 1867, when Jeremiah Robinson presented a Bureau order to John Henry for the return of one child and to Jeremiah Braxton for two more, he found himself jailed for three days because he refused to consent to indentures for his children.[49] Asserting parental authority in any way, however, was a chancy proposition for unprotected freedpeople. In September 1868, James Peter suffered a severe beating at the hands of his employer and former master for claiming the sole right to whip his own child.[50] Indeed, the outcome of Peter's efforts to claim the disciplinary prerogatives of a father was a common one in situations that challenged white dominance, for the violation of the freedpeople's right to peace, quiet, and physical safety by angry, affronted whites was a fact of life in Reconstruction Georgia.

## Freedom from Violence

The problems plaguing Georgia during the spring and summer of 1865 might have been the consequences of the unruly state of affairs that troubled the South during the early months of peace, but very early on violence had a source that went beyond the bad manners, anger, or hunger bred by years of war.[51] Violence, whether it took the form of an individual planter who whipped a worker or a brutal gang of horsemen who ran off an active Republican voter, was an integral part of white Georgia's program to regain control of the state's black population. Indeed, white Georgia used violence to curb the very rights of the freedpeople that the Bureau was committed to protect, including the right to be paid, the right to vote, the right to assemble, the right to bear arms, and ultimately the right to be treated as a free person.[52] No wonder Yankee planter Charles Stearns concluded that his white neighbors believed that they could regain their dominant position "by force, better than they can do in any other way."[53]

Often the brutal attacks against the freed community were perpetrated by groups of men dressed in women's clothing, with blackened faces, or disguised in some other manner. As often as not, however, freedpeople knew the identity of at least one of their attackers.[54] Furthermore, most black Georgians who suffered at the hands of violent whites were victimized in generally ordinary settings by individuals for whom they worked or whom they knew in some other capacity, not by bands of known or unknown vigilantes: a majority of freedpeople who reported assaults to the Freedmen's Bureau were attacked by one known person.[55]

In 1868, the number of murders and outrages perpetrated by groups of whites increased significantly because of the political excitement of that presidential election year. The riots at Camilla in southwestern Georgia, where a Republican political rally turned into a bloodbath for the participating freedpeople, and at Savannah, where a group of freedpeople were attacked at the polls, contributed significantly to those totals. Also, there were reports of Klan activity especially in Warren County in the Augusta subdistrict and across the state in Schley County in the Albany subdistrict.[56] However, when individual whites on three separate occasions used hoes to assault Angy Evans, Francis Elders, and Moseby Anderson, they probably picked up the closest available weapons in the heat of work disputes without thinking much about anything other than disciplining their fieldhands.[57]

Other white individuals lost their tempers and lashed out at freedpeople who, they believed, violated the old norms of proper race etiquette. Wilson Carter, for example, received a blow on the head with a gun from his employer because he had used "insolent language."[58] And a freedman provoked a gun-fight in Milledgeville when he failed to give up "so much of the side-walk as the white man desired."[59] In the end, ex-masters acting alone and without the cover of anonymity murdered, shot, whipped, knifed, clubbed, and pummeled freed-people who outraged white sensibilities as they challenged the authority of their ex-masters in everyday social and work situations.

In May 1868, agent John Barney made the Bureau's stand clear when he confronted a planter who threatened to whip a freedwoman. "All such acts of villany are played out, and the days for whipping colored people for amuse-ment & gratification of passion &c have passed away." He and the Bureau were there to enforce a new order. "Moral law, has superceded [sic], lynch law in this country."[60] However, given the constraints placed on the Bureau by decisions made in Washington and then in the Third Military District's headquarters, the agents and officers who were the freedpeople's first source of redress could do little to stem the tide of violence, whether perpetrated by individuals or groups. Davis Tillson, his successors, and their men knew that reports of violence de-manded the Bureau's prompt attention and, as with cases of oppression con-nected with labor disputes, they responded as promptly as possible with the means available to them.

In December 1865, Davis Tillson sent troops to Wilkes County to arrest reg-ulators there or, if that failed, to make an example of them by "shoot[ing] them on the spot."[61] During the summer of 1866, the use of military force led to the arrest of regulators in Tatnall County.[62] Later in the fall, Tillson curbed the vio-lence perpetrated by Jayhawkers in Henry County by stationing troops there.[63] The successful execution of these efforts led Tillson in November to recom-mend that cavalry be stationed in Georgia, but by that time changing circum-stances, including the new state laws concerning the ex-slaves' rights, restricted the Bureau's ability to police the state.[64]

Cases of violence against the freedpeople now necessarily required the Bu-reau to give the civil authorities every opportunity to exhibit their desire to seek justice before it would interfere. Freedpeople approached an officer or agent, swore out a complaint, and "unless the freedman exhibited upon his person proof of cruel treatment, or there is reason to fear delay will frustrate the ends of justice," could expect the papers to find their way to the appropriate Bureau officer or agent for investigation. If the Bureau man found cause to take further action, he next presented the case to the civil authorities, always careful to observe the way in which the sheriff, justice of the peace, or judge handled the complaint.[65] Sometimes the assistant commissioner's office intervened with the local authorities, firmly but courteously urging them on to "prompt & energetic action" while reassuring them that the Bureau believed that they would do justice to the freedpeople's complaints.[66]

If the civil authorities refused or were unable to act, Tillson at times called upon the governor to use his authority to influence them. Also, Bureau agents or officers could call on military force to arrest the accused and hold them "until such time as a proper judicial tribunal may be ready & willing to proceed with their trial."[67] As Davis Tillson informed the judge of Pike County court, the Bureau would always be ready to act against the perpetrators of violence, if he or his colleagues failed to do so, because "the Government of the United States is pledged to protect the freed people in their rights."[68]

On a number of occasions the assistant commissioner supported agents and officers in the field with harsh threats and, when available, detachments of troops to compensate for the lack of cooperation shown by civilian officials in arresting those who committed outrages.[69] Still, the use of military force produced mixed results. Sometimes the presence of soldiers encouraged local authorities to reassert themselves in the cause of justice, for they also might be intimidated by the presence of regulators. On too many occasions, however, the white perpetrators disappeared into the countryside, well mounted and well informed of the movements of officers and men thanks to observant friends or sympathetic civilian officials who were able to track the slow progress of the troop detachments as they moved on their prey.[70]

Even if agents and officers made their arrests, the results depended on civilian authorities, who moved quickly to retrieve prisoners from military custody, to set them free on bail, and ultimately to help them secure their liberty.[71] Indeed, of the forty-one cases of murder reported for 1865 and 1866, the courts had tried only four by the fall of 1866. The accused in those cases were acquitted. Although the courts issued warrants and tried to arrest other perpetrators, most were free to go about their business without suffering any consequences for their actions.[72]

Beyond moral suasion and threats, the best course of action open to the Bureau during the latter part of Tillson's administration and the early months of Sibley's tenure, especially since the agency could not resort to military commissions to try civilians after May 1, 1866, followed the route prescribed by the Civil Rights Act of April 1866. But even that process was seriously flawed.[73] The law provided for federal courts to appoint commissioners to assist in carrying out its intent. In Georgia, three months after the enactment of the Civil Rights Act, Tillson still found it necessary to urge the federal judge, J. Erskine, to make the appointments; as Bureau assistant commissioner, he explained, he could only do so much because of policy decisions beyond his control, and consequently he needed the assistance of the federal court, commissioners, and "a prompt and thorough enforcement of the provisions of the Civil Rights Bill."[74] However, when used to bring to justice unresolved cases of violence, the Civil Rights Act failed the Bureau and the freedpeople.

In early 1867, when the Bureau referred several cases for adjudication to the federal district court, the district attorney claimed the law did not provide him with sufficient authority to present the cases to the grand jury. Also, as late as the end of 1868, there was at least some lingering confusion among Bureau agents and United States commissioners as to what were proper cases for the commissioners' consideration under the civil rights law. Futhermore, subtle forms of discrimination rendered the law inoperative in cases where civilian courts followed the form of law without giving the freedmen the substance of justice or where juries simply refused to convict whites accused of crimes committed against blacks.[75]

Violence did not abate after Tillson left the Bureau, and with Sibley's reorganization, the patterns of justice, or rather injustice, remained the same. In the process, those patterns revealed the impossibility of bringing to justice criminals who were implementing the wishes of their communities. In November 1868, the Schley County grand jury included men who belonged to the various clandestine organizations that perpetrated the violence against the freedpeople that the court was supposedly investigating. Unsurprisingly, twenty freedpeople were indicted for quietly "carrying a gun in accordance with the constitution," whereas no whites were handed true bills. Needless to say, many freedpeople never brought their cases before the court, having been cowed by death threats if they even mentioned the violence that they had endured.[76]

Earlier, in September 1867, northwestern Georgia freedpeople witnessed justice sidetracked in a less subtle but equally effective manner. C. B. Blacker, the agent at Cartersville in Carlos de la Mesa's Rome subdistrict, discovered that a party of whites was terrorizing the freedpeople in the neighborhood of Calhoun, Georgia, "threatening to blow their brains out if they dare speak out."

He had been successful in having the sheriff arrest the culprits, who were bound over for trial, but he expressed pessimism. "When the trial comes up in court those men I have no doubt will be released and applauded for their actions; at least that is the feeling of the Gordon County officials at present." Troops might help, but only the removal of those authorities would have a lasting effect. With blue uniforms in sight, they would "lay close and keep quiet," but as soon as the troopers left the county they would "crawl out again worse than before."[77]

Blacker's assessment of the state of justice for the freedpeople was an accurate one that applied to other jurisdictions as well. In 1867, of the eighty victims of white violence recorded by the Georgia Bureau's subassistant commissioners in their official reports, only nineteen had the satisfaction of seeing the civil authorities take some positive action against their attackers. Still, of those victims, six saw the true bills found against their attackers go unexecuted, and two others lived with the knowledge that their attackers escaped from custody. By the time Bureau subassistant commissioners made their reports, authorities had brought only two perpetrators to trial, and the courts had convicted only one of those men.[78]

It was not much better in 1868. Of the 341 black victims of white violence reported by the Bureau for 1868, only 71 had the satisfaction of seeing the authorities take some kind of action against their attackers, including arrests or at least attempts to enforce true bills. In the end, however, only two whites were convicted of violence against freedpeople by the time the Georgia Bureau forwarded its consolidated report to headquarters at the end of 1868. Throughout the Bureau's existence, the most commonly reported action taken by the civil authorities in cases of white violence against blacks was that the civil authorities had taken no action at all.[79] By late 1868, many freedpeople decided that it was not worth their lives to testify against whites or even to complain to the Bureau about the violence they suffered at the hands of their ex-masters.[80]

## The Right to Bear Arms

Active white hostility, an inadequate court system, a conservative military, and an increasingly impotent Bureau almost made it essential that the freedpeople hold on to whatever firearms they had at their disposal to protect themselves and their families. Throughout Reconstruction, freedpeople kept guns in their homes and went armed into the fields where they worked or onto the streets they frequented. No doubt many a freedman like Samuel McDonald saved himself because of the practice. In July 1866, a group of men broke into Mc-Donald's Appling County home, wounded him, and then prepared to kill him. Neither the Bureau nor the army nor the courts could protect McDonald from these individuals, his undisguised neighbors. However, before the whites could complete the job, McDonald found his gun and "fired among them at which they all ran away."[81]

McDonald's effort was heroic and necessary, but the attempts of Georgia's freedpeople to organize themselves into militias revealed their understanding of the importance of collaborative efforts for protecting themselves.[82] Even before the end of the war, up and down the coast in Sherman's Reservation, black Georgians supervised by Rufus Saxton's agents mustered militias to protect their freedom and the common good.[83] The Ogeechee freedpeople apparently continued to nurture their organization even without Bureau sponsorship. So, too, did Tunis Campbell and his followers after he moved his operations to the McIntosh County mainland. Elsewhere in 1866 and 1867, freedpeople formed similar militia units and openly drilled with shouldered arms.[84] Such a fever to organize led one Bureau agent to conclude that the freedmen joined these militias "from delusion having a vague idea that it was necessary to obtain their rights."[85] This "vague idea," however, proved reasonable and in fact prescient given the conditions these freedpeople encountered in their efforts to claim their rights in a more peaceable manner. Injustice and violence only encouraged them to persist.

By the summer of 1868, freedpeople from across Georgia had gone far in organizing themselves. In Columbia County, "aggravated by the frequent outrages of persons disguised as ghosts," freedpeople formed a company of armed men "to find out whether the Ku Klux who went about at nights whipping and hanging persons were really ghosts or people upon whom powder and ball would make an impression."[86] Stewart County freedpeople were "armed and drilled"; a large number of Randolph County freedpeople organized into a militia; and Quitman and Clay County freedpeople were "rapidly organizing and for the same purpose avowed by all, mutual protection by force of arms against the merciless assaults of the whites, assaults which are becoming a daily occurrence and which are entirely overlooked by the Civil [Authorities]." The freedpeople informed Bureau agent George Ballou that they had every intention of using their weapons if pushed any further by their white neighbors. They had taken all that they could and intended to protect themselves "to the last extremity." When Ballou advised them to be moderate in their actions, they replied, "Why do you not protect us as you used to do? If you can't do it we must take care of ourselves for the courts won't do it, they won't punish a white-man for killing us."[87]

Armed freedpeople were indeed willing to protect themselves and, when they lost all faith in the legal system, take the law into their own hands. One group of freedmen "shortly after the close of the war" defended themselves from the Black Horse Cavalry, ambushing and killing and wounding several whites who were on their way to attack them.[88] In 1866, freedpeople reacted aggressively to the bad treatment of a freedwoman at the hands of a sheriff and his posse who were trying to take the prisoner back to Jones County; over forty men, at least seven armed with revolvers, attempted to rescue her "by violence."[89]

Freedpeople carried their army rifles, "making threats that they don't intend that any negroe shall be Tyed up by the thumbs," and others shot at whites who, they feared, were planning to steal from them.[90] In 1867, Athens subassistant commissioner J. J. Knox had no trouble finding twelve freedmen to arm as a sheriff's posse to track down a notorious "scape gallows"; members of that black community later armed themselves and confronted college students who had assaulted several of their number.[91] During the summer of 1868, the Stewart County freedpeople forced the release on bail of a prisoner held in Lumpkin by threatening to tear down the courthouse and burn down the town.[92]

The Bureau's stand on this type of activity was clear: freedpeople must obey the laws and would be punished if they failed to do so. Tillson believed it was justified to confiscate the weapons of individual freedpeople that had been used in an illegal manner.[93] And in 1867, Alvin B. Clark obtained a detachment of troops to arrest blacks and whites who had engaged in a "riot" and promised to arrest anyone who disturbed the peace or took the law into his own hands.[94] However, concern for the law did not mean the Bureau was unsympathetic to the freedpeople's frustration. In the case of the Jones County woman, Davis Tillson believed that if the accused freedpeople were in fact guilty of the charges of violence against civilian authority, they should be punished. However, he expressed a hope that the civil authorities would deal with the freedmen in a lenient manner because of "the very great provocation offered the freedpeople" by the sheriff and his posse.[95]

The right of law-abiding freedmen to own firearms was, as Davis Tillson recognized, a clearly defined constitutional right that no military or civilian official could abridge regardless of how unpopular it might have been among the whites who feared that, among other things, armed black men would "force the people of the South to extend to them the right of suffrage."[96] "All men, without distinction of color," Tillson advised his agents, "have the right to keep arms to defend their homes, families or themselves."[97] Consequently, when in late 1865 unauthorized Athens whites searched the houses and seized the arms of "peaceable freedmen," the city's subassistant commissioner reminded them of the pertinent articles of the Unites States Constitution that protected black citizens from their unlawful activities.[98]

In the spring of 1866, when a Morgan County planter forcibly removed a pistol from the house of a freedman, the Bureau's response was the same. "You will return the same to him immediately," the Augusta officer warned, and "also bear in mind that a coloured man has [as] much right to keep firearms in his house as a white man."[99] And in July 1866, when the agent for Glascock County disarmed freedpeople because he believed them to be responsible for taking animals from their white neighbors and for disturbing the quiet of the Sabbath with their shooting, Tillson told him that he must return the guns.[100]

Grand juries and inferior courts conveyed petitions to Assistant Commissioner Tillson to disarm freedpeople, but as far as he was concerned, "the laws of this State make no distinction between white and freedpeople." Tillson would allow his subordinates to disarm freedmen if they improperly used their weapons, but with the return of the supremacy of civil law, he advised white Georgians to take their complaints to the courts.[101]

## The Right to Assemble

As the freedmen began to organize into armed groups, the issue became one of whether they had the right to assemble with guns in tow and after 1867 how far they could go to defend their newly won political privileges. Critics of Davis Tillson interpreted his April 1866 confrontation with the Augusta teachers and freedpeople who wished to decorate the graves of Union war dead as a serious disregard for the freedpeople's right to assemble. In fact, Tillson was quite clear about the freedpeople's right to assemble peacefully, even in such apparently inconsequential areas as being able to hold "dances and amusements" without special permission.[102]

In December 1865, Tillson ordered his officer in Savannah to revoke an order permitting white fire companies to parade on the first of the new year. He did so to protect the city's freedpeople because they had already prepared a celebration.[103] More important, when Tillson learned that Warren County whites

were preventing freedmen from attending Loyal League meetings, he promised
that the Bureau would intervene if they continued to interfere with the freedmen's right of peaceable assembly.[104] And when white residents of Dougherty
County complained about the freedpeople's Equal Rights Association meetings, Tillson informed them that the "freed people have the same undoubted
right to organize & carry on any Society or Societies of any character whatever
so long as such an organization does not conflict with the existing laws of the
State of which they are citizens."[105] Legality, however, was important, for the
Bureau and Tillson would not tolerate freedpeople abandoning their work to
attend meetings; contracts limited the right to go awandering during productive agricultural hours.[106]

For the Bureau, therefore, circumstances involving contractual obligations
and potential violence limited an absolute right to assemble and especially to
assemble bearing arms. During Military Reconstruction, the agency's military
masters accepted such limitations and made it policy to prohibit both blacks
and whites from attending public meetings armed; the Bureau also disarmed
freedmen who brought weapons to polling places during elections and continued to accept the imposition of limitations designed to prevent violence.[107]

Subassistant Commissioner Douglas Risley made the Bureau's stand quite
clear. In September 1867, when Brunswick area whites complained about the
freedpeople posting armed guards at secret Union League meetings, a practice
common across the state, Risley compared those meetings to Masonic assem-
blies that employed armed guards and argued that no authority, civil or military, could violate their secrecy. However, there were limits to what the freedpeople should and could do. Risley did not object to the growth of Republican
political organizations among the freedpeople, which by their nature required
meetings; in fact, he had earlier expressed his approval because they gave the
ex-slaves a sense of power that prevented them from being manipulated by
whites. Still, he allowed that "it is a violation of existing orders for members to
meet armed in any manner." Personally, Risley believed such an order made
sense "in these times of distrust and excitement" when relations between black
and white Georgians were becoming increasingly combustible because of politics. Furthermore, no freedman should neglect their labor to attend political
meetings.[108] To the end of its days, the Bureau insisted upon abiding by the
rules and argued that freedpeople should leave their protection to the agency
and the military.[109] The Bureau could oversee white Georgia for only so long,
for the security of black rights depended on the willingness of local authorities
to do their jobs with fairness and impartiality that went wanting in the state.

## The Bureau and Civil Authorities

Davis Tillson received a sufficient number of complaints to indicate that, despite the legislature's modification of the black man's civil status, despite the federal Civil Rights Act, and despite the presence of the Freedmen's Bureau, Georgia's system of justice continued to deprive the freedpeople of more than their economic rights. Too frequently, known perpetrators remained at large, but bringing a case to trial did not guarantee that a freedman would obtain justice at the hands of the civil authorities. Once in court, if he had the good fortune of dealing with a fair judge, he had to reckon with a white jury, because freedpeople were excluded from that service.[110] And all too frequently, the very authorities who were supposed to protect the freedpeople were either derelict in their duty or worse, as in the case of the Pulaski County justice of the peace who participated in clandestine raids against the freedpeople.[111]

At the end of July 1866, Captain George Walbridge, Tillson's inspector general, confirmed this assessment after reviewing conditions in Muscogee County — conditions, he noted, that were common to other areas he had visited. The frequent complaint concerned "the dilatory & delaying manner in which the civil authorities administer justice where freedmen were concerned." The courts shrewdly "do not refuse to act but before the cases are reached the freedmen's patience is exhausted and be ready to starve while cases of white men appear to be easily reached & disposed of." The effects were all the more damaging for the impressions they made on the freedmen. Delays bred distrust and convinced blacks that there was no justice in the "white man's court."[112]

As Tillson had learned in other situations, sometimes a threat issued in the proper tone could influence civil authorities. Tillson, for example, made it clear that he would interfere with courts that refused to hear black testimony. In September 1866, Tillson learned that the judge of the Miller County court had charged the grand jury to admit black testimony only from freedmen who were involved in cases. The assistant commissioner warned the judge to pay closer attention to state law and promised to interfere with his court if he did not protect the freedpeople's right to equal treatment.[113] Also, Tillson was willing to impose himself into the judicial process when it appeared that authorities were denying a freedperson the right to a speedy trial.[114]

In July 1866, the agent at Lexington in Oglethorpe County reported a case in which the jury delivered a guilty verdict despite evidence proving the accused had not committed the larcenous act with which he had been charged. "The trial of this case convinces me of two things," wrote agent F. J. Robinson. "One is, that the *County Court* is a nuisance that should be abated—another is, that there is a class of men in the south, and they generally compose the *Petit Juries*, who will not do the negro *Justice* even when under oath." Tillson, in turn, presented the civil authorities of Oglethorpe with an ultimatum: guarantee equal justice or be subject to martial law. The unspecified result of the warning left Robinson optimistic that in the future "we shall have no complaint to make in regard to the acts of the civil authorities of this county."[115]

During Sibley's administration, even with Military Reconstruction, it remained difficult to obtain justice for the freedpeople in the civilian courts. Sibley's men continued to challenge cases in which freedpeople were denied the right to testify, and General John Pope attempted to correct the problem of all-white juries by ordering officials to select individuals from lists of registered voters, but the impact appeared to be minimal.[116] Agents and officers continued to witness injustices to the point where one described the administration of civil law in Houston and Dooly Counties as a "farce," and another believed that in the Athens region it was "exceedingly rare" for a jury to find a case in favor of a black man.[117] The only hope for freedpeople in Gordon County, according to agent C. B. Blacker, was to have all county officials removed from office.[118]

Christian Raushenberg witnessed proceedings in southwestern Georgia that, because of the various delaying tactics employed by whites involved in the cases, forced freedpeople to choose between their jobs or loitering around the courthouse waiting for their cases to come to their resolutions. Complainants missed court dates, witnesses failed to appear before the bench, and cases died "technical death in due form of law while the freedman at home curses the law and the white man."[119] Whether in the southwestern part of the state or the northeast, many freedpeople did not expect to receive justice in a civil tribunal.[120]

Despite the restrictions under which they worked and the frustrations that they experienced, Bureau men continued to do what they could to secure justice for the freedpeople. Subassistant Commissioner J. Murray Hoag's "governing rule" was "Simple justice for all," which led him to use whatever power he had to "shield the innocent."[121] Carlos de la Mesa went to court with a freedman to make sure he received a fair hearing and helped to secure the dismissal of the false charges.[122] Sibley continued Tillson's practice of petitioning Governor Jenkins to use his influence to bring the murderers of freedpeople to justice.[123] Augusta subassistant commissioner Catley interceded for a freedman who fled arrest for stealing because the accused had the idea "if he was arrested, it would follow he would be convicted."[124] And agent Andrew B. Clark intervened with a southwestern Georgia jurist to have exorbitant bail reduced for two freedmen, while complaining to his superiors about the continued use of whipping by the county court to punish freedpeople.[125]

In April 1868, Albany subassistant commissioner O. H. Howard, after a year of dealing with intransigent whites and watching his agency's power dwindle, continued to work for the freedpeople in his southwestern Georgia jurisdiction. In March 1868, a sixteen-year-old freedman accidentally shot and killed a Calhoun County white man visiting Dougherty County, having mistaken him for a bear. Calhoun County officials, without proper warrant or jurisdiction, arrested the boy. Relying only on the testimony of white men, they committed him to jail to await trial, a period that would result in months of imprisonment. Howard obtained a writ of habeas corpus and had the case reheard before the Superior Court of Dougherty County, where the boy was found not guilty.[126]

As Bureau men understood, they now lacked any authority to discipline the civilian officials who attempted to derail their efforts in these cases, but they could turn to the military to have the most obstreperous offenders removed from office.[127] Any action required more paperwork of the Bureau men. The charges agents and officers made had to be more than angry complaints; they had to be specific and documented.[128] Furthermore, General George G. Meade, the second commander of the Third Military District, did not appreciate Bureau initiative if it interfered with the civil authorities' duties and the proper channels for redress of grievances.[129] In fact, Meade criticized O. H. Howard for putting into writing his complaints about the apathetic enforcement of the laws, because such criticism reflected poorly on the general's administration.[130] In the end, although Meade's predecessor, John Pope, had removed officials from Bartow, Cobb, Lumpkin, Milton, and Muscogee Counties, the examples did not appear to have any wide-ranging or lasting impact on how local authorities viewed the Bureau, the freedpeople, or Reconstruction, especially when Meade only cautiously interfered with the civil system.[131]

As Bureau men would have admitted by the spring of 1868, the reorganization of the agency under Caleb Sibley had not succeeded in correcting the abuses that became common implements of white policy before the end of Davis Tillson's administration. Little that the Bureau did seemed to have convinced the ex-rebels to administer justice with an open mind or to treat the freedpeople in an equitable manner. The presence of the Bureau supported by the military offered some hope for securing the freedpeople's rights, and its agents and officers continued to act as advocates for justice even as their power waned, but conditions demanded that at least small detachments of soldiers be routine fixtures by the sides of all Bureau men. Even the steady use of force, however, would have produced only temporary success. As Tillson understood, a lasting change could come only through white acceptance of the goodness of the new system. But in July 1868, after serving over a year with the Bureau, Athens agent Howell Flournoy concluded that nothing had changed for the better; in fact, he lamented, he had "never seen such times."[132]

In the end, when the freedpeople lost the support of Bureau men backed by force, they often lost their chance for justice in the courts of Georgia. In October 1868, steadfast Irwinton agent H. de F. Young found that his efforts to guide freedpeople through civil court proceedings always failed, with the freedpeople having their cases dismissed by jurists who assigned them court costs; he concluded that only military force could guarantee the freedpeople justice.[133] After reporting cases of politically motivated violence and murder in October, Christian Rauschenberg saw no hope for justice in his southwestern Georgia jurisdiction even if cases went as far as a court hearing because "the juries are but too often men, imbued with the same spirit of hatred and prejudice as the criminals."[134] No wonder another agent concluded in September 1868, "They have but little if any chance before the law, as things now stand."[135]

# Epilogue

During the latter half of 1868, Carlos de la Mesa, the busy subassistant commissioner based in Rome, continued to use his diminished authority to act as a conscientious guardian of northwestern Georgia's freedpeople. Time, however, was short. De la Mesa was not only trying to solve as many of the freedpeople's problems as he could because he felt so obligated. He was also clearing his books, turning over complaints to civil authorities, and instructing the freedpeople in the procedures they would need to follow once he was gone. On November 16, he ordered his agents to do the same and to prepare to ship their official papers to Washington. Before the year ended, de la Mesa, who had first entered the Bureau's service during Tillson's administration, would be on his way home to Grafton, Massachusetts.[1]

Bureau men across the state repeated de la Mesa's activities, for the government no longer required their services in the much reduced agency.[2] In December 1868 and January 1869, Assistant Commissioner Lewis received transportation orders for the agents and officers who planned to return to their homes outside Georgia.[3] By the end of January 1869, only nine officers and civilians remained to assist him at headquarters and in the field as the Bureau spent its last months through July 1870 furthering education and processing bounty claims for black veterans.[4]

The departing Bureau men, already frustrated by months of impotence and danger, were glad to be returning to more congenial surroundings, but they left the state knowing that their work remained unfinished. Surveying his jurisdiction in Richmond, Columbia, Lincoln, and Wilkes Counties in northeastern Georgia in late 1868, P. J. O'Rourke, the Union veteran and former Pennsylvanian who would soon be on his way home to Louisville, Kentucky, warned J. R. Lewis of the freedpeople's dismal prospects. "Society is demoralized," he informed his superior. "The conditions of the Blacks is going from bad to worse, assassinations and murder stalks abroad, law and equity set at defiance and nothing but the strong military arm of the government can restore peace and order."[5]

Indeed, during 1868, the last year of extensive Bureau activity in Georgia, agents and officers worried that the agency would not leave behind much of a legacy for the freedpeople. In the Macon subdistrict, New Jersey native Daniel Losey, the agent for Houston and Dooly Counties, assessed his jurisdiction in November 1868 and concluded that the few years of Bureau activity in the state had failed to change the hearts and minds of ex-masters. Planters were scheming to keep down the price of labor and warning the freedpeople to expect stern treatment now that the Bureau was "run out." "My impression," Losey offered, "is that the freed people are going to have pretty hard times."[6]

Other Bureau men concurred with Losey's assessment. In March 1868, even when the Bureau could still resort to the power of Military Reconstruction, agent William C. Morrill offered a distressing prediction from his southwestern Georgia jurisdiction. Whites were now "more bitterly hostile to the government than at any time during or since the close of the war," he privately informed John R. Lewis. "I do not see how a State government here can be established with safety to the United States or humanity to the colored race."[7] Subassistant Commissioner Henry Catley could not predict a better future for the freedpeople in his Augusta subdistrict, where whites subjected them to political persecution throughout the summer and fall of 1868. In August 1868, Catley, who would serve out the year as the Bureau's officer in Augusta even as fear for his own safety rendered him incapable of doing his job, determined that without the presence of the federal government the freedpeople would be in worse condition than when they had been slaves.[8] And in September 1868, O. H. Howard, the Albany subassistant commissioner who would remain with the agency as an education officer, concluded, "The present aspect of affairs, warrants no reasonable hope, that there is either happiness or prosperity at hand for the freedpeople."[9]

Bureau men probably felt this way in part because Georgia's freedpeople constantly reminded them that there remained much to be done. In the process, the freedpeople confirmed that, despite decisions made in Washington, despite the agency's flaws, and despite the complaints of a few black politicians, they considered the Bureau to be their agency. As Carlos A. de la Mesa had learned, the freedpeople offered no better favorable testimony for the agency than their continued use of the Bureau even as it began to put its affairs in order. Georgia's ex-slaves insisted on reminding Bureau men that they were their advocates and arbitrators for all types of complaints ranging from the trivial to the serious. Freedpeople in the Hawkinsville area continued to turn to the Bureau to help them collect debts, and those in the counties around Columbus, Georgia, looked to the Bureau for solutions to problems concerning spouses, employers, pilfered watches, and borrowed clothing.[10] Such activity led the Hawkinsville agent to conclude as late as August 1868 that "the freedmen in this section of the county look to me for protection."[11]

The reaction of some freedpeople to the news of the agency's contraction and termination provided further witness to their understanding that the Bureau was an ally in their efforts to secure rights commensurate with their new status. In November 1867, the freedpeople in the Carnesville area "began to express their feelings of forelorn hope since they heard the Bureau was to cease next year."[12] In August 1868, when they learned that the return to civilian government would severely restrict the Bureau's authority, the freedpeople in the Butler area held a two-day "Prayer and Revival" meeting "with large attendance." Their reaction reminded the local agent that they were concerned about how they would now collect what was due to them for their labor.[13] And in January 1870, freedpeople at a meeting in Augusta expressed their desire to keep the Bureau in Georgia after they learned that it would be abolished.[14]

In time, the fears shared by Bureau men and freedpeople became the constant reality for Georgia's black population. Despite the use of moral suasion, compromise, law, and armed force, the agency had failed to convince ex-masters to allow their former slaves to be full participants in the civic and economic life of a reconstructed state. The Bureau's efforts to assist in the freedpeople's entry into electoral politics, for example, failed to make a lasting impression on those whites who believed that the political question was "whether we are to be freemen or slaves[,] whether we are to have a white man's government or [be] ruled by Radical oppressors."[15]

The Bureau could do little for the political future of the freedmen by the time Georgia embarked on another effort at Reconstruction after the expulsion of its black representatives from the state legislature in September 1868. Despite the reseating of those black lawmakers in January 1870, the freedmen's political triumph soon deteriorated into a political rout. The election of that year, accompanied by the same kinds of violent tactics that the Bureau had observed and reported on other political occasions, returned a Democratic majority.[16]

With white conservatives in charge, the "redemption" of Georgia brought about the constriction of black participation in the public political life of the state. The lack of a black political voice, for example, allowed the legislature to pass laws that were designed to keep the freedpeople in a subservient position. By the beginning of the twentieth century, through the use of such devices as cumulative poll taxes and limited registration periods, white Democrats had succeeded in discouraging approximately 90 percent of the eligible black voters of Georgia from participating in electoral politics.[17]

Politics never commanded the uniform attention of the Bureau men, especially during the critical years of the Tillson administration when Bureau guidance might have provided some assistance in organizing the freedpeople before they acquired the vote.[18] The coordination of the state's educational efforts for the freedpeople, on the other hand, was one of the Bureau's great works almost from the arrival of the agency in Georgia; not even the most conservative Bureau man could object to the elevating qualities of schooling for the freedpeople. The school buildings constructed with Bureau help remained in the hands of the freedpeople and the missionary associations after the agency closed down its operations providing at least a "seed" for future growth. However, even in this area, the accomplishments of agency were limited. It was more than symbolic that in 1875 whites stood by as Macon's Lewis High School went up in smoke, torched by an arsonist.[19] Its namesake's ideas about education were no more acceptable to most white Georgians after the efforts of the Bureau came to an end than they had been while John R. Lewis had been on duty with the agency.

As the Reconstruction of Georgia drew to a close, the freedpeople came to rely more on their own initiative, as the Bureau had hoped, and the free public school system inaugurated by the law passed in October 1870. In the end, the segregated tuition-free schools established by this law had a greater impact on black education than the Bureau-sponsored schools, at least in making available some kind of educational opportunity to the state's black children beyond the urban areas of the state. In 1880, 43 percent of Georgia's black children enrolled in public elementary schools, a substantially larger percentage than the 5 percent reached by Northern schoolteachers in each year from 1865 to 1870. In the early twentieth century, Georgia freedpeople and their decendants achieved a 70 percent literacy rate, a dramatic increase from a rate of 4 or 5 percent immediately before the war. Regardless, by the turn of the century, the segregated and inferior public educational system that would severely limit the opportunities of black Southerners was in place in Georgia.[20]

Davis Tillson had accepted the importance of education in shaping freedom, but in his mind schooling was subordinate to work in determining the future of the freedpeople. Indeed, almost all Yankee Bureau men had great expectations for the new work arrangements that they brought to Georgia's fields. Nevertheless, free labor, Tillson's "talisman power," hardly fulfilled its promise of economic independence and homesteads for the freedpeople any more than John Lewis's belief in education fulfilled its own.

During the Bureau's existence, there certainly were significant examples of communal and individual enterprise that supported Tillson's expectations. In December 1866, for example, a freedmen's colony arrived at their newly acquired 700-acre plantation at Elliot's Bluff in Camden County, and by April 1867 they had paid $300 of their $650 mortgage. At the end of 1867, Frances Butler paid each of her workers as much as $200 to $300, and they promptly left her to buy land. And by the end of 1869, a number of freedpeople in Houston County had accumulated 100 to 600 acres of land, and an enterprising company of freedpeople had purchased 1,500 acres.[21]

Toward the end of the Bureau's tenure in Georgia, John R. Lewis happily reported to Bureau education chief John Alvord, who in turn enjoyed pointing out to his superior, O. O. Howard, that there was a sufficiency of examples of black land ownership supporting the Bureau's assumptions about free labor.[22] Indeed, if crops were good, planters fair, and workers thrifty, freedpeople had a chance to taste the fruits of their hard work, just as the Bureau had promised them. By 1874, those freedpeople who had given Lewis and Alvord some hope were among a class of black Georgians who had acquired 338,769 acres of land throughout the state, a figure that steadily increased to 1,075,073 by 1900.[23]

There was, however, less room for optimism than the Bureau men would have Washington headquarters believe. Frances Butler's assessment of the land deals that her workers accepted in 1867, for example, also suggested a serious flaw in the Bureau's expectations for a reasonable and rational economic system, and it provided just one more example of how the white Georgians rejected the spirit of Reconstruction. Her workers, she explained, could only buy poor land from unscrupulous low-class whites because no gentleman would sell worthwhile property to freedpeople.[24] In postbellum Georgia, white concerns about preserving a social and economic hierarchy based on race dampened the willingness of white land owners to allow freedpeople to become like themselves, consequently limiting even successful ex-slaves' access to property.[25]

When planters did sell off property, it was generally the land that they valued least. Consequently, freedpeople's real estate holdings were small and the land itself usually marginal. Whites at similar levels of wealth were more successful in acquiring real estate, suggesting that there was more than economic dynamics at work here. In 1878 in Coweta County, Georgia, for example, of the 573 whites who reported taxable assets valued at $200 or less, 43 reported real estate holdings; of the 737 blacks reporting in that category, only 8 reported real estate holdings. The average value of the land owned by these Coweta whites was $239.18; the average value of black-owned farms was $162. In 1880 throughout the state, freedpeople held only 1.6 percent of all reported agricultural acreage.[26]

W. E. B. Du Bois's study of fifty-six counties in Georgia reveals that in 1899 over 30 percent of the blacks who owned farmland held less than ten acres, suggesting that these individuals had become economically marginalized either by choice or by circumstance. Another 27 percent did somewhat better, owning more than ten but less than forty acres. Almost 47 percent of the black land owners reported an assessed value of their farmland at less than $100, and slightly more than 31 percent reported values in the range of over $100 and under $300.[27]

After the Bureau's termination, freedpeople continued to be more likely to make some kind of rental, tenant, or share arrangement to gain some independence in their workaday lives. In Thomas County, for example, by the turn of the century blacks made up about 47 percent of the agricultural population. However, only 277 blacks owned land out of 1,202 land owners; 1,133 of the 1,777 tenants in the county were black.[28] Such arrangements placed limits on the promise of emancipation and created problems that lasted into the next century, problems that belied the intentions and the expectations of the Bureau men.

The Freedmen's Bureau of Davis Tillson, John R. Lewis, C. A. de la Mesa, and P. J. O'Rourke, then, had a limited impact on the shape of race relations and the advancement of freedpeople in Georgia after the agency's demise. The fact that it was an imperfect, short-lived institution, its functions severely limited by nineteenth-century attitudes about the propriety of encouraging such an extraordinary federal agency beyond the immediate emergency of a few postwar years, explains much of its failure to alter the economic, legal, and political landscapes of Georgia. Nonetheless, the Georgia Bureau's assistant commissioners, officers, and agents interpreted policy and dealt with the rapidly changing circumstances of Reconstruction in ways they thought would best serve the interests of all concerned.

Troubled by small resources, organizational inadequacies, a dearth of innovative ideas, and limited time in which to map out long-range programs—all the consequences of the intellectual climate that created the agency—the Bureau appeared to be an agency whose architects had designed a blueprint for institutional failure. Annoyed by black Georgians who rightly insisted on having their say in the definition of freedom, the Bureau worked with a benign paternalism that cast the freedpeople in the role of wards under the guardianship of the nation. However, although these limitations made the agency's task a formidable one, Yankee Bureau men assumed that Georgia's ex-slaves could overcome the vestiges of slavery with hard work and education, if they received equal protection under the laws of the state and the nation. Even for the much-maligned Davis Tillson, the freedman's situation had not been fixed by the first contract signed after the surrender. Unfortunately, white Georgians assumed otherwise, resisted change at every opportunity, and stymied the relatively progressive goals of the Bureau and the higher expectations of freedpeople.

Given the agency's goals, the resources at its disposal, and the understanding that it was a finite institution, Davis Tillson might have formulated the most logical plan for dealing with the problems that faced the freedpeople in 1865. His efforts to convert and co-opt white Georgians were reasonable. They realistically acknowledged the Bureau's limitations while recognizing the fact that black and white Georgians would be working out their problems without the oversight of the agency within a very short time.

Tillson's plan, however, was flawed. The assistant commissioner overestimated the power of his free-labor arguments and the reasonableness of white Georgians, and he underestimated the vehemence with which whites would oppose any effort to subvert the old racial hierarchy. As Tillson had learned after a few months' residence in Georgia, all other difficulties paled before the violent intransigence of the state's white population. Encouraged by President Johnson, cheered by the Bureau's inadequacies, emboldened by an ineffective military presence, white Georgians came to direct the course of Reconstruction to the point where even before they had reclaimed political control of the state, they had made great strides in regaining economic control of their land and labor without reference to federal policymakers and their enforcers.[29]

Certainly, the Bureau had helped the freedpeople in many specific instances of white injustice and in a broader sense by reinforcing the freedpeople's understanding that they had the right to claim equal treatment under the laws of the land. A reunited family, a secured crop, a bag of cornmeal, transportation to a better workplace, and assistance provided to a teacher who taught children how to read all touched the lives of ex-slaves in important ways, just as an agent's or an officer's confirmation of an ex-slave's sense of self-worth made it more difficult for an ex-master to act in an absolute manner when dealing with black workers. But in the end, ex-masters and ex-slaves continued to work out their long-term relationships influenced more by old prejudices, individual expectations, and the requirements of agriculture than by the Bureau's short stay in the state. The Bureau failed to convert white Georgians and therefore failed to create an atmosphere in which Yankee ideology could take root.

Early in his administration, Davis Tillson turned to bayonets to force whites to change their minds about the freedpeople, free labor, and justice, but he did not expect the military to be a permanent fixture in the state.[30] By the time the Bureau was beginning to close up its operations, however, it was a commonly held opinion among agents and field officers that only the constant presence of soldiers could protect the freedpeople and force their ex-masters to treat them fairly. R. C. Anthony, the agent stationed at Warrenton, made this plain when he worried about the whites who were obstructing him in the performance of his duty before the presidential election of 1868. "I want to see such men taken up and dealt with so that they will respect the laws," he explained, a goal that might be furthered as long as he had access to the use of troops. However, he warned that once troops left the area, whites "will make mischief here." Reasoned arguments or appeals to justice made no impression on them. "I cannot see how we are to enforce the laws at this place without troops."[31] The good-intentioned Bureau had tried to convince both freedpeople and ex-masters of the benefits of shared responsibilities and obligations, but white Georgians stubbornly shaped a Reconstruction that produced consequences unforeseen by the likes of Saxton, Tillson, Sibley, and Lewis. Eventually, as did the nation itself, Bureau men turned their backs on the freedpeople and Georgia and got on with their lives.

Caleb Sibley did further duty during Reconstruction as commander of the District of Georgia from the time he turned over the assistant commissioner's office to John R. Lewis until his retirement at the end of February 1869. He then returned north, as Georgia had nothing more to offer him. He died in Chicago in February 1875.[32]

After Rufus Saxton left the South Carolina Bureau, he returned to the regular army and to duties in the quartermaster department. His more mundane assignments did not completely dampen the idealism that had lately been so much a part of his career. While he was stationed in Atlanta, he found the time to teach in the freedmen's school there. He continued to serve with the quartermaster department until 1888, when he retired as a colonel and resided in the nation's capital until his death in February 1908.[33]

By way of contrast, Edward A. Wild fittingly engaged in a much more exotic post-Bureau career than the man who had supervised his work in Georgia. After completing his Georgia duty, he dug for silver on the West Coast and in South America, an occupation not too far afield from his earlier attempt to dig up gold in the backyards of Wilkes County's erstwhile rebels. The general met his end far from his native Massachusetts in Medellín, Colombia, in August 1891.[34]

By the time of the Bureau's demise, a few agents had already followed John Emory Bryant into politics, sharing the fortunes of the Republican Party as Reconstruction waned. As late as 1875, the former Augusta agent could issue a call to his Northern colleagues in support of free labor by recounting the continued efforts of white Georgians to reassert their complete control over their ex-slaves. Unfortunately, his concerns were no longer shared by increasingly respectable Northern Republicans. In the 1870s, Yankees like John Randolph Lewis exchanged their desire to help the freedpeople for an interest in business and capital expansion, a mutually agreeable course for the old enemies of the 1860s to pursue.[35]

John Randolph Lewis's post-Bureau career reads like a parable illustrating the shifting concerns of the nation. In the fall of 1870, not long after his retirement from the regular army as a full colonel, Lewis accepted Governor Rufus Bullock's offer to take on the duties of Georgia's first state school superintendent. It was a noble task whose success would benefit white as well as black children. The appointment might also provide Lewis with an income sufficient to replenish his personal resources now drained by his honest but less than lucrative Bureau service.[36]

The colonel's administrative experience as well as his faith in the power of education made him a good choice for implementing the particulars of the October legislation that authorized the establishment of the state's public school system. However, his position as an outsider and his association with the Bullock regime worked against him. Despite his attempt to open the doors of Georgia's common schools during the fall of 1871, he failed to achieve his goal. Funding problems, indifference, lack of confidence, and a stormy relationship with the Democratic legislature prevented Lewis from accomplishing what he once called the work of his life.

With the redemption of the state, white Democrats were able to rid themselves of their Yankee school superintendent, one of the last of the prominent carpetbaggers left in Georgia. In October 1871, Bullock absconded, avoiding the pending investigation of his administration's alleged improprieties. Asserting its power, the Democratic legislature called for a special election, which resulted in James M. Smith's assumption of the governorship. Shortly thereafter in January 1871, the new executive gave Lewis's job to Gustavus J. Orr, and the Georgia educator succeeded where the Yankee soldier and Bureau officer had failed.[37]

No doubt aware of his worn-out welcome, Lewis left the state to pursue business interests in Des Moines, Iowa, and in Buffalo, New York. However, after a decade of harsh winters, Lewis longed for the mild Southern climate. In 1880, he returned to Georgia, where his second residence nurtured activities that were far from his earlier Reconstruction duties. For the last nineteen years of his life, he conducted himself as a respectable businessman and booster rather than as a reformer.

Always a Republican, John R. Lewis served as Atlanta's postmaster during Benjamin Harrison's presidency. Never one to forget his past associations, he was an active member of the Grand Army of the Republic. Still, his concern was business, not ex-slaves. From 1883 to 1889, Lewis operated the Atlanta Rubber Company, and from 1895 to 1899 he was president of the Summit Land Company. He also acted as secretary *pro tem* for the Atlanta Cotton Exposition of 1881 and as secretary of the Cotton State and International Exposition of 1895.

Although he apparently made a respectable livelihood, great financial success seemed to elude him. He "had many hard struggles" and had "not been able to acquire much of this worlds goods," prompting him to call on his old Bureau superior, O. O. Howard, for assistance in securing an appointment for his son Fred to the military academy and again for himself as a commissioner to the Paris Exposition of 1900. As so many veterans had done before him, he explained his qualifications for this attention in part by his past service in the war as well as by his "long years of work for the elevation of the colored people, & the upbuilding of the south."[38] Lewis's son eventually earned his army commission, but his efforts to win a sinecure for himself were unsuccessful. With his health failing, the colonel decided to leave Atlanta sometime in 1898 or 1899 for Seattle, probably to be closer to his son Harry, who was a gold miner residing in Dawson City. Illness, however, forced his return to his sister's home in Chicago, where he died in February 1900.[39]

The *Atlanta Constitution* mourned the loss of the once-shunned Bureau man and carpetbagger with a flattering obituary. The paper neglected to mention, however, the Bureau service of the city's adopted son, no doubt out of respect for the deceased. The etiquette of sectional rapprochement allowed the *Constitution* to recount Lewis's valorous war record and his GAR activities, but it discouraged discussion of the Bureau in polite print. According to the paper, Lewis simply "came to Georgia to reside" after the war.[40]

Davis Tillson's post-Bureau stay in Georgia proved to be no more successful than Lewis's civilian education work in the state. Tillson put his fortune and future on the line when he embarked on his planting operation in Bryan County. His effort at earning a competency in cotton fared no better than those efforts of the freedpeople he had tried to help.

Acting as his own overseer, he supervised the planting of his land at the outset of the 1867 season. In March he was optimistic, telling Caleb Sibley that he "liked the life, although it has many cares and not a few vexations." Those "vexations," however, proved to be decisive. Excessive rains and caterpillars ruined his crop, and the coastal county's fever shook his health.[41]

Despite such hardships, Tillson continued to believe that there was money to be made in planting, or so he assured O. O. Howard, but by November 1867, Tillson had decided not to stay in Georgia to prove his point. "I should have the courage to go on planting," he explained, "but that my wife is very much dissatisfied with living in this country where we have no society and where our nearest neighbor is a mile distant."[42]

Tillson understood the consequences of his failure: he would have to look elsewhere for a way to provide for his family, and his prospects appeared to be poor. His first thought was to return to the service "in some humble position," preferably as an army paymaster.[43] The erstwhile planter never received a new commission, but he eventually improved his lot outside Georgia. Returning to his hometown of Rockland, Maine, the former engineer became involved with the lime business and developed a lucrative hundred-acre granite works on Hurricane Island. Using "powerful patent Steam Cranes" of his own design, he found that the islands of Maine much more readily yielded their rock than Georgia's soil did its cotton. In the process he earned his fortune.[44]

At some point in his post-Bureau career as a businessman, Tillson found a way to make money in the South by investing in Florida orange groves. However, unlike John R. Lewis, the former assistant commissioner devoted his civic attention to his Yankee home. An active member of the Grand Army of the Republic, he became involved in local affairs and contributed his money as well as his time to improving Rockland by expending over $100,000 on "Tillson's wharf." At the time of his death on April 30, 1895, he was "one of the best known citizens of the State," and to this day historically aware Rockland residents refer to him as "the General."[45]

The *New York Times* considered Rockland's prominent civil war veteran to be worthy of an obituary in its columns, as did the *Kennebec Journal* of Augusta, Maine, and the *Daily Eastern Argus* of Portland. The eulogists recorded Tillson's military, business, and civic careers in some detail, courteously omitting his short-lived planting venture. They also preserved his good name by neglecting to mention his postwar service in Tennessee and Georgia.[46] With Reconstruction an unpleasant memory, even Northerners chose to forget the Freedmen's Bureau.

# Abbreviations

| | |
|---|---|
| Agt | Agent |
| AMA-Ga | American Missionary Association Papers, Georgia, Amistad Research Center, Tulane University, New Orleans, Louisiana |
| BRFAL-Ga (M798) | Records of the Assistant Commissioner for the State of Georgia, Bureau of Refugees, Freedmen, and Abandoned Lands, National Archives Microfilm Publication M798 |
| BRFAL-Ga | Records of the Subordinate Field Offices for the State of Georgia, Bureau of Refugees, Freedmen, and Abandoned Lands, Record Group 105, National Archives |
| BRFAL-SC (M869) | Records of the Assistant Commissioner for the State of South Carolina, Bureau of Refugees, Freedmen, and Abandoned Lands, National Archives Microfilm Publication M869 |
| BRFAL-Tn (M999) | Records of the Assistant Commissioner for the State of Tennessee, Bureau of Refugees, Freedmen, and Abandoned Lands, National Archives Microfilm Publication M999 |
| Dept. of Ga. | Department of Georgia, United States Army Continental Command, Record Group 393, National Archives |
| Dist. (and Subdist.) of Ga. | District (and Subdistrict) of Georgia, United States Army Continental Command, Record Group 393, National Archives |
| (Ed)BRFAL-Ga (M799) | Records of the Superintendent of Education for the State of Georgia, Bureau of Refugees, Freedmen, and Abandoned Lands, National Archives Microfilm Publication M799 |
| GDAH | Georgia Department of Archives and History, Atlanta, Georgia |

| | |
|---|---|
| Ku Klux Conspiracy | *Testimony Taken by the Joint Select Committee to Inquire into the Condition of Affairs in the Late Insurrectionary States* (13 vols., serials 1484–1496; Washington, D.C.: Government Printing Office, 1872) |
| LR | Letters Received, Entered Letters Received, or Registered Letters Received |
| (LR)BRFAL (M752) | Registers and Letters Received by the Commissioner of the Bureau of Refugees, Freedmen, and Abandoned Lands, National Archives Microfilm Publication M752 |
| LS | Letters Sent |
| Official Records | *The War of the Rebellion: A Compilation of the Official Records of the Union and Confederate Armies* (70 vols. in 128; Washington, D.C.: Government Printing Office, 1880–1901) |
| RG | Record Group, National Archives, Washington, D.C. |
| (RI)BRFAL (M742) | Select Series of Records Issued by the Commissioner of the Bureau of Refugees, Freedmen, and Abandoned Lands, National Archives Microfilm Publication M742 |
| SAC | Subassistant Commissioner |
| Surgeon's Records, BRFAL-Ga | Records of the Surgeon-in- Chief for the State of Georgia, Bureau of Refugees, Freedmen, and Abandoned Lands, Record Group 105, National Archives, Washington, D.C., microfilm, University of Georgia Science Library, Athens, Georgia |
| ULR | Unregistered or Unentered Letters Received |

*Note*: Brevet, volunteer, or regular army ranks have been omitted from the notes unless they are essential for identifying the correspondents, the location of a document, or the importance of the document. Orders and circulars originated in the offices that generated the collections cited as the source of the material unless otherwise noted in the note or the text (for example, an order or circular identified as being located in the collection BRFAL-Ga [M798] originated in the assistant commissioner's headquarters).

# Notes

## Introduction

1. *Statutes at Large of the United States* (1863–1865), 13:507. For the background of the establishment of the Bureau see Bentley, *A History of the Freedmen's Bureau*, chaps. 1–3; and Belz, *A New Birth of Freedom*, 69–112. Bentley's book is the standard study of the Bureau and surpasses Peirce's monograph, *The Freedmen's Bureau*. Axinn and Levin, *Social Welfare*, 94, refer to the Freedmen's Bureau as the first federal welfare agency. I consider it a regulatory agency, especially because of the work it did supervising the new labor arrangements.

2. Rawick, ed., *The American Slave*, vol. 8: *Arkansas*, pt. 1, 68.

3. For personnel see Registers of Civilian Agents, 1865–1867; Station Books, 1: 1867–1868 and 2:1869; and Rosters of Officers and Civilian Agents, Dec. 1866, Aug. 1867–Nov. 1868, reel 35, BRFAL-Ga (M798).

4. For the size of the state and a convenient tabulation of Georgia population figures, see Spalding, "Georgia," 518, 537.

5. R. Saxton to J. E. Bryant, Aug. 15, 1865, John Emory Bryant Papers, Duke University, Durham, N.C.

6. The best survey of the recent writing on the Freedmen's Bureau may be found in LaWanda Cox's historiographical essay on Reconstruction, "From Emancipation to Segregation: National Policy and Southern Blacks," 224–28. This essay should be supplemented with Barry Crouch's *Freedmen's Bureau and Black Texans*, chap. 1. Although Crouch's primary concern is Texas, he uses his footnotes in this chapter to present an excellent assessment of the literature dealing with the Bureau. A balanced if brief recent assessment of the Bureau may be found in Eric Foner, *Reconstruction: America's Unfinished Revolution, 1863–1877*, 142–52. Crouch's book is a fine example of the benefits of placing the Bureau within its proper nineteenth-century context, but also see Richard Lowe, "The Freedmen's Bureau and Local Black Leadership," for a moderate assessment that notes that the Virginia Bureau was not as bad as its modern critics argue nor as good as its present supporters contend.

7. Howard, *Autobiography*, 2:286. Horace Greeley's *New York Tribune* contributed to this reputation and was especially troublesome to Tillson, even accusing him of saying that blacks were better off as slaves than as free men. D. Tillson to O. O. Howard, Dec. 11, 1865, reel 20, (LR)BRFAL (M752); D. Tillson to O. O. Howard, July 3, 1865, Howard Papers, Bowdoin College, Brunswick, Maine.

8. Edmund L. Drago in "Black Georgia during Reconstruction," 57, 59–62, and in *Black Politicians and Reconstruction in Georgia*, 113–16, 131, and Ruth Currie-McDaniel in her biography of Tillson's Augusta rival, *Carpetbagger of Conscience: A Biography of John Emory Bryant*, 46–47, 55–59, 68, 70–73, make this distinction, but Currie-McDaniel's assessment of Tillson especially relies too willingly on her subject's view of the assistant commissioner. For other historians who emphasize Tillson's conservatism and lack of sympathy for the freedmen see Bentley, *Freedmen's Bureau*, 69; John A. Carpenter, *Sword and Olive Branch: Oliver Otis Howard*, 127–28; Jacqueline Jones, *Soldiers of Light and Love*, 29, 55; and James L. Owen, "The Negro in Georgia during Reconstruction," 233. See especially William S. McFeely, *Yankee Stepfather*, 121–22, 202, 248–49, and Russell Duncan, *Freedom's Shore: Tunis Campbell and the Georgia Freedmen*, 29–35.

Steven W. Engerrand's Marxist interpretation of Reconstruction, "'Now Scratch or Die': The Genesis of Capitalistic Agricultural Labor in Georgia, 1865–1880," also concludes that the Freedmen's Bureau and especially Davis Tillson's contract system were instrumental in allowing the planters to dominate labor and reassert their hegemony in Georgia. In "The Freedmen's Bureau as a Legal Agent for Black Men and Women in Georgia, 1865–1868," Sara Rapport somewhat disingenuously argues that the Bureau responded sympathetically to the freedpeople's grievances because the freedpeople knew which complaints would receive favorable hearings before the agents and which would not. (As will be discussed throughout this book, freedpeople quickly learned which *agents* would respond to their complaints and brought all types of problems to them from the trivial to the great.) As far as the contract labor system was concerned, Rapport agrees with Engerrand, and both accept the assessment found in Jonathan M. Weiner, *The Social Origins of the New South: Alabama, 1860–1885*, 47–58. The Bureau compelled freedpeople to honor pro-planter contracts. Consequently, the agency and implicitly Davis Tillson "facilitated the development, at least in part, of a repressive labor system in the postbellum south" (Rapport, "Freedmen's Bureau," 31). Lewis Nicholas Wynne makes no distinction among Bureau administrations in *The Continuity of Cotton: Planter Politics in Georgia, 1865–1892*, 11–17. He concludes that the Bureau did little for the freedpeople and much for the continuity of planter hegemony, especially through its contract system.

Certainly, not all historians have condemned Tillson. The activities that damned Tillson in the eyes of the scholars mentioned above provided the sources for C. Mildred

Thompson's positive assessment of the assistant commissioner and the Georgia Bureau. Thompson, the first historian of the Georgia Bureau, argued that Tillson "plainly conceived it to be his duty as guardian of the freedmen to foster the mutual interests of the two races in so far as he was able." However, her purpose was to show that Tillson and the Georgia Bureau were not as bad as unreconstructed Southerners depicted them. Thompson, for example, praised Tillson for being an official who "took cognizance with great fairness of the interests of the white employers and did not attempt to regulate labor conditions with a view solely to guarding the rights of his wards." Although she is not wrong, her lack of access to Bureau records prevented her from seeing that Tillson was much more aggressive with employers who abused the rights of the freedpeople. See her article "The Freedmen's Bureau in Georgia in 1865–66: An Instrument of Reconstruction."

More complex and not altogether negative assessments of the Bureau may also be found in Charles L. Flynn, *White Land, Black Labor: Caste and Class in Late-Nineteenth-Century Georgia*, 32–38, and in Joseph P. Reidy, *From Slavery to Agrarian Capitalism in the Cotton Plantation South: Central Georgia, 1800–1880*, 143–77, passim. Alan Conway, *Reconstruction of Georgia*, 76–80, and Donald G. Nieman, *To Set the Law in Motion*, 163, 165, 189, present balanced views of Davis Tillson by depicting him as being fair, but there was more than fairness motivating the assistant commissioner.

9. For the activities of the Union army and a general examination of wartime contraband policy see Louis Gerteis, *From Contraband to Freedman*. Gerteis in his last chapter, J. Thomas May in "Continuity and Change in the Labor Program of the Union Army and the Freedmen's Bureau," and William F. Messner in *Freedmen and the Ideology of Free Labor: Louisiana, 1862–1865*, 184–85, emphasize the continuity between army policy and Bureau policy. May makes an especially good case for continuity in the contract system in Louisiana, but it would be wrong to apply his conclusions to Georgia even though they have merit for the state he has examined. Although some of the consequences of the Georgia Bureau's work replicated those of the army's earlier efforts in the Mississippi Valley, to emphasize continuity in army and Bureau policy would distort the agency's understanding of its purpose and would obscure the fact that the actual consequences of the Bureau's policy were not necessarily the expected results of the Bureau's intentions.

10. LaWanda Cox, in the last chapter of her book *Lincoln and Black Freedom: A Study in Presidential Leadership*, 142–84, notes that the failure of Reconstruction is generally blamed on a North that betrayed the freed slaves. She also presents an excellent exposition on the possibilities of Reconstruction.

11. Engerrand refers to "the shibboleths of capitalist ideology" in "'Now Scratch or Die,'" 13, 236. I believe that most Yankee Bureau men were not duplicitous in their pronouncements about the promise of honest work and the benefits of fair treatment. James

M. McPherson has come to a similar conclusion about wartime expressions of purpose on the part of Yankee soldiers and argues that we should take them at their word in his study *What They Fought For, 1861–1865*, 34, passim.

12. Dan T. Carter is correct in noting in *When the War Was Over* that a significant group of white Southerners tried to work out an acceptable Reconstruction settlement, but in Georgia that Reconstruction settlement for the most part was to be on their terms. White Georgians resisted outside interference, especially when it attempted to advance black rights, and even though these individuals were not all simpleminded racists, they seemed to stumble more often than not when Reconstruction measures challenged the racial hierarchy.

13. Special Field Orders, No. 15, Jan. 16, 1865, in *Official Records*, ser. 1, vol. 47, pt. 2, 60–62. For the circumstances surrounding the promulgation of the order see Howard, *Autobiography*, 2:189–91; and William T. Sherman, *Memoirs*, 2:244–52.

14. For examples of modern critical views of the Georgia Bureau's policy and particularly of Davis Tillson, who initiated the restoration process, see Duncan, *Freedom's Shore*, and McFeely, *Yankee Stepfather*. Also see McFeely's powerfully moving but somewhat romanticized *Sapelo's People*. A particularly emotional fictional account of the Georgia sea island experience that is also critical of the Bureau is Theodore Ward's play *Our Lan'*.

15. An excellent reminder of this point is Barry Crouch, "Hidden Sources of Black History: The Texas Freedmen's Bureau Records as a Case Study."

## Chapter 1. Under the Guardianship of the Nation

1. For a biography that places Howard's important Bureau activities within the context of his evangelical background, his long career of peacetime soldiering, the Civil War, black education, and Indian affairs, see John A. Carpenter, *Sword and Olive Branch*. This biography should be supplemented with such specific studies as William S. McFeely, *Yankee Stepfather*, and John and LaWanda Cox, "General O. O. Howard and the 'Misrepresented Bureau.'" See Howard's own account of his activities in his autobiography.

2. For a good, brief exploration of how individual Bureau officials in Texas, Alabama, and South Carolina stamped their agencies with their unique views and prejudices, see James D. Schmidt, "'Neither Slavery nor Involuntary Servitude,'" 226–324. The article literature on the Bureau at the state and local level is extensive, but the published monograph literature is relatively limited. For the longer published treatments see Martin Abbott, *The Freedmen's Bureau in South Carolina*; Barry A. Crouch, *Freedmen's Bureau and Black Texans*; William L. Richter, *Overreached on All Sides: The Freedmen's Bureau Administrators in Texas*; Laura Josephine Webster, *Operations of the Freedmen's Bureau in South Carolina*; and Howard A. White, *The Freedmen's Bureau in*

*Louisiana.* For examples of unpublished full-length state studies of the Bureau see Clifton L. Ganus Jr., "The Freedmen's Bureau in Mississippi"; Paul David Phillips, "A History of the Freedmen's Bureau in Tennessee"; and Randy Finley, "The Freedmen's Bureau in Arkansas."

3. Howard delayed the formal announcement of his assistant commissioners until June 13, 1865, and Thomas W. Osborn assumed command of the Florida Bureau in September 1865. O. O. Howard to R. Saxton, May 20, 1865, reel 1, (RI)BRFAL (M742); Howard, *Autobiography,* 2:215; Bentley, *Freedmen's Bureau,* 215.

4. Louise Saxton Clapp, "S. Willard Saxton: A Memorial," 3; Rufus Saxton, "The Reminiscences of a Quartermaster in the Early Days of the War"; and "Major General Rufus Saxton, U.S.A.," all in Rufus and S. Willard Saxton Papers, Yale University, Sterling Library. For additional information on Rufus Saxton's wartime experiences see Mark M. Boatner III, *The Civil War Dictionary,* 722–23; Ezra J. Warner, *Generals in Blue,* 420–21; James Grant Wilson and John Fisk, eds., *Appleton's Cyclopedia of American Biography,* 5:410; Patricia L. Faust, ed., *Historical Times Illustrated Encyclopedia of the Civil War*; and McFeely, *Yankee Stepfather,* 50–52. For a discussion of the nature of Brook Farm, where Saxton's younger brother, Willard, lived for a while, see Charles Crowe, *George Ripley: Transcendentalist and Utopian Socialist,* 143–88.

5. For a brief description of what his quartermaster duties involved during the Port Royal expedition and the praise he earned from the Union army's quartermaster general, see T. W. Sherman to R. Saxton, Sept. 27, 1861; R. Saxton to [M. C. Meigs], Nov. 9, 1861 (and Meigs's endorsement), *Official Records,* ser. 1, vol. 6, 174–75, 186–87.

6. Rufus Saxton, "The Reminiscences of a Quartermaster," 29, Saxton Papers.

7. Abbott, *Freedmen's Bureau in South Carolina,* 9; Joel Williamson, *After Slavery,* 10–11.

8. R. Saxton to E. M. Stanton, Dec. 30, 1864, *Official Records,* ser. 3, vol. 4, 1029.

9. *American Missionary* 9 (April 1865): 80.

10. E. M. Stanton to R. Saxton, June 16, 1862; E. M. Stanton to Maj. Gen. Hunter, June 16, 1862, *Official Records,* ser. 3, vol. 2, 152–53; R. Saxton to E. M. Stanton, Jan. 25, 1863, R. Saxton to E. M. Stanton, Feb. 7, Dec. 30, 1864, *Official Records,* ser. 3, vol. 4, 118–19, 1118–31; Williamson, *After Slavery,* 10–11, 55–58. For a complete examination of the Port Royal experiment and Saxton's place in it see Willie Lee Rose, *Rehearsal for Reconstruction.*

11. Capt. E. W. Cooper to Dr. LeBaron Russell, Nov. 2, 1863, Saxton Papers; R. Saxton to E. M. Stanton, Feb. 7, 1864, *Official Records,* ser. 3, vol. 4, 1024, 1025, 1031.

12. Special Field Orders, No. 15, Jan. 16, 1865, *Official Records,* ser. 1, vol. 47, pt. 2, 60–62; Howard, *Autobiography,* 2:178, 189–91.

13. Whitelaw Reid, *After the War,* 117; R. Saxton to O. O. Howard, June 14, 1865, reel 17, (LR)BRFAL (M752); R. Saxton to J. E. Bryant, May 15, 1865, John Emory Bryant Papers, Duke University.

14. R. Saxton to E. A. Wild, Aug. 11, 17, 1865, reel 1, BRFAL-SC (M869); R. Saxton to J. E. Bryant, Aug. 15, 1865, Bryant Papers.

15. R. Saxton to E. A. Wild, Aug. 11, 1865, reel 1, BRFAL-SC (M869).

16. E. A. Wild to R. Saxton, Sept. 1, 1865, reel 8, BRFAL-SC (M869).

17. In mid-June 1865 when Saxton appointed General Edward A. Wild to the Georgia Bureau to oversee most of its operations outside the Sherman Reservation, he instructed him to use the Bureau legislation as a means of settling freedpeople on land. R. Saxton to E. A. Wild, June 16, 1865, reel 1, BRFAL-SC (M869). Also see R. Saxton, Circular No. 2, Aug. 16, 1865, *House Executive Documents*, 39th Cong., 1st sess., no. 70 (serial 1256), 92–93. Earlier in June Saxton threatened planters who refused to treat their workers as free people with confiscation and the division of their property among their ex-slaves. Saxton, however, never carried out this threat, probably because he had no authority to do so. R. Saxton, General Orders, No. 1, June 20, 1865, *House Executive Documents*, 39th Cong., 1st sess., no. 70 (serial 1256), 99.

18. Saxton proposed contracts and the rental of Bureau-controlled land as an "either/ or" proposition, one not excluding the other, in August 1865, even though the reality of land redistribution had been thwarted by presidential policy. His approach to this particular problem suggests that Saxton, although perhaps overly optimistic about the prospects of the freedpeople, was not as naive or simplistic—at least in his approach to the freedpeople's economic place in a Reconstructed South—as Martin Abbott suggests. Saxton did not issue any earlier order on this matter, probably because he barely had time to become familiar with his Georgia jurisdiction before heading north on leave during the last week of June. He returned to South Carolina on August 6. R. Saxton to E. M. Stanton, Dec. 30, 1864, *Official Records*, ser. 3, vol. 4, 1022, 1025; R. Saxton, Circular No. 2, Aug. 16, 1865, *House Executive Documents*, 39th Cong., 1st sess., no. 70 (serial 1256), 92; S. W. Saxton to W. F. Eaton, June 24, 1865, Saxton Papers; R. Saxton to J. E. Bryant, Aug. 15, 1865, Bryant Papers; R. Saxton to E. A. Wild, Aug. 17, 1865, reel 1, BRFAL-SC (M869); Abbott, *Freedmen's Bureau in South Carolina*, 9.

19. R. Saxton to E. M. Stanton, Dec. 30, 1864, *Official Records*, ser. 3, vol. 4, 1022. R. Tomlinson favorably commented on Saxton's enforcement of the contracts in a letter to the *American Missionary* 9 (April 1865): 80.

20. R. Saxton, General Orders, No. 1, June 20, 1865, *House Executive Documents*, 39th Cong., 1st sess., no. 70 (serial 1256), 99.

21. R. Saxton to O. O. Howard, June 7, 1865, reel 17, (LR)BRFAL (M752).

22. R. Saxton, Circular No. 2, Aug. 16, 1865, *House Executive Documents*, 39th Cong., 1st sess., no. 70 (serial 1256), 92–93. Also reprinted in the *Savannah Republican*, Aug. 29, 1865, and in other Georgia newspapers.

23. E. A. Wild to R. Saxton, Sept. 1, 1865, reel 8, BRFAL-SC (M869); O. O. Howard to R. Saxton, Sept. 12, 1865, reel 1, (RI)BRFAL (M742); Howard, *Autobiography*, 2:235–36; Bentley, *Freedmen's Bureau*, 89–96.

24. The rationale for this change of command is discussed in chapter 2. Saxton turned over command of the South Carolina Bureau to Robert K. Scott in January 1866. Bentley, *Freedmen's Bureau*, 216.

25. D. Tillson, General Orders, No. 1, Sept. 22, 1865, reel 34, BRFAL-Ga (M798).

26. Incidentally, he also recruited the Third North Carolina Mounted Infantry, a Unionist regiment. His association with these southern Unionists might have influenced his erroneous views about how readily Southerners would accept the Yankee interpretation of Reconstruction. *Portland (Maine) Daily Eastern Argus*, May 1, 1895; *Augusta (Maine) Kennebec Journal*, May 1, 1895; *Report of the Adjutant General of the State of Maine for the Years 1864 and 1865*, 472–74; *Report of the Adjutant General for the State of Maine for the Year Ending December 31, 1866*, 17, 195; William E. S. Whitman and Charles True, *Maine in the War for the Union*, 383, 392, 397, 605; Cyrus Eaton, *History of Thomaston, Rockland and South Thomaston, Maine*, 2:433; D. Tillson to O. O. Howard, June 13, 1865, reel 18, (LR)BRFAL (M752).

27. D. Tillson to O. O. Howard, Dec. 11, 1865, reel 20, (LR)BRFAL (M752); D. Tillson to T. Rhodes, S. Jackson, and R. Malone, Apr. 3, 1866, reel 2, BRFAL-Ga (M798); "General Tillson's Speech Delivered before the Freedmen's Convention," *Augusta Loyal Georgian*, Jan. 20, 1866. In answering a complaint about a tax imposed by the city of Columbus on black and white residents, Tillson acknowledged that in theory "taxation should be accompanied by representation." But he acknowledged that exceptions "as in the case of females and residents not naturalized" provided precedents to tax blacks who lacked the franchise. Tillson also made it clear, however, that he would interfere with the local authorities if such a tax did not benefit blacks as well as whites. D. Tillson to T. Rhodes and others, Apr. 3, 1866, reel 2, BRFAL-Ga (M798).

28. Tillson's views on orderliness are clear in his critique of Colonel John Eaton's work on Presidents Island, located below Memphis, after he inspected the two-and-a-half-year-old refugee camp there. Although the schools were in good order, "The huts . . . have been located without the slightest regard to regularity convenience or neatness" and the "streets, where there are any, are crooked & narrow and yards and fences are so placed as to render any respectable system of policing impracticable." (Tillson meant "policing" in the military sense of keeping the grounds neat and clean.) At the same time, Tillson encouraged the benevolent associations to continue their work, and he made his superior aware that the schools needed additional funding to prepare for the fall term. D. Tillson to W. T. Clark, July 10, 15, 1865, reel 8, BRFAL-Tn (M999); Phillips, "Freedmen's Bureau in Tennessee," 13–14.

29. D. Tillson to W. T. Clark, July 11, 1865, reel 8, BRFAL-Tn (M999); Carpenter, *Sword and Olive Branch*, 108.

30. Tillson's commander, Clinton B. Fisk, "heartily approved" of his efforts to remove idlers and find them fair employment. At this time, Tillson also made it quite clear that the truly destitute would require government assistance. Furthermore, he recognized

that freedpeople had the right to choose their own employers, bring their complaints to the Bureau, and terminate contracts when treated cruelly by employers. D. Tillson to O. O. Howard, July 14, 1865, reel 18, (LR)BRFAL (M752); D. Tillson to W. T. Clark, July 15, Aug. 18, Aug. 30, 1865; D. Tillson, Circular No. 1, Memphis District, July 13, 1865, enclosed in D. Tillson to W. T. Clark, July 15, 1865, reel 8; W. T. Clark to D. Tillson, Aug. 27, reel 1; D. Tillson, Circular No. 5, Memphis District, Aug. 25, 1865, BRFAL-Tn (M999); W. W. Deane to Dr. Harrington, Aug. 12, 1865; D. Tillson to Bvt. Brig. Gen. Morgan, Aug. 26, 1865, vol. 133, LS, Records of the Memphis Subdistrict, BRFAL, RG 105, National Archives.

31. D. Tillson to G. Morris and others, Aug. 22, 1865, enclosed in D. Tillson to O. O. Howard, Aug. 28, 1865, reel 18, (LR)BRFAL (M752).

32. D. Tillson to J. B. Walker, Nov. 20, 1865, reel 1, BRFAL-Ga (M798).

33. Tillson had first reached this conclusion while in Memphis. D. Tillson to W. T. Clark, Aug. 18, 1865, reel 8, BRFAL-Tn (M999); D. Tillson to G. Morris and others, Aug. 22, 1865, enclosed in D. Tillson to O. O. Howard, Aug. 28, 1865, reel 18, (LR)BRFAL (M752). The views of Tillson and other Bureau officers were well within the common nineteenth-century views of environmental influences described by educational historian Carl F. Kaestle. However, in *Pillars of the Republic*, 88–89, Kaestle emphasizes nineteenth-century racial prejudice as limiting the expectations of antebellum educational reformers. His generalizations are drawn from an intellectual context that had not yet experienced changes caused by war and emancipation. Although Bureau men shared common prejudices concerning blacks, their views did not restrict their expectations of some degree of black advancement. In fact, most of Georgia's Yankee Bureau men were more likely to accept William W. Cutler III's assessment of nineteenth-century views of education: proper education could correct all flaws in American society. Cutler, "Horace Mann and Common School Reform," 331.

34. D. Tillson, Speech to the Georgia State Convention, Oct. 27, 1865, enclosed in D. Tillson to O. O. Howard, Nov. 1, 1865, reel 20, (LR)BRFAL (M752).

35. "General Tillson's Speech Delivered before the Freedmen's Convention," *Augusta Loyal Georgian*, Jan. 20, 1866.

36. Ibid.

37. John Richard Dennett, *The South as It Is, 1865–1866*, 268–69.

38. For changing views on free labor ideology, especially as the North became increasingly caught up in the industrialization of the postwar era, see Eric Foner, *Politics and Ideology in the Age of the Civil War*, 125–27.

39. "General Tillson's Speech Delivered before the Freedmen's Convention."

40. Ibid. While in Memphis, Tillson made it clear that when freedmen legally came into possession of land, even if it were leased confiscated property, they had a right to enjoy it without suffering the interference of anyone. W. W. Deane to Billey Gaffney (freedman), Aug. 12, 1865, vol. 133, LS, Records of the Memphis Subdistrict, BRFAL.

41. D. Tillson to G. Morris and others, Aug. 22, 1865, enclosed in D. Tillson to O. O. Howard, Aug. 28, 1865, reel 18, (LR)BRFAL (M752).

42. Tillson was in step with most Republicans who believed that hard work would lead to black land ownership, a truly revolutionary idea as far as the South's economic and social structures were concerned. Indeed, as Peyton McCrary argues in "Party of Revolution," Republicans, who considered their party to be a party of change, expected the South to become a land of black and white yeoman farmers.

43. For Saxton's views, see R. Saxton to E. M. Stanton, Dec. 30, 1864, *Official Records*, ser. 3, vol. 4, 1025. For Tillson's views, see D. Tillson, "Report of Operations September 22, 1865 to November 1, 1866," reel 32, BRFAL-Ga (M798).

44. Station Books, vol. 1, 1867–68, reel 35; D. Tillson to L. Thomas, Jan. 7, 1867, reel 4; D. Tillson to C. C. Sibley, Mar. 22, 1867, reel 16, BRFAL-Ga (M798); D. Tillson to O. O. Howard, Oct. 23, Dec. 1, reel 37, (LR)BRFAL (M752).

45. Station Books, vol. 1, 1867–68, reel 35, BRFAL-Ga (M798); *Savannah Daily Republican*, Jan. 24, 1867; Caleb C. Sibley, Civil War pension files, RG 15, National Archives; Boatner, *Civil War Dictionary*, 759.

46. For example, Sibley's adjutant once explained that the Bureau in all fairness could not compel employers to honor contracts if it did not require the same of the freedpeople. Endorsement of M. F. Gallagher, Jan. 17, 1868, on J. J. Knox to M. F. Gallagher, Jan. 14, 1868, box 5, LR, Athens SAC, BRFAL-Ga.

47. *Atlanta Constitution*, Feb. 10, 1900; John Randolph Lewis, Civil War pension files, RG 15, National Archives; *John Randolph Lewis: In Memoriam*; *Annual Announcement of the Pennsylvania College of Dental Surgery, Session 1858–59*; *General Catalogue of the University of Vermont and State Agricultural College, Burlington, Vermont, 1791–1900*, 240; G. G. Benedict, *Vermont in the Civil War*, 1:190, 196.

48. J. R. Lewis, Annual Report, Nov. 1, 1866, *Senate Executive Documents*, 39th Cong., 2d sess., no. 6 (serial 1276), 128, 130; J. R. Lewis to O. O. Howard, Dec. 17, 1866, reel 3, BRFAL-Tn (M999); O. O. Howard to J. R. Lewis, Sept. 14, 1866, reel 2, (RI)BRFAL (M742); Station Books, vol. 1, 1867–1868, vol. 2, 1869, reel 35; Circular No. 1, Jan. 25 1869, reel 34, BRFAL-Ga (M798).

49. For Lewis's views on the benefits and liabilities of using the contract system in Tennessee and his comments on education see J. R. Lewis, Annual Report, Nov. 1, 1866, *Senate Executive Documents*, 39th Cong., 2d sess., no. 6 (serial 1276), 128–30; J. R. Lewis to W. D. Whipple, Oct. 16, 1866; J. R. Lewis to Gen. Ord., Nov. 1, 1866; and J. R. Lewis to O. O. Howard, Nov. 24, Dec. 17, 1866, reel 3, BRFAL-Tn (M999).

50. J. R. Lewis to Bvt. Brig. Gen. W. D. Whipple, Oct. 16, 1866; and J. R. Lewis to Gen. Ord, Nov. 1, 1866, reel 3, BRFAL-Tn (M999).

51. J. R. Lewis to O. O. Howard, Dec. 17, 1866, reel 3, BRFAL-Tn (M999).

52. J. R. Lewis, Annual Report, Nov. 1, 1866, *Senate Executive Documents*, 39th Cong., 2d sess., no. 6 (serial 1276), 130–31, 140.

53. Lewis undoubtedly understood the political ramifications of education and the relationship between politically successful loyal individuals and his work, but Howard expressly forbade his subordinates to become involved in public political activities, and Lewis's speeches consequently lacked partisan content. Still, Lewis's inclinations were those of a moderate Republican, and he carried out the Bureau's duties concerning black political participation after the commencement of Military Reconstruction. He also became openly engaged in partisan politics after he left the Bureau. However, he expressed his dislike for Bryant and lobbied for and against political appointments while still on duty, as will be discussed in chapter 3. J. R. Lewis to O. O. Howard, Oct. 6, 1869, Dec. 27, 1869, O. O. Howard Papers, Bowdoin College, Brunswick, Maine. On Howard's views, see F. D. Sewall to C. C. Sibley, June 11, 1867, reel 15, BRFAL-Ga (M798).

54. Station Book, vol. 2, 1869, reel 35, BRFAL-Ga (M798); John R. Lewis, Civil War pension files; Caleb C. Sibley, Civil War pension files, RG 15, National Archives. For an assessment of Sibley's support of education, see J. W. Alvord, *Fourth Semi-Annual Report on Schools for Freedmen, July 1, 1867*, 34. For comments on Lewis's influence relative to Sibley's, see O. O. Howard to Bvt. Maj. Gen. E. Schriver, Sept. 21, 1867, reel 3, (RI)BRFAL (M742); [———] to E. P. Smith, Dec. 9, 1867; and E. A. Ware to G. Whipple, Feb. 18, 1868, reel 3, AMA-Ga.

55. J. R. Lewis to O. O. Howard, Oct. 6, 1869, Howard Papers; J. R. Lewis to W. L. Clark, Mar. 12, 1870, reel 5, (Ed)BRFAL-Ga (M799).

56. Sibley and Lewis continued to rely on contracts for regulating labor and also valued hardworking freedpeople, as will be discussed in chapter 6, but for some examples see E. Pickett [Sibley's adjutant] to J. W. Arnold, Feb. 4, 1867; J. R. Lewis to J. M. Hoag, Feb. 27, 1867, reel 5; C. C. Sibley, Report for April, May 23, 1867; Report for January, Feb. 29, 1868; Report for March, May 5, 1868; Report for December, Feb. 8, 1868, reel 32; C. C. Sibley, Circular Letter, Jan. 1, 1868, reel 34, BRFAL-Ga (M798).

57. For the content of freedmen's education see Ronald E. Butchart, *Northern Schools, Southern Blacks, and Reconstruction*, 15–16, 53–75, 137–68; Robert C. Morris, *Reading, 'Riting, and Reconstruction*, 174–212; and Joe M. Richardson, *Christian Reconstruction*, 40–44. These virtues were the same as those that educators had hoped to convey in their schools in the antebellum North. Kaestle, *Pillars of the Republic*, 75–103.

58. I. Pettibone to G. Whipple, Dec. 1, 1865, reel 1, AMA-Ga.

59. W. J. White to G. L. Eberhart, Mar. 29, 1867, reel 8, (Ed)BRFAL-Ga (M799).

60. *The Twenty-Second Annual Report of the American Missionary Association and the Proceedings at the Annual Meeting Held at Springfield, Mass., October 28th and 29th, 1868*, 44.

61. John W. Alvord, *First Semi-Annual Report on Schools and Finances of Freedmen, January 1, 1866*, 11.

62. D. Tillson to All Whom It May Concern, Nov. 4, 1865, reel 1, BRFAL-Ga (M798).

63. Earl J. Hess, *Liberty, Virtue, and Progress: Northerners and Their War for the*

*Union*, 12–13, passim; Judith N. Shklar, *American Citizenship: The Quest for Inclusion*, 77.

64. G. L. Eberhart to S. Hunt, Nov. 28, 1865, reel 1, AMA-Ga.

65. Station Books, vol. 1, 1867–1868; Station Books, vol. 2, 1869, reel 35, BRFAL-Ga (M798); E. A. Ware to O. O. Howard, Aug. 20, 1870, reel 70, (LR)BRFAL (M752); Richardson, *Christian Reconstruction*, 163–64.

66. For the place of the work ethic in American life see Daniel T. Rodgers, *The Work Ethic in Industrial America*. For a discussion of its compatibility with abolitionist thought, see Jonathan A. Glickstein, "'Poverty Is Not Slavery': American Abolitionists and the Competitive Labor Market." For the role of free labor in Republican Party ideology, see Eric Foner, *Free Soil, Free Labor, Free Men*, 11–39. Foner explains the importance of free-labor ideology during Reconstruction in his *Politics and Ideology*, 97–127. For a discussion of northern Civil War ideology, see Earl J. Hess in what is the best brief analysis of Northern wartime beliefs, *Liberty, Virtue, and Progress*. In *Emancipation and Equal Rights*, 31–32, 42, Herman Belz also identifies a moral component of the Union cause that went beyond preserving a nation and using emancipation as an expedient war measure: slavery contradicted republicanism and its basic principle of consent. Judith N. Shklar provides the fullest discussion of the central role of work in the definition of nineteenth-century citizenship in *American Citizenship*, 63–104. For the place of Democrats within this context see Jean Baker, *Affairs of Party*.

67. As Gavin Wright has noted, "Of all the conceptions of freedom that contributed to the rise of anti-slavery forces, the idea of an absolute right to quit one's work place at any time was insignificant." Wright, "The Economics and Politics of Slavery and Freedom in the U.S. South," 104. The most significant and thorough study of free-labor ideology's relationship to the widespread acceptance of the legal right to regulate labor with contract and vagrancy laws in the North may be found in Schmidt's groundbreaking work, "'Neither Slavery nor Involuntary Servitude.'" This dissertation is the first book-length study to explore court decisions that shaped contract labor law. However, although Schmidt proves that the views of men like Davis Tillson were compatible with those of many other Yankees, there is no indication that Bureau men in Georgia paid particular attention to judicial precedence in setting policy. Rather, Bureau action grew from the same broad milieu that had nurtured those legal decisions.

68. Hess, *Liberty, Virtue, and Progress*, 12–13, passim; Shklar, *American Citizenship*, 77; Kaestle, *Pillars of the Republic*, 81–82.

69. See Kirk's speech, "Educated Labor; or, Our Duty in Regard to the Americo-African Race," appended to *The Twenty-First Annual Report of the American Missionary Association and the Proceedings of the Annual Meeting Held at Homer, New York, October 17th and 18th, 1867*, 2–11.

70. The clearest statement on the racial views of antebellum Republicans is in Foner's *Free Soil, Free Labor, Free Men*, 261–300. Foner has characterized the view expressed in the text above as the "mainstream" view of the Republican Party. He also has

modified the views of historians, among them Leon Litwack, who have failed to see subtleties or variations in the degrees of racism held by antebellum Northerners, particularly within the Republican Party. Some forms of racism clearly were less virulent and certainly more flexible with regard to the place of blacks in American society than the most pathological forms expressed by the party's opponents. Foner develops these ideas for the postwar period, while also clearly explaining the hierarchy of rights that was important for dealing with the ex-slaves, in *Reconstruction*, 231. In addition, McCrary notes in "Party of Revolution," 348, that the Republicans identified their ideology with the Declaration of Independence. One should also see the earlier work of LaWanda Cox and John H. Cox, *Politics, Principle, and Prejudice*, viii, 163–64. They note that whereas Republicans were divided on the issue of suffrage for the freedmen at the outset of Reconstruction, they "substantially agreed that the freedmen should enjoy all other rights and privileges pertaining to free men and citizens." Furthermore, Cox and Cox argue that the demands the Republicans made of the South went beyond a desire to see some sort of symbolic submission and gave notice that they had no intention of leaving the South free to exploit its ex-slaves. Finally, Herman Belz, *A New Birth of Freedom*, notes the Republican Party's movement to equality before the law for the freedpeople. The most recent statement of the Republican commitment to color-blind legislation is Paul Moreno, "Racial Classifications and Reconstruction Legislation."

71. Belz, *Emancipation and Equal Rights*, 43; LaWanda Cox, *Lincoln and Black Freedom: A Study in Presidential Leadership*, 158.

72. T. F. Forbes [Tillson's adjutant] to J. D. Harris, June 9, 1866, reel 3, BRFAL-Ga (M798). That belief was why Tillson arrested white Tennesseans for whipping freedpeople and insisted that he continue to reserve the power to do so. Furthermore, that belief prompted Tillson to insist that black testimony be accepted in the civilian courts of his Memphis subdistrict. Tillson thought it proper to establish Bureau courts when the mayor of Memphis refused to honor this belief. D. Tillson to W. T. Clark, July 10, 21, 1865; D. Tillson to C. B. Fisk, July 25, 1865, reel 8, BRFAL-Tn (M999).

73. W. W. Deane to J. W. Arnold, Jan. 19, 1866, reel 1, BRFAL-Ga (M798). It is inconceivable that Deane, Tillson's adjutant, would express this official view without his superior's approval.

74. J. R. Lewis to F. A. H. Gaebel, May 28, 1867, reel 5, BRFAL-Ga (M798).

75. The North had not been purged of the influence of a racism that before the war had relegated blacks to inferior economic, legal, political, and social status. On the idea of race in nineteenth-century America, see George M. Fredrickson, *The Black Image in the White Mind: The Debate on Afro-American Character and Destiny, 1817–1914*. For the conditions under which free blacks lived in the antebellum North, see Leon F. Litwack, *North of Slavery: The Negro in the Free States, 1790–1860*. Also see Eugene H. Berwanger, *The Frontier against Slavery*, and V. Jacque Voegeli, *Free but Not Equal: The Midwest and the Negro during the Civil War*. But all of these studies must be qualified by the comments in note 70 above.

76. The words are Tillson's adjutant's, but the views are obviously the assistant commissioner's. W. W. Deane to M. P. Mayfield, Jan. 23, 1866, reel 1, BRFAL-Ga (M798).

77. *Twenty-Second Annual Report of the American Missionary Association*, 44.

78. R. Saxton, General Orders, No. 11, Aug 28, 1865, reprinted in *Savannah Daily Republican*, Sept. 5, 1865; R. Saxton, Circular No. 2, Aug. 16, 1865, *House Executive Document*, 39th Cong., 1st sess., no. 70 (serial 1256), 93. Saxton to E. M. Stanton, Dec. 30, 1864, *Official Records*, ser. 3, vol. 4, 1025.

79. R. Saxton to O. O. Howard, June 4, 1865, reel 17, (LR)BRFAL (M752).

80. On nineteenth-century perceptions of philanthropy, see Robert H. Bremner, *The Public Good*.

81. R. Saxton, Circular No. 2, Aug. 16, 1865, *House Executive Documents*, 39th Cong., 1st sess., no. 70 (serial 1256), 92.

82. C. C. Sibley, Report for May, June 11, 1868, reel 32, BRFAL-Ga (M798).

83. On January 1, 1869, Commissioner Howard discontinued most of the agency's activities, excepting its educational and veteran's claims work. The impecunious agency continued into 1870 in Georgia pursuing these tasks. Howard's entire operation stumbled along until Congress dismantled it in June 1872. Howard, *Autobiography*, 2:279; Bentley, *Freedmen's Bureau*, 49, 134, 201–2, 211–12.

84. Belz, *New Birth of Freedom*, 158; Nieman, *To Set the Law in Motion*, i–ii, 228. Also see David H. Donald's comments on constitutionalism in his survey of the era, *Liberty and Union: The Crisis of Popular Government, 1830–1890*, 175–82.

85. "General Tillson's Speech Delivered before the Freedmen's Convention," *Augusta Loyal Georgian*, Jan. 20, 1866.

86. D. Tillson to O. O. Howard, Dec. 1, 1865, reel 20, (LR)BRFAL (M752). Howard understandably but simplistically describes Tillson's approach as being based on the assumption that "if we trusted the Southern white people more, they would be disposed to do right." But shortly after Tillson voiced his concern, he forwarded to the commissioner his plan for Military Reconstruction in Georgia. Howard, *Autobiography*, 2:255; D. Tillson to O. O. Howard, Dec. 21, 1865, reel 20, (LR)BRFAL (M752).

87. D. Tillson to J. C. Johnson, Apr. 11, 1866, reel 2; D. Tillson, "Report of Operations September 22, 1865, to November 1, 1866," reel 32, BRFAL-Ga (M798). For another example of Tillson's expressed desire to work in cooperation with Georgia's officials and through established channels, see D. Tillson to C. J. Jenkins, July 13, 1866, box 60, Georgia Governors' Papers, Telamon-Cuyler Collection, University of Georgia. O. O. Howard also believed that it was important for his officers to secure the goodwill and cooperation of white Southerners. Howard, *Autobiography*, 2:255; O. O. Howard to R. Saxton, Sept. 6, 1865, reel 20, BRFAL-SC (M869).

88. Tillson used this phrase at a time when the ironclad oath guaranteed that few of his appointees would be able to secure paid agencies in his successor's Bureau. Endorsement of D. Tillson to O. O. Howard, Jan. 16, 1867, on B. Maguire to D. Tillson, Dec. 15, 1866, reel 42, (LR)BRFAL (M752).

89. D. Tillson to C. J. Jenkins, Oct. 25, 1865; D. Tillson to R. Saxton, Nov. 2, 1865, reel 1; M. Woodhull to D. Tillson, Oct. 10, 1865, reel 24, BRFAL-Ga (M798); D. Tillson to O. O. Howard, Nov. 1, 1865, reel 20 (LR)BRFAL (M752).

90. D. Tillson to O. O. Howard, Dec. 20, 1865, reel 20, (LR)BRFAL (M752).

91. D. Tillson to O. O. Howard, Feb. 1, 1866, reel 1, BRFAL-Ga (M798).

92. D. Tillson to J. Erskine, July 18, 1866, reel 3, BRFAL-Ga (M798).

93. D. Tillson to O. O. Howard, Dec. 20, 1865, reel 20, (LR)BRFAL (M752); D. Tillson, "Report of Operations September 22, 1865, to November 1, 1866," BRFAL-Ga (M798).

94. D. Tillson to [B. B.] Bowen, Sept. 6, 1866, reel 3, BRFAL-Ga (M798).

95. D. Tillson to O. O. Howard, Nov. 28, Dec. 1, Dec. 20, 1865, reel 20, (LR)BRFAL (M752).

96. D. Tillson to O. O. Howard, Feb. 2, 1866, Howard Papers. See Howard's reassurance to Tillson in O. O. Howard to D. Tillson, Feb. 28, 1866, Howard Papers.

97. As will be discussed in subsequent chapters, Tillson's and Bryant's initial views about labor, contracts, and Reconstruction were not far apart; it was only after he left the Bureau that Bryant became engaged in political activities that might have been off-putting for Tillson. Bryant's speech to the Georgia Equal Rights Association meeting in January 1866 was not very far from Tillson's speech at that meeting, except for its references to black political rights. Earlier, Tillson had expressed his opinion in a letter to Alexander Stephens that the freedpeople had no political motives. *Augusta Loyal Georgian*, Jan. 27, 1866; Elizabeth Studley Nathans, *Losing the Peace: Georgia Republicans and Reconstruction, 1865–1871*, 25.

98. Tillson's chief surgeon boarded in the same house as the teachers and informed the assistant commissioner of the teachers' intentions. City officials were willing to allow teachers and students to lay flowers on Union graves, but that compromise was not adequate for the participants who believed they should have free access to the cemetery. Emma Bryant Diary, Apr. 27, 28, 1866, Bryant Papers; M. J. Welch to S. Hunt, May 1, 1866, reel 1, AMA-Ga; D. Tillson to O. O. Howard, Apr. 29, May 7, 1866, Howard Papers; J. M. to the Editor of the *Army and Navy Journal*, [n.d.], reprinted in *Augusta Daily Constitutionalist*, June 6, 1866; *American Missionary* 10 (June 1866): 135–36. April 26 was a statewide memorial day for Confederate dead. *Columbus Daily Enquirer*, Apr. 26, 1866.

99. J. R. Davis to D. Tillson, June 7, 1866 (copy), Howard Papers.

100. D. Tillson to O. O. Howard, Apr. 29, May 7, June 15, 1866, Howard Papers; D. Tillson to Maj. Gen. C. R. Woods, June 11, 1866, reel 32 (LR)BRFAL (M752); *Augusta Daily Constitutionalist*, June 5, 1866; Charles Stearns, *Black Man of the South, and the Rebels*, 106.

101. *Augusta Daily Constitutionalist*, June 5, 1866; *New York Times*, June 18, 1866; McFeely, *Yankee Stepfather*, 248.

102. J. Thomas to D. Tillson, June 7, 1866, reel 2, (RI)BRFAL (M742); D. Tillson to

Maj. Gen. C. R. Woods, June 11, 1866, reel 32, (LR)BRFAL (M752); *Augusta Daily Constitutionalist*, June 20, 1866; Tillson referred to the "threatening letter" in his communication to the editor of the *New York Tribune*, reprinted in *Columbus Daily Enquirer*, July 1, 1866.

103. D. Tillson to G. Whipple, July 4, 1866, reel 2, AMA-Ga.

104. D. Tillson to O. O. Howard, June 16, 1866, reel 32, (LR)BRFAL (M752).

105. In July 1866 the Georgia Equal Rights Association found no evidence of wrongdoing on Bryant's part, although it did enjoin him to refrain from using the *Augusta Loyal Georgian* as a weapon for attacking Tillson. Still, Tillson persisted in gathering evidence to prove that Bryant was out to defraud freedpeople. D. Tillson to O. O. Howard, June 12, 16, 1866, reel 32; affidavit of Shade Bogian, Dec. 29, 1866 (forwarded by D. Tillson to O. O. Howard, Jan. 18, 1867), reel 42, (LR)BRFAL (M752); Trustees of the Methodist Church, Colored, at Warrenton to D. Tillson, July 6, 1866; J. C. Swayze to D. Tillson, Dec. 9, 1866, reel 29, BRFAL-Ga (M798); Report of Committee to Investigate J. E. Bryant to the Pres[ident] & Council of the GERA, [July 1866]; J. E. Bryant to H. Greeley, Jan. 21, 1867, Bryant Papers; *Columbus Daily Enquirer*, June 14, 1866; D. Tillson to the editor of the *New York Tribune*, reprinted in *Columbus Daily Enquirer*, July 1, 1866; *Augusta Daily Constitutionalist*, July 15, 1866.

106. Emma Bryant Diary, May 28, 1866, Bryant Papers; E. Pickett to W. F. White, Dec. 4, 1866, reel 4, BRFAL-Ga (M798). For White's indignant reply, see W. F. White to E. Pickett, Dec. 5, 1866, reel 29, BRFAL-Ga (M798).

## Chapter 2. A Real Blessing to the Inhabitants of the State

1. S. W. Saxton to Rev. W. F. Eaton, Sept. 14, [1865], Rufus and S. Willard Saxton Papers, Yale University, Sterling Library.

2. R. Saxton to O. O. Howard, Aug. 20, Sept. 9, 1865, reel 17, (LR)BRFAL (M752).

3. American Missionary Association, *The Nineteenth Annual Report of the American Missionary Association, and the Proceedings at the Annual Meeting, Held at Brooklyn, N.Y., October 25th and 26th, 1865*, 23; American Missionary Association, *The Twenty-First Annual Report of the American Missionary Association and the Proceedings of the Annual Meeting Held at Homer, New York, October 17th and 18th, 1867*, 12; Bullard, *An Abandoned Black Settlement*, 73.

4. R. Saxton to Maj. Gen. Q. A. Gillmore, Nov. 30, 1863, *Official Records*, ser. 1, vol. 28, pt. 1, 745; R. Saxton to J. E. Bryant, May 15, 1865, John Emory Bryant Papers, Duke University; Currie-McDaniel, *Carpetbagger of Conscience*, 31–49.

5. Eaton's, Bryant's, and Dennett's appointments were made under the authority Saxton had received from Sherman, since he was not informed by Howard of his Bureau appointment until May 20. Other individuals who received assignments under Sherman's orders and remained with the Georgia Bureau for a while were Captain Alexander P.

Ketchum (a Port Royal colleague, veteran of service with black troops, and Saxton's adjutant general who supervised the coastal and riverfront land in South Carolina near Savannah along with the approximately 150 miles of Georgia coast), the Reverend Tunis G. Campbell (a New Jersey free black who served at Port Royal and arrived on the Georgia sea island of Saint Catherines late in the war), and the Reverend William H. Tiffany (who took up his duties in the Ogeechee District near Savannah before the end of the war). The roles played by these men as well as the Reverend Eaton are discussed in chapter 7. One of Saxton's first appointments after receiving his Bureau commission was the Reverend S. W. Magill to the superintendency of freedmen schools for Savannah and its vicinity on March 30, 1865. S. W. Saxton Journal, Feb. 15, 1865; S. W. Saxton to T. G. Campbell, June 10, 1865; S. W. Saxton to S. W. Magill, order dated Mar. 30, 1865, Saxton Papers; O. O. Howard to R. Saxton, May 20, 1865, reel 1, (RI)BRFAL (M742); A. P. Ketchum to R. Saxton, Sept. 1, 1865, reel 34, BRFAL-SC (M869); *Savannah National Republican*, Sept. 29, 1865; McFeely, *Yankee Stepfather*, 49; Rose, *Rehearsal for Reconstruction*, 354; Duncan, *Freedom's Shore*, 12–20.

6. Wild was assigned to Saxton on May 31, 1865, but did not arrive at Augusta until June 30, 1865. Wild's authority was limited and always subordinate to Saxton's, despite the fact that Wild often identified himself as an assistant commissioner. Special Orders, No. 268, War Department, Adjutant General's Office, May 31, 1865, *Official Records*, ser. 1, vol. 47, pt. 3, 604; E. A. Wild to R. Saxton, July 14, 1865, reel 34; R. Saxton to E. A. Wild, June 16, Aug. 11, 1865, reel 1, BRFAL-SC (M869); R. Saxton, General Orders, No. 7, Aug. 9, 1865, *House Executive Documents*, 39th Cong., 1st sess., no. 70 (serial 1256), 107.

7. Longacre, "Brave, Radical, Wild"; Warner, *Generals in Blue*, 557–58.

8. E. A. Wild to R. Saxton, July 14, 1865, reel 34, BRFAL-SC (M869). Saxton left for the North the last week in June and returned on August 6. S. Willard Saxton to W. F. Eaton, June 24, 1865, Saxton Papers; R. Saxton to E. A. Wild, Aug. 17, 1865, reel 1, BRFAL-SC (M869).

9. M. French to [A. P. Ketchum], July 11, 1865, box 32, Records of the Assistant Adjutant General, Savannah SAC, BRFAL-Ga; R. Saxton to E. A. Wild, Aug. 17, 1865, reel 1, BRFAL-SC (M869). Also see R. Saxton to J. E. Bryant, Aug. 15, 1865, Bryant Papers. For an example of Howard's unwillingness to lay down rigid general rules for his subordinates at this time, see his Circular No. 11, July 12, 1865, reprinted in the *Savannah Daily Republican*, Aug. 11, 1865.

10. Wild noted in a letter to Saxton that upon his arrival in Georgia he lacked specific instructions concerning his duties. The letter reached Saxton's headquarters after the assistant commissioner had gone on leave. E. A. Wild to R. Saxton, July 14, 1865, reel 34; R. Saxton to E. A. Wild, Aug. 17, 1865, reel 1, BRFAL-SC (M869).

11. W. P. Russell to M. E. Strieby, Aug. 3, 1865, reel 1, AMA-Ga; J. S. Fullerton to [O. O. Howard], Aug. 11, 1865, reel 74, (LR)BRFAL (M752).

12. M. French to [A. P. Ketchum], July 11, 1865, box 32, Records of the Assistant Adjutant General, Savannah SAC, BRFAL-Ga.

13. [Col. S. B. Moe] to Capt. G. M. Brayton, July 30, 1865; J. B. Steedman to E. M. Stanton, Aug. 12, Aug. 23, 1865, Telegrams and Letters Sent, Dept. of Ga.; Capt. G. M. Brayton to Col. S. B. Moe, Aug. 4, 1865, reel 20; J. S. Fullerton to O. O. Howard, Aug. 11, 1865, reel 74, (LR)BRFAL (M752); Marion Alexander to [Mary] Clifford [Alexander], July 31, 1865, in Boggs, ed., *The Alexander Letters, 1787–1900*, 297–99.

14. J. S. Fullerton to [O. O. Howard], Aug. 11, 1865, reel 74, (LR)BRFAL (M752). Wild obviously planned to implement to the letter the confiscation laws passed during the war. On those laws, see Cimbala, "Confiscation."

15. R. Saxton to E. A. Wild, Aug. 11, 1865, reel 1, BRFAL-SC (M869); R. Saxton, General Orders, No. 7, Aug. 9, 1865, *House Executive Documents*, 39th Cong., 1st sess., no. 70 (serial 1256), 107. Saxton admitted that his subordinate was "lacking somewhat in system" when Howard ordered his removal. R. Saxton to O. O. Howard, Sept. 12, 1865, reel 17, (LR)BRFAL (M752).

16. Carl Schurz to A. Johnson, Aug. 13, 1865, in Simpson, Graf, and Muldowny, eds., *Advice after Appomattox: Letters to Andrew Johnson, 1865–1866*, 94; "Steedman's Views," in "Report of Carl Schurz," *Senate Executive Document*, 39th Cong., 1st sess., no. 2 (serial 1237), 52.

17. E. A. Wild to R. Saxton, Sept. 1, 1865, reel 8, BRFAL-SC (M869).

18. C. B. Fisk to O. O. Howard, Sept. 2, 1865, (LR)BRFAL (M752). In his excellent study of the black community in Atlanta after the war, Jerry Thornbery found Fisk's own inability to place an officer in the city another example of the difficulties confronting the agency's efforts to establish itself in Georgia that went beyond the failings of General Wild. A better explanation for this particular situation may be found in the fact that by this time Howard was making plans to establish Georgia as a separate command. The commissioner probably did not wish to confound the jurisdictions of his subordinates. Thornbery, "The Development of Black Atlanta, 1865–1885," 56–57.

19. R. Saxton to D. Tillson, Sept. 29, 1865, reel 1; R. Saxton to G. S. Eberhart, Sept. 15, 1865, reel 15, BRFAL-SC (M869); General Orders, No. 2, Oct. 6, 1865, reel 34, BRFAL-Ga (M798). Saxton also had trouble securing military cooperation in South Carolina, but he did somewhat better in securing personnel there. After two months of Bureau service, Saxton had seventeen men in the field; by the end of the year, he had twenty-four. Abbott, *Freedmen's Bureau in South Carolina*, 13–14.

20. For Howard's assessment of Saxton, see O. O. Howard, Annual Report, December 1865, *House Executive Documents*, 39th Cong., 1st sess., no. 11 (serial 1255), 2. Historians Martin Abbot, George R. Bentley, and Alan Conway believe that Saxton was more concerned with South Carolina and therefore neglected Georgia. Ruth Currie-McDaniel explains the lack of a significant Bureau network in Georgia by noting Saxton's highly selective approach to appointing agents. If anything, Saxton's jurisdiction was

too large for his personal management, but Georgia was not the victim of intentional neglect. Saxton knew he needed a large network of agents, and he very much wanted to use military men, despite their shortcomings, to expand the Bureau's presence in Georgia. Consequently, although there is some truth in these explanations, they fall short of fully describing why the Bureau was not established on a sound footing during the summer of 1865. Abbott, *Freedmen's Bureau in South Carolina,* 9; Bentley, *Freedmen's Bureau,* 68; Conway, *Reconstruction of Georgia,* 76; Currie-McDaniel, *Carpetbagger of Conscience,* 54.

21. J. S. Fullerton to O. O. Howard, July 20, 1865, Howard Papers, Bowdoin College, Brunswick, Maine.

22. Ibid. For an assessment of Fullerton's relationship to Howard, and his role in and perception of the Bureau at this time, see McFeely, *Yankee Stepfather,* 106–29. As noted in chapter 1, Saxton's speeches and circulars stressed obligations as well as rights, which Fullerton seemed to have missed and which leads one to conclude that Fullerton's sources were conservative individuals who probably feared any change in the relative balance of power in relations between black and white Georgians.

23. The Bureau was to be financed primarily through sale and rental of confiscated and abandoned property, which proved to be inadequate sources. In late August Wild complained that he had no funds to pay civilian agents, and in early September he noted that the situation had not improved. Bentley, *Freedmen's Bureau,* 74–75; E. A. Wild to R. Saxton, Aug. 23, 1865, reel 34; E. A. Wild to R. Saxton, Sept. 1, 1865, reel 1, BRFAL-SC (M869).

24. E. A. Wild to R. Saxton, Aug. 23, 1865, reel 34; R. Saxton to J. B. Steedman, Sept. 12, 1865, reel 1; R. Saxton to J. C. Beecher, Sept. 16, 1865, reel 8, BRFAL-SC (M869); R. Saxton to O. O. Howard, Aug. 20, Sept. 12, 1865, reel 17, (LR)BRFAL (M752). O. O. Howard had earlier advised his assistant commissioners that they would need to approach department commanders for staffing assistance. O. O. Howard to Assistant Commissioners, June 14, 1865, reel 1, (RI)BRFAL (M742).

25. Sefton, *Army and Reconstruction,* 21–22, 25–26, 36; Boatner, *Civil War Dictionary,* 794; J. B. Steedman, General Orders, No. 1, June 29, 1865, vol. 5/7, Dept. of Ga.; General Orders, No. 118, War Department, Adjutant General's Office, June 27, 1865, *Official Records,* ser. 1, vol. 47, pt. 3, 667.

26. *Statutes at Large of the United States* (1863–1865), 13:508; J. B. Steedman, General Orders, No. 4, July 14, 1865, vol. 5/7, Dept. of Ga. William S. McFeely dismisses Steedman as being "no friend of the Negro," but the general's relationships with the Georgia freedpeople (though certainly not on par with an abolitionist's) and with the Bureau were more complicated than that assessment would indicate. One example here should clarify this point. When Wilkes County residents asked Steedman to prevent freedpeople from holding a large meeting in October 1865, they were disappointed by his response. However, he did take the opportunity to have Davis Tillson meet the freedpeople to spread his free-labor message. Steedman's approach was clearly within the common

free-labor tradition that acknowledged the freedpeople's rights to their wages and equal treatment before the law as well as their obligations. Whether his army subordinates implemented a program that protected the freedpeople's rights during the summer of 1865 is another story. The point is that even though Steedman was known as a conservative, in principle he initially accepted the purpose of the Freedmen's Bureau. McFeely, *Yankee Stepfather*, 247; D. Tillson to O. O. Howard, Oct. 5, 1865, reel 20, (LR)BRFAL (M752). For Steedman's instructions to his local provost marshals, see Circular No. 2, Aug. 7, 1865, Headquarters, Dept. of Ga., Office of the Provost Marshal General, enclosed in J. B. Steedman to R. Saxton, Aug. 17, 1865, reel 8, BRFAL-SC (M869). For Steedman's reputation, see assessments in E. A. Wild to A. P. Ketchum, July 14, 1865, box 32, Records of the Assistant Adjutant General, Savannah SAC, BRFAL-Ga; W. P. Russell to [M. E. Strieby], July 25, 1865, reel 1, AMA-Ga.; *Macon Daily Telegraph*, July 11, Oct. 27, 1865.

27. M. French to A. P. Ketchum, July 11, 1865, box 32, Records of the Assistant Adjutant General, Savannah SAC, BRFAL-Ga. At this time, French served as a hospital chaplain and was never a regularly appointed Georgia Bureau agent. When he was mustered out of the service, General Steedman asked President Johnson to appoint the chaplain to the Bureau. Although French did not receive the appointment, in November 1865 he was sent to Tillson by O. O. Howard because Howard "believed he was doing much harm at the North but would be of great service" to the Georgia Bureau. Howard gave Tillson the option of using French if he wished, with the assurance that the Bureau would find something else for him to do if Tillson found him to be "an unsafe man" or could not find a position for him in which "he will do no injury to the cause." Tillson did not use him. French later became involved in a freedmen's camp in Charleston, South Carolina, and was a partner in a plantation on Edisto Island. Special Orders, No. 419, Ass't Adj't Gen., War Dept., Aug. 4, 1865, reel 8 , BRFAL-SC (M869); M. French to J. Johnson, Sept. 7, 1865, box 60, Georgia Governors' Papers, Telamon-Cuyler Collection, University of Georgia; J. B. Steedman to A. Johnson, Sept. 11, 1865, Letters and Telegrams Sent, Dept. of Ga.; O. O. Howard to D. Tillson, Dec. 5, 1865, reel 1, (RI)BRFAL (M742); J. B. Steedman and J. S. Fullerton to E. Stanton, June 4, 1866, in *New York Herald*, June 13, 1866. For French's background and Port Royal activities, see Rose, *Rehearsal for Reconstruction*, 26–27, passim.

28. E. A. Wild to A. P. Ketchum, July 14, 1865, box 32, Records of the Assistant Adjutant General, Savannah SAC; E. A. Wild to R. Saxton, July 14, 1865, reel 34, BRFAL-SC (M869).

29. R. Saxton to O. O. Howard, Aug. 10, 1865, reel 1 (Saxton did not send this letter, but it expresses his frustration over his inability to secure officers and agents for Bureau duty); R. Saxton to J. B. Steedman, Aug. 17, 1865, reel 8; E. A. Wild to R. Saxton, Aug. 23, 1865, reel 34; E. A. Wild to R. Saxton, Sept. 13, 1865, reel 8; R. Saxton to J. B. Steedman, Sept. 12, 1865, reel 1, BRFAL-SC (M869); R. Saxton to J. B. Steedman, Aug. 19, 1865, enclosed in R. Saxton to O. O. Howard, Aug. 20, 1865, reel 17, (LR)BRFAL (M752).

30. As early as June 1865, reflecting America's desire for quick demobilization after war, Maj. Gen. James H. Wilson complained from Macon, "The muster out is depriving me of my best officers." Consequently, the army's policy caused a shortage for Steedman. Steedman also had a legitimate worry about having his officers answer to both him and Saxton, but these concerns provide only a partial explanation for his reluctance to help staff the Bureau. T. M. Vincent to Maj. Gen. J. M. Schofield, May 29, 1865, *Official Records*, ser. 1, vol. 47, pt. 3, 588–89; Maj. Gen. J. H. Wilson to Maj. Gen. J. A. Rawlins, June 7, 1865, *Official Records*, ser. 1, vol. 49, pt. 2, 967; E. A. Wild to R. Saxton, Aug. 23, 1865, reel 34; Sept. 13, reel 8, BRFAL-SC (M869).

31. "Views expressed by Major General Steedman in conversation with Carl Schurz," in "Report of Carl Schurz on the States of South Carolina, Georgia, Alabama, Mississippi, and Florida," *Senate Executive Documents*, 39th Cong., 1st sess., no. 2 (serial 1237), 52–53; reprinted in 1969 as Schurz, *Report on the Condition of the South*.

32. Steedman also believed that civil courts should be restored as quickly as possible. E. A. Wild to A. P. Ketchum, July 14, 1865, box 32, Records of the Assistant Adjutant General, Savannah SAC, BRFAL-Ga.

33. E. A. Wild to R. Saxton, July 14, 1865, reel 34, BRFAL-SC (M869).

34. Apparently, the military men with whom Bryant had clashed earlier in July in the jurisdictional dispute did not let the matter rest. See endorsement of Bvt. Brig. Gen. E. L. Molineux, July 18, 1865, vol. 8/18A, Endorsements, Provost Marshal General; affidavit of T. J. Macgarie, July 20, 1865, LR, Provost Marshal's Office; J. E. Bryant to Capt. James [Entwisle], July 24, 1865, LR, Dept. of Ga.; and J. E. Bryant to R. Saxton, Aug. 4, 1865, reel 7, BRFAL-SC (M869). There were also complaints from the military to the headquarters of the Department of the South that Bryant was not exercising sufficient control over "idle" and "vagrant" freedpeople, again suggesting that the military and at least some Bureau men had divergent views about their roles in Reconstruction. Saxton nevertheless remained confident in his subordinate. Bvt. Brig. Gen. E. L. Molineux to Maj. W. L. M. Burger, June 26, 1865, *Official Records*, ser. 1, vol. 47, pt. 3, 665–66. S. W. Saxton to J. E. Bryant, Aug. 25, 1865, Bryant Papers.

35. J. E. Bryant to R. Saxton, Aug., 4, 1865, reel 7, BRFAL-SC (M869). Saxton's past experience with the military would support Bryant's view. In early May 1865, before Saxton was appointed assistant commissioner, the military in Savannah attempted to force him to relinquish control of educational activities in the city. Later in December 1865 Ulysses S. Grant believed that the Bureau should be somehow incorporated into the regular army structure in the South, and the Bureau lost much of its autonomy with the commencement of Military Reconstruction. Bvt. Maj. Gen. C. Grover to Asst. Adj. Gen., HQ, Dept. of the South, May 6, 13, 1865; Maj. Gen. Q. A. Gillmore to Maj. Gen. Grover, May 17, 1865, *Official Records*, ser. 1, vol. 47, pt. 3, 418, 492–93, 525; Bentley, *Freedmen's Bureau*, 109, 122.

36. Fullerton delicately omitted Steedman's hard language but noted that it was indeed profane. Fullerton also instructed Wild to restore the Toombs property. E. A. Wild

to R. Saxton, Aug. 23, 1865, reel 34, BRFAL-SC (M869); J. S. Fullerton to [O. O. Howard], Aug. 11, 1865, reel 74, (LR)BRFAL (M752).

37. As early as July 31, Fullerton warned Howard not to give Wild any more authority. U. S. Grant recommended Wild's removal at the end of August, and Fullerton suggested it on September 2, but Saxton, regretfully obeying Howard's September 11 order and wondering what Wild could have done to alienate Grant, removed his subordinate on or shortly after September 12. J. S. Fullerton to O. O. Howard, July 31, 1865, LR, Dept. of Ga.; J. S. Fullerton to R. Saxton, Sept. 2, 1865, reel 1, (RI)BRFAL (M742); R. Saxton to O. O. Howard, Sept. 12, 1865, reel 17 (LR)BRFAL (M752); Bentley, *Freedmen's Bureau*, 69.

38. Circular No. 2, Aug. 7, 1865, Office of the Provost Marshal General, Dept. of Ga., enclosed in R. Saxton to Gen. J. B. Steedman, Aug. 17, 1865, reel 8, BRFAL-SC (M869); "Steedman's Views," in "Report of Carl Schurz," *Senate Executive Documents*, 39th Cong., 1st sess., no. 2 (serial 1237), 52–53.

39. D. Young to American Missionary Association, July 3, 1865, reel 1, AMA-Ga.

40. C. Schurz to A. Johnson, Aug. 13, 1865, in Simpson et al., *Advice after Appomattox*, 95.

41. W. K. Kimball to O. O. Howard, Sept. 4, 1865, reel 24, BRFAL-Ga (M798). Carl Schurz also made this point while touring Georgia in August 1865. C. Schurz to A. Johnson, Aug. 13, 1865, in Simpson et al., *Advice after Appomatox*, 94–95.

42. R. Saxton to O. O. Howard, Sept. 9, 12, 1865, reel 17, (LR)BRFAL (M752); R. Saxton to J. B. Steedman, Sept. 12, 1865, reel 1, BRFAL-SC (M869).

43. R. Saxton to J. B. Steedman, Aug. 19, 1865, reel 1, BRFAL-SC (M869); R. Saxton to O. O. Howard, Aug. 20, 1865, reel 17, (LR)BRFAL (M752); J. S. Fullerton to R. Saxton, Aug. 24, 1865, reel 1, (RI)BRFAL (M742).

44. O. O. Howard to D. Tillson, July 17, 1865, reel 1, (RI)BRFAL (M742); O. O. Howard, Annual Report, Dec. 1865, *House Executive Documents*, 39th Cong., 1st sess., no. 11 (serial 1255), 2.

45. J. S. Fullerton to [O. O. Howard], Aug. 11, 1865, reel 74, (LR)BRFAL (M752). In July Fullerton had urged Howard to appoint an assistant commissioner for Georgia who could get along with the military people there. Otherwise, he said, the Bureau's efforts would be wasted. The commissioner could not ignore this advice because military detachments were essential for enforcing the agency's decisions. J. S. Fullerton to O. O. Howard, July 31, 1865, LR, Dept. of Ga.

46. O. O. Howard to C. B. Fisk, Aug. 31, 1865, reel 1 (RI)BRFAL (M742). Howard first offered the job to Gen. Walter Q. Gresham, a fellow veteran of the Army of the Tennessee, who refused the assignment. He also considered Gen. Absalom Baird, who would eventually serve the Bureau in Louisiana. The commissioner informed Saxton that Tillson was on his way to Georgia on September 12, 1865. Bentley believes that Andrew Johnson pushed Tillson's candidacy, noting that the president met with Howard on September 9 to discuss assistant commissioners. As early as August 12, Johnson was

aware of Tillson's activities in Tennessee. Brevet Major General J. E. Smith had reported that Tillson's "energetic management" was beneficial to both freedpeople and planters, and he had urged the president to keep Tillson in Tennessee. Bentley's view suggests that Tillson was Johnson's man. Also on September 8, D. M. Leatherwood wrote to the president praising Tillson and regretting his removal, suggesting that other Tennesseans had probably provided Johnson with similar information earlier during Tillson's residency in the state. However, Howard's and Tillson's correspondence suggest that Johnson confirmed an acceptable decision made by the commissioner and that Johnson did not force Tillson on Howard. While Tillson was no radical, he was not Johnson's toady. He did not agree with the president on all points, but as a military man he felt obliged to carry out his orders. J. S. Fullerton to O. O. Howard, July 31, 1865, LR, Dept. of Ga.; O. O. Howard to R. Saxton, Sept. 12, 1865, reel 1, (RI)BRFAL (M742); J. E. Smith to A. Johnson, Aug. 12, 1865, *Official Records*, ser. 1, vol. 49, pt. 2, 1099; D. M. Leatherwood to A. Johnson, reel 17, series 1, Andrew Johnson Papers (microfilm), Library of Congress; Bentley, *Freedmen's Bureau*, 69.

47. Tillson publicly assumed command with the issuance of his General Orders, No. 1, Sept. 22, 1865, reel 34, BRFAL-Ga (M798). Howard had announced the appointment on September 19 (Howard, *Autobiography*, 2:217). Like Edward A. Wild, Tillson was officially acting assistant commissioner, with orders to report to Saxton (who remained the assistant commissioner of South Carolina and Georgia) because of the limitations the original Bureau law placed on the number of assistant commissioners that Howard could appoint. Also, Tillson had no authority over the Sherman Reservation lands. This situation would remain until the end of 1865, when Howard relieved Tillson of his obligation to report to Saxton and gave him complete authority to deal with all Bureau affairs throughout the state. Nevertheless, Tillson's authority was greater than that of Wild, who had received his orders from Saxton. Howard's headquarters made it clear to Saxton that Tillson could act independently and carry on as if he were an assistant commissioner in his own right. Special Orders, No. 63, Bureau Headquarters, Washington, Sept. 9, 1865, reel 7, BRFAL-SC (M869); M. Woodhull to R. Saxton, Sept. 19, 1865, reel 1, (RI)BRFAL (M742); Howard, *Autobiography*, 2:217.

Special Orders, No. 119, Bureau HQ, Washington, Dec. 26, 1865, ordered Tillson to report directly to Howard. Special Orders, Bureau HQ, Washington, Feb. 24, 1866, removed the last limitation on Tillson's Georgia authority by ordering Capt. A. P. Ketchum, Saxton's officer in the Georgia Reservation lands, to turn over all records concerning his duties to Tillson. Both orders are on reel 34, BRFAL-Ga (M798).

48. D. Tillson to J. Thweatt, Oct. 17, 1865, reel 1, BRFAL-Ga (M798).

49. R. Saxton to D. Tillson, Sept. 29, 1865, reel 1, BRFAL-SC (M869). For the continued problem of rapid demobilization see M. Woodhull to D. Tillson, Dec. 28, 1865, reel 24 BRFAL-Ga (M798).

50. D. Tillson to Adjutant General, July 6, 1865; D. Tillson to C. B. Fisk, Sept. 13, 1865,

reel 8; Special Orders, No. 36, Sept. 2, 1865, reel 16, BRFAL-Tn (M999); W. Gray to D. Tillson, July 6, 1865, box 66, Memphis Subdistrict, Tennessee, BRFAL, RG 105, National Archives.

51. General Orders, No. 1, Fourth Division, Army of the Cumberland, Mar. 18, 1865, *Official Records*, ser. 1, vol. 49, pt. 2, 21; D. Tillson to Adjutant General, July 6, 1865, reel 8, BRFAL-Tn (M999); General Orders, No. 2, Oct. 6, 1865, BRFAL-Ga (M798).

52. Special Orders, No. 1, Oct. 5, 1865; Special Orders, No. 4, Oct. 12, 1865; Special Orders, No. 10, Oct. 21, 1865; Special Orders, No. 16, Nov. 9, 1865; Special Orders, No. 18, Nov. 13, 1865; Special Orders, No. 21, Nov. 24, 1865, reel 34; G. S. Eberhart, "Report of G. S. Eberhart State Superintendent of Schools Bureau of Refugees, Freedmen and Abandoned Lands for the State of Georgia from October 1, 1865 to October 1, 1866," reel 32, BRFAL-Ga (M798).

53. A. L. [Alexander] to "my darlings," Oct. 1, 1865, Alexander-Hillhouse Papers, University of North Carolina, Southern Historical Collection; D. Tillson to O. O. Howard, Oct. 5, 1865, reel 20, (LR)BRFAL (M752); and *Athens Southern Banner*, Nov. 15, 1865.

54. D. Tillson to J. Johnson, Oct. 25, 1865; D. Tillson to R. Saxton, Nov. 2, 1865, reel 1, BRFAL-Ga (M798); D. Tillson to O. O. Howard, Nov. 1, 1865, reel 20, (LR)BRFAL (M752). One might have assumed that Tillson's Tennessee experience with intransigent whites would have given him pause in taking an optimistic approach to how white Georgians would respond to the Bureau, but under the circumstances, he had no choice. Also, he continued to believe that white Southerners needed to be convinced of the efficacy of Reconstruction by participating in it.

In antebellum Georgia, justices of the peace were elected to four-year terms, two for each militia district, with counties having anywhere from four to eighteen districts. Each county had an inferior court made up of five elected justices. For the authority of the justices of the peace and the inferior court justices as well as the county ordinary and for the occupations and wealth of the inferior court justices in antebellum Georgia, see Wooster, *The People in Power*, 65–66, 158–59.

55. "General Tillson's Speech to the Freedmen's Convention," *Augusta Loyal Georgian*, Jan. 20, 1866.

56. M. Woodhull to D. Tillson, Oct. 10, Nov. 24, 1865, reel 24, BRFAL-Ga (M798).

57. D. Tillson to O. O. Howard, Nov. 1, 1865; D. Tillson to E. M. Stanton, Nov. 15, 1865, enclosed in D. Tillson to O. O. Howard, Nov. 21, 1865, reel 20, (LR)BRFAL (M752); D. Tillson to J. Johnson, Oct. 25, 1865, reel 1, BRFAL-Ga (M798).

58. Tillson might have encouraged Dennett's decision; the assistant commissioner was not pleased with the state of affairs in Savannah and was especially disturbed by the high number of rations being issued there. When Saxton discharged Eaton, he noted he had to do so because he lacked funds to pay him a salary; there is no reason to doubt that this fact was a consideration in Tillson's release of Bryant, although he was willing to keep Eaton on in an unpaid capacity. D. Tillson to R. Saxton, Oct. 14, 1865, reel 8,

BRFAL-SC (M869); W. Tiffany to H. F. Sickles, Nov. 27, 1865, box 28, ULR, Savannah SAC, BRFAL-Ga; T. G. Campbell to Rufus Saxton, Mar. 29, 1866 (and all endorsements), reel 27; D. Tillson to O. O. Howard, Oct. 21, 1865, reel 20; D. Tillson to O. O. Howard, Sept. 22, 1866, reel 37, (LR)BRFAL (M752); W. F. Eaton to D. Tillson, Sept. 25, 29, 1866, reel 26; D. Tillson, "Report of Operations September 22, 1865 to November 1, 1866," reel 32; Special Orders, No. 4, Oct. 12, 1865; Special Orders, No. 85, May 28, 1866, reel 34; Registers of Civilian Agents, 1865–1867, reel 35, BRFAL-Ga (M798); S. W. Saxton to W. F. Tiffany, Dec. 19, 1865; S. W. Saxton to W. F. Eaton, Jan. 10, 1866; S. W. Saxton to W. W. Deane, Jan. 22, 1866, Saxton Papers.

59. Bryant's discharge probably began the animosity between them. Nevertheless, Tillson's and Bryant's Reconstruction views did not significantly diverge and lead them into conflict until after Bryant left the Bureau, which supports the conclusion that the reasons for his removal were probably those stated above. (See Bryant's speech to the freedmen's convention in Augusta shortly after he left the Bureau, printed in the *Augusta Loyal Georgian*, Jan. 27, 1866, for an example of his Reconstruction views that parallel Tillson's own.) Davis had been born in New Jersey, but came to Georgia before the war, where he had accumulated no significant wealth by 1861. Register of Civilian Agents, 1865–1867; Station Books, vol. 1, 1867–1868, reel 35; D. Tillson to Maj. Gen. Brannon, Jan. 6, 1866, reel 1; J. R. Davis to E. Pickett, June 11, 1867, reel 14; J. R. Davis to O. O. Howard, Apr. 13, 1868, reel 21, BRFAL-Ga (M798); J. R. Lewis to O. O. Howard, Sept. 26, 1867, reel 49, (LR)BRFAL (M752); Richmond County Tax Digest for 1861, GDAH; Currie-McDaniel, *Carpetbagger of Conscience*, 56–57.

60. Tillson appointed at least three Union veterans. Of the thirteen identified Georgia Unionists, three were Northerners by birth, eight were native Georgians, and one was German. Some of these men or their references specifically referred to their Unionism, one is identified by a Unionist as having the "right antecedents," others are judged Unionists because they were able to take the oath required of all who assumed paid positions with the Bureau during Sibley's tenure, although one turned out to have falsely taken the ironclad oath. D. Tillson to O. O. Howard, Jan. 30, 1866, reel 20; D. Tillson to O. O. Howard, Nov. 8, 1866; C. F. Sawyer to D. Tillson, Aug. 29, 1866, reel 37; G. W. Jones to C. C. Sibley, Mar. 4, 1867; H. Loyless to N. S. Hill, Mar. 7, 1867, reel 42; J. R. Lewis to O. O. Howard, Sept. 26, 1867, reel 49, (LR)BRFAL (M752); A. P. Schurz to [————], Dec. 20, 1865, reel 31; P. Slaughter to D. Tillson, Dec. 26, 1865; J. C. Swayze to D. C. Poole, Jan. 21, 1866; J. R. Phillips to D. Tillson, Feb. 28, 1866 (and endorsement by J. C. Swayze), reel 31; J. H. Taylor to D. Tillson, Feb. 21, 1866; W. F. White to E. Pickett, June 25, 1866, reel 19; J. C. Swayze to D. Tillson, July 18, 1866, reel 29; G. M. Nolan to E. Pickett, Jan. 1, 1867, reel 30; J. B. Davenport to E. Pickett, May 7, 1867, reel 14; Registers of Civilian Agents 1865–1867; Station Books, vol. 1, 1867–1868, reel 35, BRFAL-Ga (M798).

61. A. Whitehead to D. Tillson, Nov. 20, 1865; D. Tillson, "Report of Operations September 22, 1865, to November 1, 1866," reel 32, BRFAL-Ga (M798).

62. D. Tillson to H. F. Sickles, Nov. 15, 1865, reel 1, BRFAL-Ga (M798)

63. J. H. Hand to D. Tillson, [Nov. 20, 1865], reel 31, BRFAL-Ga (M798).

64. J. J. Floyd and P. Reynolds to D. Tillson, Nov. 14, 1865, reel 31 BRFAL-Ga (M798).

65. No doubt this letter helped shape the president's opinion of Tillson, contributing—after the fact of the assistant commissioner's appointment—to the impression that Tillson was Johnson's man. H. M. Watterson to A. Johnson, Oct. 30, 1865, Harvey MaGee Watterson Papers, Georgia Historical Society, Savannah.

66. D. R. Mitchell to E. Lang, Jan. 20, 1866, box 34, LR, Thomasville SAC, BRFAL-Ga. Lang served as an agent from December 18, 1865, to May 2, 1867. Registers of Civilian Agents, 1865–1867, reel 35, BRFAL-Ga (M798).

67. Special Orders, No. 25, Dec. 1, 1865, BRFAL-Ga (M798). For examples of the petitions that came out of the local meetings that often selected and nominated potential agents to Tillson, see Citizens of Dawson County to [D. Tillson], Nov. 25, 1865; D. H. Roberts and others, Jan. 13, 1866, enclosed in W. H. Pritchett to D. Tillson, Jan. 16, 1866; S. Clements and others to [D. Tillson], Jan. 23, 1866, reel 31, BRFAL-Ga (M798).

68. All but forty-six of these were appointed in December and January. Tillson probably planned to appoint two or three agents to each county, depending on the population and size of the county. He allowed these agents to define their own territories by dividing the county along the lines of militia districts that suited their convenience. Registers of Civilian Agents, 1865–1867, reel 35; J. W. Carswell to D. Tillson, Dec. 18, 1865; P. Walden to D. Tillson, Dec. 21, 1865; C. E. Grant to D. Tillson, Jan. 1, 1866; F. J. Robinson to D. Tillson, Jan. 11, 1866, reel 31, BRFAL-Ga (M798).

69. H. Morgan to D. Tillson, Nov. 18, 1865, reel 31, BRFAL-Ga (M798).

70. Burke County Tax Digest for 1860, GDAH. The 1860 U.S. census lists only eighty-six of Burke County's 720 slaveholders as owning forty or more slaves.

71. Coweta County Tax Digest for 1860, GDAH. According to the 1860 U.S. census, only four men owned 100–200 slaves in Coweta County.

72. According to the 1860 U.S. census, of the 217 slaveholders in Franklin County, only thirteen owned more than fifteen slaves. In 1861 Willis had nineteen slaves. Franklin County Tax Digest for 1861, GDAH.

73. In November 1866, Tillson reported that he had appointed 244 agents; this is the total recorded in the registers through the end of 1866. Tillson appointed one additional agent in early January 1867. Sibley appointed three more civilian agents on January 25 shortly after Tillson left the Bureau, but given Sibley's appointment policy Tillson probably selected these civilian agents before Sibley issued their appointments. There were always fewer agents actually on duty than the total number of appointments. For example, there were about 184 on duty in April 1866, 169 in August, 174 in December. There were probably a few more agents on duty at any given time—or a few less—but the registers fail to list the appointment and termination dates of some agents, and

others probably stopped performing their duties before they resigned or were removed. No other state assistant commissioner relied on so many native whites to staff their agencies. D. Tillson, "Report of Operations September 22, 1865, to November 1, 1866," reel 32; Registers of Civilian Agents, 1865–1867, reel 35, BRFAL-Ga (M798); O. O. Howard, "Reports of the Assistant Commissioners, Dec. 21, 1866," *House Executive Documents*, 41st Cong., 2d sess., no. 142 (serial 1417), 30–31, 43, 61, 87, 101, 127, 158. The record of antebellum wealth of 71 of the 252 agents appointed by the assistant commissioner during 1865 and 1866 was preserved in county tax digests. Unfortunately, only a portion of Georgia's 132 counties are represented by the extant tax digests at the Georgia Department of Archives and History in Atlanta, Georgia. Since there is not a complete run of digests for all the available counties for any given year from 1857 through 1861, information was gathered from whichever year was available in that range. Despite these gaps, the figures are suggestive. Forty-nine (69%) of the agents listed in the extant digests had been slaveholders. Twenty-five (51%) of those slaveholders had owned more than ten slaves; thirty-five (71%) had owned more than five slaves. The recorders who maintained the antebellum tax digests also listed the value of all taxable wealth including land, town property, tools, and merchandise. Although six of Tillson's appointees located in these records had no taxable property before the war, the others had increments of wealth that ran the spectrum. Eleven agents had owned property valued at $30,000 or more, whereas eight had held taxable property worth less than $1,000. A good many agents, however, had had a significant stake in antebellum society. Fifteen had paid taxes on property worth $1,000 to $4,999, and forty-two (59%)—including those wealthiest eleven mentioned above—had owned taxable property worth $5,000 or more.

74. H. D. Williams to D. Tillson, Apr. 4, 1866, reel 29, BRFAL-Ga (M798). George N. Forbes to D. Tillson, Dec. 12, 1865; Samuel H. Crawford to D. Tillson, June 28, 1866, reel 31, BRFAL-Ga (M798).

75. Daniel S. Printemps to D. Tillson, Feb. 3, 1866, reel 28; James P. Simmons to D. Tillson, Nov. 12, 1865, reel 31, BRFAL-Ga (M798). That the candidate opposed secession suggests that perhaps Simmons and other Georgians believed that antisecessionists, even if they had eventually participated in the rebellion, would be acceptable to the federals because of that earlier opposition.

76. Alexander Stephens to D. Tillson, Dec. 28, 1865, reel 31, BRFAL-Ga (M798); 1850 census synopsis and abstract of the will of Alexander H. Stephens in Lunceford, *Taliaferro County, Georgia: Records and Notes*, 94, 372. In 1861 Jones owned $1,180 worth of taxable property. Taliaferro County Tax Digest for 1861, GDAH.

77. J. J. Wallace and others to D. Tillson, Dec. 13, 1865, reel 31, BRFAL-Ga (M798).

78. R. A. Turnipseed and A. J. Womack to D. Tillson, Dec. 18, 1865, reel 31, BRFAL-Ga (M798).

79. J. J. Floyd and P. Reynolds to D. Tillson, Nov. 14, 1865; A. W. Redding to L. Lambert, Dec. 21, 1865, reel 31, BRFAL-Ga (M798).

80. D. Tillson, Speech to the Georgia State Convention, Oct. 27, 1865, enclosed in D. Tillson to O. O. Howard, Nov. 1, 1865, reel 20 (LR)BRFAL (M752); D. Tillson to J. B. Walker, Nov. 20, 1865, reel 1, BRFAL-Ga (M798). Dan T. Carter notes the large number of "reluctant secessionists" among the postwar leadership and a willingness in 1865 to engage in some type of self-reconstruction in *When the War Was Over*. Also, William Warren Rogers notes the desire to end conflict and the quest for stability in Thomas County during this period in *Thomas County, 1865–1900*, 3–4. A desire for order or self-reconstruction, however, did not mean acquiescence to the Bureau's authority or an acceptance of its goals for Reconstruction, especially after the agency's purpose became clearer to native white Georgians.

81. D. Tillson, Speech to the Georgia State Convention, Oct. 27, 1865, enclosed in D. Tillson to O. O. Howard, Nov. 1, 1865, reel 20, (LR)BRFAL (M752).

82. R. Anderson to G. W. Selvidge, Dec. 10, 1866, reel 25; Register of Civilian Agents, 1865–1867, reel 35, BRFAL-Ga. Tillson also responded favorably to a petition from Savannah freedpeople for the appointment of Dominick O'Byrne. It did seem to matter that the freedpeople's requests were endorsed by Bureau officers or agents. Nevertheless, Tillson claimed that he considered the recommendations of the freedpeople whenever they reached him, and his actions concerning Savannah and Catoosa County as well as Clarke County, where he put black preference over white, suggest that at least on a few occasions he kept his word. J. Cox and others to D. Tillson, Dec. 12, 1865, reel 31, BRFAL-Ga (M798); "General Tillson's Speech to the Freedmen's Convention," *Augusta Loyal Georgian*, Jan. 20, 1866.

83. Tillson appointed Lyle on December 31, 1865. There are other indications that Tillson was willing to listen to the freedpeople when they were able to make themselves heard. H. B. Sprague to M. Davis, Dec. 1, 1865; M. Davis and others to H. B. Sprague, Dec. 3, 1865; John Cox and others to [D. Tillson], Dec. 12, 1865, reel 31; J. R. Smith to D. Tillson, July 4, 1866, reel 29, BRFAL-Ga (M798); Registers of Civilian Agents, 1865–1867, reel 35, BRFAL-Ga (M798); Drago, *Black Politicians*, 168.

84. Circular No. 4, Nov. 15, 1865, reel 34; D. Tillson to A. H. Hansell, Dec. 7, 1865, reel 1, BRFAL-Ga (M798). The practice of using fees to pay for services performed by certain government officials was not unknown in Georgia or elsewhere before the Civil War. It was also a practice used later by General John Pope as a means of compensating voter registrars in Georgia. Wallenstein, *From Slave South to New South*, 43; General Orders, No. 20, HQ Third Military District, May 21, 1867, in Candler, *Confederate Records*, 6:96–97.

85. Circular No. 4, Nov. 15, 1865, reel 34, BRFAL-Ga (M798).

86. For example, Colonel H. F. Sickles, subassistant commissioner at Augusta, was assigned a sergeant and two privates. Tillson charged his subassistant commissioners with traveling through their districts—or sending the men attached to their office—to inspect agents' work. Their actions generally had to be approved by the assistant

commissioner. They especially could make no expenditures without first clearing their intention with Tillson, who quickly centralized all of the agency's financial dealings under his quartermaster, Captain C. T. Watson. Special Orders, No. 12, Oct. 24, 1865; General Orders, No. 4, Nov. 3, 1865; Special Orders, No. 38, Dec. 26, 1865, reel 34, BRFAL-Ga (M798); D. Tillson to O. O. Howard, Dec. 25, 1865, reel 20, (LR)BRFAL (M752).

87. H. B. Sprague to D. Tillson, Nov. 24, 1865 (and all endorsements), reel 13, BRFAL-Ga (M798). In September 1865, shortly after Tillson assumed command, Commissioner Howard's brother informed him that Steedman believed the Georgia Bureau was working well under Tillson. Commissioner Howard later noted that the assistant commissioner and the department commander worked well together. C. H. Howard to O. O. Howard, Sept. 27, 1865, Howard Papers; Howard, *Autobiography*, 2:249; D. Tillson to O. O. Howard, Oct. 5, 1866, reel 20, (LR)BRFAL (M752).

88. M. Woodhull to D. Tillson, Dec. 28, 1865, reel 24, BRFAL-Ga (M798). Requests for army officers were not always granted because of personnel shortages. Endorsement of Bvt. Maj. Gen. John H. King, Nov. 11, 1865, on D. Tillson to Col. S. B. Moe, Nov. 1, 1865, reel 24, BRFAL-Ga (M792); D. Tillson to O. O. Howard, Apr. 18, 1866, reel 27, (LR)BRFAL (M752).

89. In December 1866 Tillson had officers from the Corps serving as subassistant commissioners stationed at Americus, Atlanta, Augusta, Brunswick, Columbus, Cuthbert, Griffin, Macon, Marietta, Rome, Thomasville, and Waynesboro. An officer had been stationed at Savannah until December 1866. For a listing of the officers and their assignments, see the roster of officers on duty in the Georgia Bureau during December 1866, reel 35, BRFAL-Ga (M798). G. T. Crabtree to D. Tillson, Dec. 25, 1865, reel 13; Dec. 25, 1865, reel 24, BRFAL-Ga (M798); D. Tillson to O. O. Howard, Apr. 18, 1866, reel 27; Nov. 19, 1866, reel 37, (LR)BRFAL (M752); Bentley, *Freedmen's Bureau*, 134; Boatner, *Civil War Dictionary*, 870.

90. T. F. Forbes to Capt. J. K. Smith, Aug. 18, 1866; T. F. Forbes to T. P. Littlefield, Sept. 28, 1866, reel 3; D. Tillson, "Report of Operations September 22, 1865 to November 1, 1866," reel 31, BRFAL-Ga (M798).

91. M. Woodhull to D. Tillson, Nov. 21, 1865, reel 24, BRFAL-Ga (M798); C. H. Howard to R. Saxton, Dec. 15, 1865, reel 34, BRFAL-SC (M869). As early as December 1865, the commissioner's brother and chief of staff, Charles H. Howard, while in Georgia on an inspection tour, admitted that he was apprehensive about Tillson's organization: "These citizen agents . . . will need to be closely watched and their operations supervised if not *revised* by U.S. officers or the negro will hardly get justice." C. H. Howard to R. Saxton, Dec. 15, 1865, reel 34, BRFAL-SC (M869).

92. J. T. Stephens to Capt. G. H. Pratt, Apr. 13, 1866, reel 29; T. F. Forbes to Capt. J. K. Smith, Aug. 18, 1866; T. F. Forbes to T. P. Littlefield, Sept. 28, 1866, reel 3; T. P. Littlefield to D. Tillson, Sept. 26, 1866, reel 8, BRFAL-Ga (M798).

93. At this time Commissioner Howard and Senator Lyman Trumbull were working

on the bill to extend the Bureau. Tillson's suggestions were probably too late to influence their work, but they do suggest that he was aware of the problems his agency and the freedpeople faced in Georgia and wished to do something about them. Howard, *Autobiography*, 2:280; McFeely, *Yankee Stepfather*, 199; Bentley, *Freedmen's Bureau*, 115–17.

94. D. Tillson to O. O. Howard, Dec. 20, 1865, reel 20, (LR)BRFAL (M752) and Tillson's draft of a plan for reorganizing the Bureau enclosed in this letter. Here Tillson agreed with Rufus Saxton about the need for troops to protect Union men. For Saxton's comments on the safety of Union men in Georgia at this time, see his February 21, 1866, testimony in *House Reports*, 39th Cong., 1st sess., no. 30 (serial 1273), pt. 3, 101. At this time Tillson also complained that the muster out of troops in late December would deprive him of the force to punish crime and carry out orders, and in March he once again complained about the need for cavalry. Tillson did not mail the letter containing this complaint because of objections from General Brannan, who believed Tillson would be exceeding his authority by calling for more troops. However, Brannan also understood that it was critical to have cavalry available to enforce Reconstruction, and he requested the troopers. C. Howard to O. O. Howard, Dec. 30, 1865, *House Reports*, 39th Cong., 1st sess., no. 30 (serial 1273), 46; D. Tillson to O. O. Howard, Mar. 19, 1866; W. W. Deane to D. Tillson, Mar. 21, 1866, reel 2, BRFAL-Ga (M798); Bvt. Maj. Gen. J. Brannan to Bvt. Brig. Gen. W. D. Whipple, Mar. 21, 1866, LR, Dept. of Ga.

95. For the definition of the civil rights of the freedpeople as well as law that authorized court contracts and a colorless apprenticeship law, both of which had bearing on the freedpeople, see *Acts of the General Assembly of the State of Georgia, Passed in Milledgeville, at the Annual Session in December 1865 and January, February, and March 1866*, 6–8, 74–75, 239.

96. General Orders, No. 17, Mar. 6, 1866, vol. 5/7, General Orders, Dept. of Ga.

97. For Tillson's instructions to his subordinates, see Circular No. 4, Apr. 6, 1866, and Circular No. 6, Apr. 9, 1866, reel 34, BRFAL-Ga (M798).

98. The March 4, 1866, issue of the *Macon Daily Telegraph* quoted Tillson as saying that the passage and approval of legislation defining the freedpeople's rights would render the Bureau an "unconstitutional institution" and that the "further continuance of Federal interference" in freedmen's affairs would become "clearly illegal." The reporter was mistaken and probably heard what he wished to hear. Tillson, despite his willingness to encourage civil authority, always assumed that the federal government could supersede civil actions that were illegal or unjust, and on numerous occasions he intervened using troops to protect the freedpeople's rights.

99. Trefousse, *Andrew Johnson*, 242–43. On Johnson's racism see Bowen, *Andrew Johnson and the Negro*, esp. 135–56.

100. The Supreme Court announced its decision in April, but the justices did not deliver their opinions until December. Nieman, *To Set the Law in Motion*, 115–16; Bentley, *Freedmen's Bureau*, 162, 252n.

101. *Macon Daily Telegraph*, Apr. 6, 1866; *Augusta Daily Constitutionalist*, Apr. 4, 1866. Numerous other commentators praised Johnson's proclamation and the return of habeas corpus; see *Augusta Daily Constitutionalist*, Apr. 7, 15, 1866; *Macon Daily Telegraph*, Apr. 7, 1866; *Athens Southern Banner*, Apr. 11, 1966; *Columbus Daily Enquirer*, Apr. 18, 1866; *Sandersville Central Georgian*, Apr. 18, 1866; Sefton, *Army and Reconstruction*, 77–81.

102. F. A. H. Gaebel to W. W. Deane, Apr. 11, 14, 1866, reel 27, BRFAL-Ga (M798).

103. J. H. Taylor to W. W. Deane, Apr. 13, 1866, reel 29, BRFAL-Ga (M798); also see J. Tillman to W. W. Deane, Apr. 15, 1866, reel 29, BRFAL-Ga (M798). Agent A. B. Nichols also discovered that his difficulties began as soon as the people in his jurisdiction learned of the president's veto. A. B. Nichols to D. Tillson, Mar. 21, 1866, reel 28, BRFAL-Ga (M798).

104. D. Tillson to O. O. Howard, Apr. 7, 1866 (telegram); D. Tillson to O. O. Howard, Apr. 7, 1866, reel 27, (LR)BRFAL (M752).

105. O. O. Howard to D. Tillson, Apr. 12, 1866, Howard Papers; Proclamation of Governor Charles J. Jenkins, Apr. 14, 1866, reprinted in D. Tillson, Circular No. 7, Apr. 18, 1866, reel 34, BRFAL-Ga (M798).

106. As for exercising military power under the Bureau bill, the president as commander-in-chief still had the authority to set the ground rules and at least try to obstruct the agency. Also, the Bureau law seemed to conflict with the Milligan case. Howard informed Tillson's successor, Caleb Sibley, that some of the Supreme Court justices did not believe that their decision would apply to states "not yet represented in Congress," and in January he pressed him to test the decision and its limits on Bureau authority by holding a military commission. Sibley questioned his authority to act in this area, the president learned of Howard's maneuver, and the matter was dropped. O. O. Howard to C. C. Sibley, Jan. 30, 1867, reel 30, BRFAL-Ga (M798); C. C. Sibley to O. O. Howard, Feb. 16, 1867, reel 2, (LR)BRFAL (M752); O. O. Howard to C. C. Sibley, Feb 20, 1867, reel 3, (RI)BRFAL (M742); Nieman, *To Set the Law in Motion*, 109, 146–47; Bentley, *Freedmen's Bureau*, 162–64.

107. Before this appointment the Bureau assistant commissioners were, according to the commissioner, subordinate to their states' army commanders "in all matters purely military," and Tillson found a reluctance on the part of his army counterpart always to act as aggressively as he would have wished. Tillson's appointment, however, was a mixed blessing for the Bureau, because the military interpreted the appointment of Bureau assistant commissioners as the clear subordination of the agency to the army hierarchy. Shortly after Tillson and the other assistant commissioners were integrated into the military chain of command, Howard, trying to hold on to what authority he had over his Bureau, ordered his assistant commissioners to continue to report directly to him and to supply duplicates to their army commanders "provided they authorize by detail or otherwise a sufficient clerical force for this purpose." O. O. Howard to D. Tillson, Apr. 12,

1866; D. Tillson to O. O. Howard, May 29, 1866, Howard Papers; O. O. Howard to R. K. Scott, June 12, 1866, reel 2; O. O. Howard to D. Tillson, May 25, 1866, reel 2; O. O. Howard to Assistant Commissioners, June 14, 1865, reel 1, (RI)BRFAL (M742); D. Tillson to R. G. Hunt, May 2, 1866, reel 2, BRFAL-Ga (M798); Bvt. Brig. Gen. W. D. Whipple to Bvt. Maj. Gen. C. R. Woods, June 21, 1866, Dist. and Subdist. of Ga.

108. T. F. Forbes to F. P. Pease, June 15, 1866, reel 3, BRFAL-Ga (M798).

109. General Orders, No. 44, July 6, 1866, Reconstruction file, GDAH; Mantell, *Johnson, Grant, and the Politics of Reconstruction*, 28. Later in December there were rumors that this order had been revoked, but Tillson reconfirmed his officers' right to enforce it. E. Pickett to F. A. H. Gaebel, Dec. 12, 1866, reel 4, BRFAL-Ga (M798).

110. J. H. Taylor to W. W. Deane, Apr. 28, 1866, reel 29; J. R. Phillips to D. Tillson, May 25, 1866, reel 28; J. T. Harmon to W. W. Deane, Dec. 1, 1866, reel 27, BRFAL-Ga (M798).

111. For the second peace proclamation and its impact on how the army viewed its role, see Sefton, *Army and Reconstruction*, 79–81.

112. Recall that during this period Congress was considering a civil rights bill as well as the Bureau's extension bill. One might judge the impact of the inspection tour on Congress's determination by noting that the Bureau bill passed through the House in May, through the Senate in June, and over the president's veto in July. O. O. Howard to D. Tillson, June 5, 1866, Howard Papers; Bentley, *Freedmen's Bureau*, 125–33, McFeely, *Yankee Stepfather*, 243–56.

113. H. V. J[ohnson] to A. Stephens, May 31, 1866, Herschel V. Johnson Papers, Duke University.

114. Steedman reportedly vowed to put an end to the Bureau's judicial role in Georgia. Steedman and Fullerton also argued for a laissez-faire approach to labor, stating that contracts in fact lowered wages and contradicted "justice and sound political economy." Georgians heard the criticism of the Bureau, however, and undoubtedly believed that it sustained their complaints and pay scales. Experience documented by the Bureau proved that with or without contracts, white employers resisted raising freedpeople's wages to the minimum set by Tillson. And Steedman and Fullerton singled out Colonel Louis J. Lambert, the Macon Bureau officer, for illegally appropriating funds. Tillson, however, had already begun an investigation of Lambert in February. Lambert claimed that all of his records and the missing money in question had been stolen. Tillson's inspector general could not make a case against Lambert because those records were missing and there were no witnesses to the alleged crime. He did, however, believe that the lack of records was suspicious and indicative of underhanded dealings. Tillson concluded that Lambert, who had already been mustered out with an honorable discharge and was residing in New York City, owed the Bureau $250. Commissioner Howard praised the Georgia Bureau for having only one case of maladministration, but there were at least two other officers who came under Tillson's scrutiny. Major G. A. Hastings

was charged with fraudulent financial dealings, but there is no indication that he was guilty of anything other than having enemies in Dougherty County. He was accused in late 1865, under investigation in early 1866, relieved in March 1866, but was free and planting in Dougherty County at the end of the year. He soon returned to his home in Bethel, Maine. Tillson personally discovered that Lieutenant J. W. Parks was "under the influence of unfortunate habits" that frequently left him "in an unfit condition" to do the Bureau's work. Tillson dismissed him shortly after discovering his failings. Tillson's actions clearly indicate that he acted decisively whenever it came to his attention that his subordinates were negligent. For comments from southwest Georgia about Steedman, Fullerton, and the Bureau's evil ways in the state see *New York Times*, May 26, 31, 1866. For Steedman and Fullerton's accusations see J. B. Steedman and J. S. Fullerton to A. Johnson, June 14, 1866, reel 22, series 1, Andrew Johnson Papers (microfilm); *Savannah Herald*, May 16, 19, 1866, quoted in *New York Times*, May 25, Aug. 10, 1866; *Savannah Republican*, Aug. 15, 1866. For the Lambert business see Howard, *Autobiography*, 2: 300–301; O. O. Howard to A. Johnson, Aug. 23, 1866, reel 2, (RI)BRFAL (M742); Special Orders, No. 29, Feb. 8, 1866; Special Orders, No. 92, June 11, 1866, reel 34; L. J. Lambert to D. Tillson, Feb. 21, 1866, reel 27; L. J. Lambert to W. W. Deane, Mar. 27, June 14, 1866; D. Tillson to N. S. Hill, June 14, 1866, reel 3, BRFAL-Ga (M798); G. Walbridge to D. Tillson, June 29, 1866 (and enclosures), reel 32, (LR)BRFAL (M752); Louis J. Lambert, Civil War pension files, RG 15, National Archives. For information on G. A. Hastings see Bvt. Brig. Gen. C. Munder to "Comd Gen Dept of Ga," Nov. 16, 1865; G. A. Hastings to W. W. Deane, Dec. 25, 1865, reel 24; Special Orders, No. 51, Mar. 20, 1866, reel 34; G. A. Hastings to D. Tillson, Dec. 7, 1866, reel 27, BRFAL-Ga (M798); Assistant Adjutant General to Capt. I. A. Watrous, Mar. 13, 1866, Letters & Telegrams Sent, Dept. of Ga.; Gideon A. Hastings, Civil War pension files, RG 15, National Archives. For Tillson's observations on Parks see D. Tillson to J. W. Parks, May 15, 1866, reel 2; D. Tillson to O. O. Howard, June 12, 1866, reel 3; Special Orders, No. 99, June 23, reel 34, BRFAL-Ga (M798).

115. *Albany Patriot*, Sept. 8, 1866; C. M. Pope to W. W. Deane, Nov. 7, 1866, reel 28, BRFAL-Ga (M798). At this time Georgians were also reading about a U.S. circuit court decision in Kentucky that nullified a Bureau judgment; editorialists drew the conclusion that if the Bureau had no power to extract monetary settlements from whites in Kentucky, it should have no power in Georgia. *Columbus Daily Sun*, Nov. 1, 1866; *Rome Weekly Courier*, Nov. 9, 1866.

116. T. Forbes to R. T. Ross, July 17, 1866, reel 3, BRFAL-Ga (M798).

117. E. Pickett to J. H. Taylor, Nov. 7, 1866, reel 4, BRFAL-Ga (M798).

118. D. Tillson to C. A. de la Mesa, July 17, 1866, reel 3; E. Pickett to C. A. de la Mesa, Nov. 7, 1866, reel 4, BRFAL-Ga (M798).

119. G. Wagner to W. W. Deane, June 21, 1866, reel 29; endorsement of W. W. Deane, Sept. 4, 1866, on affidavit of Kineaum Lausen, Aug. 17, 1866, reel 13; T. F. Forbes to

F. A. H. Gaebel, Sept. 5, 26, 1866, reel 3; endorsement of E. Pickett to F. J. Foster, Dec. 12, 1866, reel 8, BRFAL-Ga (M798).

120. D. Tillson, "Report of Operations September 22, 1865, to November 1, 1866," reel 32, BRFAL-Ga (M798). In December 1866, Tillson refused to establish a special Bureau court, and he forwarded his decision to Howard recommending congressional action. Tillson's confidence in his judicial power to use the three-man panel in November might have been boosted by an earlier confidential but unauthorized circular letter from O. O. Howard, which urged his assistant commissioners to use these panels in certain cases involving freedpeople, including labor disputes, despite Johnson's opposition. Howard claimed that by law the Bureau retained authority that was "paramount over subjects relating to Refugees, Freedmen, and Abandoned Lands." However, Donald Nieman believes that Tillson had surrendered his judicial authority during the summer of 1866 and that in early December 1866, citing Tillson's reluctance to establish the Bureau court, the assistant commissioner believed that he lacked the authority to comply with Howard's wishes. Nevertheless, his reluctance in December did not mean that he abdicated all Bureau power to seek justice for the freedpeople. As noted in chapter 1, Tillson's philosophy of Reconstruction led him to try to draw whites into the process from the outset of his administration. Consequently, he was reluctant to supersede civil procedure on a regular basis, but he was not reluctant to step in once local authorities failed to be just with the freedpeople. Endorsement of D. Tillson, Dec. 10, 1866, reel 8; O. O. Howard, Circular Letter, Sept. 16, 1866, reel 34; A. P. Ketchum to D. Tillson, Sept. 19, 1866, reel 25, BRFAL-Ga (M798); Nieman, *To Set the Law in Motion*, 120, 144–46.

121 Endorsement of D. Tillson, Dec. 6, 1866, reel 8, BRFAL-Ga (M798).

122. Endorsements of D. Tillson, Dec. 5, 6, 12, 1866, reel 8, BRFAL-Ga (M798). Tillson's endorsement book, which records orders and advice made on incoming letters that were returned to agents or officers for action, provides several examples of the assistant commissioner's vigorous activities during these final months of his administration.

123. D. Tillson, "Report of Operations September 22, 1865, to November 1, 1866," reel 32, BRFAL-Ga (M798).

124. Howard, *Autobiography*, 2:296–97; O. O. Howard to D. Tillson, June 5, 1866, Howard Papers. Tillson, unaware of the political purposes of their inspection tour, was under the impression that Steedman and Fullerton would present a report that would do Howard credit. Howard wrote to disabuse him of that notion. D. Tillson to O. O. Howard, May 29, June 9, 1866, Howard Papers. Also see "Report of General J. B. Steedman and J. S. Fullerton, July 20, 1866," reprinted in the *New York Times*, Aug. 10, 1866; and O. O. Howard to A. Johnson, Aug. 23, 1866, reel 2, (RI)BRFAL (M742).

Steedman and Fullerton gave Tillson a favorable review (Steedman informed the president that Tillson was "a good man and an excellent officer who supports your administration"), although they criticized some of his agents' efforts and generally condemned the contract system, in which, of course, Tillson placed so much stock. His-torians have used this favorable report to brand Tillson as a planter's friend and a tool of President Johnson's anti-Radical policy, which, as noted earlier, is a much too simplistic interpretation of his approach to Reconstruction. J. B. Steedman to A. Johnson, June 26, 1866, reel 22, series 1, Andrew Johnson Papers (microfilm); McFeely, *Yankee Stepfather*, 249; Currie-McDaniel, *Carpetbagger of Conscience*, 70.

The fallout from the Steedman-Fullerton tour prompted rumors that Tillson would replace Howard as commissioner. There is no indication that Tillson himself encouraged this idea. Furthermore, after learning of the president's purpose from Howard, Tillson took it upon himself to offer encouraging words to his Bureau commander. In late May, Tillson in a confidential letter wrote to Howard urging him not to resign; "Stand by the cause, I know you will come out all right." It is possible that Tillson was playing both sides; more likely than not, however, Tillson was simply smart enough to refrain from openly criticizing Johnson's policies in front of Steedman and Fullerton. Besides, by late 1866 Tillson was already making other plans. In November 1866, Tillson wished to dis-courage talk of his moving to Washington because he was planning to leave the Bureau no later than the end of December, as he informed Howard in another letter written in his own hand marked "private." D. Tillson to O. O. Howard, May 29, 1866, Howard Papers; *Washington Evening Star*, Aug. 14, 28, 1866; *Augusta Daily Constitutionalist*, Aug. 25, 1866; Emma Bryant to John Emory Bryant, Aug. 25, Sept. 23, 1866, Bryant Pa-pers; D. Tillson to O. O. Howard, Nov. [—], 1866, filed with D. Tillson to O. O. Howard, Oct. 23, 1866, reel 37, (LR)BRFAL (M752); D. Tillson to O. O. Howard, May 29, June 9, 1866, Howard Papers; McFeely, *Yankee Stepfather*, 257; Bentley, *Freedmen's Bureau*, 133. Also see "Report of General J. B. Steedman and J. S. Fullerton, July 20, 1866," reprinted in the *New York Times*, Aug. 10, 1866; and O. O. Howard to A. Johnson, Aug. 23, 1866, reel 2, (RI)BRFAL (M742).

125. *Augusta Daily Constitutionalist*, July 21, 1866; *Washington Evening Star*, July 26, 1866; Howard, *Autobiography*, 2:331; Bentley, *Freedmen's Bureau*, 133–34; McFeely, *Yankee Stepfather*, 288–90.

126. See chapter 7 for Tillson's activities in the Sherman Reservation.

127. F. D. Sewall to O. O. Howard, Dec. 6, 1866, reel 39, (LR)BRFAL (M752).

128. F. D. Sewall to O. O. Howard, Dec. 15, 1866, reel 39, (LR)BRFAL (M752). Se-wall had also unfairly and inaccurately reported that Tillson had removed only two prob-lematical agents. Tillson's actions in this area are discussed in chapter 3.

129. C. C. Sibley, Report for February, Mar. 19, 1867, reel 32; Circular No. 2, Feb. 12, 1867, reel 34, BRFAL-Ga (M798). Sibley assigned subdistrict headquarters to Savan-nah, Brunswick, Thomasville, Cuthbert, Columbus, Macon, Augusta, Athens, Atlanta, and Rome. In March 1868, the subassistant commissioner at Cuthbert received permis-sion to transfer his headquarters to Albany. Roster of Officers and Civil Agents on Duty, Apr. 1, 1868, reel 35, BRFAL-Ga (M798).

130. Roster of Officers on Duty . . . during the Month of December 1866, Jan. 1, 1867; Roster of Officers and Agents on Duty, Aug. 1, Sept. 1, 1867; Station Books, vol. 1, 1867–1868, reel 35; Circular No. 1, Jan. 25, 1869, reel 34, BRFAL-Ga (M798).

131. J. R. Lewis to O. O. Howard, Nov. 24, 1866, reel 3, BRFAL-Tn (M999).

132. O. O. Howard to C. C. Sibley, Jan. 24, 1867, reel 30, BRFAL-Ga (M798).

133. Register of Civilian Agents, 1865–1867, reel 35, BRFAL-Ga (M798).

134. C. C. Sibley to O. O. Howard, Jan. 29, 1867, reel 4; C. C. Sibley, Report for February, Mar. 19, 1867, reel 32, BRFAL-Ga (M798); O. O. Howard to C. C. Sibley, Feb. 4, 1867, reel 3, (RI)BRFAL (M742). Years later Howard wrote in his memoirs that Sibley had actually prompted the change by reporting abuses committed by the local agents. Howard had the order of events mixed up. While there had been complaints about the civilian agents, Sibley's reports came after Howard initiated the reorganization. Howard, *Autobiography*, 2:340.

135. At the end of April, Captain E. Pickett sent out several letters asking agents if they or other individuals could take the oath; see reel 16, BRFAL-Ga (M798). For Sibley's conclusion, see C. C. Sibley, Report for March, Apr. 26, 1867; C. C. Sibley, Report for May, June 27, 1867, reel 32, BRFAL-Ga (M798).

136. C. C. Sibley to O. O. Howard, Mar. 27, 1867, reel 42 (LR)BRFAL (M752). For the number of agents see the Georgia Bureau personnel rosters dated Aug. 1, 1867, through Nov. 1, 1868, reel 35, BRFAL-Ga (M798).

137. C. C. Sibley, Report for April, May 23, 1867, reel 32, BRFAL-Ga (M798).

138. Registers of Civilian Agents, 1865–1867, reel 35, BRFAL-Ga (M798).

139. C. C. Sibley, Report for May, June 27, 1867, reel 32, BRFAL-Ga (M798).

140. Howard preferred to use discharged officers and soldiers "whose Unionism is undoubted, and whose records were creditable." O. O. Howard, Annual Report, Nov. 1, 1867, *House Executive Documents*, 40th Cong., 2d sess., no. 1 (serial 1324), 674.

141. Commissioner Howard did not approve of his agents or officers participating in the convention. Dunning was required to resign to remain active in Republican politics. D. Tillson to O. O. Howard, Nov. 8, 1866, reel 37; J. R. Lewis to O. O. Howard, Sept. 26, 1867, reel 49, (LR)BRFAL (M752); Registers of Civilian Agents, 1865–1867; M. F. Gallagher to W. M. White, Oct. 28, 1867, reel 6; Station Books, vol. 1, 1867–1868, reel 35, BRFAL-GA (M798); *Atlanta Intelligencer*, Sept. 25, 1851; *Atlanta Constitution*, Sept. 16, 1868; Candler, *Confederate Records*, 6:1022.

Sibley carried over seven additional Tillson agents. One other agent, Jacob R. Davis, was a northern-born immigrant to Georgia. Like Dunning he was an urban dweller, but in 1861 he had no taxable wealth and there is no record of his wartime sentiments. However, if he was able to take the required oath, he probably had not contributed to the rebel war effort. Richmond County 1861 Tax Digest (Augusta District), GDAH; J. R. Lewis to O. O. Howard, Sept. 26, 1867, reel 49, (LR)BRFAL (M752); Registers of Civilian Agents 1865–1867; Station Books, vol. 1, 1867–1868, reel 35, BRFAL-Ga (M798).

142. F. Mosebach to G. Walbridge, Mar. 29, 1867; C. W. Chapman to F. Mosebach, March 26, 1867 (enclosed in the preceding), reel 42; J. R. Lewis to O. O. Howard, Sept. 26, 1867, reel 49, (LR)BRFAL (M752); Station Books, vol. 1, 1867–1868, reel 35, BRFAL-Ga (M798).

143. Endorsement of J. J. Knox to C. C. Sibley, Mar. 5, 1867 on H. C. Flournoy to J. J. Knox, Mar. 5, 1867, reel 42; J. R. Lewis to O. O. Howard, Sept. 26, 1867, reel 49, (LR)BRFAL (M752); H. C. Flournoy to C. C. Sibley, Oct. 5, 1868, reel 23, BRFAL-Ga (M798).

144. The August personnel figure is from the Roster of Officers and Civil Agents, Aug. 1, 1867, reel 35, BRFAL-Ga (M798). In 1868, as the number of agents dropped, the number of assistant subassistant commissioners declined to two officers. Information concerning the background of the new agents was collected from various sources, especially the Bureau records. There were probably more Northerners serving with the Bureau, and among those agents identified as Northerners there were probably additional veterans. However, their places of birth and their war records are not apparent in the sources used for this study, including army pension files. One particularly useful source is a report to O. O. Howard in which John R. Lewis conveniently listed the birthplaces and the postbellum residences at the time of their appointments for many of the newly appointed agents. J. R. Lewis to O. O. Howard, Sept. 1, 1867, reel 49, (LR)BRFAL (M752). The number of agents serving during Sibley's and Lewis's tenures is drawn from Registers of Civilian Agents, 1865–1867; Station Books, vol. 1, 1867–1868; Station Books, vol. 2, 1869, reel 35, BRFAL-Ga (M798).

145. In May 1867 White found himself forcibly evicted from the second-class railcar into the "colored" car. J. L. Eberhart to A. P. Ketchum, Jan. 1, 1867, reel 42; J. R. Lewis to O. O. Howard, Sept. 26, 1867, reel 49, (LR)BRFAL (M752); W. J. White to C. C. Sibley, June 29, 1867; G. R. Walbridge to C. C. Sibley, June 29, 1867, reel 19; Station Books, vol. 1, 1867–1868, reel 35, BRFAL-Ga (M798); Coleman and Gurr, *Dictionary of Georgia Biography*, 1:1059–60.

146. Belcher had been separated from his parents as a child and had been raised in Pennsylvania. E. Belcher to C. C. Sibley, Apr. 28, May 14, 1867, reel 14; Edwin Belcher to J. R. Lewis, Oct. 23, 1867, reel 17; Station Books, vol. 1, 1867–1868, reel 35; E. Belcher to [C. C. Sibley], Mar. 12, 1867, Register of LR, reel 11, BRFAL-Ga (M798); J. R. Lewis to O. O. Howard, Sept. 26, 1867, reel 49, (LR)BRFAL (M752); Edwin Belcher, Civil War pension files, RG 15, National Archives; Drago, *Black Politicians*, 59–62, passim.

147. For information on the Military Reconstruction law of March 2 and subsequent clarifications as well as general points on Military Reconstruction, see Stampp, *Era of Reconstruction*, 144–45; Nieman, *To Set the Law in Motion*, 196–200; Conway, *Reconstruction in Georgia*, 136–61; and Bentley, *Freedmen's Bureau*, 165.

148. For Howard's problems, see McFeely, *Yankee Stepfather*, 288–94.

149. C. C. Sibley, General Orders, No. 1, Mar. 2, 1867, reel 34, BRFAL-Ga (M798).

150. C. C. Sibley to O. O. Howard, July 8, 1867, reel 5; F. D. Sewall to C. C. Sibley, July 8, 1867, reel 18; C. C. Sibley, General Orders, No. 2, July 9, 1867, reel 34, BRFAL-Ga (M798). Another example of this relationship occurred in September 1867 when Sibley received Pope's approval for a leave of absence and then broached the subject with Howard. C. C. Sibley to O. O. Howard, Sept. 3, 1867, reel 6, BRFAL-Ga (M798).

151. O. H. Howard to C. C. Sibley, Apr. 15, 1867, box 3, LR, Albany Agt, BRFAL-Ga.

152. J. M. Hoag to T. P. Pease, Mar. 28, 1867, vol. 397, LS, Savannah SAC, BRFAL-Ga.

153. General John Pope's Report in "Report of the Secretary of War, Part 1," *House Executive Documents*, 40th Cong., 2d sess., no. 1 (serial 1324), 321–24; General G. G. Meade's Report in "Report of the Secretary of War, Part 1," *House Executive Documents*, 40th Cong., 3d sess., no. 1 (serial 1367), 79, 81; C. C. Sibley to D. G. Risley, July 3, 1867, reel 5; O. B. Gray to J. R. Lewis, Sept. 4, 1867, reel 18; J. R. Lewis to O. B. Gray, Sept. 11, 1867, reel 6; R. C. Drum to C. C. Sibley, Mar. 3, 1868, reel 20, BRFAL-Ga (M798); R. B. Bulloch to R. C. Drum, July 18, 1867 (and endorsement), Alexander Stone, File 2, GDAH; testimony of W. C. Morrill, in Ku Klux Conspiracy, vol. 7: *Georgia*, pt. 2, 1098.

154. General John Pope's Report in "Report of the Secretary of War, Part 1," in *House Executive Documents*, 40th Cong., 2d sess., no. 1 (serial 1324), 350.

155. E. Pickett to N. S. Hill, Aug. 20, 1867, enclosed in E. Pickett to N. S. Hill, July 30, box 21, LR, Macon SAC, BRFAL-Ga.

156. R. C. Drum to C. C. Sibley, Mar. 3, 1868, reel 20; C. C. Sibley to O. O. Howard, Apr. 4, 1868, reel 7, BRFAL-Ga (M798). Meade, in fact, took pride in his restrained approach to supervising Georgia's Military Reconstruction, but freedpeople in southwest Georgia were not impressed and complained about how Meade restricted the Bureau. Report of Major General G. G. Meade, Oct. 31, 1868, *House Executive Documents*, 40th Cong., 3d sess., no. 1 (serial 1367), 79–81; Formwalt, ed., "Petitioning Congress for Protection."

157. After March 5, 1868, agents needed explicit orders from the assistant commissioner to seize crops unless it was clear that those crops were being removed beyond the reach of the workers and the law. M. F. Gallagher to J. M. Robinson, Feb. 24, 1868, reel 7; Confidential Circular, Mar. 5, 1868, reel 34, BRFAL-Ga (M798); C. C. Sibley to O. O. Howard, Apr. 4, 1868, reel 53 (LR)BRFAL (M752).

158. General Orders, No. 5, HQ Third Military District, Apr. 8, 1867; General Orders, No. 20, HQ Third Military District, May 21, 1867, in Candler, *Confederate Records*, 6: 66–68, 95–97. Elizabeth Studley Nathans provides a survey history of the Republican Party in Georgia and, necessarily, of state politics during this period in *Losing the Peace*. Her study, however, must be supplemented with Currie-McDaniel, *Carpetbagger*

*of Conscience*, and Duncan, *Entrepreneur for Equality*. For a detailed treatment of black participation in Georgia politics, the role played by black leaders, and the most complete listing of Georgia black leaders, see Drago, *Black Politicians*.

159. Special Orders, No. 14, HQ Third Military District, May 3, 1867; General Orders, No. 20, HQ Third Military District, May 21, 1867, in Candler, *Confederate Records*, 6: 94, 95–96.

160. M. F. Gallagher to T. Holden, Apr. 17, 1868, reel 7, BRFAL-Ga (M798). In his study of black voter registrars , Drago mistakenly identifies the army's Bureau of Civil Affairs as being part of the Freedmen's Bureau. The confusion results from the fact that the Georgia assistant commissioner was also the Georgia military district's commander. The state's superintendent for registration, Colonel E. Hulbert, reported to Sibley as commander of the Georgia district, but he was never part of the Georgia Bureau. Brevet Colonel James F. Meline was general inspector of registration for the Third Military District, not the Military District of Georgia. The study, nevertheless, is an important extension of Drago's research on black politicians down to the grassroots level. Drago, "Georgia's First Black Voter Registrars during Reconstruction."

161. E. Hulbert, Supt. of Registration, Georgia, General Orders, No. 20, May 21, 1867, box 1, Albany SAC, BRFAL-Ga; G. R. Walbridge to D. G. Risley, July 3, 1867, reel 5, BRFAL-Ga (M798) (with copies to all assistant subassistant commissioners and subassistant commissioners).

162. Conway, *Reconstruction of Georgia*, 114; C. C. Sibley to O. O. Howard, July 25, 1868, reel 7; M. F. Gallagher to J. J. Knox, Aug. 3, 1868, reel 7; E. Whittlesey to C. C. Sibley, July 29, 1868 (filed under O. O. Howard), reel 21; Circular No. 4, Aug. 3, 1868, reel 34, BRFAL-Ga (M798); endorsement of N. S. Hill, Aug. 11, 1868 on W. R. Bell to N. S. Hill, Aug. 11, 1868, box 24, LR, Milledgeville Agt; H. Catley to M. Marbach, Sept. 4, 1868, vol. 152, LS, Augusta SAC, BRFAL-Ga; Report of O. O. Howard, Oct. 14, 1868, *House Executive Documents*, 40th Cong., 3rd sess., no. 1 (serial 1367), 1044.

During the presidential election of 1868, Bureau men reported on the conduct of the civil authorities regarding the freedpeople's right to vote. M. F. Gallagher to N. S. Hill, Nov. 9, 1868, reel 11, BRFAL-Ga (M798) (with copies to other officers).

163. After July 1868, as the army concentrated its troops in three cities, it removed detachments that had been assigned to protect and assist agents. C. C. Sibley to O. O. Howard, July 25, 1868, reel 7, BRFAL-Ga (M798). For the complement of Bureau officers and men on duty in late 1868, see Rosters of Officers and Civil Agents, Aug. 1 through Nov. 1, 1868, reel 35, BRFAL-Ga (M798). To continue the Bureau's work in education and bounty claims into 1869, Lewis expected to keep on staff fourteen men, including himself, but had to settle for the reduced figure. J. R. Lewis to O. O. Howard, Dec. 2, 1868, reel 58, (LR)BRFAL (M752); J. R. Lewis, Circular No. 1, 1869, reel 34, BRFAL-Ga (M798).

## Chapter 3. Laborious, Vexatious, and Dangerous Service

1. W. F. Eaton to G. Whipple, May 15, 26, 1865, reel 1, AMA-Ga.

2. For a discussion of their activities, see chapter 7. The black minister Henry McNeal Turner briefly served as a freedmen's agent in Atlanta, appointed by President Johnson. He resigned in the early days of Reconstruction because he did not receive, as he explained to a congressional committee, "the respect I thought was due me" from the officers with whom he had to work. He does not appear in any of Wild's or Saxton's correspondence. But, given the disorganized state of affairs in the Georgia Bureau during the summer of 1865, Turner may have made an effort to act as a representative only to run afoul of the military men in the city. Turner's association must have been brief, and to call him a Freedmen's Bureau agent, although not entirely wrong, is not exactly accurate, either. Jerry Thornbery, the historian of black postwar Atlanta, does not place him in any Reconstruction activities during the summer of 1865. In January 1866 Davis Tillson recommended that the Bureau supply Turner with transportation to facilitate his preaching to freedpeople across the state; Tillson believed that Turner would be a good influence on the freedpeople. For Turner's testimony, see Ku Klux Conspiracy, vol. 7: Georgia, 1034. Also see Thornbery, "The Development of Black Atlanta, 1865–1885." For Tillson's comment, see endorsement of D. Tillson to O. O. Howard, Jan. 13, 1866, on H. M. Turner to D. Tillson, Dec. 15, 1866, reel 8, BRFAL-Ga (M798). For a brief biography that refers to Turner as a Bureau agent, see Foner, Freedom's Lawmakers, 215.

3. W. F. Eaton to G. Whipple, May 26, Sept. 21, 1865, reel 1, AMA-Ga.

4. Sickles helped the freedmen secure school buildings in Savannah. Special Orders, No. 38, Dept. of Ga., Sept. 16, 1865, reel 7, BRFAL-SC (M869); H. F. Sickles to R. Saxton, Sept. 27, 1865, reel 24; G. L. Eberhart to W. W. Deane, Nov. 18, 1865, BRFAL-Ga (M798).

5. As early as 1864 he wrote to Saxton urging such a course of action. A. P. Ketchum to R. Saxton, Apr. 30, 1864, reprinted in Freedmen's Advocate, July and August 1864. For his activities among the reservation freedpeople see chapter 7.

6. Longacre, "Brave, Radical, Wild"; Warner, Generals in Blue, 557–58.

7. M. French to [A. P. Ketchum], July 11, 1865, box 32, Records of the Assistant Adjutant General, Savannah SAC, BRFAL-Ga.

8. Wild, however, recognized the need to identify the race of the parties involved in claims in official documents in order to explain why the Bureau became involved in the case. E. A. Wild to A. P. Ketchum, July 14, 1865, box 32, Records of the Assistant Adjutant General, Savannah SAC, BRFAL-Ga.

9. W. P. Russell to M. E. Strieby, Aug. 3, 1865, reel 1, AMA-Ga; G. M. Brayton to S. B. Moe, Aug. 4, 1865, reel 20; J. S. Fullerton to O. O. Howard, Aug. 11, 1865, reel 74,

(LR)BRFAL (M752); Marion Alexander to [Mary] Clifford [Alexander], July 31, 1865, in Boggs, ed., *Alexander Letters, 1787–1900*, 297–99.

10. Currie-McDaniel, *Carpetbagger of Conscience*, 45. Exactly in which proportions Bryant mixed concern for the freedpeople with concern for his own place is open to debate, although Currie-McDaniel is generous and sympathetic in her depiction of her subject. For Bryant's views on contracts and labor, see chapter 6 below.

11. G. N. Forbes to L. Lambert, Dec. 12, 1865; W. A. Burnside to G. H. Pratt, Dec. 18, 1865, reel 31, BRFAL-Ga (M798).

12. J. W. C. Bryan to D. Tillson, Dec. 13, 1865; J. R. Phillips to D. Tillson, Feb. 28, 1866, reel 31, BRFAL-Ga (M798).

13. J. G. McCrary to H. C. Strong, May 26, 1866, reel 28, BRFAL-Ga (M798). The desire to secure a Bureau position for profit probably was also Micajah Jones's motivation. After he lost his position in the reorganization, he urged freedpeople to petition for his restoration promising either to divide his salary with them or to donate a portion of it to them for educational purposes. W. B. Moore to E. M. L. Ehlers, July 2, 1867 (and endorsements), box 9, LR, Augusta SAC, BRFAL-Ga.

14. For some examples see C. M. Pope to [E. Pickett], Feb. 1, 1867; J. J. Bradford to E. Pickett, Feb. 1; S. Crawford to C. C. Sibley, Feb. 2, 1867; W. Haslett to C. C. Sibley, Feb. 4, 1867; J. M. Brightwell to C. C. Sibley, Feb. 4, 1867; J. G. Boynton to E. Pickett, Feb. 20, 1867; J. McWhorter to C. C. Sibley, Mar. 6, 1867, and several others on reel 30, BRFAL-Ga (M798), as well as J. M. Gray to G. L. Eberhart, Feb. 3, 1867, reel 8, (Ed)BRFAL-Ga (M799); E. F. Kirksey to F. A. H. Gaebel, Mar. 26, 1867, box 1, LR, Albany SAC, BRFAL-Ga.

15. B. Maguire to D. Tillson, Sept. 7, 1866, reel 28, BRFAL-Ga (M798).

16. This statement came from a meeting held at Athens at which John Calvin Johnson, the clerk of the inferior court, was secretary. Johnson acted as a Bureau agent from December 1865 until March 1867. *Athens Southern Banner*, June 28, 1865; H. B. Sprague to [W. W. Deane?], Dec. 29, 1865, reel 31; Registers of Civilian Agents, 1865–1867, reel 35, BRFAL-Ga (M798).

17. J. G. McCrary to H. C. Strong, May 24, 1866, reel 28, BRFAL-Ga (M798). For examples of individuals expressing their beliefs that the Bureau was primarily an agency for labor control while seeking appointments, see N. McDuffie and J. L. Warren to D. Tillson, Nov. 14, 1865; L. J. Leary to D. Tillson, Dec. 18, 1865; R. McCoan to D. Tillson, Dec. 27, 1865, reel 13; J. Entwistle to W. W. Deane, Dec. 30, 1865, reel 24, BRFAL-Ga (M798).

18. For example, see W. W. Deane to G. W. Selvidge, Jan. 9, 1866; D. Tillson to L. Lambert, Jan. 10, 1866; D. Tillson to J. Lyle, Jan. 10, 1866; D. Tillson to P. H. Heath, Jan. 15, 1866; W. W. Deane to W. F. Ross, Jan. 16, 1866; W. W. Deane to J. Dawson, Jan. 19, 1866; W. Gray to S. A. McLendon, Jan. 25, 1866; W. W. Deane to S. Crawford, Jan. 25, 1866; W. W. Deane to D. W. Pope, Jan. 26, 1866, reel 1, BRFAL-Ga (M798). For a full discussion of this problematic aspect of contracting, see chapter 6.

19. This concern for employment takes on even greater weight if one remembers the significance that Northern society placed on productive labor. For how this need for work influenced Republican politics in the Deep South during Reconstruction, see Lawrence Powell, "The Politics of Livelihood: Carpetbaggers in the Deep South." For the employment problems of Union veterans, see Larry M. Logue, *To Appomattox and Beyond*, 87–89.

20. C. W. Chapman to Senator Pomeroy, Feb. 15, 1866, Registers of LR, reel 11, BRFAL-Ga (M798); J. R. Lewis to O. O. Howard, Sept. 26, 1867, reel 49; C. W. Chapman to F. Mosebach, Mar. 26, 1867, enclosed in F. Mosebach to G. Walbridge, Mar. 29, 1867, reel 42, (LR)BRFAL (M752); Station Books, 1867–1868, vol. 1, reel 35, BRFAL-Ga (M798).

21. Alvin Clark to D. Tillson, Feb. 8, 1867, reel 31, BRFAL-Ga (M798).

22. O. O. Howard to C. C. Sibley, Feb. 22, 1867, Howard Papers; P. J. O'Rourke to G. G. Meade, Feb. 10, 1868 (and Meade's endorsement), reel 20; Station Books, vol. 1, 1867–1868, reel 35, BRFAL-Ga (M798).

23. For Max Marbach see M. Marbach to J. R. Lewis, Feb. 20, 1868, reel 20. For Alvin Clark see A. S. Bloom to Capt. O'Neal, Jan. 12, 1867, reel 31; Alvin B. Clark to D. Tillson, Feb. 8, 1867, reel 31; Alvin B. Clark to C. C. Sibley, Mar. 10, 1867, reel 42 (LR)BRFAL (M752). For Andrew B. Clark see A. B. Clark to C. C. Sibley, Feb. 22, 1867, reel 42; J. R. Lewis to O. O. Howard, Sept. 26, 1867, reel 49 (LR)BRFAL (M752); A. B. Clark to C. C. Sibley, Oct. 11, 1867, reel 17. For William Pierce see W. P. Pierce to C. C. Sibley, Sept. 18, 1867, reel 18. For all four see Station Books, vol. 1, 1867–1868, reel 35, BRFAL-Ga (M798).

24. At least twenty-four veterans or Northerners received their appointments to agencies after they had come south, many after failing at an earlier effort to make a living in what they probably had believed was a land ripe with opportunity for someone with Yankee discipline. Of Sibley's and Lewis's eighty-two agents, only fourteen were identified from various sources as having received their appointments while residing in a Union state. Although these figures are not complete, they are at least suggestive of how many Yankees first came south for economic or health reasons before they were drawn into Reconstruction. Places of residence at the time of appointment to the Bureau were culled from Bureau records.

25. For example, see G. Crabtree to D. Tillson, Dec. 25, 1865, reel 24; G. Crabtree to [————], Dec. 25, 1865, reel 13, BRFAL-Ga (M798). Generally, Tillson's subassistant commissioners, who were Yankee officers, shared the characteristics of Sibley's army veterans and officers. Of the forty officers who served as subassistant or assistant subassistant commissioners, at least twenty-three were or had been in the Veteran Reserve Corps, a total diluted by the initial appointment of army officers on detached service during 1865. By September 1, 1867, all of the Bureau's thirteen subassistant or assistant subassistant commissioners were or had been connected with the Veteran Reserve

Corp; by March 1, 1868, all but two of the twelve, and by November 1, 1868, all but three of the twelve officers had been or were connected with the Veteran Reserve Corps. Various pension files in RG 15, National Archives, and in Bureau rosters, reel 35, BRFAL-Ga (M798).

26. F. Mosebach to [F. A. H.] Gaebel, Apr. 5, 1866, LR, Albany SAC, BRFAL-Ga; Roster of Officers on Duty, Freedmen's Bureau, Georgia, Dec. 1866, reel 35, BRFAL-Ga (M798).

27. Crabtree served as Tillson's officer at Savannah and Brunswick, but after his discharge in January 1867 he began planting in Chatham County. Archer conveniently kept the marriage a secret from the North Carolina schoolteacher he met and wed while on duty with the agency. The second Mrs. Archer knew nothing about her husband's true status. She was not even aware that, as her sixth wedding anniversary approached, her husband had finally secured a divorce from his first wife. It was not until 1893 that she finally discovered the truth when, as Archer's widow, she applied for an army pension. For Crabtree, see G. Crabtree to D. Tillson, Dec. 25, 1865, reel 24; Special Orders, No. 96, June 16, 1866; No. 104, July 10, 1866, reel 34; Roster of Officers on Duty, Freedmen's Bureau, Georgia, December 1866, reel 35, BRFAL-Ga (M798); G. A. Hood to E. P. Smith, Dec. 23, 1869, reel 6, AMA-Ga; George T. Crabtree, Civil War pension files, RG 15, National Archives. For Archer, see Martin R. Archer, Civil War pension files, RG 15, National Archives; Station Books, vol. 1, 1867–1868, reel 35, BRFAL-Ga (M798).

28. Station Books, vol. 1, 1867–1868, reel 35, BRFAL-Ga (M798); Oliver B. Gray, William F. Martin, and Frederick A. H. Gaebel, Civil War pension files, RG 15, National Archives.

29. Station Books, vol. 1, 1867–1868, reel 35, BRFAL-Ga (M798); John J. Knox, Civil War pension files, RG 15, National Archives; J. J. Knox to T. D. Elliot, Dec. 30, 1867, vol. 169, LS, Athens SAC, BRFAL-Ga.

30. F. A. H. Gaebel to W. W. Deane, Mar. 31, 1866; Gaebel to D. Tillson, Aug. 5, 1866, reel 27, BRFAL-Ga (M798); *Official Records*, ser. 3, vol. 5, 563–64.

31. M. Marbach to J. R. Lewis, Feb. 20, 1868, reel 20; Station Books, vol. 1, 1867–1868, reel 35, BRFAL-Ga (M798); M. Marbach to H. Catley, Mar. 20, 1868, vol. 390, LS, Waynesboro Agt, BRFAL-Ga.

32. C. C. Richardson to W. W. Deane, Nov. 1865, reel 24, BRFAL-Ga (M798); D. G. Risley to A. P. Ketchum, May 11, 1867, vol. 204, LS, Brunswick SAC, BRFAL-Ga; D. G. Risley to E. P. Smith, Aug. 23, 1867, Oct. 21, 1867, reel 3, AMA-Ga; Douglas G. Risley, Civil War pension files, RG 15, National Archives.

33. I. Ayer to L. Matthews, Mar. 5, 1866, vol. 150, LS, Augusta SAC, BRFAL-Ga.

34. *Augusta Daily Constitutionalist*, May 27, 1865; C. A. de la Mesa to D. Tillson, Dec. 11, 1866, reel 26, BRFAL-Ga (M798); D. G. Risley to E. P. Smith, Oct. 21, 1867, reel 3, AMA-Ga.

35. H. B. Sprague to D. Tillson, Jan. 10, 1866, reel 29, BRFAL-Ga (M798). Sprague wrote this letter after he had left the Bureau.

36. Ku Klux Conspiracy, vol. 7: *Georgia*, 1081; Station Books, vol. 1, 1867–1868, reel 35, BRFAL-Ga (M798).

37. Endorsement of Andrew B. Clark to E. Pickett, May 6, 1867, on E. Pickett to A. Clark, April 25, 1867, reel 16, BRFAL-Ga (M798).

38. Alvin Clark to W. F. White, Apr. 18, 1867; Alvin Clark to C. C. Sibley, Apr. 23, 1867, vol. 334, LS, Quitman Agt; O. H. Howard to G. R. Walbridge, Mar. 12, 1867, box 3, LR, Albany Agt, BRFAL-Ga.

39. L. Gresham to D. Tillson, July 26, reel 27; P. P. Mahoney to D. Tillson, Sept. 13, 1866, reel 28; T. P. Tison to G. A. Hastings, Jan. 24, 1866; L. Schwenell to G. H. Pratt, May 15, 1866; J. B. Wilson to D. Tillson, Nov. 3, 1866; J. T. Wimberly to [W. W. Deane], Dec. 18, 1866; R. E. Wiswell to E. Pickett, Dec. 29, 1866, reel 29; G. W. York to W. W. Deane, Apr. 2, 1866, reel 31; J. W. Greene to D. Tillson, Jan. 7, 1867; W. E. Griffin to [———], Feb. 1, 1867; J. C. Johnson to C. C. Sibley, Feb. 8, 1867, reel 30; R. L. Nesbitt to F. A. H. Gaebel, Mar. 28, 1867, reel 15, BRFAL-Ga (M798).

40. E. F. Kirksey to F. A. H. Gaebel, Dec. 10, 1866, box 2, ULR, Albany SAC, BRFAL-Ga; B. Maguire to D. Tillson, Sept. 7, reel 28, BRFAL-Ga (M798).

41. D. Tillson to Judge Andrews, Jan. 24, 1866, reel 1, BRFAL-Ga (M798).

42. G. R. Walbridge to D. Tillson, Dec. 14, 1866, reel 14; J. T. Harmon to D. Tillson, Nov. 3, Dec. 18, 1866, reel 27, BRFAL-Ga (M798).

43. W. Gray to D. Tillson, Mar. 14, 1866; F. A. H. Gaebel to W. W. Deane, Apr. 11, 27, 1866, reel 27, BRFAL-Ga (M798).

44. D. Tillson to Col. Carling, Mar. 25, 1866, reel 34, BRFAL-Ga (M798). Also see E. Pickett to W. H. Mathews, Nov. 27, 1866, reel 4, BRFAL-Ga (M798).

45. Dodson and Payne to D. Tillson, Oct. 16, 1866; C. A. de la Mesa to D. Tillson, Nov. 11, 1866, reel 13; Special Orders, No. 48, Mar. 15, 1866, reel 34; Register of Civilian Agents, 1865–1867, reel 35, BRFAL-Ga (M798); E. Pickett to C. A. de la Mesa, Nov. 20, 1866, box 26, ULR, Rome SAC, BRFAL-Ga.

46. C. A. de la Mesa to D. Tillson, Oct. 19, 1866, reel 26, Oct. 8, 28, 1866, reel 13; E. Pickett to C. A. de la Mesa, Nov. 7, 1866, reel 4; Registers of Civilian Agents, 1865–1867, reel 35, BRFAL-Ga (M798).

47. A. Clark to D. Tillson, Oct. 1, 1866; J. O'Neal to D. Tillson, Oct. 15, 1866, reel 13; E. Pickett to J. O'Neal, Oct. 24, 1866, reel 4, BRFAL-Ga (M798).

48. G. R. Walbridge to D. Tillson, Dec. 14, 1866, reel 14; J. T. Harmon to D. Tillson, Dec. 18, 1866, reel 27, BRFAL-Ga (M798). Tillson sent his inspectors general on inspection tours and required his subassistant commissioners periodically to inspect the affairs of their districts, but these men were seriously overextended in their duties with little assistance—at best a few unmounted enlisted men under normal circumstances—

to alleviate their workload. Special Orders, No. 38, Dec. 26, 1865; No. 9, Jan. 1, 1866; No. 25, Jan. 31, 1866; No. 28, Feb. 6, 1866; No. 31, Feb. 12, 1866; No. 39, Mar. 2, 1866, reel 34, BRFAL-Ga (M798).

49. W. W. Deane to C. R. Woods, Aug. 14, 1866; W. W. Deane to A. Sloane, Oct. 5, 1866, reel 3; C. McC. Lord to W. W. Deane, Oct. 8, 1866, reel 28; A. M. Campbell to D. Tillson, Oct. 8, 1866, reel 25; Tillson to O. O. Howard, Oct. 19, 1866, reel 29 (and endorsement), BRFAL-Ga (M798); D. Tillson to E. Foster and A. M. Campbell, Oct. 16, 1866 (copy to O. O. Howard); J. R. Lewis to O. O. Howard, Sept. 9, 1867, reel 49, (LR)BRFAL (M752). Nolan was officially appointed in December 1866; when he was removed at the end of August 1868 because of the Bureau's contraction, he received lavish praise from his subassistant commissioner. G. M. Nolan to E. Pickett, Jan. 1, 1867, reel 30; Station Books, vol. 1, 1867–1868, reel 35, BRFAL-Ga (M798); F. Mosebach to G. M. Nolan, Aug. 29, 1868, vol. 99, LS, Atlanta SAC, BRFAL-Ga.

50. E. Yulee to D. Tillson, Nov. 12, 1866, reel 37, (LR)BRFAL (M752); E. Yulee to D. Tillson, May 3, 1866, reel 29, BRFAL-Ga (M798).

51. J. Davison to W. W. Deane, June 4, 1866, reel 26, BRFAL-Ga (M798).

52. J. Davison to D. Tillson, Dec. 26, 1865, reel 31; Jan. 8, Feb. 6, 10, Mar. 1, 1866, reel 26; W. W. Deane to J. Davison, Feb. 8, 1866, reel 1; W. Gray to D. Tillson, Mar. 14, 1866, reel 27, BRFAL-Ga (M798).

53. J. Davison to C. C. Sibley, June 4, 1867, reel 14; E. Pickett to J. Davison, June 7, 1867, reel 5, BRFAL-Ga (M798).

54. Register of Civilian Agents, 1865–1867; Station Books, vol. 1, 1867–1868, reel 35; W. F. White to E. Pickett, June 25, 1867, reel 19, BRFAL-Ga (M798).

55. J. D. Harris to L. Lambert, Feb. 20, 1866, reel 27, BRFAL-Ga (M798).

56. T. W. White to D. Tillson, Jan. 21, 1867, reel 30, BRFAL-Ga (M798).

57. C. A. de la Mesa to C. C. Sibley, Mar. 28, 1867, reel 14, BRFAL-Ga (M798).

58. Examples are numerous and will be noted throughout other chapters, but see J. C. Swayze to D. Tillson, August 28, 1866, reel 12; B. Maguire to D. Tillson, September 7, 1866, reel 28, BRFAL-Ga (M798).

59. D. Tillson to O. O. Howard, Sept. 1, 1866, reel 37, (LR)BRFAL (M752).

60. Bureau officers were well aware of the problematic lack of cavalry and its relationship to the agency's ability to function, a point also made by Yankee John Richard Dennett on his visit to Atlanta in 1865. Dennett, *The South as It Is*, 270–71.

61. T. F. Forbes to F. Mosebach, Aug. 4, 1866; T. F. Forbes to J. C. De Grafferied, Sept. 17, 1866; T. F. Forbes to F. A. H. Gaebel, Sept. 26, 1866, reel 3, BRFAL-Ga (M798). As noted earlier, in August 1865 General Brannan believed that he would need 3,000 soldiers plus a regiment of cavalry to police Georgia. J. Brannan to S. B. Moe, Aug. 1, 1865, LR, Dept. of Ga. For the number of troops stationed in Georgia during Tillson's administration see Sefton, *Army and Reconstruction*, 261–62. In December 1865, Commissioner Howard responded to Tillson's November query about

troops by suggesting that it would be sufficient to have "small columns" push into "the disaffected districts" when needed and then removed after "justice administered," not an altogether satisfactory suggestion given the lack of mobility of the infantry stationed in Georgia and the almost constant lack of cooperation exhibited by whites in many parts of the state. In April Tillson again complained to Howard about his lack of soldiers, and in May the assistant commissioner turned down a request to have troops stationed at Marietta because the department commander believed he was shorthanded. After the commencement of military reconstruction, General Pope recognized the need for cavalry to deal with mounted desperadoes in northern Georgia. M. Woodhull to D. Tillson, Dec. 14, 1865, reel 1, (RI)BRFAL (M742); D. Tillson to O. O. Howard, April 18, 1866, reel 27, (LR)BRFAL (M752); D. Tillson to G. R. Hunt and others, May 2, 1866, reel 2, BRFAL-Ga (M798); J. Pope to U. S. Grant, Apr. 7, 1867, in Candler, *Confederate Records*, 6:65.

62. F. A. H. Gaebel to W. W. Deane, Mar. 31, 1866, reel 27, BRFAL-Ga (M798).

63. Ku Klux Conspiracy, vol. 7: *Georgia*, 1086.

64. O. H. Howard, Report for August, Sept. 19, 1868, reel 58, (LR)BRFAL (M752).

65. G. S. Eberhart to C. C. Sibley, Mar. 26, 1867, reel 42, (LR)BRFAL (M752); J. R. Smith to D. Tillson, Feb. 13, July 4, 1866, reel 29; J. R. Smith to J. R. Lewis, Nov. 2, 1867, reel 19, BRFAL-Ga (M798). Smith was appointed July 19, 1866, and relieved November 24, 1868. Register of Civilian Agents; Station Books, vol. 1, 1867–1868, reel 35, BRFAL-Ga (M798).

66. J. Leonard to J. R. Lewis, Aug. 26, 1868, reel 58, (LR)BRFAL (M752).

67. M. F. Gallagher to C. K. Smith, Mar. 16, 1868, reel 7; C. A. de la Mesa to C. C. Sibley, May 16, 1868, reel 21, BRFAL-Ga (M798); C. A. de la Mesa to R. F. Finney, Dec. 5, 1867, box 16, LR, Dalton Agt; J. J. Knox to H. C. Flournoy, Feb. 4, 1868, vol. 169, LS; J. J. Knox to J. McWhorter, June 3, 1868, vol. 170, LS, Athens SAC, BRFAL-Ga.

68. O. H. Howard to J. R. Lewis, July 17, 1868; O. H. Howard to M. F. Gallagher, July 20, 1868, reel 21; C. C. Sibley to O. O. Howard, July 24, 1868, reel 7, BRFAL-Ga (M798). Also see the case of D. J. Curtis, who charged his clients illegal fees and the Bureau an extra ten dollars a month for office rent. J. R. Lewis to O. O. Howard, Sept. 26, 1867, reel 49, (LR)BRFAL (M752); Station Books, vol. 1, 1867–1868, reel 35; C. A. de la Mesa to C. C. Sibley, May 21, 1867, reel 14; J. R. Lewis, Charges and Specifications against D. J. Curtis, Mar. 9, 1868; C. A. de la Mesa to C. C. Sibley, Mar. 6, 7, 13, 1868, reel 20; Dodson and Payne to O. O. Howard, Apr. 18, 1868, reel 21; General Orders, No. 1, Apr. 2, 1868, reel 34, BRFAL-Ga (M798).

69. Andrews, *The South since the War*, 320; Anonymous to C. C. Sibley, June 22, 1867, reel 17; O. H. Howard to M. F. Gallagher, Jan. 23, 1868, reel 20; Station Books, vol. 1, 1867–1868, reel 35, BRFAL-Ga (M798); Ku Klux Conspiracy, vol. 7: *Georgia*, 1084.

70. J. M. Robinson to C. C. Sibley, Nov. [19], 1867 (and all endorsements and enclosures), reel 19; J. M. Robinson to O. O. Howard, Apr. 8, 1868, reel 21, BRFAL-Ga (M798).

71. Ku Klux Conspiracy, vol. 7: *Georgia*, 1083.

72. H. Catley, Circular addressed to the agents of the Augusta subdistrict, Feb. 4, 1868, reel 20, BRFAL-Ga (M798).

73. For example, see comments by C. C. Hicks to J. R. Lewis, Oct. 9, 1867, reel 18, BRFAL-Ga (M798); D. Losey to C. C. Sibley, June 17, 1868, vol. 332, LS, Perry Agt, BRFAL-Ga; J. A. Rockwell to "my dear brother & sister," Oct. 8, 1868, John A. Rockwell Letters, University of Georgia. For an excellent account of politically motivated violence in Georgia at this time that required extensive Bureau investigation, see Formwalt, "The Camilla Massacre of 1868."

74. Sefton, *Army and Reconstruction*, 261–62; endorsement of J. J. Knox to M. F. Gallagher, Apr. 8, 1868, on J. McWorter to J. J. Knox, Apr. 6, 1868, reel 21, BRFAL-Ga (M798).

75. O. H. Howard to C. C. Sibley, Apr. 15, 1867, box 3, LR, Albany Agt, BRFAL-Ga.

76. C. C. Sibley to O. O. Howard, Apr. 15, 1867, reel 16; J. R. Hill and others to [C. C. Sibley], Aug. 19, 1867, reel 12, BRFAL-Ga (M798).

77. J. E. Bryant to R. Saxton, Aug. 7, 1865, reel 7; E. A. Wild to R. Saxton, Aug. 23, 1865, reel 34, BRFAL-SC (M869); J. E. Bryant to D. Tillson, Oct. 19, 1865, vol. 150, LS, Augusta SAC, BRFAL-Ga; G. Curkendall to D. Tillson, Dec. 26, 1865, reel 20, BRFAL-Ga (M798); S. Willard Saxton Journal, Sept. 21, 1865, Rufus and S. Willard Saxton Papers, Yale University, Sterling Library.

78. O. H. Howard to O. O. Howard, Apr. [—], 1867, reel 42, (LR)BRFAL (M752); L. C. Mathews to D. Tillson, Mar. 13, 1866, reel 28; W. F. White to M. F. Gallagher, Oct. 10, 1867, reel 19; P. D. Claiborne to J. J. Knox, Jan. 22, 1868, reel 20; G. R. Ballou to O. O. Howard, July 13, 1868, reel 22, BRFAL-Ga (M798); Entry for July 3, 1867, Agent's Journal, vol. 226, Columbus Agt; *Thomas E. Speight* v. *Hands*, Jan. 25, 1868, Register of Complaints, Bainbridge Agt, BRFAL-Ga. Granted, agents often complained when they wanted a raise, but documents from individuals including John Emory Bryant, Tillson's conscientious agent James Davison, and a number of Sibley's officers and agents support the generalizations about heavy workloads at least among the individuals who took their appointments seriously. A good published record of a subassistant commissioner's routine is William A. Campbell, "A Freedmen's Bureau Diary by George Wagner."

79. J. Davison to W. W. Deane, June 4, 1866, reel 26, BRFAL-Ga (M798).

80. G. A. Hastings to W. W. Deane, Dec. 25, 1865, reel 24, BRFAL-Ga (M798). Hastings was also expending emotional energy on the cotton fraud charges.

81. W. Mitchell to D. Tillson, Sept. 17, 1866, reel 28, BRFAL-Ga (M798).

82. O. H. Howard to O. O. Howard, Apr. [—], 1867, reel 42, (LR)BRFAL (M752).

83. See de la Mesa's travel vouchers included in C. A. de la Mesa to C. C. Sibley, May 1, May 30, July 1, Aug. 1, Sept. 1, 1868; C. A. de la Mesa to J. R. Lewis, Nov. 2, Dec. 1, Dec. 26, 1868, vol. 342, LS, Rome SAC, BRFAL-Ga.

84. Circular Letter, Feb. 27, 1867; Circular Letter, July 31, 1867; Circular No. 15, Oct. 16, 1867, reel 34, BRFAL-Ga (M798); Jones, *Soldiers of Light and Love*, 91. Much has been made of the Bureau's connection with the Freedmen's Savings and Trust Company. Indeed, the bank sought the Bureau's favor, and the commission for cashier at the Augusta branch was forwarded to C. H. Prince through Davis Tillson. Both Jacqueline Jones and Carl Osthaus make the point about the connections, but, as Jones shows, educators, not agents, were more likely to be involved in the bank. In fact, John R. Lewis discouraged such connections because he believed that it would distract from an appointee's Bureau duties. Lewis did offer suggestions for the bank cashier positions in Macon and Atlanta, but only his Macon candidate, the Reverend T. G. Seward, received an appointment. E. A. Ware and John A. Rockwell, two American Missionary Association teachers who also had official educational positions in the Bureau, helped establish branches in Atlanta and Macon; their connections were extraordinary for Georgia. Osthaus mistakenly identifies the Savannah bank cashier, I. W. Brinckerhoff, an AMA teacher, as a Bureau agent. In the end, while Commissioner Howard and his school superintendent, John W. Alvord, pushed for cooperation between the two organizations and rendered the bank much assistance, the bank did not tax much of the Georgia Bureau's time. There were few direct connections between its officers and the bank and, at best, officers might mention it occasionally, but not frequently, in their dealings with Georgia freedpeople beyond the Augusta, Savannah, and Macon area. There were only two branches functioning in Georgia in 1866, one at Augusta and one at Savannah. Two other branches were opened as the Bureau's power and personnel were declining. A branch was opened in Macon in 1868 and one in Atlanta in 1870, meaning that most freedpeople in Georgia did not have easy access to the bank even as Bureau officers and teachers preached frugality. By the beginning of 1870, at the more recently established Atlanta and Macon branches there had been 213 and 500 depositors, respectively, since their establishment, with 213 and 432, respectively, still maintaining balances; at the older Augusta branch there had been 1,770 depositors since its establishment, with 889 current depositors on the books; and at the oldest branch in the state, Savannah, there had been 3,000 depositors, with 1,555 current depositors. M. T. Hewitt to D. Tillson, Mar. 24, 1866, reel 27, BRFAL-Ga; J. R. Lewis to O. O. Howard, Dec. 16, 1868, reel 58, (LR)BRFAL (M752); J. A. Rockwell to Alfred [P. Rockwell], Jan. 28, 1869, Rockwell Papers; J. W. Alvord, *Ninth Semi-Annual Report on Schools for Freedmen, January 1, 1870*, 66–67; Jones, *Soldiers of Light and Love*, 162; Osthaus, *Freedmen, Philanthropy, and Fraud*, 34, 63–73, 230–33.

85. C. Raushenberg to O. H. Howard, Dec. 16, 1867, reel 19, BRFAL-Ga (M798); C. C. Sibley to O. O. Howard, Feb. 20, 1868, reel 53, (LR)BRFAL (M752).

86. H. F. Mills to D. G. Risley, Oct. 11, 1867, vol. 370, LS, Stockton Agt, BRFAL-Ga; T. Holden to [C. C. Sibley?], July 31, 1867, Registers of LR, vol. 3, 183, 313–14, reel 12; G. R. Ballou to O. H. Howard, Aug. 5, 1868, reel 21, BRFAL-Ga (M798).

87. J. D. Harris to L. Lambert, Feb. 20, 1866, reel 27; C. A. de la Mesa to D. Tillson, June 26, 1866, reel 26; M. Marbach to C. C. Sibley, June 11, 1868, reel 21, BRFAL-Ga (M798); D. A. Newsome to C. C. Sibley, Sept. 6, 1867, box 9, LR, Augusta SAC; G. R. Ballou to O. H. Howard, June 27, 1868, vol. 236, LS, Cuthbert Agt, BRFAL-Ga.

88. C. A. de la Mesa to C. C. Sibley, Apr. 27, 1868, box 26, ULR, Rome Agt, BRFAL-Ga.

89. A. W. Stone to D. Tillson, May 19, June 4, 1866, reel 29, BRFAL-Ga (M798). Stone was especially upset because General Steedman on his inspection tour told him the Bureau could not exercise any judicial authority.

90. The grand jury later reconsidered their vote. W. F. Martins to W. F. White, Jan. 10, 1867, box 9, ULR, Augusta SAC, BRFAL-Ga; W. F. Martins to E. Pickett, Jan. 12, 1867, reel 30, BRFAL-Ga (M798).

91. E. F. Kirksey to F. A. H. Gaebel, Sept. 29, Oct. 13, 20, Nov. 10, Dec. 10, 1866; F. A. H. Gaebel to E. F. Kirksey, Jan. 6; E. F. Kirksey to F. A. H. Gaebel, Feb. 22, 27; F. A. H. Gaebel to E. Pickett, Mar. 1, 1867, box 2, ULR, Albany SAC, BRFAL-Ga; D. Tillson to J. T. Clarke, Dec. 20, 1866, reel 4; F. A. H. Gaebel to E. Pickett, Dec. 22, 1866, reel 27; E. F. Kirksey to F. A. H. Gaebel, Jan. 7, 1867, reel 30, BRFAL-Ga (M798).

92. D. Losey to C. C. Sibley, Sept. 7, 1868, box 25, LR, Perry Agt, BRFAL-Ga.

93. C. A. de la Mesa to J. R. Lewis, Nov. 28, 1868 (and all endorsements), reel 28; M. F. Gallagher to C. A. de la Mesa, Dec. 11, 1868, reel 7, BRFAL-Ga (M798).

94. *Augusta Daily Constitutionalist*, May 27, 28, 1865; *Macon Daily Telegraph*, Aug. 24, 1865; S. W. Saxton to A. P. Ketchum, June 24, 1865; A. P. Ketchum, by command of R. Saxton, July 6, 1865, box 32, Records of the Assistant Adjutant General, Savannah SAC, BRFAL-Ga.

95. J. E. Bryant to R. Saxton, Aug. 4, 1865, reel 7, BRFAL-SC (M869).

96. Bryant started that political relationship when he accepted the presidency of the Georgia Equal Rights Association in January 1866. *Augusta Loyal Georgian*, Jan. 27, 1866.

97. For example, see ex-agent Elias Yulee's bitter assessment of black political activity during Military Reconstruction (recall that Yulee at least believed that the freedpeople should receive economic justice during his association with the Bureau.) Yulee, *An Address to the Colored People of Georgia*, esp. 18, 27.

98. Liberty County Tax Digest for 1861, GDAH; *Savannah Republican*, July 8, 1865; *Savannah Herald* (supplement), Jan. 11, 1866; Register of Civilian Agents, reel 35; E. Yulee to D. Tillson, Aug. 20, 1866, reel 29; D. Tillson to W. B. Gaulden, Oct. 19, 1866, reel 4, BRFAL-Ga (M798).

99. G. R. Walbridge to W. W. Deane, Sept. 6, 8, 10, 1866, reel 29, BRFAL-Ga (M798). Gaulden had retried cases already determined by agent Yulee and accused him of being a liar and cheat; Yulee provided much information to Bureau headquarters concerning Gaulden's misconduct. The agent Gaulden should not be confused with the Liberty County black politician William A. Golding or Golden, as Yulee once did when he

presented Tillson with information about Gaulden's activities. Also, Gaulden already had given some indication that he believed he should continue to control and use black Georgians when he illegally bound to himself a physically mature freed girl, probably in her early- or midteens, who had been his slave, and forced her to act as his mistress for over three months, all the while her mother was trying to regain custody. Witnesses only testified to the fact that he had fondled the girl, and the county court returned her to her parents, so he escaped the penitentiary and Bureau discipline at that time. For the feud, see T. W. Quarterman to D. Tillson, July 20, Oct. 2, 1866, reel 28; E. Yulee to D. Tillson, Aug. 20, 1866; G. R. Walbridge to W. W. Deane, Sept. 6, 1866, reel 29, BRFAL-Ga (M798); E. Yulee to D. Tillson, Nov. 24, 1866 (and all endorsements), LR, Dist. of Ga.; Foner, *Freedom's Lawmakers*, 88. For the apprenticeship case, see G. Crabtree to D. Tillson, June 14, 1866, reel 13; J. K. Smith to W. W. Deane, Aug. 15, 19, 20, 27, 30, 1866; G. R. Walbridge to W. W. Deane, Sept. 8, 10, 1866; G. R. Walbridge to D. Tillson, Sept. 24, 1866, reel 29, BRFAL-Ga (M798); J. K. Smith to W. B. Gaulden, June 26, 1866, vol. 347, LS, Savannah SAC, BRFAL-Ga.

100. W. R. D. Moss to D. Tillson, Feb. 26, 1866, reel 31; W. R. D. Moss to C. C. Sibley, Feb. 14, 1867, reel 20; Register of Civilian Agents, 1865–1867, reel 35, BRFAL-Ga (M798). Also see J. Greene to D. Tillson, Aug. 19, 1866, reel 27, BRFAL-Ga (M798).

101. Since Tillson had actively sought out local officeholders for his agencies, he saw no conflict of interest if they continued their civic duties or won new offices while serving as agents. W. W. Deane to G. N. Forbes, May 9, 1866, reel 2, BRFAL-Ga (M798).

102. G. N. Forbes to L. Lambert, Dec. 12, 1865, reel 31; G. N. Forbes to D. Tillson, May 5, 1866, reel 26; M. Bethune to D. Tillson, May 7, 1867, reel 25; Register of Civilian Agents, 1865–1867, reel 35, BRFAL-Ga (M798).

103. O. O. Howard to D. Tillson, Jan. 19, 1866, reel 25, BRFAL-Ga (M798).

104. A. A. Buck to C. C. Sibley, July 22, 1867, reel 17, BRFAL-Ga (M798); D. G. Risley to Serg. J. T. Denman, Oct. 14, 1867, LS Brunswick SAC; J. Leonard to Lt. J. C. Hosmer, Oct. 28, 1867, vol. 268, LS; Lt. J. E. Hosmer to J. Leonard, Oct. 23, 28, 1867, box 19, LR, Griffin SAC, BRFAL-Ga.

105. G. R. Walbridge to D. G. Risley, July 3, 1867, reel 5; A. A. Buck to C. C. Sibley, July 22, 1867, reel 17; N. S. Hill to C. C. Sibley, July 29, 1867, reel 18; M. F. Gallagher to T. Holden, Apr. 17, 1868, reel 7; J. McWhorter to J. R. Lewis, Apr. 23, 1868, reel 21; Circular Letter, Apr. 8, 1868, reel 34; endorsement of M. F. Gallagher to J. R. Smith, Apr. 27, 1868, on statement of John Foster, Apr. 27, 1868, reel 21; G. Wagner to N. S. Hill, Nov. 11, 1868, enclosed in N. S. Hill to J. R. Lewis, Nov. 18, 1868; O. H. Howard to J. R. Lewis, Nov. 27, 1868, reel 23, BRFAL-Ga (M798); Alvin B. Clark to W. F. White, Apr. 28, 1867, vol. 334, LS, Quitman Agt; J. E. Hosmer to J. Leonard, Oct. 23, 28, 1867, box 19, LR; J. Leonard to J. E. Hosmer, Oct. 28, 29, 1867, vol. 268, LS, Griffin SAC; J. J. Knox to J. McWhorter, Nov. 5, 1867, vol. 169, LS, Athens SAC; W. F. Martins to J. E. Hosmer,

Feb. 4, 1868, vol. 328, LS, Newnan Agt; J. J. Knox to R. B. Bullock, Sept. 14, 1868, vol. 170, LS, Athens SAC, BRFAL-Ga.

106. W. F. Martins to W. Lynch, July 16, 1867, vol. 328, LS, Newnan Agt; Andrew B. Clark, August Report of Contracts, Sept. 11, 1867, box 24, Reports of Contracts, Newton Agt; J. P. Gibson to C. R. Holcombe, Sept. 21, 1867, box 20, LR, Hinesville Agt; L. L. Wheelock to [J. M. Hoag], Oct. 31, 1867, ULR, Savannah SAC; H. Catley, Reports of Contracts, Apr. 1868, box 9, Misc. Reports, Augusta SAC; M. S. Whalen to M. F. Gallagher, May 8, 1868, box 10, LR, Augusta Agt; J. Leonard to C. C. Sibley, May 12, 1868; C. W. Chapman to J. Leonard, Nov. 30, 1868, box 14, LR; W. F. White, Contract Report for August 1868, box 34, Reports & Misc. Papers, Thomasville, SAC; J. Leonard to J. R. Lewis, Aug. 26, 1868, vol. 223, LS, Columbus SAC; Andrew B. Clark to O. H. Howard, Sept. 30, 1868, box 1, LR, Albany SAC; J. L. H. Waldrop to F. Mosebach, Oct. 28, 1868, vol. 280, LS, Jonesboro Agt, BRFAL-Ga; J. Leonard to J. R. Lewis, Aug. 26, 1868; H. Catley to M. F. Gallagher, Sept. 3, 1868, reel 58, (LR)BRFAL (M752); C. C. Sibley, Report for October 1867, Nov. 11, 1867, reel 32; affidavit of Josiah Foster, May 1, 1868 (and endorsements), reel 21; C. Raushenberg to M. F. Gallagher, Oct. 6, 1868, reel 23, BRFAL-Ga (M798).

107. G. R. Walbridge to E. M. L. Ehlers, July 3, 1867, box 9, LR, Augusta SAC; G. R. Walbridge to D. G. Risley, July 3, 1867, box 12, LR, Brunswick SAC, BRFAL-Ga (and copies to other subassistant commissioners); O. B. Gray to [C. C. Sibley], Oct. 3, 1867, reel 12, BRFAL-Ga (M798).

108. M. F. Gallagher to N. S. Hill, Nov. 9, 1868 (and copies to other subassistant commissioners), reel 7; G. Wagner to N. S. Hill, Nov. 13, 1868, enclosed in N. S. Hill to J. R. Lewis, Nov. 18, 1868, reel 23, BRFAL-Ga, (M798).

109. Alvin B. Clark to J. R. Lewis, Sept. 7, 1867, reel 17, BRFAL-Ga (M798); Campbell, "A Freedmen's Bureau Diary by George Wagner," 347.

110. It is easier to determine Sibley's adequate and inadequate agents and officers than it is to divine the number of Democrats among his Unionist and Yankee appointees. Although there must have been a few, circumstances forced only Max Marbach to make to Sibley a public statement of his Democratic political affiliation. S. Mackey to J. E. Bryant, Sept. 14, 1868, reel 22; M. Marbach to C. C. Sibley, Sept. 25, 1868, reel 22, BRFAL-Ga (M798).

111. D. G. Risley to C. C. Sibley, June 24, 1867, reel 19, BRFAL-Ga (M798).

112. William Warren Rogers reports that white residents of Thomas County accused Captain White of telling freedpeople that they would be reenslaved if they failed to vote. One suspects that White made this statement, but meant to convey to the freedpeople the significance of the ballot for preserving their new status and preventing their exmasters from limiting their freedom in ways other than legal reenslavement. F. D. Sewell believed that White, whose health had been ruined during the war, was "an earnest, prudent and faithful officer of the Bureau." Rogers, *Thomas County, 1865–1900,*

15; F. D. Sewell to O. O. Howard, Dec. 15, 1866, reel 39, (LR)BRFAL (M752); William F. White, Civil War pension files, RG 15, National Archives.

113. W. C. Morrill to O. H. Howard, Sept. 30, 1868, box 2, ULR, Albany SAC, BRFAL-Ga.

114. W. C. Morrill to [J. R. Lewis], Nov. 3, 4, 1868, reel 23, BRFAL-Ga (M798); testimony of W. C. Morrill, Ku Klux Conspiracy, vol. 7: *Georgia*, 1087.

115. H. de F. Young to N. S. Hill, Nov. 11, 1868, enclosed in N. S. Hill to J. R. Lewis, Nov. 18, 1868; O. H. Howard to J. R. Lewis, Nov. 27, 1868, reel 23, BRFAL-Ga (M798).

116. J. McWhorter to J. J. Knox, May 27, 1867, box 5, LR, Athens SAC, BRFAL-Ga.

117. J. J. Knox to J. McWhorter, Oct. 22, 1867, vol. 169, LS, Athens SAC, BRFAL-Ga; endorsement of E. Whittlesey to [C. C. Sibley], Oct. 25, 1867, on W. F. White to J. R. Lewis, Oct. 16, 1867, reel 19; J. R. Davis to O. O. Howard, Apr. 13, 1868, reel 21, BRFAL-Ga (M798).

118. M. F. Gallagher to W. F. White, Oct. 28, 1867, reel 6, BRFAL-Ga (M798); S. W. Saxton to E. A. Ware, Apr. 7, 1868, O. O. Howard Papers, Bowdoin College, Brunswick, Maine.

119. Agents W. C. Carson, James Dunning, and Joseph McWhorter cut their ties with the Bureau to serve in the 1867 constitutional convention. McWhorter was reappointed in April 1868. Yankee veteran O. H. Howard was nominated, but he did not resign and did not win the election. Three other agents resigned when they decided to run for office or were elected to office. Apparently, most of Sibley's agents decided to do their Reconstruction work from their positions in the Bureau. W. C. Carson to C. C. Sibley, Dec. 2, 1867; J. Dunning to J. R. Lewis, Dec. 9, 1867, reel 17; C. C. Sibley to O. O. Howard, Mar. 18, 1868, reel 7; J. E. Cooper to E. Hulbert, Apr. 27, 1868; J. R. Davis to O. O. Howard, Apr. 13, 1868, reel 21; J. Leonard to J. R. Lewis, Nov. 2, 1868, reel 23; Station Books, vol. 1, 1867–1868, reel 35, BRFAL-Ga (M798).

120. J. J. Knox to M. F. Gallagher, Nov. 24, 1868, reel 58, (LR)BRFAL (M752).

121. T. M. Allen to [J. R.] Lewis, reel 8, (Ed)BRFAL-Ga (M799); N. S. Hill to C. C. Sibley, July 29, 1867, reel 18, BRFAL-Ga (M798).

122. F. D. Sewell to C. C. Sibley, June 11, 1867, reel 15, BRFAL-Ga (M798); G. S. Eberhart to O. O. Howard, June 17, 1867, reel 46, (LR)BRFAL (M752).

123. Andrew B. Clark to [J. R. Lewis], Nov. 3, 1868, reel 23, BRFAL-Ga (M798); J. R. Lewis to O. O. Howard, Dec. 27, 1869, Howard Papers.

124. J. R. Lewis to O. O. Howard, Oct. 6, Dec. 27, 1869, Howard Papers; J. R. Lewis to W. L. Clark, Mar. 12, 1870, reel 5, (Ed)BRFAL-Ga (M799).

125. Endorsement of C. C. Sibley [to O. O. Howard], June 18, 1867, Endorsements Sent, reel 9, BRFAL-Ga (M798).

126. H. de F. Young to M. F. Gallagher, Sept. 15, 1868, reel 58, (LR)BRFAL (M752).

127. J. W. Barney complained about his office at Carnesville; Bureau surgeon Thomas Clement complained about his accommodations near Darien. J. W. Barney to J. J. Knox,

Sept. 3, 1867, box 5, LR, Carnesville Agt; T. R. Clement to [J. V. De Hanne], Jan. 7, 1867, reel 1, ULR, Surgeon's Records, BRFAL-Ga. Also see G. R. Campbell to C. K. Smith, Dec. 4, 1865, box 9, ULR, Augusta SAC, BRFAL-Ga.

128. D. Tillson to O. O. Howard, Sept. 4, 1866, reel 37, (LR)BRFAL (M752); N. Bronson to [D. Tillson], Oct. 4, 1866, reel 11; Andrew Clark to C. C. Sibley, Oct. 11, 1867, reel 17; W. F. White to M. F. Gallagher, Oct. 10, 1867, reel 19; R. F. Finney to C. C. Sibley, Mar. 17, 1868, reel 20; J. B. Davenport to O. O. Howard, Apr. 15, 1868; J. B. Davenport to S. Hooper, Apr. 27, 1868, reel 21, BRFAL-Ga (M798); Campbell, "A Freedmen's Bureau Diary by George Wagner," 200–203.

129. O. H. Howard to M. F. Gallagher, Nov. 1, 1867, box 1, LR, Albany SAC, BRFAL-Ga.; J. M. Hoag to O. O. Howard, reel 21, BRFAL-Ga (M798); J. Murray Hoag, Civil War pension files, RG 15, National Archives; J. A. Rockwell to "My dear brother & sister," Oct. 6, 1868, Rockwell Papers; Carlos A. de la Mesa, Civil War pension file, RG 15, National Archives.

130. Ku Klux Conspiracy, vol. 7: *Georgia*, 1092.

131. C. C. Sibley to O. O. Howard, May 29, 1867, reel 5, BRFAL-Ga (M798); H. F. Mills to O. O. Howard, Dec. 2, 1867, vol. 370, LS, Stockton Agt, BRFAL-Ga.

132. T. R. Clement to [J. V.] De Hanne, Jan. 12, 1867, G. O. Dalton to J. V. De Hanne, Feb. 16, 1867, reel 1, ULR, Surgeon's Records, BRFAL-Ga; Campbell, "A Freedmen's Bureau Diary by George Wagner," 196–214, 333–59; Station Books, vol. 1, 1867–1868, reel 35; G. Wagner to O. O. Howard, July 6, 1868, reel 21, BRFAL-Ga (M798); H. de F. Young to M. F. Gallagher, Sept. 9, 1868, reel 58, (LR)BRFAL (M752).

133. J. W. Barney to [J. J. Knox], Sept. 3, 1867, box 5, ULR, Athens SAC, BRFAL-Ga; J. W. Barney to C. C. Sibley, Aug. 29, 1868, reel 58, (LR)BRFAL (M752).

134. T. A. Parsons Jr. to [Hamilton] Yancey, June 7, 1867, Benjamin C. Yancey Papers, University of North Carolina, Southern Historical Collection.

135. I. L. Harris to C. Andrews, Mar. 5, 1868, Charles Haynes Andrews Papers, University of North Carolina, Southern Historical Collection.

136. D. Tillson to O. O. Howard, June 15, 1866, Howard Papers.

137. C. A. de la Mesa to D. Tillson, Dec. 21, 1866, reel 30; D. M. Hood to Bvt. Lt. Col. Ritter, May 28, 1867, reel 19, BRFAL-Ga (M798).

138. H. C. Flournoy to J. D. Pettard, May 29, 1868, vol. 172, LS, Athens Agt, BRFAL-Ga.

139. W. C. Morrill to [J. R. Lewis], Mar. 24, 1868, reel 23, BRFAL-Ga (M798). Caleb Sibley considered Morrill "an exceedingly efficient officer" who "has labored very energetically in the interests of the freedpeople." C. C. Sibley to O. O. Howard, July 31, 1868, reel 7, BRFAL-Ga (M798).

140. J. J. Knox to M. F. Gallagher, Mar. 21, 1868, endorsement on J. W. Barney to J. J. Knox, Mar. 21, reel 20, BRFAL-Ga (M798).

141. L. Lieberman to J. R. Lewis, Aug. 28, 1868, reel 58, (LR)BRFAL (M752).

142. J. E. Bryant to J. G. Leefe, Sept. 7, 1865, vol. 150, LS, Augusta SAC, BRFAL-Ga.

143. It is significant that whites directed violence at Bureau men, for like the black and white Republican political leaders who suffered at the hands of their opponents, Bureau men were an even earlier personification of the Yankee challenge to the social and economic status quo. For the political use of violence and intimidation by white Georgians against Republicans, see Drago, *Black Politicians*, 145–55.

144. W. F. Eaton to A. P. Ketchum, July 31, 1865, box 32, Records of the Assistant Adjutant General, Savannah SAC, BRFAL-Ga; W. F. Eaton to G. Whipple, Sept. 21, 1865, reel 1, AMA-Ga.

145. For a discussion of Bryant's labor activities see chapter 6. For criticism of Bryant as well as his associate Wild, see E. B. Jones to M. Jones, June 13, 1865, in Myers, *Children of Pride*, 1274. For additional criticism of Bryant and Wild, see Ella Gertrude Clanton Thomas Diary, Oct. 8, 1865, Duke University, published in abridged form as Burr, *The Secret Eye*; Marion Alexander to [Mary] Clifford [Alexander], July 31, 1865, in Boggs, *Alexander Letters*, 299; G. M. Brayton to S. B. Moe, Aug. 4, 1865, reel 20, (LR)BRFAL (M752). For the death threats against Bryant see J. E. Bryant to J. G. Leefe, Sept. 7, 1865, vol. 150, LS, Augusta SAC, BRFAL-Ga.

146. J. E. Bryant to J. G. Leefe, September 7, 1865, vol. 150, LS, Augusta SAC, BRFAL-Ga, RG 105; *Augusta Daily Constitutionalist*, Sept. 2, 1865. A military commissioner found two of the accused not guilty but condemned a third participant to death by hanging. As late as April 1866, the convicted party remained jailed in New York State. *Augusta Daily Constitutionalist*, Nov. 11, 1865; [J. A. Cobb] to Mother [Mary A. Cobb], Apr. 21, 1866, Howell Cobb Papers, University of Georgia.

147. W. H. Tiffany to N. C. Dennett, Sept. 18, 1865, box 32, LR, Savannah Agt, BRFAL-Ga.

148. D. Tillson to O. O. Howard, Dec. 21, 1865, reel 20, (LR)BRFAL (M752).

149. W. Gray to D. Tillson, Mar. 14, 1866, reel 27, BRFAL-Ga (M798).

150. C. A. de la Mesa to D. Tillson, Jan. 6, 1867, reel 30, BRFAL-Ga (M798).

151. J. R. Phillips to D. Tillson, May 18, 25, July 20, Aug. 9, 28, 1866, reel 28, BRFAL-Ga (M798); D. Tillson to E. Foster and A. M. Campbell, Oct. 16, 1866, reel 37, (LR)BRFAL (M752). For Tillson's actions see W. W. Deane to C. R. Woods, Aug. 14, 1866; W. W. Deane to A. Sloane, Oct. 5, 1866, reel 3; C. McC. Lord to W. W. Deane, Oct. 8, 1866, reel 28; A. M. Campbell to D. Tillson, Oct. 8, 1866, reel 25, BRFAL-Ga (M798); D. Tillson to E. Foster and A. M. Campbell, Oct. 16, 1866, reel 37, (LR)BRFAL (M752); Capt. W. Mills to Bvt. Maj. C. F. Trowbridge, Nov. 21, 1866, LR, Dist. of Ga.; *Macon Daily Telegraph*, Oct. 23, 1866; *American Missionary* 10 (Dec. 1866): 272–73.

152. W. C. Riddle to D. Tillson, Aug. 16, 1866, reel 28, BRFAL-Ga (M798).

153. J. S. Dunning to E. Pickett, May 28, 1866, reel 14; G. R. Walbridge to D. Tillson, Mar. 14, 1866, reel 13, BRFAL-Ga (M798).

154. E. M. L. Ehlers to [J. R. Lewis], Sept. 9, 1867, Registers of LR, reel 12, BRFAL-Ga (M798); G. Walbridge to E. M. L. Ehlers, box 9, LR, Augusta SAC; Andrew B. Clark to O. H. Howard, June 18, 1868, vol. 323, LS, Newton Agt, BRFAL-Ga.

155. Affidavit of O. W. Sherwood, Oct. 8, 1868, reel 58, (LR)BRFAL (M752); Register of Civilian Agents, 1865–1867; Station Books, vol. 1, 1867–68, reel 35, BRFAL-Ga (M798).

156. H. W. Kearsing to H. F. Brownson, June 6, 8, 9, 24, 1868, vol. 188, Register of Complaints and Orders Sent; G. M. Brayton, Special Orders, No. 5, June 25, 1868, box 11, LR, Bartow Agt, BRFAL-Ga; H. W. Kearsing to J. R. Lewis, Apr. 17, June 6, 1868; H. W. Kearsing to J. M. Hoag, June 17, 1868; J. Mullin to C. C. Sibley, July 18, 1868 (and all enclosures but especially W. O. Moffit to H. W. Kearsing, June 27, 1868), reel 21; H. W. Kearsing to J. R. Lewis, Aug. 3, 1868, reel 30, BRFAL-Ga (M798).

157. Andrew Clark to [W. F. White], Aug. 22, 1867, reel 17, BRFAL-Ga (M798).

158. Entry for Feb. 15, 1867, Register of Complaints, vol. 174, Athens SAC, BRFAL-Ga; F. E. Sautell to E. P. Smith, Dec. 1, 1868, reel 4, AMA-Ga.

159. J. J. Knox to R. B. Bullock, Nov. 9, 1868, vol. 170, LS, Athens SAC, BRFAL-Ga.

160. F. A. Sautell to E. P. Smith, Dec. 1, 1868, reel 4, AMA-Ga; J. J. Knox to M. F. Gallagher, Nov. 24, 1868, reel 58, (LR)BRFAL (M752); E. Whittlesey to J. R. Lewis, Dec. 15, 1868, reel 23. For the white Georgia version of the incident and the assessment of Clarke County residents' feelings toward the Bureau, see Fan [Atkisson] to [M. Blackshear], Nov. 22, 1868, Baber-Blackshear Papers, University of Georgia, and the testimony of John H. Christy, given on July 24, 1871, in Ku Klux Conspiracy, vol. 6: *Georgia*, 233–35.

161. J. J. Knox to M. F. Gallagher, Nov. 24, 1868, reel 58 (LR)BRFAL (M752); Station Books, vol. 1, 1867–1868, reel 35, BRFAL-Ga (M798); John J. Knox, Civil War pension files, RG 15, National Archives. Most agents and officers who were so threatened believed that they required the protection of troops to continue their work. For example, see E. M. L. Ehlers to T. Holden, [Aug. 1, 1867], vol. 152, LS, Augusta SAC, BRFAL-Ga; Andrew Clark to [W. F. White], Aug. 22, 1867, reel 17; H. W. Kearsing to H. F. Brownson, June 6, 1868; O. H. Howard to M. F. Gallagher, June 15, 1868, reel 21, BRFAL-Ga (M798).

162. G. R. Walbridge to E. M. L. Ehlers, Aug. 1, 1867, box 9, LR, Augusta SAC, BRFAL-Ga; W. M. Moore to [C. C. Sibley], June 29, 1868, reel 21; R. C. Anthony to M. F. Gallagher, Nov. 19, 1868, reel 23, Station Books, 1:1867–1868, reel 35, BRFAL-Ga (M798).

163. C. C. Richardson to R. Saxton, Sept. 27, 1865, reel 8, BRFAL-SC (M869); Special Orders, No. 53, Mar. 23, 1866, reel 34; C. C. Richardson to D. Tillson, June 18, 1866, reel 28, BRFAL-Ga (M798). Ironically, Richardson, an ally of John Emory Bryant, eventually was murdered in 1868 by a political rival, who also happened to be a Union veteran and Republican. Currie-McDaniel, *Carpetbagger of Conscience*, 85–86.

164. J. M. Robinson to O. H. Howard, Dec. 26, 1867, box 1, LR, Albany SAC, BRFAL-Ga; Station Books, vol. 1, 1867–1868, reel 35, BRFAL-Ga (M798).

165. G. O. Dalton to J. V. De Hanne, Feb. 16, 1867, reel 1, URL; C. C. Hicks to J. R. Lewis, Oct. 22, 1867, reel 2, LR; J. M. Laing to E. A. Edwards, Oct. 26, 1867; J. M. Laing to G. O. Dalton, Nov. 13, 1867, reel 9, LS, Surgeon's Records, BRFAL-Ga; C. C. Hicks to [O. H. Howard], Oct. 22, 1867, reel 12, BRFAL-Ga (M798).

166. Andrew B. Clark to [W. F. White], Aug. 22, 1867, reel 17; Andrew B. Clark to [C. C. Sibley], Aug. 23, 1867, Register of LR, reel 12, BRFAL-Ga (M798); Andrew B. Clark to O. H. Howard, June 18, 1868, vol. 323, LS, Newton Agt, BRFAL-Ga.

167. Carlos A. de la Mesa, Civil War pension files, RG 15, National Archives.

168. C. C. Sibley to O. O. Howard, Sept. 11, 1868, reel 7, BRFAL-Ga (M798).

169. H. de F. Young to M. F. Gallagher, Sept. 9, 1868, reel 58, (LR)BRFAL (M752); H. de F. Young to M. F. Gallagher, Sept. 10, Oct. 20, 1868, reel 23, BRFAL-Ga (M798).

170. O. H. Howard to M. F. Gallagher, Oct. 3, 1868, reel 23, BRFAL-Ga (M798).

171. L. Lieberman to J. R. Lewis, Aug. 28, 1868, reel 58, (LR)BRFAL (M752); L. Lieberman to C. C. Sibley, Aug. 31, 1868, reel 22, BRFAL-Ga (M798).

172. J. W. Barney to M. F. Gallagher, Aug. 15, 1868, vol. 211, LS, Carnesville Agt, BRFAL-Ga; J. W. Barney to C. C. Sibley, Aug. 29, 1868, reel 58; J. R. Lewis to O. O. Howard, Sept. 26, 1867, reel 49, (LR)BRFAL (M752).

## Chapter 4. None but the Very Destitute

1. For a description of the war's impact on Georgia including the refugeeing process, see Clarence L. Mohr, *On the Threshold of Freedom*.

2. *Augusta Daily Constitutionalist*, May 2–4, 20, 1865; James Appleton Blackshear Diary, May 11, 1865, Emory University, Atlanta. Also see George Lamar to cousin, May 1, 1865, Howell Cobb Papers, University of Georgia; Caroline S. Jones to Mary Jones, Apr. 30, in Robert Manson Myers, ed., *Children of Pride*, 1268; *Macon Daily Telegraph*, May 11, 1865. For a southwide treatment of this disorganized state of affairs, see Dan T. Carter, *When the War Was Over*, 6–23.

3. J. M. Johnson to "My dear Maj[or]," June 10, 1865, Howell Cobb Papers; *Macon Daily Telegraph*, May 30, 31, June 2, 13, 23, Oct. 15, 1865; *Rome Weekly Courier*, Oct. 12, 26, 1865; *Columbus Daily Sun*, Sept. 2, 1865; W. P. Russell to the secretaries of the American Missionary Association, May 25, 1865, reel 1, AMA-Ga; R. Battey to Mary [Battey], July 19, 1865, Robert Battey Papers, Emory University, Atlanta; Schurz, *Report on the Condition of the South*, 29; Trowbridge, *The South*, 453, 462; A. P. Ketchum to R. Saxton, Sept. 1, 1865, reel 34, BRFAL-SC (M869).

4. J. Harper and others to President Andrew Johnson, Mar. 31, 1866, enclosed in L. D. Burwell to D. Tillson, Apr. 2, 1866, reel 25, BRFAL-Ga (M798).

5. J. M. Beiland to D. Tillson, May 20, 1866, reel 25, BRFAL-Ga (M798). For the problems planters encountered in operating their lands short of cash and supplies, also see W[illia]m Henry Stiles to Dr. D. H. Farmer, Apr. 22, 1866, series C, Mackay-Stiles Family Papers, and [Henry L. Graves] to "My Dear Cousin," Sept. 8, 1866, Graves Family

Papers, University of North Carolina, Southern Historical Collection. For white yeoman farmers, the problem of chronic poverty that resulted in the loss of land and a move to sharecropping after the war was a pressing one. Steven Hahn details the plight of these individuals in northern Georgia in *The Roots of Southern Populism*, esp. 156–68.

6. For comments on bad weather and bad crops see G. S. Lanier to brother and sister, May 18, 1866, Nancy Ann Miller Family Letters, GDAH; Elisha Lowry to John S. Dobbins, June 7, July 21, Aug. 20, Nov. 5, 1866, series I, John S. Dobbins Papers, Emory University; W. M[onroe?] to Howell [Cobb], Howell Cobb Papers; Fannie Atkisson to "My dear Coz," Aug. 19, 1866, Baber-Blackshear Papers, University of Georgia; James Green to D. Tillson, Aug. 19, 1866, reel 27; J. Davison to D. Tillson, Sept. 3, 1866, reel 26, BRFAL-Ga (M798); *Macon Daily Telegraph*, May 30, 1866; *Columbus Daily Enquirer*, June 23, 24, Oct. 18, 1866; *Augusta Daily Constitutionalist*, July 22, Aug. 4, Sept. 15, Oct. 13, 1866.

7. J. J. Knox to E. Pickett, Apr. 16, 19, 1867; G. M. Nolan to E. Pickett, Apr. 27, 1867, reel 15; W. T. Wooford to C. C. Sibley, May 15, 1867, reel 16; W. J. Bryant to C. C. Sibley, May 16; C. A. de la Mesa to C. C. Sibley, May 23, 1867, reel 14, BRFAL-Ga (M798); K. Tyner to J. J. Knox, May 18, 1867, box 5, ULR, Athens SAC, BRFAL-Ga; *Griffin Star* [n.d.], reprinted in *Savannah Daily Republican*, Apr. 5, 1867.

8. O. H. Howard to C. C. Sibley, Apr. 23, 1867, reel 15, BRFAL-Ga (M798).

9. J. W. Lawton to D. Tillson, Apr. 23, 1866, reel 27; J. W. Lawton, "Report of Surgeon J. W. Lawton, USV of the Operations of the Medical Department of the Bureau of Refugees, Freedmen and Abandoned Lands from September 1, 1865 to October 1, 1866," reel 32 (hereinafter cited as Lawton, "Report"); H. B. Sprague to W. W. Deane, Dec. 16, 1865; P. Slaughter to D. Tillson, Dec. 18, 1865, reel 24; E. P. Lumpkin to J. R. Lyle, Jan. 10, 1866, reel 27, BRFAL-Ga (M798); H. F. Sickles to J. W. Lawton, Nov. 19, 1865; S. T. Tuggle to J. W. Lawton, Jan. 1, 1866, reel 1, ULR, Surgeon's Records, BRFAL-Ga; R. M. Craighead to Rev. S. Hunt, Feb. 1, 1866; J. A. Rockwell to S. Hunt, Feb. 2, 1866, reel 1, AMA-Ga; *Augusta Daily Constitutionalist*, Jan. 26, 1866; *Columbus Daily Enquirer*, Jan. 17, 28, Feb. 21, 1866; *New York Times*, Jan. 22, Feb. 11, 1866; *Sandersville Central Georgian*, Apr. 18, 1866; D. Tillson to J. W. Lawton, Apr. 12, 1866, reel 1, ULR, Surgeon's Records, BRFAL-Ga.

10. Alvin B. Clark to J. V. De Hanne, May 29, 1867, box 26, LR, Quitman Agt, BRFAL-Ga; J. M. Laing, "Annual Report of the Operations of the Med Dep't, Bureau RF&AL Dist of Ga. Oct. 1, 1866 to Sept. 30, 1867," reel 32, BRFAL-Ga (M798).

11. J. R. Davis to O. O. Howard, Mar. 9, 1867, Howard Papers, Bowdoin College, Brunswick, Maine; J. B. Smith to J. R. Lewis, May 8, 1867, reel 16; C. C. Sibley, Report for April, May 23, 1867, reel 32; C. H. Hopkins Jr. to C. C. Sibley, Mar. 1868; A. C. Walker to C. C. Sibley, Mar. 19, 1868, reel 20, BRFAL-Ga (M798); *Bainbridge Argus*, n.d., reprinted in *Savannah Daily Republican*, May 31, 1867.

12. W. M. Mitchell to D. Tillson, Aug. 31, 1866, reel 28, BRFAL-Ga (M798); *Columbus Daily Enquirer*, Oct. 18, 1866.

13. L. D. Burwell to D. Tillson, Apr. 2, 1866, reel 25; L. T. Campbell to D. Tillson, May 21, 1866, reel 25, BRFAL-Ga (M798).

14. Statement of Jerry Goodwin, Apr. 4, 1867, box 21, LR, Macon SAC, BRFAL-Ga.

15. C. A. de la Mesa to C. C. Sibley, May 23, 1867, reel 14, BRFAL-Ga (M798).

16. M. F. Malsby to J. J. Knox, May 6, 1867, box 5, ULR, Athens SAC, BRFAL-Ga.

17. *The Statutes at Large of the United States* (1863–1865), 13:508.

18. Historians Todd L. Savitt and Gaines M. Foster both note the lack of innovation in structuring the delivery of health care to the freedpeople, an assessment that may be applied to relief in general. They are critical of the Bureau for leaving health care primarily in the hands of white Southerners, but they fail to give ample weight to the ideological and practical limits at work within the agency that made this approach almost foreordained. Savitt's and Foster's assessment of Bureau relief efforts is the most common. Savitt, "Politics in Medicine"; Foster, "The Limitations of Federal Health Care for Freedmen, 1862–1868." For a general survey of nineteenth-century philanthropy and its ideological limitations, see Robert H. Bremner, *The Public Good*.

19. Circular No. 5, Freedmen's Bureau Headquarters, Washington, D.C., May 30, 1865; Circular No. 8, Freedmen's Bureau Headquarters, Washington, D.C., June 20, 1865, *House Executive Documents*, 39th Cong., 1st sess., no. 70 (serial 1256), 180, 183.

20. R. Saxton to O. O. Howard, June 4, 1865, reel 17, (LR)BRFAL (M752).

21. *Macon Daily Telegraph*, June 16, 1865; contracts between T. F. Daniel and freedmen, June 1, 1865; N. Bussey and freedmen, Aug. 5, 1865; F. A. Bradshaw and freedmen, Aug. 10, 1865, vol. 159, Contracts, Augusta Agt, BRFAL-Ga.

22. Circular No. 2, Oct. 3, 1865, reel 34, BRFAL-Ga (M798). D. Tillson to R. Saxton, Oct. 14, 1865, reel 8, BRFAL-SC (M869); Special Orders, No. 4, Oct. 12, 1865; Special Orders, No. 10, Oct. 21, 1865, reel 34; D. Tillson, "Report of Operations from September 22, 1865, to November 1, 1866," Nov. 1, 1866, reel 32, BRFAL-Ga (M798), in which he noted the steep decrease in relief issued in Savannah by the end of October. Also see D. Tillson to H. F. Sickles, Nov. 15, 1865, BRFAL-Ga (M798), in which he compliments the Savannah subassistant commissioner for the reduction of rations and warns him to continue to be frugal.

23. W. W. Deane to G. R. Walbridge, Mar. 8, Apr. 3, 1866; W. W. Deane to W. Gray, Mar. 10, 1866, reel 2, BRFAL-Ga (M798).

24. D. Tillson to O. O. Howard, June 8, 1866, reel 32, (LR)BRFAL (M752). Also see Tillson's Circular Letter, Nov. 19, 1866, reel 34, BRFAL-Ga (M798).

25. The Army Appropriations Act of 1866 provided funds for the transportation of suffering refugees and freedpeople. Until December 1866 Tillson transported freedpeople within the state and to the borders of Georgia; on December 24, 1866, following the instructions of O. O. Howard, he provided transportation to freedpeople to points outside of Georgia where the Bureau was functioning. Tillson's transportation policy is best understood within the context of a discussion of his labor contract policy, as

described in the following chapter. D. Tillson to W. Finch, Oct. 10, 1866, reel 4; Circular No. 12, Dec. 24, 1866, reel 34, BRFAL-Ga (M798); Bentley, *Freedmen's Bureau*, 134.

26. G. Wagner to E. Pickett, Dec. 5, 1866, reel 29; F. A. H. Gaebel to E. Pickett, May 25, 1867, reel 14; J. J. Knox to E. Pickett, May 2, 1867, reel 15, BRFAL-Ga (M798).

27. N. D'Alvigny to J. W. Lawton, Nov. 26, 1865, reel 1, ULR, Surgeon's Records, BRFAL-Ga.

28. C. C. Sibley, Report for May, June 11, 1868, reel 32, BRFAL-Ga (M798).

29. J. R. Davis to O. O. Howard, Mar. 9, 1867, Howard Papers.

30. Mitchell also advocated assisting the freedpeople at Elliot's Bluff in Camden County with advances until the harvest. A. Mitchell to W. P. Fessenden, Jan. 22, 1867, reel 1, ULR, Surgeon's Records, BRFAL-Ga; Claude F. Oubre, *Forty Acres and a Mule*, 91. Mitchell lived in the South during the 1830s and then again during the 1850s and the war, when he remained a Unionist. Mitchell, however, was well aware of Yankee free-labor ideology because he was born in Maine and educated at Yale. He also spent the 1840s and early 1850s residing in his native state. A. Mitchell to [J. W. Lawton], May 28, 1866, reel 1, ULR, Surgeon's Records, BRFAL-Ga.

31. *Savannah National Republican*, Sept. 29, 1865.

32. J. M. Hoag to C. C. Sibley, May 2, 1867, reel 15, BRFAL-Ga (M798).

33. J. M. Beland to [D. Tillson], May 20, 1866, reel 25; J. H. Taylor to W. W. Deane, May 21, 1866, reel 29; and L. D. Burwell to D. Tillson, Apr. 2, 1866 (and endorsements), reel 25, D. J. Curtis to C. C. Sibley, May 18, 1867, reel 14, BRFAL-Ga (M798).

34. [D. Tillson] to L. D. Burwell, May 3, 1866, reel 2, BRFAL-Ga (M798).

35. For assistance given to Tunis Campbell's Belle Ville colony in McIntosh County, see Article of Agreement between T. G. Campbell and J. M. Hoag, Apr. 4, 1867, box 31, McIntosh County Contracts; J. M. Hoag to C. C. Sibley, Oct. 1, 1868, box 27, LR, Savannah SAC, BRFAL-Ga. For assistance given to the Elliot's Bluff settlement in Camden County, which was brought to Sibley's attention by Dr. Augustus Mitchell, see A. Mitchell to C. C. Sibley, Apr. 26, 1867, reel 15; E. Pickett to J. M. Hoag, June 6, 1867; E. Pickett to D. G. Risley, June 6, 1867, reel 5, BRFAL-Ga (M798).

36. A. P. Ketchum to R. Saxton, Sept. 1, 1865, reel 34, BRFAL-SC (M869).

37. Statement of Jerry Goodwin, Apr. 4, 1867 (and all endorsements), box 21, LR, Macon SAC, BRFAL-Ga. Goodwin, a freedman, was renting 300 acres of land and asked Sibley for provisions. For a similar request from a freedman renting 150 acres of land that evoked the same negative response from Sibley, see W. F. Martins to N. S. Hill, Apr. 4, 1867, ibid. In 1868, the Bureau supplied planters with rations to feed their workers after taking a lien on their crops in South Carolina and Louisiana, and in Florida it issued rations to freedpeople who were working at least ten acres of land. Although the Georgia Bureau distributed rations to at least one desperate planter to allow him to feed his hands, taking a lien on the crop, it implemented no general program like South Carolina's or Florida's. Bentley, *Freedmen's Bureau*, 143, 144; A. C. Walker to C. C. Sibley,

Mar. 19, 1868, reel 20; M. F. Gallagher to A. C. Walker, Mar. 20, 1868, reel 7, BRFAL-Ga (M798).

38. For example, see W. W. Deane to R. A. Heath, Feb. 5, 1866, reel 1, BRFAL-Ga (M798); C. C. Sibley, Report for December 1867, Feb. 8, 1868, reel 32, BRFAL-Ga (M798).

39. This standing policy also required planters to care for children, but children could be apprenticed. Circular No. 5, Dec. 22, 1865, reel 34; orders by W. W. Deane, directed to ex-masters J. F. Lawson and Mr. McHenry, both dated Jan. 6, 1866; W. W. Deane to J. Entwisle, Dec. 8, 1865; W. W. Deane to T. W. White, Jan. 14, 1866, reel 1; T. F. Forbes to J. W. Green, June 9, 1866; T. F. Forbes to N. G. Foster, July 27, 1866, reel 3, BRFAL-Ga (M798). Also see the exchange between Tillson and a Morgan County planter: J. B. Walker to D. Tillson, Nov. 17, 1865, reel 24; D. Tillson to J. B. Walker, Nov. 20, 1865, reel 1, BRFAL-Ga (M798).

40. Quoted in Thompson, "The Freedmen's Bureau in Georgia in 1865–66," 43–44. Also see *Southern Cultivator*, Jan. 1866, 3–4.

41. J. H. Lane to T. H. Ruger, May 19, 1868, box 60, Georgia Governors' Papers, Telamon-Cuyler Collection, University of Georgia.

42. W. F. Bowes to J. M. Laing, Nov. 12, 1868, reel 3, LR, Surgeon's Records, BRFAL-Ga.

43. The view from Bureau headquarters, which urged the Bureau to push for civilian responsibility and act only as a last resort, may be found in A. P. Ketchum to D. Tillson, Sept. 24, Oct. 6, 1866, reel 2, (RI)BRFAL (M742); F. D. Sewall to C. C. Sibley, Sept. 16, 1867, reel 18, BRFAL-Ga (M798).

44. W. Mitchell to D. Tillson, June 14, 1866, reel 32, (LR)BRFAL (M752).

45. F. A. H. Gaebel to E. Pickett, July 29, 1867, box 1, LR, Albany SAC, BRFAL-Ga.

46. J. W. Lawton to [————], Nov. 21, 1865, reel 1, LS (Unentered), Surgeon's Records, BRFAL-Ga.

47. In April 1866, Surgeon Lawton explained the small number of hospitals in the state by noting that it was best to assist county authorities in their efforts to care for the freedpeople. J. W. Lawton to D. Tillson, Apr. 23, 1866, reel 27, BRFAL-Ga (M798).

48. J. V. De Hanne to C. C. Sibley, May 18, 1867, reel 14; C. C. Sibley, Report for November 1867, Dec. 12, 1867, reel 32, BRFAL-Ga (M798).

49. Destitution was supposed to be handled at the county level by the inferior courts, the county administrative body, until in 1868 when the ordinary was given the duty to oversee the administration of poor relief. Also in 1868, the ordinary assumed jurisdiction over health matters from the county inferior court. For the development of county government and services, including poor relief and health administration and subsequent changes in official jurisdiction, see Melvin Clyde Hughes, *County Government in Georgia*, 1–17, 128–29, 140. For the limited social services that state and local governments were used to providing for its citizens, see Hughes, *County Government*, 128–29, 140. Also see Peter Wallenstein, *From Slave South to New South*.

For the inability of the traditional local infrastructure to cope with postwar destitution, see Lawton, "Report"; F. Mosebach to G. R. Walbridge, Mar. 15, 1867; O. H. Howard to C. C. Sibley, Apr. 23, 1867, reel 15; W. T. Wofford to C. C. Sibley, May 15, 1867; W. J. Bryan to C. C. Sibley, May 16, 1867; L. W. Earnest and others to C. C. Sibley, May 17, 1867, reel 14; C. Raushenberg to M. F. Gallagher, Nov. 19, 1867, reel 19; E. M. L. Ehlers to M. F. Gallagher, Dec. 23, 1867 (and all enclosures), reel 17, BRFAL-Ga (M798); B. C. Ferrell to F. Mosebach, May 9, 1867, box 20, LR, LaGrange Agt; K. Tyner to J. J. Knox, May 18, 1867, box 5, ULR, Athens SAC; J. T. Blain to D. G. Risley, June 24, 1867, box 12, LR, Brunswick SAC, BRFAL-Ga; *Columbus Daily Enquirer*, June 19, 1866.

50. M. Marbach to H. Catley, May 28, 1868, box 9, LR, Augusta SAC, BRFAL-Ga.

51. F. Moseback to C. T. Watson, June 22, 1866, vol. 222, LS, Columbus SAC, BRFAL-Ga.

52. *Augusta Daily Constitutionalist*, Jan. 26, 1866; A. P. Collins to [D. Tillson], Apr. 5, 1866; S. Collins to [D. Tillson], Apr. 22, 1866, reel 11; D. Tillson to W. Mitchell, May 30, 1860, reel 3; BRFAL-Ga (M798); D. C. Poole to H. N. Lumpkin, Feb. 2, 1866, vol. 98, LS, Atlanta SAC; F. Mosebach to Dr. J. W. Lawton, May 19, 1866, vol. 222, LS, Columbus SAC, BRFAL-Ga; Busbee, "Presidential Reconstruction in Georgia, 1865–1867," 351.

53. J. W. Lawton to D. Tillson, Apr. 23, 1866, reel 27, BRFAL-Ga (M798).

54. D. Gammage to J. B. Davenport, Oct. 21, 1867; W. F. Martins to J. R. Lewis, Oct. 25, 1867; T. Holden to J. R. Lewis, Oct. 31, 1867; W. S. Hudson to W. E. Wiggins, Nov. 6, 1867, reel 18; E. M. L. Ehlers to M. F. Gallagher, Dec. 23, 1867, reel 17, BRFAL-Ga (M798).

55. M. F. Gallagher to T. Holden, Nov. 9, 1867; M. F. Gallagher to C. Raushenberg, Nov. 25, 1867, reel 6, BRFAL-Ga (M798); O. H. Howard to C. C. Hicks, Nov. 19, 1867, box 3, LR, Albany Agt; J. Leonard to J. B. Davenport, Feb. 4, 1868, vol. 223, LS, Columbus SAC, BRFAL-Ga.

56. For the agency's efforts to relocate paupers, see M. F. Gallagher to W. F. Martins, Mar. 18, 1868; M. F. Gallagher to G. Schletfeldt, Mar. 18, 1868; M. F. Gallagher to F. Mosebach, Mar. 18, 1868; M. F. Gallagher to P. D. Claiborne, May 5, 1868; M. F. Gallagher to W. J. Bryan, May 5, 1868; M. F. Gallagher to H. D. Haskell, May 5, 1868; M. F. Gallagher to W. B. Moore, May 21, 1868, reel 7, BRFAL-Ga (M798). For the activity regarding hospitals and civil authorities, see J. M. Laing to George S. Obear, Nov. 3, 1868, reel 23, BRFAL-Ga (M798); J. M. Laing to C. C. Sibley, Aug. 31, 1868; F. D. Sewall to J. M. Laing, Dec. 22, 1868, reel 3, LR, Surgeon's Records, BRFAL-Ga. In June 1868, the Georgia medical department received orders to close all of its facilities except for one hospital. L. A. Edwards to J. W. Laing, June 26, 1868, reel 2, LR, Surgeon's Records, BRFAL-Ga.

57. G. Wagner to W. W. Deane, Sept. 3, 1866; A. Dudley and R. Covington to D. Tillson, Oct. 20, 1866, reel 1, ULR, Surgeon's Records, BRFAL-Ga.

58. A. T. Augusta to J. W. Lawton, Dec. [—], 1865, reel 1, ULR, Surgeon's Records, BRFAL-Ga. See Dr. Lawton's unfavorable assessment of white Georgia's willingness to assist aged, infirm, or destitute freedpeople in J. W. Lawton to D. Tillson, Apr. 23, 1866, reel 27, BRFAL-Ga (M798).

59. On at least one occasion, a suffering freedman died because the hospital did not admit a nonresident freedperson and the authorities preferred to allow him to shift for himself. C. T. Watson, "Annual Report of Bvt. Maj. C. T. Watson AQM—Chief Q[uarter]M[aster] RF&AL State of Georgia for the Year Ending November 1, 1866," reel 32; J. M. Hoag to C. C. Sibley, Dec. 23, 1867, reel 18, BRFAL-Ga (M798); A. T. Augustus to J. W. Lawton, Sept. 22, 1866, reel 1, ULR; T. R. Clement to J. M. Laing, Jan. 16, 1868, reel 2, LR, Surgeon's Records, BRFAL-Ga.

60. D. Tillson to J. S. Fullerton, June 4, 1866, reel 3; Gov. C. J. Jenkins to D. Tillson, Sept. 26, 1866, reel 27, BRFAL-Ga (M798); D. Tillson to O. O. Howard, Oct. 2, 1866, reel 37, (LR)BRFAL (M752).

61. C. J. Gobrecht to C. C. Sibley, Apr. 18, 1867; E. Bright to C. C. Sibley, Apr. 24, 1867; E. R. Falligant to C. C. Sibley, Apr. 25, 1867; E. Belcher to C. C. Sibley, Apr. 27, 1867, reel 14; G. M. Nolan to C. C. Sibley, June 3, 1867, reel 15; W. F. Martins to J. R. Lewis, Oct. 25, 1867, reel 18, BRFAL-Ga (M798); R. T. Finney to C. C. Sibley, June 18, 1867, box 16, LR, Dalton Agt; C. A. de la Mesa to C. C. Sibley, June 22, 1867, box 26, ULR, Rome Agt, BRFAL-Ga.

62. G. M. Nolan to C. C. Sibley, June 3, 1867, reel 15; W. Royal to C. C. Sibley, Sept. 18, 1867, enclosed in S. A. J. Collins to Maj. Gen. [John] Pope, July 25, 1867, reel 17, BRFAL-Ga (M798). For complaints about regulations, see E. Bright to C. C. Sibley, Apr. 24, 1867, reel 14, BRFAL-Ga (M798).

63. C. J. Gobrecht to C. C. Sibley, Apr. 18, 1867, reel 14; E. Pickett to Station Agent, Cartersville, Apr. 24, 1867; E. Pickett to P. D. Claiborne, Apr. 6, 1867; G. Walbridge to E. Belcher, Apr. 17, 1867; J. R. Lewis to H. M. Loyless, May 18, 1867, reel 5, BRFAL-Ga (M798); F. Mosebach to G. M. Nolan, June 10, 1867, vol. 99, LS, Atlanta SAC; R. T. Finney to C. C. Sibley, June 18, 1867, box 16, LR, Dalton Agt; C. A. de la Mesa to C. C. Sibley, June 22, 1867, box 26, ULR, Rome Agt, BRFAL-Ga.

64. F. Mosebach to G. M. Nolan, June 7, 1867, vol. 99, LS, Atlanta SAC, BRFAL-Ga.

65. Surgeon De Hanne refused to accept the expense, but Clark had warned the physician that he might have to petition the county for his pay. A. B. Clark to J. V. De Hanne, May 29, 1867, with endorsement of J. V. De Hanne, May 31, 1867, box 26, LR, Quitman Agt, BRFAL-Ga.

66. W. C. Morrill to M. F. Gallagher, July 23, 1868, reel 3, LR, Surgeon's Records, BRFAL-Ga.

67. Register of Complaints, Apr. 6, 1868, vol. 174, Athens SAC, BRFAL-Ga.

68. J. Leonard to M. F. Gallagher, May 26, 1868, LR, box 14, Columbus SAC, BRFAL-Ga. In this case, Gen. George Meade appointed new inferior court judges

under the authority of Military Reconstruction. Endorsement of John E. Horner, June 6, 1868, ibid.

69. C. A. de la Mesa to C. T. Watson, Mar. 2, 1868, vol. 342, LS, Rome SAC, BRFAL-Ga.

70. F. Ayer to Brother Dodd, [May 27?], 1866, Frederick Ayer Papers, Atlanta University. For other AMA efforts in Georgia, see Joe M. Richardson, *Christian Reconstruction*, 63, 65.

71. A. B. Clark to J. V. De Hanne, May 29, 1867, box 26, LR, Quitman Agt, BRFAL-Ga.

72. C. Raushenberg to the Inferior Court, Dougherty County, July 7, 11, 17, 20, 23, 24, 1868, vol. 124, LS, Albany Agt, BRFAL-Ga.

73. B. Maguire to W. W. Deane, Jan. 28, May 9, 1866, reel 28, BRFAL-Ga (M798); B. Maguire to J. W. Lawton, Mar. 7, 1866, reel 2, ULR, Surgeon's Records, BRFAL-Ga.

74. J. V. De Hanne to M. L. Bowes, Feb. 23, 1867; W. F. Martins to E. Pickett, Mar. 2, 1867, reel 15, BRFAL-Ga, (M798).

75. Howard, *Autobiography*, 2:256, 258; Abbott, *Freedmen's Bureau in South Carolina*, 38; Bentley, *Freedmen's Bureau*, 134. During Tillson's tenure the Bureau received a significant amount of irregular and damaged goods from the Quartermaster Department as well as clothing from northern relief organizations. It also had on hand captured rebel property. The Bureau distributed this clothing "without reference to color, though the greater portion has been given to the freed-people." C. T. Watson, "Annual Report," reel 32, BRFAL-Ga (M798). Although clothing obviously relieved the immediate suffering of many individuals, it was the distribution of food, the chief focus herein, that caused the greatest problem to those who passed it out. It was the distribution of food that had or could have had an impact on the rooting of free labor in the state.

76. J. E. Bryant to W. Saxton, June 11, 1865, J. E. Bryant Papers, Duke University.

77. E. A. Wild to R. Saxton, Sept. 1, 1865, reel 8, BRFAL-SC (M869). In O. O. Howard's Circular No. 8, issued June 20, 1865, the commissioner defined a ration for an adult by quoting the War Department's General Orders, No. 30, 1864. A recipient of the Bureau's largess ideally would receive sixteen ounces of fresh beef or ten ounces of pork or bacon (presumably once a week), sixteen ounces of flour or soft bread or twelve ounces of hard bread twice a week, sixteen ounces of cornmeal five times a week, and various portions of beans, peas or hominy, sugar, vinegar, candles, soap, salt, and pepper. In addition, women and children received portions of rye coffee or tea. Children under fourteen received half rations. In reality, Georgians in need were fortunate to receive meat and corn. Commissioner Howard's Circular No. 11, issued April 3, 1867, informed his subordinates that a ration consisted of one bushel of corn and eight pounds of meat per month for adults and half of that amount for children. *House Executive Documents*, 39th Cong., 1st sess., no. 70 (serial 1256), 183; *House Executive Documents*, 40th Cong., 2d sess., no. 1 (serial 1324), 644; Howard, *Autobiography*, 2:257.

78. Poorly kept records prevented Davis Tillson from ascertaining the exact number of rations distributed by Bureau officers in Georgia during Saxton's tenure. D. Tillson, "Report of Operations from September 22, 1865, to November 1, 1866," reel 32, BRFAL-Ga (M798).

79. Watson planned to follow orders from O. O. Howard and sell some of this property, but he noted that many of the buildings were "temporary" structures erected by the Confederate government during the war. At the time that Watson made his report, the Bureau had collected over $15,000 from the sale and rental of property. Once appropriations were available, money also came into the Bureau's regular fund from the Washington headquarters. The Bureau also had a contingency fund made up of fines, bonds for good behavior, and a Savannah school tax; the agency kept a modest refugees' and freedmen's fund and a smaller school fund. All told, during a little over a year of Bureau work, Watson oversaw $78,873.64 in receipts and disbursements for the Bureau, and beginning in July 1866 he also served as the post quartermaster for Augusta. Watson earned $2,400, twice as much as the Bureau's subassistant commissioners, which suggests the importance of his position. Dealing with significant sums of money opened Watson to charges of "irregularity" in the summer of 1867. The investigation by J. R. Lewis cleared him with Bureau headquarters, and Watson, who received an appointment in the regular army, remained with the Georgia agency until its end. Watson, "Annual Report," reel 32; C. C. Sibley to O. O. Howard, Apr. 3, 1867, reel 5; Circular No. 1, Jan. 25, 1869, reel 34; Station Books, vol. 1, 1867–1868; vol. 2, 1869, reel 35, BRFAL-Ga (M798); F. D. Sewall to C. C. Sibley, July 10, 1867, reel 46 (and all enclosures); J. R. Lewis to O. O. Howard, Sept. 26, 1867, reel 49, (LR)BRFAL (M752); E. Whittlesey to C. C. Sibley, Aug. 2, 1867, reel 3, (RI)BRFAL (M742); Charles T. Watson, Civil War pension files, RG 15, National Archives; Bentley, *Freedmen's Bureau*, 134.

80. D. Tillson to W. Mitchell, May 30, 1866; D. Tillson to O. O. Howard, June 8, 1866; D. Tillson to W. D. Whipple, June 8, 1866, reel 3 BRFAL-Ga (M798).

81. D. Tillson to A. R. Aininger, July 2, 1866, reel 3; D. Tillson, "Report of Operations September 22, 1865, to November 1, 1866," reel 32, BRFAL-Ga (M798).

82. D. Tillson to W. D. Whipple, June 16, 1866; D. Tillson to O. O. Howard, June 19, 1866; C. T. Watson to D. Tillson, June 14, 1866, reel 29, BRFAL-Ga (M798). Also see A. A. Buck to D. Tillson, June 6, 1866; J. B. Austin and others to D. Tillson, June 11, 1866, reel 25, BRFAL-Ga (M798).

83. T. F. Forbes to G. J. Barnsley, July 5, 1866; T. F. Forbes to N. G. Foster, July 27, 1866; E. Pickett to G. B. Stovall, Aug. 9, 1866, reel 3; E. Pickett to W. W. Deane, Aug. 4, 1866, reel 28, BRFAL-Ga (M798). Tillson compiled reports of individuals by county who required rations, so he was serious about the screening process. Obviously, Tillson believed that there were legitimate cases of need in the state but that there remained individuals who would take advantage of easy bread. D. Tillson to O. O. Howard, July 14, 1866, reel 32, (LR)BRFAL (M752).

84. C. T. Watson to D. Tillson, June 14, 15, 1866, reel 29; L. D. Burwell to D. Tillson, June 19, 1866, reel 25; D. Tillson to S. Eldridge, July 13, 1866, reel 3; General Orders, No. 4, June 22, 1866, reel 34; Station Books, vol. 1, 1867–1868, reel 35, BRFAL-Ga (M798); D. Tillson to O. O. Howard, Sept. 1, 1866, reel 37, (LR)BRFAL (M752); Eugene Pickett, Civil War pension files, RG 15, National Archives. Presumably the special agents, who received a salary from the federal government, were required to take the test oath as their successors were required during the relief crisis of 1867. E. Pickett to J. J. Knox, Apr. 21, 1867, reel 5, BRFAL-Ga (M798).

85. D. Tillson to Stuart Eldridge, July 13, 1866; D. Tillson to A. R. Aininger, July 13, 1866, reel 3; E. Pickett to D. Tillson, Aug. 4, 1866, reel 28, BRFAL-Ga (M798).

86. Quoted in S. Thomas to D. Tillson, Aug. 15, 1866, reel 25, BRFAL-Ga (M798).

87. E. Pickett to W. W. Deane, Aug. 30, 1866; E. Pickett to D. Tillson, Sept. 10, 1866, reel 28, BRFAL-Ga (M798); A. P. Ketchum to D. Tillson, Sept. 24, 1866, reel 2, (RI)BRFAL (M742).

88. D. Tillson to O. O. Howard, Sept. 29, Oct. 2, 1866, reel 3, BRFAL-Ga (M798).

89. D. Tillson, "Report of Operations from September 22, 1865, to November 1, 1866," reel 35; T. F. Forbes to N. S. Hill, Oct. 1, 1866; T. F. Forbes to A. B. Nickols, Oct. 4, 1866, reel 3, BRFAL-Ga (M798). Tillson also could feed freedpeople in the Bureau hospitals. E. Pickett to G. McWhorter, Oct. 17, 1866, reel 4, BRFAL-Ga (M798).

90. Circular Letter from the Office of the Commissary General of Subsistence, Nov. 19, 1866, reel 34; E. Pickett to G. W. Selvidge, Nov. 26, 1866, reel 4, BRFAL-Ga (M798); O. O. Howard to D. Tillson, Nov. 16, 1866, reel 2, (RI)BRFAL (M742).

91. D. Tillson, "Report of Operations from September 22, 1865, to November 1, 1866," reel 35; D. Tillson to W. Finch, Oct. 10, 1866, reel 4, BRFAL-Ga (M798). In his report, Tillson distinguished between freedpeople and refugees who received rations.

92. C. C. Sibley, Report for February, Mar. 19, 1867; C. C. Sibley, Report for March, Apr. 26, 1867, reel 32, BRFAL-Ga (M798).

93. E. Belcher to C. C. Sibley, May 1, 1867, reel 14, BRFAL-Ga (M798).

94. J. Leonard to E. Pickett, Mar. 6, 1867, reel 15, BRFAL-Ga (M798).

95. Howard noted that he shifted money that had been allocated for transportation. O. O. Howard, Annual Report, Nov. 11, 1867, *House Executive Documents*, 40th Cong., 2d sess., no. 1 (serial 1324), 641, 643; Howard, *Autobiography*, 2:351.

96. E. Bright to C. C. Sibley, Feb. 8, Mar. 7, Mar. 26, 1867; C. J. Gobrecht to C. C. Sibley, Apr. 18, 1867, reel 14; J. R. Lewis to J. Leonard, Feb. 22, 1867; J. R. Lewis to J. [Mills?], Mar. 13, 1867, reel 5; C. C. Sibley, Report for April, May 23, 1867, reel 32, BRFAL-Ga (M798).

97. E. Pickett to J. J. Knox, Apr. 21, 1867, reel 5; J. J. Knox to E. Pickett, May 3, reel 15, BRFAL-Ga (M798). For Pickett's activities see several letters dated April, May, June, and July on reel 5, BRFAL-Ga (M798).

98. J. Leonard to C. C. Sibley, May 1, 1867, reel 15, BRFAL-Ga (M798).

99. E. Pickett to J. Walsh, Apr. 3, 1867, reel 6; E. Bright to C. C. Sibley, Apr. 24, 1867; E. Belcher to C. C. Sibley, Apr. 27, 1867, reel 14, BRFAL-Ga (M798); P. D. Claiborne to J. J. Knox, Apr. 5, 1867, box 5, LR; J. W. Simmons to J. J. Knox, May 12, 1867, box 5, ULR, Athens SAC, BRFAL-Ga.

100. A. A. Buck to C. C. Sibley, July 22, Aug. 14, 1867, reel 17; General Orders, No. 4, October 26, 1867, reel 34; C. B. Blacker to C. C. Sibley, Nov. 2, 1867, reel 20, BRFAL-Ga (M798); C. C. Sibley to O. O. Howard, July 22, 1867, reel 46, (LR)BRFAL (M752).

101. Register of Civilian Agents, 1865–1867; Station Books, vol. 1, 1867–1868, reel 35; Case of G. W. Selvidge, May 14, 1867; Special Orders, No. 72, May 18, 1867, reel 16, BRFAL-Ga (M798). As Special Orders, No. 72, indicates, the Bureau never brought Selvidge to trial after the investigation.

102. C. A. de la Mesa to C. C. Sibley, May 15, 1867, reel 30, BRFAL-Ga (M798).

103. G. R. Walbridge to C. C. Sibley, June 24, July 24, 1867, reel 19, BRFAL-Ga (M798).

104. The complete figures for May are reported in C. C. Sibley, Report for July, Sept. 6, 1867, reel 32, BRFAL-Ga (M798).

105. J. R. Lewis, who was acting assistant commissioner briefly while Sibley was on leave, reported these figures in his Report for August, Oct. 14, 1867, reel 32, BRFAL-Ga (M798). The figures cited here do not include patients in the Bureau's hospitals, who routinely received rations along with their medical care. Bvt. Brig. Gen. E. Whittlesey, who oversaw the entire Bureau relief operation for Howard, reported that from April through the end of August the Georgia Bureau distributed 349,772 pounds of pork and 1,987,917 pounds of corn. His figures for the total number of recipients of this aid are slightly higher than Lewis's and Sibley's figures. O. O. Howard, Annual Report, Nov. 11, 1867, *House Executive Documents*, 40th Cong., 2d sess., no. 1 (serial 1324), 649.

106. E. Pickett to G. J. Lewis, July 27, 1867, reel 6, BRFAL-Ga (M798).

107. J. R. Lewis, Report for August, Oct. 14, 1867; C. C. Sibley, Report for October, Nov. 26, 1867, reel 32; F. D. Sewall to C. C. Sibley, Sept. 16, 1867, reel 18, BRFAL-Ga (M798).

108. Busbee, "Presidential Reconstruction," 349; J. W. Lawton, "Report." When Saxton forwarded the list of officers on duty to Tillson on September 29, he noted two additional surgeons, one listed as being stationed in Savannah. R. Saxton to D. Tillson, Sept. 29, 1865, reel 1, BRFAL-SC (M869).

Lawton noted that the freedpeople were willing to contribute to the support of their hospitals, but he decided that it would be best if the Bureau hospitals were funded by the government, and he redirected the freedpeople's contributions to education. Lawton, "Report."

109. J. E. Bryant to R. Saxton, June 5, 1865, Bryant Papers; J. E. Bryant to R. Saxton, Aug. 4, 1865, reel 7, BRFAL-SC (M869).

110. Lawton, "Report"; J. W. Lawton to C. W. Horner [chief medical officer of the Bureau], June 30, 1866, reel 1, ULR, Surgeon's Records, BRFAL-Ga.

111. Ibid. The second Bureau law gave the agency the authority to distribute medical stores. *Statutes at Large of the United States* (1866), 14:174.

112. Station Books, vol. 1, 1867–1868, reel 35; J. M. Laing, "Annual Report of the Operations of the Med Dep't, Bureau RF&AL Dist of Ga. Oct. 1, 1866 to Sept. 30, 1867," reel 32, BRFAL-Ga (M798).

113. P. Slaughter to D. Tillson, Nov. 1, 1865, reel 24; Lawton, "Report"; Laing, "Annual Report . . . Oct. 1, 1866 to Sept. 30, 1867," reel 32, BRFAL-Ga (M798).

114. Returns of Medical Officers, Dec. 1866, Feb. 1867, reel 7, Surgeon's Records, BRFAL-Ga. From December 1865 through May 1868, the Bureau never had fewer than ten doctors on its rolls, including the chief surgeon. During the latter half of 1868, as the Bureau began to reduce its services, the medical department dropped from eight physicians in July to six in November and finally to three in December. Returns of Medical Officers, July 1868, Nov. 1868, Dec. 1868, reel 7, Surgeon's Records, BRFAL-Ga.

115. Shortly after Caleb Sibley assumed command, the chief medical officer of the Bureau informed him that regular and volunteer medical officers on duty with the Bureau were to be relieved by order of the secretary of war. L. A. Edwards to C. C. Sibley, Feb. 14, 1867, reel 30, BRFAL-Ga (M798).

116. O. O. Howard, Annual Report, Dec. 1865, *House Executive Documents*, 39th Cong., 1st sess., no. 11 (serial 1255), 20; O. O. Howard, Annual Report, Nov. 1, 1867, *House Executive Documents*, 40th Cong., 2d sess., no. 1 (serial 1324), 633; O. O. Howard, Annual Report, Oct. 14, 1868, *House Executive Documents*, 40th Cong., 3d sess., no. 1 (serial 1367), 1025.

117. J. V. De Hanne to C. C. Sibley, May 18, 1867, reel 14; J. A. Laing, "Annual Report . . . Oct. 1, 1866 to Sept. 30, 1867," reel 32, BRFAL-Ga (M798); G. O. Dalton to J. V. De Hanne, Feb. 2, 1867, reel 1, ULR; J. M. Laing to E. A. Edwards [chief medical officer of the Bureau], Oct. 26, 1867, reel 9, LS, Surgeon's Records, BRFAL-Ga.

118. J. A. Laing, "Annual Report . . . Oct. 1, 1866 to Sept. 30, 1867"; C. C. Sibley, Report for June, Aug. 1, 1867, reel 32, BRFAL-Ga (M798).

119. J. M. Laing to G. O. Dalton, Nov. 13, 1867, reel 9, LS; O. H. Howard to J. M. Laing, Jan. 25, 1868, reel 2, LR, Surgeon's Records, BRFAL-Ga; O. H. Howard to M. F. Gallagher, Jan. 17, Jan. 25, 1868, reel 20, BRFAL-Ga (M798).

120. J. A. Laing, "Annual Report . . . Oct. 1, 1866 to Sept. 30, 1867," reel 32, BRFAL-Ga (M798).

121. A. Mitchell to J. W. Lawton, June 29, July 18, 1866; A. Mitchell to W. P. Fessenden, Jan. 22, 1867; T. R. Clement to J. V. De Hanne, Jan. 7, Jan. 12, 1867, reel 1, ULR, Surgeon's Records, BRFAL-Ga.

122. Mitchell believed that a Yankee uniform worn without the backing of bayonets would surely invite assassination. A. Mitchell to J. W. Lawton, July 18, 1866; A. Mitchell to W. P. Fessenden, Jan. 22, 1867, reel 1; G. O. Dalton, Mar. 18, 1867, reel 2, ULR, Surgeon's Records, BRFAL-Ga.

123. Returns of Medical Officers, Oct. 1866, reel 7, Surgeon's Records, BRFAL-Ga. Apparently Tillson and his successors had no problems with hiring black physicians to care for freedpeople at the same pay rate as their white counterparts. These are the only three black physicians whom I have identified, but the Bureau also used freedpeople as nurses and orderlies in its hospitals in Georgia.

124. J. V. De Hanne to C. C. Sibley, May 18, 1867, reel 14, BRFAL-Ga (M798).

125. Laing, "Annual Report . . . Oct. 1, 1866 to Sept. 30, 1867," reel 32; A. Mitchell to C. C. Sibley, May 24, 1867, reel 15, BRFAL-Ga (M798).

126. Lawton, "Report."

127. See Laing, "Annual Report . . . Oct. 1, 1866 to Sept. 30, 1867," reel 32 and J. V. De Hanne to C. C. Sibley, May 18, 1867, reel 14, BRFAL-Ga (M798) for the praise. See F. H. Matlock to J. W. Lawton, July 21, 1866, and N. D'Alvigny to [J. W. Lawton], Sept. 20, 1866, reel 1, ULR, Surgeon's Records, BRFAL-Ga, for complaints from Macon and Atlanta, respectively.

128. J. W. Lawton to D. Tillson, Apr. 23, 1866, reel 27; Lawton, "Report"; A. P. Collins to [D. Tillson], Apr. 5, 1866; S. Collins to [D. Tillson], Apr. 22, 1866, reel 11, BRFAL-Ga (M798); D. C. Poole to H. N. Lumpkin, Feb. 2, 1866, vol. 98, LS, Atlanta SAC; F. Mosebach to Dr. J. W. Lawton, May 19, 1866, vol. 222, LS, Columbus SAC, BRFAL-Ga; *Augusta Daily Constitutionalist*, Jan. 26, 1866.

129. Laing, "Annual Report . . . Oct. 1, 1866 to Sept. 30, 1867," reel 32, BRFAL-Ga (M798).

130. O. O. Howard, Annual Report, Oct. 14, 1868, *House Executive Documents*, 40th Cong., 3d sess., no. 1 (serial 1367), 1024.

131. Lawton, "Report."

132. *Macon Daily Telegraph* [n.d.], quoted in *Rome Weekly Courier*, Feb 1, 1866.

133. Lawton, "Report."

134. C. C. Sibley, Report for May, June 27, 1867, reel 32, BRFAL-Ga (M798).

135. Circular No. 12, Aug. 31, 1867, reel 34, BRFAL-Ga (M798).

136. C. C. Sibley, Report for October, Nov. 26, 1867; C. C. Sibley, Report for November, Dec. 28, 1867, reel 32, BRFAL-Ga (M798).

137. O. O. Howard, Annual Report, Oct. 10, 1867, *House Executive Documents*, 40th Cong., 3d sess., no. 1 (serial 1367), 1026.

138. M. F. Gallagher to W. F. Martins, Mar. 18, 1868, and numerous similar letters written in May, reel 7, BRFAL-Ga (M798).

139. J. M. Laing to G. S. Obear, Nov. 3, 1868, reel 23, BRFAL-Ga (M798).

140. F. D. Sewall to C. C. Sibley, Oct. 1, 1868, reel 23, BRFAL-Ga (M798).

141. F. J. Gould to J. M. Laing, Oct. 10, 1868, reel 3, LR, Surgeon's Records, BRFAL-Ga.

142. J. M. Laing, "Report of Surgeon-in-Chief James M. Laing from Oct. 1 to Dec. 31, 1868," Jan. 10 [1869], reel 32, BRFAL-Ga (M798).

143. Howard, *Autobiography*, 2:226.

144. D. Tillson to Lyman Abbott, Apr. 26, 1866, reel 2, BRFAL-Ga (M798).

145. S. W. Saxton to H. G. Judd, Aug. 12, [1865], Rufus and S. Willard Saxton Papers, Yale University, Sterling Library.

## Chapter 5. The Seed Sown in This Land

1. *Statutes at Large of the United States* (1863–1865), 13:507.

2. Circular No. 2, May 19, 1865, *House Executive Documents*, 39th Cong., 1st sess., no. 70 (serial 1256), 178–79.

3. W. W. Deane to H. F. Sickles, Nov. 1, 1865; D. Tillson to H. F. Sickles, Nov. 15, 1865, reel 1, BRFAL-Ga (M798).

4. E. A. Ware to J. H. Caldwell, Sept. 10, 1867; E. A. Ware to H. F. White, Sept. 10, 1867, reel 1; E. A. Ware to J. W. Barney, Mar. 4, 1868, reel 2, (Ed)BRFAL-Ga (M799).

5. For example, in 1867 the American Missionary Association paid teachers' salaries but required the freedpeople or some other benefactors to assume all other expenses totaling approximately thirty dollars each month. J. R. Lewis to W. F. White, Aug. 1, 1867, reel 1, (Ed)BRFAL-Ga (M799).

6. D. Tillson to T. P. Pease, Mar. 25, 1866, reel 34, BRFAL-Ga (M798).

7. *The Biographical Encyclopedia of Pennsylvania of the Nineteenth Century*, 564.

8. Eberhart had actually been appointed by Saxton before Tillson's arrival in Georgia. G. L. Eberhart to R. Saxton, Sept. 7, 1865, reel 7; R. Saxton to G. L. Eberhart, Sept. 15, 1865, reel 1; Special Orders, No. 18, Oct. 2, 1865, reel 36, BRFAL-SC (M869); F. D. Sewell to G. L. Eberhart, July 20, 1867, reel 3, (RI)BRFAL (M742); Station Books, vol. 1, 1867–68, reel 35, BRFAL-Ga (M798).

9. G. L. Eberhart to S. Hunt, Nov. 28, 1865, reel 1, AMA-Ga. Between late December 1865 and mid-April 1866, for example, Eberhart visited Madison, Atlanta, Marrietta, Macon, Columbus, Greensboro, Athens, Savannah, Albany, and Thomasville at least once. Special Orders, No. 39, Dec. 27, 1865; No. 23, Jan. 29, 1866; No. 35, Feb. 17, 1866; No. 55, Mar. 27, 1866; No. 57, Mar. 29, 1866; No. 65, Apr. 11, 1866, reel 34, BRFAL-Ga (M798).

10. G. L. Eberhart to J. J. Knox, Apr. 1, 1867, box 5, LR, Athens SAC, BRFAL-Ga.

11. Lewis refused to pay the rent on a technicality. The Bureau would subsidize rent at this time only if the need had been reported in advance. However, he was clear about the necessity of black initiative and the consequence if it were not forthcoming. J. R. Lewis to L. Burkett, Aug. 11, 1869, reel 4, (Ed)BRFAL-Ga (M799).

12. D. G. Risley to H. F. Mills, July 23, 1867; D. G. Risley to O. O. Howard, Sept. 2, 1867, vol. 201, LS, Brunswick SAC, BRFAL-Ga; D. G. Risley to G. Whipple, July 24, 1867, reel 3; D. G. Risley to E. P. Smith, Aug. 6, 1868, reel 4, AMA-Ga.

13. O. O. Howard, Annual Report, Nov. 1, 1867, *House Executive Documents*, 40th Cong., 2d sess., no. 1 (serial 1324), 650–51; *Statutes at Large of the United States* (1866), 14:176.

14. J. R. Lewis to D. Swope, Aug. 7, 1867; J. R. Lewis to R. C. Merriwether, Aug. 7, 1867; E. A. Ware to H. Stephens, Jan. 28, 1868, reel 1; E. A. Ware to W. A. Golden, Sept. 10, 1868, reel 2, (Ed)BRFAL-Ga (M799). The use of voluntary associations to raise money for educating the poor was not unknown in the cities of the North, but school funding during the antebellum era came from a number of sources. Tillson at first advised that students who were able should pay a small fee, but the general feeling was against charging tuition. Eberhart also urged freedpeople to contribute to a fund to defray the costs of schools, but individual teachers at times charged tuition. After 1868 the American Missionary Association schools generally charged tuition at the rate of a dollar per month for each pupil. D. Tillson to Lyman Abbott, Apr. 26, 1866, reel 2, BRFAL-Ga (M798); G. L. Eberhart to S. Hunt, Dec. 31, 1865, reel 1, AMA-Ga; Jones, *Soldiers of Light and Love*, 130. For methods of funding rural and urban schools in the antebellum North, see Kaestle, *Pillars of the Republic*, 10–12, 37, 148–51, 183–85, passim.

15. W. J. White to G. L. Eberhart, Mar. 29, 1867, reel 8, (Ed)BRFAL-Ga (M799). The Georgia Bureau also provided transportation for the educational activities of the Reverend Henry McNeil Turner, the African Methodist Episcopal minister and former Union army chaplain, but unlike White, the agency never formally carried Turner on its rosters as a special agent for education, as a review of the Bureau's station books and rolls on reel 35, BRFAL-Ga (M798) reveals. Turner's work as an educational organizer was linked to his desire to politicize the freedpeople. A. P. Ketchum to C. C. Sibley, Jan. 27, 1867, reel 30; W. W. Deane to H. M. Turner, reel 1, BRFAL-Ga (M798); Drago, *Black Politicians*, 24–27; Jones, *Soldiers of Light and Love*, 72.

16. J. S. Eberhart to A. P. Ketchum, Jan. 1, 1867, reel 42, (LR)BRFAL (M752); E. A. Ware to E. D. Cheney, Aug. 23, 1867, reel 1, (Ed)BRFAL-Ga (M799); J. W. Alvord, *Third Semi-Annual Report on Schools for Freedmen, January 1, 1867*, 15; J. W. Alvord, *Fourth Semi-Annual Report on Schools for Freedmen, July 1, 1867*, 32; J. W. Alvord, *Fifth Semi-Annual Report on Schools for Freedmen, January 1, 1868*, 28–29; Jones, *Soldiers of Light and Love*, 54; Reidy, *From Slavery to Agrarian Capitalism*, 175, 181; Nathans, *Losing the Peace*, 26–29; Currie-McDaniel, *Carpetbagger of Conscience*, 57–76.

17. *Savannah Daily Republican*, May 7, 1867; E. Pickett to N. S. Hill, July 14, 1867, reel 5, BRFAL-Ga (M798); J. R. Lewis to D. Swope, Aug. 7, 1867; E. A. Ware to J. H. Caldwell, Sept. 10, 1867, reel 1, (Ed)BRFAL-Ga (M799).

18. F. Mosebach to O. B. Gray, July 16, 1867, box 23, LR, Marietta SAC, BRFAL-Ga. Also see D. G. Risley to H. F. Mills, July 23, 1867, vol. 201, LS, Brunswick SAC, BRFAL-Ga.

19. C. B. Blacker to J. R. Lewis, Nov. 16, 1867, reel 17, BRFAL-Ga (M798); M. R. Archer to A. J. Comar, Aug. 25, 1868; M. R. Archer to D. Fowler, Aug. 25, 1868, vol. 242, LS, Dahlonega Agt, BRFAL-Ga.

20. Alvin B. Clark to W. F. White, Oct. 23, 1867, box 33, LR, Quitman Agt, BRFAL-Ga.

21. C. B. Blacker to J. R. Lewis, Nov. 16, 1867, reel 17, BRFAL-Ga (M798); W. O. Moffit to O. O. Howard, Jan. 1, Feb. 1, 1868, vol. 188, LS, Bartow Agt, BRFAL-Ga.

22. Rockwell, a member of a wealthy Connecticut family, served the American Missionary Association and the Bureau without pay. He became connected with the Georgia Bureau because of O. O. Howard's intercession. For his work as an agent-at-large for education, White earned the same salary as Sibley's other agents, $100 per month. Both received their appointments in January 1867. Special Orders, No. 3, Commissioner, Freedmen's Bureau, Jan. 7, 1867, reel 34; Register of Civilian Agents, 1865–1867; Station Books, vol. 1, 1867–1868, reel 35, BRFAL-Ga (M798); Richardson, *Christian Reconstruction*, 165.

23. L. Lieberman to G. Adams, Aug. 8, 1868, vol. 277, LS, Hawkinsville Agt, BRFAL-Ga; L. Lieberman to J. R. Lewis, Aug. 28, 1868, reel 58, (LR)BRFAL (M752); L. Lieberman to C. C. Sibley, Aug. 31, 1868, reel 22, BRFAL-Ga (M798).

24. M. R. Archer to D. Fowler, Aug. 25, 1868; M. R. Archer to A. J. Comer, Aug. 25, 1868, vol. 242, LR, Dahlonega Agt, BRFAL-Ga.

25. H. L. Haskell to J. Leonard, Aug. 31, 1868, LR, Columbus SAC, BRFAL-Ga; J. J. Knox to M. F. Gallagher, Aug. 8, 1868, reel 21, BRFAL-Ga (M798).

26. C. A. de la Mesa to C. C. Sibley, Aug. 7, 1868, vol. 342, LS, Rome SAC, BRFAL-Ga; C. A. de la Mesa to J. R. Lewis, Oct. 26, 1868, reel 23, BRFAL-Ga (M798).

27. Alvin B. Clark to W. F. White, Oct. 23, box 33, LR, Quitman Agt; C. A. de la Mesa to C. C. Sibley, Aug. 7, 1868, vol. 342, LS, Rome SAC, BRFAL-Ga; D. G. Risley to E. P. Smith, Mar. 16, 1868, reel 4; W. L. Clark to [E. P.] Smith, Feb. 10, Oct. 26, 1868, reel 3, AMA-Ga; W. L. Clark to E. A. Ware, Jan. 9, 1869, Edmund Asa Ware Papers, Atlanta University Center.

28. After Sherman liberated Savannah, black ministers organized the Savannah Educational Association, which by May 1865 served 600 children, although the AMA teacher S. W. Magill ran a school for some 500 black children, too. Saxton appointed Magill as superintendent for schools for freedmen in the Savannah area, but the Savannah Education Association resisted Magill's efforts to impose white teachers on their children. During the summer of 1865 in Macon, black ministers inaugurated the education movement, with the city's four black churches sponsoring schools. By late 1866, five Macon churches housed freedpeople's schools. S. W. Saxton to S. W. Magill, order dated Mar. 30, 1865, Rufus and S. Willard Saxton Papers, Yale University, Sterling Library; A. P. Ketchum to R. Saxton, Sept. 1, 1865, reel 34, BRFAL-SC (M869); C. Grover to Asst. Adj. Gen., HQ, Dept. of the South, May 6, 13, 1865, *Official Records*, ser. 1, vol. 47, pt. 3, 418, 492–93; *American Missionary* 9 (Mar. 1865): 51; 10 (Feb. 1866): 33; *The Twentieth Annual Report of the American Missionary Association, and the Proceedings at the Annual Meeting Held at Galesburg, Ill., October 31st and November 1st, 1866*, 31; Jones, *Soldiers of Light and Love*, 73–76; Reidy, *From Slavery to Agrarian Capitalism*, 172.

29. Thornbery, "The Development of Black Atlanta, 1865–1885," 57, 70–71.

30. C. F. Springer to E. A. Wild, Sept. 16, 1865; E. T. Kimble to G. L. Eberhart, Oct. 16, 1865; M. Jones to Superintendent of Freedmen's Schools, Oct. 31, 1865, reel 8, (Ed)BRFAL-Ga (M799).

31. Alvord, *Third Semi-Annual Report*, 14, 17; Alvord; *Fourth Semi-Annual Report*, 33.

32. J. W. Alvord, *Sixth Semi-Annual Report on Schools for Freedmen, July 1, 1868*, 28.

33. J. R. Lewis to O. O. Howard, June 23, 1869, reel 3 (Ed)BRFAL-Ga (M799).

34. J. W. Alvord, *Tenth Semi-Annual Report on Schools for the Freedmen, July 1, 1870*, 6. The educational alliance between the freedpeople, the Bureau, and Northern educational societies certainly was impressive, but it never reached a proportionately large number of freed children. Bureau resources were limited, and its philosophical intentions were explicit. Also, Jacqueline Jones notes that white Northern teachers, most of whom probably received some kind of Bureau assistance in establishing themselves in Georgia and who were certainly the type of teachers whom the agency favored assisting, only taught 5 percent of the black school-age population each year from 1865 through 1870. Even if one acknowledges that some Bureau assistance went to black teachers and their white Georgia neighbors, that figure cannot increase by much more. The policies of the Bureau as well as educational societies such as the American Missionary Association were not formulated to bring educational opportunities to every corner of the state. Jones, *Soldiers of Light and Love*, 198.

35. Some freedpeople probably sensed that even their Northern friends, who perceived schooling as a means by which they could transform their charges into good Yankees, were hostile to their customs and rhythms. For examples of complaints from schoolteachers about the freedpeople's ways, see M. J. Conkling to E. P. Smith, Jan. 3, 1868; S. E. Russel to E. P. Smith, Nov. 12, 1867, reel 3, AMA-Ga. Also, freedpeople preferred not to turn over the education of their children to white Georgians, whose strongest motivation for teaching seems to have been to avoid poverty. For example, see ETC to "My dear Marion," Apr. 24, 1866, Baber-Blackshear Papers, University of Georgia; E. A. Ware to B. Sears, Aug. 13, 1868, reel 2, (Ed)BRFAL-Ga (M799); D. G. Risley to G. Whipple, June 6, 1867, reel 3, AMA-Ga.

36. E. A. Ware to A. Clark, Oct. 7, 1868, reel 2, (Ed)BRFAL-Ga (M799).

37. J. R. Lewis to J. G. Mitchell, Nov. 23, 1869, reel 4, (Ed)BRFAL-Ga (M799).

38. J. R. Lewis to O. O. Howard, July 17, 1869, reel 3, (Ed)BRFAL-Ga (M799). Also see J. W. Alvord, *Ninth Semi-Annual Report on Schools for Freedmen, January 1, 1870*, 27. Some of the hardly literate letters received by the Bureau from a few of the black teachers undoubtedly confirmed Lewis's fears. For example, see J. A. Woodson to W. L. Clark, June 6, 1868, box 11, LR, Bainbridge Agt, BRFAL-Ga.

39. G. L. Eberhart to S. Hunt, May 15, 1866, reel 1, AMA-Ga; J. J. Knox to E. Pickett, May 17, 1867, reel 15, BRFAL-Ga (M798); J. R. Lewis to W. L. Clark, Oct. 9, 1869, reel 4; J. R. Lewis to O. O. Howard, Mar. 30, 1870, reel 5, (Ed)BRFAL-Ga (M799); Alvord, *Ninth Semi-Annual Report*, 29.

40. E. A. Ware to O. O. Howard, June 30, 1870, reel 68, (LR)BRFAL (M752). Ware expected to pay these students from Bureau funds, but the Bureau closed in July 1870.

41. J. R. Lewis to O. O. Howard, Apr. 7, 1869, reel 62, (LR) BRFAL (M752). The AMA had been offering a teacher training program in Atlanta since 1867, and the school

facilities that Lewis supported were completed in 1869. Richardson, *Christian Reconstruction*, 114; Alvord, *Ninth Semi-Annual Report*, 29.

42. Jones, *Soldiers of Light and Love*, 63–76.

43. For the views of Georgia's preacher-politicians, see Drago, *Black Politicians*, esp. 16–100.

44. Other scholars disagree with this positive assessment of education. Ronald E. Butchart is especially critical of education as a tool for liberating the freedpeople; he views it as a distraction from genuine reform. It is true that Yankees like Eberhart believed that education would make freedpeople productive workers, but that view has a positive, dynamic side to it when placed within the context of nineteenth-century Yankee beliefs. Butchart's assessment of education misreads this side of Yankee ideology. G. L. Eberhart, Circular Letter No. 2, Nov. 1, 1865, *House Executive Document*, 39th Cong., 1st sess., no. 70 (serial 1256), 66; Butchart, *Northern Schools, Southern Blacks, and Reconstruction*, 74, 260.

45. Jones, *Soldiers of Light and Love*, 54, 76.

46. H. Cobb to [Mary Ann Cobb], Sept. 4, 1867, Howell Cobb Papers, University of Georgia.

47. Rawick, *American Slave*, vol. 12: *Georgia*, pt. 2, 191.

48. *American Missionary* 11 (May 1867): 99.

49. S. W. Saxton to E. A. Ware, Apr. 7, 1868, Saxton Papers; testimony of Thomas M. Allen in Ku Klux Conspiracy, vol. 7: *Georgia*, pt. 2, 612. Also see W. H. Robert to D. Tillson, May 30, 1866, reel 28, BRFAL-Ga (M798).

50. E. A. Ware to E. D. Cheney, Aug. 23, 1867, reel 1, (Ed)BRFAL-Ga (M799).

51. John Richard Dennett, *The South as It Is*, 269.

52. G. O. Dalton to J. V. De Hanne, June 10, 1867, reel 2, ULR, Surgeon's Records, BRFAL-Ga; G. S. Eberhart to O. O. Howard, June 17, 1867, reel 46, (LR)BRFAL (M752). After Eberhart returned to Pennsylvania, he earned a reputation as a "warm advocate of the principle governing the Republican party." *Biographical Encyclopedia of Pennsylvania of the Nineteenth Century*, 564.

53. E. A. Ware to E. P. Smith, Sept. 9, 1867; E. A. Ware to J. M. McKiver, Sept. 13, 1867; E. A. Ware to A. Cooper, Sept. 13, 1867, reel 1; E. A. Ware to E. D. Chaney, Sept. 13, 1867, reel 1, (Ed)BRFAL-Ga (M799).

54. C. W. Parker to G. L. Eberhart, Apr. 8, 1867; W. H. Robert to G. L. Eberhart, June 1, 1866, reel 8; (Ed)BRFAL-Ga (M799); E. A. Ware to J. M. McKiver, Sept. 13, 1867; E. A. Ware to A. Cooper, Sept. 13, 1867, reel 1, (Ed)BRFAL-Ga (M799); H. W. Kearsing to C. C. Sibley, June 9, 1868, vol. 188, LS, Bartow Agt, BRFAL-Ga; G. L. Eberhart to S. Hunt, May 23, 1866; D. Jencks to S. Hunt, Apr. 23, 1866, reel 1; G. L. Eberhart to S. Hunt, June 4, 1866, reel 2; E. E. Athington to E. P. Smith, Aug. 1, 1868; R. H. Gladding to E. P. Smith, Oct. 5, 1868, reel 4, AMA-Ga; J. A. Rockwell to A. [P. Rockwell], Jan. 28, 1869, John A. Rockwell Papers, University of Georgia; Alvord, *Third Semi-Annual*

*Report*, 15; *American Missionary* 11 (May 1867): 99; Jones, *Soldiers of Light and Love*, 107–11; Richardson, *Christian Reconstruction*, 40–46.

55. *American Missionary* 10 (May 1866): 113.

56. Jones estimates that 4 or 5 percent of Georgia blacks were literate in 1860. Jones, *Soldiers of Light and Love*, 59, 60.

57. J. R. Lewis to O. O. Howard, July 17, 1869, reel 3, (Ed)BRFAL-Ga (M799); J. C. Swayze to D. Tillson, July 20, 1866, reel 29; D. C. Clinch to O. O. Howard, Apr. 5, 1867 (and all endorsements), reel 14; P. J. O'Rourke to J. R. Lewis, Dec. 4, 1868, reel 30, BRFAL-Ga (M798); W. S. Clark to E. P. Smith, Nov. 19, 1867; F. Randall to E. P. Smith, Dec. 6, 1867; L. J. Kelley to E. P. Smith, Jan. 25, 1868, reel 3; R. H. Gladding to E. P. Smith, Oct. 5, 1868; D. G. Risley to E. P. Smith, Oct. 24, Nov. 3, 1868, reel 4, AMA-Ga; Alvin B. Clark to W. F. White, Oct. 23, 1867, box 33, LR, Thomasville SAC; W. Royal to D. G. Risley, June 30, 1868, vol. 373, LS, St. Mary's Agt, BRFAL-Ga; F. Butler to W. Kelly, Jan. 17, [1869], Frances Butler Leigh Letterbook, James W. Wistar Family Papers, Historical Society of Pennsylvania, Philadelphia; Butchart, *Northern Schools, Southern Blacks, and Reconstruction*, 190.

58. S. H. Champrey to E. P. Smith, Jan. 30, 1869, reel 4, AMA-Ga.

59. D. C. Jenks to S. Hunt, Dec. 21, 1865, reel 1; F. Randall to E. P. Smith, Oct. 8, 1867, AMA-Ga; H. L. Cole to D. Tillson, Jan. 17, 1866, reel 25; W. Harris to D. Tillson, Mar. 22, 1866, reel 27; G. L. Eberhart to D. Tillson, Dec. 17, 1866, reel 14; E. Armstrong to [C. C. Sibley], Sept. 5, 1867, reel 12, BRFAL-Ga (M798); G. R. Walbridge to J. R. Phillips, May 9, 1866, vol. 98, LS, Atlanta SAC; J. J. Knox to E. A. Ware, Nov. 13, 1868, vol. 170, LS, SAC, BRFAL-Ga; Alvord, *Ninth Semi-Annual Report*, 28; Stearns, *Black Man*, 67, 132.

60. W. J. White to G. L. Eberhart, May 27, 1867, reel 8; E. A. Ware to R. L. Rust, May 1, 1868, reel 2, (Ed)BRFAL-Ga (M799); F. A. H. Gaebel to W. W. Deane, June 29, 1866, reel 27; D. Tillson to A. R. Aininger, July 11, 1866, reel 3; J. R. Lewis to E. Pickett, July 23, 1867; N. S. Hill to C. C. Sibley, Dec. 13, 1867, reel 18; P. J. O'Rourke to J. R. Lewis, Dec. 4, 1868, reel 30, BRFAL-Ga (M798); I. Harris and others to Agent at LaGrange, May 13, 1868, box 20, LR; H. L. Haskell to J. E. Hosmer, May 25, 1868, vol. 288, LS, LaGrange Agt; J. J. Knox to E. A. Ware, Nov. 13, 1868, vol. 170, LS, Athens SAC, BRFAL-Ga.

61. Ku Klux Conspiracy, vol. 6: *Georgia*, 10, 524; D. Hough to G. L. Eberhart, Oct. 22, 1865, reel 8, (Ed)BRFAL-Ga (M799); J. C. Swayze to D. Tillson, May 13, 1866, reel 29; E. M. L. Ehlers to T. F. Forbes, Aug. 9, 1866, reel 26; Eberhart, "Report . . . from October 1, 1865, to October 1, 1866," reel 32, BRFAL-Ga (M798); W. J. Bryan to F. Mosebach, Dec. 27, 1868, box 7, LR, Atlanta SAC, BRFAL-Ga. Subassistant Commissioner Mosebach noted that some of the better citizens of Jonesboro objected to the burning of the schoolhouse there, offering a reward for the arrest of the culprits and a building for a temporary schoolhouse. However, he also noted that while the better

sort vocally condemned the act, "at the same time I know that many . . . at heart rejoice at it." F. Mosebach to C. C. Sibley, May 13, 1867, reel 15, BRFAL-Ga (M798).

62. J. W. Alvord, *Second Semi-Annual Report on Schools for Freedmen, July 1, 1866*, 5.

63. W. L. Clark to E. A. Ware, Jan. 9, 1869, Ware Papers; Circular No. 1, Jan. 25, 1869, reel 34, BRFAL-Ga (M798).

64. For examples of schools closing down for want of resources, see G. L. Eberhart, "Report . . . from October 1, 1865, to October 1, 1866," reel 32, BRFAL-Ga (M798); J. A. Rockwell to A. [P. Rockwell], Jan. 28, 1869, Rockwell Letters.

65. T. M. Harris to G. L. Eberhart, Apr. 16, 1867, reel 8, (Ed)BRFAL-Ga (M799).

66. W. L. Clark to Mr. Woodworth, July 7, 1868, reel 4, AMA-Ga. Also see A. O. Mitchell to J. V. De Hanne, Feb. 9, 1867, reel 1, ULR, Surgeon's Records, BRFAL-Ga.

67. H. F. Mills to C. C. Sibley, Nov. 1, 1867, vol. 370, LS, Stockton Agt, BRFAL-Ga; J. A. Rockwell to A. [P. Rockwell], Jan. 28, 1869, Rockwell Letters.

68. W. P. Russell to [M. E.] Strieby, Aug. 3, 1865, reel 1, AMA-Ga.

69. John W. Alvord, *First Semi-Annual Report on Schools and Finances of Freedmen, January 1, 1866*, 4.

70. Bentley, *Freedmen's Bureau*, 171; G. L. Eberhart to C. H. Howard, Nov. 30, 1865 (and all endorsements), reel 13, BRFAL-Ga (M798).

71. W. W. Deane to H. F. Sickles, Nov. 1, 1865; D. Tillson to H. F. Sickles, Nov. 15, 1865, reel 1, BRFAL-Ga (M798).

72. G. L. Eberhart to W. W. Deane, Nov. 18, 1865, reel 7, BRFAL-SC (M869); *Twentieth Annual Report of the American Missionary Association*, 32.

73. W. W. Deane to G. A. Hastings, Nov. 18, 1865, reel 1; G. L. Eberhart to W. W. Deane, May 15, 1866 (and all endorsements), reel 13; Elmer B. Adams to O. O. Howard, Jan. 19, 1866, reel 25, BRFAL-Ga (M798).

74. Endorsement of A. P. Ketchum, May 19, 1866, on G. L. Eberhart to W. W. Deane, May 15, 1866, reel 13, BRFAL-Ga (M798).

75. Special Orders, No. 32, Dec. 13, 1865, reel 34, BRFAL-Ga (M798).

76. *Statutes at Large of the United States* (1866), 14:92, 176.

77. E. P. Smith to G. L. Eberhart, Oct. 3, 1866 (and all endorsements and enclosures), reel 13; D. Tillson to L. Abbott, Apr. 26, 1866, reel 2; BRFAL-Ga (M798); E. A. Ware to W. L. Clark, Dec. 21, 1868, reel 2, (Ed)BRFAL-Ga (M799). Also see J. R. Lewis to W. L. Clark, Nov. 2, 1869, reel 4, (Ed)BRFAL-Ga (M799). In 1866 Tillson rightly believed that poor whites—an obvious pool of students for Bureau-assisted schools—would not attend school with freedpeople. But by December 1868, E. A. Ware noted that in some parts of Georgia whites were attending school with freedpeople. The exact extent of this type of integration is unknown, but Jacqueline Jones notes that few whites took advantage of AMA schools. She also notes that integrated schools were not a goal of the Georgia freedpeople. She concludes that "integrated schools were never a viable option" in Georgia during Reconstruction. Jones, *Soldiers of Light and Love*, 81, 204–5.

78. E. Pickett to W. Coking, July 17, 1867. reel 5; A. W. Caldwell to J. R. Lewis, Aug. 28, 1867, reel 17; E. A. Ware to J. R. Lewis, Sept. 19, 1867, reel 19, BRFAL-Ga (M798); J. R. Lewis to F. H. Randall, Oct. 7, 1869, reel 4, (Ed)BRFAL-Ga (M799).

79. L. Lieberman to G. Adams, Aug. 8, 1868, vol. 277, LS, Hawkinsville Agt, BRFAL-Ga.

80. L. Lieberman to J. R. Lewis, Aug. 28, 1868, reel 58, (LR)BRFAL (M752); L. Lieberman to C. C. Sibley, Aug. 31, 1868, reel 22; E. A. Ware to J. R. Lewis, Sept. 19, 1867, reel 19, BRFAL-Ga (M798); J. R. Lewis to W. F. White, Aug. 1, 1867; J. R. Lewis to J. H. Caldwell, Aug. 7, 1867, reel 1, (Ed)BRFAL-Ga (M799).

81. C. T. Watson to D. G. Risley, July 29, 1867, box 12, LR, Brunswick SAC; M. F. Gallagher to D. G. Risley, Dec. 3, 1868, reel 7, BRFAL-Ga (M798).

82. Alvord, *Third Semi-Annual Report*, 17.

83. C. C. Sibley, Report for June, Aug. 1, 1867, reel 32; C. C. Sibley, Report for July, Sept. 6, 1867, reel 32, BRFAL-Ga (M798).

84. Alvord, *Sixth Semi-Annual Report*, 26.

85. Bentley, *Freedmen's Bureau*, 172; J. R. Lewis to W. L. Clark, Nov. 2, 1869, reel 4, (Ed)BRFAL-Ga (M799).

86. J. W. Alvord, *Eighth Semi-Annual Report on Schools for Freedmen, July 1, 1869*, 33; Alvord, *Ninth Semi-Annual Report*, 29; Alvord, *Tenth Semi-Annual Report*, 22. The Bureau actually kept in its possession and carried on its property returns only a few of these schools. In December 1868, only fourteen remained on the Georgia Bureau's property returns with three more being completed by the agency. The state school superintendent recommended that the agency turn all of these structures over to the trustees or the benevolent societies that held the deed to the property on which they stood, excepting three (Macon, Savannah, and Bainbridge), where "there is danger of dissensions arising among the local trustees holding the land, and also of outside influence being brought to bear on them, which would prove injurious to the best interests of Education." E. A. Ware to J. R. Lewis, Dec. 14, 1868, reel 58, (LR)BRFAL (M752).

87. W. O. Moffit to O. O. Howard, Jan. 1, Feb. 1, 1868, vol. 188, LS, Bartow Agt, BRFAL-Ga.

88. G. L. Eberhart, Circular Letter No. 2, Nov. 1, 1865, reprinted in *Rome Weekly Courier*, Nov. 30, 1865.

89. G. L. Eberhart, "Report . . . from October 1, 1865, to October 1, 1866," reel 32, BRFAL-Ga (M798). Eberhart agreed with Tillson that the use of white teachers would make black education more acceptable to white Georgians and therefore more secure for the freedpeople. E. Chaney to G. L. Eberhart, Dec. 6, 1865, reel 8, (Ed)BRFAL-Ga (M799); D. Tillson to L. Abbott, Apr. 26, 1866, reel 2, BRFAL-Ga (M798).

90. C. H. Howard to O. O. Howard, Dec. 30, 1865, *House Executive Documents*, 39th Cong., 1st sess., no. 70 (serial 1256), 353; C. C. Jones Jr. to M. Jones, Dec. 3, 1866, in Myers, *Children of Pride*, 1363.

91. For example, see the Augusta subassistant commissioner's assessment of the prospects for soliciting financial assistance from those whites who had the resources to make a difference. H. Catley, Contract Report for April 1868, box 9, Contract Reports, Augusta SAC, BRFAL-Ga.

92. L. J. Kelley to E. P. Smith, Jan. 25, 1868, reel 3, AMA-Ga. Also see J. R. Lewis to O. O. Howard, July 17, 1869, (Ed)BRFAL-Ga (M799).

93. *Columbus Daily Enquirer*, Aug. 8, 1866; C. Smith to G. L. Eberhart, Apr. 27, 1866, reel 8, (Ed)BRFAL-Ga (M799); E. Attaway to D. C. Barrow, Dec. 12, 1866, Colonel Davis Crenshaw Barrow Papers, University of Georgia. Northern educators and Bureau personnel should not have been surprised by the reluctance of white Georgians to support a statewide school system for freedpeople. Even if white Georgians put aside their racist ideas and accepted Yankee arguments about the benefits of black education, they had already shown their reluctance to establish a publicly funded common school system for white children. For the abortive antebellum attempts, see Dorothy Orr, *A History of Education in Georgia*, chap. 5.

94. *Albany Patriot*, July 29, 1865; *Macon Daily Telegraph*, July 4, 1866; *Sandersville Central Georgian*, Mar. 6, 1867.

95. C. W. Robbins to C. C. Sibley, July 15, 1867, reel 19, BRFAL-Ga (M798).

96. D. F. Clinch to O. O. Howard, Apr. 5, 1867 (and all endorsements), reel 14, BRFAL-Ga (M798).

97. Alvord, *Eighth Semi-Annual Report*, 33; Alvord, *Ninth Semi-Annual Report*, 29; J. W. Alvord to O. O. Howard, Jan. 17, 1870, in John W. Alvord, *Letters from the South*, 15; Alvord, *Tenth Semi-Annual Report*, 23.

98. Of these schools, the Bureau supported only four, whereas the freedpeople supported twenty-five. Northern benevolence sustained the rest. E. D. Chaney to G. L. Eberhart, Dec. 6, 1865, reel 8, (Ed)BRFAL-Ga (M799); Eberhart, "Report . . . from October 1, 1865, to October 1, 1866," reel 32, BRFAL-Ga (M798).

99. G. L. Eberhart to A. P. Ketchum, Jan. 1, 1867, reel 42, (LR)BRFAL (M752).

100. E. A. Ware to F. A. H. Gaebel, Sept. 12, 1867; E. A. Ware to D. [McGu?], Sept. 11, 1867; E. A. Ware to W. C. Child, Sept. 13, 1867; E. A. Ware to W. A. Hallock, Sept. 13, 1867; E. A. Ware to B. Griffith, Sept. 14, 1867; E. A. Ware to Secretary, Presbyterian Board of Publications, Sept. 14, 1867 (and several other letters written on or around these dates), reel 1, (Ed)BRFAL-Ga (M799).

101. W. F. Eaton to G. Whipple, May 15, 1866, reel 1, AMA-Ga.

102. E. A. Ware to E. P. Smith, Sept. 9, 1867, reel 1, (Ed)BRFAL-Ga (M799); W. F. Eaton to G. Whipple, May 15, 1866, reel 1, AMA-Ga.

103. E. A. Ware to E. P. Smith, Sept. 23, 1868; E. A. Ware to R. L. Rust, Mar. 17, 1868, reel 2, (Ed)BRFAL-Ga (M799). The presidential campaign of 1868 and the political excitement that accompanied it discouraged school attendance among those

students and teachers who feared violence and delayed the opening of a number of Georgia's schools. Alvord, *Seventh Semi-Annual Report*, 23.

104. E. A. Ware to E. D. Cheney, Aug. 23, 1867; E. A. Ware to B. S. Green, Sept. 12, 1867; E. A. Ware to E. Heyson, Aug. 19, 1867, reel 1, (Ed)BRFAL-Ga (M799).

105. E. A. Ware to B. Sears, Feb. 3, 1869, reel 2; J. R. Lewis to O. O. Howard, June 23, 1869, reel 3, (Ed)BRFAL-Ga (M799); Alvord, *Eighth Semi-Annual Report*, 32; Alvord, *Ninth Semi-Annual Report*, 29; Alvord, *Tenth Semi-Annual Report*, 22.

106. J. R. Lewis to B. Sears, Oct. 18, 1869, reel 4, (Ed)BRFAL-Ga (M799).

107. J. R. Lewis to O. O. Howard, June 23, 1869, reel 3, (Ed)BRFAL-Ga (M799).

108. E. A. Ware to D. Losey, July 15, 1870, reel 5, (Ed)BRFAL-Ga (M799). Those educators paid with Peabody money were among 367 Yankee teachers who served the freedpeople of Georgia between 1865 and 1873. The American Missionary Association sponsored 290 (79%) of the total, thanks to its aggressive early start in Georgia and its vigorous pursuit of the dominant position in what it considered its exclusive field. Its nearest competitor was the Freedmen's Aid Society of the Methodist Episcopal Church, which sponsored only thirty-one teachers. Georgia's school superintendents believed that Northern educators were better suited by training and sentiment for freedmen's education than either black or white Georgians. Jacqueline Jones estimates that, despite this preference, about 150 native Georgians taught school to freedpeople, 50 of whom received support from Northern aid societies. However, some of these, she explains, had strong ties to the North. Jones, *Soldiers of Light and Love*, 16, 78–79, 209. J. T. Chalfant to G. L. Eberhart, May 8, 1867, reel 8; E. A. Ware to Dr. B. Sears, Aug. 13, 1868, reel 2; J. R. Lewis to O. O. Howard, July 17, 1869, reel 3; Mar. 30, 1870, reel 5; J. R. Lewis to B. Sears, Mar. 12, 1870, reel 5, (Ed)BRFAL-Ga (M799); Alvord, *Seventh Semi-Annual Report*, 22; Alvord, *Eighth Semi-Annual Report*, 30, 33.

109. Alvord, *First Semi-Annual Report*, 4.

110. Jones, *Soldiers of Light and Love*, 89–90.

111. Alvord, *Sixth Semi-Annual Report*, 26–27; Alvord, *Seventh Semi-Annual Report*, 22.

112. Jones, *Soldiers of Light and Love*, 89–90, 191.

113. G. L. Eberhart to E. A. Cooley, Dec. 23, 1865, (Ed)BRFAL-Ga (M799); Jones, *Soldiers of Light and Love*, 16, 73–76.

114. Ronald E. Butchart discusses the Bureau's close relationship with the AMA in *Northern Schools, Southern Blacks, and Reconstruction*, 100–107; Jones focuses on the favored place of the AMA in Georgia, *Soldiers of Light and Love*, 92–103; and Joe Richardson confirms it in his study of the AMA, *Christian Reconstruction*, 37, 75–84.

115. Later, when Howard reorganized the Bureau to serve its reduced functions and John R. Lewis performed the duties of school superintendent from January 1869 to May 1870, Ware held the position of assistant superintendent of schools of the

Atlanta subdistrict. *National Cyclopedia of American Biography*, 5:380–81; J. R. Lewis to G. L. Eberhart, Aug. 12, 1867, reel 1, (Ed)BRFAL-Ga (M799); Special Orders, No. 48, Apr. 17, 1867, reel 34; Station Books, vol. 1, 1867–1868; vol. 2, 1869, reel 35, BRFAL-Ga (M798); Richardson, *Christian Reconstruction*, 80, 163–64.

116. For a specific comment about the Methodists' jealousy of Ware's position in the Bureau see E. M. Cravath to E. A. Ware, Mar. 28, 1868, Ware Papers. Also see Jones, *Soldiers of Light and Love*, 101.

117. E. A. Ware to O. O. Howard, Apr. 4, 1868, reel 2, (Ed)BRFAL-Ga (M799).

118. For example, see J. R. Lewis's views of the counterproductive nature of sectarian rivalry in Alvord, *Seventh Semi-Annual Report*, 22.

119. Circular No. 1, Jan. 25, 1869, reel 34, BRFAL-Ga (M798).

120. With the Bureau's contraction, at this time Ware was serving the agency as an assistant superintendent of schools in Atlanta, where he was at the center of AMA activities. J. R. Lewis to J. S. Lowell, Jan. 22, 1870, reel 4, (Ed)BRFAL-Ga (M799); Jones, *Soldiers of Light and Love*, 101.

121. Richardson, *Christian Reconstruction*, 80; I. Pettibone to S. Hunt, Oct. 23, 1866, reel 2, AMA-Ga; E. M. Cravath to E. A. Ware, Mar. 28, 1868, Ware Papers.

122. Bureau chief surgeon Lawton boarded at the same house with the teachers and told Tillson that the timing was designed to be an act of defiance aimed at white Augustans as much as it was to be a tribute to the Union dead. For the various sides of the controversy, see D. Tillson to O. O. Howard, Apr. 29, May 7, 1866, Howard Papers, Bowdoin College, Brunswick, Maine; Emma Bryant Diary, Apr. 27, 28, 1866, John Emory Bryant Papers, Duke University; M. J. Welch to S. Hunt, May 1, 1866, reel 1, AMA-Ga; unsigned letter to the editor of the *Army and Navy Journal*, reprinted in the *Augusta Daily Constitutionalist*, June 6, 1866; Stearns, *Black Man*, 106.

123. For the teacher's insult, see G. L. Eberhart to S. Hunt, June 4, 1866, reel 2, AMA-Ga. For the teacher on her colleagues, see J. A. Shearman to Mr. Whiting, Feb. 6, 1867, reel 2, AMA-Ga. For Tillson's unflattering characterization of the teachers, see J. Bryant to G. Whipple, June 12, 1866, reel 2, AMA-Ga. Bryant does not note to whom Tillson made this remark or from whom he heard it; he begs confidentiality. Bryant is a prejudiced source on most things regarding Tillson, but this particular accusation, given the heated circumstances, rings true even though Tillson denied it. The whole affair did not bring out the best in either of the men. Also, it appears that this business prompted less than aboveboard behavior by all parties involved. Commissioner Howard requested that any correspondence from Tillson to the American Missionary Association be shared with him. D. Tillson to G. Whipple, July 4, 1866, reel 2, AMA-Ga (and Whipple's endorsement to "Dear General"); D. Tillson to O. O. Howard, June 12, 1866 (and all enclosures), Howard Papers; Emma Bryant Diary, June 5–8, 1866, Bryant Papers.

124. S. E. Russell to G. Whipple, May 1, 7, 1868; S. E. Russell to E. P. Smith, May 1,

1868; D. G. Risley to S. E. Russell, July 7, 1868; D. G. Risley to E. P. Smith, Mar. 16, Aug. 6, 1868; A. B. Wilkins to E. P. Smith, Jan. 1, 1869; E. A. Ware to E. P. Smith, Jan. 4, 1869, reel 4, AMA-Ga; J. M. Hoag to [J. R. Lewis], Dec. 8, 1868, reel 23, BRFAL-Ga (M798); J. R. Lewis to D. G. Risley, Jan. 5, 1869, reel 2, (Ed)BRFAL-Ga (M799).

125. G. L. Eberhart to E. A. Cooley, Dec. 23, 1865, reel 8, (Ed)BRFAL-Ga (M799); D. Tillson to O. O. Howard, Apr. 29, 1866, Howard Papers; Jones, *Soldiers of Light and Love*, 75.

126. W. P. Russell to [M. E.] Strieby, Mar. 20, 1866, reel 1; I. Pettibone to E. P. Smith, Dec. 18, 1866, reel 2, AMA-Ga.

127. Circular Letter No. 2, Nov. 1, 1865, reprinted in *Rome Weekly Courier*, Nov. 30, 1865.

128. *Savannah Daily Republican*, May 7, 1867.

129. Circular Letter No. 2.

130. G. L. Eberhart to S. Hunt, May 23, June 4, 1866, reel 1, AMA-Ga.

131. For a comment on the missionary fervor of AMA teachers, which an AMA official admitted was at times mistaken, see E. P. Smith to E. A. Ware, July 22, 1868, Ware Papers.

132. Shearman at least had the nerve to confront Eberhart with a list of charges. J. A. Shearman to E. P. Smith, Apr. 23, July 1, 1867, reel 3, AMA-Ga; J. Shearman to G. L. Eberhart, July 1, 1867, and J. A. Shearman to J. R. Lewis, July 2, 1867, both enclosed in J. E. Bryant to J. R. Lewis, July 9, 1867, reel 17, BRFAL-Ga (M798). Also see the testimony of Thomas M. Allen, a black Baptist preacher and politician, in Ku Klux Conspiracy, vol. 7: *Georgia*, 612–13. For other victims of Shearman's pen as well as her criticism of male AMA school superintendents, see Jones, *Soldiers of Light and Love*, 105, 174, 175, 180. Joe M. Richardson sees "a good sense of humor" in Miss Shearman's sharp pen, but the examples he uses tend to reinforce an impression that she was an acerbic-tongued complainer (Richardson, *Christian Reconstruction*, 172, 174). It is also possible that Shearman, who seemed to know all about the private affairs of every other teacher and spent much time informing AMA headquarters about them, might have learned about and resented the fact that Eberhart supported the reappointment of Augusta teacher Hattie Foote. Foote was the subject of gossip concerning alleged "criminal intercourse" with Bureau surgeon Lawton. Eberhart believed such an accusation was slanderous and unjust and argued for Foote's reappointment. For Eberhart's defense, see G. S. Eberhart to S. Hunt, Sept. 22, 1866, reel 2, AMA-Ga. For Shearman's proclivity for gossip, see Jones, *Soldiers of Light and Love*, 179–80. Shearman soon left Georgia and turned up in Lexington, Virginia, where she continued to teach freedpeople and suffer the insults of white Southerners, including students at Washington College. Never one to remain silent about the injustices heaped upon her, she brought them to the attention of the New York press, and thus she helped to bring the college's president, Robert E. Lee, under criticism for not controlling his student charges. For this episode, see Emory M. Thomas, *Robert E. Lee*, 388–89.

133. Shearman appreciated the fact that Bryant respected her and her opinions. J. A. Shearman to E. P. Smith, May 29, 1867; J. E. Bryant to E. P. Smith, July 9, 1867, reel 3, AMA-Ga.

134. G. L. Eberhart to S. Hunt, July 19, 1866; G. L. Eberhart to G. Whipple, Nov. 13, 1866, reel 2, AMA-Ga. One never knows with Eberhart. Despite his apparent alliance with Tillson against the Bryant faction, in January 1867 he claimed to be glad to see the assistant commissioner go. Eberhart probably deserved at least some of the criticism leveled at him by Shearman and Bryant. G. L. Eberhart to E. P. Smith, Jan. 28, 1867, reel 2, AMA-Ga.

135. *Savannah Daily Republican*, May 7, 1867; E. A. Ware to E. P. Smith, May 8, 1867; J. A. Shearman to E. P. Smith, May 23, 1867, reel 3, AMA-Ga; J. A. Shearman to G. L. Eberhart, July, 1, 1867, and J. A. Shearman to J. R. Lewis, July 7, 1867, both enclosed in J. E. Bryant to J. R. Lewis, July 8, 1867, reel 17, BRFAL-Ga (M798); J. E. Bryant to E. P. Smith, July 9, 1867, reel 3, AMA-Ga. Bryant's biographer, Ruth Currie-McDaniel, describes this confrontation. She finds Bryant blameless and accepts all criticism of Eberhart at face value. Although Eberhart was not a perfect man, his initial opposition to Bryant might very well have been based on his concerns about the intrusion of politics into educational matters as well as his concern for how Bryant used the freed-people's donations to his publishing enterprise. As late as 1870, John Alvord, Commissioner Howard's chief education officer, noted that state politics disrupted the educational association's internal harmony, which most likely diminished its effectiveness. Also, sometime during the summer of 1867 John A. Rockwell, Bureau agent-at-large for education and AMA teacher, allegedly called Bryant a "schemer." However, as noted earlier, Eberhart himself was scolded by Commissioner Howard in June 1867 for making too political a speech, and the man was not above trying to manipulate things to his advantage. E. A. Ware to E. P. Smith, May 8, 1867; J. E. Bryant to G. Whipple, Aug. 6, 1867, reel 3, AMA-Ga; F. D. Sewall to C. C. Sibley, June 11, 1867, reel 15, BRFAL-Ga (M798); J. W. Alvord to O. O. Howard, Jan. 17, 1870, in Alvord, *Letters from the South*, 16. For Currie-McDaniel's interpretation, see *Carpetbagger of Conscience*, 63–64.

136. J. R. Lewis to G. L. Eberhart, Aug. 5, 1867, reel 1, (Ed)BRFAL-Ga (M799).

137. Eberhart's removal was certainly hurried along by this conflict, but he also received an unfavorable report in the spring of 1867 from Howard's chief education officer. Also, Eberhart's recordkeeping, always a great concern in the Bureau, was inadequate. "Inextricable confusion" were the words Lewis used to describe the state in which he had found Eberhart's records. Because of this poor recordkeeping, Eberhart failed to leave behind much information on black emigration from Georgia to homestead lands, a project that Tillson had assigned to him. Alvord, *Fourth Semi-Annual Report*, 32; J. R. Lewis to G. L. Eberhart, Aug. 9, 1867, reel 1, (Ed)BRFAL-Ga (M799).

138. C. W. Sharp to E. P. Smith, Nov. 16, 1868, reel 4, AMA-Ga.

139. S. Vannest to E. P. Smith, Dec. 27, 1867, reel 3, AMA-Ga; Rawick, *American Slave*, vol. 12: *Georgia*, pt. 1, 262.

140. [————] to E. P. Smith, Dec. 9, 1867, reel 3, AMA-Ga; J. A. Rockwell to A. [P. Rockwell], May 4, 1868, Rockwell Papers.

141. Alvin B. Clark to W. F. White, Oct. 23, 1867, box 33, LR, Quitman Agt, BRFAL-Ga; E. A. Ware to E. D. Cheney, Nov. 4, 1868, reel 2, (Ed)BRFAL-Ga (M799). Lack of housing could lead to the closing of a school. For example, see I. Pettibone to E. P. Smith, Feb. 25, 1867, reel 2, AMA-Ga.

142. G. A. Hoods to E. P. Smith, Dec. 2, 1869, reel 6, AMA-Ga.

143. A. O. Mitchell to J. V. De Hanne, Feb. 9, 1867, reel 1, ULR, Surgeon's Records; H. Emerson to L. North, Apr. 24, May 29, 1868, box 13, LR, Brunswick Agt; Register of Complaints, Feb. 12, 14, 1867, vol. 174, Athens SAC, BRFAL-Ga; J. R. Lewis to J. M. Hoag, June 4, 1869, reel 3, (Ed)BRFAL-Ga (M799).

144. E. A. Ware to F. Randall, Nov. 27, 1867; E. A. Ware to E. P. Smith, Nov. 27, 1867; E. A. Ware to E. Woods, Jan. 14, 1868, reel 1, (Ed)BRFAL-Ga (M799).

145. J. A. Woodson to W. L. Clark, June 6, 1868, box 11, LR, Bainbridge Agt, BRFAL-Ga.

146. H. W. Kearsing to C. C. Sibley, June 9, 1868, vol. 188, LS, Bartow Agt, BRFAL-Ga.

147. W. L. Clark to E. P. Smith, Jan. 8, 1868, reel 3, AMA-Ga; Circular No. 1, Jan. 25, 1869, reel 34, BRFAL-Ga (M798); W. L. Clark to E. A. Ware, Jan. 9, 1869, Ware Papers.

148. I. Harris and other freedmen to the Agent at LaGrange, May 13, 1868, LR, Box 20; H. L. Haskell to J. E. Hosmer, May 25, 1868, vol. 288, LS, LaGrange Agt, BRFAL-Ga.

149. N. S. Hill to W. Brannan, July [—], 1866, vol. 296, LS, Macon SAC, BRFAL-Ga.

150. J. R. Phillips to G. R. Walbridge, May 6, 1866, box 7, LR; G. Walbridge to J. R. Phillips, May 9, 1866, vol. 98, LS, Atlanta SAC, BRFAL-Ga.

151. F. A. H. Gaebel to W. W. Deane, July 7, 17, 1866, reel 27, BRFAL-Ga (M798).

152. F. Mosebach to C. C. Sibley, May 13, 1867, reel 15, BRFAL-Ga (M798).

153. J. R. Lewis to J. Ayecock, May 24, 1867, reel 5, BRFAL-Ga (M798).

154. J. R. Lewis to E. Pickett, July 28, 1867, reel 18, BRFAL-Ga (M798).

155. N. S. Hill to C. C. Sibley, Dec. 13, 1867, reel 18, BRFAL-Ga (M798).

156. E. A. Ware to R. P. Lindsay, Oct. 1, 1869, reel 4, (Ed)BRFAL-Ga (M799). Also see Alvord, *Ninth Semi-Annual Report*, 28.

## Chapter 6. The Talisman Power

1. *Augusta (Maine) Kennebec Journal*, Aug. 11, 1865.

2. D. Tillson to O. O. Howard, Feb. 1, 1866, reel 1, BRFAL-Ga (M798).

3. Howard admitted that the Bureau chose the contract system, the best possible means for implementing free labor "for the present at least," from several alternatives (*Kennebec Journal*, Aug. 11, 1865). Too frequently historians of southern Reconstruction assume that the army and the Bureau created the contract system for the

freedpeople as an innovation and a departure from northern practices; in fact, there was a long tradition in the North of using yearly contracts in agricultural labor, particularly in the Midwest, a crucial point for understanding Reconstruction that is admirably explored by James D. Schmidt in "'Neither Slavery nor Involuntary Servitude,'" 7–69. For the treatment of farmhands in the antebellum Midwest and a brief description of the type of contract terms used, see David E. Schob, *Hired Hands and Plowboys*, 207–33, esp. 222–27.

4. A. C. McKinley to R. D. B. Taylor, May [4], 1865, Col. Davis Crenshaw Barrow Papers, University of Georgia; J. M. Johnson to "My dear Maj[or]," June 10, 1865, Howell Cobb Papers, University of Georgia; J. Hill to A. Johnson, May 10, 1865, Joshua Hill Folder, File 2, GDAH; H. N. Howland to Capt. Imhoff, June 27, 1865, *Official Records*, ser. 1, vol. 49, pt. 2, 1041–42; *Turnwold Countryman*, May 23, June 6, 13, 1865; *Macon Daily Telegraph*, May 28, June 21, 1865; *Augusta Daily Constitutionalist*, May 25, June 21, 1865; *Atlanta Intelligencer* [May 1865], quoted in *Albany Patriot*, May 27, 1865; *National Anti-Slavery Standard*, July 15, 1865; Rawick, *American Slave*, vol. 12: *Georgia*, pt. 2, 77, 237; vol. 13: *Georgia*, pt. 3, 101. Both Leon F. Litwack and James L. Roark note that ex-masters did not waste much time feeling guilty over the institution that they had fought to preserve. The evidence from white Georgia's reaction to freedom supports their view. Roark, *Masters without Slaves*, 97; Litwack, *Been in the Storm So Long*, 189.

5. J. A. Wilson to W. D. Whipple, May 15, 1865, *Official Records*, ser. 1, vol. 49, pt. 2, 784; Robertson, ed., *Diary of Dolly Lunt Burge*, 112–13.

6. *Albany Patriot*, June 10, 1865.

7. J. M. Johnson to "My dear Maj[or]," June 10, 1865; J. A. Cobb to father [Howell Cobb], June 29, July 18, 1865; [Mary A. Cobb] to husband [Howell Cobb], Sept. 15, 1865; H. Cobb to wife [Mary A. Cobb], Sept. 15, 1865, Howell Cobb Papers; R. G. Lamar to G. B. Lamar, Aug. 17, 25, Gazaway Bugg Lamar Papers, University of Georgia; Eva B. Jones to Mary Jones, June 13, 1865; Rev. J. Jones to Mary Jones, Aug. 21, 1865, in Myers, *Children of Pride*, 1274, 1293; R. [Battey] to Mary [Battey], July 19, 1865, Robert Battey Papers, Emory University, Atlanta; Maj. A. Porter to A. L. Alexander, Aug. 17, 1865, Alexander-Hillhouse Family Papers, University of North Carolina, Southern Historical Collection; *Turnwold Countryman*, May 30, June 13, 1865; *Macon Daily Telegraph*, May 31, 1865; *Augusta Daily Constitutionalist*, Oct. 15, 1865.

8. J. M. Johnson to "My dear Maj[or]," June 10, 1865, Cobb Papers; Memorial, Citizens of Chatham County, May 26, 1865, enclosed in Gen. Q. A. Gilmore to E. M. Stanton, May 29, 1865, *Official Records*, ser. 1, vol. 47, pt. 3, 594–96. For another prediction of violence see W. W. Gordon to wife [Elinor Kenzie Gordon], June 5, 1865, Gordon Family Papers, University of North Carolina, Southern Historical Collection. See *Macon Daily Telegraph*, June 20, 1865, for rumors of an insurrection at Savannah and M. French to J. B. Steedman, Sept. 5, 1865, reel 1, AMA-Ga, for comments on the fear of

insurrection in central and southern Georgia during the summer of 1865. The fear of an uprising at the end of 1865 was experienced throughout the South; see Carter, "The Anatomy of Fear."

9. G. W. Lamar to G. B. Lamar, Aug. 17, 1865, Lamar Papers; E. R. Harden to mother, Nov. 13, 1865, Edward R. Harden Papers, Duke University; J. S. Dobbins to [Elisha] Lowry, Jan. 29, 1866, ser. 1, John S. Dobbins Papers, Emory University, Atlanta; Stearns, *Black Man*, 114. Decades after emancipation when some black Georgians recalled their freedom experience, they remembered their ability to walk away from their old slave homes. Rawick, *American Slave*, vol. 8: *Arkansas*, pt. 1, 68; vol. 12: *Georgia*, pt. 1, 218.

10. Mary Jones to son [C. C. Jones Jr.], Aug. 18, 1865, Charles Colcock Jones Jr. Collection, University of Georgia. There was a belief among the ex-slaves encountered by the Reverend Mansfield French that there would be a general division of lands at Christmas. M. French to J. B. Steedman, Sept. 5, 1865, reel 1, AMA-Ga. Also see Proclamation by James Johnson, Provisional Governor to the People of Georgia, [July 13, 1865], box 60, Georgia Governors' Papers, Telamon-Cuyler Collection, University of Georgia; *Macon Daily Telegraph*, Sept. 30, 1865; C. C. Richardson to W. W. Deane, Nov. 28, 1865, reel 24, BRFAL-Ga (M798); C. L. Gaulden to C. C. Richardson, Dec. 19, 1865, vol. 375, LR; C. C. Richardson to C. L. Gaulden, Dec. 19, 1865, vol. 379, LS, Thomasville SAC, BRFAL-Ga. The rumor of free land surfaced again in the spring of 1867 in southwest Georgia and in the summer of 1868 along the coast, but federal officials generally convinced freedpeople that if they wanted land they would have to work for it. O. H. Howard, Circular to the Freedpeople of Dougherty, Lee, and Terrell Counties, June 10, 1867, reel 20, BRFAL-Ga (M798); C. R. Holcolmbe to J. M. Hoag, Sept. 5, 1868, box 28, ULR, Savannah SAC Commissioner, BRFAL-Ga.

11. A. P. Ketchum to R. Saxton, Sept. 1, 1865, reel 34, BRFAL-SC (M869). For a similar assessment see the testimony of Sidney Andrews, Apr. 19, 1866, *House Reports*, 39th Cong., 1st sess., no. 30 (serial 1273), pt. 3, 174.

12. General Orders, No. 1, June 20, 1865, *House Executive Documents*, 39th Cong., 1st sess., no. 70 (serial 1256), 99; Laura E. Buttolph to Mary Jones, June 30, 1865, in Myers, *Children of Pride*, 1277.

13. *Augusta Daily Constitutionalist*, May 27, 28, 1865. One ex-slave remembered going into Augusta "to see if twas true we wuz free." He heard "the man" confirm this fact, telling the freedpeople to "Work wheh you want." Rawick, *American Slave*, vol. 13: *Georgia*, pt. 4, 238.

14. Thornbery, "The Development of Black Atlanta," 58.

15. *Macon Daily Telegraph*, Aug. 10, 18, 24, 1865; M. French to J. B. Steedman, Sept. 5, 1865, reel 1, AMA-Ga.

16. Newspapers beyond the Augusta hinterlands published these regulations, and planters beyond Richmond County used them as guidelines. For the regulations see

*Macon Daily Telegraph*, June 16, 1865, and *Albany Patriot*, June 17, 1865. For an example of a contract based on them from Greene County to the west of but not far from Augusta, see W. G. Daniel to C. McCarthy, Sept. 13, 1865, Two or More Citizens File, Dept. of Ga.; for an example from Decatur County, located across the state in the far southwest corner, see contract between McQueen McIntosh and freedmen, July 8, 1865, box 11, LR, Bainbridge Agt, BRFAL-Ga.

17. *Macon Daily Telegraph*, June 16, 1865, and the *Albany Patriot*, June 17, 1865. Bryant made his remark about self-supporting freedpeople to Saxton later in September, but his labor views were consistent and generally compatible with those of his nemesis Davis Tillson even after he left the Bureau. For Bryant's views see Bryant to R. Saxton, Sept. 6, 1865, John Emory Bryant Papers, Duke University, and his speech to the freedmen's convention at Augusta printed in the *Augusta Loyal Georgian*, Jan. 27, 1866. That same speech, however, also marks an important difference with Tillson, for while Bryant argued for the acceptance of free-labor principles, he also publicly acknowledged that black industry could convince white Georgians to recognize the freedmen's claim to the privilege of suffrage.

18. O. O. Howard was opposed to fixing wage rates. The commissioner believed that his office could not take into consideration regional variations in the economy, so he refrained from issuing a Bureau directive committing all of his assistant commissioners to one wage schedule. More important, however, was his fear that any kind of an established rate would lower the maximum pay for the freedmen rather than raise the minimum. In August, Rufus Saxton made no more specific suggestion than that a crop-sharing arrangement, whereby the planter received half and the workers divided the other half, would be equitable and acceptable, although he did note that freedpeople also were entitled to housing, food, medical care, and fuel. O. O. Howard to Brig. Gen. Molineau, June 28, [1865], reel 1, (RI)BRFAL (M742); O. O. Howard to R. Saxton, June 20, 1865, reel 8, BRFAL-SC (M869); Circular No. 11, July 12, 1865, reprinted in *Savannah Daily Republican*, Aug. 11, 1865; *Brunswick (Maine) Telegraph*, July 21, 1865; General Orders, No. 11, Aug. 28, 1865, *House Executive Documents*, 39th Cong., 1st sess., no. 70 (serial 1256), 113; Bentley, *Freedmen's Bureau*, 80–81; Abbott, *Freedmen's Bureau in South Carolina*, 68–69.

19. Circular No. 2, Aug. 16, 1865, *House Executive Documents*, 39th Cong., 1st sess., no. 70 (serial 1256), 92–93. This circular, as were most Bureau circulars and orders, was reprinted in local newspapers. *Savannah Daily Republican*, Aug. 29, 1865.

20. *Macon Daily Telegraph*, May 19, 1865.

21. *Augusta Daily Constitutionalist*, May 28, 1865.

22. *Albany Patriot*, June 24, 1865.

23. *Macon Daily Telegraph*, Aug. 10, 1865. Also see *Macon Daily Telegraph*, Aug. 29, 1865.

24. W. H. S[tiles] to wife, July 1, 1865, series A, Mackay-Stiles Family Papers, Univer-

sity of North Carolina, Southern Historical Collection; D. Young to the American Missionary Association, July 3, 1865, reel 1, AMA-Ga; Rev. J. Jones to Mary Jones, July 26, Aug. 21, 1865, in Myers, *Children of Pride*, 1282, 1297; *Augusta Daily Constitutionalist*, June 1, 1865; *National Anti-Slavery Standard*, July 15, 1865; *Savannah Daily Republican*, Aug. 7, 1865; *Macon Daily Telegraph*, Sept. 16, 1865. Local military commanders had authority to approve contracts during the summer of 1865. Maj. W. L. M. Burger to Capt. C. C. Dyer, June 3, 1865, *Official Records*, ser. 1, vol. 47. pt. 3, 619.

25. Generalizations concerning the summer contracts for the remainder of 1865 are based on an examination of forty-two contracts, most of them selected from the contracts in the files of the Augusta and the Savannah Freedmen's Bureau districts, the most fully functioning agencies at this time, located in BRFAL-Ga. Fifteen of the forty documents were approved by John Emory Bryant and are located in volume 159 of the Augusta agent's records, BRFAL-Ga. Eighteen were approved by army provost marshals. Most of these are located in box 32, Savannah Subassistant Commissioner, BRFAL-Ga. One was found in the Two or More Citizens File, Dept. of Ga. Contracts from private manuscript collections, some of them approved by provost marshals, one of them approved by an officer acting as a Bureau official, supplement these. The contracts were entered into between June 1 and September 12, with the majority being executed in August. The contracts represent labor arrangements in twenty-one Georgia counties.

26. Contract between David S. Johnston and freedmen, July 15, 1865, enclosed in F. C. Genth to O. H. Howard, Dec. 20, 1867, box 24, LR, Newton Agt; contract between Nathan Bussey and freedmen, Aug. 5, 1865; contract between Richard Powell and freedmen, Aug. 7, 1865; contract between Edmund Lee and freedmen, Aug. 12, 1865, vol. 159, Contracts, Augusta Agt; contract between John Hamilton and Jack, Aug. 10, 1865, box 32, Records of the Assistant Adjutant General, Savannah SAC, BRFAL-Ga; contract between John M. McCrary and freedmen, Aug. 9, 1865, John Mathew McCrary Papers, Atlanta History Center; contract between G. J. Orr and freedmen, Aug. 14, 1865, Orr Family Papers, Emory University, Atlanta.

27. Contract between Ellis H. Goff and freedmen, June 1, 1865; contract between Elizabeth C. Harden and freedmen, June 1, 1865, vol. 159, Contracts, Augusta Agt, BRFAL-Ga. Also see contract between William K. Wilkinson and freedmen, Aug. 8, 1865, Wilkinson Family Papers, GDAH; contract between Benjamin C. Yancey and freedmen, July 22, 1865, Benjamin C. Yancey Papers, University of North Carolina, Southern Historical Collection.

28. Contract between E. McCord and freedmen, July 1, 1865; contract between Ransom Harwell and freedmen, July 31, 1865; contract between L. P. Murray and freedmen, Aug. 11, 1865, vol. 159, Contracts, Augusta Agt, BRFAL-Ga. Also see contract between G. J. Orr and freedmen, Aug. 14, 1865, Orr Family Papers; contract between McQueen McIntosh and freedmen, July 8, 1865, box 11, LR, Bainbridge Agt, BRFAL-Ga. For examples of complaints about impudent freedpeople during the summer of

1865, see Minerva Leah Rowles McClatchey Diary, July [1865], GDAH; *Macon Daily Telegraph*, Aug. 18, 1865.

29. G. W. Lamar to brother [Gazaway B. Lamar], Aug. 17, 1865, Lamar Papers; Rev. J. Jones to Mary Jones, Aug. 21, 1865, in Myers, *Children of Pride*, 1293.

30. Contract between John Mathew McCrary and freedmen, Aug. 9, 1865, McCrary Papers.

31. W. H. Stiles to "my dear wife," July 1, 1865; "Mother" [Elizabeth Anne Stiles] to "my dear children," Aug. 20, 1865, ser. A, Mackay-Stiles Family Papers; W. H. Stiles to R. Saxton [Sept. 25. 1865], box 32, LR, Savannah Agent, BRFAL-Ga.

32. *Macon Daily Telegraph*, June 28, 1865. As the Yankee planter Charles Stearns later noted, Georgians "were quite willing for the Bureau to punish their refractory hands, but utterly unwilling to be placed in the same category with their former slaves." And Captain A. P. Ketchum believed that planters would accept contracts out of self-interest but that they would complain constantly and never fully embrace free-labor ideology. Indeed, as early as July 1865, a planter in Greene County made it quite clear that he did not expect the freedpeople in his employ to take advantage of the counsel of northern intruders; he threatened to kill one freedman, or at least "'*clinch his . . . teeth,*'" to keep him from complaining to Yankees. Stearns, *Black Man*, 109; A. P. Ketchum to R. Saxton, Sept. 1, 1865, reel 34, BRFAL-SC (M869); Capt. C. McCarthy to Bvt. Brig. Gen. C. H. Grosvenor, July 24, 1865, Two or More Citizens File, Dept. of Ga.

33. The *Southern Cultivator* noted that August was a good time to do odd jobs, "the farm work not being so pressing." Quoted in *Athens Southern Banner*, Aug. 9, 1865.

34. D. Young to Rev. M. E. Strieby, Aug. 3, 1865, reel 1, AMA-Ga; A. P. Ketchum to R. Saxton, Sept. 1, 1865, reel 34, BRFAL-SC (M869); *National Anti-Slavery Standard*, Sept. 9, 1865.

35. J. E. Bryant to R. Saxton, Aug. 4, 1865, reel 7, BRFAL-SC (M869).

36. W. F. Eaton, "A List of Planters in Southern Georgia who have sent away the Freedmen unpaid to the islands and the names of the Freedmen up to August 15th 1865," Aug. 24, 1865, box 26, Misc., St. Simons Agent, BRFAL-Ga. Also see W. F. Eaton to A. P. Ketchum, Aug. 3, 1865, box 32, Records of the Assistant Adjutant General, Savannah SAC, BRFAL-Ga.

37. Burr, *Secret Eye*, 275–77.

38. C. H. Howard, Inspection Report for South Carolina, Georgia, and Florida, Dec. 30, 1865, *House Executive Documents*, 39th Cong., 1st sess., no. 70 (serial 1256), 357.

39. D. Tillson to J. E. Godfrey, Oct. 12, 1865, reel 1, BRFAL-Ga (M798). For other examples see D. Tillson, endorsement, Oct. 11, 1865, on C. S. Cheves to D. Tillson, Oct. 7, 1865, reel 24; D. Tillson to [J. M. Miller], Nov. 4, 1865, reel 1, BRFAL-Ga (M798).

40. D. Tillson to O. O. Howard, Oct. 5, 1865, reel 20, (LR)BRFAL (M752); H. B. Sprague to D. Tillson, Nov. 24, 1865, reel 13, BRFAL-Ga (M798). Also see *Macon Daily Telegraph*, Oct. 12, 1865; *Athens Southern Banner*, Nov. 15, 1865. Tillson's visit to

Wilkes County went over well because he condemned the previous administration's activities in that county. A. L. A[lexander] to "my darlings," Oct. 1, 1865, Alexander-Hillhouse Family Papers.

41. D. Tillson to O. O. Howard, Nov. 1, 1865, reel 20, (LR)BRFAL (M752).

42. For a positive review of Tillson's speech and "the kind, conciliatory and gentlemanly manner in which he communicated his views" (which undoubtedly influenced President Johnson's view of the assistant commissioner), see H. M. Watterson to A. Johnson, Oct. 30, 1865, Harvey MaGee Watterson Papers, Georgia Historical Society, Savannah.

43. Sidney Andrews, *The South since the War: As Shown by Fourteen Weeks of Travel and Observation in Georgia and the Carolinas*, 281; also see 282–87.

44. *Macon Daily Telegraph*, Oct. 12, 1865; *Athens Southern Banner*, Nov. 15, 1865.

45. C. H. Howard to Mother [Eliza Gilmore Howard], Oct. 31, 1865, Charles H. Howard Papers, Bowdoin College, Brunswick, Maine; C. C. Richardson to W. W. Deane, Nov. 28, 1865; S. Draws to D. Tillson, Dec. 26, 1865, reel 24; R. McCoan to D. Tillson, Dec. 27, 1865, reel 31, BRFAL-Ga (M798); W. Young to A. A. Buck, Dec. 8, 1865, box 35, LR, Waynesboro Agt; S. Oliver to Capt. Campbell, Dec. 14, 1865, box 9, ULR, Augusta SAC; T. C. Arnold to H. F. Sickles, Dec. 27, 1865, box 28, ULR, Savannah SAC, BRFAL-Ga; C. H. Howard to O. O. Howard, Dec. 30, 1865, *House Executive Documents*, 39th Cong., 1st sess., no. 70 (serial 1256), 350; Reid, *After the War*, 146–47. Nancy Cohen-Lack argues that in 1865 Texas freedpeople believed that contracts were simply another form of bondage; her study, however, is limited in its scope and does not account for change over time. While this view of contracts was initially true among some of Georgia's freedpeople and remained so among others, it altered over time as the freedpeople adjusted to the system. Cohen-Lack, "A Struggle for Sovereignty."

46. S. Oliver to Capt. Campbell, Dec. 14, 1865, box 9, ULR, Augusta SAC; T. C. Arnold to Col. H. F. Sickles, Dec. 27, 1865, box 28, ULR, Savannah SAC, BRFAL-Ga.

47. C. H. Howard to Mother [Eliza Gilmore Howard], Oct. 31, 1865, Charles H. Howard Papers.

48. Circular No. 2, Oct. 3, 1865, reel 34; C. C. Richardson to W. W. Deane, Nov. 28, 1865, reel 24, BRFAL-Ga (M798).

49. Freedpeople across the state crowded into Georgia's cities throughout the summer and fall of 1865. There they found a wide range of nonagricultural jobs that provided alternatives to planting cotton as well as a degree of freedom that might have compensated for the fact that those menial urban jobs open to them were not paying top dollar. For details about black urban life in Georgia see Blassingame, "Before the Ghetto"; McLeod, *Workers and Workplace Dynamics in Reconstruction-Era Atlanta*; Reidy, "Masters and Slaves, Planters and Freedmen," 280–353; Thornbery, "The Development of Black Atlanta, 1865–1885." As McLeod demonstrates, there were serious limits to economic advancement defined by the low-status, low-paying jobs open to

blacks in an urban setting. Those limits as well as the ultimate disappointment experienced by the freedpeople, however, should not obscure the fact that the freedpeople who moved to the cities were making decisions about their futures and attempting to take control of their lives.

50. Circular No. 2, Oct. 3, 1865, reel 34, BRFAL-Ga. Tillson's concerns were valid, for urban poverty and crowding contributed to the spread of sickness among the freedpeople.

51. H. Casey to D. Tillson, Oct. 3, 1865; J. McK. Gunn to D. Tillson, Oct. 14, 1865; J. G. Barney to D. Tillson, Nov. 1, 1865; P. Slaughter to D. Tillson, Nov. 1, 1865; E. M. Hill to D. Tillson, Nov. 7, 1865; W. Willingham et al. to D. Tillson, Nov. 16, 1865; A. C. Walker to D. Tillson, Nov. 24, 1865; M. McQ. McIntosh to D. Tillson, Dec. 6, 1865; J. Matthews to D. Tillson, Dec. 6, 1865; G. Curkendale to W. Gray, Dec. 7, 1865; J. D. Harris to D. Tillson, Dec. 18, 1865; J. T. Stephens to D. Tillson, Dec. 19, 1865, reel 24, BRFAL-Ga (M798).

52. Circular No. 5, Dec. 22, 1865, reel 34, BRFAL-Ga (M798). Tillson was acting within the bounds of Yankee legal traditions concerning vagrancy, although Tillson, of course, was working outside of traditional legislative and judicial institutions at this time because of the special circumstances of Reconstruction. See Schmidt, "'Neither Slavery nor Involuntary Servitude,'" 70–112.

53. D. Tillson's speech to the Georgia State Convention, Oct. 27, 1865, enclosed in D. Tillson to O. O. Howard, Nov. 1, 1865, reel 20, (LR)BRFAL (M752).

54. Certainly Howard's and Congress's disapproval of compulsory labor in any form contributed to Tillson's withdrawal of his order, but in Tillson's independent opinion, the freedmen were signing fair contracts whereas employers were proving to be the intransigent parties. Also, intelligence from individuals like his former subordinate Lt. Col. Homer B. Sprague reinforced the assistant commissioner's impression that whites were clinging to old notions of mastery. Amy Dru Stanley's failure to note this shift in policy after asserting that the Georgia Bureau initiated a compulsory contract system based on her reading of reports and circulars published in Congressional documents illustrates the danger of drawing conclusions about the Bureau without reading the complete record at least at the assistant commissioner's level. H. B. Sprague to D. Tillson, Jan. 10, 1866, reel 28; F. A. Billingslea to D. Tillson, Jan. 23, 1866, reel 25; Circular No. 3, Feb. 1, 1866, reel 34, BRFAL-Ga (M798); D. Tillson to O. O. Howard, Feb. 1, 1866, reel 20, (LR)BRFAL (M752); Stanley, "Beggars Can't Be Choosers," 1284–85.

55. For Tillson's growing awareness of inadequate work arrangements, see D. Tillson to R. Saxton, Dec. 30, 1865, reel 1, BRFAL-Ga (M798); "Tillson's Speech," *Augusta Loyal Georgian*, Jan. 20, 1866; D. Tillson, "Report of Operations September 22, 1865 to November 1, 1866," reel 32, BRFAL-Ga (M798). For a comment on the varied nature of contracts signed for the remainder of the 1865 season and the confusion this caused for one of Tillson's subordinates, see G. A. Hastings to W. W. Deane, Dec. 24, 1865, reel 24, BRFAL-Ga (M798).

56. Circular No. 2, October 3, 1865, reel 34, BRFAL-Ga (M798).

57. Tillson's Tennessee experience had convinced him that a uniform wage guideline would be beneficial. To protect the freedpeople's ability to collect that set wage, Tillson's Bureau would not approve the contracts of employers who did not actually own real property unless they posted a bond to secure the freedpeople's earnings. It does not appear probable that Tillson was able to enforce with any degree of regularity the requirement of bond from nonlandholders who leased plantations, but his intention to secure the freedpeople's earnings was clear. Circular No. 5, Dec. 22, 1865, reel 34; W. W. Deane to J. W. Arnold, Jan. 19, 1866, reel 1, BRFAL-Ga (M798); D. Tillson to W. T. Clark, July 15, 1865, reel 8, BRFAL-Tn (M999).

58. For Tillson's stand on his wage rates, see D. Tillson to G. W. Selvidge, Jan. 26, 1866, reel 1, BRFAL-Ga (M798); Trowbridge, *The South*, 495–97.

59. Circular No. 1, Jan. 5, 1866, reel 34, BRFAL-Ga (M798).

60. While this approach might appear to be a compromise on his wage scale, it allowed him to deal with unapproved contracts at settlement time that might have escaped Bureau notice. Also, in all likelihood, there were planters and freedpeople in the county who had accepted the Bureau's terms for upper Georgia. A. H. Teasely to D. Tillson, Feb. 4, 1866, reel 29; W. W. Deane to A. H. Teasley, Feb. 8, 1866, reel 1, BRFAL-Ga (M798).

61. In January Tillson learned that the legislature was considering a bill that would hold all contracts binding, whether or not the parties signed them under Bureau supervision. Tillson objected on the grounds that the law would be unjust; it would sanction unfair contracts made by employers who had taken advantage of the freedpeople. He informed Governor Charles Jenkins that even if the legislature passed the bill, he would continue to void contracts. Jenkins agreed to do his best to stop the bill from taking effect, which he did, but he believed that Tillson was being unreasonable in asking planters to pay a price for labor far above the average wage of past years. Also, he argued, some freedpeople were worth more than others, and the planters would be the best judges of the differences in the quality of their laborers. Eventually, the planters won this concession. D. Tillson to C. J. Jenkins, Jan. 23, 1866, reel 1; C. J. Jenkins to D. Tillson, Jan. 30, 1866, reel 27, BRFAL-Ga (M798); D. Tillson to O. O. Howard, Feb. 12, 1866, reel 20, (LR)BRFAL (M752); *Augusta Daily Constitutionalist*, Jan. 23, 1866; Candler, *Confederate Records*, 4:483–85, 492–94.

62. O. O. Howard to D. Tillson, Jan. 23, 1866, reel 2, (RI)BRFAL (M742); D. Tillson to O. O. Howard, Feb. 1, 1866, reel 20 (LR)BRFAL (M752). Generals Steedman and Fullerton also criticized Tillson's contract system as a violation of laissez-faire. The *Savannah Daily Republican* of August 15, 1866, reported that the officers believed that Bureau contracts limited the freedpeople, who were competent to negotiate their own labor arrangements, and claimed that the freedpeople would have been able to contract for upwards of 50 percent more than promised under Bureau supervision. They

were wrong. Also see *New York Times*, Aug. 10, 1866; *Columbus Daily Enquirer*, Aug. 14, 1866.

63. W. W. Deane to G. W. Selvidge, Jan. 9, 1866; D. Tillson to L. Lambert, Jan. 10, 1866; D. Tillson to J. Lyle, Jan. 10, 1866; W. W. Deane to J. Dawson, Jan. 19, 1866; D. Tillson to J. R. Lyle and J. C. Johnson, Jan. 19, 1866; W. Gray to S. A. McLendon, Jan. 25, 1866; W. W. Deane to S. Crawford, Jan. 25, 1866; W. W. Deane to D. C. Poole, Jan. 29, 1866; W. W. Deane to D. W. Pope, Jan. 26, 1866, reel 1, BRFAL-Ga. Circular No. 3, Feb. 1, 1866, reel 34, BRFAL-Ga (M798) restates Tillson's position concerning unfair contracts.

64. The civilian agents who approved substandard contracts claimed that labor was on the open market within their jurisdictions, that the contracting freedpeople received all they deserved according to their abilities as workers, that the arrangements made for freedmen were comparable to what white workers could earn, that the freedmen would rather work for low wages in familiar surroundings than go elsewhere for top pay, or that their counties were too poor to support the rate required by Tillson. F. J. Robinson to D. Tillson, Feb. 4, 1866, reel 27; J. R. Lyle and J. C. Johnson to D. Tillson, Jan. 13, 1866, reel 27; A. H. Teasley to D. Tillson, Feb. 4, 1866; J. H. Blount to D. Tillson, Feb. 12, 1866, reel 25; W. Serrine to D. Tillson, Mar. 1, 1866, reel 29, BRFAL-Ga (M798).

65. J. Davison to D. Tillson, Dec. 26, 1865, reel 31; Jan. 8, Feb. 6, 10, Mar. 1, 1866, reel 26; W. W. Deane to J. Davison, Feb. 8, 1866, reel 1; W. Gray to D. Tillson, Mar. 14, 1866, reel 27, BRFAL-Ga (M798).

66. W. Gray to W. M. Haslett, Jan. 22, 1866, reel 1; W. Gray to D. Tillson, Jan. 30, 1866, reel 27; F. J. Robinson to D. Tillson, Jan. 13, 1866; A. T. Reeve to D. Tillson, Jan. 31, 1866, reel 28; D. Tillson to S. B. Moe, Jan. 31, 1866; D. Tillson to W. Gray, Jan. 31, 1866, reel 1, BRFAL-Ga (M798).

67. O. M. Gray to D. Tillson, Feb. 27, 1866, reel 27, BRFAL-Ga (M798). According to one white Georgian, Bureau intervention in Elbert County was unnecessary to achieve this end. W. H. Mattox complained to the governor of Georgia that Major Gray had not given the citizens of Elbert County a fair chance, but at the same time he argued that Tillson's wage expectations were too high for the county. Still, he assured the governor, Elbert's people were "reliable & honest, as any of God's creation" and that the majority of planters were paying their workers one-third of the crop plus lodging. Even if this assessment was correct, the response of the Bureau to the perceived injustice is important in assessing the agency's commitment to just work arrangements for the freedpeople. W. H. Mattox to C. J. Jenkins, Feb. 16, 1866, box 53, Executive Department Correspondence, GDAH.

68. W. Gray to M. P. Wingfield, Mar. [15], 1866, reel 2, BRFAL-Ga (M798).

69. G. H. Pratt to D. Tillson, Feb. 1, 1866, reel 28; W. Gray to M. P. Wingfield, Mar. [15], 1866; W. W. Deane to M. P. Wingfield, Mar. 15, 1866, reel 2, BRFAL-Ga (M798).

70. W. C. Riddle to D. Tillson, Mar. 14, 1866, reel 28; F. A. H. Gaebel to W. W. Deane,

July 2, 1866, reel 27; C. A. de la Mesa to D. Tillson, Sept. 15, 1866, reel 13, BRFAL-Ga (M798). Also see orders issued by Subassistant Commissioner Frederick Mosebach printed in the *Columbus Daily Sun*, Jan. 10, 1867.

71. Stearns, *Black Man*, 105.

72. H. B. Sprague to D. Tillson, Jan. 10, 1866, reel 28, BRFAL-Ga (M798). Also see E. R. Harden to mother, July 19, 1866, Edward R. Harden Papers.

73. Generalizations concerning contracts for 1866 are based on an examination of 106 documents selected from the Georgia Bureau's records. Unlike the files of some other state Bureau offices, Georgia's contract records are not complete or gathered into a central file. Twenty-five counties provide contracts for this period for this study. although the majority are from eastern Georgia, either along the coast or around Augusta.

74. This threat probably accounted for some of agent James Davison's success. Tillson's policy was to try to secure the highest possible rates for workers without written contracts. W. W. Deane to J. Davison, Jan. 19, 1866, reel 1, BRFAL-Ga (M798).

75. *Columbus Daily Enquirer*, Mar. 22, 1866. In September 1866, a Rome, Georgia, editorialist also suggested this method for dealing with the Bureau and, showing his lack of faith in the agency to make free labor work, urged employers to draw up pledges of "mutual protection" to enforce labor agreements; several months earlier a planter in Albany called for a meeting of employers to agree on uniform contract terms, a way by which they could subvert the system. *Albany Patriot*, Dec. 16, 1865; *Rome Weekly Courier*, Sept. 28, 1866.

76. *Acts of the General Assembly of the State of Georgia, Passed in Milledgeville, at an Annual Session in December 1865 and January, February, and March, 1866*, 74–75.

77. C. A. de la Mesa, July 18, 1866, reel 26, BRFAL-Ga (M798).

78. J. Davison to D. Tillson, Jan. 14, 1867, reel 30, BRFAL-Ga (M798).

79. De la Mesa, however, shared Tillson's views about mutual responsibilities and obligations. After a year of planting, Dent changed his view of de la Mesa and praised his fairness in dealing with blacks and whites. Mathis, Mathis, and Purcell, *John Horry Dent Farm Journals and Account Books*, Jan. 11, 15, 18, 22, 1867; Dec. 31, 1867, vol. 7, reel 1 (hereinafter cited as *Dent Journals*).

80. *Columbus Daily Enquirer*, Aug. 14, 1866. This critic, however, believed that a contract system should be enforced more rigorously on the ex-slaves to make them productive members of society.

81. S. W. Swanson and others to D. Tillson, Feb. 8, 1866, reel 31, BRFAL-Ga (M798).

82. Fannie A[tkisson] to My dear Coz, Feb. 25, 1866, Baber-Blackshear Papers, University of Georgia.

83. J. C. Swayze to D. Tillson, Feb. 8, 1866, reel 29, BRFAL-Ga (M798). For additional white complaints about the Bureau during Tillson's tenure see *Southern Cultivator*, Jan. 1866; *New York Times*, Jan. 16, 1866; *Macon Daily Telegraph*, Mar. 4, Apr. 15, 19,

May 15, 1866; *Augusta Daily Constitutionalist*, June 13, 1866; *Sandersville Central Georgian*, June 6, 1866; Helen J. Salter to [A. H.] Stephens, Apr. 5, 1866, ser. 1, Alexander Stephens Papers, Emory University, Atlanta.

84. Circular No. 2, October 3, 1865, reel 34, BRFAL-Ga (M798).

85. D. Tillson, "Report of Operations September 22, 1865, to November 1, 1866," reel 32, BRFAL-Ga (M798). The *New York Times* of Jan. 29, 1866, reported that planters in more fertile areas outside of Georgia were paying as much as fifteen dollars a month plus lodging, food, and clothing. O. O. Howard adopted a similar program for the Bureau in December 1865. Howard was undoubtedly aware of Tillson's efforts—the Georgia assistant commissioner regularly corresponded with Howard and kept him abreast of affairs in Georgia. However, as William Cohen notes, there is no evidence that Tillson's efforts directly influenced Howard's plans and Howard appeared to be moving in that direction before Tillson arrived in Georgia. Cohen estimates the the the Bureau moved upwards of fifty or sixty thousand freedpeople throughout the South between the end of May 1865 and the end of September 1868. Cohen, *At Freedom's Edge*, 44–77; for Howard's initial efforts see 55–59.

86. G. Curkendall to W. Gray, Dec. 5, 1865; W. F. Avent to D. Tillson, Dec. 8, 1865; B. Maguire to W. Gray, Dec. 8, 1865; G. Curkendall to W. W. Deane, Dec. 11, 1865, reel 24; G. Curkendall to D. Tillson, Jan. 1, 1866, reel 25; W. Gray to P. Slaughter, Dec. 6, 1865; W. Gray to G. Curkendall, Dec. 6, 1865; W. W. Deane to D. C. Poole, Jan. 17, 1866; W. W. Deane to G. Walbridge, Feb. 19, 1866, reel 1, BRFAL-Ga (M798).

87. Circular No. 2, Oct. 3, 1865; Special Orders, No. 40, Mar. 3, 1866, reel 34, BRFAL-Ga (M798); W. Gray to G. Curkendall, Dec. 6, 1865, reel 1; B. Maguire to W. Gray, Dec. 8, 1865, reel 24; C. C. Richardson to W. W. Deane, Feb. 8, 1866, reel 28; G. Walbridge to D. Tillson, Feb. 22, 1866, reel 29; W. Gray to D. Tillson, Mar. 14, 1866, reel 27, BRFAL-Ga (M798); D. Tillson to G. Curkendall, Nov. 9, 1865; G. Curkendall to W. Gray, Dec. 6, 1865, vol. 98, LS; W. Gray to G. Curkendall, Dec. 9, 1865, LR, Atlanta SAC, BRFAL-Ga.

88. D. Tillson to G. R. Walbridge, Mar. 12, 1866, box 27, LR, Atlanta SAC, BRFAL-Ga.

89. D. Tillson to O. O. Howard, Nov. 28, 1865, reel 20, (LR)BRFAL (M752); Capt. F. Wells to W. W. Deane, Dec. 8, 1865, reel 24, BRFAL-Ga (M798).

90. The freedpeople had cause to worry because Elbert County was home to Jayhawkers who had already proved their willingness to use violence. W. Gray to D. Tillson, Jan. 30, 1866, reel 27; F. J. Robinson to D. Tillson, Jan. 13, 1866; A. T. Reeve to D. Tillson, Jan. 31, 1 ;66, reel 28, BRFAL-Ga (M798).

91. W. Gray to D. Tillson, Mar. 14, 1866, reel 27, BRFAL-Ga.

92. C. A. de la Mesa to D. Tillson, Sept. 15, 1866, reel 13; N. S. Hill to W. W. Deane, Oct. 11, 1866, reel 27; M. H. Mathews to D. Tillson, Nov. 17, 1866, reel 28; H. Dodd to F. W. Coleman, Nov. 24, 1866, reel 14; W. M. Haslett to D. Tillson, Dec. 17, 1866,

reel 27, BRFAL-Ga (M798); *Columbus Daily Enquirer*, Sept. 4, 30, Oct. 16, 1866; *New York Times* [n.d.], quoted in *Macon Daily Telegraph*, Nov. 13, 1866.

93. M. H. Mathews to D. Tillson, Nov. 17, 1866, reel 28; E. M. L. Ehlers to E. Pickett, Jan. 4, 1867, reel 30, BRFAL-Ga (M798).

94. W. W. Deane to J. C. Swayze, Feb. 5, 1866, reel 1; W. W. Deane to M. P. Wingfield, Mar. 15, 1866, reel 2; J. R. Lyle to D. Tillson, Oct. 4, 1866, reel 27; T. F. Forbes to J. R. Lyle, Oct. 6, 1866, reel 3; D. Tillson to W. Finch, Oct. 10, 1866; G. Walbridge to J. D. Allen, Nov. 9, 1866, reel 4; Circular No. 12, Dec. 24, 1866, reel 34 (for Tillson's desire to have "indisputable evidence" that the freedpeople would have good homes), BRFAL-Ga (M798). Also see various contracts signed in January and February 1866, vol. 159, Contracts, Augusta Agt, BRFAL-Ga; L. D. Burwell to D. Tillson, Nov. 1, 1866 (and all enclosed contracts), reel 25, BRFAL-Ga (M798).

95. Officials also refused to honor a Bureau discount on fares until Major Gray intervened. W. Gray to D. Tillson, Mar. 14, 1866, reel 27, BRFAL-Ga (M798).

96. D. Tillson, "Report of Operations September 22, 1865, to November 1, 1866," reel 32, BRFAL-Ga (M798).

97. For example, see contract between G. M. Holt and J. H. Phinizy and freedmen, Jan. 15, 1866; contract between G. W. Hancock and Oscar Dennis and freedmen, Feb. 1, 1866, vol. 159, Contracts, Augusta Agt, BRFAL-Ga.

98. Few freedpeople moved beyond the South, however, even during the "exodusters" migration to Kansas. Cohen describes the limits that the rural South placed on the advantages that the freedpeople could gain by moving to better-paying jobs. Still, while ultimately these limits severely restricted black economic advancement, they did not stop the freedpeople from trying to better themselves by using whatever means they could. Brooks, *Agrarian Revolution in Georgia, 1865–1912*, 15–17; Cohen, *At Freedom's Edge*, 60–68, 105, 169–70.

99. D. Tillson to J. L. Donaldson, Jan. 16, 1866, reel 20, (LR)BRFAL (M752). D. Tillson, "Report of Operations September 22, 1865 to November 1, 1866," reel 32, BRFAL-Ga (M798). There were other postwar changes that contributed at least temporarily to the labor shortage, including the desire of freedmen to keep their wives and children out of the fields. Jane L[e] C[onte] H[ardin] to brother, Dec. 13, 1865, Le Conte Family Papers Addition, University of California, Berkeley, Bancroft Library; *Macon Daily Telegraph*, Apr. 19, 1866; Litwack, *Been in the Storm So Long*, 244–45. For a full treatment of the freedwoman's Reconstruction experience see Jones, *Labor of Love*, 44–78.

100. Trowbridge, *The South*, 498.

101. G. H. Pratt to W. W. Deane, Feb. 14, Mar. 1, 1866, reel 28; G. Walbridge to D. Tillson, Feb. 22, 1866, reel 29, BRFAL-Ga (M798). For additional comments on the problem see J. McWhorter to D. Tillson, Jan. 17, 1866, reel 29, BRFAL-Ga (M798); *Sandersville Central Georgian*, Mar. 7, 1866; *Columbus Daily Enquirer*, Mar. 25, 1866;

*Augusta Daily Constitutionalist*, Apr. 4, 1866; *Macon Daily Telegraph*, Apr. 19, 1866; *Rome Weekly Courier*, Sept. 28, 1866; W. S. Thomson to [W. A. Thomson], July 27, 1866, William Sydnor Thomson Papers, Emory University, Atlanta. Bureau surgeon George Dalton noted at the beginning of 1867 that there had been an exodus from the Albany area. G. O. Dalton to J. V. De Hanne, Feb. 7, 1867, reel 1, ULR, Surgeon's Records, BRFAL-Ga.

102. The Georgia Bureau would allow these individuals to recruit workers if they hired them at the agency's prescribed rate and absorbed the cost of transportation because the agency had no intention of hampering the freedpeople's right to responsible freedom of movement. W. W. Deane to D. C. Poole, Jan. 20, 1866, reel 1, BRFAL-Ga (M798).

103. D. Tillson to Bvt. Maj. Gen. J. L. Donaldson, reel 20, (LR)BRFAL (M752); W. W. Deane to D. C. Poole, Jan. 20, 1866, reel 1; W. W. Deane to F. J. Robinson, Mar. 23, 1866, reel 2, BRFAL-Ga (M798). That influence appeared to be insufficient, at least in the case of the Central Railroad, whose president "respectfully" declined giving reduced fares. W. W. Wodly to D. Tillson, Apr. 16, 1866, reel 29, BRFAL-Ga (M798).

104. Apparently, Tillson was being cautious with the renewed transportation effort; on October 29, Howard's office issued brief guidelines for requesting transportation with no reference made as to whether these requests were to be confined to in-state movement. D. Tillson to W. Finch, Oct. 10, 1866, reel 4; S. Eldridge, Circular Letter, Oct. 29, 1866, reel 34; endorsement of D. Tillson to O. O. Howard, Dec. 18, 1866, reel 8; D. Tillson, "Report of Operations September 22, 1865 to November 1, 1866," reel 32; Circular No. 12, Dec. 24, 1866, reel 34, BRFAL-Ga (M798); Cohen, *At Freedom's Edge*, 72.

In November, the Bureau had temporarily suspended transportation issuances because of abuses perpetrated by those to whom the agency issued them and because railroads refused to recognize the agency's general transportation orders. Also, at least one railroad official complained that the railroads were bearing the burden of labor relocation because the government's rates were too low and payment even at these rates failed to arrive promptly. G. Walbridge to G. R. Campbell, Nov. 9, 1866; E. Pickett to Willy & Whitehead, Nov. 20, 1866, reel 4; R. S. Rhodes to O. O. Howard, Nov. 29, 1866, reel 28, BRFAL-Ga (M798).

105. C. C. Sibley to Col. J. A. Mower, Jan. 24, 1867, reel 4, BRFAL-Ga (M798). Also see J. Davison to D. Tillson, Jan. 14, 1867; T. W. White to C. C. Sibley, Feb. 1, 1867, reel 30; E. Pickett to J. M. McClintock, Feb. 1, 1867, reel 4, BRFAL-Ga (M798); J. M. Harris to G. L. Eberhart, Feb. 18, 1867, reel 8, (Ed)BRFAL-Ga (M799).

106. Testimony of W. C. Morrill, Nov. 6, 1871, Ku Klux Conspiracy, vol. 7: *Georgia*, 1098. Morrill served as a Bureau agent in southwest Georgia from April 1868 through December 1868. Station Books, vol. 1, 1867–1868, BRFAL-Ga (M798).

107. In January 1870, O. O. Howard's chief education officer observed that freedpeople from central Georgia were "rapidly going" to plantations in the Mississippi valley. J. W. Alvord to O. O. Howard, Jan. 18, 22, 1870, in John W. Alvord, *Letters from the*

*South*, 19, 27. Also see O. H Howard to E. Pickett, Aug. 26, 1867 (and endorsements), box 3, LR, Albany Agt; J. S. Dunning to F. Mosebach, Sept. 7, 1867, box 7, LR, Atlanta SAC, BRFAL-Ga; *LaGrange Reporter*, Mar. 1, 1867, quoted in *Savannah Daily Republican*, Mar. 6, 1867; W. S. Thomson to [W. A. Thomson], Feb. 12, 1867, William Sydnor Thomson Papers; testimony of H. M. Turner, Nov. 3, 1871, Ku Klux Conspiracy, vol. 7: *Georgia*, 1042; Cohen, *At Freedom's Edge*, 249–52.

108. G. H. Pratt to D. Tillson, Jan. 15, 1866, reel 29, BRFAL-Ga (M798).

109. W. H. Mattox to C. J. Jenkins, Feb. 16, 1866, box 53, Executive Department Correspondence, GDAH.

110. H. Dodd to F. W. Coleman, Nov. 24, 1866, box 21, LR, Macon SAC, BRFAL-Ga. Also see G. Walbridge to D. Tillson, Dec. 14, 1866, reel 14, BRFAL-Ga (M798).

111. H. Cobb Jr. to [Howell Cobb], Jan. 3, 1866, Cobb-Erwin-Lamar Collection, University of Georgia.

112. *Turnwold Countryman* [n.d.], quoted in *Augusta Daily Constitutionalist*, Apr. 17, 1866.

113. *Macon Telegraph*, [n.d.], quoted in *Columbus Daily Enquirer*, Mar. 23, 1866. Clearly, in Howell Cobb Jr.'s case Bureau-supported competition forced an employer to rethink his approach to labor. John Cobb, fearful of losing workers to labor brokers, urged his father to make certain that Tillson had approved his contracts. Other Georgians urged their neighbors to work harder at retaining black labor by making working conditions better for the freedpeople. Later in 1868 Agent Morrill discovered that reducing the number of freedpeople in Schley County had the effect of convincing the whites there to treat the freedpeople better. J. A. Cobb to [H. Cobb], Feb. 22, 1866, Howell Cobb Papers; *Newnan Herald*, [n.d.], quoted in *Columbus Daily Sun*, Nov. 4, 1866; *Columbus Daily Sun*, Nov. 29, 1866; Testimony of W. C. Morrill, Nov. 6, 1871, Ku Klux Conspiracy, vol. 7: *Georgia*, 1098.

Tillson's concerns for the sanctity of legitimate contracts made no allowances for labor agents' enticing away hands bound by legitimate contracts, and the Georgia legislature passed a law in December 1866 that made it a misdemeanor to entice away servants already legitimately employed. *Acts of the General Assembly of the State of Georgia, Passed in Milledgeville, at the Annual Session, in November and December, 1866*, 153–54.

114. G. H. Pratt to D. Tillson, Jan. 15, 1866; A. T. Reeve to D. Tillson, Jan. 31, 1866, reel 28, BRFAL-Ga (M798); H. Dodd to F. W. Coleman, Nov. 24, 1866, box 21, LR, Macon SAC, BRFAL-Ga.

115. J. W. Arnold, Mar. 7, 1866, reel 11, BRFAL-Ga (M798).

116. W. Gray to D. Tillson, Mar. 14, 1866, reel 27, BRFAL-Ga (M798). An army officer not associated with the Bureau believed that the "orderly and well-disposed" citizens of Putnam County had been "considerably provoked of late" by labor contractors who tried to entice away freedpeople with legitimate contracts. The editor of the *Turnwold Countryman* believed Gray's report was exaggerated and argued that any "restive"

individuals that Gray encountered were justified in resisting with what he believed to be "unauthorized and illegal interference" with valid contracts. Lt. G. W. Graffam to Lt. C. E. Moore, Mar. 27, 1866, LR, Dept. of Ga.; *Turnwold Countryman*, Apr. 3, 1866.

117. J. C. Swayze to Wiley [Goodman], Mar. 23, 1866; G. H. Pratt to W. Goodman, Mar. 26, 1866, box 20, LR, Jackson Agt, BRFAL-Ga.

118. Affidavit of Harriett Hill, enclosed in C. Axt to D. Tillson, Feb. 5, 1866, reel 25, BRFAL-Ga (M798).

119. *Columbus Daily Enquirer*, June 26, 1866.

120. *Macon Daily Telegraph*, May 10, 1866.

121. *New York Times* [n.d.] quoted in *Macon Daily Telegraph*, Nov. 13, 1866. Also see *Macon Daily Telegraph*, Oct. 25, 1866; *Columbus Daily Sun*, Nov. 4, 29, 1866.

122. As early as January 1866, the *New York Times* was printing accusations that Tillson had forced freedpeople to break their contracts and emigrate to Mississippi against their will. In November 1866, Tillson warned O. O. Howard that if the Georgia Bureau resorted to supplying transportation to indigent freedpeople to move them to jobs out of state, he would "certainly" be accused of fraud; in other words, Tillson understood that any delivery of services that involved shifting funds from one place to another was an obvious target of public scrutiny. D. Tillson to O. O. Howard, Feb. 12, 1866, reel 20; D. Tillson to O. O. Howard, Nov. 18, 1866; J. Abbott to D. Tillson, Dec. 4, 1866, reel 37, (LR)BRFAL (M752); O. O. Howard to D. Tillson, Nov. 7, 1866, reel 2, (RI)BRFAL (M742); R. S. Rhodes to O. O. Howard, Nov. 29, 1866, reel 28; Affidavit of J. C. Swayze, Dec. 4, 1866, reel 29; D. Tillson to C. J. Jenkins, Dec. 4, 1866, reel 4, BRFAL-Ga (M798).

123. D. Tillson to J. F. Stevens, Jan. 31, 1866, reel 1; W. W. Deane to M. P. Wingfield, Mar. 15, 1866, reel 2; D. Tillson to J. R. Lyle, Oct. 2, 1866, reel 3; G. Walbridge to J. D. Allen, Nov. 9, 1866, reel 4, BRFAL-Ga (M798); D. Tillson to O. O. Howard, Feb. 12, 1866, reel 20, (LR) BRFAL (M752).

124. D. Breck to D. Tillson, Mar. 7, 1866 (including all endorsements and enclosures), reel 13, BRFAL-Ga (M798).

125. Civilian agents collected up to five dollars a hand as well as a fee for approving their contracts. Brien Maguire of Wilkes County, for example, made $170 recruiting thirty-three hands for an employer with the approval of Tillson's office. For examples of Tillson's supervisory efforts see W. Gray to J. Jones, Jan. 23, 1866, reel 1, 1866; D. C. Poole to D. Tillson, Feb. 4, 1866, reel 13; J. Leonard to W. W. Deane, Sept. 17, 1866; J. Leonard to E. Pickett, Oct. 31, 1866, reel 27, BRFAL-Ga (M798).

126. A. J. White to D. Tillson, Nov. 6, 1866, reel 29; G. Walbridge to Capt. G. R. Campbell, Nov. 9, 1866; D. Tillson to W. H. Morgan, Dec. 3, 1866, reel 4, BRFAL-Ga (M798).

127. D. Tillson to D. C. Poole, Feb. 7, 1866, reel 1; D. C. Poole to D. Tillson, Feb. 24, 1866 (and all enclosures and endorsements), reel 13; W. W. Deane to J. Leonard, Sept. 8, 1866, reel 3; J. Leonard to W. W. Deane, Sept. 17, 1866, reel 27; T. F. Forbes to J. R. Lyle, Oct. 6, 1866; D. Tillson to J. Leonard, Oct. 6, 1866; D. Tillson to N. S. Hill, Oct. 9,

1866, reel 3; W. W. Deane to J. R. Lyle, Oct. 14, 15, 1866, reel 4, BRFAL-Ga (M798); F. D. Sewall to O. O. Howard, Dec. 15, 1865, reel 39, (LR)BRFAL-Ga (M752); D. Tillson to E. M. L. Ehlers, Oct. 9, box 19, ULR, Griffin SAC; E. Pickett to N. S. Hill, Nov. 12, 1866; N. S. Hill to E. Pickett, Nov. 14, 1866, box 21, LR, Macon SAC, BRFAL-Ga.

128. Registers of Civilian Agents, 1865–1867, reel 35; C. Peeples to D. Tillson, Sept. 15, 1866, reel 28; J. C. Swayze to D. Tillson, July 18 (and all enclosures), Nov. 15, Dec. 27, 1866, reel 29; G. Walbridge to G. Campbell, Nov. 9, 1866, reel 4; A. J. White to D. Tillson, Nov. 6, 1866, reel 29; E. M. L. Ehlers to Capt. E. Pickett, Dec. 2, 1866; E. M. L. Ehlers to G. R. Walbridge, Dec. 5, 1866 (and all enclosures); G. R. Walbridge to D. Tillson, Dec. 14, 1866, reel 14; E. Pickett to J. C. Swayze, Dec. 17, 1866, reel 4; G. R. Walbridge to J. C. Swayze, Feb. 25, 1867, reel 5, BRFAL-Ga; *Augusta Daily Constitutionalist*, Aug. 9, 1866; *Griffin Herald*, Dec. 12, 1866, quoted in *Columbus Daily Sun*, Dec. 15, 1866. For a discussion of Swayze's post-Bureau career, see Abbott, "Jason Clarke Swayze."

129. F. D. Sewall to O. O. Howard, Dec. 6, 15, 1866, reel 39, (LR)BRFAL (M752); O. O. Howard to D. Tillson, Dec. 20, 1866, Howard Papers. Tillson had opened his records to Sewall and had become frustrated over what he believed was the inspecting officer's inability to understand the situation. Ruth Currie-McDaniel argues that Tillson was the source of the abuse of transportation in Georgia based on Sewall's report, because there were implications that Tillson knew about irregularities and might have benefited from his position. There is no evidence of wrongdoing on Tillson's part, a conclusion with which William Cohen's findings concur. Currie-McDaniel also misses the fact that Howard still believed labor redistribution was useful. Howard must have believed that the benefits of transporting freedpeople to good jobs outweighed any of the problems connected with the process; shortly after receiving Sewall's recommendations, he promulgated new guidelines for continuing the redistribution of destitute laborers. Currie-McDaniel, *Carpetbagger of Conscience*, 73; Cohen, *At Freedom's Edge*, 66, 72.

130. J. J. Knox to W. M. Brown, July 5, 1867, vol. 169, LS, Athens SAC, BRFAL-Ga.

131. O. H. Howard, Circular to the Freedmen of Dougherty, Lee, and Terrell Counties, June 10, 1867, reel 20, BRFAL-Ga (M798). Also see O. H. Howard to the Freedmen in the Subdistrict of Albany, Jan. 17, 1868, reel 20, BRFAL-Ga (M798).

132. O. H. Howard, Circular to the Freedmen of Dougherty, Lee, and Terrell Counties, June 10, 1867, reel 20, BRFAL-Ga (M798). Also see O. H. Howard to T. Willingham, Apr. 6, 1867, vol. 121, LS, Albany Agt, BRFAL-Ga.

133. W. F. White to J. J. Bradford, Mar. 1, 16, 1867, vol. 381, LS, Thomasville SAC, BRFAL-Ga. Also see Alvin B. Clark to J. Hodges, Apr. 13, 1867, vol. 334, LS, Quitman Agt, BRFAL-Ga.

134. C. C. Hicks to O. H. Howard, Jan. 3, 1868, vol. 122, LS, Albany Agt, BRFAL-Ga.

135. Endorsement of M. F. Gallagher, Feb. 3, 1868, on J. J. Knox to M. F. Gallagher, Jan. 22, 1868, box 5, LR, Athens SAC, BRFAL-Ga.

136. W. F. White to J. J. Bradford, Mar. 16, 1867, vol. 381, LS, Thomasville SAC, BRFAL-Ga.

137. C. A. de la Mesa to C. B. Blacker, May 25, 1868, vol. 342, LS, Rome SAC, BRFAL-Ga.

138. W. F. White to J. J. Bradford, Mar. 16, 1867, vol. 381, LS, Thomasville SAC; Alvin B. Clark to H. B. Holliday, Apr. 13, 1867, vol. 334, LS, Quitman Agt; endorsement of F. A. H. Gaebel on contract between D. L. Ferguson and freedmen, May 19, 1867, enclosed in F. A. H. Gaebel to E. Pickett, May 20, 1867, box 1, LR, Albany SAC; endorsement of E. Pickett, June 8, 1867, on G. Wagner to J. R. Lewis, June 6, 1867, box 14, ULR, Columbus SAC; endorsement of M. F. Gallagher, Feb. 3, 1868, on J. J. Knox to M. F. Gallagher, Jan. 22, 1868, box 5, LR, Athens SAC, BRFAL-Ga; F. Mosebach, Circular No. 1, Jan. 13, 1868, in F. Mosebach, Report of Orders and Circulars, Jan. 31, 1868, reel 20, BRFAL-Ga (M798).

139. C. C. Sibley, Report for February, Mar. 19, 1867, reel 32, BRFAL-Ga (M798).

140. W. S. Thomson to [W. A. Thomson], Mar. 4, 1867, William Sydnor Thomson Papers.

141. C. C. Sibley, Report for February, Mar. 19, 1867, reel 32, BRFAL-Ga (M798). John R. Lewis had earlier concluded that the old fee system, abolished now in the early part of 1867, had discouraged planters from bringing contracts to Bureau agents for approval, but even with Sibley's reorganization in place and Georgia's fee system discontinued, planters continued to show their reluctance to have the Yankee Bureau tamper with their work arrangements. J. R. Lewis to O. O. Howard, Nov. 24, 1866, reel 3, BRFAL-Tn (M999).

142. E. Pickett to J. W. Arnold, Feb. 4, 1867; J. R. Lewis to J. M. Hoag, Feb. 27, 1867, reel 5, BRFAL-Ga (M798). It must be emphasized that the Bureau in Sibley's mind remained the judge of what was a fair contract and that there were officers who continued Tillson's practice of trying to secure for dissatisfied freedpeople with unwritten agreements wages comparable to the highest wages in the county. E. M. L. Ehlers to W. B. Moore, Aug. 5, 1867, vol. 152, LS, Augusta SAC, BRFAL-Ga.

143. J. G. H. Waldrop to D. Tillson, Jan. 10, 1867; J. G. Brown to C. C. Sibley, Jan. 28, 1867, reel 30, BRFAL-Ga (M798).

144. Andrew B. Clark, Contract Reports for September and October 1867, box 24, Reports of Contracts, Newton Agt, BRFAL-Ga.

145. C. Raushenberg to E. Pickett, Aug. 20, 1867, box 1, LR, Albany SAC, BRFAL-Ga.

146. F. A. H. Gaebel to E. Pickett, Mar. 8, 1867, reel 14, BRFAL-Ga (M798).

147. Alvin B. Clark, Contract Report for April and May 1867, box 26, Misc. Reports, Quitman Agt, BRFAL-Ga.

148. Andrew B. Clark, Contract Reports for September and October 1867, box 24, Reports of Contracts, Newton Agt, BRFAL-Ga.

149. Circular Letter, January 1, 1868, reel 344, BRFAL-Ga (M798); C. Raushenberg to O. H. Howard, Sept. 1, 1868, vol. 124, LS, Albany Agt, BRFAL-Ga.

150. D. Losey, Contract Report for November 1868; Contract Report for December 1868, box 25, Reports Rec'd, Perry Agt, BRFAL-Ga.

151. D. G. Risley to C. C. Sibley, June 24, 1867, reel 19, BRFAL-Ga (M798).

152. Contracts between John M. McCrary and freedmen, Aug. 9, 1865, McCrary Papers; G. J. Orr and freedmen, Aug. 14, 1865, Orr Family Papers; Nathan Bussey and freedmen, Aug. 5, 1865; Richard Powell and freedmen, Aug. 7, 1865, vol. 159, Contracts, Augusta Agent; John Hamilton and Jack, Aug. 10, 1865, box 32, Records of the Asst. Adj. Gen., Savannah SAC, BRFAL-Ga. For examples of planters who encountered freedpeople who insisted on dealing directly with them in the contracting process, see T. J. Mount to J. A. Cobb, Aug. 27, 1865, Cobb-Erwin-Lamar Collection, and Leigh, *Ten Years on a Georgia Plantation*, 85–90.

153. This generalization is based on a complete reading of the Georgia Freedmen's Bureau files. The Georgia Bureau did not preserve a complete record of all the contracts that its agents supervised, unlike some other state Bureaus, and the contract record tends to favor some counties over others. Eric Foner notes that this development in contracting was encouraged by the Freedmen's Bureau's insistence on dealing with heads of households. Indeed, the printed form contracts that some agents and officers used seemed to be designed to suit such arrangements. However, as Fanny Butler learned in 1869, the freedmen had something to do with this shift as they insisted on being given individual contracts. Foner notes that black men were at this time asserting themselves as heads of households. By the end of the Reconstruction era on the Barrow plantation in Oglethorpe County, for example, freedpeople found the control of a foreman "irksome, each man feeling the very natural desire to be his own 'boss,' and to farm himself." Workers then moved their houses onto their plots of land, breaking up the old slave quarters. But if freedpeople were accepting the economic individuality that was part of the free-labor message, sufficient ties remained to hold together their communities. Churches and schools, for example, required group action and projected powerful community identities. Even less formal community functions like the Saturday night frolic acted as social glue. Leigh, *Ten Years on a Georgia Plantation*, 127; *Scribner's Monthly*, April 1881, 830–36; Georgia Writers' Project, *Drums and Shadows*, 100; Eric Foner, *Reconstruction*, 86–88.

154. The literature on the rise of sharecropping and tenant farming and the debate concerning their relationship to market forces and race is extensive, but see Woodman, "Sequel to Slavery: The New History Views the Postbellum South"; Woodman, "Economic Reconstruction and the Rise of the New South, 1865–1900"; Higgs, *Competition and Coercion;* Ransom and Sutch, *One Kind of Freedom: The Economic Consequences of Emancipation*; Royce, *The Origins of Southern Sharecropping*; Jaynes, *Branches without Roots*. Jaynes is correct in noting that various types of share arrangements or payments were common by 1866 and that because of credit conditions few employers could pay their workers on a weekly or monthly schedule (45–53). Freedpeople might have initially favored wages paid on a more frequent basis than the postharvest payments

noted by Jaynes because of the flexibility and control over their lives that cash in the pocket could give the freedpeople. However, in Georgia, when circumstances made this type of arrangement impracticable, freedpeople proved to be quite adaptable and saw some value in being able to claim shares of their employers' crops.

155. Rawick, *American Slave*, vol. 12: *Georgia*, pt. 1, 181–82.

156. E. W. Douglas to S. Hunt, Feb. 1, 1866, reel 1, AMA-Ga.

157. O. O. Howard to Secty of War J. Schofield, Oct. 24, 1868, reel 5, (RI)BRFAL (M742).

158. *Columbus Sun* [n.d.], reprinted in *Macon Daily Telegraph*, Oct. 10, 1865. Also see Rawick, *American Slave*, vol. 8: *Arkansas*, pt. 1, 68.

159. H. Cobb to wife [Mary A. Cobb], [Dec. 1865], Howell Cobb Papers. Also see C. C. Jones Jr. to Mary S. Mallard, Jan. 2, 1867, in Myers, *Children of Pride*, 1366.

160. Contract between Angus Gillus and Moses, Jan. 31, 1866, box 31, Emanuel County Contracts, Savannah SAC, BRFAL-Ga.

161. Contract between J. G. Cone and John Cone, Jan. 1, 1866, box 31, Bullock County Contracts, Savannah SAC, BRFAL-Ga.

162. J. W. Arnold to [W. W. Deane], Dec. 22, 1966, reel 25, BRFAL-Ga (M798).

163. W. E. Wiggins to T. D. Elliot, Dec. 30, 1867, vol. 288, LS, LaGrange Agt, BRFAL-Ga. Wiggins believed the freedpeople to be ignorant as well as distrustful, but he did believe that the Bureau's presence was reassuring, and he kept the freedpeople at work.

164. W. B. Moore to H. Catley, May 31, 1868, reel 21, BRFAL-Ga (M798).

165. W. L. Clark, Contract Report for November 1868, box 11, Misc. Reports, Bainbridge Agt, BRFAL-Ga. Also see Andrew B. Clark, Contract Report for January 1868, box 24, Reports of Contracts, Newton Agt; H. Catley, Contract Report for February 1868, Contract Report for May 1868, box 9, Reports on Contracts, Augusta SAC; G. R. Ballou, Contract Report for September 1868, box 16, Contract Reports, Cuthbert Agt; D. Losey, Contract Report for October 1868, box 25, Reports Rec'd, Perry Agt, BRFAL-Ga.

166. By early January 1868, John Dent argued that shares placed the planter in a precarious position, trusting the freedpeople to stay the season while advancing them necessities, the balance of which could dissolve into a loss if the freedpeople abandoned the crop. He argued for the use of money wages, but noted that "the freedmen wont listen to it." *Dent Journals*, vol. 7, Jan. 4, 1868, reel 1. Of sixty-five contracts examined primarily from the Bureau records for the 1867 season, twenty-seven stipulated wages and twenty-nine stipulated some form of share arrangements. Of thirty-seven contracts examined for the 1868 season, twenty-three stipulated some form of share arrangements. Although this sample of contracts is small, it suggests a trend that is clarified by contract reports from various officers and agents of the Bureau. In the Augusta subdistrict, during March and April 1867, of the 934 employees represented by 229 registered contracts, 545 were working for wages and 620 for shares. In the Thomasville subdistrict

for the same two months, most of the contracts promised the freedpeople a part of the crop. In Alvin B. Clark's southern Georgia jurisdiction, of the 169 employees listed on contracts registered during January 1868, only seven worked for wages; in February, out of an additional 141 hands, only three had agreed to accept wages. And on February 1, 1868, William O. Moffit, the agent in charge of Johnson and Emanuel Counties, reported that of the 160 employees for whom he had approved contracts, three-fourths were working for a part of the crop. As noted, freedpeople generally interpreted any kind of share arrangement as giving them a special claim on the crop; planters, of course, would not concede to this view, and most probably continued to claim complete control of the crops their workers tended. W. F. Martins, Contract Reports for March and April 1867, box 9, Reports on Contracts, Augusta SAC; W. F. White, Contract Reports for March and April 1867, box 34, Reports and Misc. Papers, Thomasville SAC; Alvin B. Clark, Contract Reports for January and February 1868, box 26, Misc. Reports, Quitman Agt; W. O. Moffit to J. M. Hoag, Feb. 1, 1868, vol. 188, LS, Bartow Agt, BRFAL-Ga. Also see D. Losey, Contract Reports for January, February, March, and April 1868, box 25, Reports Rec'd, Perry Agt, BRFAL-Ga.

167. F. A. H. Gaebel to W. W. Deane, May 23, 1866, reel 27, BRFAL-Ga (M798).

168. J. L[e] C[onte] H[arden] to brother, Dec. 13, 1865, Le Conte Family Papers Addition.

169. O'Neal and Liles to A. B. Clark, Nov. 1, 1867, box 26, LR, Quitman Agt, BRFAL-Ga.

170. O. H. Howard, Report for August, Sept. 19, 1868, reel 58, (LR)BRFAL (M752).

171. F. J. Foster to D. Tillson, Dec. 19, 1866, reel 26, BRFAL-Ga (M798).

172. Andrew B. Clark to O. H. Howard, May 23, 1868, box 15, LR, Cuthbert Agt, BRFAL-Ga.

173. Endorsement of M. F. Gallagher, Jan. 17, 1868, on J. J. Knox to M. F. Gallagher, Jan. 14, 1868, box 5, LR, Athens SAC, BRFAL-Ga.

174. J. M. Gatewood to D. Tillson, Jan. 29, 1866, reel 27, BRFAL-Ga (M798); P. E. Arnold to G. R. Walbridge, Mar. 19, 1866, box 7, LR, Atlanta SAC; F. Mosebach to W. A. Adams, Apr. 12, 1867, vol. 223, LS, Columbus SAC; E. M. L. Ehlers to E. Pickett, July 11, 1867 (and endorsement), box 9, ULR, Augusta SAC; C. Raushenberg to W. P. Pierce, Feb. 17, 1868; C. Raushenberg to J. W. Flint, Mar. 6, 1868, vol. 124; O. H. Howard to D. A. Vason, Mar. 11, 1867; O. H. Howard to C. P. Sibley, Mar. 25, 1867, vol. 121; O. H. Howard, Order, June 17, 1868, vol. 122, LS, Albany Agt; Andrew B. Clark to T. W. Fleming, May 13, 1868, vol. 323, LS, Newton Agt, BRFAL-Ga. When freedpeople wrongly left an employer, agents sought assistance from their colleagues in other jurisdictions to force their return to their rightful employers. C. Raushenberg to W. P. Pierce, Feb. 17, 1868, vol. 124, LS; Andrew B. Clark to O. H. Howard, May 27, 1867, box 3, LR, Albany Agt, BRFAL-Ga.

175. O. H. Howard, Report for August, Sept. 19, 1868, reel 58, (LR)BRFAL (M752).

176. Endorsement of O. H. Howard, Apr. 9, 1867, on affidavit of Henry Bright, Apr. 1, 1867, box 1, LR, Albany SAC, BRFAL-Ga.

177. G. R. Ballou, Contract Report, August 1868, box 16, Misc. Rec'd, Cuthbert Agt, BRFAL-Ga.

178. Tillson and his successors always believed that the freedpeople had first claim on the crops they had worked. This was important since it meant that the Bureau worked to see that the freedpeople were paid before all other creditors. Unfortunately, it was also a policy that might have encouraged creditors to drag their cases before county courts in order to circumvent the Bureau's requirements. In 1873 the Georgia legislature gave the first lien to landlords. Endorsement of E. Pickett, Nov. 21, 1866, on J. H. Taylor to [D. Tillson], Nov. 8, 1866, reel 13; endorsement of E. Pickett on C. M. Pope to D. Tillson, Nov. 26, 1866, reel 8; C. A. de la Mesa to C. C. Sibley, Dec. 19, 1867, reel 17, BRFAL-Ga (M798); endorsement of E. Pickett, Nov. 20, 1866, on T. W. White to D. Tillson, Nov. 17, 1866, box 24, LR, Milledgeville Agt; Alvin B. Clark to H. B. Holiday, Apr. 13, 1867, vol. 334, LS, Quitman Agt; Andrew B. Clark to O. H. Howard, Nov. 27, 1867, box 24, LR, Newton Agt; endorsement of F. A. H. Gaebel, July 20, 1867, on C. Raushenberg to F. A. H. Gaebel, July 20, 1867, box 1, LR, Albany SAC; O. H. Howard to Whom It May Concern, Aug. 15, 1867, vol. 122, LS; endorsement of J. R. Lewis to O. H. Howard, Sept. 13, 1867, on O. H. Howard to E. Pickett, Sept. 7, 1867; O. H. Howard to C. C. Hicks, Dec. 7, 1867, box 3, LR, Albany Agt; A. Leers to J. M. Hoag, Sept. 30, 1868, box 28, ULR, Savannah SAC, BRFAL-Ga; Drago, *Black Politicians*, 122.

179. For example of planters discharging or refusing to sign contracts with freed-people because of their Republican politics, see J. W. Duer to E. Hulbert, Oct. 30, 1867; G. H. Clower to J. R. Lewis, Nov. 26, 1867, reel 17; C. C. Sibley, Report for October, Nov. 11, 1867, reel 32, BRFAL-Ga (M798); J. W. Barney to J. J. Knox, Nov. 13, 1867, vol. 211, LS, Carnesville Agt; L. L. Wheelock to J. M. Hoag, Nov. [—], 1867, box 28, ULR, Savannah SAC; H. W. Kearsing to C. C. Sibley, June 8, 1868, vol. 188, LS, Bartow Agt; J. L. H. Waldrop to F. Mosebach, Oct. 28, 1868, vol. 280, LS, Jonesboro Agt, BRFAL-Ga; J. Leonard to J. R. Lewis, Aug. 26, 1868, reel 58, (LR)BRFAL (M752).

180. For comments on the bad weather that hurt agriculture during Tillson's administration see W. F. Martins to D. Tillson, July 25, 1866; W. Mitchell to D. Tillson, Aug. 31, 1866, reel 28; J. L. H. Waldrop to D. Tillson, Aug. 17, 1866, reel 29; J. Davison to D. Tillson, Sept. 3, 1866, reel 26, BRFAL-Ga (M798); Thompson, *Reconstruction in Georgia: Economic, Social, Political, 1865–1872*, 74–75; Conway, *Reconstruction of Georgia*, 121–22.

181. Circular No. 8, July 17, 1866, reel 34, BRFAL-Ga (M798); S. Crawford to D. Tillson, June 28, 1866, reel 13; J. C. Swayze to D. Tillson, July 20, 1866, reel 29; W. C. Brantly to D. Tillson, July 25, 1866, reel 25; T. F. Forbes to C. R. More, July 18, 1866; E. Pickett to L. Collins, July 23, 1866; T. F. Forbes to A. J. Miller, Aug. 8, 1866; T. F. Forbes to H. Loring, Aug. 11, 1866; T. F. Forbes to J. M. Brightwell, Aug. 11, 1866; T. F. Forbes to J. T. Reade, Sept. 17, 1866; T. F. Forbes to J. W. Brinson, Sept. 21, 1866; T. F. Forbes to J. Neil, Sept. 24, 1866; E. Pickett to B. McGuire, Sept. 24, 1866; E. Pickett to Mrs. Lampkin, Sept. 26, 1866, reel 3, BRFAL-Ga (M798).

182. P. J. O'Rourke to J. R. Lewis, Dec. 4, 1868, reel 30, BRFAL-Ga (M798). For other examples of similar lay-by problems during 1867 and 1868 see Sgt. J. L. LeRoy to C. C. Sibley, July 12, 1867, reel 18; J. R. Lewis to W. B. Moor, Aug. 8, 1867, reel 6; endorsement of C. N. Holcombe, Aug. 22, 1867, on W. A. Way to C. C. Sibley, Aug. 11, 1867, reel 19; E. Belcher to C. C. Sibley, Sept. 11, 1867, reel 17; M. S. Whalen to M. F. Gallagher, June 26, 1868, reel 21; J. H. Sullivan to H. Catley, Oct. 31, 1868, reel 23, P. I. O'Rourke to J. R. Lewis, Dec. 4, 1868, reel 30, BRFAL-Ga (M798); O. H. Howard to J. McCullum, July 5, 1867 (and several other letters around this date), vol. 122; C. Raushenberg to W. C. Goodwin, Aug. 31, 1868; C. Raushenberg to O. H. Howard, Sept. 1, 1868, vol. 124, LS, Albany Agt; affidavit of Ben Brown, Sept. 20, 1867, box 33, LR, Thomasville SAC; affidavit of Edward Neils, Sept. 4, 1867, box 19, Misc. Papers, Halcyondale Agt; Andrew Clark to B. Keaton, Nov. 23, 1867, vol. 322, LS, Newton Agt; H. G. Flournoy to T. D. Elliot, Jan. 9, 1868, vol. 171, LS, Athens Agt; H. W. Kearsing to H. F. Brownson, July 31, 1868, vol. 188, LS, Bartow Agt; G. Ballou, Report for October 1868, box 16, Misc. Contract Reports, Cuthbert Agt, BRFAL-Ga.

183. Affidavit of Henderson Crawford, Apr. 11, 1866, reel 11; C. A. de la Mesa to D. Tillson, July 18, Dec. 11, 1866, reel 26; J. G. Brown to D. Tillson, July 11, 1866, reel 25; affidavit of Billy Beltley, Aug. 2, 1866, reel 11; J. H. Taylor to D. Tillson, Oct. 28, 1866, reel 29; J. H. Taylor to D. Tillson, Nov. 8, 1866, reel 13; M. F. Gallagher to G. Wagner, Dec. 27, 1867, reel 6, BRFAL-Ga (M798); W. F. White to J. Reynolds, Nov. 16, 1866, vol. 151, LS; W. F. White to E. Pickett, Nov. 19, 1866, box 9, ULR, Augusta SAC; W. F. White, Contract Report for July 1867, box 34, Reports and Misc. Papers, Thomasville SAC; F. C. Genth to C. C. Sibley, Jan. 2, 1868, vol. 258, LS; F. C. Genth to M. F. Gallagher, Jan. 28, 29, 1868, box 18, LR, Fort Gaines Agt, BRFAL-Ga.

184. E. M. L. Ehlers to E. Pickett, May 23, box 9, LR, Augusta SAC, BRFAL-Ga; E. M. L. Ehlers, Augusta Subdistrict, Circular No. 1, May 27, 1867, reel 4, BRFAL-Ga (M798).

185. H. M. Loyless to D. Tillson, Aug. 13, 1866, reel 27, BRFAL-Ga (M798).

186. H. de F. Young to M. F. Gallagher, Oct. 16, 1868, reel 23, BRFAL-Ga (M798).

187. O'Neal and Liles to Alvin B. Clark, July 23, 1867, box 26, LR, Quitman Agt; G. R. Ballou to M. F. Gallagher, July 1, 1868, vol. 236, LS, Cuthbert Agt, BRFAL-Ga; O. H. Howard to M. F. Gallagher, Nov. 11, 1868; O. H. Howard to C. C. Sibley, Nov. 19, 1868, reel 58, (LR)BRFAL (M752).

188. G. Walbridge to D. Tillson, July 30, 1866, filed with J. C. Swayze to D. Tillson, July 18, 1866, reel 27; D. Tillson, "Report of Operations September 21, 1865 to November 11, 1866," reel 32, BRFAL-Ga (M798); O'Neal and Liles to Alvin B. Clark, July 23, 1867, box 26, LR, Quitman Agt, BRFAL-Ga; O. H. Howard to M. F. Gallagher, Nov. 11, 1868, reel 58, (LR)BRFAL (M752).

189. J. D. Ashton to [W. F.] Martins, Dec. 6, 1866, reel 37, BRFAL-Ga (M798). Also see O'Neal and Liles to Alvin B. Clark, July 23, 1867, box 26, LR, Quitman Agt, BRFAL-Ga.

190. G. R. Ballou to M. F. Gallagher, July 1, 1868, vol. 236, LS, Cuthbert Agt, BRFAL-Ga.

191. This conclusion is based on the records and busy routine of Rome subassistant commissioner Carlos de la Mesa, the repetitive letters to employers written by Albany agent C. C. Hicks, and a general reading of the Bureau files. C. A. de la Mesa to W. W. Smith, Jan. 1, 1868, and several other letters in vol. 342, LS, Rome SAC; C. C. Hicks to W. Vason, Dec. 26, 1867, and numerous letters into 1868 in vol. 122, LS, Albany Agt, BRFAL-Ga.

192. J. Neal to D. Tillson, Apr. 3, 1866, reel 28, BRFAL-Ga (M798); Andrew B. Clark to J. Sapp. Dec. 16, 1867, vol. 322, LS, Newton Agt; C. A. de la Mesa to C. C. Sibley, Apr. 27, 1868, box 26, ULR, Rome Agt; M. Marbach to J. Kilpatrick and W. Baxter, May 20, 1868; M. Marbach to C. Carpenter, Sept. 28, 1868, vol. 390, LS, Waynesboro Agt; A. Pokorny to J. Devine, July 6, 1868, vol. 195, LS, Butler Agt; A. Pokorny to J. Leonard, Oct. 31, 1868, box 14, LR, Columbus SAC, BRFAL-Ga.

193. W. L. Clark to W. F. White, Mar. 19, 1868, box 11, LR, Bainbridge Agt, BRFAL-Ga.

194. W. L. Clark to W. F. White, Mar. 19, 1868; W. L. Clark to C. C. Sibley, May 14, 1868 (and all endorsements, which show the dispute not settled until August), box 11, LR, Bainbridge Agt, BRFAL-Ga. For an example of the Georgia assistant commissioner giving an agent the authority to settle a complaint without the employer present, see endorsement of M. F. Gallagher, May 16, 1868, on W. C. Morrill to M. F. Gallagher, May 8, 1868, box 4, LR, Americus Agt, BRFAL-Ga.

195. Entry for May 20, 1867, Journal, vol. 226, Columbus Agt; C. A. de la Mesa to J. R. Lewis, Sept. 27, 1867, box 26, ULR, Rome SAC; Andrew B. Clark to S. Walton, Nov. 22, 1867, vol. 322; Andrew B. Clark to A. J. Stephens, Jan. 31, 1868, vol. 323, LS, Newton Agt; C. B. Blacker to C. Dodd, Jan. 10, 1868; C. B. Blacker to Monford, Jan. 27, 1868, vol. 214, LS, Cartersville Agt; M. Marbach to W. Barton, Apr. 11, 1868, vol. 390, LS, Waynesboro Agt; W. C. Morrill to M. F. Gallagher, Apr. 30, 1868, box 4, LR, Americus Agt; W. P. Pierce to H. Long, May 7, 1868; W. P. Pierce to O. H. Howard, May 22, 1868, vol. 367, LS; O. H. Howard to W. P. Pierce, May 30, 1868, box 17, Dawson Agt; W. L. Clark to C. C. Sibley, May 14, 1868 (and all endorsements and enclosures), box 11, LR, Bainbridge Agt; O. H. Howard to W. P. Pierce, May 30, 1868, LR, Dawson Agt; A. Pokorny to J. Leonard, Oct. 31, 1868, box 14, LR, Columbus SAC; W. C. Morrill to O. H. Howard, Nov. 30, 1868, box 2, ULR, Albany SAC, BRFAL-Ga; J. H. Sullivan to H. Catley, July 13, 1868, reel 21, BRFAL-Ga (M798); Stearns, *Black Man*, 527.

196. C. A. de la Mesa to D. Tillson, Dec. 11, 1866, reel 26, BRFAL-Ga (M798).

197. T. F. Forbes to S. Peirce, Oct. 1, 1866, reel 3, BRFAL-Ga (M798). Tillson's policy was not an outright ban on peonage, but it would have had that effect if he had been able to enforce it. Also note that the Georgia Bureau's stand on peonage was in effect months before Congress passed its peonage law in March 1867. Foner, *Reconstruction*, 277.

198. E. Pickett to R. J. Triggle, Feb. 19, 1867, reel 5, BRFAL-Ga (M798). Also see J. McWhorter to J. J. Knox, Apr. 8, 1867, box 5, ULR, Athens SAC, BRFAL-Ga.

199. J. Davison to W. W. Deane, June 4, 1866, reel 26, BRFAL-Ga (M798).

200. D. Tillson to J. T. Clarke, Dec. 20, 1866, reel 4, BRFAL-Ga (M798).

201. J. H. Taylor to W. W. Deane, Oct. 28, 1866, reel 29; E. Pickett to J. H. Taylor, Nov. 7, 1866, reel 4, BRFAL-Ga (M798). Also see endorsements of E. Pickett, Dec. 5, 12, 1866, reel 8, BRFAL-Ga (M798).

202. J. M. Beeland to D. Tillson, Apr. 27, May 4, May 6, 1866, reel 25; T. F. Forbes to J. M. Beeland, Apr. 28, 1866, reel 2, BRFAL-Ga (M798). For other examples of Tillson's threats to use military force see T. F. Forbes to T. P. Pease, July 13, 1866; T. F. Forbes to J. M. Dell, July 30, 1866; T. F. Forbes to J. K. Smith, Aug. 1, 1866; T. F. Forbes to M. J. Moody, Aug. 1, 1866; T. F. Forbes to justices of the Inferior Court and sheriff of Tatnall County, Aug. 10, 1866, reel 3; E. Pickett to J. J. Bradford, Nov. 20, 1866, reel 4, BRFAL-Ga (M798).

203. Bvt. Maj. J. O'Neal to E. Pickett, Nov. 5, 1866 (and endorsement), LR, Dist. of Ga.

204. W. W. Deane to Bvt. Maj. Gen. C. R. Woods, Aug. 14, 1866; W. W. Deane to A. Sloane, Oct. 5, 1866, reel 3; C. McC. Lord to W. W. Deane, Oct. 8, 1866, reel 28; A. M. Campbell to D. Tillson, Oct. 8, 1866, reel 25; J. R. Phillips to W. W. Deane, Oct. 16, 1866, reel 28, BRFAL-Ga (M798); D. Tillson to E. Foster and A. M. Campbell, Oct. 16, 1866 (copy to O. O. Howard), reel 37, (LR)BRFAL (M752). Needless to say, Henry County residents believed that the Bureau was unjustly persecuting them and protested Tillson's actions. *Columbus Daily Enquirer*, Oct. 14, 1866.

205. G. Walbridge to W. W. Deane, Aug. 4, 1866, reel 29, BRFAL-Ga (M798).

206. For examples of Tillson's responses, see T. F. Forbes to F. Mosebach, Aug. 4, 1866; T. F. Forbes to J. C. De Grafferied, Sept. 17, 1866; T. F. Forbes to F. A. H. Gaebel, Sept. 26, 1866, reel 3, BRFAL-Ga (M798).

207. This generalization of procedures is based on a complete reading of the records of Sibley's agents, but for Sibley's description of how things should proceed see C. C. Sibley to O. O. Howard, Apr. 4, 1867, reel 53, (LR)BRFAL (M752). There were certainly inconsistencies and variations in how agents and officers approached settlement problems, but for an example of Bureau procedure passed from the assistant commissioner's office to an agent, see endorsement of E. Pickett, Apr. 18, 1867, on G. M. Nolan to J. Leonard, Mar. 28, 1867, box 23, LR, McDonough Agt, BRFAL-Ga.

208. C. R. Holcombe to C. C. Sibley, Mar. 23, 1868, reel 20, BRFAL-Ga (M798). Also see C. A. de la Mesa to C. C. Sibley, May 30, 1868, vol. 342, LS, Rome SAC, BRFAL-Ga.

209. F. A. H. Gaebel to E. Pickett, May 16, 1867, reel 14, BRFAL-Ga (M798).

210. C. Raushenberg to M. F. Gallagher, Dec. 4, 1867, reel 19, BRFAL-Ga (M798).

211. W. O. Moffit to C. C. Sibley, Jan. 13, 1868; W. O. Moffit to O. O. Howard, Feb. 1, 1868, vol. 188, LS, Bartow Agt, BRFAL-Ga. Sibley's men had his authorization to seize

and hold crops before the resolution of a settlement if it appeared that an employer was planning to ship them beyond the reach of the complainants and the involved agent. C. C. Sibley to O. O. Howard, Apr. 4, 1866, reel 52, (LR)BRFAL (M752). There were numerous instances of the Bureau's efforts to speed settlements for the freedpeople by threatening or actually seizing crops, but for some additional examples see C. Raushenberg to F. A. H. Gaebel, July 20, 1867 (and endorsements), box 1, LR, Albany SAC; J. L. H. Waldrop to F. Mosebach, Oct. 21, 1867 (and endorsement), box 20, LR, Jonesboro Agt; J. M. Robinson to H. Johnson and Co., Dec. 12, 1867, and other letters dated this month, vol. 136, LS, Americus Agt; H. Catley to H. C. Bryson, Jan. 9, 1868, vol. 152, LS, Augusta SAC; J. Leonard to J. B. Davenport, Jan. 10, 1868, vol. 223, LS, Columbus SAC; W. P. Pierce to G. L. Wallace, Jan. 1, 1868, and other letters dated this month, vol. 367, LS, Dawson Agt; W. F. Martins to W. Wilson, Jan. 24, 1868, vol. 328, LS, Newnan Agt; T. M. Aubry to W. F. Martins, Feb. 22, 1868, box 24, LR, Newton Agt; G. M. Nolan to F. Mosebach, Mar. 2, 1868 (and endorsement), box 23, LR, McDonough Agt; A. Leers to C. C. Sibley, Mar. 25, 1868, vol. 348, LS, Savannah Agt; L. Lieberman to sheriff of Pulaski Co., Apr. 29, 1868, vol. 277, LS, Hawkinsville Agt, BRFAL-Ga; M. F. Gallagher to C. Raushenberg, Nov. 14, 1867; M. F. Gallagher to J. R. Smith, Dec. 20, 1867; M. F. Gallagher to G. Wagner, Dec. 27, 1867, reel 6; M. F. Gallagher to J. M. Robinson, Feb. 24, 1868, reel 7; Andrew B. Clark to M. F. Gallagher, Jan. 15, 1868, reel 20, BRFAL-Ga (M798).

212. F. Mosebach to J. H. Graham, Feb. 28, 1867, vol. 222, LS, Columbus SAC; entry for Jan. 5, 1868, Journal, vol. 226, Columbus Agt, BRFAL-Ga.

213. A. Leers to J. M. Hoag, Sept. 30, 1868, box 28, ULR, Savannah SAC, BRFAL-Ga.

214. A. Leers to C. C. Sibley, Mar. 25, 1868, box 27, LR, Savannah SAC, BRFAL-Ga.

215. E. M. L. Ehlers to O'Dowd and Mulherin, Dec. 13, 1867, vol. 152, LS, Augusta SAC, BRFAL-Ga. For another example see E. M. L. Ehlers to F. Phinizy & Co., Nov. 23, 1867, vol. 152, LS, Augusta SAC, BRFAL-Ga.

216. J. M. Hoag to W. F. White, Feb. 3, 1868, box 34, LR, Thomasville SAC, BRFAL-Ga.

217. C. Raushenberg to M. F. Gallagher, Mar. 4, 1868 (and all endorsements), reel 20, BRFAL-Ga (M798).

218. C. Raushenberg to M. F. Gallagher, Dec. 23, 1867, box 15, LR, Cuthbert Agt; J. Leonard to J. B. Davenport, Jan. 10, 1868, vol. 223, LS, Columbus SAC, BRFAL-Ga; M. F. Gallagher to G. Wagner, Dec. 27, 1867, reel 6, BRFAL-Ga (M798). The Columbus Bureau also kept busy tracking down cotton shipped into the city from Alabama by planters who were trying to avoid paying their workers there. See entries for January and February 1868, Journal, Columbus Agt, BRFAL-Ga; J. B. Healy to Maj. Gen. J. Pope, Nov. 9, 1867, reel 18; M. F. Gallagher to G. Wagner, Nov. 20, 1867, reel 6, BRFAL-Ga (M798). For other examples of this type of activity see D. Losey to N. S. Hill, Dec. 27, 1867, box 25, LR, Perry Agt; C. W. Chapman to A. Pokorny, May 25, 1868, vol. 225, LS, Columbus Agt, BRFAL-Ga; M. F. Gallagher to G. Wagner, Dec. 27,

1867, reel 6; M. F. Gallagher to J. M. Robinson, Feb. 24, 1868, reel 7, BRFAL-Ga (M798).

219. M. F. Gallagher to J. M. Robinson, Feb. 24, 1868, reel 7, BRFAL-Ga (M798); C. C. Sibley to O. O. Howard, Apr. 4, 1868, reel 53, (LR)BRFAL (M752).

220. J. Leonard to N. S. Hill, Dec. 5, 1867; endorsement of J. R. Lewis to J. Leonard, Dec. 18, 1867, on the preceding, box 19, ULR, Griffin SAC, BRFAL-Ga. Sibley reported that on several occasions the military gave him permission to sell crops to satisfy the claims of freedpeople; the district military authorities also confirmed Bureau policy that recognized the freedmen's right to first claim on the crops they raised. C. C. Sibley to O. O. Howard, Apr. 4, 1868, reel 53, (LR)BRFAL (M752); M. F. Gallagher to J. R. Davis, Mar. 20, 1868, reel 7; C. Raushenberg to M. F. Gallagher, Mar. 21, 1868 (and endorsements), reel 20, BRFAL-Ga (M798).

221. H. B. Larson to Alvin B. Clark, Nov. 23, 1867, box 26, LR, Quitman Agt, BRFAL-Ga.

222. C. A. de la Mesa to C. C. Sibley, Dec. 16, 1867, vol. 341; C. A. de la Mesa to C. C. Sibley, Jan. 11, Feb. 11, 1868; C. A. de la Mesa to Bvt. Lt. Col. Ritter, Jan. 11, 1868; F. A. de la Mesa to C. C. Sibley, Jan. 14, 15, 1868, vol. 342, LS, Rome SAC, BRFAL-Ga.

223. Report of Major General G. G. Meade, Oct. 31, 1868, *House Executive Documents*, 40th Cong., 3d sess., no. 1 (serial 1367), 74–75; W. L. Clark to C. C. Sibley, Apr. 28, 1868; endorsement of M. F. Gallagher, May 6, 1868, on the preceding, box 11, LR, Bainbridge Agt; W. L. Clark to W. F. White, May 8, 1868, box 34, LR, Thomasville SAC, BRFAL-Ga.

224. As noted earlier, the army's forces were severely limited and concentrated in Georgia's chief towns. Sefton, *Army and Reconstruction*, 261–62.

225. M. F. Gallagher to Croswell Bros., Feb 7, 1868, reel 7, BRFAL-Ga (M798).

226. T. Holden to E. M. L. Ehlers, July 15, 1867, box 35, LR, Warrenton Agt; D. A. Newsom to C. C. Sibley, Sept. 6, 1867, box 9, ULR, Augusta SAC; D. A. Newsom to C. C. Sibley, Sept. 3, 1867, box 35, LR, Woodville Agt; F. Mosebach to G. M. Nolan, Nov. 2, 1867, vol. 99, LS, Atlanta SAC; Andrew B. Clark to O. H. Howard, Dec. 27, 1867, vol. 322; Andrew B. Clark to M. F. Gallagher, Apr. 15, 1868, vol. 323, LS, Newton Agt; W. P. Pierce to W. G. Parks, Jan. 7, 1868, vol. 367, LS, Dawson Agt; H. Kearsing to J. M. Hoag, June 29, 1868, box 11, LR, Bartow Agt, BRFAL-Ga; M. F. Gallagher to [Cossell] Bros., Feb. 7, 1868, reel 7, BRFAL-Ga (M798).

227. For example, see Max Marbach's lament of how no one in the Waynesboro region paid attention to him or his summonses. M. Marbach to H. Catley, June 2, 1868, reel 21, BRFAL-Ga (M798).

228. F. Mosebach to P. D. Claiborne, Aug. 7, 1868, vol. 99, LS, Atlanta SAC, BRFAL-Ga.

229. J. H. Sullivan to H. Catley, Sept. 10, 1868, reel 23, BRFAL-Ga (M798); C. Raushenberg to O. H. Howard, Sept. 1, 1868, vol. 124, LS, Albany Agt, BRFAL-Ga.

230. H. G. Flournoy to T. D. Elliot, Jan. 9, 1868, vol. 171, LS, Athens Agt, BRFAL-Ga. Any number of agents' complaint registers will confirm this statement, but see esp.

vol. 344, Register of Complaints, Rome Agt, BRFAL-Ga, which covers a period from June 1866 through the end of November 1868.

231. [A. Pokorny] to J. Leonard, Aug. 31, 1868, vol. 195, LS, Butler Agt, BRFAL-Ga.

232. W. C. Morrill to M. F. Gallagher, Aug. 5, 1868, vol. 136, LS; W. F. Martins to F. Mosebach, Aug. 17, 1868, box 7, LR, Atlanta SAC; C. Raushenberg to O. H. Howard, Sept. 1, 1868, vol. 124, LS, Albany Agt, BRFAL-Ga.

## Chapter 7. The People Go to Their Work Early and Gladly

1. Mohr, "Before Sherman: Georgia Blacks and the Union War Effort, 1861–1864"; Heard, "St. Simons Island during the War between the States."

2. Special Field Orders, No. 15, January 16, 1865, *Official Records*, ser. 1, vol. 47, pt. 2, 60–62; Sherman, *Memoirs*, 1: 249–50.

3. The starting point for understanding the land question is Oubre, *Forty Acres and a Mule*, supplemented by LaWanda Cox, "The Promise of Land for the Freedmen," and McFeely, *Yankee Stepfather*, 45–64, 84–148, 211–44. Manuel Gottlieb's older study, "The Land Question in Georgia during Reconstruction," is still useful for conceptualizing questions concerning the sea islands. It is less useful as an account of what actually occurred on the Georgia sea islands, and at points it is erroneous in its description of the Georgia situation. Gottlieb did not have access to the Bureau's records, which are essential for understanding not only the land question but all aspects of Reconstruction touching black and white Southerners.

4. *Savannah National Republican*, Sept. 29, 1865; R. Saxton to J. E. Bryant, May 15, Aug. 15, 1865, John Emory Bryant Papers, Duke University; R. Saxton to O. O. Howard, June 14, 1865, reel 17, (LR)BRFAL (M752); R. Saxton to E. A. Wild, June 16, Aug. 11, 17, 1865, reel 1, BRFAL-SC (M869); *Statutes at Large of the United States* (1863–1865), 13:508; Bullard, *Abandoned Black Settlement*, 73n.

5. Ketchum began his duties after Sherman issued Special Field Orders, No. 15. He supervised the coastal and riverfront land in South Carolina near Savannah along with the approximately 150 miles of Georgia coast. A. P. Ketchum to R. Saxton, Sept. 1, 1865, reel 34, BRFAL-SC (M869); McFeely, *Yankee Stepfather*, 49; Rose, *Rehearsal for Reconstruction*, 354. Records of Land Titles Issued to Freedmen, reel 36, BRFAL-Ga (M798).

6. W. F. Eaton, Monthly Report of Lands for August, Aug. 31, 1865; T. G. Campbell, Monthly Report of Lands for November 15 through December 15, 1865, reel 33, BRFAL-SC (M869).

7. Register of Land Titles Issued to Freedmen, reel 36, BRFAL-Ga (M798); Magdol, *A Right to the Land*, 104–5.

8. In November 1865, Tiffany reported that he had enrolled thirty-seven guardsmen with twelve on regular or active duty. By this time some guardsmen had absconded with

six weapons ("blackguards," Tiffany called them, pun intended). The guards had been armed earlier with old weapons given to them by the army at Savannah. Through the summer of 1865 agent Tiffany reserved the right to act alone as the arbitrator of disputes between the freedpeople in his jurisdiction. In the fall he began to use a referee and jury in his trials. W. H. Tiffany to A. P. Ketchum, Aug. 25, 1865, box 32, Records of the Assistant Adjutant General; W. H. Tiffany to H. F. Sickles, Nov. 27, 1865, box 28, URL, Savannah SAC, BRFAL-Ga; *Savannah National Republican*, Sept. 29, 1865.

9. W. F. Eaton to R. Saxton, October 24, 1865, reel 20, BRFAL-SC (M869); *New York Herald*, June 2, 1866; Ku Klux Conspiracy, vol. 7: *Georgia*, 854, 937.

10. J. W. Alvord, "Negro Industry."

11. Apparently these guardsmen received at least some of their weapons from Captain A. P. Ketchum. *Savannah National Republican*, Sept. 29, 1865; W. H. Tiffany to N. C. Dennett, Sept. 12, 1865, box 32, LR; W. H. Tiffany to H. F. Sickles, Nov. 2, 1865, box 28, ULR, Savannah SAC, BRFAL-Ga. Willie Lee Rose also notes that where blacks acted in leadership roles ex-slaves were less likely to accept unquestioningly white direction. Rose, *Rehearsal for Reconstruction*, 314–15.

12. W. H. Tiffany to H. F. Sickles, Nov. 7, 1865, box 30, Complaints, Charges, and Specifications, Savannah SAC, BRFAL-Ga.

13. W. F. Eaton to R. Saxton, Oct. 24, 1865, reel 20, BRFAL-SC (M869).

14. *Savannah National Republican*, Sept. 29, 1865. Tiffany's description of the Ogeechee plantations, though not explicit, suggests that the freedmen were working their old homes. Clarence Mohr in his study of slavery in wartime Georgia examines the impact of slave removal by owners or "refugeeing." He explains that there was a greater degree of continuity on the river rice planations than elsewhere along the coast because even when planters removed their slaves from the area, the slaves returned periodically to work the rice fields. Given these circumstances, the Ogeechee freedmen's actions support Philip D. Morgan's conclusions about the impact of the task system on slave life in the low country. According to Morgan, slaves who worked by the task developed responsibility, solidarity, and cooperative work habits in spite of the individualized nature of tasking. They also accumulated privileges that led to a degree of autonomy. Mohr, *On the Threshold of Freedom*, chap. 4; Morgan, "Work and Culture: The Task System and the World of Lowcountry Blacks, 1700 to 1800"; Morgan, "The Ownership of Property by Slaves in the Mid-Nineteenth-Century Low Country."

15. W. F. Eaton, Monthly Report of Lands for August, Aug. 31, 1865; T. G. Campbell, Monthly Report of Lands for November 15 through December 15, 1865, reel 33, BRFAL-SC (M869). Again, Clarence Mohr discusses how the slaves' removal by their masters, called refugeeing, broke down the old system of discipline, instilled new ideas in the slaves, and encouraged black independence. But when circumstances forced black sea islanders to work for white employers, some preferred to return to the task

system, which gave them freedom unknown to gang labor. Mohr, *Threshold of Freedom*, 111–19.

16. S. F. Du Pont to his wife, May 24, 1862, in Hayes, *Samuel Francis Dupont*, 2:70–71.

17. W. F. Eaton to A. P. Ketchum, Aug. 31, 1865; W. F. Eaton, Monthly Report on Lands for November, Nov. 30, 1865, reel 33, BRFAL-SC (M869); F. Littlefield to S. Hunt, Feb. 1, 1866, reel 1, AMA-Ga; D. Tillson to O. O. Howard, Feb. 12, 1866, reel 20, (LR)BRFAL (M752).

18. T. G. Campbell to A. P. Ketchum, Sept. 30, 1865, box 32, Records of the Assistant Adjutant General, Savannah SAC, BRFAL-Ga.

19. W. F. Eaton to R. Saxton, Dec. 1, 1865, reel 34, BRFAL-SC (M869); W. F. Eaton to A. P. Ketchum, July 31, 1865, box 32, Records of the Assistant Adjutant General, Savannah SAC, BRFAL-Ga.

20. W. F. Eaton, Monthly Report for August, Aug. 31, 1865; W. F. Eaton, Monthly Report for October, Oct. 31, 1865; T. G. Campbell, Monthly Report of Lands for November 15 through December 15, 1865, reel 33; W. F. Eaton to R. Saxton, Dec. 1, 1865, reel 34, BRFAL-SC (M-869); *Savannah National Republican*, Sept. 29, 1865; W. H. Tiffany to H. F. Sickles, Nov. 27, 1865, box 32, ULR, Savannah SAC, BRFAL-Ga.

21. W. H. Tiffany to H. F. Sickles, Nov. 27, Dec. 12, 1865, box 28, ULR, Savannah SAC, BRFAL-Ga.

22. In mid-December 1865 an army sergeant criticized Tiffany's work in the Ogeechee district and suggested that he could "get the mills out of debt" if he regularly visited the plantations to force freedmen to use the mills. Whether he had the opportunity to prove his point is unclear, but it appears that by February 1866 many Chatham County freedpeople, at least within the observation of American Missionary Association teacher Frances Littlefield, were paying a toll of seven bushels for every one hundred milled. A related problem arose when the home guards learned that Tiffany was leaving and they had yet to be paid in full. Those guarding the rice mills stole rice to make up for what they believed was their rightful pay. After Tiffany left the region, Subassistant Commissioner H. F. Sickles believed that about $1,800 was owed to about forty of the home guard. W. F. Tiffany to H. F. Sickles, Nov. 27, 1865; J. J. Thomas to H. F. Sickles, Dec. 16, 1865, box 28, ULR, Savannah SAC, BRFAL-Ga; H. F. Sickles to W. W. Deane, Jan. 1, 1866, reel 29, BRFAL-Ga (M798); F. Littlefield to S. Hunt, Feb. 1, 1866, reel 1, AMA-Ga.

23. W. Williams to O. O. Howard, Sept. 18, 1865, reel 13, BRFAL-Ga (M798); W. F. Eaton to R. Saxton, Oct. 12, 1865, reel 20; W. F. Eaton to R. Saxton, Dec. 1, 1865, reel 34, BRFAL-SC (M869); W. F. Eaton to A. P. Ketchum, May 19, 1865, box 32, Records of the Assistant Adjutant General, Savannah SAC, BRFAL-Ga.

24. W. H. Tiffany to A. P. Ketchum, July 31, Aug. 7, 1865, box 32, Records of the Assistant Adjutant General, Savannah SAC; W. H. Tiffany to N. C. Dennett, Sept. 12, 18,

1865; W. H. Tiffany to L. M. Birge, Sept. 30, 1865, box 32, LR, Savannah Agt; W. H. Tiffany to H. F. Sickles, Nov. 27, 1865, box 28, ULR, Savannah SAC, BRFAL-Ga.; W. F. Eaton to G. Whipple, May 15, 1866, reel 1, AMA-Ga.

25. Maj. Gen. Q. A. Gilmore to Brig. Gen. L. Thomas, May 24, 1865, reel 17, (LR)BRFAL (M752); R. Saxton to A. P. Ketchum, June 13, 1865, box 32, Records of the Assistant Adjutant General, Savannah SAC, BRFAL-Ga; E. A. Wild to R. Saxton, July 14, 1865, reel 34; R. Saxton to J. B. Steedman, Aug. 18, 1865, reel 1, BRFAL-SC (M869); J. S. Fullerton to R. Saxton, Aug. 28, 1865, reel 1, (RI)BRFAL (M742); S. W. Saxton to W. F. Eaton, June 21, 1865, Rufus and S. Willard Saxton Papers, Yale University, Sterling Library.

26. J. S. Fullerton to R. Saxton, Aug. 28, 1865, (RI)BRFAL (M742). In June 1865, when Saxton appointed Wild to the Bureau, he expected to settle freedpeople on abandoned property, but he had no idea what was available at that time; by the end of the summer, as far as Wild could ascertain, there was nothing available. R. Saxton to E. A. Wild, June 16, 1865, reel 1; E. A. Wild to R. Saxton, Sept. 1, 1865, reel 8, BRFAL-SC (M869).

27. Howard, *Autobiography*, 2:235–36; O. O. Howard to R. Saxton, Sept. 12, 1865, reel 1, (RI)BRFAL (M742); Circular No. 15, Sept. 12, 1865, *House Executive Documents*, 39th Cong., 1st sess., no. 70 (Serial 1256), 193; Bentley, *Freedmen's Bureau*, 89–98; McFeely, *Yankee Stepfather*, 134–35.

28. C. H. Howard to O . O. Howard, Sept. 27, 1865, Howard Papers. Throughout the remainder of 1865, Saxton refused to accept the restoration of the grant lands. He was finally relieved of his Bureau command on January 9, 1866. For a complaint from a South Carolina planter touching on this matter, which probably contributed to Saxton's demise, see W. H. Trescott to A. Johnson, Dec. 1, 1865, in Scrapbook, 1834–1926, Saxton Papers. Also see McFeely, *Yankee Stepfather*, 221–22, 226–27.

29. Testimony of H. S. Wells, February 24, 1866, *House Reports*, 39th Cong., 1st sess., no. 30 (serial 1273), pt. 3, p. 111.

30. General Orders, No. 145, War Department, Oct. 9, 1865, *House Executive Documents*, 39th Cong., 1st sess. no. 11 (serial 1255), 6, 7; Bentley, *Freedmen's Bureau*, 98.

31. Special Field Orders, No. 1; Special Field Orders, No. 2, Oct. 19, 1865, *House Executive Documents*, 39th Cong., 1st sess., no. 11 (serial 1255), 7–8; Howard, *Autobiography*, 2:239.

32. E. A. S[tiles] to [W. H. Stiles], Oct. 30, 1865, ser. A, Mackay-Stiles Papers, University of North Carolina, Southern Historical Collection.

33. William Trescot, a South Carolina planter, made this complaint to the president, but one might assume that Saxton's policies made the same impression on Trescott's Georgia counterparts, especially given their later complaints about A. P. Ketchum's work. W. H. Trescott to A. Johnson, Dec. 1, 1865, Scrapbook, 1834–1926, Saxton Papers.

34. A. P. Ketchum to D. Tillson, Jan. 11, 1866, reel 25, BRFAL-Ga (M798); E. M. Stanton to O. O. Howard, Oct. 25, 1865; O. O. Howard to E. M. Stanton, Nov. 3, 1865; H. M. Stinson to A. P. Ketchum, Nov. 23, 1865, *House Executive Documents*, 39th Cong., 1st sess., no. 11 (serial 1255), 8–10; C. H. Howard to O. O. Howard, Sept. 27, 1865, Howard Papers, Bowdoin College, Brunswick, Maine; Joseph F. Waring, application for restoration of property, Jan. 13, 1866, Joseph Frederick Waring Papers, Georgia Historical Society, Savannah; Bentley, *Freedmen's Bureau*, 98–100; Abbott, *Freedmen's Bureau in South Carolina*, 60. Ketchum continued to work in the reservation until March 1866, when he turned over his books to Davis Tillson and left to assume a new position in Washington. A. P. Ketchum to W. W. Deane, Mar. 22, 1866, reel 25, BRFAL-Ga (M798).

35. A. P. Ketchum to D. Tillson, Jan. 11, 1866, reel 25, BRFAL-Ga (M798); D. Tillson to O. O. Howard, Jan. 16, 1866, reel 20, (LR)BRFAL (M752).

36. D. Tillson to H. F. Sickles, Dec. 6, 1865, reel 1; H. F. Sickles to D. Tillson, Dec. 7, 1865, reel 24; endorsement of D. Tillson to O. O. Howard, Mar. 12, 1866, reel 8, BRFAL-Ga (M798); D. Tillson to O. O. Howard, Dec. 7, 1865; W. H. Tiffany to H. F. Sickles, Dec. 8, 1865; H. F. Sickles to W. W. Deane, Jan. 2, 1866, reel 20, (LR)BRFAL (M752); W. H. Tiffany to H. F. Sickles, Dec. 12, 1865, box 28, ULR, Savannah SAC, BRFAL-Ga; E. A. Cooley to S. Hunt, Dec. 20, 1865, reel 1, AMA-Ga. For a complete and favorable appraisal of Bradley see Joseph P. Reidy, "Aaron A. Bradley: Voice of Black Labor in the Georgia Lowcountry."

37. A. P. Ketchum to R. Saxton, Apr. 30, 1864, reprinted in *Freedman's Advocate*, July and August 1864.

38. Howard, *Autobiography*, 2:240; C. H. Howard to O. O. Howard, Sept. 27, 1865, Howard Papers; J. F. Waring, application for restoration of property, Jan. 1, 1866; J. F. Waring to O. O. Howard, Jan. 15, 1866, Waring Papers; Bentley, *Freedmen's Bureau*, 98–100; Abbott, *Freedmen's Bureau in South Carolina*, 60; Oubre, *Forty Acres and a Mule*, 57, 59–60.

39. A. P. Ketchum to D. Tillson, Jan. 11, 15, 1866, reel 25, BRFAL-Ga (M798); A. P. Ketchum, Monthly Report of Lands for October, Oct. 31, 1866; A. P. Ketchum, Monthly Report of Lands for November, Nov. 31, 1866, reel 33, BRFAL-SC (M869); Order of A. P. Ketchum, Nov. 2, 1865, box 32, Records of the Assistant Adjutant General, Savannah SAC, BRFAL-Ga.

40. D. Tillson to O. O. Howard, Dec. 15, 1865, Howard Papers. While he was in charge of the Port Royal experiment, Saxton had shown his reluctance to pursue policies that were contrary to the freedmen's interests and on occasion dragged his feet in implementing them. Rose, *Rehearsal for Reconstruction*, 274–75, 329–30.

41. D. Tillson to O. O. Howard, Jan. 16, Feb. 12, 1866, reel 20, (LR)BRFAL (M752); T. G. Campbell, Monthly Report of Lands for November 15 through December 15, 1865, reel 33, BRFAL-SC (M869).

42. W. King to D. Tillson, Jan. 16, 1866, reel 27, BRFAL-Ga (M798). Problems for the Bureau in the reservation were probably intensified by black Union veterans native to the reservation who now returned undoubtedly expecting to share in the material rewards of freedom. In his study of slavery in Civil War Georgia, Clarence Mohr notes that at least 376 blacks born in coastal Georgia counties enlisted from 1862 to 1865 in the South Carolina volunteer units that became known as the 21st, 33d, and 34th U.S. Colored Infantry. Joseph Reidy in his essay on A. A. Bradley also notes that Georgia blacks joined Massachusetts volunteer units that recruited on the coast, and they settled in the Savannah area after their discharge from the service. These veterans must have returned home too late to take advantage of Sherman's January 1865 field order. The 21st and 33d U.S. Colored Infantry, for example, were mustered out on December 13, 1865. An indication of the role that veterans could play in coastal affairs may be seen in the active role taken by Robert Bowling, Robert Wilson, Joseph Harmon, and J. F. Wilson, black veterans who in 1868 organized a militia unit in Savannah. Further generalizations on the role of black veterans in the reservation must await an extensive examination of their pension records located in the National Archives. Such an examination should help clarify their distribution throughout the reservation, their expectations, and the degree of their militancy. Mohr, *On the Threshold of Freedom*, 87–89; Reidy, "Aaron A. Bradley," 281; Circular No. 54, War Department, Adjutant General's Office, Dec. 19, 1865, *Official Records*, ser. 3, vol. 5, 578; Robert Bowling et al. to Gov. [Rufus B.] Bullock, August 13, 1868, box 89, File II: Reconstruction, GDAH.

43. D. Tillson to O. O. Howard, Dec. 15, 1865, Howard Papers; D. Tillson to O. O. Howard, Jan. 16, reel 20, (LR)BRFAL (M752).

44. J. B. Weems to D. Tillson, Oct. 12, 1865; E. B. Adams to D. Tillson, Nov. 14, 1865, reel 24; D. Tillson to J. A. Andrew, Jan. 19, 1866, reel 1; W. S. King to D. Tillson, Feb. 2, 1866, reel 27, BRFAL-Ga (M798). For the type of enterprise that Tillson envisioned, see Powell, "The American Land Company and Agency."

45. D. Tillson to O. O. Howard, Nov. 28, Dec. 2, 1865, reel 20 (LR)BRFAL (M752); D. Tillson to G. A. Hastings, Nov. 15, 30, 1865; D. Tillson to O. O. Howard, Nov. 30, 1865, reel 1; G. A. Hastings to D. Tillson, Nov. 25, 1865; L. Williams and others to D. Tillson, [Dec. 23, 1865], reel 24; G. A. Hastings to D. Tillson, Jan. 7, 1866, reel 27, BRFAL-Ga (M798); Cimbala, "A Black Colony in Dougherty County."

46. Tillson placed G. L. Eberhart in charge of implementing the act in Georgia. Although Eberhart actively promulgated the law, he kept poor records, making it difficult to judge his success. Also, imperfections in the law—the law promised transportation with only one month's rations to the migrants, an understandable but grossly inadequate stake unless the freedpeople had their own resources—and problems at the destinations of the Georgia emigrants limited the law's impact. D. Tillson, "Report of Operations from September 22, 1865, to November 1, 1866," reel 32; E. C. Powell to O. O. Howard, Sept. 22, 1866; E. C. Powell to D. Tillson, Sept. 24, 1866; E. O. C. Ord to

D. Tillson, Oct. 31, 1866, reel 28; D. Tillson to E. C. Powell, Oct. 9, 1866, reel 3; endorsement of D. Tillson, Dec. 4, 1866, on L. Speed and others to G. L. Eberhart, Nov. 27, 1866, reel 16, BRFAL-Ga (M798); G. L. Eberhart to O. O. Howard, Nov. 15, 1866, reel 8 (Ed)BRFAL (M799); D. Tillson to O. O. Howard, Oct. 9, 1866, reel 37; F. D. Sewell to O. O. Howard, Dec. 15, 1866, reel 39 (LR)BRFAL (M752); W. F. White to G. L. Eberhart, Dec. 6, 1866, vol. 151, LS; W. F. White to Assistant Commissioner [Mississippi], Dec. 25, 1866 (and endorsements), box 9, ULR, Augusta SAC, BRFAL-Ga; Bentley, *Freedmen's Bureau*, 134, 145; Oubre, *Forty Acres and a Mule*, 90–91, 103–4, 107.

47. Hyman, *A More Perfect Union*, 177–80.

48. For a critical comment in an 1867 issue of the *Nation* on the unhappy effects land redistribution might have, see Eric Foner, "Thaddeus Stevens, Confiscation, and Reconstruction," in *Politics and Ideology*, 143. For William Tiffany's comment on seed rice and seed corn see the *Savannah National Republican*, Sept. 29, 1865. Frances Littlefield, an American Missionary Association teacher residing in Chatham County, and Davis Tillson noted the negative impact of having little in the way of seed and other capital to initiate planting in the reservation, but Tillson saw this problem as a reason for moving the freedpeople into contract arrangements where he believed they could accumulate the necessary resources. Also, it is interesting to note that Manuel Gottlieb in his article on the land question believed land alone would not have brought prosperity to the freedpeople; rather, he concluded that land and assistance were necessary. F. Littlefield to S. Hunt, Feb. 1, 1866, reel 1, AMA-Ga; D. Tillson to O. O. Howard, Mar. 5, 1866, reel 27, (LR)BRFAL (M752); Gottlieb, "Land Question in Georgia during Reconstruction," 387.

49. D. Tillson to O. O. Howard, Dec. 15, 1865, Howard Papers; D. Tillson to O. O. Howard, Jan. 16, 1866, reel 20, (LR)BRFAL (M752); O. O. Howard to D. Tillson, Jan. 23, 1866, reel 2, (RI)BRFAL (M742); D. Tillson to O. O. Howard, Feb. 6, 1866, *House Executive Documents*, 39th Cong., 1st sess., no. 70 (serial 1256), 329; D. Tillson, Report of Operations from September 22, 1865 to November 1, 1866, reel 32, BRFAL-Ga (M798). At the time that Howard was reviewing Tillson's plan he was working on a bill concerning land grants to the former slaves with Senator Lyman Trumbull. McFeely, *Yankee Stepfather*, 205–36.

50. D. Tillson to C. J. Jenkins, Feb. 12, 1866, reel 1, BRFAL-Ga (M798).

51. D. Tillson to O. O. Howard, Feb. 12, 1866, reel 20, (LR)BRFAL (M752); D. Tillson to Col. Carling, Mar. 18, 1866, reel 34, BRFAL-Ga (M798); D. Tillson to O. O. Howard, Feb. 20, 1866, *House Executive Documents*, 39th Cong., 1st sess., no. 70 (serial 1256), 331–32; Powell, *New Masters*, 100. A reporter described a similar trip through these channels from Savannah to the islands in the *New York Herald*, June 2, 1866.

52. T. G. Campbell, Monthly Report of Lands for November 15 through December 15, 1865, reel 33, BRFAL-SC (M869); Register of Land Titles Issued to Freedmen, reel 36, BRFAL-Ga (M798); D. Tillson to O. O. Howard, Feb. 12, 1866, reel 20; endorsement of D. Tillson, Apr. 13, 1866, on T. G. Campbell to R. Saxton, Mar. 26,

1866, reel 27, (LR)BRFAL (M752). For the requirements of Sherman's special field orders, refer to *Official Records*, ser. 1, vol. 47, pt. 2, 62. If this order were strictly interpreted, only Saxton could issue the possessory titles. However, Tillson accepted Saxton's delegation of authority to A. P. Ketchum and also the titles that Ketchum signed under Saxton's name. For an example see Special Field Orders, No. 7, Mar. 16, 1866, reel 34, BRFAL-Ga (M798).

53. D. Tillson to O. O. Howard, Feb. 12, 1866, reel 20; D. Tillson to O. O. Howard, Mar. 5, 1866, reel 22, (LR)BRFAL (M752); D. Tillson, "Report of Operations from September 22, 1865 to November 1, 1866," reel 32, BRFAL-Ga (M798). Campbell was not above mixing self-interest with his work for the freedpeople, but for a much more sympathetic and overly positive view of the black leader see Duncan, *Freedom's Shore*.

54. W. F. Eaton to R. Saxton, Sept. 10, 1865, reel 7; W. F. Eaton, Monthly Report of Lands for August, Aug. 31, 1865; W. F. Eaton, Monthly Report of Lands for October, Oct. 31, 1865, reel 33, BRFAL-SC (M869); D. Tillson to O. O. Howard, Dec. 15, 1865, Howard Papers; D. Tillson to O. O. Howard, Feb. 12, 1866, reel 20, (LR)BRFAL (M742); Special Field Orders, No. 1, Feb. 14, 1866; Special Field Orders, No. 3, Feb. 14, 1866, reel 34, BRFAL-Ga (M798); D. Tillson to O. O. Howard, Feb. 20, 1866, *House Executive Documents*, 39th Cong., 1st sess., no. 70 (serial 1256), 331–32. Evidently Commissioner Howard found Tillson's orders acceptable; the South Carolina assistant commissioner issued a similar directive for the reservation area within his jurisdiction one month later. D. Tillson to J. B. Steedman, May 16, 1866, reel 2, BRFAL-Ga (M798); Abbott, *Freedmen's Bureau in South Carolina*, 61–62.

55. *New York Herald*, June 13, 1866; S. D. Dickson to D. Tillson, June 25, 1866, reel 26; Register of Land Titles Issued to Freedmen, reel 36, BRFAL-Ga (M798); T. S. Mallard to "Robert," July 31, 1866, Rev. John Jones Family Papers, University of Georgia. Thomas Spalding had died in 1851, but the register of land titles and other Bureau papers referred to his property as the estate of Thomas Spalding. His son Charles Spalding supervised the property when it was not leased by Yankee entrepreneurs. C. Spalding to D. Tillson, Jan. 14, 1867, reel 30, BRFAL-Ga (M798). For information on the Spalding family see Myers, *Children of Pride*, 1682–83.

56. *Macon Daily Telegraph*, June 6, 1866; N. Bronson to W. W. Deane, Sept. 13, 1866, reel 25; D. Tillson, "Report of Operations from September 22, 1865 to November 1, 1866," reel 32, BRFAL-Ga (M798).

57. D. Tillson to O. O. Howard, Feb. 12, 1866, reel 20; Mar. 5, 1866, reel 27, (LR)BRFAL (M752). Later Tillson characterized Tunis Campbell as a man of "great plausibility; and remarkable cunning," which seems to have been his general opinion of the leaders of the freedpeople in the reservation. Campbell also made an unfavorable impression on Ira Pettibone of the American Missionary Association. D. Tillson, "Report of Operations from September 22, 1865 to November 1, 1866," reel 32, BRFAL-Ga (M798); I. Pettibone to Strieby, Apr. 30, 1866, reel 1, AMA-Ga.

58. W. F. Eaton to D. Tillson, Apr. 25, 1866, reel 26; W. W. Deane to W. F. Eaton, May 3, 1866, reel 2, BRFAL-Ga (M798); F. J. Foster to M. Cummings, Dec. 17, 1866, vol. 347, LS, Savannah SAC, BRFAL-Ga.

59. D. Tillson to O. O. Howard, Feb. 21, 24, 1866, Howard Papers.

60. W. F. Eaton to D. Tillson, Apr. 25, 1866, reel 26; W. W. Deane to W. F. Eaton, May 3, 1866, reel 2, BRFAL-Ga (M798).

61. W. F. Eaton to D. Tillson, May 17, Sept. 1, 1866, reel 26; W. W. Deane to Marston and Rowe, May 14, 1866, reel 2; D. Tillson to Marston and Rowe, June 2, 1866, reel 3, BRFAL-Ga (M798).

62. The fact that Tillson was able to secure a salary for Perry was unusual—he argued that the agent would end up saving the Bureau more than what it cost to employ him— but it also suggests the importance to Tillson of having someone he could trust on the coast. D. Tillson to O. O. Howard, Jan. 30, 1866, reel 20, (LR)BRFAL (M752); Special Field Orders, No. 2, Feb. 14, 1866, reel 34; Registers of Civilian Agents, 1865–1867, reel 35, BRFAL-Ga (M798).

63. Special Orders, No. 85, May 28, 1866, reel 34, BRFAL-Ga (M798); D. Tillson to O. O. Howard, Sept. 22, 1866, reel 37, (LR)BRFAL (M752). For a sympathetic account of Campbell's dismissal, which acknowledges that it is unclear whether the agent actually committed those dishonest practices, see Duncan, *Freedom's Shore*, 32–33.

64. Registers of Civilian Agents, 1865–1867, reel 35, BRFAL-Ga (M798); W. F. Tiffany to H. F. Sickles, Nov. 27, 1865, box 28, ULR, Savannah SAC, BRFAL-Ga.

65. A. P. Ketchum to W. W. Deane, Feb. 24, 1866, reel 32; Mar. 22, 1866, reel 25, BRFAL-Ga (M798).

66. W. F. Eaton to D. Tillson, Sept. 25, 29, 1866, reel 26, BRFAL-Ga (M798). Tillson had earlier developed a favorable opinion of Eaton. There is no indication that he had changed his mind or that he wished Eaton to be removed from the Bureau. D. Tillson to O. O. Howard, Dec. 15, 1865, Howard Papers.

67. Registers of Civilian Agents, 1865–1867, reel 35; Special Field Orders, No. 7, Mar. 16, 1866; Special Field Orders, No. 9, Mar. 27, 1866, reel 34, BRFAL-Ga (M798); list of payments to A. G. Bass, "overseer," Oct. 30, 1862, Feb. 5, 1863, Jan. 13, 1864, June 11, 1866, Journal of William Cooke, University of Georgia Library; Myers, *Children of Pride*, 1683.

68. Registers of Civilian Agents, 1865–1867, reel 35; D. Tillson to J. B. Steedmen, May 16, 1866, reel 2; S. D. Dickson to D. Tillson, June 25, 1866, reel 26; J. K. Smith to W. W. Deane, Aug. 30, 1866, reel 13, BRFAL-Ga (M798).

69. Leigh, *Ten Years on a Georgia Plantation*, 33; Testimony of Toby Maxwell, [1872], box 110, File II: Tunis G. Campbell, GDAH. Toby Maxwell was referring to a store that McBride and Dixon had established on St. Catherines.

70. S. D. Dickson to D. Tillson, June 25, 1866, reel 26, BRFAL-Ga (M798).

71. S. D. Dickson to D. Tillson, June 25, 1866; S. D. Dickson to W. G. Dickson, Aug. 18, 1866, enclosed in W. G. Dickson to W. W. Deane, Aug. 22, 1866; J. C. Dickson to

D. Tillson, Sept. 22, 1866, reel 26; Special Orders, No. 130, Sept. 5, 1866, reel 34; C. Spalding to D. Tillson, Jan. 14, 1867, reel 30, BRFAL-Ga (M798).

72. T. F. Forbes to G. T. Crabtree, Sept. 5, 1866, reel 3; Special Orders, No. 130, Sept. 5, 1866, reel 34; C. Spalding to D. Tillson, Jan. 14, 1867, reel 30, BRFAL-Ga (M798); D. Tillson to O. O. Howard, Sept. 22, Oct. 10, 1866, reel 37 (LR)BRFAL (M752).

73. J. K. Smith to W. Flye, July 25, 1866, vol. 347, LS, Savannah SAC, BRFAL-Ga; J. K. Smith to W. W. Deane, Aug. 30, 1866, reel 13; Sept. 7, 1866, reel 29; N. Bronson to W. W. Deane, Sept. 13, 1866, reel 25, BRFAL-Ga (M798).

74. J. R. Cheves to D. Tillson, Sept. 14, 1866 (and endorsement from Tillson's office), reel 25, BRFAL-Ga (M798). Cheves's choice of word to describe the crowd of freedmen is interesting. Historically, *landsturm* refers to militia, but literally it means a storm on the land.

75. *Statutes at Large of the United States* (1866), 14:173–76.

76. D. Tillson to O. O. Howard, Oct. 23, 1866, reel 37, (LR)BRFAL (M752); Circular Letter, Oct. 22, 1866; Circular No. 11, Nov. 8, 1866, reel 34 ; D. Tillson to O. O. Howard, Nov. 17, 1866, reel 4, BRFAL-Ga (M798).

77. Schedule of Warrants for Land Given by the Assistant Commissioner of Georgia, reel 36, BRFAL-Ga (M798). Also see Register of Land Titles Issued to the Freedmen, reel 36, BRFAL-Ga (M798).

78. D. Tillson to J. B. Steedman, May 30, 1866, reel 3; Special Field Orders, No. 4, Feb. 23, 1866, roll 34, BRFAL- Ga (M798); *New York Herald*, June 13, 1866; Bullard, *Abandoned Black Settlement*, 80n.

79. D. Tillson to editor, *Savannah Daily Republican*, Jan. 23, 1867; Register of Land Titles Issued to the Freedmen, reel 36, BRFAL-Ga (M798). Tillson annotated Ketchum's record book with remarks concerning the listed grant holders and their status at the end of 1866 or the beginning of 1867. One may assume that he was careful, especially since he had been so disturbed by the register's inadequacies. Still, one cannot be certain that Bradley was the sole cause of the dearth of warrants listed here. At the same time, Bradley had earlier urged freedpeople in the Ogeechee district to hold on to land on a plantation that was to be restored, prompting a Bureau investigation. W. H. Tiffany to H. F. Sickles, Dec. 13, 1865, box 28, ULR, Savannah SAC, BRFAL-Ga.

80. J. W. Magill to D. Tillson, Dec. 18, 1866, reel 28; C. C. Sibley to R. W. Bard, Jan. 25, 1867, reel 4; R. W. Bard to J. C. Hosmer, Feb. 8, 1867, reel 30; endorsement of J. M. Hoag, May 30, 1867, on J. C. Simmons to J. M. Hoag, Apr. 12, 1867, reel 16, BRFAL-Ga (M798).

81. J. M. Hoag to C. C. Sibley, May 20, 1867, reel 15, BRFAL-Ga (M798). For examples of restoration orders see Special Orders, No. 13, Jan. 31, 1867; No. 80, May 31, 1867; No. 119, July 31, 1867; No. 192, Dec. 31, 1867; No. 2, Jan. 6, 1868; No. 9, Jan. 22, 1868, reel 34, BRFAL-Ga (M798).

82. C. H. Hopkins to [J. M.] Hoag, Mar. 12, 1867, reel 15; G. R. Walbridge to C. A. Reynolds, Mar. 26, 1867, reel 5; C. R. Holcombe to C. C. Sibley, July 31, 1867, reel 18, BRFAL-Ga (M798); *Savannah Daily Republican*, Apr. 18, 1867.

83. Twenty-four of the thirty grant holders on Cheves's place received warrants; on Sapelo, seven of the twelve grant holders recorded on the Kenan place and nine of the fourteen recorded on the Spalding place received warrants. Register of Land Titles Issued to Freedmen, reel 36, BRFAL-Ga (M798).

84. A. A. Bradley to Sen. B. Wade, Jan. 3, 1867, reprinted in *Savannah Daily Republican*, Jan. 24, 1867; E. E. Howard to J. E. Bryant, Jan. 26, 1867, Bryant Papers; Magdol, *A Right to the Land*, 105.

85. It should also be noted that the Bureau's concern for the freedpeople of St. Catherines continued into the next Bureau administration when Caleb Sibley, in consideration of the small 1866 crop, absolved them of a $1,300 debt owed to the agency. It appears that the freedpeople, however, never received all that they should have; in November 1867, J. Murray Hoag, the Savannah subassistant commissioner, pointed out to Sibley that the firm still was indebted to the freedpeople and that Winchester was dead, Schuyler was bankrupt, and the only "monied partner," a Mr. Ballard, was far away in Cincinnati. C. C. Sibley to Bryan, Hartridge & Co., Apr. 24, 1867; E. Pickett to Bryan, Hartridge & Co., Apr. 27, 1867; C. C. Sibley to J. Murray Hoag, Apr. 27, 1867; E. Pickett to Bryan, Hartridge & Co., May 12, 1867, reel 5; Bryan, Hartridge & Co. to Assist[ant] Adj[utant] General, F[reedmen's] B[ureau] G[eorgi]a, Apr. 29, 1867; Bryan, Hartridge & Co. to C. C. Sibley, Apr. 25, May 11, May 13, 1867, reel 14; J. M. Hoag to C. C. Sibley, May 4, 1867, reel 15; J. M. Hoag to C. C. Sibley, Nov. 18, 1867, reel 18, BRFAL-Ga (M798); D. Tillson to C. C. Sibley, Apr. 9, 1867; J. M. Hoag to C. C. Sibley, May 11 (including E. Pickett's endorsement, May 14), Nov. 18, 1867, box 27, LR, SAC, BRFAL-Ga.

86. F. J. Foster to M. Cummings, Dec. 17, 1866, vol. 347, LS, Savannah SAC, BRFAL-Ga.

87. D. Tillson, "Report of Operations from September 22, 1865 to November 1, 1866," reel 32, BRFAL-Ga (M798).

88. Foner, "Thaddeus Stephens," 141–47. Foner also notes here that by 1867 Northerners expressed fear that confiscation would discourage businessmen from investing in the South.

89. Manuel Gottlieb notes that, except for the coastal counties, Georgia did not produce an aggressive black leadership, but Edmund Lee Drago provides a much better analysis of the reasons behind this apparent lack of aggression in his thorough study of Georgia's black leaders. He offers ample explanation as to why fieldhands could not expect politicians to support significant attempts at land reform. Many black politicians were preachers who assumed an accommodating stance when dealing with whites. Black politicians placed their highest priority on political and civil rights, not on economic reform. Drago suggests that there might have been a class difference when he notes that black politicians were more prosperous than their constituents, but he also shows that they were closer to the black worker than were their South Carolina counterparts. Black

politicians, given their backgrounds and beliefs, readily accepted the free-labor message of the Bureau while emphasizing their own quest for civil and political rights. Even if Georgia Republicans had followed through with a confiscatory tax program, the odds would have been against land redistribution among the state's black residents. As Eric Foner notes, throughout the South forfeiture for taxes did not necessarily permanently deprive the owner of his land, and often land sold at tax auctions found its way into the possession of white farmers, speculators, and businessmen. William C. Harris in his study of Reconstruction Mississippi also discovered that even though a significant amount of land was subject to tax sale, officials allowed owners and tenants to continue to work the property, and uncertainties concerning the titles made the purchase of such land far from a safe or secure investment. Gottlieb, "Land Question in Georgia," 369; Drago, *Black Politicians*, 37–39, 86–88, 90–93, 96, 97; Eric Foner, *Nothing but Freedom*, 69–70; Harris, *The Day of the Carpetbagger*, 334, 486, 506–7.

90. For examples of arrangements that gave coastal freedmen land to plant on their own in exchange for a dollar sum, a specific amount of produce, cotton, or some other commodity, a portion of the crop, or labor on the leasor's lands, see contracts between William R. Nelson and freedmen, Jan. 16, 1866 (Chatham County), which allowed the freedmen to cultivate from ten to twenty acres of land on the property that they worked during the preceding year for one-fourth of the gross harvest (it also gave the freedmen one acre of land, probably for gardens, to work rent-free); contract between C. W. Broughton and Starling, Jan. 31, 1866 (McIntosh County), which gave Starling as much land as he could cultivate well in return for 100 pounds of ginned cotton as rent; contract between Walter B. Heyward and freedmen, Mar. 14, 1866 (Chatham County), which gave the freedmen ten acres each plus one-acre garden plots in return for one-third of the crop; contract between W. A. Way and freedmen (for the 1867 season) (Liberty County), which gave the freedmen "as much land as they desire for planting their own crops" in return for cultivating land for Way; contract between John Mullen and freedmen, Jan. 1, 1867 (McIntosh County), which leased a 130-acre tract of land on Harris Neck for $1.50 an acre plus fencerails; contract between James N. Winn and David Byrne, Jan. 7, 1867 (McIntosh County), which leased land in a rice-growing area for the return of 250 bushels of corn and 6,000 pounds of fodder; contract between Lewis Tattnal Turner and Cassius Hunter, July 15, 1867 (Chatham County), which leased to Hunter land on Whitemarsh Island "not exceeding Eleven acres" for $60; contract between Lewis Tattnal Turner and John Dixon, July 15, 1867 (Chatham County), which leased to Dixon thirteen acres of Whitemarsh Island land for $60; and contract between Lewis Tattnal Turner and Sampson Wiggins, July 15, 1867 (Chatham County), which leased to Wiggins six acres and a house for $30, all in box 31, Contracts, Savannah SAC, BRFAL-Ga.

91. Two other freedpeople leased an unspecified amount of property described as "half of nursery," as did another who also leased ten acres. Some of the freedpeople also rented a house or part of one. J. F. Waring to O. O. Howard, Jan. 15, 1866; lease

arrangements between J. F. Waring and freedpeople, Seaside Plantation, Skidaway Island, Jan. 8, 1866, Waring Papers.

92. For some examples of freedmen who received portions of land to work as part of their compensation see T. Q. Fleming and freedmen, Jan. 1, 1866 (Liberty County), which allowed each adult to claim the use of half-acre garden plots; contract between William Harrison and Peter Law and Jenny Bacon, Jan. 8, 1866 (Liberty County), which gave Law and Bacon one day each week to cultivate rent-free as much land as they could; contract between James M. Couper and freedmen (for the 1867 season) (McIntosh County), which among other things gave the Champneys Island freedmen two acres for each family to work on its own; and contract between Jacob Waldburg and freedmen, Jan. 20, 1868 (Liberty County), which gave these St. Catherines freedmen permission to tend garden plots near their houses. All of the above are found in box 31, Contracts, Savannah SAC, BRFAL-Ga. Also see contract between J. P. Stevens and freedmen, Jan. 1, 1868 (Liberty County), which gave the freedmen garden plots (box 20, Contracts, Hinesville Agt, BRFAL-Ga) and contract between Mary Jones and freedmen, Feb. 12, 1867 (Liberty County), which compensated the freedmen in part with the permission to use "as much Land for agricultural purposes as they may be able to plant cultivate and tend" (Charles C. Jones Jr. Collection, University of Georgia). In 1867 Fanny Butler discovered that her employees preferred to work in gangs by the task. Leigh, *Ten Years on a Georgia Plantation*, 55–56.

93. Leigh, *Ten Years on a Georgia Plantation*, 85–90, 127. Leigh's problems did not abate, as her memoirs attest, but also see [Frances Butler] to P. G. Hollis, Feb. 14, [1869]; Frances Butler to Mr. Duncan, June 2, 1869, Frances Butler Leigh Letterbook, James W. Wistar Family Papers, Historical Society of Pennsylvania, Philadelphia.

94. At the end of 1867, Leigh paid out between two hundred and three hundred dollars to each worker. At the end of 1868 she noted that for the 1869 season she would be paying her workers twelve dollars a month plus rations. And in 1877 she editorialized that "with good management, good wages paid regularly, and no outside interference, there need be no trouble whatever with Southern labor." Leigh, *Ten Years on a Georgia Plantation*, 78–79, 127, 226–27.

95. O. W. Dimick to E. P. Smith, Mar. 7, 1868, reel 4, AMA-Ga.

96. Leigh, *Ten Years on a Georgia Plantation*, 54n, 124–25, 156; Bullard, *Abandoned Black Settlement*, 107.

97. The Savannah press named the incident and contended that the supporters of Rufus Bullock instigated the affair. *Atlanta Constitution*, Jan. 5, 8, 10, 1869. Drago provides details in *Black Politicians*, 123–24.

98. D. G. Risley to Mrs. M. Downes, May 19, 1867; D. G. Risley to Mr. Manoe, Jan. 29, 30, 1868, vol. 201, LS; G. W. Anderson to D. G. Risley, Feb. 5, 1868, box 12, LR, Brunswick SAC, BRFAL-Ga. Even when squatters avoided eviction, they eventually had to come to terms with the people who made the laws of the state. White Georgians limited the squatters' prospects for gleaning a livelihood from property owned by whites

by passing hunting, fishing, gathering, and trespassing laws during the 1870s that restricted what had once been customary uses of rural lands. Flynn, *White Land, Black Labor*, 115–25.

99. Trowbridge, *The South*, 535.

100. As noted in chapter 4, the Bureau would give very limited and selective help to freedpeople working their own land, while requiring that they pay back the advance after they harvested and marketed their crops.

101. A. Mitchell to C. C. Sibley, Apr. 26, 1867; J. M. Hoag to C. C. Sibley, May 2, 1867, reel 15, BRFAL-Ga (M798).

102. For Frances Butler's comments on the quality of the land purchased by the freedmen, see Leigh, *Ten Years on a Georgia Plantation*, 78–79.

## Chapter 8. The Same Footing before the Law

1. D. Tillson to R. J. Dawson, Apr. 9, 1866, reel 2, BRFAL-Ga (M798).

2. Raushenberg is quoted in O. H. Howard to M. F. Gallagher, Nov. 14, 1868, reel 23, BRFAL-Ga (M798).

3. C. C. Richardson, Circular Letter, Jan. 17, 1866, vol. 379, LS, Thomasville SAC, BRFAL-Ga.

4. General Orders, No. 8, Aug. 11, 1865; Circular No. 2, Aug. 16, 1865, *House Executive Documents*, 39th Cong., 1st sess., no. 70 (serial 1256), 93, 108–11. Earlier in February 1865, Saxton's associate, Mansfield French, had urged black men to settle down with one wife, instead of the multiple mates he assumed they had freely chosen in slavery. Gutman, *The Black Family in Slavery and Freedom, 1750–1925*, 418.

5. In August 1865, Mansfield French had devised an elaborate set of rules for Saxton that dealt with ex-slaves who had more than one spouse, but Saxton's Bureau did not appear to be overly concerned with enforcing these rules nor could it actively supervise them because of its limited personnel. Tillson was never so specific and accepted the Georgia legislation as his guide in these matters: Georgia ex-slaves had to choose one spouse without delay or suffer the consequences of the law. Bureau agents could live with this law, but if a freedperson left behind children when moving on to another spouse and the earlier spouse complained to the Bureau, the agency believed that child support was in order. For French's guidelines, see Gutman, *Black Family in Slavery and Freedom*, 419. For the Georgia law, which went into effect in March 1866, see *Acts of the General Assembly of the State of Georgia, Passed in Milledgeville, at the Annual Session in December 1865 and January, February, and March 1866*, 240.

6. Circular No. 5, Dec. 22, 1865; Circular No. 5, Apr. 9, 1866, reel 34, BRFAL-Ga (M798).

7. Endorsement of D. Tillson to P. Slaughter, Oct. 13, 1865; endorsement of D. Tillson to G. Curkendall, Dec. 8, 1865; endorsement of D. Tillson to Col. Thomas, Jan. 26, 1866; endorsement of D. Tillson to O. Brown, Apr. 11, 1866; endorsement of D. Tillson

to W. F. Martins, Dec. 20, 1866; endorsement of W. F. Martins to E. Pickett, Dec. 23, 1866, reel 8; J. H. Cochrane to [D. Tillson], Oct. 9, 1865, reel 11, BRFAL-Ga (M798); C. G. Campbell to [J. R. Davis], July 4, 1866, box 10, URL, Augusta Agt; M. Marbach to J. Inman, May 13, 1868, vol. 390, LS, Waynesboro Agt; B. Sparrow to [L. Lieberman], Aug. 1, 1868 (and all endorsements), box 19, ULR, Hawkinsville Agt; entry for Jan. 20, 1868, vol. 316, Register of Complaints, McDonough Agt, BRFAL-Ga; L. R. Lewis to C. Sterling, July 1, 1860, reel 3, (Ed)BRFAL-Ga (M799).

8. Circular No. 6, Apr. 9, 1866, reel 34, BRFAL-Ga (M798).

9. The Bureau's view of family authority obviously followed standard nineteenth-century attitudes of the father-headed family. In this case, however, the father's right to delegate control of his family to others in the workplace was to be supervised by the paternalistic oversight of the Bureau, lest ex-masters take advantage "of the ignorance of the Freedpeople." W. W. Deane [Tillson's adjutant] to M. P. Mayfield, Jan. 23, 1866, reel 1, BRFAL-Ga (M798).

10. J. E. Bryant to E. Bryant, May 29, 1865, John Emory Bryant Papers, Duke University.

11. For the Rachael Lumpkin incident, see the entry dated August 3, 1867, in the section for the Rome subdistrict in List of Freedmen Assaulted or Murdered in 1867, reel 32, BRFAL-Ga (M798). Such reports of spousal murder were rare, with only one other case finding its way into the Bureau's yearly reports on violence when Alfred Butler killed his wife in the Macon subdistrict on August 18, 1868. John R. Lewis, Report of Outrages Committed upon Freedpeople in the State of Georgia from January 1, 1868, to November 15, 1868, reel 59, BRFAL (M752). The following examples of marital difficulties are not offered to diminish the importance of the commitment black men and women made to one another. Rather, they are cautionary tales, offered to keep in proper perspective the reality of human relationships and to avoid overromanticizing the freedpeople's postwar lives. In fact, marital complaints made up only a small portion of any agent's or officer's caseload. For example, the Milledgeville agent recorded 164 cases between June 6, 1867, and August 17, 1868. Most involved contract disputes and settlements; only eleven involved marital disputes (Register of Complaints, vol. 319, Milledgeville Agt, BRFAL-Ga). Whether the small number reflects the real numbers of marital difficulties or whether freedwomen, as Catherine Clinton reasonably speculates, hesitated to approach Bureau men with their personal problems, and thus underreported such problems, is a matter open for discussion. Clinton also is probably correct to note that freedwomen brought their marital complaints to the Bureau only when they were desperate, but she wrongly suggests that the hesitation came from the fact that the agents were "allied by color with former masters" (Clinton, "Bloody Terrain: Freedwomen, Sexuality, and Violence During Reconstruction," 319). Freedpeople brought these private problems to the Bureau, and the Bureau tried to resolve them favorably for the wronged party; such activity implies a working relationship between the agency and the freedpeople worth noting.

12. Affidavit of Mary Allen, Nov. 1, 1867, reel 17; J. B. Davenport to [Georgia Bureau headquarters], July 2, 1867, reel 12, BRFAL-Ga (M798).

13. Entries for Jan. 4, 12, Mar. 7, May 5, 21, Nov. 1, 1866, vol. 392, Register of Complaints, Washington Agt, BRFAL-Ga.

14. Entries for June 6, July 12, Aug. 1, 1867, Jan. 6, 13, 21, 22, Mar. 31, Apr. 7, May 13, 19, 1868, vol. 319, Register of Complaints, Milledgeville Agt, BRFAL-Ga.

15. Entry for Aug. 1, 1866, vol. 319, Register of Complaints, Milledgeville Agt, BRFAL-Ga; Grossberg, *Governing the Hearth*, 249–50.

16. Entry for Jan. 12, 1866, vol. 392, Register of Complaints, Washington Agt; entry for May 19, 1868, vol. 319, Register of Complaints, Milledgeville Agt, BRFAL-Ga.

17. Entry for June 4, 1868, vol. 264, Register of Complaints, Crawfordsville Agt, BRFAL-Ga.

18. Entries for Jan. 4, May 5, 21, 1866, vol. 393, Register of Complaints, Washington Agt, BRFAL-Ga.

19. Richard Paul Fuke examines how Maryland freedpeople understood the economic importance of controlling the labor of their children in "Planters, Apprenticeship, and Forced Labor." Rebecca Scott notes the economic importance that freedpeople and ex-masters attached to the labor of children in "The Battle over the Child." Herbert Gutman, *Black Family in Slavery and Freedom*, 402–12, examines the freedpeople's efforts to combat illegal apprenticeships in Maryland and the assistance given them by sympathetic Bureau officials. Scott points out that in North Carolina, "contradictory signals from their superiors . . . complicated the decision making process" and confused the issue of the Bureau's role in apprenticeship disputes for agents (Scott, "Battle over the Child," 111). That was not the case in Georgia, where policy was clear.

20. As noted earlier, freedpeople bartered their children's labor for land that they could cultivate independent of their employers. Contract between J. G. Cone and John Cone, Jan. 1, 1866, box 31, Bullock County Contracts; contract between Angus Gillus and Moses, Jan. 31, 1866, box 31, Emanuel County Contracts, Savannah SAC; contract between Joseph Head and Jefferson Wise, Aug. 18, 1866, box 19, Contracts, Griffin SAC, BRFAL-Ga.

21. T. Holden to [J. R. Davis], May [—], 1867, box 10, ULR, Augusta Agt, BRFAL-Ga.

22. The agent ordered the boy to work with his father until he turned twenty-one. Entry for Jan. 27, 1868, vol. 319, Register of Complaints, Milledgeville Agt, BRFAL-Ga.

23. During the summer of 1866, for example, a father who had abandoned his wife and child over a decade earlier kidnapped his son and his former wife's daughter and bound them out to an Emanuel County planter. The Bureau supported the mother's claim, recognizing that she had a right to what the eldest child could earn because she had raised him. Caleb Sibley removed the citizen agent who was a party to this illegal apprenticeship agreement after his inspector general reported the irregularities in the case. W. F. Martins to W. W. Deane, Aug. 20, 1866 (and all enclosures and endorsements), reel 15; G. R. Walbridge to T. P. Littlefield, Feb. 27, 1867, reel 5; Registers of

Civilian Agents, 1865–1867, reel 35, BRFAL-Ga (M798). Also see F. A. H. Gaebel to E. Pickett, May 25, 1867, reel 14, BRFAL-Ga (M798).

24. G. R. Walbridge to C. C. Sibley, Feb. 19, 1867, filed with W. F. Martins to W. W. Deane, Aug. 20, 1866, reel 15, BRFAL-Ga (M798).

25. W. H. S[tiles] to wife [E. A. Stiles], Sept. 12, 1865, ser. A, Mackay-Stiles Papers, Southern Historical Collection, University of North Carolina. As antebellum masters, white Georgians had always had absolute control of their workers' children. There had been no need to have any legal mechanism beyond the law of slavery to keep children on the plantation performing whatever duties their owners prescribed. However, after freedom, ex-masters could look back to the apprenticeship laws that they had designed to control antebellum free blacks. In Georgia, antebellum law allowed whites to bind free black children until they turned twenty-one, if they could prove that the children were "not being raised in becoming and proper manner." The antebellum law is quoted in Berlin, *Slaves without Masters*, 226.

26. In 1865 and 1866, the freedmen's refugee camp on the outskirts of Atlanta sheltered a large number of parentless children (at one point in 1866 there were one hundred orphans in the shantytown). In 1867, there were twenty orphans in the Marietta freedmen's community near Atlanta. R. M. Craighead to E. P. Smith, May 5, 1867, reel 3, AMA-Ga; R. M. Craighead to J. R. Lewis, May 11, 1867, reel 14; C. C. Sibley, Report for May, June 27, 1867, reel 32, BRFAL-Ga (M798); F. Mosebach to G. M. Nolan, Sept. 9, 1867; F. Mosebach to J. S. H. Waldrop, Sept. 11, 1867; F. Mosebach to J. J. Knox, Sept. 16, 1867, vol. 99, LS, Atlanta SAC, BRFAL-Ga; Thornbery, "The Development of Black Atlanta, 1865–1885."

27. Circular No. 3, Oct. 14, 1865, reel 34; Indenture of Apprenticeship for Fanny Reed with John Elkins, Apr. 6, 1866, reel 13, BRFAL-Ga (M798); indenture of apprenticeship for Jack, Bill, and Martha Darden with David Darden, Jan. 13, 1866, box 15, Labor Contracts, Crawfordsville Agt, BRFAL-Ga.

28. *Acts of the General Assembly of the State of Georgia, Passed in Milledgeville, at the Annual Session in December 1865 and January, February, and March 1866*, 6–8; C. C. Sibley, Report for February, Mar. 19, 1866, reel 32, BRFAL-Ga (M798).

29. Emily to O. B. Green [*sic*] [Gray], Feb. 19, 1867, box 23, LR, Marietta SAC; affidavit of Henry Parnell, Mar. 26, 1867, box 33, LR, Thomasville SAC, BRFAL-Ga.

30. For some examples see J. Dunning to D. Tillson, Feb. 3, 1866; E. Kimble to G. L. Eberhart, Mar. 25, 1866, reel 13; W. F. Martins to W. H. C. Pace, June 27, 1867, enclosed in W. F. Martins to E. Pickett, July 9, 1867, reel 18, BRFAL-Ga (M798); affidavit of Adam Middlebrook, Nov. 25, 1867, box 21, LR, Macon SAC; W. O. Moffit to J. M. Hoag, Feb. 17, 1868, filed in J. R. Smith to N. S. Hill, Jan. 6, 1867, box 11, LR, Barton Agt, BRFAL-Ga.

31. C. B. Blacker to C. C. Sibley, June 16, 1868, box 13, LR, Cartersville Agt, BRFAL-Ga.

32. G. R. Walbridge to C. C. Sibley, Feb. 19, 1867, filed with W. F. Martins to W. W. Deane, Aug. 20, 1866, reel 15, BRFAL-Ga (M798).

33. O. B. Gray to E. Pickett, Mar. 4, 1867, box 23, LR, Marietta SAC, BRFAL-Ga.

34. F. A. H. Gaebel to E. Pickett, Apr. 3, 1867, box 1, LR; F. A. H. Gaebel to F. Mosebach, Apr. 30, 1867, vol. 120, LS, Albany SAC, BRFAL-Ga.

35. E. Belcher to C. C. Sibley, Sept. 23, 1867, vol. 367, LS, Dawson Agt, BRFAL-Ga; Drago, *Black Politicians*, 112.

36. Circular No. 6, Apr. 9, 1866, reel 34; W. W. Deane to W. H. Pritchell, Apr. 30, 1866, BRFAL-Ga (M798).

37. J. C. de Graffereid to W. W. Deane, Aug. 14, 1866, reel 26; T. F. Forbes to J. C. de Graffereid, Aug. 29, 1866, reel 3, BRFAL-Ga (M798).

38. D. Tillson to Judge Gamby, Nov. 3, 1866, reel 4, BRFAL-Ga (M798).

39. E. Pickett to H. M. Loyless, Dec. 5, 1866, reel 4, BRFAL-Ga (M798). Also see D. Tillson to P. W. Alexander, Apr. 2, 1866, reel 2, BRFAL-Ga (M798).

40. J. C. Johnson to D. Tillson, Nov. 19, 1866, reel 27; E. Pickett to J. C. Johnson, Nov. 26, 1866, reel 4, BRFAL-Ga (M798).

41. C. C. Sibley, Report for February, Mar. 19, 1867, reel 32; M. F. Gallagher to J. Middleton, Nov. 13, 1867, reel 6, BRFAL-Ga (M798); F. Mosebach to J. M. Blalock, May 20, 1867, vol. 99, LS, Atlanta SAC; J. M. Hoag to F. W. Flanders, June 7, 1867, vol. 397, LS, Savannah SAC; G. Wagner to M. F. Gallagher, Apr. 7, 1868, box 19, URL, Griffin SAC, BRFAL-Ga.

42. Bellamy filed a grievance against Mosebach, but after an investigation, the assistant commissioner supported the officer's actions. F. Mosebach to E. Pickett, Feb. 14, 1867, reel 30; F. L. Bellamy to C. C. Sibley, Feb. 19, 1867, reel 14; F. L. Bellamy to C. C. Sibley, Nov. 26, 1867 (and all endorsements), reel 17, BRFAL-Ga (M798).

43. D. Tillson to Col. W. W. Pritchell, Apr. 3, 1866, reel 2, BRFAL-Ga (M798). Also see endorsement of W. W. Deane to L. J. Lambert, Jan. 27, 1866, reel 8, BRFAL-Ga (M798).

44. Herbert Gutman makes a strong case for the importance of kinship obligations that extended beyond the nuclear family and explores the role that relations played in attempts to reunite families after the war. Gutman, *Black Family in Slavery and Freedom*, 204–29.

45. Entry for May 7, 1868, vol. 319, Register of Complaints, Milledgeville Agt, BRFAL-Ga.

46. Jack Gill to J. R. Lewis, Sept. 21, 1867 (and all endorsements and enclosures): N. P. Hotchkis to [H. C.] Flournoy, Oct. 8, 1867 (and all endorsements), box 23, LR, Marietta SAC, BRFAL-Ga. Also see E. Pickett to J. McWhorter, Feb. 4, 1867, reel 5, BRFAL-Ga (M798), which instructed a grandfather to take his claim to court.

47. E. Walker to "headquarters at Savannah Ga," Mar. 11, 1867, box 27, LR; J. M. Hoag to A. Drake, Mar. 24, 1867; J. M. Hoag to E. Walker, June 18, 1867; J. M. Hoag to A. Drake, June 18, 1867, vol. 397, LS, Savannah SAC, BRFAL-Ga.

48. Emily to O. B. Green [*sic*] [Gray], Feb. 19, 1867, box 23, LR, Marrietta SAC, BRFAL-Ga.

49. Affidavit of J. Robinson, Apr. 27, 1867, reel 14, BRFAL-Ga (M798).

50. J. R. Lewis, "Report of Outrages Committed upon Freedpeople in the State of Georgia from January 1st, 1868, to November 15, 1868," reel 58, (LR)BRFAL (M752) (hereinafter cited as Lewis, "Report of Outrages"). James Peter's case is listed under Albany Subdistrict, September 1868.

51. Carter, *When the War Was Over*, 6–23.

52. Examples are numerous, but see F. Mosebach to J. McNeal, Mar. 6, 1867, vol. 223, LS, Columbus SAC; W. F. White to W. C. Carson, Aug. 21, 1867, box 11, ULR, Bainbridge Agt; H. Catley, Contract Report for September 1868, box 9, Contract Reports, Augusta SAC, BRFAL-Ga; Petition of Spencer Fields and others, Aug. 1867, reel 17; L. Lieberman to N. S. Hill, June 29, 1868, reel 21; O. H. Howard to M. F. Gallagher, Nov. 14, 1868, reel 23, BRFAL-Ga (M798); entries for April 1868, May 1868, Oct. 24, 1868, Atlanta Subdistrict, and Oct. 16, 1868, Macon Subdistrict, in J. R. Lewis, "Report of Outrages"; and P. J. O'Rourke to J. R. Lewis, Dec. 4, 1868, reel 58, (LR)BRFAL (M752). At this time, as freedmen became increasingly active in politics, Ku Klux Klan violence became an important aspect of Democratic Party efforts to regain political control of the state. For an excellent discussion of the Klan and politics in Georgia, see Drago, *Black Politicians*, 144–47 and passim. Also see Rable, *But There Was No Peace*; Trelease, *White Terror*, 226–42; Flynn, *White Land, Black Labor*, 30–58.

53. Stearns, *Black Man*, 452. See Crouch, "A Spirit of Lawlessness," for a good analysis of the types of violence, their perpetrators, and their purposes in Texas. Crouch illustrates that violence during this period was the consequence of white efforts to assert political, economic, and social control of ex-slaves.

54. Of the 147 freedpeople who complained of being victimized by a group of three or more men from 1865 through 1868, sixty-one (41%) had been attacked by whites whose identities were known, and the remaining eighty-six had been attacked by unknown or unnamed whites. These figures—and all others describing violence in Reconstruction Georgia—are only suggestive. They provide a very restricted picture of the true extent of racial violence because so many victims failed to report such crimes. Attacks by known perpetrators might actually have been even more terrifying to the freedpeople than those of ghostly nightriders and might have dissuaded the freedpeople from reporting the crimes; the perpetrators were clearly signaling to their victims that they had no fear of suffering punishment for their actions at the hands of local law or the Yankees. See the various reports on murders and outrages on reel 32, BRFAL-Ga (M798), as well as J. R. Lewis, "Report of Outrages."

55. From the Bureau's establishment into mid-November 1868, of the 463 reported cases of white violence directed against freedpeople, 272 (or almost 59 percent) involved individual white perpetrators who were known by name. Add to these acts of

violence those crimes committed by two known whites, and the total accounts for over 64 percent of the 298 reported cases. In 1865, 1866, and 1867, violent acts perpetrated by three or more individuals, a figure that suggests at least some forethought and co-ordination among the attackers, comprised only about 17 percent of the total reported murders and outrages for these years (21 out of 122 instances of assaulted freed-people). Bureau reports from which these figures were drawn appear on reel 32, BRFAL-Ga (M798).

56. Although there were only twenty-one freedpeople listed as being attacked by known or unknown groups of whites between 1865 and 1867, 126 of the 341 cases of white on black violence reported during 1868, or almost 37 percent, account for the largest portion of that type of violence in any given year included in the Bureau reports. The reports from which these figures come are admittedly incomplete and flawed. For example, Edmund Drago notes that there were riots in the towns Elberton and Augusta in November 1868, and the Bureau records report only one case for Richmond County, the site of Augusta (Drago, *Black Politicians*, 150). Either no other individuals were in-jured in the disturbances or the injured parties did not make it into the reports. Also, Bureau men in tabulating their reports could give specific reasons for the attacks on freedpeople in only about 23 percent of all reported cases for 1865–1868, excluding those cases that the agents or officers noted as being "unprovoked" (105 cases out of 463). Bureau men knew that their figures were incomplete; there were undoubtedly more cases of unrecorded violence. Regardless of their weaknesses, the Bureau reports give some indication of the nature of violence in Georgia during the early years of Re-construction. These reports may be found on reel 32, BRFAL-Ga (M798). The report for 1868 on that reel is incomplete; the version used here is J. R. Lewis, "Report of Out-rages." For a comment on the Warren County problem and how it interfered with the agricultural progress of the freedpeople, see R. A. Anthony to M. F. Gallagher, Oct. 30, 1868, reel 23, BRFAL-Ga (M798). For the Camilla massacre, see Formwalt, "The Camilla Massacre of 1868," and Wynne and St. Julien, "The Camilla Race Riot and the Failure of Reconstruction in Southwest Georgia." For the Savannah affair, see J. M. Hoag to J. R. Lewis, Nov. 9, 1868; C. T. Sawyer to J. R. Lewis, Nov. 12, 1868, reel 23; and Drago, *Black Politicians*, 150.

57. Outrages dated August 3, 8, 1868, Athens; Oct. 22, 1868, Columbus Subdistrict, J. R. Lewis, "Report of Outrages."

58. Outrage dated Aug. 17, 1868, Albany Subdistrict, J. R. Lewis, "Report of Out-rages." It was possible that organized group violence was grossly underreported for var-ious reasons. Nevertheless, I would assume that the proportion of acts committed by three or more whites to those committed by one or two whites is reflected in the reports because the total manuscript record suggests the preponderance of a more personal kind of violence. In other words, although organized political violence admittedly had a significance that extended beyond its victims, it was not as common as the encounters

that developed out of the ordinary and daily interaction of freedpeople asserting their rights and ex-masters trying to protect their assumed privileges. Both Joseph P. Reidy and Charles L. Flynn Jr. acknowledge this fact, but Flynn's original analysis of the Ku Klux Klan in Georgia as well as Edmund L. Drago's important study of Georgia's black leaders and the violence directed at these politically active individuals tend to shift attention away from what might be considered "common" violence. Reidy, *From Slavery to Agrarian Capitalism*, 139–40; Flynn, *White Land, Black Labor*, 13; Drago, *Black Politicians*, 144–47 and passim. Also see Crouch, "A Spirit of Lawlessness," 217–32.

59. J. D. Rogers to N. S. Hill, Nov. 26, 1867, filed with T. W. White to C. C. Sibley, Nov. 25, 1867, box 22, LR, Macon SAC, BRFAL-Ga.

60. J. W. Barney to J. Scott, May 15, 1868, vol. 211, LS, Carnesville Agt, BRFAL-Ga.

61. D. G. Cotting to D. Tillson, Nov. 21, 1865; W. M. Reese to D. Tillson, Nov. 27, 1865, reel 24; D. Tillson to W. A. [Jones], Nov. 24, 1865; D. Tillson to Commanding Officer Washington, Wilkes Co., Dec. 2, 1865, reel 1, BRFAL-Ga (M798); D. Tillson to O. O. Howard, Nov. 28, 1865, reel 20, (LR)BRFAL (M752).

62. N. Bronson, "Report of Persons Murdered in District of Savannah, Georgia [1865–1866]," reel 32, BRFAL-Ga (M798).

63. W. W. Deane to Bvt. Maj. Gen. C. R. Woods, Aug. 14, 1866; W. W. Deane to A. Sloane, Oct. 5, 1866, reel 3; A. M. Campbell to D. Tillson, Oct. 8, 1866, reel 25; C. McC. Lord to W. W. Deane, Oct. 8, 1866; J. R. Phillips to W. W. Deane, Oct. 16, 1866, reel 28, BRFAL-Ga (M798); D. Tillson to E. Foster and A. M. Campbell, Oct. 16, 1866 (copy to O. O. Howard), reel 37, (LR)BRFAL (M752).

64. D. Tillson, "Report of Operations September 22, 1865, to November 1, 1866," reel 32, BRFAL-Ga (M798).

65. Ibid.; G. Wagner to W. W. Deane, June 21, 1866, reel 29; E. Pickett to J. W. Arnold, Nov. 7, 1866, reel 4, BRFAL-Ga (M798).

66. T. F. Forbes to "His Honor Judge of the County Court Columbia Co. Ga.," Sept. 6, 1866; D. Tillson to W. W. Shields, Sept. 22, 1866, reel 3, BRFAL-Ga (M798).

67. D. Tillson, "Report of Operations from September 22, 1865, to November 1, 1866," reel 32, BRFAL-Ga (M798); endorsement of D. Tillson to C. J. Jenkins, Dec. 27, 1866, reel 8; T. F. Forbes to F. A. H. Gaebel, Sept. 5, 1866, reel 3; endorsement of E. Pickett to J. Leonard, Dec. 6, 1866, on A. Griffin to D. Tillson, Nov. 13, 1866, reel 13, BRFAL-Ga (M798). Tillson was able to hold prisoners until civil authorities acted under the authority of Grant's General Orders, No. 44, issued on July 6, 1866. Headquarters of the Army, General Orders, No. 44, July 6, 1866, Reconstruction File, GDAH.

68. Endorsement of D. Tillson to Judge of County Court, Pike County, Sept. 26, 1866, on E. M. L. Ehlers to W. W. Deane, Sept. 3, 1866, reel 13, BRFAL-Ga (M798).

69. D. Tillson, "Report of Operations from September 22, 1865 to November 1, 1866," reel 32, BRFAL-Ga (M798). As noted earlier, Tillson did not hesitate to send troops to address the problem of violence when they were available. In September 1866,

an officer requested twenty to thirty men to curb "*Black Hawk* cavalry" in Heard County. Through Tillson's intervention, the post commander at Macon dispatched an officer and fifteen men to arrest the parties. W. Comstock to W. Mills, Sept. 13, 1866 (and all endorsements), LR, Dist. and Subdist. of Ga. For additional examples of Tillson's response see T. F. Forbes to T. P. Pease, June 15, 1866; D. Tillson to J. D. Powell, Sheriff, DeKalb Co., June 31, 1866; T. F. Forbes to Judge of the County Court, Columbia Co., Sept. 6, 1866, reel 3; E. Pickett to F. A. H. Gaebel. Nov. 3, 1866, reel 4; G. R. Walbridge to W. W. Deane, Aug. 31, 1866, reel 29, BRFAL-Ga (M798); C. A. de la Mesa to Bvt. Lt. Col. J. Ritter, Jan. 14, 1867, vol. 342, LS, Rome SAC, BRFAL-Ga; D. Tillson to Sheriff, DeKalb Co., June 11, 1866, vol. 10/27, LS; Maj. J. D. Wilkens to W. W. Deane, Oct. 29, 1866; Capt. W. Mills to Bvt. Maj. C. F. Trowbridge, Nov. 21, 1866; Capt. V. L. Dykeman to G. R. Walbridge, Dec. 5, 1866, LR, Dist. and Subdist. of Ga.

70. G. Wagner to W. W. Deane, June 14, 1866; C. A. de la Mesa to D. Tillson, Nov. 9, 1866, reel 26; Report of Sergeant R. A. Pelen, Feb. 1, 1866; L. C. Mathews to D. Tillson, Mar. 13, 1866, reel 28; J. K. Smith to W. W. Deane, July 26, 1866, reel 29; Capt. C. McC. Lord to E. Pickett, Jan. 14, 1867, reel 30; D. Tillson, "Report of Operations from September 22, 1865 to November 1, 1866," reel 32, BRFAL-Ga (M798). For an example of the long and lengthy journeys of a detachment sent out to arrest individuals, see G. W. Graffam to C. E. Moore, Mar. 27, Apr. 4, 1866, LR, Dept. of Ga. In March 1866 Lieutenant Graffam and his men traveled 226 miles from Augusta into Putnam County, 40 of them on foot over nearly impassable muddy roads to make his arrests. A day after Graffam made his report, he left with a detachment of cavalry to make more arrests twenty miles from Augusta, but spent several days traveling because the residences of the individuals were spread over the countryside. Unlike other detachments, however, Graffam's successfully completed its duties on both occasions. No wonder Subassistant Commissioner Louis Lambert complained about the need for cavalry; in cases of emergency, he had to requisition horses from the nearest stable for infantrymen to ride. Trowbridge, *The South*, 463–64.

71. G. Walbridge to W. W. Deane, Aug. 31, 1866, reel 29; D. Tillson, "Report of Operations from September 22, 1865 to November 1, 1866," reel 32, BRFAL-Ga (M798).

72. The Savannah subassistant commissioner's report included one case of attempted murder, which if included in the figure above would bring the total to forty-two and would add an additional case to those in which the perpetrator was actually arrested, in this instance by the military. Reports from various subassistant commissioners for 1865–1866, reel 32, BRFAL-Ga (M798).

73. Nieman, *To Set the Law in Motion*, 115–20. For the law, see *Statutes at Large of the United States* (1866), 14:27–29.

74. D. Tillson to J. Erskine, July 18, 1866, reel 3, BRFAL-Ga (M798).

75. J. W. Greene to D. Tillson, Aug. 17, 1866, reel 27; J. O'Neal to W. W. Deane, Oct. 15, 1866; F. Mosebach to E. Pickett, Dec. 6, 1866, reel 28; W. C. Morrill to [J. R. Lewis],

Nov. 2, 1868, reel 23, BRFAL-Ga (M798); N. S. Hill to J. R. Lewis, Dec. 3, 1868, vol. 297, LS, Macon SAC, BRFAL-Ga; Nieman, *To Set the Law in Motion*, 109–15, 137, 139. As Nieman notes, Senator Lyman Trumbull designed the law primarily as a means for combating the overt discrimination of the early black codes.

76. W. C. Morrill to [J. R. Lewis], Nov. 2, 1868, reel 23, BRFAL-Ga (M798); P. J. O'Rourke to J. R. Lewis, Dec. 4, 1868, reel 58, (LR)BRFAL (M752).

77. C. B. Blacker to C. C. Sibley, Sept. 3, 1867, vol. 214, LS, Cartersville Agt, BRFAL-Ga.

78. Again, the reports from which these totals are drawn are not complete, but they do reflect a trend. If anything, the problems experienced by the freedpeople were underreported. It should also be noted that the outcome for eight of the cases is unknown or was not reported and that fourteen victims "settled" their complaints out of court. The reports do not indicate the circumstances surrounding these settlements, but given the conditions of the times, one may assume that at least some of these settlements were less than wholeheartedly embraced by the victims. The cases are drawn from the various subassistant commissioners' reports on murders and outrages for 1867 on reel 32, BRFAL-Ga (M798).

79. Of the 463 cases of white violence against the freedpeople, the Bureau reported 211 instances (almost 46%) of inaction by the civil authorities, 71 instances (about 15%) of unknown action, and 24 instances (about 5%) of cases settled out of court.

80. H. Catley to R. C. Anthony, Nov. 17, 18, 1868, vol. 152, LS, SAC Augusta, BRFAL-Ga; P. J. O'Rourke to J. R. Lewis, Dec. 4, 1868, reel 58, (LR)BRFAL (M752).

81. Affidavit of Samuel McDonald, July 10, 1866, enclosed in J. K. Smith to W. W. Deane, July 26, 1866, reel 29, BRFAL-Ga (M798).

82. For examples of freedpeople carrying guns with them, see J. A. Davis to O. H. Howard, June 11, 1867, box 3, LR, Albany Agt; entry for July 19, 1867, vol. 226, Journal, Columbus Agt, BRFAL-Ga; M. Jones to M. S. Mallard, Mar. 15, 1867, in Myers, *Children of Pride*, 1376.

83. *Savannah National Republican*, Sept. 29, 1865; *New York Herald*, June 2, 1866; Ku Klux Conspiracy, vol. 7: *Georgia*, 854, 937.

84. For references to armed groups of Ogeechee freedmen, see *Savannah Daily Republican*, Nov. 11, 1867, reprinted in *Sandersville Central Georgian*, Dec. 4, 1867, and *Savannah Republican* [n.d] reprinted in *Atlanta Constitution*, Jan. 5, 1869. For Campbell, see E. Pickett to E. Yulee, Dec. 19, 1866, reel 4, BRFAL-Ga (M798), and Duncan, *Freedom's Shore*, 67, 97. For references to other organizations see S. B. Pearce to W. W. Deane, June 10, 1866, reel 28; E. Pickett to E. Yulee, Dec. 19, 1866, reel 4; M. F. Gallagher to H. de F. Young, Aug. 28, 1868, reel 7, BRFAL-Ga (M798); E. M. L. Ehlers to Editors *Griffin Star*, Aug. 13, 1866, vol. 267, LS, Griffin SAC; N. Tift, T. H. Johnston, and J. A. Davis to O. H. Howard, June 11, 1867, box 3, LR, Albany Agt.; W. E. Wiggins to G. Wagner, June 11, 1867, box 20, LR, LaGrange Agt.; D. Gammage to J. B. Daven-

port, Oct. 24, 1867, LR, Columbus SAC; Alvin B. Clark to Corporal Holland, Nov. 18, 1867; Alvin B. Clark to Lt. S. H. Sarson, Nov. 18, 1867, vol. 334, LS, Quitman Agt, BRFAL-Ga; *Columbus Daily Enquirer*, Aug. 19, 1866.

85. J. B. Davenport to G. Wagner, Nov. 11, 1867, enclosed in D. Gammage to J. B. Davenport, Oct. 24, 1867, box 14, LR, Columbus SAC, BRFAL-Ga.

86. H. Catley to M. F. Gallagher, Aug. 27, 1868, reel 21, BRFAL-Ga (M798).

87. G. R. Ballou to O. H. Howard, Aug. 13, 1868, reel 58, (LR)BRFAL (M752). For a report of a similar tense situation in Jackson County from the Athens agent, see H. C. Flournoy to C. C. Sibley, Oct. 5, 1868, reel 23, BRFAL-Ga (M798).

88. Rawick, *American Slave*, vol. 12: *Georgia*, pt. 1, 192–93.

89. *Macon Journal and Messenger*, Apr. 18, 1866, reprinted in *Columbus Daily Enquirer*, Apr. 19, 1866; D. Tillson to N. S. Hill, Apr. 23, 1866, reel 2, BRFAL-Ga (M798); M. A. Cocker to S. B. Moe, Apr. 25, 1866, LR, Dept. of Ga.

90. T. W. Brock to [D. Tillson], May 18, 1866, reel 25, BRFAL-Ga (M798); *Columbus Daily Enquirer*, Mar. 1, 1866.

91. J. J. Knox to E. Pickett, Mar. 7, 1867, reel 15, BRFAL-Ga (M798); J. J. Knox to M. F. Gallagher, Dec. 11, 1867, vol. 169, LS, Athens SAC; H. G. Flournoy to T. D. Elliot, Jan. 9, 1868, vol. 171, LS, Athens Agt., BRFAL-Ga; Mary Ann R. to [Mary Ann Cobb], Dec. 15, 1867, Cobb-Erwin-Lamar Papers, University of Georgia.

92. G. R. Ballou to O. H. Howard, Aug. 13, 1868, reel 58 (LR)BRFAL (M752). Also see C. C. Sibley to O. O. Howard, Report for November 1867, Dec. 28, 1867, reel 32; R. C. Anthony to J. R. Lewis, Nov. 2, 1868, reel 23, BRFAL-Ga (M798); Rawick, *American Slave*, vol. 12: *Georgia*, pt. 1, 193.

93. Circular No. 5, Dec. 22, 1865, reel 34, BRFAL-Ga (M798).

94. Alvin B. Clark to Corporal Holland, Nov. 18, 1867, vol. 334, LS, Quitman Agt, BRFAL-Ga.

95. D. Tillson to N. S. Hill, Apr. 23, 1866, reel 2, BRFAL-Ga (M798).

96. *Albany Patriot*, Dec. 9, 1865. For other white concerns see *Macon Daily Telegraph*, Apr. 3, 13, 1866.

97. Circular No. 5, Dec. 22, 1865, reel 34, BRFAL-Ga (M798). Military commanders after the war also did not allow white efforts to disarm the freedpeople as a class, except in Louisiana. Sefton, *Army and Reconstruction*, 43.

98. Circular No. 1, Athens Subdistrict, Dec. 12, 1865, reprinted in *Athens Southern Banner*, Dec. 20, 1865.

99. Capt. W. Shields to J. Henson, Apr. 44, 1866, vol. 151, LS, Augusta SAC, BRFAL-Ga.

100. J. O'Neal to D. Tillson, July 10, 1866, reel 28; T. F. Forbes to W. Mitchell, May 7, 1866, reel 2; T. F. Forbes to J. O'Neal, July 18, 1866, reel 3, BRFAL-Ga (M798).

101. L. J. Leary to D. Tillson, Apr. 29, 1866; H. F. Horne and others, Justices of Inferior Court, Liberty County, to D. Tillson, Aug. 28, 1866, reel 27; W. W. Deane to

L. J. Leary, May 8, 1866, reel 2; D. Tillson to H. F. Horne and others, Sept. 11, 1866, reel 3, BRFAL-Ga (M798).

102. F. Mosebach to F. G. Wilkins, Aug. 4, 1866, vol. 222, LS, Columbus SAC, BRFAL-Ga.

103. W. W. Deane to H. F. Sickles, Dec. 30, 1865, reel 1, BRFAL-Ga (M798).

104. Special Orders, No. 12, Jan. 15, 1866, reel 34, BRFAL-Ga (M798).

105. Citizens of Dougherty County to [H. G. Strong], July 17, 1866, reel 26; T. F. Forbes to W. C. Watson and others, July 28, 1866, reel 3, BRFAL-Ga (M798).

106. Tillson was clear that his officer could interfere with the freedpeople only if they were indeed violating contracts, and he reminded the officer that under other circumstances he had no authority to interfere. W. W. Deane to E. M. L. Ehlers, Aug. 16, 1866, reel 3, BRFAL-Ga (M798). Also see E. M. L. Elhers to Editors *Griffin Star*, Aug. 13, 1866, vol. 267, LS, Griffin SAC, BRFAL-Ga; E. M. L. Ehlers to W. W. Deane, Aug. 14, 19, 1866, reel 26, BRFAL-Ga (M798).

107. Endorsement of G. Wagner, Oct. 28, 1867, on D. Gammage to J. B. Davenport, Oct. 24, 1867, box 14, LR, Columbus SAC; Alvin B. Clark to Corporal Holland, Nov. 18, 1867, vol. 334, LS, Quitman Agt, BRFAL-Ga; G. Wagner to [C. C. Sibley], Oct. 30, 1867, reel 12; Circular Letter, Georgia Bureau Headquarters, April 8, 1868, reel 34; M. F. Gallagher to H. de F. Young, Aug. 25, 1868, reel 7, BRFAL-Ga (M798).

108. D. G. Risley to C. C. Sibley, June 24, 1867, reel 19, BRFAL-Ga (M798); D. L. Clinch and others to D. Risley, Sept. 7, 1867, box 12, LR; D. G. Risley to E. Wright, Sept. 9, 1867; D. G. Risley to the Freedmen of Camden County, Sept. 9, 1867; D. G. Risley to D. L. Clinch and others, Sept. 9, 1867, vol. 201, LS, Brunswick SAC, BRFAL-Ga. For other examples of freedpeople using armed guards or attending political meetings armed, see J. A. Shearman to Mr. Smith, Mar. 7, 1867, reel 2, AMA-Ga; J. G. Park to G. G. Meade, Apr. 6, 1868, reel 20; L. Lieberman to C. C. Sibley, July 27, 1868, reel 21; M. F. Gallagher to H. de F. Young, Aug. 25, 1868, BRFAL-Ga (M798).

109. M. F. Gallagher to H. de F. Young, Aug. 25, 1868, reel 7; H. Catley "To the Colored Voters," Aug. 30, 1868, enclosed in H. Catley to J. R. Lewis, Aug. 28, 1868, reel 21, BRFAL-Ga (M798).

110. Nathans, *Losing the Peace*, 53.

111. N. S. Hill to J. R. Lewis, Dec. 3, 1868, vol. 297, LS, Macon SAC, BRFAL-Ga.

112. G. R. Walbridge to D. Tillson, July 30, 1866, reel 29, BRFAL-Ga (M798).

113. D. Tillson to [B. B.] Bowen, Sept. 6, 1866, reel 3, BRFAL-Ga (M798). Also see Circular No. 4, Nov. 15, 1865, reel 34, BRFAL-Ga (M798).

114. Tillson threatened to free a black prisoner being held without a trial. E. Pickett to Judge County Court, Chatham County, Nov. 26, 1866, reel 4, BRFAL-Ga (M798).

115. F. J. Robinson to D. Tillson, July 12, 1866, reel 32, (LR)BRFAL (M752); T. F. Forbes to F. J. Robinson, July 13, 1866, reel 3; F. J. Robinson to D. Tillson, July 18, 1866, reel 28, BRFAL-Ga (M798).

116. W. F. Martins to C. C. Sibley, Sept. 15, 1867 (and endorsements), reel 18,

BRFAL-Ga (M798); C. C. Hicks to O. H. Howard, box 1, LR, Albany SAC, BRFAL-Ga; Nieman, *To Set the Law in Motion*, 203; Drago, *Black Politicians*, 95–97.

117. D. Losey to C. C. Sibley, Nov. 25, 1867, vol. 332, LS, Perry Agt; J. J. Knox to T. D. Elliot, Dec. 30, 1867, vol. 169, LS, Athens SAC, BRFAL-Ga.

118. C. B. Blacker to C. C. Sibley, Sept. 3, 1867, enclosed in petition of Spencer Fields and others, Aug. 25, 1867, reel 17, BRFAL-Ga (M798).

119. C. Raushenberg quoted in O. H. Howard to M. F. Gallagher, Nov. 14, 1868, reel 23, BRFAL-Ga (M798).

120. J. W. Barney to J. J. Knox, Nov. 13, 1867, vol. 211, LS, Carnesville Agt, BRFAL-Ga. Also see H. Catley to B. Tankersley, June 16, 1868, vol. 152, LS, Augusta SAC, BRFAL-Ga, and the comments of George Ballou quoted in O. H. Howard to M. F. Gallagher, Nov. 14, 1868, reel 23, BRFAL-Ga (M798).

121. J. M. Hoag to J. P. Gibson, vol. 397, LS, Savannah SAC, BRFAL-Ga.

122. C. A. de la Mesa to C. C. Sibley, Dec. 9, 28, 1867, box 26, ULR, Rome SAC, BRFAL-Ga.

123. C. C. Sibley to C. J. Jenkins, Nov. 13, 1867, reel 6, BRFAL-Ga (M798).

124. H. Catley to B. Tankersley, June 16, 1868, vol. 152, LS, Augusta SAC, BRFAL-Ga.

125. J. Dickey to M. McKay, May 10, 1868 (and endorsements), box 1, LR, Albany SAC; Andrew B. Clark to M. F. Gallagher, Apr. 15, 1868, box 24, Newton Agt, BRFAL-Ga.

126. O. H. Howard to M. F. Gallagher, Apr. 16, 1868 (and all enclosures and endorsements), reel 21, BRFAL-Ga (M798). Howard had been with the Bureau since March 1867. Station Book, vol. 2, 1868, reel 35, BRFAL-Ga (M798).

127. C. C. Sibley, Confidential Circular, Mar. 5, 1868, reel 34, BRFAL-Ga (M798).

128. J. R. Lewis to C. B. Blacker, Sept. 11, 1868, reel 6, BRFAL-Ga (M798).

129. R. C. Drum to C. C. Sibley, Mar. 3, 1868, reel 20, BRFAL-Ga (M798); C. C. Sibley to O. O. Howard, Apr. 4, 1868, reel 53, (LR)BRFAL (M752).

130. O. H. Howard to O. O. Howard, June 9, 1868, reel 53, (LR)BRFAL (M752).

131. The removal of thirteen officials from several Georgia counties during General Pope's command of the Third Military District had not impressed Georgia's other sheriffs, deputies, ordinaries, and judges or improved the dispensation of justice throughout the state. General Meade, who took charge of the Third Military District in January 1868, if anything used his authority even more carefully than had Pope. In the three states under his jurisdiction he had convened only thirty-two military commissions over a ten-month period with results far from being as drastic as his maligners would have people believe. The hearings resulted in fifteen convictions of which only one remained standing, and two other cases were under presidential review with the others being countermanded or remitted. "Report of General John Pope, Oct. 1, 1867," *House Executive Documents*, 40th Cong., 2d sess., no. 1 (serial 1324), 370–72; "Report of General G. G. Meade, Oct. 31, 1868," *House Executive Documents*, 40th Cong., 3d sess., no. 1 (serial 1367), 79–81.

132. H. G. Flournoy to T. D. Elliot, vol. 172, LS, Athens Agt, BRFAL-Ga.

133. H. de F. Young to M. F. Gallagher, Oct. 16, 1868, reel 23, BRFAL-Ga (M798).

134. C. Raushenberg to M. F. Gallagher, Oct. 15, 1868, reel 23, BRFAL-Ga (M798).

135. [O. T. Lyon], Contract Report for Sept. 1868, box 26, Monthly Reports of Contracts, Quitman Agt, BRFAL-Ga.

## Epilogue

1. C. A. de la Mesa to C. C. Sibley, July 1, Sept. 1, 1868; C. A. de la Mesa to J. R. Lewis, Nov. 1, Dec. 1, 26, 1868; C. A. de la Mesa to agents of the subdistrict, Nov. 16, 1868, vol. 342, LS, Rome SAC, BRFAL-Ga; O. O. Howard to J. R. Lewis, Dec. 16, 1868, reel 23, BRFAL-Ga (M798).

2. For example see Campbell, "A Freedmen's Bureau Diary of George Wagner," 359; F. Mosebach to J. R. Lewis, vol. 2, LS, Atlanta SAC, BRFAL-Ga; J. R. Lewis to O. O. Howard, Nov. 12, 1868, reel 7, BRFAL-Ga (M798). For an overview of the Bureau's contraction at this time see Bentley, *Freedmen's Bureau*, 209–10.

3. E. Whittlesey to J. R. Lewis, Dec. 15, 16, 18, 19, 24, 1868; Jan. 6, 1869, and others forwarded during these months on reel 23, BRFAL-Ga (M798). A few Yankee Bureau men remained in Georgia to make lives for themselves, at least for a time. However, most eventually left the state. Places of death or last-known residences were located in various sources but especially in the Civil War pension files of RG 15 for twenty-nine of the forty subassistant commissioners and assistant subassistant commissioners who served with the Bureau in Georgia. All but three died in Georgia. Two others died in Florida and one in Texas. The record is not sufficiently complete to make generalizations about those Yankees who served as agents in Georgia.

4. O. O. Howard, Annual Report, Oct. 14, 1868, *House Executive Documents*, 40th Cong., 3d sess., no. 1 (serial 1367), 1044; J. R. Lewis to O. O. Howard, Dec. 15, 1868, reel 58; Jan. 26, 1869, reel 62, (LR)BRFAL (M752); Circular No. 1, Jan. 25, 1869, reel 34, BRFAL-Ga (M798). E. A. Ware closed the Bureau to outside business on July 15, 1870, but continued to straighten up the agency's affairs into August. E. A. Ware to D. Losey, July 15, 1870, reel 5, (Ed)BRFAL-Ga (M799); E. A. Ware to O. O. Howard, Aug. 20, 1870, (LR)BRFAL (M752).

5. P. J. O'Rourke to G. G. Meade, Feb. 10, 1868, reel 20; [C. C. Sibley] to O. O. Howard, Feb. 6, 1868, reel 7; P. I. O'Rourke to J. R. Lewis, Dec. 4, 1868, reel 30; E. Whittlesey to J. R. Lewis, Dec. 16, 1868, reel 23, BRFAL-Ga (M798).

6. D. Losey to C. C. Sibley, June 17, 1868, vol. 332, LS; D. Losey, Contract Reports for Nov. 1868, Dec. 1868, box 25, Reports Rec'd, Perry Agt, BRFAL-Ga; J. R. Lewis to O. O. Howard, Sept. 26, 1867, reel 49, (LR)BRFAL (M752); Station Books, vol. 1, 1867–1868, reel 35, BRFAL-Ga (M798); J. R. Lewis to D. Losey, Jan. 6, 1869, reel 2; E. A. Ware to D. Losey, July 15, 1870, reel 5, (Ed)BRFAL (M799).

7. W. C. Morrill to [J. R. Lewis], Mar. 24, 1868, reel 23, BRFAL-Ga (M798).

8. H. Catley, Contract Reports for July, August, September 1868, box 9, Contract Reports, Augusta SAC, BRFAL-Ga; H. Catley to M. F. Gallagher, Nov. 1, 1868, reel 23, BRFAL-Ga (M798).

9. O. H. Howard to C. C. Sibley, Sept. 19, 1868, reel 58, (LR)BRFAL (M752); Circular No. 1, Jan. 25, 1869, reel 34, BRFAL-Ga (M798).

10. L. Lieberman to N. S. Hill, Apr. 4, 1868, box 19, URL, Hawkinsville Agt; and the numerous entries in agent C. W. Chapman's journal for late 1868, vol. 226, Journal, Columbus Agt, BRFAL-Ga.

11. Endorsement of L. Lieberman to C. C. Sibley, Aug. 10, 1868, on L. Lieberman to N. S. Hill, June 29, 1868, reel 21, BRFAL-Ga (M798).

12. J. J. Knox, Contract Report for Nov. 1867, box 6, Contract Reports, Athens SAC, BRFAL-Ga.

13. [A. Pokorny] to J. Leonard, Aug. 31, 1868, vol. 195, LS, Butler Agt, BRFAL-Ga.

14. J. W. Alvord to O. O. Howard, Jan. 17, 1870, in John W. Alvord, *Letters from the South*, 16.

15. W. H. Parsons to H. Yancey, Nov. 1, 1868, Benjamin C. Yancey Papers, Southern Historical Collection, University of North Carolina.

16. Drago, *Black Politicians*, 49–65; Nathans, *Losing the Peace*, 127–212; Stearns, *Black Man*, 287–304.

17. Drago, *Black Politicians*, 155–57; Flynn, *White Land, Black Labor*, 84–114; Dittmer, *Black Georgia in the Progressive Era*, 94–95.

18. Michael W. Fitzgerald notes the importance of the Bureau's support of the Union League in Alabama even before the March 1867 Reconstruction Acts. In Mississippi, Fitzgerald explains, the League lacked Bureau sympathy and failed to become as well organized as its Alabama counterpart. One might speculate that if Tillson had been more concerned about Republican politics—more like John Emory Bryant or John Randolph Lewis—during his crucial administration and if he had had the resources to appoint Yankee agents who shared such views, the freedpeople might have had a better chance at helping the Republican Party take hold in the state. Aside from the fact that Tillson would have lacked those resources regardless of his personal views, the prejudices of white Republicans and the strength of the white reactionary movement in the state make such speculation almost pointless (Fitzgerald, *The Union League Movement in the Deep South*, 37–71). For the problems black politicians had with their white Republican counterparts, see Drago, *Black Politicians*, passim.

19. Jones, *Soldiers of Light and Love*, 197.

20. Ibid., 60, 191–208; Harlan, *Separate and Unequal*, 210–69.

21. A. Mitchell to C. C. Sibley, Apr. 26, 1867, reel 15, BRFAL-Ga (M798); C. Ormes and A. Wilson to L. North, July 15, 1868, box 13, LR, Brunswick Agt, BRFAL-Ga; Frances Butler Leigh, *Ten Years on a Georgia Plantation*, 78–79; J. W. Alvord to O. O. Howard, Jan 18, 1870, in Alvord, *Letters from the South*, 19.

22. J. W. Alvord, *Ninth Semi-Annual Report on Schools for Freedmen, January 1, 1870*, 28; J. Alvord to O. O. Howard, Jan. 13, 17, 18, 21, 1870, in Alvord, *Letters from the South*, 19.

23. W. E. B. Du Bois, "The Negro Landholder in Georgia," 665.

24. Leigh, *Ten Years on a Georgia Plantation*, 78–79.

25. Testimony of Rufus Saxton, Feb. 21, 1866, *House Reports*, 39th Cong., 1st sess., no. 3 (serial 1273), pt. 3, p. 101; D. Tillson to O. O. Howard, Nov. 28, 1865, reel 20, (LR)BRFAL (M752); W. F. Eaton to G. Whipple, May 15, 1866, reel 1, AMA-Ga; P. J. O'Rourke to J. R. Lewis, Dec. 4, 1868, reel 30; J. D. Watkins to N. S. Hill, Dec. 24, 1866, reel 29; BRFAL-Ga (M798); G. W. Anderson to D. G. Risley, Feb. 5, 1866, box 12, LR, Brunswick SAC, BRFAL-Ga; Stearns, *Black Man*, 514, 522.

26. Ransom and Sutch, *One Kind of Freedom*, 83–87, esp. Table 5.4.

27. Du Bois, "Negro Landholder in Georgia," 670–71.

28. Rogers, *Thomas County, 1865–1900*, 33.

29. W. E. B. Du Bois's assessment of the Bureau still rings true today. Among its failures, he notes its inability to encourage a climate of goodwill between whites and blacks, and he points out that it would be wrong to discount white attachment to slavery. W. E. B. Du Bois, "The Freedmen's Bureau," 354–65.

30. Tillson believed that ill-disposed Georgians "ought to have for a time at least the experience and education of military law." Eventually, after the state had been "educated and elevated," the "whole matter may be safely left to the people." D. Tillson to O. O. Howard, Dec. 21, 1865, (LR)BRFAL (M752).

31. R. C. Anthony to J. R. Lewis, Nov. 1, 1868, reel 23, BRFAL-Ga (M798).

32. Caleb C. Sibley, Civil War pension file, RG 15, National Archives.

33. J. A. Rockwell to Alfred [P. Rockwell], Jan. 28, 1869, John A. Rockwell Letters, University of Georgia; Warner, *Generals in Blue*, 421.

34. Edward Longacre, "Brave, Radical, Wild," 19; Warner, *Generals in Blue*, 558.

35. Foner, *Politics and Ideology*, 97–127; Woodward, *Reunion and Reaction*.

36. In July 1869 Lewis complained to O. O. Howard that he could not even afford transportation costs to visit the North because of the strain his three-and-a-half-year stint with the Bureau had placed on his income. At this point in his service, Lewis had not been home in thirty-one months. J. R. Lewis to O. O. Howard, July 29, 1869, Howard Papers, Bowdoin College, Brunswick, Maine.

37. A. D. Mayo, "The Final Establishment of the American Common School System in North Carolina, South Carolina, and Georgia," *House Executive Documents*, 58th Cong., 3d sess., no. 5 (serial 4804), 999–1090, but especially pages 1061–64. For the travails of Lewis's political sponsor, see Duncan, *Entrepreneur for Equality*.

38. J. R. Lewis to O. O. Howard, Jan. 20, 1890, Feb. 19, 1891, Mar. 31, Apr. 19, 1897, Howard Papers.

39. J. R. Lewis to O. O. Howard, Mar. 31, 1879, O. O. Howard Papers; *Atlanta Constitution*, Feb. 10, 1900; *John Randolph Lewis: In Memoriam* ([Atlanta]: Grand Army of the Republic, Department of Georgia, 1900); *City of Atlanta: A Descriptive, Historical and Industrial Review of the Gateway City of the South, Being the World's Fair Series on Great American Cities*, 83–84; Cooper, *The Cotton States and International Exposition and South, Illustrated* 145–46; Garrett, *Atlanta and Environs*, 2:198; Coleman, ed., *A History of Georgia*, 215, 239. For the importance of the Grand Army of the Republic in the lives of Union veterans, see McConnell, *Glorious Contentment*.

40. *Atlanta Constitution*, Feb. 10, 1900. For the Yankee perception of the process of reunion, see Silber, *The Romance of Reunion*.

41. D. Tillson to C. C. Sibley, Mar. 22, 1867, reel 16, BRFAL-Ga (M798); D. Tillson to O. O. Howard, Nov. 7, 1867, Howard Papers.

42. D. Tillson to O. O. Howard, Nov. 7, 1867, Howard Papers. As Lawrence N. Powell notes in his study of Yankee planters, Tillson was not alone in his failure. By the end of 1867, the bad postwar seasons "ruined nearly every Yankee who grew cotton in the South in these years." See his *New Masters*, 146. To place Tillson's wife's experience into context, see Currie-McDaniel, "Northern Women in the South, 1860–1880."

43. D. Tillson to O. O. Howard, Nov. 7, 1867, Howard Papers.

44. D. Tillson to J. L. Chamberlain, Joshua Lawrence Chamberlain Papers, Bowdoin College, Brunswick, Maine; D. Tillson to O. O. Howard, Apr. 29, 1871, Howard Papers.

45. *Augusta (Maine) Daily Kennebec Journal*, May 1, 1895; Priscilla B. Adams, director, Shore Village Museum, Rockland, to the author, May 3, 1980. Tillson also remains a part of Rockland's townscape in the name of a street that parallels the waterfront and on a plaque on a Civil War monument—a cannon now somewhat ingloriously located in front of the local Dunkin' Donuts—that he had erected. He is buried in the town cemetery in the family mausoleum, which is made of the granite stone that helped to make his fortune.

46. *New York Times*, May 1, 1895; *Kennebec Journal*, May 1, 1895; *Portland (Maine) Daily Eastern Argus*, May 1, 1895. Apparently, this was something of a trend. Rufus Saxton's entries in two well-known biographical encyclopedias published at the end of the century fail to mention his Bureau service. See Wilson and Fisk, *Appleton's Cyclopedia of American Biography*, 5:410, and *The National Cyclopedia of American Biography*, 4:219.

# Bibliography

## Primary Sources

**MANUSCRIPTS**

*Amistad Research Center, Tulane University, New Orleans*
    American Missionary Association, Georgia. Papers. (Microfilm consulted at University of Georgia Library, Athens, and Duane Library, Fordham University, The Bronx, N.Y.)

*Atlanta History Center*
    McCrary, John Mathew. Papers.
    McNaught, William. Papers.
    Perry, Jesse M. Family correspondence.

*Atlanta University Center*
    Ayer, Frederick. Papers.
    Ware, Edmund Asa. Papers.

*Bowdoin College, Brunswick, Maine*
    Chamberlain, Joshua Lawrence. Papers.
    Howard, Charles H. Papers.
    Howard, Oliver Otis. Papers.

*Duke University, Durham, N.C.*
    Alexander, Adam Leopold. Papers.
    Bryant, John Emory. Papers.
    Bridges, Charles E. Papers.
    Brodnax, Samuel Houston. Papers.
    Harden, Edward R. Papers.
    Johnson, Herschel V. Papers.
    Moore, N. B. Farm journal.
    Smith, William Ephraim. Papers.
    Thomas, Ella Gertrude Clanton. Diary.

*Emory University, Atlanta*
  Battey, Robert. Papers.
  Blackshear, James Appleton. Diary.
  Dobbins, John S. Papers.
  Orr Family Papers.
  Reconstruction miscellany.
  Stephens, Alexander. Papers.
  Thomson, William Sydnor. Papers.
*Georgia Department of Archives and History, Atlanta*
  Campbell, Tunis G. File.
  County Tax Digests, 1857–1861.
  Executive Department. Correspondence.
  Hill, Joshua. File.
  McClatchey, Minerva Leah Rowles. Diary.
  Miller, Nancy Ann. Family letters.
  Reconstruction File.
  Stone, Alexander. File.
  Wilkinson Family Papers.
*Georgia Historical Society, Savannah*
  Watterson, Harvey MaGee. Papers.
  Waring, Joseph Frederick. Papers.
*Historical Society of Pennsylvania, Philadelphia*
  Leigh, Frances Butler. Letterbook. James W. Wistar Family Papers.
*Library of Congress*
  Fessenden, William Pitt. Papers (microfilm).
  Johnson, Andrew. Papers (microfilm).
*National Archives*
  Assistant Commissioner for the State of Georgia, Bureau of Refugees, Freedmen, and
    Abandoned Lands. Records. National Archive microfilm publication M798, Record
    group 105. (Microfilm consulted at Robert Woodruff Library, Emory University,
    and Duane Library, Forham University.)
  Assistant Commissioner for the State of South Carolina, Bureau of Refugees, Freed-
    men, and Abandoned Lands. Records. National Archives microfilm publication
    M869, Record group 105.
  Assistant Commissioner for the State of Tennessee, Bureau of Refugees, Freedmen,
    and Abandoned Lands. Records. National Archives microfilm publication M999,
    Record group 105.
  Civil War pension files. Record group 15.
  Commissioner of the Bureau of Refugees, Freedmen, and Abandoned Lands. Select
    series of records issued. National Archives microfilm publication M742, Record
    group 105.

Commissioner of the Bureau of Refugees, Freedmen, and Abandoned Lands. Registers and letters received. National Archives microfilm publication M752, Record group 105.

Department of Georgia, U.S. Army. Continental Commands, 1821–1920. Record group 393.

District and Subdistrict of Georgia, U.S. Army. Continental Commands, 1821–1920. Record group 393.

Memphis Subdistrict, Bureau of Refugees, Freedmen, and Abandoned Lands. Records. Record group 105.

Records of the Assistant Adjutant General, State of Georgia, Bureau of Refugees, Freedmen, and Abandoned Lands. Records. Record group 105.

Superintendent of Education for the State of Georgia, Bureau of Refugees, Freedmen, and Abandoned Lands. Records. National Archives microfilm publication M799, Record group 105.

Surgeon-in-chief for the State of Georgia, Bureau of Refugees, Freedmen, and Abandoned Lands. Records. Record group 105. (Microfilm consulted at University of Georgia Science Library, Athens.)

*University of California, Berkeley, Bancroft Library*

Le Conte Family Papers Addition.

*University of Georgia, Athens*

Baber-Blackshear Papers.

Barrow, Col. Davis Crenshaw. Papers.

Brown, Joseph E. Papers. Felix Hargrett Collection.

Cobb, Howell. Papers.

Cobb-Erwin-Lamar Collection.

Cooke, William. Journal.

Georgia Governors' Papers. Telamon-Cuyler Collection.

Jones, Charles Colcock Jr. Collection.

Jones, Rev. John. Family papers.

Lamar, Gazaway Bugg. Papers.

Latimer Plantation Record Book.

Rockwell, John A. Letters.

*University of North Carolina, Chapel Hill, Southern Historical Collection*

Alexander-Hillhouse Family. Papers.

Anderson, Edward Clifford. Papers.

Andrews, Charles Haynes. Papers.

Arnold-Screven Family. Papers.

Bacon, Augusta Octavious. Papers.

Bryan, George W. Papers.

Gordon Family. Papers.

Graves Family. Papers.

Horn, Daniel Alexander. Diaries and papers.

Lawton, Alexander Robert. Papers.

Mackay-Stiles Family. Papers.

Yancey, Benjamin Cudworth. Papers.

*Yale University, Sterling Library, New Haven, Conn.*

Saxton, Rufus and S. Willard. Papers.


PUBLIC DOCUMENTS: FEDERAL

Alvord, John W. *Semi-Annual Reports on Schools for Freedmen.* Washington, D.C.: Government Printing Office, 1866–1870.

Du Bois, W. E. B. "The Negro Landholder in Georgia." *U.S. Department of Labor Bulletin* 35 (July 1901): 647–777.

*Statutes at Large of the United States of America, 1789–1873.* 17 vols. Washington, D.C.: Government Printing Office, 1850–1873.

U.S. Congress. *Testimony Taken by the Joint Select Committee to Inquire into the Condition of Affairs in the Late Insurrectionary States.* Vols. 6, 7: *Georgia.* Serials 1489, 1490. Washington, D.C.: Government Printing Office, 1872.

U.S. Department of the Interior. Census Office. *Agriculture of the United States in 1860: Compiled from the Original Returns of the Eighth Census under the Direction of the Secretary of the Interior.* By Joseph C. G. Kennedy. Washington, D.C.: Government Printing Office, 1864.

U.S. House. *Executive Documents.* 39th Cong., 1st sess., 1865. No. 11. Serial 1255.

———. 39th Cong., 1st sess., 1865. No. 70. Serial 1256.

———. 39th Cong., 2d sess., 1866. No. 1. Serial 1285.

———. 40th Cong., 2d sess., 1868. No. 1. Serial 1324.

———. 40th Cong., 3d sess., 1868. No. 1. Serial 1367.

———. 41st Cong., 2d sess., 1870. No. 142. Serial 1417.

———. 58th Cong., 3d sess., 1905. No. 5. Serial 4804.

———. *Reports.* 39th Cong., 1st sess., 1865. No. 30. Serial 1273.

U.S. Senate. *Executive Documents.* 39th Cong., 1st sess., 1865. No. 2. Serial 1237.

———. 39th Cong., 2d sess., 1866. No. 6. Serial 1276.

*War of the Rebellion: A Compilation of the Official Records of the Union and Confederate Armies.* Series 1, vols. 6, 28, 47, 49; series 3, vols. 2, 4, 5. Washington, D.C.: Government Printing Office, 1895, 1897.


PUBLIC DOCUMENTS: STATE

Candler, Allen D., comp. *The Confederate Records of the State of Georgia.* Vols. 4, 6. Atlanta: Chas. P. Byrd, 1910, 1911.

Georgia General Assembly. *Acts of the General Assembly of the State of Georgia, Passed in Milledgeville, at the Annual Session in December 1865 and January, February, and March 1866.* Milledgeville, 1866.

———. *Acts of the General Assembly of the State of Georgia, Passed in Milledgeville, at the Annual Session in November and December 1866.* Macon, 1867.

Maine Adjutant General's Office. *Report of the Adjutant General of the State of Maine for the Years 1864 and 1865.* Augusta, 1866.

———. *Report of the Adjutant General of the State of Maine for the Year Ending December 31, 1866.* Augusta, 1867.

NEWSPAPERS AND PERIODICALS

*Albany Patriot*
*American Missionary*
*Athens Southern Banner*
*Atlanta Constitution*
*Atlanta Intelligencer*
*Augusta Daily Constitutionalist*
*Augusta (Maine) Kennebec Journal*
*Augusta Loyal Georgian*
*Brunswick (Maine) Telegraph*
*Columbus Daily Enquirer*
*Columbus Daily Sun*
*Freedmen's Advocate*
*Macon Daily Telegraph*
*National Anti-Slavery Standard*
*New York Herald*
*New York Times*
*New York Tribune*
*Portland (Maine) Daily Eastern Argus*
*Rome Weekly Courier*
*Sandersville Central Georgian*
*Savannah Daily Republican*
*Savannah Herald*
*Savannah National Republican*
*Southern Cultivator*
*Turnwold Countryman*
*Washington Evening Star*

## Published Sources

Abbott, Martin. *The Freedmen's Bureau in South Carolina, 1865–1872*. Chapel Hill: University of North Carolina Press, 1967.

Abbott, Richard H. "Jason Clarke Swayze, Republican Editor in Reconstruction Georgia, 1867–1873." *Georgia Historical Quarterly* 79 (summer 1995): 337–66.

Alvord, John W. *Letters from the South Relating to the Condition of the Freedmen Addressed to Major General O. O. Howard, Commissioner, Bureau R., F., and A. L.* Washington, D.C.: Howard University, 1870.

———. "Negro Industry." *American Missionary* 9 (November 1865): 249.

American Missionary Association. *Annual Reports* (Nineteenth through Twenty-third). New York: American Missionary Association, 1865–1869.

Andrews, Sidney. *The South since the War: As Shown by Fourteen Weeks of Travel and Observation in Georgia and the Carolinas*. Boston: Ticknor and Fields, 1866.

Axinn, June, and Herman Levin. *Social Welfare: A History of the American Response to Need*. 2d ed. New York: Longman, 1982.

Baker, Jean H. *Affairs of Party: The Political Culture of Northern Democrats in the Mid-Nineteenth Century*. Ithaca, N.Y.: Cornell University Press, 1983.

Belz, Herman. *Emancipation and Equal Rights: Politics and Constitutionalism in the Civil War Era*. New York: W. W. Norton, 1978.

———. *A New Birth of Freedom: The Republican Party and Freedmen's Rights, 1861–1866*. Westport, Conn.: Greenwood Press, 1976.

Benedict, G. G. *Vermont in the Civil War: A History of the Part Played by Vermont Soldiers and Sailors in the War for the Union, 1861–1865*. 2 vols. Burlington, Vt.: Free Press Association, 1886.

Bentley, George R. *A History of the Freedmen's Bureau*. Philadelphia: University of Pennsylvania Press, 1955. Reprint, New York: Octagon Books, 1974.

Berlin, Ira. *Slaves without Masters: The Free Negro in the Antebellum South*. New York: Pantheon Books, 1974.

Berwanger, Eugene H. *The Frontier against Slavery*. Urbana: University of Illinois Press, 1967.

*Biographical Encyclopedia of Pennsylvania of the Nineteenth Century*. Philadelphia: Galaxy, 1874. Reprinted as pub. no. 3 on reel 1 of *Pennsylvania County and Regional Histories*. New Haven, Conn.: Research, 1973.

Blassingame, John W. "Before the Ghetto: The Making of the Black Community in Savannah, Georgia, 1865–1880." *Journal of Social History* 6 (summer 1973): 463–88.

Boatner, Mark M., III. *The Civil War Dictionary*. Rev. ed. New York: David McKay, 1988.

Boggs, Marion Alexander, ed. *The Alexander Letters, 1787–1900*. Savannah, Ga.: privately printed for George J. Baldwin, 1910.

Bowen, David Warren. *Andrew Johnson and the Negro*. Knoxville: University of Tennessee Press, 1989.

Bremner, Robert H. *The Public Good: Philanthropy and Welfare in the Civil War Era*. New York: Alfred A. Knopf, 1980.

Brooks, Robert Preston. *The Agrarian Revolution in Georgia, 1865–1912*. Madison: University of Wisconsin Press, 1914. Reprint, New York: AMS, 1971.

Bullard, Mary R. *An Abandoned Black Settlement on Cumberland Island, Georgia*. South Dartmouth, Mass.: Mary R. Bullard, 1982.

Burr, Virginia Ingraham, ed. *The Secret Eye: The Journal of Ella Gertrude Clanton Thomas, 1848–1889*. Chapel Hill: University of North Carolina Press, 1990.

Busbee, Westley Floyd, Jr. "Presidential Reconstruction in Georgia, 1865–1867." Ph.D. diss., University of Alabama, 1973.

Butchart, Ronald E. *Northern Schools, Southern Blacks, and Reconstruction: Freedmen's Education, 1862–1875*. Westport, Conn.: Greenwood Press, 1980.

Campbell, William A., ed. "A Freedmen's Bureau Diary by George Wagner." Parts 1 and 2. *Georgia Historical Quarterly* 48 (June, September, 1964), 196–214, 333–59.

Carpenter, John A. *Sword and Olive Branch: Oliver Otis Howard*. Pittsburgh: University of Pittsburgh Press, 1964.

Carter, Dan T. "The Anatomy of Fear: The Christmas Day Insurrection Scare of 1865." *Journal of Southern History* 42 (August 1976): 345–64.

———. *When the War Was Over: The Failure of Self-Reconstruction in the South, 1865–1867*. Baton Rouge: Louisiana State University Press, 1985.

Cimbala, Paul A. "A Black Colony in Dougherty County: The Freedmen's Bureau and the Failure of Reconstruction in Southwest Georgia." *Journal of Southwest Georgia History* 4 (fall 1986): 72–89.

———. "Confiscation: Federal Confiscation." In *Encyclopedia of the Confederacy*, ed. Richard N. Current, 1:389–91. New York: Simon and Schuster, 1993.

*City of Atlanta: A Descriptive, Historical and Industrial Review of the Gateway City of the South, Being the World's Fair Series on Great American Cities*. Louisville, Ky.: Inter-State, 1892–93.

Clinton, Catherine. "Bloody Terrain: Freedwomen, Sexuality, and Violence during Reconstruction." *Georgia Historical Quarterly* 76 (summer 1992): 313–32.

Cohen, William. *At Freedom's Edge: Black Mobility and the Southern White Quest for Racial Control, 1861–1915*. Baton Rouge: Louisiana State University Press, 1991.

Cohen-Lack, Nancy. "A Struggle for Sovereignty: National Consolidation, Emancipation, and Free Labor in Texas, 1865." *Journal of Southern History* 58 (February 1992): 57–98.

Coleman, Kenneth, ed. *A History of Georgia*. Athens: University of Georgia Press, 1977.

Coleman, Kenneth, and Charles Stephen Gurr, eds. *Dictionary of Georgia Biography*. 2 vols. Athens: University of Georgia Press, 1983.

Conway, Alan. *The Reconstruction of Georgia*. Minneapolis: University of Minnesota Press, 1966.

Cooper, Walter G. *The Cotton States and International Exposition and South, Illustrated*. Atlanta: Illustrator Co., 1896.

Cox, John, and LaWanda Cox. "General O. O. Howard and the 'Misrepresented Bureau,'" *Journal of Southern History* 19 (November 1953): 427–56.

Cox, LaWanda. "From Emancipation to Segregation: National Policy and Southern Blacks." In *Interpreting Southern History: Historiographical Essays in Honor of Sanford W. Higginbotham*, ed. John B. Boles and Evelyn Thomas Nolan, 199–253. Baton Rouge: Louisiana State University Press, 1987.

———. *Lincoln and Black Freedom: A Study in Presidential Leadership*. Columbia: University of South Carolina Press, 1981.

———. "The Promise of Land for the Freedmen." *Mississippi Valley Historical Review* 45 (December 1958): 413–40.

Cox, LaWanda, and John H. Cox. *Politics, Principle, and Prejudice, 1865–1866: The Dilemma of Reconstruction America*. New York: Free Press, 1963.

Crouch, Barry A. *The Freedmen's Bureau and Black Texans*. Austin: University of Texas Press, 1992.

———. "Hidden Sources of Black History: The Texas Freedmen's Bureau Records as a Case Study." *Southwestern Historical Quarterly* 83 (January 1980): 211–26.

———. "A Spirit of Lawlessness: White Violence, Texas Blacks, 1865–1868." *Journal of Social History* 18 (winter 1984): 217–32.

Crowe, Charles. *George Ripley: Transcendentalist and Utopian Socialist*. Athens: University of Georgia Press, 1967.

Currie-McDaniel, Ruth. *Carpetbagger of Conscience: A Biography of John Emory Bryant*. Athens: University of Georgia Press, 1987.

———. "Northern Women in the South, 1860–1880." *Georgia Historical Quarterly* 76 (summer 1992): 284–312.

Cutler, William W., III. "Horace Mann and Common School Reform." In *American Reform and Reformers: A Biographical Dictionary*, ed. Randall M. Miller and Paul A. Cimbala. Westport, Conn.: Greenwood Press, 1996.

Dennett, John Richard. *The South as It Is, 1865–1866*. Edited by Henry M. Christman. New York: Viking Press, 1965. Reprint, Athens: University of Georgia Press, 1986.

Dittmer, John. *Black Georgia in the Progressive Era, 1900–1920*. Urbana: University of Illinois Press, 1977.

Donald, David Herbert. *Liberty and Union: The Crisis of Popular Government, 1830–1890*. Boston: Little, Brown, 1978.

Drago, Edmund L. "Black Georgia during Reconstruction." Ph.D. diss., UC Berkeley, 1975.

———. *Black Politicians and Reconstruction in Georgia: A Splendid Failure*. Baton

Rouge: Louisiana State University Press, 1982; 2d ed., Athens: University of Georgia Press, 1992.

———. "Georgia's First Black Voter Registrars during Reconstruction." *Georgia Historical Quarterly* 78 (winter 1994): 760–93.

Du Bois, W. E. B. "The Freedmen's Bureau." *Atlantic Monthly* 87 (March 1901): 354–65.

Duncan, Russell. *Entrepreneur for Equality: Governor Rufus Bullock, Commerce, and Race in Post–Civil War Georgia*. Athens: University of Georgia Press, 1994.

———. *Freedom's Shore: Tunis Campbell and the Georgia Freedmen*. Athens: University of Georgia Press, 1986.

Eaton, Cyrus. *History of Thomaston, Rockland, and South Thomaston, Maine; from Their first Explorations, A.D. 1605; with Family Genealogies*. 2 vols. Hallowell, Me.: Masters, Smith, 1865.

Engerrand, Steven W. "'Now Scratch or Die': The Genesis of Capitalistic Agricultural Labor in Georgia, 1865–1880." Ph.D. diss., University of Georgia, 1981.

Faust, Patricia L., ed. *Historical Times Illustrated Encyclopedia of the Civil War*. New York: Harper and Row, 1986.

Finley, Randy. "The Freedmen's Bureau in Arkansas." Ph.D. diss., University of Arkansas, 1993.

Fitzgerald, Michael W. *The Union League Movement in the Deep South: Politics and Agricultural Change during Reconstruction*. Baton Rouge: Louisiana State University Press, 1989.

Flynn, Charles L., Jr. *White Land, Black Labor: Caste and Class in Late-Nineteenth-Century Georgia*. Baton Rouge: Louisiana State University Press, 1983.

Foner, Eric. *Free Soil, Free Labor, Free Men: The Ideology of the Republican Party before the Civil War*. New York: Oxford University Press, 1970.

———. *Freedom's Lawmakers: A Directory of Black Officeholders during Reconstruction*. New York: Oxford University Press, 1993.

———. *Nothing but Freedom: Emancipation and Its Legacy*. Baton Rouge: Louisiana State University Press, 1983.

———. *Politics and Ideology in the Age of the Civil War*. New York: Oxford University Press, 1980.

———. *Reconstruction: America's Unfinished Revolution, 1863–1877*. New York: Harper and Row, 1988.

Formwalt, Lee W. "The Camilla Massacre of 1868: Racial Violence as Political Propaganda." *Georgia Historical Quarterly* 71 (fall 1987): 399–426.

———, ed. "Petitioning Congress for Protection: A Black View of Reconstruction at the Local Level." *Georgia Historical Quarterly* 73 (summer 1989): 305–22.

Foster, Gaines M. "The Limitations of Federal Health Care for Freedmen, 1862–1868." *Journal of Southern History* 48 (August 1982): 349–72.

Fredrickson, George M. *The Black Image in the White Mind: The Debate on Afro-American Character and Destiny, 1817–1914*. New York: Harper and Row, 1971.

Fuke, Richard Paul. "Planters, Apprenticeship, and Forced Labor: The Black Family under Pressure in Post-Emancipation Maryland." *Agricultural History* 62 (fall 1988): 57–74.

Ganus, Clifton L., Jr. "The Freedmen's Bureau in Mississippi." Ph.D. diss., Tulane University, 1953.

Garrett, Franklin M. *Atlanta and Environs: A Chronicle of Its People and Events*. 3 vols. New York: Lewis Historical, 1954.

Georgia Writers' Project. *Drums and Shadows: Survival Studies among the Georgia Coastal Negroes*. Athens: University of Georgia Press, 1940, 1986.

Gerteis, Louis S. *From Contraband to Freedman: Federal Policy toward Southern Blacks, 1861–1865*. Westport, Conn.: Greenwood Press, 1973.

Glickstein, Jonathan A. "'Poverty Is Not Slavery': American Abolitionists and the Competitive Labor Market." In *Antislavery Reconsidered: New Perspectives on the Abolitionists*, ed. Lewis Perry and Michael Fellman, 195–218. Baton Rouge: Louisiana State University Press, 1979.

Gottlieb, Manuel. "The Land Question in Georgia during Reconstruction." *Science and Society* 3 (summer 1939): 356–88.

Grossberg, Michael. *Governing the Hearth: Law and the Family in Nineteenth-Century America*. Chapel Hill: University of North Carolina Press, 1985.

Gutman, Herbert G. *The Black Family in Slavery and Freedom, 1750–1925*. New York: Pantheon Books, 1976.

Hahn, Steven. *The Roots of Southern Populism: Yeoman Farmers and the Transformation of the Georgia Upcountry, 1850–1890*. New York: Oxford University Press, 1983.

Harlan, Louis R. *Separate and Unequal: Public School Campaigns and Racism in the Southern Seaboard States, 1901–1915*. Chapel Hill: University of North Carolina Press, 1958.

Harris, William C. *The Day of the Carpetbagger: Republican Reconstruction in Mississippi*. Baton Rouge: Louisiana State University Press, 1979.

Hayes, John D., ed. *Samuel Francis Dupont: A Selection from His Civil War Letters*. 3 vols. Ithaca, N.Y.: Cornell University Press, 1969.

Heard, George A. "St. Simons Island during the War between the States." *Georgia Historical Quarterly* 22 (September 1938): 249–72.

Hess, Earl J. *Liberty, Virtue, and Progress: Northerners and Their War for the Union*. New York: New York University Press, 1988.

Higgs, Robert. *Competition and Coercion: Blacks in the American Economy, 1864–1914*. Cambridge: Cambridge University Press, 1977.

Howard, Oliver Otis. *Autobiography of Oliver Otis Howard, Major General, United States Army*. 2 vols. New York: Baker and Taylor, 1908.

Hughes, Melvin Clyde. *County Government in Georgia*. Athens: University of Georgia Press, 1944. Reprint, Westport, Conn.: Greenwood Press, 1975.

Hyman, Harold M. *A More Perfect Union: The Impact of the Civil War and Reconstruction on the Constitution*. New York: Alfred A. Knopf, 1973.

Jaynes, Gerald David. *Branches without Roots: Genesis of the Black Working Class in the American South, 1862–1882*. New York: Oxford University Press, 1986.

*John Randolph Lewis: In Memoriam*. [Atlanta]: Grand Army of the Republic, Department of Georgia, 1900.

Jones, Jacqueline. *Labor of Love, Labor of Sorrow: Black Women, Work, and the Family from Slavery to the Present*. New York: Basic Books, 1985.

———. *Soldiers of Light and Love: Northern Teachers and Georgia Blacks, 1865–1873*. Chapel Hill: University of North Carolina Press, 1980.

Kaestle, Carl F. *Pillars of the Republic: Common Schools and American Society, 1780–1860*. New York: Hill and Wang, 1983.

Leigh, Frances Butler. *Ten Years on a Georgia Plantation since the War*. London: Richard Bentley, 1883. Reprint, New York: Negro Universities Press, 1969.

Litwack, Leon F. *Been in the Storm So Long: The Aftermath of Slavery*. New York: Alfred A. Knopf, 1979.

———. *North of Slavery: The Negro in the Free States, 1790–1860*. Chicago: University of Chicago Press, 1961.

Logue, Larry M. *To Appomattox and Beyond: The Civil War Soldier in War and Peace*. Chicago: Ivan R. Dee, 1996.

Longacre, Edward. "Brave, Radical, Wild: The Contentious Career of Brigadier General Edward A. Wild." *Civil War Times Illustrated* 19 (June 1980): 9–19.

Lowe, Richard. "The Freedmen's Bureau and Local Black Leadership." *Journal of American History* 80 (December 1993): 989–98.

Lunceford, Alvin Mell, Jr. *Taliaferro County, Georgia: Records and Notes*. Spartanburg, S.C.: Reprint, 1988.

McConnell, Stuart. *Glorious Contentment: The Grand Army of the Republic, 1865–1900*. Chapel Hill: University of North Carolina Press, 1992.

McCrary, Peyton. "The Party of Revolution: Republican Ideas about Politics and Social Change, 1862–1867." *Civil War History* 30 (December 1984): 330–50.

McFeely, William S. *Sapelo's People: A Long Walk into Freedom*. New York: W. W. Norton, 1994.

———. *Yankee Stepfather: General O. O. Howard and the Freedmen*. New Haven, Conn.: Yale University Press, 1968.

McLeod, Jonathan W. *Workers and Workplace Dynamics in Reconstruction-Era Atlanta: A Case Study*. Los Angeles: UCLA Center for Afro-American Studies, 1989.

McPherson, James M. *What They Fought For, 1961–1865*. Baton Rouge: Louisiana State University Press, 1994.

Magdol, Edward. *A Right to the Land: Essays on the Freedmen's Community.* Westport, Conn.: Greenwood Press, 1977.

Mantell, Martin E. *Johnson, Grant, and the Politics of Reconstruction.* New York: Columbia University Press, 1973.

Mathis, Ray, Mary Mathis, and Douglas Clare Purcell, eds. *John Horry Dent Farm Journals and Account Books, 1840–1892.* Microfilm ed. University: University of Alabama Press for the Historic Chattahoochee Commission, 1977.

May, J. Thomas. "Continuity and Change in the Labor Program of the Union Army and the Freedmen's Bureau." *Civil War History* 17 (September 1971): 245–54.

Messner, William F. *Freedmen and the Ideology of Free Labor: Louisiana, 1862–1865.* Lafayette: Center for Louisiana Studies, University of Southwestern Louisiana, 1978.

Mohr, Clarence L. "Before Sherman: Georgia Blacks and the Union War Effort, 1861–1864." *Journal of Southern History* 45 (August 1979): 331–52.

———. *On the Threshold of Freedom: Masters and Slaves in Civil War Georgia.* Athens: University of Georgia Press, 1986.

Moreno, Paul. "Racial Classifications and Reconstruction Legislation." *Journal of Southern History* 61 (May 1995): 271–304.

Morgan, Philip D. "The Ownership of Property by Slaves in the Mid-Nineteenth-Century Low Country." *Journal of Southern History* 49 (August 1983): 399–420.

———. "Work and Culture: The Task System and the World of Lowcountry Blacks, 1700 to 1800." *William and Mary Quarterly*, 3d ser., 39 (October 1982): 563–99.

Morris, Robert C. *Reading, 'Riting, and Reconstruction: The Education of Freedmen in the South, 1861–1870.* Chicago: University of Chicago Press, 1981.

Myers, Robert Manson, ed. *The Children of Pride: A True Story of Georgia and the Civil War.* New Haven, Conn.: Yale University Press, 1972.

Nathans, Elizabeth Studley. *Losing the Peace: Georgia Republicans and Reconstruction, 1865–1871.* Baton Rouge: Louisiana State University Press, 1968.

*National Cyclopedia of American Biography.* 49 vols. New York: James T. White, 1907.

Nieman, Donald G. *To Set the Law in Motion: The Freedmen's Bureau and the Legal Rights of Blacks, 1865–1868.* Millwood, N.Y.: KTO Press, 1979.

Orr, Dorothy. *A History of Education in Georgia.* Chapel Hill: University of North Carolina Press, 1950.

Osthaus, Carl R. *Freedmen, Philanthropy, and Fraud: A History of the Freedman's Savings Bank.* Urbana: University of Illinois Press, 1976.

Oubre, Claude F. *Forty Acres and a Mule: The Freedmen's Bureau and Black Land Ownership.* Baton Rouge: Louisiana State University Press, 1978.

Owen, James L. "The Negro in Georgia during Reconstruction, 1865–1872: A Social History." Ph.D. diss., University of Georgia, 1975.

Peirce, Paul S. *The Freedmen's Bureau: A Chapter in the History of Reconstruction.* Iowa City: State University of Iowa, 1904. Reprint, St. Clair Shores, Mich.: Scholarly Press, 1970.

Pennsylvania College of Dental Surgery, Session 1858–59. *Annual Announcement.* Philadelphia: J. H. Jones, 1858.

Phillips, Paul David. "A History of the Freedmen's Bureau in Tennessee." Ph.D. diss., Vanderbilt University, 1964.

Powell, Lawrence N. "The American Land Company and Agency: John A. Andrew and the Northernization of the South." *Civil War History* 21 (December 1975): 293–308.

———. *New Masters: Northern Planters during the Civil War and Reconstruction.* New Haven, Conn.: Yale University Press, 1980.

———. "The Politics of Livelihood: Carpetbaggers in the Deep South." In *Region, Race, and Reconstruction: Essays in Honor of C. Vann Woodward*, ed. J. Morgan Kousser and James S. McPherson, 315–47. New York: Oxford University Press, 1982.

Rable, George C. *But There Was No Peace: The Role of Violence in the Politics of Reconstruction.* Athens: University of Georgia Press, 1984.

Ransom, Roger L., and Richard Sutch. *One Kind of Freedom: The Economic Consequences of Emancipation.* Cambridge: Cambridge University Press, 1977.

Rapport, Sara. "The Freedmen's Bureau as a Legal Agent for Black Men and Women in Georgia, 1865–1868." *Georgia Historical Quarterly* 73 (spring 1989): 26–53.

Rawick, George P., ed. *The American Slave: A Composite Autobiography.* Vol. 8: *Arkansas Narratives.* Vols. 12–13: *Georgia Narratives.* Westport, Conn.: Greenwood Press, 1972.

Reid, Whitelaw. *After the War: A Southern Tour, May 1, 1865, to May 1, 1866.* Cincinnati: Moore, Wilstach and Baldwin, 1866. Reprint, New York: Harper and Row, 1965.

Reidy, Joseph P. "Aaron A. Bradley: Voice of Black Labor in the Georgia Lowcountry." In *Southern Black Leaders of the Reconstruction Era*, ed. Howard N. Rabinowitz, 281–308. Urbana: University of Illinois Press, 1982.

———. *From Slavery to Agrarian Capitalism in the Cotton Plantation South: Central Georgia, 1800–1880.* Chapel Hill: University of North Carolina Press, 1992.

———. "Masters and Slaves, Planters and Freedmen: The Transition from Slavery to Freedom in Central Georgia, 1820–1880." Ph.D. diss., Northern Illinois University, 1982.

Richardson, Joe M. *Christian Reconstruction: The American Missionary Association and Southern Blacks, 1861–1890.* Athens: University of Georgia Press, 1986.

Richter, William L. *Overreached on All Sides: The Freedmen's Bureau Administrators in Texas, 1865–1868.* College Station: Texas A&M University Press, 1991.

Roark, James L. *Masters without Slaves: Southern Planters in the Civil War and Reconstruction*. New York: W. W. Norton, 1977.

Robertson, James I., Jr., ed. *The Diary of Dolly Lunt Burge*. Athens: University of Georgia Press, 1862.

Rodgers, Daniel T. *The Work Ethic in Industrial America, 1850–1920*. Chicago: University of Chicago Press, 1978.

Rogers, William Warren. *Thomas County, 1865–1900*. Tallahassee: Florida State University Press, 1973.

Rose, Willie Lee. *Rehearsal for Reconstruction: The Port Royal Experiment*. Indianapolis: Bobbs-Merrill, 1964. Reprint, New York: Oxford University Press, 1978.

Royce, Edward. *The Origins of Southern Sharecropping*. Philadelphia: Temple University Press, 1993.

Savitt, Todd L. "Politics in Medicine: The Georgia Freedmen's Bureau and the Organization of Health Care, 1865–1866." *Civil War History* 28 (March 1982): 45–64.

Schmidt, James D. "'Neither Slavery nor Involuntary Servitude': Free Labor and American Law, ca. 1815–1880." Ph.D. diss., Rice University, 1992.

Schob, David E. *Hired Hands and Plowboys: Farm Labor in the Midwest, 1815–1860*. Urbana: University of Illinois Press, 1975.

Schurz, Carl. *Report on the Condition of the South*. New York: New York Times and Arno Press, 1969.

Scott, Rebecca. "The Battle over the Child: Child Apprenticeship and the Freedmen's Bureau in North Carolina." *Prologue* 10 (summer 1978): 101–13.

Sefton, James E. *The United States Army and Reconstruction, 1865–1877*. Baton Rouge: Louisiana State University Press, 1967.

Sherman, William Tecumseh. *Memoirs of General William T. Sherman*. 2 vols. Edited by William S. McFeely. New York: D. Appleton, 1875; reprint, New York: Charles L. Webster, 1891; reprint, New York: Da Capo Press, 1984.

Shklar, Judith N. *American Citizenship: The Quest for Inclusion*. Cambridge, Mass: Harvard University Press, 1991.

Silber, Nina. *The Romance of Reunion: Northerners and the South, 1865–1900*. Chapel Hill: University of North Carolina Press, 1993.

Simpson, Brooks D., LeRoy P. Graf, and John Muldowny, eds. *Advice after Appomattox: Letters to Andrew Johnson, 1865–1866*. Special vol. 1 of *The Papers of Andrew Johnson*. Knoxville: University of Tennessee Press, 1987.

Spalding, B. Phinizy. "Georgia." In *The Encyclopedia of Southern History*, ed. David C. Roller and Robert W. Twyman. Baton Rouge: Louisiana State University Press, 1979.

Stampp, Kenneth M. *The Era of Reconstruction, 1865–1877*. New York: Alfred A. Knopf, 1965.

Stanley, Amy Dru. "Beggars Can't Be Choosers: Compulsion and Contract in Postbellum America." *Journal of American History* 78 (March 1992): 1265–93.

Stearns, Charles. *The Black Man of the South, and the Rebels; or, The Characteristics of the Former, and the Recent Outrages of the Latter.* New York: American News, 1872. Reprint, New York: Negro Universities Press, 1969.

Thomas, Emory M. *Robert E. Lee: A Biography.* New York: W. W. Norton, 1995.

Thompson, C. Mildred. "The Freedmen's Bureau in Georgia in 1865–66: An Instrument of Reconstruction." *Georgia Historical Quarterly* 5 (March 1921): 40–49.

———. *Reconstruction in Georgia: Economic, Social, Political, 1865–1872.* New York: Columbia University Press, 1915. Reprint, Savannah, Ga.: Beehive Press, 1972.

Thornbery, Jerry John. "The Development of Black Atlanta, 1865–1885." Ph.D. diss., University of Maryland, 1977.

Trefousse, Hans L. *Andrew Johnson: A Biography.* New York: W. W. Norton, 1989.

Trelease, Allen W. *White Terror: The Ku Klux Klan Conspiracy and Southern Reconstruction.* New York: Harper and Row, 1971.

Trowbridge, John Townsend. *The South: A Tour of Its Battlefields and Ruined Cities, a Journey through the Desolated States, and Talks with the People.* Hartford, Conn.: L. Stebbins, 1866.

University of Vermont and State Agricultural College. *General Catalogue, 1791–1900.* Burlington: Free Press Association, 1901.

Voegeli, V. Jacque. *Free but Not Equal: the Midwest and the Negro during the Civil War.* Chicago: University of Chicago Press, 1967.

Wallenstein, Peter. *From Slave South to New South: Public Policy in Nineteenth-Century Georgia.* Chapel Hill: University of North Carolina Press, 1987.

Ward, Theodore. *Our Lan'.* In *Black Drama in America: An Anthology*, ed. Darwin T. Turner, 115–203. Greenwich, Conn.: Fawcett, 1971.

Warner, Ezra J. *Generals in Blue: Lives of the Union Commanders.* Baton Rouge: Louisiana State University Press, 1964.

Webster, Laura Josephine. *The Operations of the Freedmen's Bureau in South Carolina.* Northampton, Mass.: Smith College, 1916.

White, Howard A. *The Freedmen's Bureau in Louisiana.* Baton Rouge: Louisiana State University Press, 1970.

Whitman, William E. S., and Charles True. *Maine in the War for the Union: A History of the Part Borne by Maine Troops in the Suppression of the American Rebellion.* Lewiston, Me.: Nelson Dingley Jr., 1865.

Wiener, Jonathan M. *Social Origins of the New South: Alabama, 1860–1885.* Baton Rouge: Louisiana State University Press, 1978.

Williamson, Joel. *After Slavery: The Negro in South Carolina during Reconstruction, 1861–1877.* Chapel Hill: University of North Carolina Press, 1965.

Wilson, James Grant, and John Fisk, eds. *Appleton's Cyclopedia of American Biography.* 8 vols. New York: D. Appleton, 1894.

Woodman, Harold D. "Economic Reconstruction and the Rise of the New South,

1865–1900." In *Interpreting Southern History: Historiographical Essays in Honor of Sanford W. Higginbotham*, ed. John B. Boles and Evelyn Thomas Nolan, 254–307. Baton Rouge: Louisiana State University Press, 1987.

―――. "Sequel to Slavery: The New History Views the Postbellum South." *Journal of Southern History* 43 (November 1977): 523–54.

Woodward, C. Vann. *Reunion and Reaction: The Compromise of 1877 and the End of Reconstruction*. Boston: Little, Brown, 1951.

Wooster, Ralph A. *The People in Power: Courthouse and Statehouse in the Lower South, 1850–1860*. Knoxville: University of Tennessee Press, 1869.

Wright, Gavin. "The Economics and Politics of Slavery and Freedom in the U.S. South." In *The Meaning of Freedom: Economics, Politics, and Culture after Slavery*, ed. Frank McGlynn and Seymour Drescher, 85–111. Pittsburgh: University of Pittsburgh Press, 1992.

Wynne, Lewis Nicholas. *The Continuity of Cotton: Planter Politics in Georgia, 1865–1892*. Macon, Ga.: Mercer University Press, 1986.

Wynne, Lewis Nicholas, and Milly St. Julien. "The Camilla Race Riot and the Failure of Reconstruction in Southwest Georgia." *Journal of Southwest Georgia History* 5 (fall 1987): 15–37.

Yulee, Elias. *An Address to the Colored People of Georgia*. Savannah, Ga.: Republican Job Office, 1868.

# Index